GERMANY
1945

GERMANY
1945

From War to Peace

RICHARD BESSEL

SIMON &
SCHUSTER

London · New York · Sydney · Toronto

A CBS COMPANY

First published in Great Britain by Simon & Schuster UK Ltd, 2009
A CBS COMPANY

1 3 5 7 9 10 8 6 4 2

Simon & Schuster UK Ltd
1st Floor
222 Gray's Inn Road
London WC1X 8HB

www.simonsays.co.uk

Simon & Schuster Australia
Sydney

A CIP catalogue record for this book
is available from the British Library.

ISBN: 978-0-74323-955-4

Typeset in Bembo by M Rules
Printed and bound in the UK by CPI Mackays, Chatham ME5 8TD

CONTENTS

ACKNOWLEDGEMENTS

Although my name stands on the title page, this book could not have been written without the support of many institutions, colleagues and friends. In particular, I would like to express my gratitude to the University of Freiburg, where I taught in 2003–2004 and where I spent my research leave in 2005. They say that in Freiburg one is 'spoiled by the sun'. While I was in Freiburg I too was spoiled, not so much by the weather (it rained a lot when I was there) as by the welcome I received, in particular from Franz Brüggemeier. Much of this book was drafted while I was in Freiburg, where I benefited from the collegial atmosphere of the Historisches Seminar, from the impressive resources of the University Library, from the efficiency of the staff at the Federal Military Archive, and from discussions with the students who participated in my seminar on the subject of this book.

I also want to thank Bernd Wegner, who once again was my congenial host at the Helmut-Schmidt Universität in Hamburg, where I was able to take advantage of that university's excellent library resources. Furthermore, I would like to express my thanks to the Institut für soziale Bewegungen at the Ruhr-Universität in Bochum, and to its director Klaus Tenfelde, for the time I spent there in 2004. I also owe a debt of gratitude to friends and colleagues who have helped me clarify my understanding of what happened in Germany in 1945, in particular to Nick Stargardt, Benjamin Ziemann, Paul Betts, Alon Confino, Alf Lüdtke, and Jürgen Förster.

A special word of thanks must go to the Alexander von Humboldt Foundation, both for support over the years that made possible my earlier research and for funding my time in Freiburg in 2005. As those who have been privileged to be part of its world-wide network know so well, the Humboldt Foundation is a model of an organization whose purpose is to promote scholarship: consistently helpful, unbureaucratic, dedicated to enabling people to bring their projects to fruition, and aware that time taken to complete lengthy and complicated applications to fund research is time taken away from doing research.

Richard Bessel
Stony Stratford
July 2008

LIST OF ABBREVIATIONS

AfsB	Archive for Social Movements, Bochum
BAB	German Federal Archive, Berlin
BA–MA	German Federal Archive, Military Archive, Freiburg
CCG	(British) Control Commission for Germany
CCS	Combined Chiefs of Staff
CDU	Christian Democratic Union
CIC	Counter Intelligence Corps
DP	Displaced Person
EKD	Protestant Church in Germany
ETOUSA	European Theater of Operations, United States Army
GDR	German Democratic Republic
GIFAC	German Inter-regional Food Allocation Committee
JCS	Joint Chiefs of Staff
KPD	Communist Party of Germany
KTB	War Diary of the Supreme Command of the Wehrmacht
LHA–SA	Land Main Archive Saxony-Anhalt, Magdeburg
MLHA	Mecklenburg Land Main Archive, Schwerin
NA	National Archives, Washington
NKVD	People's Commissariat of Internal Affairs
NSDAP	National Socialist German Workers Party
OKW	Supreme Command of the Wehrmacht
OMGUS	Office of Military Government, United States
POW	Prisoner of War
PWD	Psychological War Department

RM	Reichsmark
SA	Storm Sections
SHAEF	Supreme Headquarters, Allied Expeditionary Force
SMAD	Soviet Military Administration of Germany
SPD	Social Democratic Party of Germany
SS	Protection Squads
UNRRA	United Nations Relief and Rehabilitation Administration
USFET	United States Forces in the European Theater

N

NORWAY

FINLAND

Oslo

Helsinki

Stockholm

SWEDEN

ESTONIA

North

Baltic Sea

COURLAND *Riga*

LATVIA

Sea

DENMARK

Memel

LITHUANIA

SCHLESWIG
HOLSTEIN

Königsberg

Stettin

Gdynia

EAST
PRUSSIA

Hamburg

Danzig

NETHERLANDS

Hannover

POMERANIA

R. Vistula

Warsaw

Dortmund

Berlin

Poznań

Antwerp

R. Oder

LOWER
SILESIA

Łodz

BELGIUM

Cologne

R. Elbe

Dresden

Breslau

Lublin

R. Rhine

*Frankfurt
am Main*

UPPER
SILESIA

LUXEMBOURG

Prague

Kraków

Strasbourg

Nuremberg

FRANCE

Freiburg

R. Danube

Vienna

Munich

Berne

BAVARIA

Salzburg

Budapest

SWITZERLAND

HUNGARY

Milan

ROMANIA

ITALY

Trieste

YUGOSLAVIA

Adriatic Sea

Florence

GERMAN OCCUPIED EUROPE

1 JANUARY 1945

– – – *Front lines*

German occupied territory

Allied and liberated territories

Non-combatant countries

Mediterranean Sea

Rome

0   100   200   300 miles

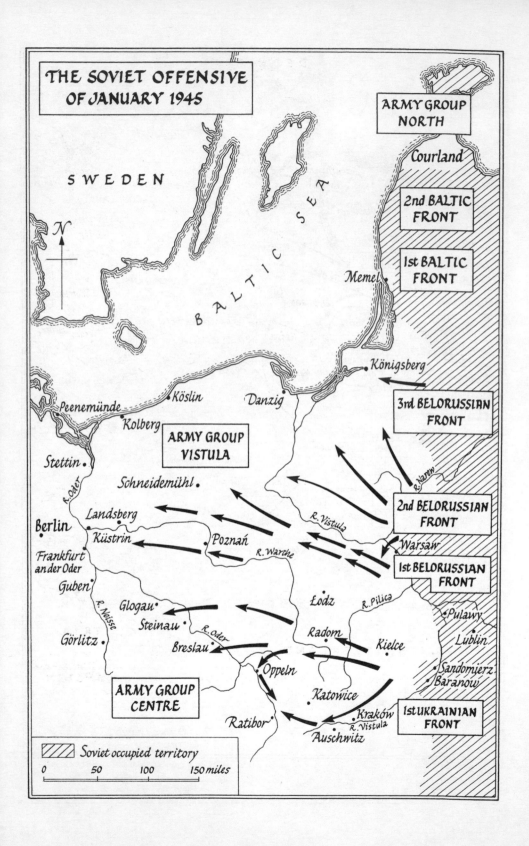

THE SOVIET OFFENSIVE
OF JANUARY 1945

ARMY GROUP
NORTH

Courland

2nd BALTIC
FRONT

1st BALTIC
FRONT

S W E D E N

N

B A L T I C   S E A

Memel

Königsberg

3rd BELORUSSIAN
FRONT

Peenemünde   Köslin   Danzig

Kolberg

R. Narew

Stettin

ARMY GROUP
VISTULA

Schneidemühl

R. Oder   Landsberg   R. Vistula   2nd BELORUSSIAN
                                                                                   FRONT

Berlin   Warsaw
          Küstrin   Poznań
Frankfurt   R. Warthe   1st BELORUSSIAN
an der Oder   FRONT

Guben

R. Neisse   Glogau   Łódz   R. Pilica   Pulawy

Görlitz   Steinau   R. Oder   Radom   Kielce   Lublin

          Breslau   Sandomierz

          Oppeln   Baranow

ARMY GROUP   Katowice
CENTRE
                              Kraków   1st UKRAINIAN
     Ratibor   R. Vistula   FRONT

                         Auschwitz

///// Soviet occupied territory

0   50   100   150 miles

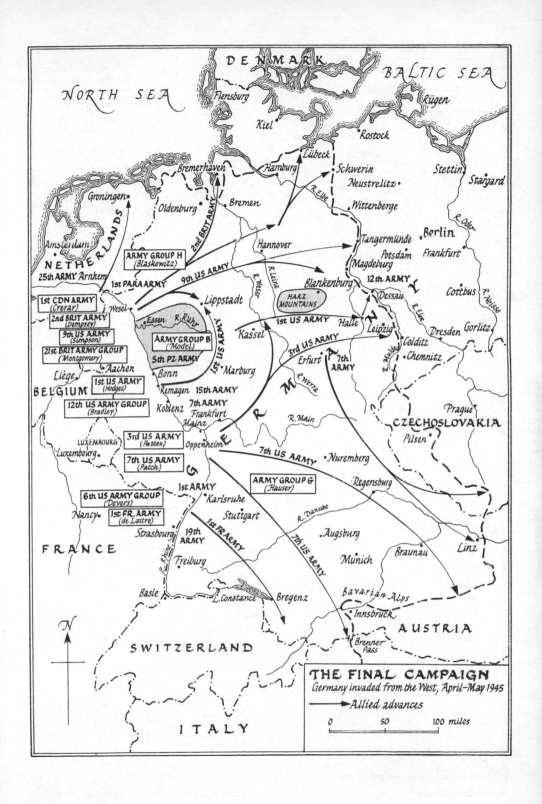

THE FINAL CAMPAIGN
Germany invaded from the West, April–May 1945
→ Allied advances

0   50   100 miles

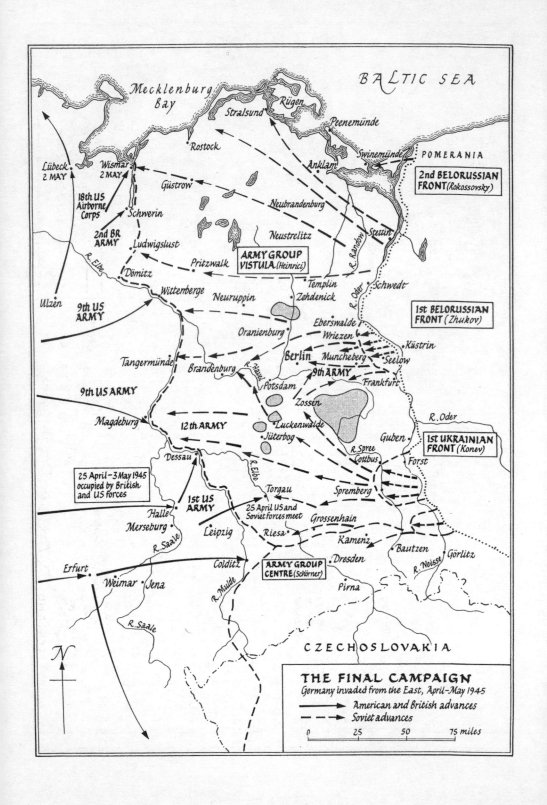

BALTIC SEA

Mecklenburg Bay

Rügen

Stralsund

Peenemünde

Rostock

Anklam

Swinemünde

POMERANIA

Lübeck
2 MAY

Wismar
2 MAY

Güstrow

Neubrandenburg

2nd BELORUSSIAN FRONT (Rokossovsky)

18th US
Airborne
Corps

Schwerin

Neustrelitz

Stettin

2nd BR
ARMY

Ludwigslust

Pritzwalk

R. Elbe

Dömitz

Wittenberge

Neuruppin

Templin

Zehdenick

Schwedt

**ARMY GROUP
VISTULA** (Heinrici)

R. Randow

R. Oder

1st BELORUSSIAN FRONT (Zhukov)

9th US
ARMY

Ulzen

Oranienburg

Eberswalde

Wriezen

Küstrin

Tangermünde

Brandenburg

Berlin

Muncheberg

Seelow

R. Havel

Potsdam

9th ARMY

Frankfurt

9th US ARMY

Magdeburg

12th ARMY

Zossen

Luckenwalde

R. Oder

Jüterbog

Guben

1st UKRAINIAN FRONT (Konev)

Dessau

R. Spree

Cottbus

Forst

25 April–3 May 1945
occupied by British
and US forces

R. Elbe

Torgau

Spremberg

**1st US
ARMY**

25 April US and
Soviet forces meet

Grossenhain

Halle

Merseburg

Leipzig

Riesa

Kamenz

Bautzen

Görlitz

R. Saale

Colditz

Dresden

R. Neisse

Erfurt

Weimar

Jena

**ARMY GROUP
CENTRE** (Schörner)

Pirna

R. Mulde

R. Saale

CZECHOSLOVAKIA

N

THE FINAL CAMPAIGN
Germany invaded from the East, April–May 1945

American and British advances

Soviet advances

0   25   50   75 miles

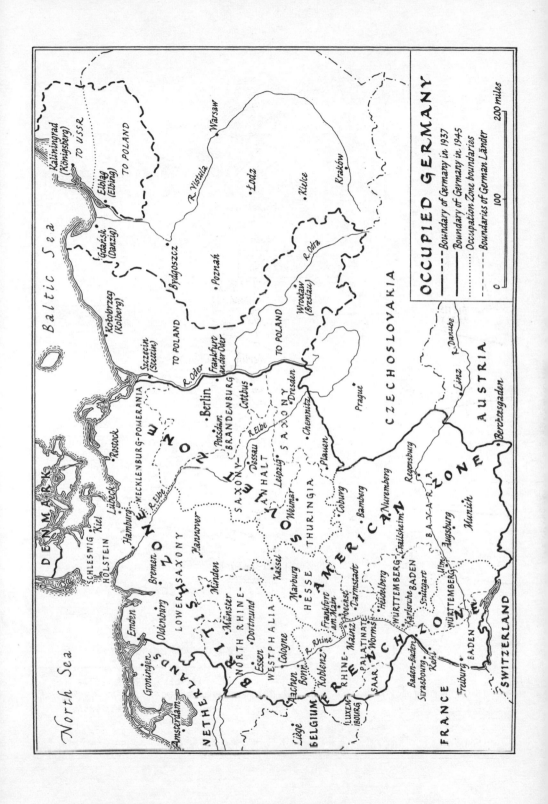

North Sea

Baltic Sea

DENMARK

TO USSR
Kaliningrad (Königsberg)
Elbląg (Elbing)
TO POLAND
Gdańsk (Danzig)
Kotobrzeg (Kolberg)
Szczecin (Stettin)
TO POLAND
R. Oder
Frankfurt an der Oder
TO POLAND
Warsaw
R. Vistula
Łódź
Kielce
Kraków
Poznań
Bydgoszcz
Wrocław (Breslau)
R. Ostra

SCHLESWIG HOLSTEIN
Kiel
Lübeck
Rostock
Hamburg
MECKLENBURG-POMERANIA
R. Elbe

SOVIET ZONE

Berlin
Potsdam
BRANDENBURG
Cottbus
Dessau
ANHALT
SAXONY
Leipzig
Dresden
Chemnitz
R. Elbe
Weimar
THURINGIA
Plauen
Coburg
Bamberg

CZECHOSLOVAKIA
Prague

NETHERLANDS
Groningen
Amsterdam
Emden
Oldenburg
Bremen
LOWER SAXONY
Hannover
Minden
Münster
NORTH RHINE-WESTPHALIA
Dortmund
Essen
Cologne
Bonn
Aachen
LUXEMBOURG
Liège
BELGIUM

BRITISH ZONE

Kassel
Marburg
HESSE
Frankfurt am Main
Darmstadt
Wiesbaden
Worms
RHINE-PALATINATE
Mainz
Koblenz
R. Rhine
SAAR

AMERICAN ZONE

Crailsheim
WÜRTTEMBERG-BADEN
Heidelberg
Stuttgart
Nuremberg
Regensburg
BAVARIA
Augsburg
Ulm
Munich
Linz
R. Danube
Berchtesgaden

FRENCH ZONE
Strasbourg
Karlsruhe
Baden-Baden
Kehl
WÜRTTEMBERG
BADEN
Freiburg
FRANCE
SWITZERLAND
AUSTRIA

OCCUPIED GERMANY

- – – – Boundary of Germany in 1937
- — — Boundary of Germany in 1945
- ———— Occupation Zone boundaries
- ········· Boundaries of German Länder

0   100   200 miles

To the memory of my father, who was there

1

INTRODUCTION:
TO HELL AND BACK

The mood of catastrophe — for us wearers of the star [of David], nine-tenths joyful, one-tenth fearful — but even when it comes to fear people say 'Better a terrible end [than no end at all]! — is growing stronger. Victor Klemperer[1]

Now I hope that everything goes back to the way it was. It is wonderful when one can lie down in bed in the evening in peace. Hopefully the war will soon be over, the soldiers will be able to come home. Gerda J.[2]

At midnight on New Year's Eve, as 1945 began, German radio broadcast Adolf Hitler's last New Year's message to the German people. To a nation that faced certain defeat, he yet again asserted his faith in ultimate victory, concluding with his 'unshakeable belief that the hour is near in which victory finally will come to that which is the most worthy of it: the Greater German Reich'.[3] Popular reactions to Hitler's message were astonishingly positive, although laced with disappointment that the leader had not offered any details of how victory might be achieved, whether through new weapons or new offensives, or how the Allied bombing campaign which was causing such destruction to Germany's cities might be halted.[4] Less than two weeks later, on 12 January, the great Soviet offensive began, and sealed the fate of the 'Thousand-Year Reich'. By the end of January, the Wehrmacht had suffered its highest ever monthly total of casualties as the numbers of German military dead reached their peak of over 450,000 – far in excess of the 185,000 Wehrmacht members who died in January 1943, the month of the defeat at Stalingrad.[5] Never before had so many people been killed in Germany in so short a time. This bloodbath opened the year 1945; with it, what Marlis Steinert has described as Germans' 'last flicker of hope' arising from Hitler's New Year's message was extinguished.

In late March 1945 an intelligence report, apparently drafted by the Security Service of the SS, described German popular opinion in the blackest of terms. The last remaining, desperate hopes of avoiding defeat had evaporated. The collapse of the German fronts in east and west, the Allied bombing, the 'chaotic transport disarray', had led to a 'general hopelessness':

> A large proportion of the population has become accustomed to living only day-to-day. They make the most of any comforts of life that present themselves. Any otherwise trivial excuse is used to justify drinking up the last bottle which originally was saved for the victory celebration, for the end of the blackout, for the return of a husband or son. Many are getting used to the idea of making an end of it all. Everywhere there is great demand for poison, for a pistol and other means of ending one's life. Suicides due to real depression about the catastrophe which is expected with certainty are an everyday occurrence. Numerous conversations with families, with relatives, friends and acquaintances are dominated by planning how one also could get by under enemy occupation. Savings are being set aside, hiding places are being sought out. Especially the elderly torment themselves day and night with sombre thoughts and no longer are able to sleep for worry. Things that no one dared to imagine only a few weeks previously are today the subject of open discussions in public-transport vehicles and among complete strangers.[6]

Six weeks later those 'things that no one dared to imagine only a few weeks previously' had come to pass: The Wehrmacht surrendered unconditionally and Allied armies occupied the whole of Germany. Instead of the victory in which Hitler had asserted his 'unshakeable belief', Germans experienced total defeat. Never before in modern world history had a country been defeated so thoroughly as was Nazi Germany. At the end of the Nazi 'assault on the roots of civilization',[7] Germany lay in ruins – politically, socially, economically and morally.

For decades, historians have examined in impressive detail the catastrophic course of modern German history in order to explain how a developed and cultured nation could abandon democratic and civilized values, launch brutal wars of imperialist plunder and racist violence, engage in organized campaigns of mass murder unparalleled in human history, and carry the barbarous Nazi programme through to a catastrophic and suicidal end. In short, we have been concerned, rightly, to explain how humanity in central Europe slid into the abyss of tyranny, violence, war and genocide. However, that is far from the whole story, and in recent years increasing attention has been paid to the end of Nazi Germany as well as its beginning. For as important as it is to understand how people got themselves into the horrors of Nazism and war, it is at least as important to understand how they emerged from the other side, to understand how they managed to get out.

The hole from which the Germans had to climb in 1945 was incredibly deep. After Nazi Germany had subjected people across the European continent to horrific violence, particularly in the closing stages of the war the Germans themselves were subjected to deadly violence on a massive scale. Germany had been the target of a bombing campaign which was unprecedented in its destructive power, reached its peak in early 1945 and claimed the lives of nearly half a million people.[8] The bombing, the evacuations from cities endangered by the Allied air assault, the westward flight of millions of Germans ahead of the Red Army and the subsequent expulsion of millions more following the Wehrmacht's surrender, left at least a quarter of the German population homeless. The Nazi concentration camp empire had degenerated into a series of collection points in which almost no provision was made for the needs or indeed survival of prisoners herded into them, with predictably horrific consequences. The Nazi political system collapsed, and what had remained of it in the spring of 1945 was abolished by the Allied occupying powers. Millions of German soldiers had been killed or wounded, and millions more were in Allied prisoner-of-war camps. The country's transport system was largely at a standstill; electricity and gas supplies were cut; telecommunications systems no longer functioned; water and sewerage systems were severely damaged; food supply was precarious and many people faced the prospect of severe malnutrition; disease was rampant and medical services were severely disrupted. Far from being Europe's masters, Germans now were ruled by occupying armies. A people which had been schooled in racism and conquered a continent, subjecting its inhabitants to murderous violence on a massive scale, now had to make the transition to life in postwar society in the most inauspicious circumstances.

That transition forms the hinge on which the history of twentieth-century Germany and Europe turns: from the most terrible outburst of human violence in world history to the beginning of a period characterized (at least in Western Europe) by peace and prosperity. After the experience of destruction, defeat, disease, death and destitution on an unimaginable scale, Germans took their first steps along a path that would lead to stable democratic government, prosperity beyond the dreams of most people before the Second World War, and peaceful civilized behaviour.

Germany did indeed go to hell and, in 1945, began to come back; the peaceful second half of the twentieth century rested on the ashes of the first.

How is this remarkable transition – the turning point of Europe's twentieth century as well as of the lives of millions of individuals – to be explained? The search for an answer to this question – and the central argument of this book – needs to begin with the enormity of the violence which overwhelmed Germany during the last year of the war.[9]

At the beginning of 1945 Germany witnessed the greatest killing frenzy that the world has ever seen, as military casualties reached their peak, the Allied bombing campaign was at its most intense, and millions of Germans fled westwards ahead of the Red Army. The violence which Germans now experienced in their daily lives was a profound shock, which pushed into the background their memories of the earlier phases of the war when they had the upper hand and were more often the perpetrators of violence than its victims. The effects of the shock of violence, of the trauma which 1945 signified for millions of Germans, can hardly be overestimated.

This has to be understood in the context of the rise and fall of the Nazi racial state. The people's shock at becoming the victims of violence on so massive a scale and of total military defeat was all the greater after the experience of a dictatorship which had propagated German racial superiority and been so stunningly successful in subjugating others. Popular reactions to what occurred in 1945, as well as the views of those still running the Nazi regime as it crumbled, had been conditioned by tremendous faith in the leader, widespread complicity in the crimes of the regime (from which millions of people had profited directly and indirectly),[10] and broad agreement with many of the ideological assumptions that had underpinned the regime: that democratic government in the form of the Weimar 'system' had been a chaotic failure; that Germans and their culture were superior to other peoples and their cultures, especially those of eastern Europeans; that – in the words of a propaganda volume published just after the Wehrmacht's 1939 campaign in Poland – Germany's fighting forces consisted of the 'soldiers of the best army in the world';[11] and that Germans could share in what Friedrich Meinecke, doyen of the German historical profession and later founding rector of the Free University in Berlin, had described to a colleague just after the conquest of France in 1940 as his 'joy, admiration and pride at this army'.[12] The rapid economic recovery and stunning diplomatic successes of the 1930s, the astonishing military triumphs during the first half the war, and the fact that Germans had been able to eat relatively well during the conflict thanks to their brutal exploitation of a conquered continent, made the complete military collapse and extreme violence visited upon them in 1945 – the sudden transition from power to impotence – all the more devastating. As a consequence, remarkably little remained of a movement and an ideology which had held Germany in its grip for twelve years.

Thus, in 1945 Germans were transformed from active protagonists to passive observers of their fate. People who had become accustomed to ruling others now found themselves powerless and subject to the rule of foreign powers. The occupation and administration of Germany by the Allies, with important decisions taken out of German hands, were central to the remarkable shift in German mentalities that occurred in 1945. Their emergence from Nazism and war into a peaceful and prosperous postwar world had much to do with the fact that for years after May 1945 the Germans were not allowed to govern themselves. This formed a striking contrast with what had occurred after the armistice of November 1918. Then, the Germans had been defeated militarily, but unfortunately they were not made impotent. They were not stripped of their state, their army, their political institutions; their country – except for relatively small amounts of territory in the east and west – was not occupied by foreign armies; and they still were able to govern themselves, which they proceeded to do remarkably badly. After their unconditional surrender in May 1945 and the occupation of the entire country by foreign armed forces, however, things were very different: little opportunity remained for Germans actively to shape their future beyond the day-to-day struggle for survival.

The violence and upheaval of the last months of war and the first months of occupation left Germans disorientated in other regards as well. The fixed points in the lives of millions of people had been obliterated, both physically and emotionally. Altogether roughly 26 million Germans had lost their homes, whether through bombing, flight, or expulsion. Those who still possessed a home often had to endure severe overcrowding or to inhabit buildings which were severely damaged. This meant more than the loss of a physical environment, with all the practical problems that signified; it also signified the loss of familiar points of reference – of community, of social and cultural networks. It meant, as Fritz Stern expressed it in a lecture given in Berlin in 1995 on 'lost Heimat', not simply 'the loss of possessions, of one's livelihood' but, more importantly, 'the human-spiritual loss' of safety and security, of something that 'also puts its stamp on the largely "unconscious self-confidence" or – to use the modern expression – on identity'.[13]

The cataclysm of 1945 shook the 'unconscious self-confidence' of millions of Germans. Collective identities, social solidarities and the sense of place and security were undermined. The terror of the Nazi regime, which had been aimed not just against others but, increasingly, against Germans themselves during the last months of the war in order to prevent the crumbling of resistance to the Allies and any challenges to the dying regime, made collective action all but impossible. The destruction of infrastructure, which paralysed transport, post and telecommunications, increasingly restricted people's sphere of activity to their own immediate vicinity. The smashing of Germany's cities and the movement of millions of citizens from their homes destroyed communities, occupational connections and social networks. Everyday problems, the scramble to find food and shelter, were overwhelming. Family connections were broken, with millions of men dead, missing or in prisoner-of-war camps, and with millions of survivors left desperately searching for their relatives.

It was not only what actually happened to Germans but also how they reacted to their predicament that corroded collective bonds and 'unconscious self-confidence'. The loss of family, friends, homes, limbs and years of their lives, in the service of a criminal and lost cause, left behind an ocean of bitterness. At the same time, the fact that so many people had been complicit in, and profited from, the actions of a racist and murderous regime, and were in danger of being called to account by the victorious Allies, raised the question of guilt and the problem of having to deal with one's own often chequered past. And the imposition of Allied rule brought with it new insecurities, ranging from fear of violence by occupation soldiers to fear of arrest by occupation authorities. Altogether, the German population was battered physically, economically and psychologically to an extent unprecedented in living memory.

How individuals experienced the events of 1945 depended to a great extent on their age at the time. Of course, the bombing, the privations, the flight and expulsion from the east, and the Allied occupation affected the young as well as the old; those born and socialized under the Kaiser as well as those born during the Weimar period and socialized under the Nazis, and those who still were children when the war ended. Yet the place of 1945 in individual biographies differed significantly depending upon whether one had been born in, say, 1880, 1900, 1920 or 1935.

Those born in the 1880s could view the cataclysm of 1945 against the background of a childhood and socialization in the relatively stable and prosperous Wilhelmine Empire, a seemingly peaceful and secure world which had been shattered by the First World War, defeat in 1918 and the crises of the Weimar Republic, followed by the dizzying hopes and terrible catastrophes of Nazi rule. This was a cohort who, in a more stable world, would have been looking forward to a peaceful retirement in 1945. Those born in the years after 1900 had a rather different perspective. They included the men who constituted the 'generation of the unbound',[14] those who had been able to take advantage of the extraordinary opportunities offered by the Third Reich and to make astonishing careers in murder and war. They were people who, in more settled times, would have been entering into positions of responsibility and authority during the late 1940s. The experiences and perspectives of those born around 1920, in the aftermath of the First World War, were different yet again. These were the people who suffered most acutely as a result of Nazism and war. This group consisted of birth cohorts half of whose male members would not survive their twenties and whose female members consequently stood relatively poor chances of finding a male life partner after the dust settled in 1945. Born in the crisis-ridden Weimar Republic and coming of age under Hitler, this was the generation for whose survivors the shock of 1945 was perhaps most severe – people who were robbed of their young-adult years, whether due to military service, captivity as prisoners of war, war-related disability, or the absence of life partners.

Finally, those born in the mid-to-late 1930s experienced the war as children; their childhood world and earliest memories often consisted of bombing, homelessness, flight and fear.[15] This was the generation of Manfred Uschner, born in 1937 and during the 1980s a leading Socialist Unity Party functionary (as Private Secretary of the Politburo member Hermann Axen) in the German Democratic Republic. As a seven-year-old Uschner had witnessed his grandmother being burned alive in the bombing of Magdeburg on 16 January 1945, an experience which, he asserted, had 'burned itself into us for ever' and about which nearly a half a century later he would write: 'I have never shaken loose from it.'[16]

For older Germans, the experience of 1945 was profoundly affected by memories of 1918. Frequent comparisons were made between what was happening at the end of the Second World War and what had happened at the end of the First. In the last weeks of the Second World War many Germans were convinced that – as one muttered in an air-raid shelter in Berlin at the end of March 1945 – 'if our soldiers were as clever as in 1918, the war already would be over'.[17] And after it was over, many no doubt shared the opinion expressed in June 1946 by Dr Rudolf Paul, Minister-President of Thuringia and himself born in 1893, that 'the collapse of 9 November 1918 was a tempest in a teacup compared with the typhoon of the year 1945'.[18] The scale and intensity of the violence, the extent of the destruction, and the totality of the defeat made 1945 very different from 1918.

The 'typhoon' of 1945 was no freak storm. It was the consequence of the determination of the Nazi leadership to ensure that there would be no repeat of the armistice that had ended Germany's First World War. This time, they vowed, Germany would fight to the bitter end. It did not matter that there was no hope of avoiding catastrophic defeat: the final bloody battles would set the stage for future struggle; the greater the destruction the greater would be the inspiration for future generations. However, rather than provide inspiration for the next war, the 'typhoon' of 1945 did just the opposite: instead of inspiring a new generation of warriors, it left a population remarkably disposed towards pacifism. The shock of the cataclysm in 1945 made possible a transition very different than that which followed the First World War. The story of that shock and that transition is the subject of this book.

2

A WORLD IN FLAMES

I believe that the year 1945 will be a very stormy one for us. Joseph Goebbels[1]

The sacrifices that were made on both sides from January 1945 were senseless. Albert Speer[2]

On New Year's Day 1945, Joseph Goebbels observed in his diary:

Day and night heavy enemy attacks again have taken place, especially on Koblenz, Kassel and Cologne. The city of Koblenz has been hit especially hard in recent weeks, and Cologne slowly is being transformed into a complete pile of rubble. These Rhenish cities are to be most deeply pitied. Their remaining population is leading a truly hellish existence. I have received a dreadful report about the last heavy night attack on Heilbronn from a colleague whom I sent there. The city is 70 to 80 per cent destroyed. It exists without water, without gas, without electricity. The mood in the city is very grave. Again and again one has to ask oneself the question: How long will our people endure these terrible bombardments without sinking into lethargy? We can be happy that the current situation at the front is not contributing further to such a development of morale. The situation at the front currently is halfway bearable again. But I believe that where it is calm, that is the calm before the storm.[3]

Goebbels was right. Less than two weeks later the Soviet Army launched the greatest offensive in military history, an offensive that would break the temporary stalemate in the east, bring massive casualties, and destroy any remaining belief that Nazi Germany might avoid total defeat. In January 1945 the roof caved in on the Third Reich.

Never has there been a killing frenzy to match what occurred in Germany at the beginning of 1945. After years during which the armed forces of Nazi Germany had spread violence, devastation and mass murder across the European continent, the most destructive war ever fought well and truly came home to the Reich. As the Nazi empire contracted, with Allied armies closing in from both east and west, and as German defences against attack from the air became increasingly ineffective, the full violence of war was concentrated on what remained of what the Nazis referred to as 'Greater Germany'. The last months of the war were, for Nazi Germany, by far the most bloody. In January, when Soviet armies launched the greatest offensive of the Second World War, that brought them from the Vistula to the Oder in only a couple of weeks, German casualties reached their peak: In that single month more than 450,000 German soldiers lost their lives – more, by a considerable margin, than either the United Kingdom or the United States lost in all theatres during the entire war. In each of the next three months – February, March and April – the number of German military dead exceeded 280,000.[4] That is to say, more than a quarter of Germany's entire military losses during the Second World War occurred in 1945; during the last four months of the war more Germans were killed than in 1942 and 1943 put together, and they were killed largely within Germany.

Allied casualties – the overwhelming majority of which were Soviet soldiers battling their way into the Reich from the east – were probably even greater than those of the Germans; in the battle for Berlin the Soviet Army, whose tactics were hardly designed to minimise its own losses, suffered more than 300,000 casualties in the space of only three weeks.[5] Altogether, it is likely that more than a million people died violent deaths in the first month of 1945 alone. But that was not all! Fleeing for their lives ahead of the advancing Red Army were millions of Germans, many of whom perished in the bitterly cold winter weather. At the same time the Allied bombing of German cities and towns reached its most intense phase. With German air defences no longer able to offer effective protection and the whole of Germany now within range of Allied bombers, a greater tonnage of bombs was dropped monthly than ever before. Both towns and countryside now came within range of low-flying Allied fighter planes, which were able to strafe German soldiers and civilians alike almost at will and inflicted further casualties on a terrorized population.[6] And it was not just their military opponents who were spilling the blood of German 'racial comrades' (*Volksgenossen*). In the shrinking territory remaining under German control, the increasingly desperate police, judiciary, SS and Wehrmacht were applying deadly terror in ever greater measure against both foreign workers and Germans in order to maintain discipline, to stifle 'defeatism', and to prevent a repetition of what had occurred in 1918. During the final months and weeks of the 'Thousand-Year Reich', Germany was engulfed in violence and became a world in flames.

The bloodshed of the first four months of 1945 was not just a continuation of the horrors which had descended upon Germany during 1944. It marked a qualitative as well as a quantitative change. During the last months of the war the Germans continued to fight, but without any hope of winning the war or even of somehow achieving a bloody stalemate. Outnumbered and outgunned, the Wehrmacht fought on without serious consideration of replacing losses of men and materiel, or of what might happen afterwards. Warfare was continued not out of any strategic considerations, but for its own sake. German cities now faced a fate that Nazi aggression had inflicted on the cities of others across Europe: evacuation, artillery bombardment, street fighting, occupation by foreign troops. The ability of German forces to resist the Allied onslaught was dwindling rapidly on all fronts – in the air, almost to the vanishing point. During the final months and weeks of war, as Allied forces largely destroyed the German transport and communications infrastructure, broke the back of the Wehrmacht, cutting military units off from one another, and eventually sliced Nazi-controlled territory in two, the fighting took on a quite different character.

Nevertheless, as the year 1945 dawned it still seemed possible for Germans to hope that the war somehow might be fought to a stalemate. At the beginning of 1945, on land the National Socialist regime still had roughly 7.5 million men under arms.[7] The Nazi 'Fortress Europe' had shrunk considerably during 1944, but almost all of 'Greater Germany' and a fair amount of foreign territory still remained under German control. To the west, the last major German offensive, the Operation 'Watch on the Rhine' launched in the Ardennes on 16 December (the 'Battle of the Bulge'), had been checked; and Aachen had been the first German city to fall to the Allies when the Americans took it on 21 October 1944, after bitter street fighting. Nonetheless, the Western Allies had not yet made substantial inroads into German territory or managed to cross the Rhine. To the east, with the Soviet Army having been stalled along the Vistula for months, German forces still held much of Poland and had repeatedly demonstrated their skill in defensive military operations. They remained capable of achieving temporary tactical successes along a 900-kilometre front that stretched from the Carpathian mountain range in the south to the Baltic Sea in the north. On the seas, the sailors of the German Navy – in marked contrast to their counterparts in the autumn of 1918 – showed few signs of unwillingness to continue fighting or to follow orders, much less of revolutionary sentiment;[8] the Supreme Commander of the Navy, Admiral Karl Dönitz, had some justification for his boast to Hitler in November 1944 that the Navy 'is precisely 180 degrees different than in the [First] World War'.[9] The fighting over the previous half year had led to exceptionally heavy losses, especially since the Allied landings in Normandy on 6 June 1944 and the Soviet summer offensive which had been launched with 2.4 million men on 23 June; German forces had been driven back steadily in both east and west; France largely had been liberated by the year's end, and some 30 Wehrmacht divisions had been cut off in Courland and Memel along the eastern Baltic and could be supplied only by sea. However, the German armed forces still displayed remarkable tenacity and ability to wage defensive war, and German lines more or less still held.

Thus, at the beginning of 1945, even after the failure of the Ardennes Offensive, some among the German leadership imagined that the Wehrmacht might be able to hold the Allies at bay and induce them to negotiate a settlement. One example, and a revealing sign of the extent to which German military leaders had lost touch with reality, was a proposal on 5 January by Reinhard Gehlen, head of the 'Section Foreign Armies East' (*Abteilung Fremde Heere Ost*), the intelligence-gathering organization collecting information about enemy forces in the east. Gehlen proposed strengthening the eastern front by 20 to 30 divisions to enable the Wehrmacht to mount an offensive and thus force Stalin to the negotiating table.[10] Other initiatives may have been less fantastic, but were no less doomed to failure. On 1 January 1945, German forces spearheaded by divisions of the Waffen-SS mounted a major offensive in Hungary ordered by Hitler. Their objective: to break the encirclement of Budapest, which had been surrounded by Soviet forces the week before,[11] and to secure oil resources without which, as Hitler put it, 'a continuation of the war no longer is possible'.[12] The fact that 'a continuation of the war' no longer made any sense was beside the point: Nazi Germany would keep fighting, regardless of the strategic implications and regardless of the cost. In incredibly bloody fighting, and after committing further reinforcements to check Soviet counterattacks, the German forces made surprising, if temporary, progress; the battles in Hungary, that continued into March and were described by Stalin himself as comprising 'one of the heaviest offensives of the entire war', caused difficulties to the Soviet Army similar to those which the Ardennes Offensive had caused the Americans.[13] In the end, however, the inevitable result in Hungary was the same as in the Ardennes. The Nazi regime demonstrated that it still commanded a military force capable of inflicting serious damage on its opponents; yet it could not change the course of the war, and throwing so many irreplaceable troops and so much materiel into the offensive in effect served to hasten the day of Germany's unconditional surrender.

The fate of Nazi Germany was sealed in January 1945. Until that time, while Allied bombing already had exacted a terrible toll on German cities and towns – Aachen had fallen to the Americans, some (relatively small) portions of German territory were already occupied by Allied forces, and eastern portions of East Prussia had been overrun by the Soviet Army – the Wehrmacht was still fighting for the most part on foreign soil. That was the way Germany's wars had been fought for most of living memory: the First World War ended while German forces still were standing on French and Belgian soil in the west and occupying huge areas in the east after the Treaty of Brest-Litovsk; and the Franco-Prussian War had been fought in northern France, not in the Rhineland. For Germans, war on the ground was something that happened in foreign countries – until 1945. Then, precipitously, the full force of war came to Germany itself.

The fighting in 1945 was characterized by, on the one hand, the overwhelming superiority of the Allied armed forces, and on the other by the increasingly desperate predicament of a Wehrmacht whose supplies were depleted and whose mobility was diminishing rapidly. While the Wehrmacht managed with rather impressive skill to maintain a potent fighting machine in early 1945 – their administrative and organizational bureaucracy maintained an effective working routine to an astonishing degree almost to the last[14] – it did so by employing tactics which could serve only to prolong the agony and killing for a few more weeks. Seventeen-year-old recruits were thrown into battle with only rudimentary training; reserves were sent into the front line; all remaining resources were expended in a futile attempt to stem the massive tide of Allied force. The Wehrmacht leadership committed itself to an utterly hopeless struggle, throwing its soldiers into battles which they could not hope to win and into positions where they only could be annihilated, thus ensuring that the maximum destruction would be visited on German cities and towns and on the civilian population. In the absence of any military rationale for prolonging the war, the Wehrmacht continued fighting, in effect sentencing both soldiers and German civilians to death and destruction on a monstrous scale. Few military leaders protested. In military terms, the war which German forces waged during the first four months of 1945, after the Ardennes Offensive had ground to a halt, amounted to a negation of the basic requirements of military leadership.

The radicalization of Nazi war at the front was paralleled by a radical-ization of attempts to mobilize the home front, as the two melded into one. Faced with the imminent invasion of the Reich itself, the Nazi regime looked to a sort of *levée en masse* whereby the civilian popula-tion, alongside the Wehrmacht, would defend 'fortress' cities to the last drop of blood. In the absence of any coherent military options which might stem the tide, the regime referred increasingly to its ideology of eternal struggle to be taken up by a supposedly united, fanatical war-rior people. The embodiment of this was the '*Volkssturm*', called into being by Hitler in the autumn of 1944 as the Allies were making their first advances into German territory.[15] Supposedly embodying the spirit of the *Landsturm* which had battled against the French in 1813 – Hitler's call was made public on 18 October 1944, the anniversary of the 'Battle of the Nations' against Napoleon in 1813 – the *Volkssturm* was to bring all men between the ages of 16 and 60 capable of bearing arms into an 'army of millions of idealists' who would prefer death to surrendering the 'freedom' of the German people.[16] What this was supposed to mean was described in graphic detail by Heinrich Himmler, in a speech for a swearing-in ceremony of men into the *Volkssturm* in East Prussia at the end of October 1944:

> Our opponents must know that every kilometre that they want to advance into our country will cost them rivers of blood. They will step onto a field of living mines consisting of fanatical uncompromising fighters. Every block of flats in a city, every vil-lage, every farmstead, every forest will be defended by men, boys and old men and, if need be, by women and girls. Furthermore, in the territory that they believe they have con-quered, the German determination to resist will rise up behind them and, like the werewolves, fearless volunteers will do damage to the enemy and cut off his lifelines.[17]

This was the Nazi vision of battle in the last months of the war. The old men and young boys of the *Volkssturm* ('and, if need be, [. . .] women and girls') were expected to confront the overwhelming might of the Soviet, American, British and Canadian armies with hand-held anti-tank weapons, and to die alongside the remaining soldiers of the Wehrmacht for the sake of the Nazi 'people's community' (*Volksgemeinschaft*). If they could not reverse the tide of war, then they were to set a shining example for future generations – and expunge the disgrace of the surrender in 1918 – by dying in combat.[18] That was the vision which Hitler presented in his last proclamation to Germany's soldiers on the occasion of the last 'Heroes Remembrance Day' on 11 March 1945:

> It is therefore my unalterable decision, and it must be our general irreversible will, not to give posterity a bad example like those who came before us did. The year 1918 therefore will not be repeated. [. . .]
>
> In large parts of the east and in many areas of the west we already are experiencing what is in store for our people. What we therefore have to do is clear to everyone: to continue to offer resistance and to strike at our enemies until they tire and finally crack in the end![19]

And it was a vision which framed the chilling order given in March 1945 for the 'preparations for the defence of the Reich capital':

> The Reich capital will be defended to the last man and the last bullet. [. . .]
>
> The enemy, who is to be granted not a minute's peace, must be chewed up and bled to death in the closely-meshed net of nests of resistance, strongholds and resistance blocks. Any house or any stronghold that is lost is to be retaken immediately with a counterattack. [. . .]
>
> The precondition for a successful defence of Berlin, however, is that every block of flats, every house, every floor, every hedgerow, every shell-hole is defended to the utmost!

It does not matter that every defender of the Reich capital masters the technique of using weapons down to the last detail, but much more that every fighter is inspired and permeated by the fanatical will TO WANT TO FIGHT.[20]

This was a call, in effect, not so much for the defence of the Reich capital as for its destruction.

Not surprisingly, the stream of orders demanding that each and every town, street, position and house be held at any cost, led to a growing gulf between the military leadership issuing the orders and the men whose lives were to be sacrificed in the futile fighting that would follow.[21] The response, certainly in the west and south of Germany, and by March and April increasingly in the east as well, was one of save-yourself-if-you-can, of 'defeatism', 'shirking', 'desertions' and remaining separated from one's unit in the hope of surviving until the war ended.

To counter such understandable responses to Nazi demands for sacrifice, the regime intensified its terror against its own soldiers. In mid-February the Reich Justice Minister, Otto Thierack, ordered the creation of summary courts martial in areas threatened by Allied troops (which soon were to comprise virtually the entire country); their competence extended to all offences 'which threaten German fighting strength or determination to fight'.[22] For the military, on 9 March a 'Führer Decree' ordered the creation of 'Flying Courts Martial of the Führer', consisting solely of officers and with their own execution squads.[23] During the last weeks of the war, the Army High Command effectively did away with the distinction between desertion and merely being absent without leave; in mid-March Field Marshal von Rundstedt (Supreme Commander in the West) and Field Marshal Model (Supreme Commander of the Army Group B) ordered that all those 'found without reason away from their units on roads, in villages, among civilian treks, at field-dressing stations without being wounded and claim to be separated from their unit and searching for it, are to be sentenced by summary court martial and to be shot'.[24] The flying courts martial set up to enforce this regime were in reality little more than roving death squads, and officers tempted to

act responsibly and protect the men under their command by ordering tactical retreat were themselves threatened with the death penalty.
As the conflict neared its end, soldiers and civilians willing to give up
the fight had more to fear from their own regime than they did from
the enemy.[25] The spectre of 1918 was to be banished and the ideal of
Nazi sacrifice was to be secured through terror.

Nevertheless, the military situation did not match remotely the
rhetoric and images conjured up by the Nazi regime. Despite the draconian punishments aimed at preventing a repeat of 1918, during the
final months of the Second World War more German soldiers deserted
than at the end of the First.[26] The *Volkssturm*, intended to embody the
fanatical will of a civilian population fighting shoulder to shoulder
with its army, was incapable of offering serious resistance. Not just
the *Volkssturm*, whose military value was virtually nil, but also the
Wehrmacht increasingly lacked the necessary hardware. Whether
in terms of armaments, logistics, ammunition, communications, or
food and fuel, the Wehrmacht no longer possessed the requirements
of a modern army capable of waging war effectively.[27] Telecommunications between headquarters and theatres of battle were cut
repeatedly.[28] Between June 1944 and March 1945 the Wehrmacht lost
three and a half million rifles, and by early 1945 the shortages of rifles
and machine guns had become critical.[29] Fuel supply was a chronic
problem, making it impossible for the Wehrmacht to use the hardware
remaining at its disposal. By February, it was receiving less than a
fifth of the normal railway shipments of munitions; stocks of weapons
were being depleted and it was difficult to distribute what replacement
stocks there were; and army units increasingly found themselves without heavy weapons or adequate quantities of ammunition.[30] German
soldiers increasingly were left without the most basic requirements, as
the members of one infantry division, charged with defending the
town of Cleve (along the Lower Rhine near the Dutch border), found
towards the end of 1944: the lack of motor vehicles undermined
efforts to bring up artillery ammunition; a switch to horse-drawn
vehicles failed due to the lack of horses; weapons and communications
equipment were in desperately short supply; and radio links were
non-existent.[31]

In memoirs written in Allied captivity during the winter of 1945/46, General Erich Dethleffsen, Chief of the Command Group in the General Staff of the Army from 23 March to 23 April 1945, described what he found when he reported for his new duties in late March:

> There was, at the moment that I had familiarised myself with my new functions, scarcely anything left to 'lead'. The initiative lay completely with the enemy. Operational reserves did not exist, movement [of units] remained possible only to a limited degree given the largely destroyed rail network.[32]

For the German military, just about everything was breaking apart: communications, supply, and authority.

With reports of military catastrophe cascading in after the collapse of the Ardennes Offensive and the Soviet breakthrough on the eastern front, the Wehrmacht was thrown back on hasty, desperate improvization. This resulted in some temporary tactical successes as German units sometimes managed to stall the progress of the Allies and, on occasion, even to score minor victories, while Allied forces regrouped and amassed supplies for their next offensive. The available documentation of Wehrmacht operations in early 1945 reveals the huge increase in losses of soldiers and equipment. The military value of many units, filled with very young or very old recruits lacking combat experience and without internal cohesion, was limited, and consequently they served as little more than cannon fodder.[33] It was obvious therefore that fighting could continue for only a few weeks or, at most, a few months, before the inevitable collapse. Consideration was not given to the longer-term viability of the Wehrmacht or to the maintenance of a war-fighting capability even for the medium term. Military strategy in the conventional sense had gone completely out the window. The essence of Nazism had overwhelmed the ethos of the German military. The Wehrmacht no longer existed to win military victories but instead to sacrifice its soldiers in an apocalyptic final struggle.

Pointless though this 'strategy of self-annihilation' may have been, it did not mean that the Wehrmacht was unable to cause enormous bloodshed; they still proved very effective in defensive tactics. German soldiers remained capable of inflicting serious losses on their opponents and were, despite everything, generally more effective in combat man-for-man than were British or American ground troops and, by a greater margin, than their Soviet opponents.[34] Although outnumbered and outgunned, German soldiers were able to inflict more casualties per man on their enemies than Allied soldiers were able to inflict on the Germans. This ability and determination to keep killing until the bitter end and, particularly, to inflict huge casualties on the Soviet Army during the last weeks of the war, helped to fuel the furious revenge of Soviet troops when they arrived in Germany (most notably the orgy of rape which accompanied the arrival of Soviet soldiers in central Europe – in particular in Budapest, Vienna and Berlin – at the end of April and beginning of May 1945). But the fact that the Wehrmacht was so comprehensively outnumbered, outgunned and outsupplied, and unable to move effectively, coupled with the determination of its leadership to throw as many men as possible into combat, ensured that there would be astronomical numbers of casualties on all sides until the Germans finally surrendered.

The huge numbers of casualties were not limited to members of the Wehrmacht, but extended to the hapless auxiliaries who were drafted to make real the Nazi fantasies of a people in arms stopping the invader. Lacking serious military training, effective combat experience and adequate weaponry, the *Volkssturm* contributed to the huge casualty figures. The hopeless condition of the *Volkssturm* was reflected in the description by one member of a battalion hurriedly thrown onto the Oder front at the beginning of February 1945:

The equipment consists of brown uniforms and coats with Italian steel helmets; snow jackets no longer are available, so that the men stand out against the snow especially clearly. The consequences are losses that could be avoided, also losses due to strafing. In addition, our own troops shot at the battalion, assuming that we were Russians. The footwear – in so far as it is not private property and good – consists of military boots that let in any moisture. There are only two field kitchens for the entire battalion.

The armament consists of rifles. Machine guns and other heavy weapons no longer are available. 1200 oval and stick hand grenades have been sent without fuses, which despite constant efforts could not be obtained. They therefore are useless.

As military action began immediately after we were transported, there was no training whatsoever with any weapon or in the field. 60 per cent of the men are completely untrained, the remainder are old soldiers.[35]

They were little more than cannon fodder, and displayed little enthusiasm to join the hopeless struggle despite exhortations to defend their towns 'to the last man and to the last bullet'. One *Volkssturm* unit after another failed to fight when Allied soldiers arrived.[36] Not surprisingly, as the war drew to a close, Germans drafted into *Volkssturm* units were reluctant to die or suffer lasting injury (and to increase the damage done to their own communities) for an obviously lost cause. A description of the *Volkssturm*'s last stand in Aalen in Württemberg (to the east of Stuttgart) in April 1945 makes this abundantly clear:

On 17 April the *Volkssturm* was called up. Out of 120 men from each company roughly 20–25 presented themselves, the rest stayed at home despite the threat of rope and bullet. Colonel Fischer threatened the commander of the *Volkssturm* with court martial, but in vain as even he could not magic one up.

The weaponry of the Ahlen *Volkssturm* consisted of four French machine guns without suitable ammunition and 30 rifles, some of Czech and some of Italian origin, as well as a number of hand-held anti-tank weapons. It was a crime to order such a badly armed unit against an opponent with modern equipment. [. . .]

The *Volkssturm* did not go into action. When they asked what they should do, the answer came: 'Await further orders.'

On Sunday afternoon only roughly 25 men of the entire *Volkssturm* were still in position, the rest already had sidled off. [. . .]

On 22 April news came of the advance of the Americans. Their tanks rolled by [. . .] and met with no resistance except in Lippach.

The *Volkssturm* in the approaches to Ahlen had wound itself up and had gone home.[37]

The men in the Wehrmacht, however, could not simply go home when Allied soldiers arrived. They had to face the full hopelessness of Germany's military position as the blows against the 'Thousand-Year Reich' came thick and fast in 1945. In the West the Ardennes Offensive had been checked by Christmas Eve; by the end of January, American forces once again were in possession of the territory they had held when the German offensive had begun. What had been launched as a reckless offensive designed to recapture Antwerp and, as Hitler had put it, 'to make it clear to the enemy that . . . he can never count on our capitulation, never, never',[38] ended in a fiasco which effectively used up the reserves of the Army and the Luftwaffe. In the east on 12 January the Soviet Army took advantage of the weakened state of a Wehrmacht which had diverted resources for its failed operations in the west: Soviet armies launched the first of a series of vast offensives over virtually the entire front from the Baltic to the Carpathian mountains; by the end of the month they had driven forward from the Vistula to the Oder.

The forces still at Hitler's disposal, however tough and skilful they may have been, were handicapped increasingly by problems of supply. During these final months of the war, as German transport and communications were so disrupted and fuel supply so diminished that the ability of the Wehrmacht to fight effectively was undercut, the hopes of the Allied advocates of massive aerial bombing finally were realized. While the suffering the bombardment caused to innocent civilians was enormous, and although its continuation and intensification in 1945 has been condemned as 'manifest insanity' (Angus Calder) and as 'morally and militarily wrong' (Toby Thacker),[39] the campaign appeared finally to justify the assertions of Arthur Harris, Chief of Britain's Bomber Command, that the merciless bombing of Germany would make a decisive contribution to Allied victory. It was the conditions that resulted which, more than anything else, in late January 1945 at last convinced Albert Speer that no realistic hope existed for an armistice settlement; that Nazi Germany's war was lost and that military collapse was inevitable.[40] The railways, which had been Germany's principal means for transporting men and supplies over long distances, were paralysed by the bombing. By February/March they were scarcely functioning at all.[41] Now that the ability of the Luftwaffe, lacking the necessary fuel to get its remaining aircraft off the ground, to offer resistance to Allied incursions had disappeared, Allied bombers were largely unopposed: in March 1945 the bombing reached its peak, with the British and Americans dropping over 133,000 tons of bombs in a single month.[42] German forces could not easily – if at all – move supplies and replacements to the front; troop units were pinned down due to constant strafing by Allied fighters and acute lack of fuel; and the destruction of communications systems made it increasingly difficult for German forces to coordinate their operations.

That said, it was the vast Soviet offensive of January 1945 that broke the back of the Wehrmacht and removed, both among the Nazi leadership and among the population at large, any serious hope of avoiding defeat. Involving five Soviet Army groups altogether (the First, Second and Third Belorussian Fronts and the First and Fourth Ukrainian Fronts), it was the greatest offensive operation of the Second World War, and the first which resulted in the Allied conquest of large swathes of German territory. Facing the massed troops of the Red Army were the battered forces of the Wehrmacht's Army Group Centre and Army Group A. The numbers of troops involved on the Soviet side were staggering. The Soviet First Belorussian Front (under the command of Marshal Georgi Zhukov) and First Ukrainian Front (under Marshal Ivan Koniev) had 2.2 million men with 7000 tanks and armoured vehicles at their disposal in central Poland; facing them were the 400,000 troops of the Wehrmacht's Army Group A, a depleted force which could muster only a single division to defend each 24 kilometres of front and a mere 300 tanks altogether.[43] To the north 1.67 million men and 3800 tanks and armoured vehicles of the Second and Third Belorussian Fronts (under the command of Marshals Konstantin Rokossovsky and Alexandr Vasilevsky respectively) were poised to smash through East Prussia.

In his memoirs, General Heinz Guderian, the man who, after being named Chief of the German General Staff on 21 July 1944 (the day after the bomb plot of 20 July) had promised Hitler to stop the Red Army at the borders of East Prussia and who in his New Year's message to the army expressed his 'unshakeable belief in the Leader',[44] claimed that 'the superiority of the Russians amounted to 11:1 in infantry, 7:1 in tanks, 13:1 in artillery'.[45] Guderian may have been exaggerating somewhat the advantage of the Russians in an attempt to minimize his own responsibility for the German military disaster of January 1945; other estimates put the Soviet superiority in tanks, for example, at just over three to one.[46] But that was superiority enough, and the Wehrmacht's position was made even worse by the fact that the men and supplies which the Germans still possessed could not necessarily be moved up to the front. According to Albert Speer, the extreme fuel shortages contributed 'essentially to the rapid collapse of the German front' when the Russians drove forward through Poland towards the Oder.[47]

What Hitler, who had vetoed Guderian's requests to bolster the eastern front against a possible Soviet offensive, initially had dismissed as 'the greatest bluff since Ghengis Khan'[48] turned into a military avalanche. After a massive artillery barrage in the early morning hours, at 8:00 a.m. on Friday, 12 January the 'long-awaited major attack of the enemy'[49] on the eastern front began. Soviet forces launched assault after assault along a vast front, aiming to drive first from the Vistula to the Oder and then from the Oder to the Elbe, thus bringing the war to a speedy conclusion. On 12 January the First Ukrainian Front attacked with overwhelming force from their bridgehead at Sandomierz and Baranóv in southern Poland, pushing forward by 15 kilometres on the first day;[50] 24 hours later the Third Belorussian Front opened its attack in the north, along the eastern frontier of East

Prussia; and on the following day, 14 January, the First and Second Belorussian Fronts began the main thrust of the offensive to the north and south of Warsaw, in the central area of the German-Soviet front. By 15 January, the day on which Hitler left for Berlin from what had been his 'Eagle's Nest' headquarters in the west during the Ardennes campaign,[51] Soviet forces had broken through German lines at every point where they attacked; the main fighting forces of the Wehrmacht's Army Group A had been either bypassed, surrounded or annihilated. Within three days the Soviet offensive had become a German rout, and along a 250-kilometre front to the north of Warsaw a coherent German front no longer existed.[52] The weather, with freezing conditions but little snow on the ground, proved ideal for the attacking Soviet tanks,[53] whose formations rushed forward, sometimes by as much as 70 to 80 kilometres in a single day; by 17 January Soviet forces had advanced between 130 and 180 kilometres west of their initial positions – double the operational plans and expectations of the Soviet High Command when the offensive had begun[54] – and the Wehrmacht had vacated Warsaw.

Hitler reacted to the crisis in a characteristic manner, ordering that every tactical movement be reported to him in good time so that he could intervene in operations down to divisional level and compel German units not to surrender any ground.[55] The front was to be held at any price, German troops surrounded by enemy forces were to fight to the last breath, and 'fortress' cities were to be defended to the end. No tactical retreat was permitted. But the tactics which had saved the Wehrmacht from collapse at the gates of Moscow in the winter of 1941/42 were pointless in the winter of 1944/45. German forces were so outnumbered and outgunned that Hitler's determination to hold the line no matter what could at best only postpone the inevitable for a short period – and at a terrible cost in human life. Nothing could stop the onslaught. After only a week, the Wehrmacht's defensive positions had been smashed or bypassed; on 18 January, Marshal Zhukov was able to report that the Germans were unable to offer effective resistance, and ordered his tank units to accelerate the charge forward.[56]

★

On 19 January Lodz and Krakow fell to the Russians, and Soviet forces had reached the old Reich border in the Upper Silesian industrial region. On 20 January Zhukov's forces were at the gates of Posen (Poznań), and on 22 January Koniev's troops had reached the Oder near Steinau. By 23 and 24 January they had reached the Oder both upstream and downstream from Breslau, established bridgeheads on the western side of the river at Steinau and at Oppeln, and thus denied the Germans the possibility of holding the line at the Oder. Further north Zhukov's troops, having smashed their way through the German lines between Bromberg and Posen, reached the former borders of the Reich between Krenz and Unruhstadt on 26 January. On the following day, in the south of Poland, troops of the 28th and 106th Corps of the First Ukrainian Front liberated the camps at Auschwitz.[57]

By the end of the month, along the central part of the eastern front, the Soviet Army had captured the entire Upper Silesian industrial region to the south and the towns of Schwiebus, Schwerin and Landsberg to the north almost without a fight. With the loss of this industrial region (which, unlike the Ruhr, largely had escaped heavy bombing, and whose loss, according to Speer at the time, spelled the immediate reduction of Germany's war production by a quarter),[58] the writing was on the wall. Without Upper Silesian coal, Guderian noted in his memoirs, 'the continuation of the war had become a question of a few months'.[59] However, this realization did not prevent Guderian from ordering at the end of January that defensive barriers be set up between the Oder and Berlin, and in mid-February that preparations be made for blowing up the bridges across the Elbe.[60] At the same time, on 30 January, units of the First Belorussian Front reached the Oder to the south of Küstrin, where they managed to establish a bridgehead over the river on the following day. Near the village of Kienitz, to the north of Küstrin, Russian infantry and artillery were crossing the iced-over river.[61] By the beginning of February Soviet forces were laying siege to Frankfurt on the Oder and to Küstrin.[62] After the war, General Vassili Chuikov (who had commanded Soviet troops at Stalingrad and whose Eighth Guards Army made rapid progress across Poland in January 1945) asserted that, but for timidity at Soviet headquarters and lack of adequate supplies, the Red Army could have stormed on from Frankfurt and Küstrin to take Berlin in February.[63] Although Chuikov's opinion was not widely shared, there can be little doubt about the magnitude of what Soviet forces had achieved. In less than three weeks the forces of the First Belorussian Front had pushed forward some 570 kilometres, averaging over 30 kilometres per day.[64] However, the Soviet pause to resupply and consolidate gains allowed the Wehrmacht to construct defences between the front and Berlin which would greatly hinder the Red Army's progress over the next couple of months.

The progress of Soviet forces on their northern flank, in East Prussia, was not the immediate success that it was in central Poland and the south. However, after a week of bitter conflict during which German forces managed to maintain a military front through tenacious fighting and tactical withdrawals, there too the Wehrmacht was driven back.[65] On 18 January the troops of the Third Belorussian Front achieved their decisive breakthrough between Breitenstein and Schillen, and in the days which followed, one East Prussian town after another fell to the invaders: on 21 January Tilsit fell to the Red Army; on the 22nd Soviet forces occupied Allenstein; and on the 23rd the Russians were in Insterburg. The Red Army also reached Tannenberg, the site of Imperial Germany's victory over the Russians in August 1914 – but not before the Germans hastily blew up the huge Tannenberg Memorial and salvaged the remains buried there of Paul von Hindenburg, the hero of the 1914 battle and the man who, as Reich President, had appointed Hitler to head a government in 1933.[66] By the 26th, Soviet forces had reached the Baltic coast, cut East Prussia's land link with the remainder of Germany, and encircled the Wehrmacht's Fourth Army on the Frische Haff (the coastal lagoon which stretched southwest of Königsberg). Soviet forces now were only 20 kilometres away from Königsberg, and began to aim their artillery at the East Prussian capital. On the same day the Soviet Army arrived at Hitler's former military headquarters, the massive 'Wolf's Lair' complex near Rastenburg (which the Germans had blown up two days before), and had reached the defences around Königsberg.

On 29 January the Russians surrounded the East Prussian capital, and by mid-February almost the whole of East Prussia, with the exception of the region immediately around Königsberg, was in Soviet hands.

When Stalin met with Roosevelt and Churchill at Yalta in the Crimea from 4 to 11 February, he therefore could negotiate with his Western Allies from a position of considerable strength: the Wehrmacht had been dealt a decisive defeat, the Germans had been driven out of Poland, the Upper Silesian industrial region had been conquered, and the Red Army stood a mere 65 kilometres from Berlin. The German Army High Command now sought approval to evacuate the Courland and East Prussia and to withdraw troops from other fronts (Northern Italy, Norway and Yugoslavia) in order to defend the Reich in the east. Hitler would have none of it. Instead, to head his army groups he now named generals who he felt could be relied upon to follow his orders to hold out regardless of the circumstances: in East Prussia Colonel General Lothar Rendulic (who took command of the new Army Group North, cobbled together largely from the remnants of the Fourth Army); in Silesia Colonel General Ferdinand Schörner (who took command of the Army Group Centre, and who, despite – or perhaps because of – his high standing with Hitler as an uncompromising and ideologically driven commander, received approval for a tactical withdrawal from Upper Silesia at the end of January);[67] and in Pomerania at the head of the newly cobbled-together Army Group Vistula, the Reichsführer-SS Heinrich Himmler.

Himmler, who lacked any experience as a field commander, soon proved out of his depth and was replaced on 20 March as head of the Army Group Vistula by General Gotthard Heinrici. Schörner, however, rose to the occasion. Fanatically committed to the Nazi cause, slavish in his relationship to Hitler, and harsh towards those under his command, Schörner had risen rapidly through the ranks during the war. After commanding units in Greece in 1941 and southern Ukraine in 1944, on 20 July 1944 he was placed in command of the Army Group North, and in January 1945 became head of the new Army Group Centre. In the last months of the war Schörner distinguished himself by making liberal use of the death penalty against deserters and 'cowards' in order to stiffen morale in a desperate attempt to prevent Soviet troops from advancing on Berlin; as he reported to Hitler in March, he had to 'intervene harshly, in order to help overcome the consequences of an unremitting siege psychosis'.[68] Vice had its rewards, however short-lived they may have been: Schörner was made a Field Marshal on 5 April 1945 (the last Field Marshal to be appointed by Hitler), and in his testament Hitler named his favourite general to be the last Supreme Commander of the Army.

In the wake of the defeats in early 1945 the Wehrmacht frantically improvized: individual divisions were moved from other fronts to shore up the east, units were moved back and forth in order to plug gaps along the eastern front, and new divisions were cobbled together with 17-year-old recruits who had been given rudimentary military training and with older men from the *Volkssturm*.[69] Despite acute supply and transport difficulties, and lacking reserves, the fact that the Soviet Army paused at the Oder in order to consolidate the gains it had made in January allowed the Wehrmacht more or less to stabilize its front. At the beginning of February Himmler, as the new com-mander of the Army Group Vistula, was charged with preparing a comprehensive line of defence along the Oder, to prevent further Soviet advances onto its west bank and to beat back the bridgeheads which the Soviet Army already had established over the river.[70] This set the stage for two months of bloody fighting along the Oder, during which the Wehrmacht managed, in some places, to achieve minor tactical successes (such as the recapture of the Silesian towns of Lauban and Striegau in March).[71] Nevertheless, their successes in sta-bilizing their battered eastern front could only be temporary, until the next Soviet onslaught which would bring the Russians to Berlin.

In the west Germany's military situation was little better than in the east. The Ardennes campaign, although it had been a very unpleasant surprise for the Allies, succeeded only in leaving the Wehrmacht dan-gerously exposed along Germany's western frontier. Of the half million men who had been committed to the offensive, the Germans had suffered nearly 100,000 casualties,[72] and they had lost nearly all their tanks and a large proportion of their aircraft. (On 1 January 1945 the Luftwaffe sent 1035 aircraft out to attack Allied airfields in southern Holland and Belgium; while they managed to destroy about 180 Allied aircraft and to damage another 100, the Germans lost 277 planes – losses which could not be made good and which meant that never again would the Luftwaffe be able to mount a major operation.)[73] Altogether, the Wehrmacht suffered at least 130,000 casualties, including 19,000 dead, in the fighting in the Ardennes and Alsace, while U.S. forces took some 140,000 casualties, including 16,000 dead.[74] The Americans could make good their losses; two weeks after the battle the Americans had more soldiers, tanks and aircraft along Germany's western border than they had had in mid-December, before the Ardennes Offensive had been launched.

The Germans, however, could not replace what they had lost. Although the Wehrmacht continued to offer dogged resistance, by the end of January the armies under Eisenhower's command were back where they had been before the 'Battle of the Bulge' began. While they still could inflict damage on the Allies, the strength of the German forces defending their country's western borders had been broken.

The Western Allies now were poised for the push into the Reich. The next great barrier was the Rhine. The plan, agreed by the Combined Chiefs of Staff meeting in Malta on 1 February, was for British, Canadian and U.S. forces under Bernard Montgomery's command to cross the Rhine north of the Ruhr region and thence move towards Berlin; the remaining American armies, with French forces, were to clear the Rhineland and push forward south of the Ruhr. The renewed Allied offensives began on 8 February. Initially, however, progress was slow. After extensive bombing of the towns of Cleve and Goch and then a massive artillery barrage 'exceeding any the British had employed previously in this war',[75] the armies under Montgomery's command moved forward through the Reichswald Forest near the Dutch border. Although no longer capable of mounting major offensive operations and crippled by the total control of the air enjoyed by the Americans and British, the Wehrmacht still proved remarkably adept at defensive tactics, constructing numerous lines of defence in the forest and flooding the area. After a month of vicious fighting, the Allies achieved success, but not before the Wehrmacht had inflicted heavy casualties on the advancing British and Canadians and hardly a house in Cleve was left standing. The fighting in and around Cleve illustrates how mistaken it is to believe that by this stage of the war the Wehrmacht fought tenaciously only in the east, or that only the Russians were prepared to level German towns in their path. In early 1945 the fighting was incredibly bloody and destructive in the west as well as the east.

In Alsace and south-western Germany the Americans too found the going tough during February.[76] Even General George Patton, whose aggressive tank tactics had been so successful in the Ardennes, made slow progress as the American Army moved into the hilly woodlands of the Eifel towards Prün and Bitburg during February. The same was true of the fighting along the Germans' 'Westwall' fortifications in the Saar-Mosel Triangle, and it was not until the beginning of March that American forces were able to take the city of Trier. As the thousands of graves at the U.S. military cemetery by the Franco-German border near St Avold (the largest American military cemetery for the dead of the Second World War) testify, the Wehrmacht continued to kill large numbers of Americans in the early months of 1945.

Nevertheless, the Allies' vast superiority in men and materiel proved decisive, and by the end of February they had managed to push German forces back all along the west bank of the Rhine. The race to cross the river was on: Allied units charged ahead in the hope of finding a river crossing intact, and German defenders worked feverishly to blow up bridges before the Allies could cross them.[77] Although the Germans succeeded in causing further damage to their own country, it was only a matter of time before the Rhine would be breached. The moment came, famously and unexpectedly, on the afternoon of 7 March when troops of the 9th Armored Division of the American First Army arrived at the Rhine overlooking Remagen to the south of Bonn – by this time the Wehrmacht on the left bank of the Rhine was in full retreat – and to their amazement found the Ludendorff railway bridge over the river damaged but still usable. Troops of the American

27th Armored Infantry quickly crossed the bridge before the Germans could blow it up.[78] Within 24 hours 8000 American soldiers had crossed the river and established a bridgehead on the right bank. In the days that followed, thousands more American troops crossed this last major geographical obstacle standing between them and the heart of the Reich; by the time the bridge at Remagen finally collapsed some weeks later, eight bridges newly constructed by Allied forces were in use over the Rhine.[79] German forces were facing a military disaster in the west scarcely less serious than the one they faced in the east.

Had the Germans succeeded in destroying the bridge at Remagen before American troops could cross it, no doubt the Rhine soon would have been breached somewhere else. Indeed, the Americans had considered Remagen far from the best location from which to establish a bridgehead on the far side of the river. Nevertheless, Hitler reacted to the events at Remagen with characteristic fury. He used the occasion to replace Field Marshal Gerd von Rundstedt as commander of German forces in the west with Field Marshal Albert Kesselring (who had distinguished himself by his brutality when commanding German forces in Italy) on 10 March, and to order a flying court martial into action. This flying court martial did its job, which was not to determine the facts of what had happened, but to carry out sentences that would exercise, in Goebbels' words, an 'educative influence'. Between 11–13 March the court sentenced to death five officers implicated in the failure to blow up the bridge; four were shot immediately, while the fifth owed his survival to the fact that he was taken prisoner by the Americans.[80] In this way the men of the Wehrmacht were spurred on to destroy countless bridges as Allied armies swept into Germany. This campaign of destruction could not affect the outcome of the war, but it would cause enormous difficulties for the German people after the inevitable surrender.

By the time that Kesselring had replaced von Rundstedt, German forces in the west were 'so weak and widely dispersed, their communications so badly disrupted and the means of communication so disjointed and uncertain, that no overall commander could now exercise effective control over the whole front'.[81] Nothing now could hold back the Allied advance. By 7 March Cologne, which had been Germany's fourth largest city but by 1945 was little more than a bombed-out shell, was in American hands; on the following day Bonn and Bad Godesberg had been taken; and by the 10th, British and American forces were spread along the western bank of the Rhine from the Dutch border to Koblenz. A few days later, beginning on the 15th, American forces were moving through the Saar region and the Palatinate; on 22 March American troops crossed the Rhine at Oppenheim and pushed forward towards Groß-Gerau to the south of Frankfurt, by which time the Remagen bridgehead was 50 kilometres wide. On 24 March, after three days of massive Allied bombing to destroy the Germans' road and rail communications in the area, forces under Montgomery crossed the Rhine at Wesel, to the north of the Ruhr region; by 25 March there was no longer German resistance on the west bank of the Rhine. One after another, west German cities were occupied by Allied troops: Mainz on 22 March, Darmstadt on the 25th, Mannheim, Wiesbaden and Frankfurt on the 29th. Allied armies rushed forward – Montgomery's troops from the north and Hodges' U.S. First Army from the south (which by 27 March had reached Marburg, 110 kilometres east of the Rhine) – and on 1 April British and American forces met at Lippstadt. They had surrounded the entire Ruhr region, and with it Germany's largest industrial centre and 21 Wehrmacht divisions with over 300,000 troops.

With Soviet forces massing for their drive to Berlin from the east and with the Western Allies streaming into Germany from the west, it made little sense for German forces to keep fighting. Yet keep fighting they did. The person who was overheard to mutter in a Berlin air-raid shelter at the end of March, 'if our soldiers were as clever as in 1918, the war already would be over' was right. The same judgement could have been levelled at the German military leadership. In 1918 their counterparts – including the man who became the chief propagandist for 'total war', Erich Ludendorff – recognized that their strategic position had become hopeless, faced the fact that their war could not be won, and demanded that the German government seek an armistice.[82] In stark contrast, in a military situation which, during the first four months of 1945, was far worse, Germany's armed forces committed themselves to a suicidal strategy of self-destruction, of fighting on without any real hope of victory. The Wehrmacht leadership, keen to demonstrate their loyalty to Hitler after the failed bomb plot of 20 July 1944 (in which a number of officers had been involved) were prepared to fight on German territory and to the end, regardless of the consequences for the men under their command.[83]

As the Third Reich collapsed, the Wehrmacht leadership displayed no more consideration for the civilian population than they did for their soldiers. In eastern Germany, where the Soviet breakthrough in January had led to a human avalanche as millions of Germans fled westwards to escape the advancing Russians, the Wehrmacht did little or nothing to help. Notwithstanding the subsequent protestations of officers who justified their decisions in the last months and weeks of the war as an attempt to save the German people and the men under their command from capture by the enemy from the east, the actions of the German armed forces in early 1945 tell a different story.

By the beginning of 1945 nearly 10 million Germans – in large measure urban dwellers seeking refuge from the bombing, or ethnic Germans from eastern Europe who had moved westwards as the Red Army approached – had been evacuated from their homes. Consequently, there was general agreement between the Nazi Party and Wehrmacht leadership that 'thereby the capacity of Germany with regard to both housing space and provisions was reaching its limits', and that at least in the west 'if necessary, leaving the population behind in territory to be occupied by the enemy must be accepted'.[84] In the east, where the impending problem was far greater, the Wehrmacht in late 1944 had displayed little interest in preparing evacuation plans for the civilian population; and when the dam broke in January 1945, with some 3.5 million Germans fleeing westwards by the end of the month, there was no evidence of a fundamental change in attitude. As Heinrich Himmler, in his role as Commander of the Army Group Vistula, put it when he justified his decision to prohibit evacuation measures in Brandenburg, 'we are organizing defence and not running away'.[85] Hitler and Dönitz, the Commander of the Navy (and soon to become Hitler's successor) agreed: the highest priority for both shipping and the railways was to meet the needs of the military, not to transport terrified civilians westwards.[86] Although in many places German soldiers helped fleeing civilians, the callousness of their officers contributed to the deaths of hundreds of thousands of German civilians, who were left to flee westwards on foot and often were overtaken by the Red Army.

Things got no better as the end approached. In early March, retreating German troops in the Danzig region were described as having 'callously forced' civilians fleeing from the Russians off the roads and leaving them to their fate.[87] On 15 March, Albert Speer (who knew that 'the sacrifices that were made [. . .] from January 1945 were senseless') distributed an order by Hitler making brutally clear the priorities for the use of scarce transport capacity:

> In cases of evacuation the following sequence is to be applied: Wehrmacht for operational purposes, coal, food being cleared out. Even transports of refugees can be taken only after the total fulfilment of these requirements, if empty space that really is unused is available.[88]

Coal took precedence over people. And only three weeks before the German surrender, on 16 April, the Chief of Staff of the Armed Forces High Command, Wilhelm Keitel, rejected a proposal by representatives of the International Red Cross to provide safe zones for the civilian population in Berlin with the words: 'Rejection, because [it is] only an attempt to discover if the will to resist still exists!! Agreement would be the first step towards becoming soft.'[89] The priority of the Nazi regime and its armed forces was not to protect German women and children, but to fight to the very end.

The last three months of the war saw huge Allied encirclements, in which German armies and *Volkssturm* conscripts trapped inside 'fortress' cities were ordered to continue fighting to the last bullet. During February Soviet forces advanced into Pomerania from the south and cut off the Wehrmacht's Second Army in Danzig and West Prussia, to the east. On 22 February, after a murderous artillery bombardment, the Red Army took the citadel of Posen (Poznań), the birthplace of Paul von Hindenburg and the major railway junction between Berlin and Warsaw.[90] By the time that the Germans in the city capitulated, 28,000 of the 40,000 men who had been defending Posen were either dead or wounded. In March it was the turn of Kolberg on Pomerania's Baltic Sea coast, a town of particular symbolic importance. The apocalyptic scenes in Goebbels' last great film epic, *Kolberg*, showing the city besieged and blasted by French artillery during the Napoleonic Wars, became reality: on 7 March, a little more than a month after the film had been given its premier viewing (on 30 January, to Wehrmacht soldiers defending the fortress at La Rochelle on the Atlantic and in Berlin), Kolberg was surrounded by Soviet troops and declared a 'fortress'. Yet film did not imitate life, nor did life imitate film: whereas in the film the town's defenders prevailed against overwhelming odds, in 1945, as in 1806/07, the town fell to the enemy. On 18 March, after 68,000 civilians, over 1200 wounded, and more than 5000 soldiers had been evacuated by sea, the Soviet Army entered this 'fortress'.

At the end of March Danzig fell to the Russians, and the Wehrmacht withdrew to the Hela Peninsula and to the mouth of the Vistula, where Hitler ordered that they hold their positions at all costs. That they did, and when the war ended in May there still were some 200,000 German soldiers and refugees on Hela and at the mouth of the Vistula.[91] In the Courland and East Prussia a similar story unfolded. The 'Courland Army' (previously Army Group North) fought on, supplied by sea, until 8 May, when its 200,000 surviving soldiers finally surrendered. In East Prussia the Wehrmacht's Fourth Army had also been ordered by Hitler to fight to the last man. When its commander, Friedrich Hoßbach, ordered a tactical retreat in January to prevent his soldiers from becoming surrounded, he was dismissed by Hitler. His successor, Walter Weiß, proved more compliant, and proudly reported to Hitler at the end of March that his army had held out for ten weeks against a superior enemy and was 'defending every metre of German soil'.[92] As a consequence the Fourth Army was almost completely destroyed, and not until 25 March did Hitler approve its withdrawal from the Frische Haff northwards to the Samland (the peninsula north of Königsberg). Hitler ordered that from there only the badly wounded be evacuated by sea from East Prussia; the rest were sent back into action. By this time, Königsberg lay in ruins. German forces in the city surrendered on 9 April; and although the 'Fortress Commandant', General of the Infantry Otto Lasch, did not capitulate until the Russians had reached his command bunker, on the following day Hitler sentenced him to death in absentia.[93] Even after the fall of the East Prussian capital, the Wehrmacht still fought on in the Samland, and German forces in the port of Pillau did not surrender to the Soviet Army until 25 April.

The numbers of casualties in 1945 – German and Allied, military and civilian – were magnified by the determination of Hitler and Himmler to declare German cities threatened by Allied soldiers as fortresses which were to be held no matter what the cost. This was the tactic that supposedly would reverse Germany's fortunes at the eleventh hour. What had happened to the Wehrmacht at Stalingrad now was supposed to happen to the Allies across Germany; if the Soviet Union's war had its turning point in the merciless street-by-street fighting along the Volga, then Nazi Germany would achieve a similar outcome as the Allied invaders bled to death on the streets of German towns and cities. The war, in the Nazi leadership's vision, would end in a gigantic battle of attrition, in which a fanatically committed German people would grind down Allied armies and break the will of Allied soldiers to keep fighting.[94] Nazi Germany would never surrender. Instead of capitulating as they had in 1918, the Germans implacably would wear down the invader – or else go down in flames so as to set an example for future generations which someday might take up the struggle once again.[95] Thus, during the first four months of 1945, town after German town was surrounded by Soviet forces, to face the prospect of the most destructive imaginable final battle before the inevitable capitulation of 'fortresses' where civilians were trapped, where massive artillery fire from the surrounding forces caused huge casualties among soldiers and civilians alike, and where the Wehrmacht and the ill-trained and ill-equipped *Volkssturm* units were expected to fight to their last breath.

What this meant was illustrated by the fate of Breslau, the capital of Silesia and the largest city in eastern Germany. When, only two weeks after their great January offensive had been launched, Soviet forces reached the Oder both upstream and downstream from the Silesian capital, which now occupied a key position in the defence of south-eastern Germany against the Soviet onslaught, Breslau was to become a battleground. On 22 January the front pages of the city's newspapers carried an announcement by the Silesian Nazi Party Gauleiter and 'Reich Defence Commissar', Karl Hanke, that Breslau had been declared a 'fortress'; that the city's women and children were being evacuated; that the 'men of Breslau' were to 'take their position in the defence of our fortress Breslau', and that 'the fortress will be defended to the bitter end'.[96] (At the same time, however, Hanke – who himself remained in the 'Fortress Breslau' – moved the regional government offices to the comparative safety of Hirschberg and Waldenburg in the foothills of the Sudeten mountains.)[97] It was not long before the 'men of Breslau' would have their opportunity to fight and die. Soon after the Red Army broke out from its bridgeheads at Steinau and Ohlau on 8 February, the entire northern Silesian plain was in Russian hands; and during the night of 15/16 February Breslau was surrounded completely by Soviet forces. By then, the city's population numbered fewer than a third of the 600,000 people who had lived there before the war, and fewer than a fifth of the nearly one million people – many fleeing the Russians from further east – who had crowded there in mid-January. For the city's defence, the German 'fortress commandant', Hans von Ahlfen, could call on approximately 45,000–50,000 men in total – *Volkssturm* formations together with hastily assembled Wehrmacht units, and Waffen-SS reservists; facing them were thirteen divisions of the Soviet Army's First Ukrainian Front under Marshal Koniev.[98]

Just days after surrounding the Silesian capital, Koniev's forces made their first thrust towards the city centre. Soviet tanks attacked from the south and moved up their heavy artillery; house after house was set alight with incendiary grenades, which took a terrible toll on the civilian population. The Germans were able to repel this assault and to stabilize the front, but their successes served only to prolong the suffering. The city was pounded daily by Soviet artillery, and corpses became a regular feature on the city's streets. Cut off from the rest of the Reich, all railway transport having ceased in mid-February, Breslau could be supplied only by air, from the airport at Gandau just outside the city. However, realizing that it was only a matter of time until the Russian advance made the use of Gandau impossible, in March the Germans set about constructing a makeshift airstrip along the Kaiserstraße, a wide boulevard to the east of the old city centre: buildings along the Kaiserstraße were detonated; men, women and children were put to work shifting the rubble, while Soviet artillery was aimed at the intended landing strip and Russian fighter planes strafed the area.[99] In the event, the improvized landing strip proved of little value, and when Gandau was lost at the beginning of April it spelled the end of the evacuation of the wounded from Breslau.[100] Altogether, the German forces defended the beleaguered city for nearly three months. On 6 April, referring to the 140,000 'desperate' civilians trapped in the besieged city, the last 'fortress commandant' General Hermann Niehoff (who had replaced von Ahlfen on 9 March) requested permission to surrender, a request brusquely refused by Hitler, and then went on loyally to continue the senseless struggle for another month.[101] 'Fortress Breslau' did not surrender until 6 May, a week after Hitler had killed himself and four days after Berlin had fallen to the Red Army. By the time Niehoff finally capitulated to the Russians, two thirds of the city had been destroyed, 20,000 houses had disappeared, roughly 6000 German and 8000 Soviet soldiers, and at least 10,000 civilians (including 3000 suicides) were dead.[102]

The agony of the inhabitants of eastern Germany's other major city, Königsberg, was scarcely less terrible. The east Prussian capital had been cut off by the forces of the Soviet Army's Third Belorussian Front at the end of January, becoming the first major German city to be besieged by the Russians. Königsberg was indeed a fortified city already: it was encircled by 14 forts, each containing roughly 800 defenders, but these fortifications with their stone walls dating from the previous century were hardly capable of withstanding the sort of assault mounted by the five Soviet armies under Ivan Chernyakovsky's command.[103] The tens of thousands of civilians trapped inside the fortress were called upon to produce makeshift weapons for Königsberg's ill-equipped defenders; the city was prepared for street-to-street fighting, with trenches dug and the cellars of buildings fortified. Constant artillery barrages made everyday tasks extraordinarily dangerous: over a thousand Soviet bombers, accompanied by hundreds of support aircraft and fighters, constantly dropped explosives; buildings were being destroyed and fires were breaking out throughout the besieged city. In this utterly hopeless situation the 'Fortress Commandant', General Lasch, had little to offer the 35,000 soldiers under his command other than death:

> Comrades! [. . .] The Fatherland demands of us an unconditional and final engagement. Only if we resolutely and properly stand side by side in this spirit do we have a future. Lack of discipline, however, brings the danger of our complete and dishonourable annihilation. [. . .] We want to fight as the Fatherland expects of us. Then we can be certain that we will gain something by fighting: if not our life, then our honour![104]

The language of sacrifice and 'honour' was all that remained – but that was insufficient to prevent Lasch from being condemned to death in absentia after finally capitulating to the Russians on 9 April. By that time, the city where Prussia's kings once had been crowned, had been reduced to rubble, with thousands of its inhabitants dead or injured and 130,000 survivors (compared to a pre-war population of more than 300,000) facing more horror under Soviet rule.

Such stubborn, suicidal tactics ensured that the last months of the war were the bloodiest, and that the most extreme violence and bloodshed occurred within Germany. The fighting in early 1945 was incredibly destructive, with huge Allied offensives supported by massive firepower rolling over German positions, alternating with periods of dogged stationary fighting in German cities and towns where the defenders had been ordered to hold out at all costs. The Wehrmacht remained capable of limited tactical successes almost to the end, managing to mount offensive operations in Hungary in early March and to defend the Seelow Heights to the west of the Oder – where in mid-April the 129,000 men of the German 9th Army managed to hold back and inflict serious casualties on the more than 900,000 soldiers of Marshal Zhukov's First Belorussian Front.[105] Yet such successes came at a huge price. German forces were able to postpone the inevitable only by throwing everything they still had into battle. But 'everything' was not much: It was only a matter of a weeks until the Germans could fight no more.

That the Wehrmacht nevertheless continued to fight despite its mounting logistical problems, its almost total lack of resources, and the widespread realization that the war was lost – and despite the utter senselessness of the continued carnage – had a number of causes. No doubt there were some who continued to place their faith in an apocalyptic Nazi ideology and in the Leader, although such people were becoming increasingly rare; and ever more numbers were prepared openly to blame Hitler for the disastrous war (with some expressing the opinion that only Hitler himself still believed in a miracle).[106] And no doubt, too, fear of the Soviet invader spurred on many who expected to be killed in any case once the 'Bolshevik hordes' arrived to take revenge for the crimes committed by Germans in the USSR. But there were more immediate causes. In the extreme conditions of early 1945, people's horizons became limited to day-to-day survival. The sense of comradeship, not wanting to let down one's fellow soldiers, and of sharing a common fate as their world came crashing down, assumed tremendous importance.[107] At the same time, the alternatives to continuing to fight were removed when military commanders led their men into positions where they were surrounded by enemy forces and had nowhere to run, and as the regime's terror against its own troops intensified.

In particular, Wehrmacht 'justice' against its own soldiers, already incredibly harsh, became even more draconian in the war's final months.[108] The military leadership grew increasingly desperate to prevent their men from deserting – a possibility open to many more German soldiers now that so many were fighting within Germany, where they spoke the language and could find refuge among the civilian population. In early February the Chief of Staff of the Army Group Vistula admitted that 'in the Wehrmacht we find ourselves in a leadership crisis of the greatest extent: The officer corps no longer has firm control of the troops. Among the troops themselves there are manifestations of disintegration of the worst kind. It is no isolated occurrence that soldiers remove their uniforms and attempt by all possible means to obtain civilian clothing in order to get away.'[109] With hundreds of thousands of German civilians fleeing westwards from East Prussia, Pomerania and Silesia ahead of the Russians, it became increasingly tempting for soldiers to shed their uniforms and join the treks of refugees. Military police combed the territory behind the front lines for deserters and were given powers of summary court martial; tens of thousands of soldiers were caught and immediately sent back into battle; hundreds were summarily executed, some without any trial whatsoever.[110] The aim was to exact revenge on alleged cowards and to terrorize into submission the rest, who effectively had no legal protection against their own army. The executions were well publicized among the troops – as for example when the soldiers in the Military District X (Hamburg) were informed that 'on 27 March 1945, 21 soldiers, who the court martial has sentenced to death for desertion, were shot in Hamburg', and that 'every shirker and coward will face the same fate without mercy'.[111] A few weeks later the last shred of legal trapping was stripped from the campaign against allegedly defeatist elements within the Wehrmacht when, in his 'Call to the Soldiers of the Eastern Front' on 15 April, Hitler ordered: 'Whoever gives you orders to retreat, without you knowing him exactly, is to be arrested at once and if necessary bumped off immediately – whatever rank he holds.'[112] The Supreme Commander and Head of State made it clear that neither legality nor military hierarchy were to be respected. German soldiers were expected to fight and to die, and if they hesitated they were to be killed by their comrades.

Although by April 1945 the reach of Hitler's orders was shrinking daily, the harsh measures had their effect. While many German soldiers managed to escape the Wehrmacht in the last weeks of war, most continued to fight, in the west as well as in the east even though, as the Army command in the west had admitted in mid-February, they were exhausted and 'generally fed up'.[113] Morale remained 'depressed, but not bad', according to the Commander of the Army Group South in March,[114] and the Wehrmacht kept fighting. A repetition of November 1918, the great obsession of the Nazi and military leadership (many of whom had witnessed the collapse of 1918 as junior officers), did not materialize. According to a Wehrmacht report, drafted on 19 March, of an inspection visit in the area around the Remagen-Siegburg bridgehead over the Rhine: 'Apart from exceptional cases – there really are no signs of a revolution-soldier in the mould of 1918.' Nevertheless, while the 'old fighters' allegedly remained 'steadfast' and while 'the Army from the general to the foot-soldier is bearing a constant burden that really deserves appreciation', the report noted that many exhausted and dispirited soldiers were reacting passively to their dire predicament:

> An unwelcome phenomenon that already has spread widely is the apathetic and tired soldier who fights only when he is directed by an officer but then quickly collapses again. He is often completely listless, neither courts martial nor punishments nor the harshest orders impress him.
>
> The next type is the coward and deserter who just allows himself to be overrun without shooting.[115]

Despite draconian orders threatening execution, soldiers who became separated from their units failed to display 'the desire to join up with the fighting troops' but instead showed an 'intention to wander from one post to another at least for a few days'.[116] Matters were made yet more difficult for the army leadership by the fact that 'given the apparent hopelessness of the struggle' German civilians displayed little enthusiasm for having the Wehrmacht make a last stand near them: 'The population is worn down by the air terror and also does not want the final battle in their town.'[117] In his memoirs, Albert Speer described how Field Marshal Kesselring, then Wehrmacht Supreme Commander in the west, reported to Hitler that 'the populace was playing a negative role in the struggle against the advancing American forces':

More and more often the people did not allow our own troops to enter the villages. Deputations would go to the officers to beg them not to cause the destruction of localities by defending them. In many cases the troops had yielded to these desperate pleas.[118]

Hitler's answer was that the population of threatened areas should be forcibly evacuated. After some discussion, according to Speer, Hitler concluded, 'We can no longer afford to concern ourselves with the population.'[119]

Not surprisingly, there was little popular enthusiasm for the Nazi apocalypse. The carnage and destruction occurring on German soil for the sake of an obviously lost cause put the goals of the military leadership increasingly at odds with the hopes and interests of the German population, and contributed significantly to the disintegration of popular support for, and belief in, the legitimacy of the Nazi government. An armed force which, until early 1945, might have been regarded as defending the German nation against a bloodthirsty enemy, increasingly was looked on as a threat whose continued operations often served to undermine what little security German civilians still possessed. And yet, the fighting continued. Civilians did not rebel, and soldiers did not turn on their leaders; generally they kept fighting when they had to, but with increasing passivity in the hope that soon the war would be over and they might survive.

The apocalyptic rhetoric of the Nazi leadership notwithstanding, it was in January 1945 that the German people finally abandoned hope of avoiding total defeat and Allied occupation. Although Germans had made enormous sacrifices during the first five years of the war, as military casualties mounted (particularly in the east) and as German cities were pounded by British and American bombers (particularly in the west), there remained the hope that Germany somehow might avoid 'unconditional surrender' – a hope which had motivated the plotters of 20 July 1944. However, with the collapse of the eastern front in 1945, the last glimmer of such hope was snuffed out. It was at this point that the Allied bombing contributed to breaking German civilian morale, as its British proponents had long predicted it would and as Goebbels now admitted that it had;[120] there no longer seemed any point in attempting to withstand the terrible toll of the bombing – prolonging the war would only increase the damage done before the inevitable surrender. As the casualties and suffering of the German people mounted to levels never before experienced, it became obvious to everyone – even to Albert Speer, whose efforts to maintain production of the materials required for war had been essential to sustain the slaughter of the last and most bloody year of the conflict – that there was no rational purpose in making further sacrifice.

During April the Wehrmacht finally collapsed. It was then, in the spring of 1945, that the very last act in the history of the Nazi regime was played out. The inevitable finally happened: the overwhelming superiority of the Allies on the ground and their complete control of the air, the inability of the Germans to move their troops effectively or to make good the losses of men and supplies, acute shortages of weapons and ammunition, and the loss of large portions of the Reich itself finally led to the complete collapse of the German military effort. Heinrich Himmler's order of 12 April 1945, demanding yet again the defence of 'every village and every city with all means', now had little effect: the Allies were marching through Germany at so rapid a pace, and the numbers of Germans prepared to support the pointless destruction of their country was diminishing so quickly, that the resonance of such demands for self-destruction had become minimal.[121] Finally the Nazi regime was disintegrating under the pressure of comprehensive military defeat. The Nazi war machine was now an empty shell, and all that was left of Hitler's 'Greater German Reich' was a country in shock. The military campaigns within Germany during the first four months of 1945 were of such force, of such overwhelming violence, that they delivered a profound shock to the German people. It was a shock which framed the ways in which Germans emerged from the nightmare of the Second World War to put their experiences of Nazism and war behind them.[122]

*

On 6 March the last German military offensive of the Second World War, 'Operation Spring Awakening' was launched in Hungary.[123] By mid-March it was halted, and on 16 March Soviet forces mounted their counter offensive. Within days German lines had been broken and German formations crushed, forcing the Wehrmacht to retreat to the Austrian border. By 3 April the Russians were at the southern suburbs of Vienna, and ten days later the Soviet Army captured the Austrian capital. In the west, at the beginning of April British and American forces had surrounded the Ruhr region. With his forces overwhelmed and without adequate supplies, but ordered by Hitler to treat the entire Ruhr region as a 'fortress', Field Marshal Walther Model shot himself on 17 April; Germany's largest industrial region, the heart of the German war economy, was captured and 317,000 Wehrmacht troops were taken prisoner. With American forces now racing eastwards across Germany, on 16 April the Russians had launched their massive offensive to take Berlin. A week later, on 23 April, they reached the southern city limits of the Reich capital. On 25 April, the day that Soviet forces had surrounded Berlin completely, Russian and American soldiers met near Torgau on the Elbe. The Third Reich was cut in half, the Wehrmacht command was split in two, and the fate of the Reich capital was sealed.

3

MURDER AND MAYHEM

How incomprehensible the Germans are, that they are still killing one another at the last minute, destroying their country with their own hands. Ursula von Kardorff[1]

In his posthumous memoir, Hugo Gryn, who later became a prominent rabbi in Britain, described the march on which, as an adolescent, he was forced to participate from Lieberose (a camp some 30 kilometres north of Cottbus) to the Sachsenhausen concentration camp, north of Berlin, in early February 1945:

> By this time, the hunger was very great and it was bitterly cold. Then we had to evacuate Lieberose and go to Sachsenhausen on foot. When we left Lieberose, we were marched some distance away, stopped, and then we heard lots of firing and then [there was] smoke. They killed and set on fire everybody who could not move out. This march was dreadful. Snow, mud. And when dusk came, turn left or turn right, walk into the nearest field, get down. In the morning, get up, except for those who could not get up, then we would move forward, wait a while, hear the shots and move on.[2]

Of the 1400 men who started on the march on 2 February, Gryn recollected, only 900 arrived at Sachsenhausen on 10 February. The

remainder of the roughly 3000 prisoners at Lieberose had been massacred before the march began.

The trek from Lieberose to Sachsenhausen, a distance of roughly
130 kilometres, was only one of the many death marches which took
place across Germany during the last months of the war as the Nazi
regime was stripped to its essentials: violence and murder.[3] As the territories under Nazi rule shrank back to, and then within, the borders
of Germany, and as those who once had terrorized the whole of
Europe brought their recently developed skills back home to the
Reich, the criminal violence of the regime continued while its
administrative structures disintegrated. In its final blood-soaked
months, the crumbling Nazi regime inflicted further violence and suffering on those still within its grasp: the inhabitants of the prisons and
the concentration camp empire, the foreign labourers who had been
compelled to work in the German war economy, and those Germans
unwilling to sacrifice themselves in desperate campaigns staged to
delay the inevitable capitulation.

Unlike the Nazi campaigns of mass murder through 1944 – the
attempt to murder Europe's entire Jewish population, the onslaught
against the Gypsies, the deliberate starvation of millions of Soviet
prisoners of war, the massacre of civilians across occupied Europe and
eastern Europe in particular – the terror and killings in Germany in
early 1945 were the consequence of the regime's breakdown rather
than of its cohesion. And they took place against the background of
a widespread public recognition that Germany's war was lost. The
erosion of public order drove the Nazi police state to lash out against
foreign labourers who appeared to pose a growing threat of crime,
and against 'racial comrades' who dared to admit that the war was lost;
the destruction of Germany's infrastructure meant that the already
inadequate provisioning of the concentration camps and prisons collapsed; huge numbers of prisoners were being herded into camps
inside what remained of German territory, and the breakdown of
social and health services meant that the German victims of the
bombing and fighting were left to depend largely on their own
resources.

★

The most terrible aspect of the murder and mayhem of the last months of Nazi rule was the final chapter of the history of the concentration camps. The German military collapse at the beginning of 1945 created huge problems in running the camps, and led to the worst conditions and highest death rates seen in the concentration camps (as opposed to the extermination camps, whose sole purpose had been to kill human beings) during the entire war. First in the east, with the Soviet offensive beginning in mid-January 1945, and then in the west as the Americans, British and Canadians crossed the Rhine and streamed eastwards, camp after camp was liberated by Allied armed forces. The Germans, for their part, were keen to cover their tracks and hastily evacuated camps and prisons in order to prevent the inmates being freed by the rapidly advancing Allied armies. Prisoners, already gravely weakened by their treatment, were put on trains in the dead of winter and transported, often in goods wagons, without food or sanitary facilities, or – as Germany's rail system broke down – were forced onto what became death marches, often without any particular end to the march in sight. The number of victims was enormous. Towards the end of the war the number of prisoners in the SS concentration camp empire had mushroomed as more and more were used as slave labour in the German war economy. In January 1945, when the evacuations from Auschwitz, Groß Rosen in Lower Silesia (about 60 kilometres south west of Breslau) and Stutthof near Danzig, began, there were 714,211 prisoners in the Reich (some 511,537 men and 202,674 women, of whom roughly 200,000 were Jews) – nearly 200,000 more than during the previous summer.[4] Guarding them were some 40,000 SS personnel. Of the approximately 700,000 prisoners in the camps in January, somewhere between 200,000 and 350,000 died during the winter and early spring of 1945.[5] Starvation, freezing to death, disease, and shooting by guards on death marches claimed the lives of tens of thousands just weeks, and then days, before the camps in which they had suffered were liberated.

Throughout the concentration camp empire, conditions deteriorated drastically during the last months of the war as the numbers of prisoners grew and supplies dried up. In Buchenwald, to the north of

Weimar, where large numbers of evacuees arrived from Auschwitz and Groß Rosen in early 1945, nearly 14,000 people died between January and the beginning of April.[6] In Mauthausen, 25 kilometres upstream from Linz in Austria, the highest monthly death rates during the camp's entire existence were recorded for the period January–April 1945 – some four times the death rate over the preceding nine months; roughly 45,000 prisoners died there between the onset of winter in 1944/1945 and the beginning of the following summer.[7] (Mauthausen, the first concentration camp to have been established outside the borders of the 'old Reich', also had received evacuees from Auschwitz and Groß Rosen in early 1945.) Particularly dreadful were conditions in the Mittelbau–Dora camp complex near Nordhausen in Thuringia, where prisoners had been forced to work in huge underground tunnels assembling, among other things, V-1 flying bombs and V-2 rockets.[8] During the last months of the war some 60,000 prisoners, many of whom were evacuees from Auschwitz and Groß Rosen, were sent to Mittelbau–Dora. Weak, desperately ill captives were transported in open railway carriages in the middle of winter, and prisoners barely strong enough to walk were forced on death marches as the SS disposed of those described as 'weak' and 'not capable of work'.[9] Shortly after his liberation in 1945, a prisoner who had been forced to unload the dead and dying from rail cars as they arrived at Mittelbau–Dora described the scene:

> These people were evacuated from a camp in Poland before the Russian offensive. They were transported from Poland to central Germany in open goods wagons for 20 days without food. On the way they froze, starved or were shot. Men, women and children of all ages were among them. When we took hold of the dead, arms, legs or heads often came off in our hands, as the corpses were frozen.[10]

Between mid-January and mid-February 1945 the number of prisoners at the main Mittelbau–Dora camp increased by 50 per cent; housing provision was primitive; death due to undernourishment and disease common. And, if that were not enough, the camp administration reacted to the worsening conditions by stepping up the terror: in March 1945, 150 prisoners were hanged.[11]

No less dreadful was what happened to the prisoners of Neuengamme in Hamburg – hardly the most notorious of the camp complexes – which encompassed 57 satellite camps and had roughly 50,000 prisoners in its clutches (including some 14,000 in the main camp) when its evacuations began at the end of March. Prisoners were sent off on hastily organized railway transports or on foot to 'reception camps' – 9000 to the prisoner-of-war camp at Sandborstel near Bremervörde, 8000 to the concentration camp at Bergen-Belsen and 5000 to the satellite camp just established at Wöbellin near Ludwigslust. Many perished or were shot by guards on the way; many more died of hunger and disease after they arrived at the reception camps. (Some 1000 died at Wöbellin and 3000 at Sandborstel; the number of the Neuengamme prisoners who died at Bergen-Belsen is unknown.)[12] However, the most terrible fate was reserved for the last 10,000 prisoners from Neuengamme. After the camp was finally closed on 19 April, the remaining prisoners were either taken by rail or marched by the SS to the Lübeck Bay, where (together with some other prisoners who had been evacuated from Auschwitz and Stutthof) they were loaded onto 'floating concentration camps': the freighters *Athen* and *Thielbek* in Lübeck harbour and the former luxury liner *Cap Arcona* berthed at nearby Neustadt. Due to over-crowding and lack of food or water, conditions on the ships were terrible in the extreme, but worse was to come. On 3 May, the Royal Air Force, assuming the ships to be troop transports, bombed them. The roughly 2000 prisoners on the *Athen* were lucky; the boat suffered only minor damage. However, the *Thielbek* with roughly 2800 on board and the *Cap Arcona* with its 4600 prisoners were hit. Only 450 of the prisoners on these two ships survived. The remaining 7000 either burned to death on board, drowned, or were shot while trying to escape the inferno – only days before they would have been liberated by the advancing British Army.[13]

It was not only the inmates of the concentration camps who faced deteriorating conditions and brutal evacuations in early 1945. Once the Red Army began its offensive in January 1945, German authorities had to decide what to do with the roughly 35,000 inmates held in prisons and gaols in the east of the Reich.[14] Death rates among ordinary prisoners forced onto marches were not so high as among the much larger numbers of people evacuated from the concentration camps. However, conditions were awful enough: thousands of prisoners were herded, mostly on foot, towards penal institutions in central and western Germany in freezing weather, without proper clothing or shoes and without sufficient food (sometimes with no food at all). A prison governor described the fate of prisoners on a forced march in late January and February from the prison at Preußisch Stargard, to the south of Danzig:

> The weather conditions were disastrous. The progress of the
> trek was hindered by the heavy snowfall, the cold, the mass of
> refugees and army vehicles as well as the flooding back of masses
> of troops, prisoners of war etc. Every road was jammed, so that
> the treks sometimes had to wait for hours in one spot, just to
> move a few hundred metres forward.[15]

Like the hapless concentration camp prisoners, the captives of the prison system were constantly on the move during the last weeks of the Nazi regime. Many died of exposure, exhaustion or hunger, or were shot by their guards along the way.

Not only concentration camp and prison guards but also the police took part in this final orgy of murder. In the autumn of 1944, Himmler had authorized local police commanders that, 'should the uncertainty at the front continue or even grow', the 'danger' this posed was 'to be removed', i.e. prisoners were to be 'fetched from the gaols and liquidated'.[16] These were not empty words. In Cologne the Gestapo began selecting foreign prisoners for execution in late October 1944, and the killings continued until the beginning of March 1945. In the last weeks of the war, people whose court cases were still pending were executed. Altogether hundreds of prisoners were killed, hanged in the courtyard of the Cologne Gestapo headquarters An assembly-line routine was established: the local Gestapo would prepare a list of prisoners on a Wednesday evening, the list would be confirmed by the Gestapo command by Thursday evening, and on Friday morning the listed prisoners would be executed one by one, after which the corpses were taken away by the city's refuse service to be dumped in a mass grave in Cologne's Western Cemetery. The killings continued until the Americans reached the city, and the last of the planned mass executions, scheduled to take place on 4 March, was called off only because of the heavy bombing that had taken place the night before.[17]

As Allied troops approached, prisoners were removed hastily from prisons, internment camps, 'worker education camps' and the like. During the first three months of 1945 hundreds of prisoners along Germany's western border were evacuated, often half-starved, suffering debilitating disease, randomly attacked by their guards, and – if they managed to survive the march – dumped in desperately overcrowded and filthy prisons or camps. At the end of many a march, those who had survived were executed. The overwhelming majority of the victims were foreigners.[18] The evacuations not only provided an occasion for doing away with Germany's prison population; they also proved an ideal means of spreading disease. For example, between 10 and 15 February the Gestapo camp at Brauweiler near Cologne was evacuated and over 200 prisoners marched off to the prison at Siegburg, which already was terribly overcrowded and where there was a virulent typhus epidemic. When prisoners were subsequently evacuated from Siegburg, they took the disease with them, infecting further prisoners when they arrived at the next station on their path.[19]

As the prospect of defeat and surrender drew nearer, imprisoned foreign labourers increasingly became targets of police violence. By August 1944 over 7.6 million foreign labourers (more than 5.7 million civilians and more than 1.9 prisoners of war) had been brought to the Reich from across Europe to serve the Nazi war economy, and made up over a quarter of the entire labour force.[20] During the last months of the war, as Allied armies advanced and as there was less work to keep foreign labourers occupied in factories without the fuel or raw materials needed to maintain production, foreign workers became less and less inclined to do as they were told. Concern was expressed (for example, in a Wehrmacht report on civilian morale in Berlin at the beginning of 1945) about drunken foreigners carousing on trains, 'hanging about by day' in bars 'apparently without anything to do', and engaging 'in brisk black-market activity'.[21] Foreign workers, according to a report from Swabia in southern Germany, were behaving in a 'more provocative, insolent, arrogant' manner, and 'the employers often no longer dare to reprimand the foreigners for fear of revenge'.[22] Many barracks for foreign labourers had been destroyed by Allied bombing, leaving their erstwhile inhabitants to fend for themselves as best they could, and the Gestapo grew increasingly anxious about the activities of 'foreigner gangs' and 'terrorists' – labourers who had gone underground and lived from stealing among the ruins of bombed-out cities.[23] Although often motivated by sheer hunger, those whom the Gestapo referred to repeatedly as 'terror gangs' seemed to confirm Nazi ideas about the inherently dangerous nature of foreigners and the need to deal harshly with the threat they posed. Looters were shot, and local Nazi Party functionaries were keen to let the public know about it, especially when those executed were foreigners.[24]

Communication between Berlin and the rest of the country became more difficult to maintain as the telephone and postal systems collapsed, effectively allowing local officials greater latitude in responding to threats, both real and perceived. On 6 February Ernst Kaltenbrunner, the last chief of the Reich Security Main Office, decreed that heads of police offices throughout the Reich could themselves decide 'about special treatments with regard to crimes deserving death'. Local Security Police commanders were allowed wide discretion when it came to executing foreign workers (especially in the case of Russian workers, where they were authorized to decide on their own). Lack of firmness was not to be tolerated: 'From all police offices [I] expect the highest state of readiness, responsibility, robust action, no hesitation. Ruthlessly eliminate any defeatism in one's own ranks with the harshest measures.'[25] The fact that the Third Reich was collapsing did not motivate its leaders to reassess their suicidal course: it spurred them on to further acts of murder.

This campaign of terror was particularly intense as Allied forces approached the Ruhr region, where huge numbers of foreign labourers lived in an increasingly bombed-out industrial landscape. In late January the head of the Security Police in Düsseldorf, Walter Albath, made clear to Gestapo offices throughout the region what was expected: 'The current overall situation will induce [anti-social] elements and foreign workers and also former German Communists to engage in subversive activity. The greatest vigilance therefore is required.' Albath left no doubt what this meant: 'in all cases that come to light' they were 'to strike immediately and brutally'.[26] During the late winter and early spring of 1945 – when controls over foreign labourers were eroding, when there was little to keep the work force busy in factories where production largely had ceased, and when hungry gangs of foreign labourers, emboldened by the imminent defeat of the 'master race', were roaming Germany's streets – hundreds of foreign workers who had landed in Gestapo and police gaols, often for theft of food and for looting, were massacred.[27] In Ratingen a 'special police court' was established in mid-March on the orders of the Gestapo head in Düsseldorf, Hans Henschke, and promptly set about its work: on 12 March it sentenced to death for 'gang criminality' 35 'eastern workers', who were dispatched in a bomb crater to the south of Essen with bullets to the back of the head.[28] A week later Henschke was at work again, this time ordering the execution of a further 30 'eastern workers' near Wuppertal. Police gaols were emptied and prisoners marched to nearby forests where they were shot. In Gelsenkirchen on 28 March, 11 'eastern workers' were shot by the local police in the city forest on the orders of the Gestapo in Münster; in Bochum between 25 March and 9 April at least 26 people, most of them workers from eastern Europe, were shot in the cellar of the police offices on the recommendation of the local Gestapo; and in Dortmund altogether more than 230 men and women, most of them Russian workers and prisoners of war, were shot in the back of the neck by the Gestapo between 7 March and 8/9 April 1945.

Such executions by police were by no means confined to the Ruhr. During the last couple of months of the war, police across Germany were on the rampage against 'community aliens'. On 24 March members of the Gestapo office in Darmstadt removed the 14 remaining prisoners from the gaol attached to the local court in Bensheim and executed them in a nearby forest. Two days later a police commando shot 81 Russian women and six men in the course of the 'evacuation' of the 'Workers' Educational Camp' in Hirzenheim near Frankfurt as the American Army approached. (These camps had been set up, under the control of the Gestapo, for the supposed work-shy; towards the end of the war they effectively were transformed into 'extended police prisons' for the growing numbers of people being scooped up by the Nazi police state.)[29] On 31 March a commando of the Security Police at the Kassel-Wilhelmshöhe railway station rounded up and shot 78 Italian workers suspected of having plundered a Wehrmacht food-supply train. The Gestapo chief in Hannover, Johannes Rentsch, proved particularly zealous, authorizing local Gestapo chiefs to execute Russian forced labourers without further ado: in Ahlem, to the west of Hannover, Gestapo officers murdered 82 imprisoned labourers and prisoners of war at the beginning of March, and on 6 April a further 154 Soviet forced labourers imprisoned in the police gaol and the 'Workers' Education Camp' at Lahde fell victim. In Kiel between January and the end of April 1945, the Gestapo murdered at least 200 prisoners; in Frankfurt on the Oder the Gestapo liquidated over 750 prisoners from the penitentiary in Sonnenburg, including some 200 foreigners. On 12 April the Leipzig Gestapo shot 52 prisoners, most of them eastern European labourers, in nearby Lindenthal, and five days later did the same to some 300 concentration camp prisoners in Abtnaundorf. Throughout Germany the pattern was repeated: prisoners were selected, transported to some isolated place of execution, shot and dumped in mass graves. This 'naked terror of the final phase of war' was not simply a response to orders emanating from the centre; it persisted beyond the point where any direct link remained with the Nazi leadership in Berlin – for example, in Schleswig-Holstein, which had been cut off from Berlin at the end of March but where the Gestapo and SS continued to murder prisoners.[30]

It has been estimated that altogether over ten thousand people were executed in this way within the Reich during the last months of the war.[31] Roughly 90 per cent of the victims were foreigners, the majority of them foreign labourers from Eastern Europe.[32] The remainder were a few German Jews who had managed to survive the deportations to the death camps, Communist resisters, and Germans who for some reason or other had been considered suspicious. Many things fuelled this last wave of murder: prejudice against eastern Europeans whose behaviour may have appeared to confirm racist stereotypes; hatred of people whose countrymen were pounding Germany into the ground; grudges and thirst for vengeance; the growing radicalization of German police, to whom acts of brutality became almost second nature; and a feeling among Gestapo and SS members, who saw little future for themselves in a postwar world, that they might as well take as many people down with them as possible. In some respects these murders paralleled the execution of German 'defeatists' and deserters during the last weeks of the war. Yet they had another, racial dimension: the foreigners most frequently targeted – generally from eastern Europe, branded as criminal, often ragged and in ill health, disorderly and constituting a threat to Germans now that the Nazi state was crumbling – were of precisely those groups which the Nazi regime had sought to exterminate. Although in some instances German police moderated their behaviour as Allied armies approached, in others they continued to murder prisoners even as Allied artillery shelled the towns in which they were working.[33] Often, the perpetrators of this last outburst of Nazi violence were people who had learned their trade in Nazi-occupied eastern Europe – many of the commanders of the Security Police responsible for the wave of murder within Germany in early 1945 had been heads of Security Police squads in the east (for example, in the General Government in Poland)[34] – and now were employed to 'strike immediately and brutally' to shore up the home front in the 'final struggle'. The Nazis' war of extermination had come home.

Not all the killing was done by people in uniform or ordered by officials. The war, and years of racist dictatorship, had also eroded standards of civilized behaviour among many 'ordinary' people. In the last weeks of the war, the murder of 'others' became almost fortuitous, an action demanding little thought. To take one example, an account of an almost routine act of murder in the Ruhr region:

At the beginning of April 1945, as American troops already stood at the Rhine-Herne-Canal near Oberhausen, the miner C. and a certain K. were in a bunker in Oberhausen. A woman appeared and said that a flat in the Ruhrortstraße was being looted by Russian workers. C., K. and a few other men went to the flat, but found no one there. A Russian worker was discovered on a railway embankment nearby. He was seized by C. and K. and brought to the police. They [the police] claimed that the matter was not their affair. No one seemed concerned about whether the Russian worker had been looting or not. A Wehrmacht officer declared that he did not have any people available to shoot the Russian. K. showed a real desire to kill the worker: '. . . the Russian must be shot; if the Wehrmacht does not do it, then he, K., would do it himself.' Subsequently C. and K. went with the Russian worker, whom they held by the arms, to the Sports Ground Concordia. They were accompanied by 'other people, especially by adolescents'. K. shot the alleged looter in the sports ground in front of a bomb crater.[35]

Vigilante action, not just against foreign labourers but also what the Nazi leadership referred to as 'popular justice against Anglo-American murderers' – the lynching of British and American bomber crews who bailed out over German territory[36] – reflected both the diminishing reach of the state and the brutalization of everyday life.

The terror in the areas remaining under German control in early 1945 was aimed not just against hapless prisoners and foreign labourers who found themselves in the wrong place and the wrong time. It was targeted against German 'racial comrades' as well. As Allied armies smashed their way into the Reich and it became obvious that Germany's war was lost, 'defeatism' and looting by Germans as well as foreigners became increasingly serious concerns for a Nazi leadership determined to fight on to the bitter end. The spectre of 1918, when Germany's armies supposedly had been 'stabbed in the back' at home, was never out of the minds of Adolf Hitler and the Nazi (and military) leadership. A repetition of November 1918 was to be prevented through terror. Germans who appeared to be 'defeatist', who sought to avoid fighting and dying in the futile final battles, were to be hunted down and killed. Minor infractions could result in execution, as in the case in early February of an unfortunate town council official in Silesia accused of having 'left his official post near the front line at a time of danger without sufficient reason and without the knowledge of his superiors'. The man was sentenced by a special court and executed.[37]

On 15 February 1945 the terror aimed against Germans was given an ostensibly legal framework when Reich Justice Minister Otto Thierack issued a decree establishing summary courts martial in 'defence districts threatened by the enemy'. The jurisdiction of these courts martial extended to all offences 'which jeopardize German combat strength or determination' – a category so broad as to include almost anything.[38] Chaired by a professional judge sitting alongside a Nazi Party official and an officer drawn from the Wehrmacht, the Waffen-SS or the police, these courts were designed to operate almost completely outside what was left of a legal framework. Three decisions were open to it: to execute the accused, to release him or her, or to hand the accused over to a regular court. With these summary courts martial, the last shreds of legal protection for the accused were swept away. Empowered to hand out death sentences to anyone who allegedly undermined the war effort, these courts were, as Martin Bormann noted with satisfaction, 'a weapon for the annihilation of all parasites of the people'.[39] While some judges, to their credit, evaded serving in these courts, others did as they were expected.

Although we lack a systematic investigation of how these summary courts martial operated, it appears that they did the job for which they had been designed. Hastily constituted, they sprang into action as Allied armies approached, and severe measures were applied to stop local inhabitants from surrendering their towns in an effort to prevent the death and destruction which, inevitably, would result from continued fighting. Judges and assessors were hastily called to serve on the courts, which wasted little time on legal niceties before handing out draconian sentences. For example, the summary court martial set up in Lohr (between Aschaffenburg and Schweinfurt) had as its chairman a local court official, serving together with two lay assessors: a lieutenant who had been wounded and happened to be convalescing in Lohr with his in-laws and a junior officer who also had been wounded and was employed as an instructor in a local training school for the *Volkssturm*. The prosecutor was a lieutenant who had been discharged from the Wehrmacht as unfit for duty after suffering a severe head wound and who then headed the *Volkssturm* training school. The two lay assessors and the prosecutor had attempted to avoid serving on the court, but were compelled to do so on military orders. However, their initial reluctance to get involved did not prevent them at the beginning of April – after a hearing lasting barely 45 minutes – from sentencing a local doctor to death for having tried to secure the surrender of the town to the approaching Americans without fighting.[40] The results of this quasi-judicial murder campaign frequently were displayed for all to see. For example, as the war neared its end and the Americans approached Lohr, the SS hanged six local notables.[41]

In the east it was no different. For example, in Stargard in Pomerania on 17/18 February, shortly before the town was conquered by the Soviet Army, the last ever edition of the *Stargarder Tageblatt* announced in a banner headline, which could serve as an epitaph for the Third Reich, 'On Adolf-Hitler-Square the hanged are swinging in the wind'.[42] Over 60 years later (in the interview in which he revealed his membership, as a 17-year-old, in the Waffen-SS) Günter Grass recalled: 'The first dead that I saw were not Russians, but Germans. They were hanging from the trees, many of them were my age.'[43]

Hundreds of Germans were executed in the last weeks of the war for displaying insufficient enthusiasm for continuing the war or for trying to bring the fighting to a stop.[44] Not all of these cases necessarily were processed through Thierack's special courts, because some functionaries of the regime and SS members found resorting even to this summary process too laborious. In the chaos of the last days of the Reich, true believers lashed out at their 'racial comrades', but the shape this took depended greatly on local circumstances. Where local Nazi Party bosses were particularly fanatical and the fighting on the ground particularly intense, the local population was especially at risk. One such case was that of Heilbronn, in south-western Germany. Heilbronn had been bombed heavily in December 1944, and from the 3rd to the 12th of April 1945 there was bitter and enormously destructive fighting on the ground before the Americans finally overcame German military resistance. The district Nazi Party leader Richard Drauz (later described as the 'butcher of Heilbronn') proved remarkably bloodthirsty, and unleashed an utterly lawless wave of terror against the local population, leading to a shooting spree by local Nazis. This left 14 people, including a local-government official and his wife, dead for allegedly having displayed white flags from their homes.[45] Another case was that of Erwin Helm, a career army officer who had advanced to the rank of major. During the last stages of the war, Helm became the leader of a 'snatch squad' of the Wehrmacht's Seventh Army and then got his own 'court' which left a bloody trail across southern Germany. Helm drove around in a grey Mercedes bearing the sign 'flying court martial' and leaving behind numerous soldiers and civilians executed, often without even the pretence of judicial proceedings.[46] During these last days of the Reich, the Nazi 'racial community' was held together by terror and murder, and as the Allies arrived many Germans had more to fear from their own regime than from their external enemies. As the intelligence staff of the U.S. Sixth Army Group, which had occupied large portions of Baden, Württemberg and western Bavaria, observed at the end of April 1945, German civilians had to protect their homes and property not so much against the Allies as against Nazi fanatics unwilling to accept defeat.[47]

German soldiers were no less likely to become victims of Nazi terror than were German civilians. As the Wehrmacht crumbled and its lines of communication were destroyed, the opportunities increased for German soldiers to leave their units, cast off their uniforms, hide among the civilian population and try to sit out the final stages of the lost war. Not surprisingly, the number of soldiers who deserted rose substantially.[48] And not surprisingly, ruthless measures were taken to prevent desertion: military police and SS units patrolled behind the lines, and any soldier who was apprehended and unable to provide the necessary identification or who was suspected of desertion faced the rope or the firing squad.[49]

The more brutal the retaliation, the more pleased was the Nazi leadership. Thus, in January 1945, Himmler commended the commander of the 'fortress' city of Schneidemühl (200 kilometres east of Berlin), not least because he had shot retreating German soldiers and hung signs from the corpses announcing 'that is what happens to all cowards'.[50] Orders distributed to the Nazi Party Gauleiters on 9 March to 'strengthen the front' by capturing deserters, stipulated that all Wehrmacht soldiers discovered away from their military units and who had not been wounded were to be shot.[51] The leadership was determined that there would be no repetition of the end of the First World War, when, according to Hitler in Mein Kampf, 'tens of thousands of deserters [. . .] were able to turn their backs on the front without special risk'. Hitler had been adamant that 'the deserter must know that his desertion brings with it the very thing that he wants to escape. At the front a man can die, as a deserter he must die. Only by such a draconian threat against any attempt at desertion can a deterring effect be obtained, not only for the individual, but for the whole army.'[52] Wehrmacht 'justice' treated those accused of desertion with remarkable severity, and some 15,000 were executed. (By contrast, a mere 18 German soldiers had been executed for desertion in the First World War, and only one American soldier and no British soldiers were executed for desertion during the Second World War.)[53]

The mayhem of the last months of the Third Reich was facilitated and exacerbated by the destruction of Germany's infrastructure by Allied bombing and the battles fought on German territory. Communication – which was necessary for the regime to maintain its grip on the population – became increasingly difficult. Many services that people in developed countries tend to take for granted no longer existed: telecommunications, the postal service, the railways, local public transport, road networks, gas and electricity supply, and water and fuel supply, largely ceased to function. In the heavily bombed city of Siegen, for example, the gas supply had been cut in mid-December

1944 and gas remained unavailable for the remainder of the war; electricity supply ceased on 15 March 1945 and was not restored; the supply of running water was largely disrupted from the beginning of March, leaving people to get their water from street pumps; and railway traffic ceased completely in mid-March 1945.[54]

The collapse of infrastructure meant that civil administration, schools and the police, as well as military units, increasingly were cut off from the central authorities, from one another, and from the people they were meant to rule. As the Third Reich approached its end, directives from Berlin or from regional centres no longer necessarily reached their intended recipients. At the local level, those in government or Party offices and in police stations were left increasingly to their own devices, for good or ill. While some local functionaries used their new-found freedom to distance themselves from the more insane orders of the leadership, others seized the opportunity to lash out against fellow citizens who failed to display sufficient commitment to the Nazi cause. The collapse of infrastructure also led people – both Germans and the millions of others who had been brought, generally against their will, to the Reich – to behave in ways which brought them increasingly to the attention of the Nazi police state. This was true particularly with regard to food: rations were cut repeatedly in early 1945, and even what notionally could be purchased according to the reduced ration schedules, was no longer available.[55] Consequently, Germans looked increasingly to the black market towards the end of the war, and engaged in looting. Civilians, soldiers and foreign labourers looted shops and homes, railway cars, left-luggage offices at railway stations, wine cellars, coal stores, and government installations as civil order broke down and police no longer were able to protect property.[56] Crime, which had risen during the war, now increased substantially, and the police were less and less able to suppress it.[57] The bombing created new opportunities for theft, from the ruins of businesses and dwellings; as the black market grew, Germans were drawn into illegal activity. With parents working long hours, serving in the armed forces or dead, and with schools closed in order to provide shelter for refugees or taken over by the Wehrmacht,[58] young people were drawn into activities branded as illegal; and as the infrastructure disintegrated, it became increasingly difficult for the police to impose order. They could murder, but they no longer necessarily could control.

Unlike the circumstances which prevailed during the previous years of Nazi rule, the savagery let loose by the regime during the first four months of 1945 was not the product of its tight control of German society. Instead, it was an expression of the breakdown of order, which brought a willingness, and indeed desire, to engage in violence and an utter disregard for the lives of individual human beings. The horrors of the death marches and the appalling conditions in vastly over-crowded concentration and transit camps in early 1945, as well as the terror meted out to German soldiers, civilians and foreign labourers during the last months of the Reich, arose from the inability to deal with the consequences of collapse, or to respect the most basic human values. After twelve years of Nazi rule, violence had become second nature to the regime; in the end violence was all that it had left to offer.

In 1945 the connection between the regime and the people appears to have broken almost completely. The vast majority of Germans no longer shared the perspectives offered by the Nazis and increasingly sought just to survive as best they could. While Hitler and those clos-est to him welcomed and sought death – and expected Germans to do the same – most people still in Nazi-controlled territory wanted to emerge in one piece from the escalating nightmare. The violence of the Third Reich no longer offered rewards for Germans, who now distanced themselves from their regime. No longer was there any sense in continuing to support the war effort, since to continue the war served only to postpone the inevitable at a huge cost in life and property. The destruction of other countries – or at least the profiting from the exploitation and destruction of other peoples and coun-tries – may once have provided a basis for popular support for 'Hitler's People's State'.[59] In the end, however, when all that the regime could offer its people was increasingly vicious and random violence from which no one could be safe – this link between people and regime was severed.

The end of the Third Reich spelled the end of dictatorial control over the lives of Germans. This neither occurred suddenly, when the German armed forces finally surrendered in May 1945, nor meant that the Nazi regime was incapable of extinguishing hundreds of thousands of lives in its final months. The murder and mayhem of the final months resulted from the regime lashing out in desperation, with its remaining fanatical supporters tied to their apocalyptic ideology while its hapless subjects were compelled to look after themselves, often in the most dreadful circumstances. With the collapse of the regime, the bases for the Nazis' attempt to mobilize the German population for campaigns of violence, conquest, domination and murder, were swept away. Their last measures cost many people their lives, but they failed to prevent Germans from trying to avoid death. In the end, as the Third Reich collapsed, collective dreams and nightmares gave way to individual fears and hopes.

The violence dispensed by an increasingly desperate Nazi regime during its last months not only cost huge numbers of concentration camp prisoners, foreign labourers, German soldiers and civilians their lives. It also contributed to the transformation of Germany into a nation of self-proclaimed victims, where it was everyone for him or her self. The murder and mayhem of the first four months of 1945 helped to distance the population from National Socialism, as Germans were exposed to what other people across the European continent knew only too well. Nazism was no longer identified with economic recovery, order, conquest and strength, but rather with fear and wanton murder. In a sense, the final terror campaigns achieved their purpose: to a considerable extent German society was atomised in 1945, which helped to prevent a repetition of what had occurred at the end of the First World War. The chaos, desperation, fear and violence of early 1945 reduced people's horizons and concerns to their own small worlds. The larger universe faded away as Germany went down to defeat. In this 'zero hour' the Nazi past was largely left behind and personal survival became all-important. This perhaps was the last achievement of Nazism, and it was achieved through violence, brutality and murder.

4

FLEEING FOR THEIR LIVES

Nothing at all was prepared. The population fled aimlessly in all directions. E. Müller[1]

We believed that we soon would return. No one imagined the scale of the tragedy. Former mayor of Löbau, Neumark District[2]

When they emerged from the Second World War, Germans remembered not so much the suffering that their regime had inflicted on others from 1939 onwards as they did the suffering they themselves experienced in 1945. Of all the hardships which Germans endured at the end of the war, it was the removal of millions from their homes which perhaps cast the darkest shadow. During the last months of the war and in its aftermath, the German people, whose own regime had brutally removed populations from their homes across Nazi-occupied Europe, became victims of one of the greatest forced removals of people in the history of the world.[3] Millions lost their homes in the east – in the former eastern German provinces of East and West Prussia, Pomerania, Silesia and the eastern portions of Brandenburg; in the Sudetenland, in Romania, Yugoslavia, Poland, Hungary and the Baltic countries – either having fled or been expelled and moved westwards into what became the four occupation zones of Germany. (Austria, it should be noted, became home to relatively few of the refugees and expellees after the war – roughly 430,000 altogether.)[4] The first postwar German census, carried out on 29 October 1946 in the four occupation zones, recorded 5,645,000 expellees from the former eastern regions of the Reich.[5] When one adds those expelled from Czechoslovakia (primarily from the Sudetenland, where some 3.3 million Germans had lived before the war and from which nearly 3 million refugees came to postwar Germany), from pre-1939 Poland, Hungary, Yugoslavia, Rumania and the Baltic, and those who went to postwar Austria, the total approaches 12 million.[6]

This huge forced removal fundamentally altered the human and social geography of the German people as well as the economic and political geography of their country. It spelled the end of German settlement in regions that had been inhabited by German speakers for hundreds of years and that had formed the old heartlands of Prussia and of the East Elbian land-owning aristocracy. It cut millions of Germans off from their Heimat, from the communities and connections which had sustained them and from which they had drawn a sense of identity, and it altered the religious and cultural map of Germany. It changed the face of German-speaking Europe and created a sense of victimhood among millions of Germans who had lost homes that they were never to see again.

The Potsdam Agreement reached by the victorious 'Big Three' in the summer of 1945 stipulated blandly that 'any transfers [of population] that take place should be effected in an orderly and humane manner'.[7] However, the manner in which the transfer of the German population was carried out by the Poles and the Czechs was hardly humane. Early estimates of casualties among the Germans who fled or were expelled from their homes in the east exceeded a million dead; according to rough calculations made by the West German government in the 1950s, as of late 1950 1,390,000 people who had lived in the former eastern regions of Germany were unaccounted for, presumed dead, as a consequence either of the fighting in the last months of war, of the deportations carried out by the Soviet authorities, or of the dreadful conditions that had accompanied the move westwards.[8] Altogether, it has been estimated that by 1944–1945 some 16.5

million Germans were living in the areas of eastern Europe (excluding the Soviet Union) to be affected by the exodus. By 1950 something over 11.5 million had left, as a result either of flight or of expulsion; of the remainder, some 2.2 million were unaccounted for by the Germans and presumed dead (with the remainder having stayed more or less where they were.)[9] Claims that more than a million died are probably overestimates, made by a West German government keen during the 1950s to emphasize the suffering of the German people; more recent calculations have put the number at about 500,000 – which itself is hardly an insignificant figure.[10]

The story of German flight and expulsion from eastern Europe did not begin with the Soviet military offensive of January 1945. Neither were all those who were displaced from the east long-standing inhabitants of the areas they vacated, nor did all those who moved westwards in the later stages of the war do so amidst the panic of early 1945. To begin with, some of those who fled or were expelled from the east, beginning in early 1945, had themselves resettled – or been resettled – during the war, to live in dwellings which had been taken from Poles whom the Germans had forcibly removed. A substantial number of ethnic Germans were resettled during the war, particularly from the Baltic countries after the USSR took them over in 1940; in January 1944 roughly 352,000 of these ethnic Germans from the Baltic were in occupied Poland. In addition, an even larger number of Germans from the Reich had taken up the Nazi challenge to settle and 'Germanize' the conquered east, and in January 1944 these numbered some 472,000 in occupied Poland.[11] Thus at least some of the Germans forcibly removed from their homes in 1945 and 1946 had profited from the forced removal of others, in particular in occupied Poland, during earlier stages of the war.

Furthermore, the movement of Germans from their homes within Germany did not begin suddenly in January 1945. On the one hand, millions had been evacuated during the war from cities threatened by Allied air attacks or had lost their homes due to the bombing. Many of these evacuees were moved eastwards, to regions from which they then would be removed at the end of the war: during the war an estimated 825,000 Germans were sent from areas endangered by the bombing to the eastern provinces, 450,000 of these to Silesia alone.[12] On the other hand, the successes of the Red Army during the second half of 1944 led many Germans to flee westwards from areas where they had settled (or been settled during the war) in the Baltic, in Poland, in Romania, and then from East Prussia as Soviet forces reached that province in the autumn of 1944. Thus on the eve of the great migration westwards, the population of eastern Germany included 'racial comrades' evacuated both from territories further to the east and from cities in the west.

For those lucky enough to have left eastern Germany behind before January 1945, the experience generally bore little resemblance to what their compatriots would experience in the months that followed. One such was the historian Wolfgang Schieder, who was born in Königsberg in 1935 and who, in an interview in March 1999, described his move from East Prussia to Bavaria:

> I lived in Königsberg until I was nine, then I had to leave from there – like all the Germans. It is easy to assume that the flight from East Prussia had a traumatic effect on me, but that was not the case. Already at the beginning of 1944 my parents had me, together with my younger siblings, brought to the countryside in West Prussia, where my grandmother owned a farm. In the autumn of 1944 I went by train via Berlin on endless journeys to Bavaria. As a child I did not experience that as dramatic but rather as something incredibly exciting. I did not feel the loss of Heimat which had afflicted an entire generation of German refugees and expellees, and naturally I therefore did not have any revisionist dreams later. I felt myself at home in Bavaria relatively quickly, although at the beginning I did not speak the dialect and, in the village where we had landed, was of the 'wrong' confession.[13]

Schieder's childhood home of East Prussia had been the first part of the Reich reached by the Soviet Army and the first German province

whose population faced mass evacuation. In the initial waves of evacuation from East Prussia – the first in late July/early August 1944 and
the second in October, as Soviet forces occupied sections of north-
eastern East Prussia – roughly one quarter of the population (in
the main women and children, the elderly and the ill), left the
province.[14] What occurred in October 1944 was of tremendous
importance for events in early 1945, for it framed expectations
everywhere of what would happen if and when the Russians arrived.
The name which was seared into German consciousness was
Nemmersdorf, a village in the district of Gumbinnen in north-eastern
East Prussia. Nemmersdorf was occupied by Soviet forces on 20
October as they marched into the districts of Gumbinnen and
Goldap; when Wehrmacht units re-occupied the area a few days
later, they found that numerous German civilians had been killed.
The Nazi propaganda machine made the most of the scene, giving it
prominent and graphic coverage: the 'gruesome Bolshevik crimes in
East Prussia', including pictures of mutilated corpses of German victims, were featured prominently in German news propaganda so as to
arouse the greatest possible fear.[15] The propaganda worked. The
atrocities in Nemmersdorf became almost legendary, with descriptions of how the Russians left behind a scene (according to later
testimony of a member of a *Volkssturm* unit charged with clearing
up Nemmersdorf in the wake of the short-lived Soviet occupation
in 1944) of mutilated dead bodies, of naked women nailed to doors, of
infants whose heads had been smashed, of dozens of corpses of women
and children 'almost without exception murdered in a bestial manner'.[16]
The immediate effect was panic. Not only did the temporary Soviet
occupation of north-eastern East Prussia lead to substantial flight by
Germans in the autumn of 1944, but the images of Nemmersdorf
fuelled fears which drove millions to flee westwards ahead of the Red
Army in early 1945.

East Prussia therefore occupies a special place in the history of the
removal of Germans from what had been eastern Germany. As a consequence of the evacuations from the eastern districts of East Prussia
in 1944, roughly a half a million people already had left the province
by the beginning of 1945, in generally well-organized programmes,

for Pomerania or for Saxony and Thuringia further to the west. Whereas in March 1944 the total population of East Prussia (not including the *Regierungsbezirk* West Prussia) had been 2,346,000, at the end of 1944 only 1,754,000 remained in those parts of the province still under German control.[17] This meant that when the Soviet Army conquered the north-east of East Prussia the area was largely devoid of people; hundreds of years of German settlement there had come to an end. In many places elsewhere in the province, however, the population increased as refugees found temporary sanctuary. For example, the numbers of people in the Braunsberg district, along the Baltic coast between Königsberg and Elbing, grew between September and December 1944 from 66,000 to 97,000.[18]

The wave of flight from East Prussia in the wake of the Soviet offensive in January 1945 was quite different from what had gone before. This time the evacuations were chaotic. Despite the exposed position of the province, the East Prussian Nazi leadership had not prepared for the eventual evacuation of the remainder of the civilian population. Like his counterparts in Danzig-West Prussia (Albert Foerster) and in Lower Silesia (Karl Hanke), the East Prussian Nazi Party Gauleiter and 'Reich Defence Commissar', Erich Koch, stubbornly refused to countenance evacuation orders. According to the mayor of Insterburg (in the north-east of the province, and East Prussia's third-largest town after Königsberg and Allenstein):

> . . . preparations for evacuation in the event of enemy danger were neither made nor permitted. The Gauleiter [Koch] asserted repeatedly that not only the Wehrmacht but, above all, the [civilian] men now called up by him would hold fast to the soil of the Heimat, and that no enemy would be able to penetrate the province again.[19]

Koch, the Insterburg mayor claimed, had 'repeatedly asserted that there was no danger for the population. [. . .] The Wehrmacht and the *Volkssturm* would [. . .] smash any enemy attack.'[20] Consequently, instead of a planned evacuation, when the Red Army appoached there was panic. With the Russians at the gates, the civilian population did not wait for orders: 'Almost nowhere did a timely and organized evacuation take place, on the contrary the departure of the East Prussian population constituted a disorderly flight which was triggered at the last moment and which was completely chaotic.'[21]

From the 19th to the 26th of January hundreds of thousands of East Prussians streamed westwards. However, for many it was too late. The unexpectedly rapid Soviet advance in the south of the province – Allenstein was occupied by Soviet forces on 21 January – severed rail links and cut the overland routes of escape. The East Prussian population also received scant assistance from the military. Although the commander of the Wehrmacht's Fourth Army, General Friedrich Hoßbach, ordered – without Hitler's permission and against the dictator's expressed wishes – that the forces under his command attempt to break out to the west, he displayed little concern for the fate of the civilian population. According to Hoßbach, the treks of civilians hampered the attempts of the Wehrmacht to break through to the west; consequently, he ordered that they 'must get off the roads', and on 24 January he noted callously that 'the civilian population has to remain behind . . . That sounds cruel, but unfortunately it cannot be helped'.[22] (This contrasts sharply with the image that Hoßbach projected in his memoirs, where he referred to the military commander's 'moral obligation' and asserted that 'in the deliberations for the conduct of the struggle for East Prussia the fate of the population could no longer remain neglected'.)[23] As a result, most of the East Prussians who fled overland at this time ended up in the hands of the Soviet forces. Only a small proportion managed to reach the western bank of the Vistula.

Left in the lurch by both the Nazi Party and the Wehrmacht, the civilian population faced a terrible choice. Cut off from the Reich by land, they now had only two paths of escape westwards: over the ice on the Frische Haff and along the Frische Nehring (the sandy spit of land that paralleled the East Prussian coast) along the Baltic, or by ship from the port of Pillau, to the north of Königsberg. Tens of thousands tried to flee over the ice while temperatures reached 20–30 degrees below zero; many fell victim to the freezing weather or to strafing from Soviet aircraft, while German police combed groups of fleeing people for adolescents and middle-aged men who were pressed into *Volkssturm* units. By the end of February – as the ice over the Frische Haff was breaking up – some 450,000 had escaped via this path.

The sea route remained open longer. Ships began ferrying evacuees out of the province from Pillau on 25 January. One woman from Königsberg who managed to escape by sea from Pillau later described the scene:

It was bitterly cold, the temperature was between 20 and 28 degrees below zero. Since Pillau had not been prepared for such an onslaught, a large proportion of the poor people had to camp out under the stars, and therefore many of the people [who had] gathered, especially children, already froze to death there. As soon as a ship berthed in the harbour it was stormed. Any organization dissolved.[24]

Another refugee described what happened at Pillau on the last Sunday in January, when 28,000 people from Königsberg arrived at the harbour desperately hoping to board a ship heading westwards:

At the harbour everyone was pushing towards the ships. There were terrible scenes. Human beings became animals. Women threw their children into the water [against the moored boats] just in order to keep up or in order that they not be crushed to death in the crowd. The general confusion was now made even greater when completely disorganized military units streamed into the city and into houses, looted, intermingled with the refugees and also pushed to get themselves onto the ships. In order to get through the cordons to the harbour, soldiers took children from their mothers and claimed that they wanted to bring their families on board! Others put on women's clothing and thus attempted to get away on the ships.[25]

Civilized behaviour became a luxury which no longer could be afforded: social solidarity dissolved amidst chaos, fear and violence. In the end, the Nazi 'racial community' was little more than a collection of desperate individuals seeking to save their own skins.

Amidst such scenes the ship transports continued – under repeated air attacks which took the lives of many refugees – during March and April. By the time that Pillau finally fell to the Red Army, over 450,000 refugees and a further 141,000 wounded had escaped from East Prussia by sea. (Many, however, were taken only as far as Danzig, where they soon found themselves in a situation similar to the one they had left.)[26] The numbers evacuated from ports further west were even greater, as refugees in West Prussia and eastern Pomerania headed towards coastal towns which still were in German hands: some 900,000 refugees in January and a further 85,000 refugees and 300,000 wounded and soldiers thereafter were evacuated westwards to Germany or Denmark from Danzig, Gdingen (Gdynia) and Hela. Altogether, the evacuation of Germans from East and West Prussia and Pomerania comprised one of the greatest sea-borne evacuations in history. Seven hundred and ninety ships were employed in a massive logistical effort by the German Navy to evacuate what in the end totalled 2,186,500 people from eastern Germany between January and May 1945.[27]

For those who managed to get on board a boat, the nightmare was not necessarily over. The Soviet Navy managed to sink over 200 of the refugee ships. The most prominent casualties of the Soviet submarine campaign were the one-time 'Strength through Joy' luxury cruise ship *Wilhelm Gustloff* and the passenger liner *General Steuben*. The *Wilhelm Gustloff* was sunk after leaving Gdingen (Gdynia) on 30 January, the twelfth anniversary of Hitler's coming to power, with over 10,000 people on board (some 8800 civilians, a large portion of whom were children, and 1500 members of the Wehrmacht), of whom altogether only 1239 were rescued; the *General Steuben* was sunk on 10 February with a loss of some 3000 lives.[28] The sinking of the *Wilhelm Gustloff*, with a loss estimated to have been more than 9000 lives, and that of the refugee transport *Goya* on 16 April 1945 with a loss of perhaps as many as 7000 people, were the greatest maritime disasters in world history – each resulting in many times more casualties than the 1513 people who died with the sinking of the *Titanic*.

★

The desperate predicament of the German refugees did not awaken much sympathy from the Nazi regime. In West Prussia and Pomerania, where roads became jammed with people fleeing westwards from East Prussia and whose own populations also soon would take flight as the Red Army approached, the German leadership put further obstacles in their path. The bridges across the Vistula were reserved for military traffic, leaving the refugees to make their way over the ice across the river. In Pomerania the Nazi Party Gauleiter, Franz Schwede-Coburg, tried to turn back his 'racial comrades' fleeing from further east, but was overruled by the military.[29] While Danzig and West Prussia were being overwhelmed with refugees from East Prussia, at the end of February the Nazi leadership there ordered a halt to evacuations. Soon thereafter, on the 1st of March, the Red Army reached the Baltic Sea coast to the east of Köslin, cutting German-held Pomerania in two; as in East Prussia, now in West Prussia and eastern Pomerania the only remaining escape route was the sea.

Evacuation from landlocked Silesia, home to some 4,718,000 people in early 1944 (over 100,000 more than in 1939, despite wartime losses),[30] posed different logistical problems. Of the 4.7 million Silesians, roughly 1.6 million fled south into the Sudetenland and the Czech 'protectorate', while another 1.6 million fled westwards in Germany; the remaining 1.5 million were unable to escape before the region was occupied by the Red Army.[31] Yet, although they were spared the rigours of fleeing by sea, the contours of the human tragedy which unfolded in Silesia were similar to what happened in East Prussia and Pomerania. In Silesia too the population had been urged to stand fast; the Nazi Party leadership, in particular the radical Gauleiter and Reich Defence Commissar in Breslau, Karl Hanke, maintained until the last moment that the German population was in no immediate danger.[32] Indeed, in Cosel in Upper Silesia the district Nazi Party leader informed local officials as late as 19 January that 'everything is to remain as it is' since, he assured them, the Russians would not cross the Oder; anyone who expressed views to the contrary was to be shot immediately.[33] Although detailed evacuation plans had been drawn up for Silesia during the second half of 1944, actual preparations were not made until the last moment; but with the railways by then vastly overburdened and many railway lines severed, most plans no longer could have been put into practice anyway.[34]

In Upper Silesia the first orders for evacuation were not issued until the Soviet offensive was well underway, and the evacuations – of women and children and the elderly – did not begin until 19–21 January. The men were expected to remain and work in the factories of this industrial region or in administration; however, many of them fled nevertheless, despite orders by Upper Silesian Gauleiter Fritz Bracht to stay put.[35] In any event, the evacuation orders came too late: on 22 January Soviet forces crossed the Oder near Brieg, cutting railway links between Upper Silesia's industrial cities (Gleiwitz, Kattowitz, Beuthen, Hindenburg) and Breslau, and making it impossible to transport evacuees westwards into Saxony and Thuringia as originally envisaged. Instead, they went south into the Sudetenland, where they found temporary refuge until they were removed after May 1945.[36]

In Lower Silesia, the rapid advance of the Soviet Army and reports of atrocities by Soviet soldiers led to panicked flight, towards Saxony to the west or Bohemia to the south. Altogether, roughly 85 per cent of the civilian population of rural Lower Silesia east of the Oder, which had numbered some 700,000, abandoned their homes. Those who failed to get away in time faced rough treatment at the hands of Soviet troops. In the town of Striegau, where only about half the German inhabitants had managed to flee, the remaining 15,000 were left to face the fury of the Red Army. According to the later account of a Polish forced labourer:

Dreadful news increased the fear. There were reports about murders of old people and of men that made the blood curdle in one's veins. It was reported that women of all ages were raped, that the breasts of nursing mothers were cut off, that the bellies of pregnant women were cut open and the unborn ripped out of their bodies. There were stories that deep wells were filled with the bodies of living people, that people had their eyes gouged out with bayonets or had their tongues cut out, that Germans were herded in their droves into barns or houses and there were burned alive, that militia [*Landsturm*] men who were captured were driven into captivity with heavy tanks or lorries, and people spoke of many other things that made one shudder.[37]

Such stories resonated with German prejudices about Slavs, images which had been served up for years in Nazi propaganda. They also found confirmation in the reports of the Wehrmacht's intelligence service on 'foreign armies east' during early 1945, which noted that Soviet soldiers were 'continuing to loot and murder in German villages and towns' and that the Red Army leadership no longer seemed 'in a position to stem the desire to annihilate which has resulted from the years of hate propaganda against the Germans'.[38] These reports, although clearly influenced by an ideology which regarded Russians and other Soviet nationalities as lower forms of humanity, were not simply expressions of Nazi fantasies about Slav 'sub-humans'. When, for example, Wehrmacht units managed to recapture Striegau (some 50 kilometres south-west of Breslau) in mid-March, they found a town littered with the corpses of murdered civilians.[39]

As in East and West Prussia and Pomerania, in Silesia the widespread panic was accompanied by desperate efforts to obtain a place on any available means of transport heading westwards. This led to gruesome scenes, most notably in Breslau. First, the city was overwhelmed with refugees from the right bank of the Oder, where Gauleiter Hanke already had authorized evacuation. Paul Peikert, a priest who remained in Breslau throughout the siege in 1945, described the waves of human misery passing through the city from the rural regions to the east of the Oder:

As the Russian army came closer the evacuation began of the entire population of Silesia on the right bank of the Oder. For days now, day and night, Breslau presented a gruesome picture of the fleeing population. Never-ending columns of horse-drawn or cow-drawn farmers' wagons, as well as the handcarts of women workers or the columns of prisoners of war, foreigners, Russians, French, Serbs, etc. with small sleds on which they moved their baggage. [. . .] Mostly they are elderly people and children who sit on the wagons or younger women who have had to cultivate their fields alone with the help of prisoners of war. In addition, this mass of refugees arrives in harsh winter weather, 13–15 degrees and more below zero. Children freeze and are laid out on the roadside by their relatives. It is reported that entire lorry loads of such frozen children are being delivered to the local mortuaries. My cleaning woman reported today that she herself saw eight corpses of children and the corpse of an old man in the roadside ditch along her stretch of the Strehlener Chaussee. [. . .] Many of these refugees are being delivered to local hospitals with frozen limbs.[40]

Then came the turn of the Breslauers themselves. As the Red Army closed in on the Silesian capital during the second half of January, the Nazi Party *Gauleitung* on 19 January finally gave the order for evacuation. A large portion of the civilian population fled, their actions and reactions differing little from those of their counterparts in East Prussia and Pomerania.

The consequences of the hasty evacuation were horrific: panic among crowds desperately trying to get aboard the last trains out of the city reportedly led to 60–70 children being crushed to death at the main railway station;[41] the exodus of tens of thousands of the city's inhabitants in freezing temperatures led to huge numbers of casualties, with search parties burying hundreds of children and adults who had frozen to death;[42] and when the weather thawed in the spring, some 90,000 corpses were found in ditches alongside the roads travelled by Germans fleeing westwards.[43]

Of all the regions of Germany east of the Oder-Neiße, the area whose population suffered proportionally the greatest number of casualties was the 'Neumark', the eastern portion of Brandenburg.[44] There, of a German population of 644,834 before the outbreak of war in 1939 (and about 660,000 in 1944, including some 110,000 people – most of whom had been evacuated from Berlin – who had arrived in the province between March 1943 and the end of 1944), an estimated

257,000 – roughly two fifths – had died by 1945 as a result of military action, flight and expulsion. As elsewhere in eastern Germany, the flight from eastern Brandenburg was precipitate. Altogether, the period during which evacuation was possible – between the time the German authorities allowed the population to flee and the time that the entire region was occupied by the Soviet Army – was a mere two weeks.[45] Evacuation from the regions to the east of Brandenburg had started within days of the beginning of the Soviet January offensive: from the 'Warthegau', which had become home to some 670,000 Germans, it started in mid-January; and from the region of the old province of Posen (Poznań) Germans fled between the 20th and the 23rd of January. However, the flight of the population of eastern Brandenburg did not get underway until the end of January, and by that time for many it was too late.

Responsibility for the delay once again lay with the Nazi Party leadership, which was charged with organizing the evacuations. Having convinced themselves that Soviet forces were unlikely to advance rapidly to Berlin, Party leaders remained unwilling to allow people to flee until the last minute. Even at the end of January the Nazi Party authorities in eastern Brandenburg prohibited the flight of the civilian population, with the exception of the roughly 100,000 Berliners who had been evacuated to this supposedly safe province during 1943 and 1944 in order to escape the bombs falling on the Reich capital. Years later, Hans Runger, a farmer from the village of Bärfelde in the district of Soldin in Brandenburg, described his experiences at the beginning of 1945, starting his account with the observation that 'until 1945 our village was spared the effects of war'. Then, at the end of January, refugee treks passed through on their way westwards from the 'Warthegau' and West Prussia. On 29 January, Russian tanks were a mere 12 kilometres distant; the villagers could hear shooting and 'just about everyone became uneasy'. Nevertheless, reported Runger:

> The word from official Party offices remained only that the Soldin district will not be evacuated. So no one dared to flee, although many had their wagons ready for departure. The men

conferred with one another and decided to follow along with retreating German military units. However, we waited in vain for the German military. They simply had withdrawn to Pomerania.

Then suddenly and unexpectedly on 31 January, between 2:15 and 3:00 in the afternoon, the Russians entered Bärfelde.[46]

In the days that followed, Soviet tanks were stationed in the village, German civilians were shot, women and girls were raped by drunken Soviet soldiers, and half the village was burned down; Soviet infantry passed through the village and looted whatever they could. Germans were ordered to clear the streets of dead horses and spent war materiel, and German men who had been members of the Nazi Party were deported.

When Soviet forces moved into eastern Brandenburg simultaneously from both the north and the south at the end of January, there was panic among the Germans. However, a large proportion of the rural population was unable to flee, due to the speed of the Soviet advance. The population in the towns fared a bit better, as some had been able to escape on special trains to the west. But it was not long before that avenue of escape was blocked as well. On 28 January, as Soviet forces raced to the Oder, the rail line via Frankfurt on the Oder was cut, and three days later the same thing happened to the rail line via Küstrin. Many German civilians paid dearly for the refusal of local Nazi Party leaders to allow a timely evacuation of their communities.

Just about all the Germans who fled or were expelled from the east lost most if not all of their property. The first wave of looting was by soldiers. In both east and west, soldiers of all armies preyed on the helpless civilian population. In the west, soldiers of a Wehrmacht facing imminent defeat stole from their civilian 'racial comrades', as did soldiers of the Western armies moving into Germany.[47] In the east, Soviet forces advancing into Germany gladly plundered the property of their hated enemy, a prospect made all the more inviting since Germans were abandoning their homes as quickly as possible. At the same time, the arrival of Soviet forces often heralded an orgy of looting and rape, accompanied not infrequently by murder; many civilians were killed for the most trivial of reasons, for an item of clothing or a watch. Three decades later, the German Federal Archive registered the cases of some 23,200 people from Germany east of the Oder–Neiße who had been killed either in their native villages and towns or in flight, and that figure was far from complete; altogether it is estimated that the total number of Germans killed in former German areas east of the Oder–Neiße exceeded 120,000, the vast majority as a result of attacks by Soviet soldiers.[48] Later, after the German surrender, many Poles and Czechs in the regions to be vacated by Germans also took what they could from the erstwhile members of the 'master race'.[49] Germans who had fled from the east therefore generally arrived in central and western Germany impoverished and traumatized.

The mass flight of Germans westwards was a profound shock: the horrors that the Nazi regime had perpetrated against others across Europe now were visited on Germans themselves; homes were lost, communities torn apart, social networks disrupted, and respect for human life and dignity eroded. The shock was all the greater for the Germans in the eastern Prussian provinces and in the Sudetenland, who had suffered far less from Allied bombing hitherto than had their fellow citizens in western and central Germany. Indeed, until 1945 the Sudetenland had been almost a haven of peace surrounded by the horrors of war, where people experienced neither the food shortages nor the bombing that had threatened Germans elsewhere, nor the fighting of the last months of the war which turned much of Germany into a wasteland.[50] In the testimony about flight and expulsion collected by the German Federal Government, some of which was published during the 1950s, stories usually stress the sudden approach of the Russians and loss of Heimat. The abrupt transition was deeply shocking even where the evacuations had proceeded smoothly.

The experience of the inhabitants of Löbau, in the rural district of Neumark in West Prussia, was fairly typical. Years later, the then mayor of Löbau noted that 'the last Christmas holidays in the Heimat passed peacefully. [. . .] Housebuilding for those bombed out of their homes and other measures continued apace alongside the construction of military defences, so that we had the impression that there

was nothing to fear'. Then in the middle of January everything
suddenly changed:

The Russian winter offensive began. The *Volkssturm* was called
up and trained and assigned to the villages along the line of fortifications. On the morning of 18 January we mayors and
administrative officials of the district of Neumark had gathered in
the district government office [*Landratsamt*] in Neumark for a
conference, when at around 11 o'clock Evacuation Level 1 [. . .]
was announced for the district. According to the evacuation
plan the population now was to be evacuated except for those
who, due to special obligations to maintain vital institutions of
government, the post office and the railways, were to remain
behind until Evacuation Level II. The conference with the
Landrat was broken off immediately.

The population was informed according to plan and the
departure of the trek was fixed for the morning of 19 January
1945. The shops were instructed to sell their stocks freely [i.e.
without reference to ration cards]. The order had to be
rescinded, however, as some of the population proved disorderly and tried primarily to purchase alcohol. For most people
the evacuation order was unexpected despite the fears that
already existed. It was possible, however, to avoid a panic, as
the front was still roughly 80–100 km. distant. The Poles
remained quiet. During the night of 19 January a considerable
number of the town's population was able to be evacuated by
train [. . .]. The remainder of the town's population used
horse-drawn vehicles that had been requisitioned from the villages and special trains, buses and lorries provided on 19
January 1945 but which departed partly empty since the population already had gone. Scheduled train service continued up
to the evening of 20 January 1945. The treks gathered at specific assembly points and by the afternoon of 19 January 1945
were brought to the marching route which had been specified
and laid down in writing. [. . .] There was a biting wind with
snow flurries and ice. The mood was depressed. We hoped

nevertheless that the Vistula would offer enough protection and believed that we soon would return. No one imagined the scale of the tragedy.[51]

Shortly thereafter, the Soviet Army occupied the district. The Germans were never to return.

Like most treks, the well-organized exodus from Löbau consisted disproportionately of the most vulnerable members of society. The fact that most able-bodied men either were in the armed forces or already fallen in battle – by the time that the mass flight began in January 1945 some 3,645,000 German soldiers had been killed[52] – necessarily meant that the treks would consist largely of women, children and the elderly. This created additional difficulties, since the proportion of those able to carry heavy burdens and to withstand the rigours of tramping westwards during winter was relatively small.

It was the Nazi Party Gauleiters who, in their capacity as 'Reich Defence Commissars', had been placed in overall charge of organizing the treks; district and local Nazi Party leaders were responsible for organizing the evacuations locally. With the disruption of communications and transport, and the growing isolation of Hitler and his entourage in Berlin, the Party assumed responsibility locally and regionally for emergency measures during the last-ditch defence of the country. Party officials were to work together with the state administration and local Wehrmacht commanders; the Party's welfare organization, the *Nationalsozialistische Volkswohlfahrt*, was made responsible for looking after the evacuees and securing places for them to sleep as they travelled westwards. (However, the evacuees themselves were responsible for providing the food they would need for the journey.)[53] The allocation of these responsibilities to Party bosses was part of a remarkable expansion of the power and importance of the Nazi Party as the German government crumbled during the last months of the Third Reich.[54] As German rule in the eastern regions of the Reich disintegrated, increasingly the Party rather than the state exercised authority.

As in Löbau, the order to evacuate usually was not issued until the last minute. It was felt that to initiate evacuations in good time would

undermine the troops fighting to defend their homeland. The consequences of delay could be – and frequently were – terrible. At best,
there might not be enough time to organize adequate transport,
assemble sufficient food for the journey or to make the necessary
arrangements for places to stay as the treks moved westwards. At
worst, delay could mean that civilians attempting to flee would be
caught in the firing line or be overrun by Russian tanks.

The dominant image of the treks is of columns of horse-drawn
wagons, piled high with people's worldly possessions and with
refugees (more often than not, women) tramping alongside, making
their way across desolate countryside in bitterly cold weather. A typical trek consisted of a convoy of perhaps as many as 50 horse-drawn
wagons from a particular village, carrying food, clothing, crockery,
and fodder for the horses. They made slow progress, covering barely
30 to 40 kilometres per day[55] – which, given the delay in their getting
underway, added to the danger that they might be overtaken by Soviet
military forces charging into Germany. Not all treks immediately
headed westwards; some merely moved out of their village for what
they assumed would be a short interval. For example, a trek from a
landed estate (Repplin) in the district of Pyritz (10 kilometres south-
east from Stargard in Pomerania) initially decamped to a neighbouring
village in order to await military developments, since 'everyone was of
the firm belief that they soon would be able to return to Repplin';
some of the trek members even walked back to their village to see
what had happened since they had left, and discovered that the estate
house had been looted. It was not until the district Party leadership
gave the order to leave three days later that the trek headed off westwards in the direction of Stralsund.[56] When the evacuations began it
was still possible to use the railways to travel westwards; by March,
however, that no longer was the case as lines had been cut, the railway
system had largely been paralysed by Allied bombing and shortage of
coal, and the trains still running were devoted almost exclusively to the
needs of the military. Motor vehicles, even where they were available,
did not offer much of an alternative, as they frequently had to be
abandoned when they broke down or when it became impossible to
find fuel. As Bernadetta Nitschke has observed in her study of the

expulsions from Poland, 'many motorised transports therefore ended as marches on foot'.[57]

Generally the treks were comprised of the inhabitants of a particular village, who kept largely together as they travelled westwards.[58] Village communities became trek communities, consisting mainly of women, children and the elderly, sometimes together with prisoners of war and foreign labourers who had been working in the village. Essentially the treks were villages on the move, and – the numerous horror stories which filled the documentary collections compiled in the 1950s notwithstanding – many journeys proceeded remarkably smoothly, with the refugees effectively handed on and looked after in one town after another as they travelled westwards. One such was the trek which, on 3 February 1945, left the estate village of Sallenhin/Schönigsthal, in the district of Pyritz to the south-east of Stettin, consisting of 367 people, 32 wagons, 65 horses and three further groups of wagons. As they made their way westwards, they were directed from one staging post to the next. On 17 February the trek reached the village of Vanselow near Demmin, where both people and animals were able to rest for a couple of days on a landed estate before moving on towards Stralsund. On the 23rd they arrived at Leblin, in the north of the island of Rügen, where the travellers were dispersed among the surrounding villages and farms wherever there was space. At the end of the month, the men from the trek below the age of 65 received their reward for having survived the journey: they were drafted into the local *Volkssturm*.[59]

Another successful example concerned the evacuation of the village of Sandow, in the district of Pyritz in Pomerania. Preparations for evacuation had been made at the end of January, when Germans fleeing from the 'Wartheland' began passing through. On 2 February the front neared Sandow and the military, expecting heavy fighting, recommended that the local population leave. When the local Nazi Party leader refused, claiming that the district Party had not authorized evacuation, the estate owner in the village, Count Wilhelm von Schlieffen, assumed responsibility. At 5:30 in the morning of 4 February the trek left Sandow. The initial hope was to sit out developments in another village some 25 kilometres away, but this soon proved illusory. Nonetheless, the participants on this trek were relatively fortunate. Only three people died during the journey, while a further 20 villagers left the trek along the way to seek out friends and relatives. The remainder succeeded in reaching the island of Rügen, 20 days after their journey had begun.[60] The trek from Sandow demonstrates a number of typical characteristics: hasty departure, initial hope that it might not be necessary to leave the area, and the fading authority of local representatives of the Nazi Party as the estate owner, the embodiment of the traditional village elite, took charge.

Most treks of village populations were led not by local Party leaders but by men who had occupied traditional positions of authority in their communities: estate owners, estate managers, mayors, farmers' leaders, teachers and priests. Insofar as they set out westwards before Soviet forces were on top of them, village communities were able to remain intact as they fled, whereas those who fled from the towns – if they did not find a place on the railways or Wehrmacht transports – often set out on their own. On foot with a handcart, or perhaps on a bicycle, they became easy targets for robbery, while treks of villagers, with their horse- or ox-drawn carts, often remained together as a coherent community.[61] The threats and challenges they faced on the way created, in the words of a former West Prussian estate owner and trek leader, 'a community in adversity which did not break apart and in which one helped one another'.[62] The social pressure to meet the needs of the group rather than just to look out for oneself, often created the basis for social discipline – in sharp contrast to the awful scenes where individuals in towns desperately sought places for themselves on boats or trains leaving for the west. Of course, not everyone maintained exemplary discipline or consistently put the common good before individual need – particularly when the food supply was so critical as to threaten survival. But selfishness had its limits: 'In order to live, one had to steal if need be, but whoever was dishonest over and above that was condemned.'[63] The experience of the trek often cemented bonds which remained strong for years. On Rügen, for example, many trek communities retained their sense of collective identity well after the end of the war.[64] Indeed, it was not uncommon for groups of refugees, often looked down upon and discriminated against by their new neighbours, to organize among themselves and to select former trek leaders as their 'refugee representatives' in their new places of settlement.[65]

Nothing so undermined the authority and legitimacy of the Nazi Party as the behaviour of its officials as the Red Army drew near to eastern German towns and villages. Assigned the task of stiffening resistance to the invader in an obviously hopeless and suicidal cause, Party bosses lost their grip on a population that could see the Third Reich dissolving around them. Those men who had been loudest in exhorting their 'racial comrades' to defend the homeland to the last breath against the Slavic hordes, were often the first to abandon their communities – and were more likely to have access to motor vehicles when most civilians had to make the hazardous trek westwards with horse-drawn carts or on foot. One woman teacher, who had been evacuated once already (from Suwalki) during the previous summer as the Red Army approached and then was posted to a kindergarten near Lötzen in East Prussia, described what happened to her in January 1945:

> And there I am running my kindergarten all obediently and along comes this friend Hanni . . . who worked in Lötzen in an office somewhere. Hanni comes home and says: 'Are you crazy? Still doing the kindergarten? Where do you think the *Kreisleiter* is? Where do you think your *NSV-Leiter* is? Empty! Empty! They all left long ago. Taken the last car and off they went! The offices are all empty, the whole Nazi bureaucracy has long gone and you sit here!'[66]

Another witness described what happened in Randsdorf, near the industrial city of Beuthen, in Upper Silesia:

> The village was not evacuated according to plan, although there had been enough time. One day before the Russians pushed into the village, I went first to the mayor, then to the district [Nazi Party] leader, in order to get a permit to evacuate. Both refused

me permission to leave the village. Yet the following night both of them fled.[67]

There were similar scenes across eastern Germany.

The loss to millions of Germans of their homes in the east, the experience of precipitate and dangerous flight, and the sorry sight of poor refugees trudging across the country in search of somewhere to settle, contributed mightily to the collapse in support for the Nazi regime. As another German woman (a settler in Kutno in occupied Poland where the order to evacuate came suddenly in the night of 16 January) noted subsequently, the evacuation order 'destroyed the last link between the Party and the population'.[68] She felt that the population had been kept in the dark until the moment when the hasty departure was announced, and then were left to fend for themselves; in her case, the trek was overtaken by Soviet forces and she spent a year in Soviet captivity.[69] According to a German army intelligence report in mid-March 1945, the German retreat left a 'general feeling of hopelessness, fear for one's life and bitterness against the National Socialist leadership' in its wake; anger was provoked especially by Party leaders 'who brought themselves and their families to safety when Soviet forces approached without caring for the racial comrades entrusted to them by their leaders'.[70]

In his chronicle of the siege of the 'fortress Breslau' Paul Peikert also noted that 'the mood of the population' became 'increasingly bitter'.[71] In Peikert's view, the evacuation order by Gauleiter Hanke on 19 January was nothing less than a 'crime against the German people [. . .] a rush into death'.[72] Where once the Nazi regime had enjoyed the overwhelming support of the German people, it now was seen to have betrayed them and left them to face mortal danger. This in turn provided a way for Germans to divest themselves of association and identification with Nazism. The sufferings of 1945, and particularly the fate of millions of Germans in the east, purged them of their identification with Nazism. They no longer saw themselves as its supporters or beneficiaries; now they counted themselves among its victims.

★

The millions of refugees and expellees who arrived in central and western Germany in 1945, and in the years that followed, were settled largely in rural regions – hardly surprising given the destruction of housing in German cities caused by Allied bombing. The regions which received the greatest numbers were those across northern Germany: Mecklenburg in the east, Schleswig-Holstein and Lower Saxony in the west.[73] Proportionally, the greatest concentration was in Mecklenburg where, in 1950, 47 per cent of the population consisted of 'resettlers' (the official term adopted by the German Democratic Republic) and where in many districts the refugees and expellees outnumbered the native population. In the American Occupation Zone, many were settled in rural Bavaria, where large numbers of people expelled from the Sudetenland found a new home. The areas where the fewest refugees and expellees settled were the heavily bombed large cities and industrial areas such as the Ruhr region and Hamburg, and the French Occupation Zone in the far southwest of the country, where only 1.9 per cent of the population were refugees/expellees in 1946. (The French, who had not been a party to the Potsdam Agreement, agreed subsequently to take 150,000 refugees from Austria, and until 1948 effectively closed the borders of their zone to all refugees except those joining relatives, or who had previously arranged employment.)[74]

Flight and expulsion from the east had profound effects upon the communities which received the uprooted. For example, the British Military Government estimated that in early August 1945 the population in the rural district of Celle was some 70 per cent greater than it had been before the war; according to a census taken on 1 October, the district contained a native population of 58,721 alongside 31,944 refugees and people who had been bombed out of their homes; in nine villages in the Celle rural district newcomers outnumbered natives.[75] In the rural northern districts of the Soviet Occupation Zone the influx was even greater. In the district of Demmin, for example, where the town of Demmin itself had been largely destroyed during the fighting in 1945, the *Landrat* estimated in November 1945 that 'to the roughly 53,000 inhabitants of the district roughly 54,000 resettlers already have been added'.[76] The social and cultural fabric of many rural communities changed hugely with the sudden influx of destitute people from the east.

Not surprisingly, the newcomers were not always welcomed with open arms. Despite what they had been through, their arrival provoked tensions and misunderstandings. On the one side, the refugees usually arrived impoverished and often traumatized; on the other, the inhabitants of the communities compelled to receive their compatriots from the east were preoccupied with their own problems – the loss of family members, food shortages, high levels of crime, overcrowding, and dealing with the new occupation regimes. That so many refugees regarded the loss of their Heimat as temporary, and did not imagine that they would have to build a new existence in their new communities, did nothing to make the processes of integration easier. Nor, for that matter, did the suspicions that the newcomers aroused among the natives – not least among those who regarded the refugees as badly behaved and partly responsible for the steep rise in theft that characterized the immediate postwar period.[77] To refer once again to the rural district of Celle: in November 1945 the *Landrat* reported to the British authorities the 'enormous difficulties' caused by the 'overwhelming influx of evacuees and refugees'. 'That so many people are living together in such close quarters', he wrote, 'naturally leads to discontent on the one side as well as on the other, especially when one side, or indeed both sides, are not prepared to adapt'.[78] Mutual suspicion, not mutual solidarity, often prevailed.

For millions of Germans the expulsion was the greatest upheaval of their lives. Not only the expulsion itself but also the experience of losing one's home and having to build a new life in a different and often unwelcoming environment left deep wounds. Decades would elapse before these wounds began to heal, before the dream of a return to their old Heimat faded, before their children grew up as citizens of the Federal Republic of Germany or the German Democratic Republic rather than thinking of themselves as uprooted East Prussians, Silesians, Pomeranians or Sudeten Germans. In the years after their forced removal from the east, the stories of what had happened to them would be repeated constantly within families, where

parents who were refugees told their children, born into a postwar
East or West Germany, of the hardships they had had to endure when
they lost their homes. No doubt the stories and memories of the lost
Heimat deeply affected postwar generations, but not so as to fill them
with a sense of Silesian or East Prussian identity somehow inherited
from their parents or with a longing for the lost German East, but
rather to amplify their fear of war.[79] Decades later an office worker in
Hamburg, born in 1950 to a mother who came from Silesia, related
the following in a life-history interview:

Yes, my mother – and my grandmother as well – constantly
talked about their Heimat, about the beauty of their Heimat.
And they often spoke about the flight. They had to leave their
house from one day to the next. Then they were in flight. My
mother said that they picked up a boy along the way. He had lost
his parents. What exactly became of him I do not know any
longer. I think they handed him over to the Red Cross. But I
don't know exactly. It may be that I thought of the Red Cross
because then constant messages of people searching for the missing came over the radio. They spoke of refugee children who
were searching for their parents: name, height, eye colour, etc.
That was terrible for us all back then, the idea of searching for
parents and siblings. In any case this thing must have preoccupied
me a lot, as my best friend and I, we constantly imagined how
awful it would be if we ourselves would have had to flee. If we
were to flee, in no case must we lose one another and so forth.
But if that should happen nonetheless, then we would have to
notify the Red Cross without fail, so that we could find one
another. Back then I dreamt very often that I had to leave our
home, our beautiful house, that I was in flight and had lost my
parents.[80]

5

THE LAST DAYS OF THE REICH

It is difficult to make plausible to the people one's own conviction that this war inevitably must be seen through to the bitter end.
Wilfried von Oven[1]

One experienced the collapse of the former regime, as far as I could observe, almost with a feeling of liberation from a heavy burden.
A parish priest in Franconia[2]

In April and May 1945, the nightmare of the Third Reich reached its grotesque conclusion. During the previous months the Nazi regime had been disintegrating and its military position deteriorating by the day, and casualties had reached unprecedented heights. However, the regime was still able to function, albeit with increasing difficulty. During its final weeks and days this changed: Allied armies now occupied a large and rapidly expanding portion of the Reich itself, while territory remaining under German control was cut in two. German administrative structures virtually ceased to function: Hitler and his immediate entourage had taken to living permanently underground; military orders were issued which bore only a fleeting relationship to reality. While the German population greeted the invading Allies with white flags, die-hard Nazi fanatics liquidated 'defeatists'; some Nazi leaders (Himmler and Göring) looked to secure a separate peace, while others (most prominently, Hitler and Goebbels) looked to suicide rather than face surrender. By the middle of April 1945 it had become difficult to speak of a functioning German state at all.

In the end, it was the military collapse that determined everything else. The Soviet offensives of January, and the American, British and Canadian offensives in February and March, had broken the back of the Wehrmacht and brought huge swathes of German territory – including the country's main heavy industrial areas of Upper Silesia, the Ruhr and the Saar – under Allied control. The Wehrmacht – without reserves, lacking air cover, and unable to make good its losses, to move its troops or supply them adequately[3] – was less and less able to stem the Allied advance. By the beginning of April the Germans' western front was crumbling: On 1 April Allied forces had reached Münster and Bielefeld, American troops were in the suburbs of Kassel, and the Ruhr region was surrounded; two days later Münster had been taken and Osnabrück reached, and the Americans were in Thuringia in central Germany and had taken Gotha, while Soviet forces were a mere ten kilometres from Vienna (which was occupied on the 13th). However, the Western Allies did not charge on to Berlin.

In a decision which has provoked considerable debate since, the Supreme Allied military commander, Eisenhower, chose in mid-April not to head for Berlin – as Montgomery had wanted – but instead 'to hold a firm front on the Elbe' and 'to make a powerful thrust in the Danube valley to join with the Russians and break up the southern redoubt'.[4] Eisenhower's decision 'to stop on the Elbe and clean up my flanks' and 'to await the advance of the Russian forces', and his concern to prevent the Germans from fighting on from a base in the Alps, left the Red Army with the bloody task of taking the Reich capital.

While the Western Allies were racing across Germany, Stalin convened his military commanders in Moscow on 1 April in order to finalize plans to take Berlin before the British or the Americans could do so. The Soviet offensive was to begin no later than 16 April, and by the middle of the month Soviet forces were poised for the final assault on the Reich capital.[5] The Germans were well aware that a Soviet offensive to take Berlin was imminent. However, by this stage there was little that the Nazi leadership had to offer the German people but fear and threats. On the eve of the attack, Hitler issued what was to be his last 'Order of the Day' to his soldiers on the eastern front:

Soldiers of the German Eastern Front!
For the last time the Jewish–Bolshevik arch-enemy has lined up his masses for attack. He is trying to smash Germany and to exterminate our people. You soldiers from the East yourselves know already to a great extent what fate threatens German women, girls and children above all. While the old men and children will be murdered, the women and girls will be reduced to becoming barracks whores. The rest will march to Siberia.

We have been planning for this threat, and since January of this year everything has been done in order to build up a strong front. A powerful artillery is greeting the enemy. The losses of our infantry have been replenished by countless new units. Alarm units, reactivated units and the *Volkssturm* are reinforcing the front. This time the Bolshevist will experience the old fate of Asia i.e. he must and will bleed to death in front of the capital of the German Reich.

Whoever does not do his duty at this moment is acting as a traitor to our people. The regiment or division that abandons their position is behaving so disgracefully that they will have to be ashamed in front of the women and children who endure the bombing terror in our cities. [. . .] Whoever gives you orders to retreat without your knowing him well is to be arrested immediately and, if necessary, to be bumped off [*umzulegen*] straight away – no matter what rank he holds. If every soldier on the eastern front does his duty in the coming days and weeks, the last onslaught of Asia will break apart, just as despite everything the breakthrough of our opponents in the west also will fail in the end.

Berlin remains German, Vienna will be German again, and
Europe will never be Russian.

Form a blood brotherhood not for the defence of the empty
notion of a Fatherland but for the defence of your Heimat, your
wives, your children and thereby of our future.

At this hour the entire German people look to you, my eastern fighters, and hope only that your steadfastness, your
fanaticism, through your weapons and under your leadership, the
Bolshevik onslaught suffocates in a bloodbath. At the moment in
which fate has removed the greatest war criminal of all times
[President Roosevelt, who died on 12 April] from this earth, the
turning point of this war will be decided.[6]

The hopeless struggle was to continue, spurred on by fear of the
Russians, by the illusion that the Soviet attack on Berlin would be
ground down as had the German attack on Stalingrad two and a half
years earlier, and by savage repression of anyone who showed signs of
wavering. The stage was set for the blood-soaked end of the Third
Reich.

Five days later, on 20 April 1945, as the Soviet operation to take
Berlin was underway, Adolf Hitler celebrated his last birthday. It was
a bizarre occasion. The leaders of the Nazi regime gathered together
for the last time: Martin Bormann, Joseph Goebbels, Hermann
Göring, Heinrich Himmler, Robert Ley, Joachim von Ribbentrop
and Albert Speer, along with the heads of the armed forces and a
number of Nazi Party Gauleiters. While those assembled in the Reich
Chancellery offered congratulations to their leader, air-raid sirens
sounded in the background.[7] Four days earlier the Red Army had
launched its final offensive to take Berlin, breaking out from the
bridgehead it had established along the Oder at Küstrin; and by the
time Hitler's entourage were raising champagne glasses to toast their
leader's fifty-sixth birthday, the American 7th Army had fought its way
into Nuremberg (where the Nazi Party rallies had been staged before
Germany went to war), Soviet tanks had reached the outskirts of the
capital, and the sound of artillery could be heard in the Reich

Chancellery. As if to provide appropriate birthday greetings, British (by night) and American (by day) bombers mounted raids on Berlin, including a daytime raid on the government quarter.[8]

In her account, drafted in 1947 but not published until 2002, Hitler's personal secretary Traudl (Gertraud) Junge, described how 'the Führer received birthday wishes from the faithful':

> They all came, shook his hand, promised to be loyal, and tried to persuade him to leave the city. 'My Führer, the city will soon be surrounded. You will be cut off and unable to reach the south. There's still time to take command of the southern armies if you go by way of Berchtesgaden.' Goebbels, Ribbentrop, Himmler, Dönitz – they all tried, but in vain. Hitler intended to stay and await developments. Out in the park, he pinned decorations on boys of the Hitler Youth, children who had distinguished themselves in battle against Russian tanks. [. . .]
>
> In the evening we sat crammed together in the little study. Hitler was silent, staring into space. We too asked him if he wouldn't leave Berlin. 'No, I can't,' he replied. 'I should feel like a Tibetan lama turning an empty prayer mill. I must bring things to a head here in Berlin – or go under!' We said nothing, and the champagne we were drinking to Hitler's health tasted insipid.
>
> For Hitler had now said out loud what we had long seen, with terror, as a certainty: he himself no longer believed in victory. He retired early, and the birthday party broke up.[9]

By this time, the Nazi leader and his entourage were living in the infamous bunker in the grounds of the Reich Chancellery. The bunker complex had its origins before the war. No sooner had Hitler been installed as head of government than he began ordering alterations to the Chancellery, and through the 1930s various air-raid bunkers were built: first underneath the old Reich Chancellery, then in the garden behind the Chancellery, and then underneath the new Reich Chancellery designed by Albert Speer.[10] During the war the complex was extended further, and the gardens of the Chancellery became a building site. The work on what became a sprawling under-ground complex had largely been completed by the time Hitler returned to Berlin from the western front in January 1945.

Initially, the bunker was intended to serve as a temporary refuge for Hitler and his entourage during air raids. However, by mid-April it had become the permanent home of the dictator and his staff after bombing had wrecked the living quarters above ground in the Chancellery. The bunker contained underground living quarters for Martin Bormann, the Party secretary who had amassed enormous power as gatekeeper to Hitler, for the last Army Chief of Staff, General Hans Krebs, who replaced Heinz Guderian in this post in March 1945, for Hitler's chief military adjutant General Wilhelm Burgdorf, his personal pilot General Hans Baur, and Hermann Fegelein, who served as Heinrich Himmler's liaison officer at Hitler's headquarters and who had married Eva Braun's sister. In addition, the bunker complex had come to house 'countless officers, secretaries, guards, orderlies, radio oper-ators, cartographers, and other personnel', as well as becoming a refuge for victims of the bombing, pregnant women and some 200 children.[11]

Hitler's own bunker – the 'Führer Bunker' – consisted of some twenty small rooms under eleven metres of concrete, and was reached by stairs leading down from a modest opening at ground level in the Reich Chancellery garden.[12] By all accounts, the atmosphere in the bunker was strange and oppressive, a function of the unnatural under-ground existence, the hopeless military situation, and Hitler's own peculiar habits. Hitler had 'an odd daily schedule', and usually slept into the afternoon.[13] Since the activities within the bunker revolved around the dictator, this lent a strange rhythm to life in an already strange environment. What is more, Hitler's physical condition had deteriorated greatly by the last weeks of his life. Among those who described the environment of the bunker and the shocking physical appearance of the man who until recently had ruled most of Europe was Major General Erich Dethleffsen. Dethleffsen had been appointed on 23 March to replace Hans Krebs as Chief of the *Führungsgruppe* in the Army General Staff (after Krebs took over from Guderian as Army

Chief of Staff); in this capacity he had to accompany Krebs when the latter made his daily reports to Hitler. In memoirs, written while a prisoner of war in Allendorf, in the district of Marburg, during the winter of 1945/46, Dethleffsen described his first encounter with his 'Führer' in the bunker:

Before I drove to the Reich Chancellery for the first time, an officer of the operational section told me that I had to be prepared to see in Hitler a completely different person than was known to me through photos and film or perhaps from earlier encounters. An exhausted old man. The reality surpassed the warning by far. Previously I had seen Hitler fleetingly only twice, at an act of state at the memorial to the fallen in 1937 and at his birthday parade in 1939. The Hitler of that time was in no respect comparable with the wreck of a person to whom I reported on 25 March 1945 and who wearily extended to me a limp, trembling hand. [. . .] Physically he presented a terrible picture. He dragged himself along slowly and laboriously from his living quarters into the conference room of the bunker, throwing the upper part of his body forward and pulling his legs along afterwards. He lacked a sense of balance; if he was stopped on this short distance (20 to 30 metres), he would have to sit on one of the benches placed along both walls for this purpose or hold on to his conversation partner. He had lost control of his right arm, the right hand trembled constantly. [. . .] The eyes were bloodshot; although all written material intended for him was typed on special 'Führer typewriters' with letters three times the normal size, he could read only with glasses. Saliva often trickled from the corners of the mouth – a picture of misery and of horror.[14]

Nevertheless, according to Dethleffsen, 'mentally Hitler was, compared with his physical decline, still fresh'. When Gotthard Heinrici reported to Hitler after being appointed Himmler's successor as Commander of the Army Group Vistula in late March, his observations were similar:

He gave me the impression of a man who was seriously physically ill. This changed completely as soon as discussion with
him got underway. Immediately he became lively, answered with
clear considered arguments and proved himself to be most
extremely strong-willed and convinced of the correctness of his
views. He was not a man who wanted to let himself be led by
others, but held the reins himself firmly in his grasp.[15]

Although a physical wreck and with his world crashing down around
him, Hitler nevertheless remained remarkably clear-headed about
what was occurring, and his personality continued to have a remarkable effect upon those with whom he came into direct contact. He
retained a phenomenal memory for detail, in particular technical
details, which lent his arguments a power to convince even in the
hopeless situation facing the German military and political leadership.

However, Hitler's arguments, his assertion that fighting spirit and
fanaticism could overcome impossible odds, had taken on the quality
of a broken record. When Heinrici reported to Hitler on the eve of
the Soviet offensive to take Berlin and described the enormous difficulties facing the vastly outnumbered German forces, the dictator
responded that 'he was conscious of the existing shortcomings, but
belief and trust in success would make up for them. If everyone were
convinced not only that this battle must be won but also that it will be
won, then it would become the greatest defensive success of the war
and the bloodiest defeat for the enemy.'[16] Hitler maintained a stubborn
refusal to reconsider his strategic and political goals, even as the world
was caving in on him and on the 'Thousand-Year Reich' that he had
created. This posture had to be maintained if Germany were to go
down fighting, and Hitler considered no alternative. He remained, in
the words of Heinrici, 'the incarnation of an unyielding attitude'.[17]
According to Dethleffsen:

He did not deviate one step from the course he had laid out, not
even when all the requirements for ever achieving the goal had
been lost. [. . .]
He rejected with grim obstinacy every attempt to describe the

true situation to him and to make it clear to him that the strength of the troops was exhausted, that their value was constantly declining due to the enormous losses and the hasty and therefore incomplete training of replacements, that no reserves either of supplies or of men were available – in short, that the military end was approaching.[18]

On the night of 20/21 April Dethleffsen was sent to the bunker to report to Hitler about the Soviet breakthrough near Cottbus, some 120 kilometres south-east of Berlin. The breakthrough signalled the final collapse of the Wehrmacht's eastern front and the imminent encirclement of Berlin. This was the only time that Dethleffsen was alone with Hitler: 'Hitler took the bad news calmly; but again he found only one word to explain the Soviet success: "treason".'[19]

By this point Hitler was intent on committing suicide. He had no future after defeat, and he knew it. At times he clung to the illusory hope that the alliance against Germany would crumble; that the British and Americans 'would not leave him in the lurch as the champion of western culture and civilization against the barbarity of the east' but instead would offer an armistice and material assistance so that he could continue the struggle against the USSR.[20] When news arrived that Roosevelt had died, it had been greeted in the bunker with jubilation and a short-lived belief that the war in the west would come to an end. At other times, however, Hitler was brutally realistic, and resigned to what was happening. According to Dethleffsen, after being challenged on the night of 20/21 April by Walter Hewel (the permanent representative of the Foreign Ministry on Hitler's staff in the bunker) that it was high time for a political initiative, Hitler blurted out: 'I don't do politics any more. Politics makes me sick. When I am dead you will have to do plenty of politics.'[21] Indeed, Hitler had never 'done politics' in the conventional sense of the term; he had always played *va banque*. Now the game was up.

While Hitler was issuing orders from his underground lair, conditions on the surface were deteriorating rapidly. When, shortly before the battle for Berlin began, Dethleffsen travelled through the city in order to attend the military briefings in the bunker, he saw a strange, ghostly landscape:

> For kilometres we drove through rubble. Traffic had ceased almost entirely. On the streets there was scarcely a person left to be seen. In the main arterial roads barricades had been built out of rails which had been ripped up and tramcars which had been pushed over. The streets were partly dug up in order to erect positions for defensive weapons. The city of millions was barely still viable, [and] prepared itself for a defence that was taken very seriously by large sections of the population, especially by the adolescent youth, while every soldier who assessed the situation soberly could only be convinced of its senselessness.[22]

As the Red Army approached, the main sign of life was the queues of people at grocery shops, stocking up for the coming siege.[23] Fear and confusion reigned, and once the 'Battle for Berlin' began, few of the city's remaining inhabitants had a clear idea of what was happening around them – other than that the sound of artillery announced the arrival of the Russians. As public transport ceased to function and with the telephone network largely out of commission, moving from one section of the city to another became increasingly hazardous and people's horizons shrunk. Once street fighting began, their horizons contracted still further as they took to the cellars of their ruined blocks of flats. Berlin's newspapers had ceased publication in mid-April. The government's international broadcasting service, the 'Deutschlandsender', had stopped transmitting on 19 April, the 'Reichssender Berlin' ceased operating on the 24th,[24] and Germans listened to the BBC, despite the risk involved and the constant power cuts which made this difficult.[25] Rumours abounded, some deliberately planted by a desperate, collapsing regime trying with exhortation and threat to keep people fighting in a hopeless situation.[26] The wheels of government largely stopped turning, and people were thrown back on their own resources to survive as best they could until the fighting was over.

*

For the German military, co-ordinating operations during the last weeks of the Third Reich became ever more difficult. Already by late March Hitler was holed up in the bunker with his loyal and fanatical military adjutant General Wilhelm Burgdorf, while Field Marshal Wilhelm Keitel and General Alfred Jodl (Chief of the Wehrmacht High Command and Chief of Staff respectively) had their headquarters and a small staff in Dahlem in the south-west of Berlin. However, much of the army command was situated in a camp kitted out with bunkers near Zossen (to the south of Berlin), and a portion of the Army General Staff had been transferred to Bavaria.[27] By the second half of April, when the area still under German military control had been split in two, proper co-ordination and command had become impossible.

That, however, did not prevent the German military leadership from continuing the struggle. Daily conferences, at which the chiefs of the general staffs of the army, navy, and air force reported on developments over the previous twenty-four hours, took place in the late afternoons in the bunker beneath the Reich Chancellery garden. A large number of people would crowd into the bunker's small conference room: Field Marshal Keitel and officers assigned to various generals, often Reich Marshal Göring, Reichsleiter Martin Bormann (who remained constantly at Hitler's side), Admirals Voss (Vice-Admiral and naval liaison officer at Hitler's headquarters) and Wagner, General Burgdorf, Admiral von Puttkammer, Colonel von Below (Luftwaffe), Major-General Eckhard Christian, SS-Obergruppenführer Hermann Fegelein, two or three young officers who functioned as personal adjutants to Hitler, frequently Albert Speer and Heinrich Himmler, the permanent representative of the Foreign Office Walter Hewel, sometimes Goebbels, and numerous stenographers.[28] They all stood around the table in the centre of the room; only Hitler and the stenographers would be seated. There was a constant coming and going, and after hearing reports from the assembled officers Hitler would issue his orders for the following day.

As the end drew closer, the relationship of these orders to the reality of the military situation became ever more tenuous. While the army leadership calculated that the looming Soviet offensive would come from the Oder in an attempt to take Berlin directly, Hitler was convinced that the main attack would come from the south; in his opinion, a direct attack from the Oder would be designed essentially to pin down German troops while a Soviet thrust could be made on Prague.[29] He was proved to be very wrong. Stalin's priority – his obsession – was to capture Berlin, not Prague. The main Soviet attack would indeed come from the Oder, and lead to the capture of the Reich capital less than three weeks later.

After the successes of its January offensive, during March and the first half of April the eastern front in Germany was relatively quiet. While fighting raged around various surrounded 'fortresses' (Breslau, Königsberg, Glogau) in eastern Germany and while the Germans' last offensive, in Hungary, failed in March, and while the Western Allies crossed the Rhine, surrounded the Ruhr and began their race across central Germany, along the Oder the Russians were making preparations for the final assault on the capital. They gathered some 16,700 artillery guns and thousands of tonnes of shells, and brought forward all available reinforcements, combat engineers and bridge-building troops; 190 Soviet divisions were made ready for the attack.[30] To face this extraordinary force, the Wehrmacht could call only upon exhausted, outnumbered units without sufficient ammunition, artillery or reserves; in some places, the German front was held not by Wehrmacht soldiers but by members of the *Volkssturm* militia, Hungarians in the SS, and 'Vlasov soldiers' (Russian soldiers fighting for Germany under the command of General Andrei Vlasov).[31] The final Soviet offensive was about to begin.

On 16 April the gigantic Soviet force of 2.5 million troops, 6,250 tanks and some 42,000 pieces of artillery and mortars began the assault on what remained of the Wehrmacht defending the path to Berlin.[32] As the Germans had expected – their reconnaissance had observed the Soviet build-up along the Oder – after a massive artillery barrage the Red Army attacked westwards along the entire front. While the Soviet Second White Russian Front (under the command of Marshal Konstantin Rokossovsky) pushed forward north of Berlin (towards

Prenzlau, Neustrehlitz and Neubrandenburg), Soviet forces further south aimed at capturing the Reich capital. From the Küstrin bridge-head in the centre of the front, the Soviet First White Russian Front (under the command of Marshal Georgi Zhukov) smashed its way westwards in two bold drives: one towards Oranienburg just to the north of Berlin, with the aim of either turning south towards Potsdam or else continuing to drive westwards, the other directly towards Berlin itself. From the south, the forces of the First Ukrainian Front (under the command of Marshal Ivan Koniev) drove into the Lausitz towards Forst, Cottbus and Spremberg, then turning northwards in the direction of Berlin and Potsdam (with other forces aiming further south towards Dresden). Berlin was to be both surrounded and attacked frontally from the east and the south.

The German military leadership may have foreseen the attack but – overstretched, fatigued, without sufficient fuel or ammuni-tion, and decimated by the effects of enemy artillery and air attacks – they were powerless to contain it for long. Initially, the Wehrmacht managed to hold back Soviet forces, except for a breakthrough of tank companies from Görlitz to Bautzen in the south and some Russian gains between Frankfurt on the Oder and Eberswalde. Soviet units met particularly determined opposition from well-placed German defences on the Seelow Heights to the west of Küstrin. Here Gotthard Heinrici, a master of defensive tactics, had calculated accurately when and where the Russians would attack and pulled his forces back the night before; consequently the Soviet artillery bom-bardment which preceded the attack did little damage to the Germans but served to impede the Soviet advance. German resistance to the frontal attack on the Seelow Heights, which claimed the lives of at least 33,000 soldiers under Zhukov's command, was the last tac-tical success of the Wehrmacht in the Second World War.[33] But that success was fleeting: German lines held for a mere three days. On 19 April the exhausted and outnumbered defenders were overcome, and Soviet forces broke through on both sides of the railway line from Küstrin to Berlin. Heinrici's requests for permission to withdraw his forces to prevent their destruction – a move which amounted to an admission that the Wehrmacht's eastern front had been broken –

were refused.[34] The Germans threw in what reserves they still had, including an inadequately trained division of 16- and 17-year-old members of the Labour Service, and tanks either previously captured from the enemy or used for training – but managed to hold back the Russians for only a few more hours.[35] There no longer was a coherent front line between the Oder and the eastern suburbs of Berlin.

To the south, the German position was no better. After the troops of the First Ukrainian Front crossed the river Neiße, the German lines there too crumbled, and Koniev's armies moved across the Spree Forest, which stretches out to the south-east of Berlin. Before long, Koniev's forces had surrounded the Wehrmacht's 9th Army under General Theodor Busse, which was destroyed at the end of the month in and around the village of Halbe with a loss of at least 40,000 lives.[36] By the 20th, Soviet troops had reached the village of Baruth, some 60 kilometres south of Berlin, and were turning northwards towards Zossen. Now the headquarters of the Army High Command was threatened, and hasty preparations were made for its evacuation from Zossen to Potsdam-Eiche and to an air-raid training school in Berlin-Wannsee. The following day, what had been the headquarters of the German Army fell largely intact to Soviet forces.[37] Berlin lay a mere 40 kilometres to the north.

At this point, on Sunday 22 April, with Zossen captured and with Soviet forces in the outskirts of Berlin between Frohnau and Pankow in the north and Lichtenberg, Mahlsdorf and Karlshorst in the east, Hitler openly acknowledged the truth of the military position and announced that he would remain in Berlin to the end.[38] Soviet troops had broken through the ring of defences around Berlin and at the city's northern suburbs. With fighting raging in the eastern suburbs, with Soviet forces at Jüterbog and thus about to capture the Wehrmacht's largest and most important ammunition supply centre, the military situation that Krebs, Jodl and Keitel outlined to Hitler was hopeless. Krebs informed Hitler that the attack which was to have been undertaken by a new 'combat group' under the command of the SS General Felix Steiner against Soviet forces to the south east of Berlin, an attack which supposedly would turn the tide, never took place: the 'Steiner Combat Group' and its offensive had been fictions.[39] At this the dictator finally cracked. He ordered everyone from the conference room except for Keitel, Jodl, Krebs and Burgdorf. To the amazement of his small audience, Hitler now admitted out loud that the war was lost. 'Betrayal' was everywhere! According to his Luftwaffe adjutant, Nicolaus von Below, the 'Führer':

> [. . .] then unleashed a furious tirade against the Army commanders and their 'long-term treachery'. I was sitting near the door in the annexe and heard almost every word. It was a terrible half-hour. After this outburst, however, he had at least made up his mind about his destiny, He ordered Keitel and Jodl to report to Dönitz in northern Germany and continue the war from there. He, Hitler, would remain in Berlin and take his own life.[40]

With the Reich capital soon to be surrounded and the impossibility of successfully defending Berlin blindingly obvious;[41] with communications with the various Wehrmacht units increasingly difficult (the main communications cable to the south had been cut in Thuringia), the choice – as Keitel put it in his memoirs, hastily written before his execution at Nuremberg – was clear: either surrender in Berlin before the city became a battlefield, or fly out that evening to Berchtesgaden.[42]

Hitler would do neither. As he had stated repeatedly, and despite attempts to dissuade him, he would stay in Berlin and die there. He was determined to commit whatever military units seemed available to defend the capital.[43] He ordered that the units of the 12th Army under the command of General Walther Wenck between Wittenberg and Brandenburg cease fighting against the Western allies and commit to the defence of Berlin; the SS Tank Corps under the command of General Steiner in the regions around Oranienburg and the Wehrmacht's 9th Army in the Königswusterhausen-Beeskow district (southeast of Berlin) were ordered to join the defence of the capital. According to Keitel, Hitler declared:

I am not going to leave Berlin; I will defend the city to the end. Either I am in command of this battle for the Reich capital [. . .] or I go down in Berlin with my soldiers and fall in battle for the symbol of the Reich.

[. . .] I am staying here in Berlin! I already have announced that to the German people and the Reich capital on the radio an hour ago. [This was a reference to Goebbels' broadcast announcement that Hitler was staying in Berlin 'in the immediate vicinity of the front line'.] I can no longer go back.

I am staying here, that is certain. [. . .] Now it also will be necessary to negotiate with our enemies and Göring can do that better than I in any case. Either I win the battle of Berlin or I die in Berlin. That is my irrevocable decision.[44]

Hitler was convinced both that the war was lost and that his presence in Berlin would inspire German troops to fight on nevertheless. Confidence and belief in him would keep the fighting going; therefore he had to stay in the city.[45] It was the last, most extreme and futile exercise of his charismatic authority – to ensure that fighting would continue and that more people would be killed, before he took his own life. Hitler remained true to form to the end: burning his bridges, viewing the choices before him in apocalyptic 'either/or' terms, displaying utter disregard for the loss of life and suffering that this course would entail. 'I can no longer go back.' This was his motto, and he was determined that there would be no way back for the German people either.

Joseph Goebbels too decided to remain in the Reich capital, announcing over the radio that Berlin had become a 'front city', that he would stay in the embattled capital and that 'my wife and my children also are here and remain here'.[46] Six weeks earlier, in mid-March, Goebbels had noted in his diary that 'we have to lead the German people back to the basic theses of how we wage war and make it clear to them that they have no other choice but to fight or to die.'[47] Now, in the final hour, they would be given no choice; they were to die. The Second World War was not to end in surrender as had the First; if Germany was going to lose this war, the nation would go down fighting in such a way as to inspire future generations.[48] As Dönitz put it (while in Allied captivity during the summer of 1945), 'the truth of Clausewitz, that a rebirth can only arise one day from an honourable struggle and ending', still held good.[49]

As the end approached, the spectre of the collapse and revolution of 1918 remained fixed in the minds of the Nazi leadership. Keitel, for example, echoed his master's opinion that the reverses suffered by the Wehrmacht were due to a lack of will and looked back with disgust at the collapse in 1918, when any soldier who no longer wanted to fight allegedly got away with it, placing a red cockade on his cap and turning on his officers.[50] On 26 April the Commander of the Third Tank Army, General Hasso von Manteuffel, reported by telephone to the Chief of Staff of the Army Group Vistula that a number of units were in a state of 'complete dissolution', adding that 'I have not seen such pictures as those today even in 1918'.[51] Von Manteuffel knew how to deal with such problems. The day before this telephone conversation he had ordered that, should units that came under enemy fire or attack then abandon their positions without a fight, 'all heavy weapons and artillery should direct their fire on these gangs'.[52]

Although some military commanders and members of Hitler's entourage remained committed to continuing the fight to the very end, not everyone was prepared to follow the example of Hitler and Goebbels and to embrace death. The news that Hitler had decided to remain in Berlin spread rapidly among the Nazi leadership, who began to consider what would happen after their 'Führer' was dead.[53] Himmler, who had been informed by Fegelein of Hitler's outburst on the 22nd, now sought contact with Eisenhower, in the strange hope that the SS might join with the Americans in a struggle against the Soviet Union. Göring, from Berchtesgaden, sent a telegram to Hitler on the 22nd asking if his decision to remain in Berlin meant that he, the Reich Marshal, now would succeed the 'Führer' (as had been spelled out for the case that Hitler become incapacitated, in the decree of 29 June 1941).[54] Göring's telegram was followed by another a few hours later, ordering von Ribbentrop to Berchtesgaden as soon as the succession took effect – a move used by Göring's rivals at Hitler's side,

Goebbels and Bormann, to convince the dictator that Göring's behaviour amounted to an attempt at a *coup d'état*. Predictably, Hitler viewed Göring's initiative as treason, and ordered the Reich Marshal's arrest.

While Himmler and Göring unrealistically sought a negotiated peace, Hitler remained committed to continuing the war. Although it was clear to him that complete military collapse was imminent, this did not stop him from ordering continued operations to defend the capital. However, the available units of the 12th Army that he now called to the defence of Berlin consisted of only five or six 'children's divisions' and a few further units formed of soldiers thrown together after they had been separated from their own formations; and the 9th Army, far from being able to relieve Berlin as Hitler had hoped, was surrounded and fighting for its survival. In the centre of the city, Hitler appointed SS Brigadier General Wilhelm Mohnke, a member of his personal guard since 1933, to assume command of the 'citadel' – the defences surrounding the government quarter. To face the Soviet onslaught, Mohnke had some 4000 SS men and some smaller Wehrmacht and Hitler Youth units at his disposal.[55] These meagre forces were supposed somehow to stop the Red Army.

On 23 April, Soviet units reached the southern boundary of Berlin itself, cutting off the Wehrmacht's 9th Army, which had been defending Frankfurt and Guben along the Oder, and at the same time reached the River Havel to the north of Spandau. By this time the Wehrmacht High Command was leading a nomadic existence. Already forced to abandon its headquarters at Zossen, once Hitler had decided to remain in Berlin the remnants of the Wehrmacht High Command assembled in Krampnitz, to the north of Potsdam; then, in the night of 23/24 April, the approach of Soviet tanks made necessary another move, this time to Neu-Roofen (to the north of Berlin, between Rheinsberg and Fürstenberg). Travel by the military leadership to and from the bunker became ever more difficult as the Russians advanced.[56] The chain of command was quite literally breaking apart.

By this time, the rapid American advance across central Germany and the Soviet advance into Saxony promised to cut in half the area still controlled by the Nazi regime. That this would happen had been obvious for days, and on 15 April (the same day that he made his last

'Call to the Soldiers of the German Eastern Front') Hitler issued a
'Führer Order' stipulating that, should the land link in central
Germany be cut, the Wehrmacht command would be split, with two
separate general staffs.[57] To head these commands Hitler named two
men known for their uncompromising adherence to the Nazi line
whom he felt could be counted on to fight to the end. As Supreme
Commander for the northern region (to whom the Supreme
Commander of the Army Group Vistula in the east and the Supreme
Commander Northwest in the west, as well as the Wehrmacht commanders in Denmark and Norway, were to be subordinated) he
named Grand Admiral Karl Dönitz; as Supreme Commander for the
southern region (to whom the Supreme Commander of the Army
Group South and Centre in the east and the Supreme Commander of
the Army Group G for the west, as well as the commanders in the
southeast and southwest, were to be subordinated) he named Field
Marshal Albert Kesselring, who had commanded German forces in
Italy from 1943 to 1945. After his last meeting with Hitler at the
Reich Chancellery, on 21 April, Dönitz (who 'displayed his determination solely to execute what was ordered by the Führer')[58] moved to
the small town of Plön in Holstein, some 30 kilometres south-east of
Kiel. There he began to set up the administrative apparatus which
would serve for a few weeks as a caretaker successor government after
Hitler's suicide and the surrender of Berlin. With Dönitz in charge of
German forces in the north and Kesselring in charge of German
forces in the south, from 23 April Hitler's own military command was
limited to the defence of the Reich capital.[59]

It was at this point that the Wehrmacht essentially gave up the struggle against the Western Allies. Hitherto, German forces had fought
tenaciously in the west as well as in the east, and the Western Allies
had faced tough fighting and taken heavy casualties. Now that
changed: in the last weeks of the war, what remaining military
strength the Germans possessed would be concentrated against the foe
from the east: 'every available force' was 'to be engaged against the
Bolshevik arch enemy. Compared with this, even substantial losses of
territory to the Anglo-Americans recede into the background.'[60]

On 25 April the noose was tied around Berlin. Soviet forces had joined up from the north and the south near Ketzin, to the west of Berlin. The Reich capital was surrounded; Potsdam was encircled and cut off, and for the first time Soviet artillery shells hit the Reich Chancellery.[61] Hitler described the battle for Berlin as the 'German battle of fate'; on the 25th he radioed to Dönitz that 'compared with this all other tasks and fronts [are] of secondary importance'.[62] But it was far too late for this 'battle of fate' to be anything other than an exercise in pointless sacrifice. The only way in and out of Berlin now was by air; and with the air field at Gatow under artillery fire this meant using the broad avenue leading westwards from the Brandenburg Gate, the East-West Axis, as a landing strip.[63] On the same day that the Russians had encircled Berlin, over 300 British Lancaster bombers attacked the Obersalzberg, destroying Hitler's 'Berghof' retreat in the Bavarian Alps, and American and Soviet troops met up face-to-face at Torgau on the Elbe for what became one of the war's great photo opportunities. The 'Greater German Reich' had been split in two.

Within Berlin, fighting was raging around the Görlitz and Silesian railway stations (to the south-east and east of the city centre respectively) and in the area between Tegel and Siemensstadt to the north-west. On the 26th there was fighting in the south-west, in Zehlendorf and Steglitz, and to the south of the city centre around the Tempelhof air field. While this was happening, the State Secretary in the Reich Propaganda Ministry, Werner Naumann, informed his listeners over the radio: 'At the head of the defenders of Berlin stands our Leader. This fact by itself already is giving the battle for Berlin an unparalleled and decisive significance.'[64] However, Hitler was not exactly heading the battle; instead, he remained underground as the battle came to him. On the 27th the fighting in Berlin reached Charlottenburg, to the west of the city centre, and Zhukov's troops had reached the centre at the Hallisches Tor to the south and the Alexanderplatz to the east. The Russians were barely two kilometres from the bunker.

By this point, Hitler was grasping at straws. He ordered the 12th Army under General Walther Wenck and the 9th Army under

General Theodor Busse to relieve Berlin, but to no avail. Portions of the 12th Army tried to relieve Potsdam, but lacked the necessary strength and got bogged down near Ferch; the 9th Army remained trapped south-east of Berlin and, as Dethleffsen later observed, was falling apart.[65] Attempts by the 9th Army to break out failed. According to its own leadership on 28 April, the 'physical and mental condition of officers and men as well as the situation regarding ammunition and fuel allow neither a well-planned break-out attack nor holding out for long'. Nevertheless, the utter hopelessness of the military situation did not prevent Busse from going on to report that 'for the 9th Army it goes without saying that the fight continues to the end'.[66] Nor did it mean that Hitler, with Keitel (as ever) in agreement, had given up the idea of relieving Berlin, this time from the north with two divisions of the Army Group Vistula. However, the Army Group Vistula was in no condition to offer much relief to anyone: its Chief of Staff, General von Trotha, reported to Dönitz on 27 April that it was 'no longer in a position to check the Russian enemy, but is badly battered and is streaming back to the west through Mecklenburg and the northern portion of Brandenburg'.[67] In the face of this, the Commander of the Army Group, Heinrici, disregarded orders to relieve the capital: his forces lacked the strength, and he 'no longer carried out orders that did not correspond to reality'.[68] With the 9th Army surrounded, and given the depleted condition of the German units, 'above all their inadequacy for major offensive tasks', the resources needed for such operations no longer existed;[69] the orders from the Wehrmacht High Command (Keitel and Jodl) to commit forces to rescuing Hitler in Berlin had 'completely lost a basis in reality'. Heinrici's troops were unable to offer serious resistance to the Russians, whose tanks now broke through German lines almost at will: 'There no longer was a real determination to fight among these thrown-together units. Everyone saw the end of the war coming and no longer still was willing to risk his life at this time.'[70]

In Heinrici's opinion, the struggle was 'already lost'. Soviet forces had broken through towards Bernau, the 9th Army was pinned down; new recruits were untested; the morale of German troops was plummeting; supplies of fuel and ammunition were inadequate. Heinrici now was convinced that Berlin should be declared an open city in order to spare its inhabitants further suffering. However, he received no support from Dönitz, who insisted instead that 'the battle is indeed unavoidable, as otherwise the population will be carried off by the enemy to Russia without any attempt being made to save them from such a fate'.[71] For the man soon to become Hitler's successor, at issue was not whether the operation had any prospect of success but rather what impression would be created for posterity. In the event, Heinrici opted to withdraw his divisions to the lakes north of Berlin, where better defensive positions might be formed. His assessment of his position was dire – lack of fuel, constant air attack, and roads congested with refugee treks made movement almost impossible – and he chose to spare the lives of his soldiers rather than sacrifice them in Hitler's last battle. Soviet forces then broke through at Prenzlau, and on 28 April Heinrici was dismissed.[72]

Belated outbursts of sanity did not prevent the Wehrmacht High Command from asserting that relief was on its way, and on the 28th it reported that 'while the capital is being defended in a grandiose struggle unique in modern history, our troops on the Elbe have turned their backs on the Americans in order to relieve the defenders of Berlin'.[73] This described the state of the front facing the Americans more accurately than it did the prospects for relieving the capital. By this point the battle for the centre of Berlin already had begun, with the East-West Axis under artillery fire and Russian troops advancing house-by-house in bitter street fighting. Sunny weather favoured Allied air activity over the city; telephone connections were cut; there was only intermittent communication between Hitler and the military formations he theoretically commanded. To the last (in a radioed message), Hitler continued to demand information about attempts to relieve the city, but Keitel now could respond only that there was no further hope of relief for Berlin or for opening an escape route to the west.[74] German military commanders were becoming increasingly reluctant to order their men to fight; the Reich Chancellery was, as Bormann put it in a telegram to Munich 'already a pile of rubble';[75] and Soviet troops were only a few hundred metres from the bunker.

★

Nothing now could save the capital of the Third Reich or its leader, and Hitler's lieutenants knew it. On 28 April news arrived of a Reuters report that Himmler had been trying to arrange negotiations for surrender with the Allies, using the Swedish diplomat Count Folke Bernadotte (the Vice-President of the Swedish Red Cross) as an intermediary. The man whose career had been built on loyalty to Hitler, whose SS had as its motto 'my honour is loyalty', had sought to negotiate a surrender behind Hitler's back. According to Hannah Reitsch, who had flown Robert Ritter von Greim, Göring's successor as 'Supreme Commander of a Luftwaffe that no longer existed', to the bunker a few days before, Hitler flew into a rage at the news and subsequently looked 'like someone whose life had already been extinguished'.[76] Betrayal also surfaced closer to home when Hermann Fegelein (Eva Braun's brother-in-law and Himmler's liaison officer at Hitler's headquarters), having resolved not to die in Berlin, abandoned his post and his uniform. After Fegelein was found, drunk, it was learned that he had been aware of Himmler's contacts with Bernadotte.[77] Court-martial proceedings already underway against Fegelein were broken off and on 29 April, a beautiful spring day, Hitler ordered that the man who would have become his own brother-in-law be shot forthwith. Hitler's bride-to-be was shocked – her sister was heavily pregnant – and was reported as convinced that 'in this case he would have killed even his own brother'.[78] Fegelein was sentenced to death and immediately executed by firing squad.

By this time most of Berlin was in the hands of the Russians, who were taking the first steps towards forming a Soviet administration for the city. On the 28th, while the Wehrmacht High Command still was speaking of the 'heroic struggle of the city of Berlin', the head of the Soviet occupation authority in Berlin, General Nikolai Bersarin, issued his 'Order Nr. 1' to the city's population.[79] In each administrative district of the city, Soviet military commands were to be established; members of the Nazi Party, Nazi organizations, police formations, the Wehrmacht, SA and SS were to register with the occupying authorities; electricity and water works, public transport workers, hospitals, food shops and bakeries were to resume operation, while the banks were to remain shut. Although the fighting still raged in the immediate vicinity of the bunker, for much of the population of Berlin the postwar era already had begun.

This did not mean that peace and security had arrived. For many Berliners the postwar era began with rape. The end of April brought not only energetic Soviet attempts to get the city's services up and running; it also saw an explosion of sexual violence by Soviet soldiers. Women were raped in cellars, in their flats, in front of children and German men; women were gang-raped and groups of women were divided up to be raped by soldiers. No woman was safe from sexual humiliation – old women as well as young girls were raped. The great wave of rape began when the Red Army captured substantial portions of the city and continued until the battle for Berlin came to an end i.e. during the last week of April and the first week of May.[80] Although Marshal Zhukov had ordered his troops repeatedly to make no contact with the civilian population at their own initiative, in fact they were allowed quite free rein during this period. On 22 April the German propaganda sheet *Pänzerbär, ein Kampfblatt für die Verteidiger Großberlins* had informed its readers: 'This Soldateska roams from house-to-house and steals watches and jewellery, demands schnapps and cigarettes at gun-point. In the evening the Asiatic lechers scour flats for young German women and girls, [and] violate them in the most brutal violent manner.'[81] For many Germans the behaviour of Soviet troops confirmed the images long purveyed in bloodcurdling Nazi propaganda.

Berlin was far from the only place where Soviet soldiers raped large numbers of women. Their conduct during their first incursions into East Prussia and their advance across eastern Germany earlier in 1945 had been similar. Furthermore, this behaviour was not confined to Soviet troops. The behaviour of some of the soldiers in French uniform who marched into Baden and Württemberg in south-western Germany behind the Americans in April 1945 was not much better. The French arrival in the Reutlingen district, for example, was accompanied by large numbers of rapes: in Gönningen, 24 April was a day of plunder and rape during which 'the Moroccans attacked many women and in addition demonstrated their great liking for jewellery and watches'; in Gomaringen, after three days of sexual violence by French soldiers 75 women aged between 14 and 60 were treated medically after being raped; in Bronnen, while the first French soldiers had left a good impression, later a 'black unit' arrived in the village, searched 'every house from cellar to attic', stole money, watches, cutlery and food, discovered stores of alcohol at a local inn, and beat the men and raped the women 'in the presence of their husbands or children'; and in Reutlingen itself the arrival of the 'second wave' of soldiers ushered in a 'reign of terror with looting and rape'.[82] In Freudenstadt in the Black Forest, hundreds of women reported being raped after the French arrived in mid-April and proceeded to destroy much of the town;[83] in the university town of Tübingen, which French forces had occupied without a fight on 19 April, the Women's Clinic treated hundreds of patients who had been sexually assaulted, 'including children of 12 years of age up to old women of over 70 years';[84] and in Konstanz, on the Bodensee at the Swiss border, which had also been occupied by French forces, large numbers of women – 115 in August 1945 alone – approached the city's Women's Clinic to seek abortions, claiming that their pregnancies had been the product of rape.[85]

But it was in Berlin that the greatest and most concentrated outburst of sexual violence occurred. As in most communities within Germany by this time, in Berlin the overwhelming majority of the German population was female; of the much-depleted civilian population in the capital in 1945, over 63 per cent were female.[86] Belated calls for the evacuation of some 500,000 women and children before the battle for the city began could not be heeded,[87] and the largely female civilian population was forced to lead an underground existence in bunkers and air-raid shelters as the fighting raged. One woman, born in 1932, described nearly 40 years later what happened when Soviet soldiers entered the air-raid shelter in which she, then a 13-year-old, had sought refuge:

And they took me out with them. And now I always thought, because my mother, she also never explained things to us, because I once asked her what rape is, then she said: then people are shot. . . . And I just said: 'now go ahead and shoot, now go ahead and shoot'. But in any case after the thing [i.e. the rape] I had to go back into the cellar. And that was terrible for me to see the people again. . . . And then they called me out again. Then I knew what they wanted. And I simply sat down . . . I said: 'I want to go to my mummy, I want to go to my mummy.' I said that non–stop until he let me go.[88]

Another, born on 1928, described what she experienced:

I counted them, there were eight Russians, yes . . . and I have to tell you, I did not cry, I didn't do anything, I whimpered, yes, because I, back then one heard, rape and then a shot in the back of the head and I was incredibly afraid. Yes, and the first one, he had me quasi, they tore the clothes from my body, yes therefore I had nothing more on, nothing more at all . . . and the last one, he had me, and you know, I screamed, but afterwards I had no tears anymore, and the last one . . . then I thought how many more still are coming, and then I constantly thought and when this is over then there will be a shot in the back of the head anyway.[89]

This, and not some heroic final struggle to inspire future generations, was the experience of tens of thousands of Berliners at the end of April 1945.

Hitler and his shrinking entourage were ignorant of what was happening to the civilian population, and they did not much care. Those remaining in the bunker complex were concerned with themselves – either with how to save their own skins or how to maintain a posture of fanaticism as their ship was sinking. On Sunday 29 April, news came that Mussolini had been captured and shot and that his corpse, together with that of his mistress, had been hung upside down at a petrol station in Milan to be abused by an angry crowd. This was, for Hitler, confirmation of his worst fears about what might happen to him were he to be captured. Outside the bunker, the street fighting had reached the Potsdamer Straße and the Belle-Alliance-Platz, only a few hundred metres to the south. The depleted Wehrmacht still was reporting how 'in bitter house-to-house and street fighting, troops of all branches of the Wehrmacht, Hitler Youth and the *Volkssturm*' were offering a 'shining symbol of German heroism' and how the invaders were being 'brought to a standstill by the defenders'.[90] However, it was just a matter of hours before Soviet troops would be in the government quarter itself. When asked by Hitler, at the midday situation conference on the 29th how much longer his troops defending the government quarter could hold out, Mohnke replied: 'At most twenty to twenty-four hours.'[91] Shortly thereafter, in response to Hitler's final curt demand for information about the progress of the military units around Berlin, Keitel radioed that German 'attacks on Berlin have not advanced anywhere'.[92] To the last Hitler and Bormann demanded that military leaders 'take action with lightning speed and hard as steel against all traitors'.[93] It did not matter that this made little sense with the end of the regime at most only a few days away: the bloodshed had to continue.

Inside the bunker Hitler was taking the final steps to end his own life and that of his regime. First he had his dog, Blondi, poisoned with cyanide and her five puppies shot. Then, shortly after midnight on 30 April, Hitler married Eva Braun, less than 48 hours after having ordered the execution of her sister's husband. Afterwards he dictated his personal and political testament to his youngest secretary, Traudl Junge. On the following day – with Soviet troops in Schöneberg, fighting their way through the Tiergarten and beginning their assault on the Reichstag building just a couple of hundred metres from the bunker – Hitler finally took the step which he had resolved to take for some time and which, Göring later admitted, had been expected.[94] In the early afternoon he said his good-byes to his staff in the bunker, and retreated into his study, followed by 'Eva Hitler née Braun'. Then he shot himself. His bride took poison. Afterwards, Hitler's valet Heinz Linge, aided by three SS guards, carried the dictator's corpse up to the surface; Martin Bormann, and then Hitler's chauffeur Erich Kempka, carried that of Eva Braun. The dead pair were laid out on the ground near the door to the bunker, doused with petrol and set alight.[95] That same day American troops entered Hitler's private flat in Munich's Prinzregentenplatz.

In his political testament, Hitler appointed a new government to take charge after his death – 'a government composed of honourable men, a government which will fulfil its pledge to continue the war by every means'.[96] As his successor, as 'Reich President', Hitler named Grand Admiral Karl Dönitz, who was also given the War Ministry portfolio and remained Commander-in-Chief of the Navy. At the head of a new Reich government he appointed Goebbels as Chancellor, and as Party Minister Martin Bormann (whom Hitler also named as the executor of his will) – thus rewarding his two most loyal lieutenants and men who soon would follow their 'Führer' to their deaths. As Commander-in-Chief of the Army Hitler named the last field marshal he had promoted, the ruthless Ferdinand Schörner; as Interior Minister he chose the fanatical Gauleiter of Munich/Upper Bavaria, Paul Giesler. As head of the SS and Chief of the German Police, he named the Gauleiter of Lower Silesia and organizer of the last-ditch defence of the 'Fortress Breslau', Karl Hanke. There was no mention of Albert Speer. Göring and Himmler, who according to Hitler had 'done immeasurable harm to the country and the whole nation by secret negotiations with the enemy', were dismissed from all their offices and expelled from the Nazi Party. Concluding his political testament, Hitler made his last appeal to the successor government – to adhere to 'scrupulous observance of the laws of race and to merciless opposition to the universal poisoner of all peoples, International Jewry'. The allotted task of the next government was to maintain the commitment to the central tenets of Nazism: war and racism.

It was not until the following day that Dönitz was told of Hitler's death and that the news was made public. After having been informed (by telegram from Bormann on 30 April at 6:35 p.m.) that he was to succeed Hitler, but believing the 'Führer' still to be alive, Dönitz responded in the early morning hours of 1 May. His language was unmistakably National Socialist:

My Führer! My loyalty to you will be unalterable. I therefore will make every attempt to relieve you in Berlin. Should fate

nonetheless compel me to lead the German Reich as your designated successor, I will conduct this war to the end in such a
way as demanded by the unparalleled heroic struggle of the
German people.[97]

It was not until a few hours later, at just before 11:00 a.m., that a
telegram from Bormann to Dönitz arrived at Plön, containing the
message 'testament in force' and instructing Dönitz to 'hold back
from publication'.[98] By delaying the news, Bormann and Goebbels
may have sought to gain time to negotiate surrender to the Red
Army without consulting the new head of state – a vain hope. A few
hours later, shortly after 3:00 p.m., Dönitz received a second telegram,
this time from Goebbels, informing the Grand Admiral: 'Führer
passed away yesterday at 15:30.'[99] Now Dönitz knew that Hitler was
dead, and the phrase 'passed away', rather than 'fallen' made it clear
that the 'Führer' had taken his own life. At 22.26 that night the news
of Hitler's death was broadcast on the radio, according to which 'fighting to the last breath against Bolshevism' he had 'fallen for Germany'.[100]
On the following day the Wehrmacht report of 2 May claimed: 'At the
head of the heroic defenders of the Reich capital the Führer has fallen.
[. . .] This example "faithful unto death" is binding for all soldiers.'[101] It
was characteristic of both the man, and the regime he led, that the official announcement of his death was a lie.

The lie was repeated by Dönitz, now Hitler's successor as head of the
crumbling state that had been the Third Reich, who spoke in his proclamation to the Wehrmacht of Hitler's 'heroic death'. According to the
Wehrmacht's report, Hitler had fallen 'at the head of the heroic defenders of the Reich capital'. Desperate to forestall a complete military
collapse and to salvage what he could from a hopeless situation, Dönitz
was understandably reluctant to inform those under his command that
the man to whom they had sworn their loyalty had abandoned them.

On the 30th of April Keitel had issued an order to armed forces
commanders asserting that 'the Führer is personally leading the defence
of the Reich capital' and that 'the fate of Berlin will be the fate of the
Führer'.[102] He then laid out the case for maintaining the struggle against
the Russians in future:

The sole precondition for the continued existence of the German Reich and people is our political and military coherence. The supreme law for the German Wehrmacht remains the unconditional obedience to the new head of state, whose orders are passed on by the Wehrmacht High Command.

For the time being the continuation of the struggle remains the only possibility for saving millions of German soldiers from destruction as a result of Bolshevik arbitrary acts. No commander, no commandant, no officer has the right to act on his own initiative and against orders. Whosoever nevertheless dares to act on his own initiative or lays down his weapons is to be executed as a traitor to the German people.

Keitel remained his master's voice even as his master had killed himself. With Hitler dead, the question remained of how what was left of the Third Reich could be held together in its final days. The answer remained: continue the struggle! In another order issued on 30 April, Keitel asserted: 'The struggle to win time politically must be continued, any attempt to wind things up politically or militarily must be smashed with ruthless force. Only thus can we bring relief to the people and deliverance from anarchy.'[103]

With Hitler dead, the remainder of the bunker community now had to make choices. For some, the choice was to follow the leader and to kill themselves. Most prominent were the two men who had remained loyal to Hitler to the end and who had assumed central roles in the apocalyptic decision-making of the last days of the Reich: Joseph Goebbels and Martin Bormann. After Hitler had signed his testament, Goebbels contributed his own addendum, in which he justified his decision to disobey Hitler's wish that he (Goebbels) leave Berlin to head the new government. Employing purple prose to the last, he swore that he could not 'abandon the Führer in his darkest hour'; in deciding to remain and die with his leader he would be 'performing the best service for the German people for, in the difficult times ahead, good examples are more important than men'.[104] A family man to the end, Goebbels added that 'my wife and children join with me in this refusal [to leave Berlin]'; accordingly he, together with his wife Magda, arranged first for their six children to be poisoned during the evening of 1 May, and then they too bit into vials of poison. Martin Bormann, who disappeared and later was tried in absentia at Nuremberg, appears to have killed himself by poison the following day in the nearby Invalidenstraße.

Goebbels and Bormann were not the only members of Hitler's final inner circle to commit suicide. The Chief of the Army General Staff General Hans Krebs, Hitler's chief adjutant General Wilhelm Burgdorf, Franz Schädle, who had headed Hitler's military escort, and the State Secretary in the Reich Propaganda Ministry Werner Naumann also took their own lives. The majority of the entourage, however, sought to escape. A few, including Traudl Junge, succeeded; others either died in the inferno that raged around Berlin's government district or were captured by Soviet forces and shipped off to imprisonment in the USSR.[105]

The struggle in Berlin did not continue for long after the announcement of Hitler's death. In the early morning hours of 2 May, General Helmuth Weidling, the last commander of Wehrmacht forces in Berlin, told his troops to stop fighting. Weidling had been informed by Krebs that Hitler had killed himself and that 'the strictest secrecy had to be maintained about the suicide of the Führer'. This deeply shocked him – 'I was deeply upset. This therefore was the end!'[106] – and in his order to his troops he dispensed with the fiction of the Führer's 'heroic death':

On 30.4.45 the Führer took his own life and thereby abandoned those who had sworn him loyalty. At the Führer's command you believe that you must still fight for Berlin, although the lack of heavy weaponry and munitions, and the overall situation shows the struggle to be pointless. . . . In agreement with the High Command of the Soviet troops, I therefore demand you end the fighting immediately.[107]

Hitler's death finally freed his soldiers from the need to fight on regardless of the consequences. At 3:00 p.m. on 2 May the remaining troops in Berlin under Weidling capitulated. In Berlin, at least, the fighting was over, although elsewhere it continued for some days.

While the Battle for Berlin still was raging, Jodl had told Heinrici that negotiations 'do not take place and are not possible as long as the Führer is alive'.[108] Now with Hitler dead, the purpose of the caretaker administration under Dönitz – Keitel and Jodl had arrived in Plön in the afternoon of 1 May – was to surrender. At this point, the Wehrmacht still had 4.2 million men in the field.[109] However, they no longer were capable of offering any effective resistance to the Allies, and the idea of fighting on from an Alpine redoubt was rendered impractical by, among other things, the lack of sufficient food supplies.[110] Dönitz was motivated by two concerns: first, to avoid if possible total and unconditional surrender, in order to preserve the Reich and the German army (as had occurred at the end of the First World War) in the hope of making common cause with the west against 'Bolshevism'; and second, to delay the inevitable capitulation in order to enable as many German soldiers as possible to avoid being taken prisoner by the Red Army.[111] The first aim was quite unrealistic, and reflected the extent to which Dönitz shared the illusions held among the Nazi leadership during the last months of the Reich. However, with regard to the second aim Dönitz was, under the circumstances, rather successful.

Upon being named (much to his surprise) Hitler's successor as head of state, Dönitz's 'overall view' – as he put it when interrogated in Luxembourg in July 1945 – was: 'In the west to end the war immediately, in the east on the contrary to win some time in which the armies and the population from the eastern territories could rescue themselves in the western territories occupied by the Anglo-Americans.' While the fighting in the west was practically over in any case – Dönitz was informed on 1 May that in the west Germany 'was almost completely occupied by the American armies' and that 'a coherent resistance probably no longer is being mounted' – this meant continuing to wage war in the east. Dönitz sought 'to make peace immediately' in the west while continuing to fight in the east in order to 'rescue the German people'.[112] As Heinrici observed, this was almost without parallel in the history of war: 'fighting one enemy in order to lead the troops into the hands of another, his ally'.[113] Although Eisenhower flatly rejected the idea of a separate peace in the west, this strategy, while it led to further loss of life by allowing the fighting to carry on during the first week of May, enabled some 1.8 million German soldiers to surrender to the Western Allies rather than be captured by the Russians. Despite the great mass of the Wehrmacht having fought against the Red Army on the eastern front during the Second World War, when the conflict ended only 30 per cent of the 10 million German soldiers who were prisoners of war found themselves in Soviet captivity.[114]

With Goebbels dead and no trace of Bormann, Dönitz formed the last Nazi government on the 5th of May. In selecting his cabinet, he tried to present the acceptable face of the Third Reich, in the hope that his government might be treated by the Western Allies as a partner in liquidating the war and preparing for peace. When, later, Dönitz was interrogated in captivity at Mondorf in Luxembourg during July 1945, he maintained that he was 'the legal Head of State and deliberately had formed a small government of non-political people. We were what still embodied the German state.'[115] When forming his 'small government', Dönitz excluded Himmler (who showed up at Mürwick in the hope of being included in the new administration), Ribbentrop (whose style of diplomacy was hardly what was required in the circumstances), and Alfred Rosenberg (who was frequently drunk).[116] Nevertheless, the new 'government' was to a considerable degree a continuation of the old. Heading the cabinet and responsible for foreign affairs was Johann Ludwig Graf Schwerin von Krosigk, who had served Hitler as Reich Finance Minister since 1933; Albert Speer was given the economics and production portfolio; Herbert Backe remained in charge of food and agriculture; Franz Seldte (who had been Reich Minister of Labour throughout Hitler's time in power) was responsible for the labour and social affairs portfolio; and Julius Dorpmüller remained responsible for transport and post.[117] Keitel and Jodl remained at the head of the Wehrmacht, and the Nazi Party was not disbanded. Altogether, the package was not quite so apolitical as Dönitz claimed.

Dönitz hoped that his 'caretaker Reich Government' would provide for an orderly and gradual transfer of administrative responsibility to the Allies. Allegedly apolitical experts, so the logic went, would be better able than Allied military commanders to rescue the country from the catastrophe overwhelming its economy, transport facilities and financial system. Accordingly, members of the new government held quite unrealistic expectations about how they might effect the postwar transition. According to Dönitz, for example, Dorpmüller asserted that 'he could restore the whole of Germany's system of transportation and communications to full working order in six weeks'.[118] However, the Allies were not interested. Indeed, the suggestion that the Organization Todt be employed to repair bridges and the transport network and to clear away rubble was brusquely rejected by the Allies, and when Backe and Dorpmüller were called to Reims for consultations they were unceremoniously arrested.[119] The task allotted to Dönitz's 'caretaker government' was not to manage a postwar transition but to sign Germany's unconditional surrender.

By the beginning of May, events were quite beyond the control of Dönitz's 'caretaker government'. What remained of the Wehrmacht was collapsing like a house of cards. From the Wehrmacht units facing Soviet forces in the northeast, along the Baltic, came the following assessment on the 4th of May:

Troops are succumbing more and more to enemy superiority. [. . .] Non-arrival of ammunition almost completely rules out further co-ordinated engagements. Those units not being attacked are so stripped of men and ammunition that even with weak forces the enemy can break through to the mouth of the Vistula at any time. [. . .]

Under these circumstances the Vistula region no longer can be held. Our own troops are headed for certain annihilation.[120]

North of Berlin the remnants of the Army Group Vistula found movement almost impossible due to lack of fuel and constant aerial attack and with the roads full of fleeing refugees.[121] Nothing now could stop Soviet forces from reaching the Elbe to the north west of

Berlin. A few small German units still put up a fight against the Red Army, but 'otherwise everyone was heading for the west'.[122]

As Dönitz observed during his interrogation in July 1945, by this point 'the only front which had not yet been overrun lay in East Freesia and Schleswig-Holstein facing the English army under Montgomery'.[123] The sole enclave in the west remaining under German government control was that around Dönitz's own head-quarters – an area rapidly filling up with homeless refugees[124] – and it was only a matter of days before this would be overrun as well. A British attack and breakthrough from a bridgehead established in late April at Lauenburg on the Elbe, a breakthrough which brought British troops to Lübeck on 2 May, now compelled Dönitz to relocate. The place chosen was a naval school at Mürwick, just outside Flensburg, to which Dönitz removed his 'government' during the night of 2/3 May. (On 3 May the Wehrmacht High Command, which had just moved to Neustadt in Holstein a couple of days before, also relocated to Flensburg-Mürwick.)

Dönitz's overall aim, as his military commanders were informed, remained the 'continuation of the struggle against Bolshevism in order to rescue as many people of German blood as possible'.[125] This meant negotiating with the Western Allies, while as many Germans as possible could be transported by sea from Courland and East Prussia (something which, it was hoped, would be accepted by the Western powers) and fighting continued against the Red Army. In north-west Germany the British advance into Schleswig-Holstein and the American advance into Mecklenburg left Dönitz no alternative but surrender.

> From the Baltic to the Elbe the British and Americans were standing astride the roads leading from Mecklenburg to Holstein, which were choked with columns of refugees and the retreating troops of the Vistula Army. The gateway to the west was no longer open, and it depended upon British acquiescence whether or not the troops and refugees would be allowed to escape from the pursuing Russians into the British zone in Schleswig-Holstein. It had been solely for the purpose of

keeping this gateway into Schleswig-Holstein open for the refugees that the fight against the Western Allies had continued on the Elbe. Now that Schleswig-Holstein was in British hands, there was no point in persisting. I therefore gave orders that surrender negotiations, in accordance with our prepared plan, should forthwith be initiated. Friedeburg was to go in the first instance to Montgomery and the offer to surrender north-west Germany to him. Then, when that had been accepted, he was to go on to Eisenhower and offer the surrender of the rest of the western theatre.[126]

The aim was to conclude a separate peace with the Western Allies.

In the southern theatre as well, once Hitler was out of the way German forces bowed to the inevitable. There too the Wehrmacht was falling apart and civil administration collapsing, and in places the local population was expressing open hostility to the Wehrmacht (with reports of old Bavarian flags being raised in Bavaria).[127] On 2 May the capitulation was announced of German forces in Italy, the Army Group South-West under General Heinrich von Vietinghoff-Scheel, who had initiated surrender negotiations on his own initiative on 29 April.[128] Although the Supreme Commander of the remnants of the Wehrmacht in the south, the hard-line Field Marshal Albert Kesselring, initially responded by ordering the arrest of Vietinghoff-Scheel and his chief of staff, by 3 May after the news of Hitler's suicide had been made public, he had relented and was asking Dönitz's approval for negotiating the surrender of his sector to the Western Allies.[129] Dönitz readily approved.[130] As he later put it in his memoirs, 'the more territory that was taken over by the Americans and not the Russians, the better pleased we were'.[131] On 4 May the Army Group G (southern portion of the western front) capitulated in Haar, to the east of Munich, and on 6 May, in Berchtesgaden, Kesselring surrendered the Army Group C (alpine fortress).

In the north the aim now was 'to gain time for the Reich Government to negotiate with Montgomery about the north-western area'.[132] On the morning of 3 May Dönitz gave the order for Hamburg to be relinquished to the British, after which British forces

quickly occupied the 'open city', and sent his successor as Commander-in-Chief of the Navy, Admiral Hans-Georg von Friedeburg,
to meet with Montgomery and agree terms of surrender. But Dönitz,
through Friedeburg, was not yet offering unconditional surrender on
all fronts, and it was unclear how Montgomery would respond. In the
event, Montgomery did not reject the German offer out of hand. He
indicated that he would not transfer German prisoners to the
Russians, and British air attacks ceased. When Friedeburg arrived
back at Mürwick on the 4th, he reported that Montgomery was willing to accept the separate surrender of north Germany but had
stipulated that German forces in Holland and Denmark had to lay
down arms as well. Furthermore, all German naval vessels, both military and civilian, had to be surrendered. After some consideration –
Dönitz was concerned that giving up the ships would hinder efforts to
rescue refugees from the Russians – Friedeburg was authorized to
agree to Montgomery's terms.

On 4 May Friedeburg signed the surrender document at
Montgomery's headquarters. With his mind fixed on the enemy in the
east, Dönitz could be pleased (as he later put it) that 'the first step
towards a separate surrender to the West had been accomplished without our having been forced to abandon German soldiers and civilians
to the mercy of the Russians'.[133] Accordingly, fighting ceased in
north-western Germany, Holland and Denmark at 8.00 a.m. on 5
May. The Wehrmacht announced publicly:

> This ceasefire was agreed at the order of Grand Admiral Dönitz
> after almost six years of honourable struggle, since the war
> against the Western powers has lost its meaning and is leading
> only to the loss of precious German blood, above all through the
> bombing campaign. The resistance to the Soviets, however, will
> be continued in order to protect as many German people as
> possible from the Bolshevik terror.[134]

At the same time orders were issued that 'the struggle against the
Soviets nevertheless is to be continued with all means'.[135] Keitel
echoed his new Commander-in-Chief: 'If we lay down our arms in

northern Germany, Denmark and Holland, this is occurring because the struggle against the Western powers has lost its meaning. In the east, however, the struggle continues, in order to rescue as many German people as possible from Bolshevism and enslavement.'[136] This in effect provided the psychological bridge between the previous insistence upon continuing the 'honourable struggle' to the last breath and acceptance that, finally, the time had arrived to cease fighting.

Having secured a ceasefire with Montgomery, Friedeburg's next task was to fly to Reims to offer Eisenhower 'in the same manner the separate surrender of our forces in the American sector'.[137] Eisenhower, however, was not prepared to play that game. The Allied Supreme Commander was blunt, and 'flatly refused to discuss the matter with him'.[138] Instead, Eisenhower demanded complete, immediate and unconditional surrender on all fronts i.e. in the east as well as in the west, and that German soldiers stay where they were, surrender and hand over their weapons. Friedeburg responded that he was not authorized to agree to this, and that he would have to obtain authorization from Dönitz. Dönitz played for time, convinced that it would be impossible to keep soldiers facing the Russians where they were without landing them in Soviet captivity, and hoping to use any breathing space gained to move as many troops as possible from east to west. On 6 May he sent Jodl to Reims, to attempt again to secure a separate peace in the west but now with authorization to agree a complete cessation of hostilities (subject to final confirmation from Dönitz). Eisenhower remained adamant: the surrender had to be signed immediately, to take effect from midnight on 9 May; otherwise, Allied air raids would resume. At 1:00 a.m. on 7 May Jodl radioed a message to Dönitz: 'Eisenhower insists that we sign today. If not, the Allied fronts will be closed to persons seeking to surrender individually, and all negotiations will be broken off. I see no alternative – chaos or signature.'[139] Dönitz agreed. The hopeless military situation, the imminent 'complete annihilation of sections of the front', and the prospect of a resumption of the bombing left him no choice.[140] At 2:41 a.m. Jodl signed. At midnight on the night of 8/9 May, the Second World War in Europe would come to an end.

On the 9th of May, the capitulation ceremony was played out

again, this time in Berlin and this time with a full surrender document. Just after midnight, at 00:16, on 9 May, Allied representatives on the one side (A.W. Tedder for the British, Georgi Zhukov for the Russians, Jean de Lattre de Tassigny for the French, and Carl Spaatz for the Americans) and German representatives on the other (representing the three armed forces: Keitel for the Army, von Friedeburg for the Navy and Colonel-General Hans-Jürgen Stumpff for the Luftwaffe) assembled at Zhukov's headquarters in the eastern Berlin suburb of Karlshorst to sign the capitulation document. As the ceremony had been scheduled to begin earlier, the document bore the date 8 May. Although fighting continued to the east of Prague until the 11th, and although all German forces in Yugoslavia did not surrender until the 15th, Nazi Germany's war was over.

After more than five and a half years of war, Germans who were able to tune in to the 'Reichssender Flensburg' heard their 'government' announce that the conflict had come to an end. In a message broadcast 'to the German people' at 12:45 on 7 May the 'leading minister' of Dönitz's government, Schwerin von Krosigk announced:

> On the orders of Grand Admiral Dönitz the Supreme Command of the Wehrmacht today has declared the unconditional capitulation of all fighting troops. [. . .]
>
> After a heroic struggle of unparalleled severity lasting almost six years, Germany's strength has been overcome by the overwhelming power of our opponents. The continuation of this war would have meant only senseless bloodshed and pointless destruction. A government which possesses a sense of responsibility for the future of our people had to draw the conclusion from the collapse of [our] physical and material forces and to request a cessation of hostilities from the opponent.
>
> It was the most noble aim of the Grand Admiral and of the government supporting him, after the sacrifices that the war has demanded, to preserve the lives of as many German people as possible in its last phase. This aim accounts for the fact that the war was not ended immediately and not simultaneously in the west and in the east.

In a message notably devoid of apocalyptic Nazi rhetoric, Schwerin von Krosigk appealed to values which were seen to transcend political differences:

> We must light the path through the darkness of the future and be guided by three stars which always were the pledge of true German character: unity and law and freedom.
>
> We want to safeguard and rescue one thing from the collapse of the past: the idea of the people's community that during the years of war found its finest expression in the comradeship out at the front, in the reciprocal readiness to help in all emergencies at home. [. . .] Only if we preserve this unity and do not again break apart into conflicting groups and classes can we survive the difficult time to come.
>
> We must make law the basis of the life of our people. Justice shall be the supreme law and the uppermost guiding principle among our people. We must recognise and respect the law as the basis of relations between peoples out of inner conviction. [. . .]
>
> We will combine pride in the heroic struggle of our people with determination as part of Christian-Western culture to make a contribution in sincere work for peace that corresponds to the best tradition of our people.
>
> May God not forsake us in misfortune, and bless our difficult undertaking.[141]

The message was a shock. It had been years since Germans heard their leaders speak in such language – and the radio station Prague I, which still was in German hands, described the broadcast as an Allied propaganda trick and demanded that the fighting continue.[142]

However, it *was* all over. At 12:30 the following day, using a rather more familiar rhetoric, Dönitz broadcast his message to 'German men and women' with the news that millions wanted to hear: 'On 8 May at 11:00 p.m. the weapons will be silent.'[143]

With a little over three million men still in the army in the field (of whom some 1,850,000 were on what was left of the eastern front),[144] on 9 May the Wehrmacht announced the surrender in its last communiqué, broadcast just after eight in the evening from the 'Reichssender Flensburg':

> Since midnight the weapons on all fronts are now silent. On the orders of the Grand Admiral, the Wehrmacht has given up the fight which has become hopeless. Thus the heroic struggle which lasted nearly six years has come to an end. It brought us great victories but also heavy defeats. In the end the German Wehrmacht was honourably defeated by a huge superior force.
>
> The German soldier, true to his oath and with the greatest dedication, has performed deeds which never will be forgotten. The home front supported him to the last with all its powers and suffering the greatest sacrifices.
>
> The unique achievement of the front and the home front will find its ultimate appreciation in a future just verdict of history.
>
> Our opponents too will not refuse their respect for the achievements and sacrifices of German soldiers on land, at sea and in the air. Every soldier therefore can hand over his weapons with honour and pride and begin work courageously and confidently for the eternal life of our people in the darkest hour of our history.
>
> In this dark hour the Wehrmacht is thinking of its comrades who remain with the enemy.
>
> The dead obligate us to unconditional loyalty, to obedience and discipline with regard to a Fatherland bleeding from countless wounds.[145]

This was the final message, and a necessary step towards cutting loose from the spell of Nazism and the experiences of war: German soldiers had fought an honourable fight, performed astounding feats and endured terrible hardships; they could be proud of what they had done. A few days later, stressing that members of the Wehrmacht should bear themselves proudly when coming into contact with the British and Americans, Dönitz asserted:

We have nothing to be ashamed of. What the German
Wehrmacht achieved in combat and the German people
endured during these six years is unparalleled in history and in
the world. It is a heroism such as there has never been. We soldiers stand here without blemishes on our honour.[146]

Given the enormity of the losses and destruction, the effects of twelve
years of Nazi politics and propaganda, and the shock of what happened in 1945, it is difficult to imagine that the representatives of
Germany's caretaker government could have expressed themselves
very differently.

Whether this resonated with the great mass of people who now had
to rebuild their lives amidst the rubble is another matter. No doubt
most of those who heard the broadcast of the Wehrmacht's final communiqué shared the feelings of Klaus Kahlenberg, the man who read
it out over the airwaves – feelings of 'relief that the war was over'.[147]
The countless widows, orphans, homeless evacuees and refugees that
Nazism and war had left in their wake may have had their own opinion about the 'just verdict of history', and the notion that German
soldiers were 'without blemishes on [their] honour' no doubt would
have met with some scepticism among the millions of people across
the European continent who had been on the receiving end of the
'war of annihilation' carried out by Germany's armed forces.
Nevertheless, in his memoirs Dönitz wrote of the last Wehrmacht
communiqué: 'I thought then, and I still think, that those words are
both appropriate and just.'[148]

While the oft-recounted events in Berlin in April and early May 1945,
and the developments which surrounded the surrender of German
forces stood at the centre of the drama of the last days of the Third
Reich, they form only part of the story. The end of Nazi rule occurred
at different times and in different circumstances across the country.
Some areas had been in Allied hands for weeks or even months by the
time that the surrender documents were signed in Reims and in
Berlin-Karlshorst; in other places fighting continued for days after
Hitler's death had been announced and Berlin had been surrendered to

the Red Army. In Aachen Nazi rule had ended in the autumn of 1944 and the Red Army had entered Upper Silesia in January 1945; in the 'fortress Breslau', however, the fighting did not cease until 6 May. Throughout Germany during April and early May confusion reigned and rumours abounded. What was happening in Berlin – for all its importance to the course of the war – was disconnected increasingly from what occurred in the remainder of 'Greater Germany'.

Across Germany, communities had faced the prospect of devastation as Allied forces approached. Given the overwhelming firepower at the disposal of the Allies, German attempts to hold a city or town 'to the last bullet' did little more than to ensure its destruction. However, whereas in the west it became increasingly common for German forces to surrender a location to the British or Americans with little or no fight, in the east resistance to the Red Army was more likely to remain tenacious. Thus the stark contrast between the German decision to allow British forces to occupy Hamburg on 3 May without a fight, and the bitter resistance of the 'fortress Breslau' against the Soviet forces until 6 May (despite that the fact that the military commanders knew that holding the city, which still contained 40,000 civilians at the end of April, was impossible).[149] In effect, this reflected the strategy articulated by Dönitz during the first week of May – that an accommodation be sought with the Western Allies while the fight against the Red Army continued.

In many places, particularly in the western half of the country, the war came to an end less with a bang than with a whimper. German armed forces may have fought to the bitter end in Berlin and Breslau, but in countless cities and towns they did not. One example was what occurred in Freiburg, in the far south-west of Germany. When this university city came under artillery fire on 21 April, *Volkssturm* members and Wehrmacht soldiers quickly fled. One eyewitness, Max Meister, described what happened after German soldiers had set up an anti-tank gun ('not a pleasant neighbour', as Meister put it) near his garden as the French approached:[150]

The gun delivers not a shot. When it is quiet I take up my observation post again. The artillery piece has been abandoned.

Then I see the leader of the artillery unit approaching. He repeatedly calls after the crew. No one appears. The men have taken themselves out of harm's way. He dismantles the sighting mechanism, throws it over the garden fence and leaves on the double. I go out. No doubt about it: this is flight, without an enemy in sight far and wide. Even the knapsacks have been left behind. The explosive charges lie unused on a stack of hay. This once was – only a short time ago – the first army of the world.

By the following day the war was over in Freiburg:

In the Hauptstraße there are no French, but there are witnesses who can give an account of enemy tanks and infantry passing through in the evening hours and during the night. The resistance must have been extremely limited.

A few minutes later a scene awaits me that slots in beside the painful events of the day before: the police station stands open. To my relief the inscription has been removed that covered the garden fence for months: 'The people arise and the storm breaks', which equated the *Volkssturm* in so painful a manner with the uprising of the Wars of Liberation. The [police] station has been abandoned with obvious haste. [. . .] Everything is left standing and lying around. [. . .]

Returning home I see that the knapsacks of the artillery crew have been opened. A neighbour says that one or another of the crew came back in unconvincing civilian clothing in order to take away the most valuable items of their belongings. The complete disintegration of the troop is confirmed.

In the course of the morning friends from the neighbourhood come and relate their experiences. The picture becomes clear. Freiburg was not seriously defended. The city commandant and his adjutant were natives of Freiburg. In contrast with the mayor and Party officials they did what they could to spare the city needless suffering: the self-surrender of the Wehrmacht – its last service to Germany. The bridges over the [River] Dreisam that were supposed to have been blown up, although the little river is no military obstacle, remain undamaged.[151] [. . .] At six in the evening the white flag was raised from the cathedral.

Particularly in western and southern Germany, where the American army was making rapid advances in late April, the end of Nazi rule often arrived without a fight. Carl Friedrich Wilhelm Behl (a long-time friend and biographer of Gerhart Hauptmann and editor of Hauptmann's collected works) described in his diary what happened as U.S. forces arrived at the village of Berndorf (near Kemnath, to the east of Bayreuth) in late April. After a noisy night bombardment:

> I was surprised when in the morning, from the small hill behind our inn which offers a view towards Kemnath, I saw the town lying intact before me. Immediately we ventured forth to investigate the situation. As we got higher, we already saw the first white flags waving from the houses. As we heard, the last German military units already had withdrawn during the night and courageous women were said to have removed the anti-tank barriers.[152]

The Jewish-born diarist Victor Klemperer, who had spent most of the war in Dresden but was in a village (Unterbernbach) to the north of Aichach (near Augsburg) in late April 1945, described how the war ended when the Americans arrived there on the 28th:

> We were sitting reading in our attic in the morning. Suddenly the already familiar artillery fire turned into explosions very close by and the sharp reports of individual shots. Eva [Klemperer's wife] also heard the whistle of a bullet – evidently there was now fighting going on at the edge of our wood, in front of our village, our corner. We hurried downstairs. [. . .] For quite a while we stood and sat pressed into a corner of the kitchen, which appeared safest to us. Gradually the shooting abated and our courage grew. We wanted to cross over to the Asam shelter [i.e. the shelter of the Asam family] – renewed

shooting forced us to look for cover against the outside wall of the Asam shelter; not until some time had passed did we risk the final couple of steps. [. . .] After that we sat in the shelter, sometimes I stuck my head out, but without discovering anything [. . .] at about two o'clock we ventured home again and made ourselves a coffee. The attack rolled over our village, more exactly, it had rolled *around* it: only at the edge of 'our' strip of wood had a last, small group of soldiers offered resistance for a couple of minutes, before they too fled. The war lay behind us, even as we thought it was before us.[153]

In the end it was rather anti-climactic – so much so that Klemperer's wife had to remind him during the following week to include this account in his otherwise richly detailed diary.

As the end approached, Germans had little desire to see their town, village or neighbourhood defended to the last and thus destroyed. In mid-April, the inhabitants of the village of Bünz-wangen, in the district of Göppingen, faced the imminent arrival of the Americans:

At this time there still were German soldiers in the village, not combat units but members of the Luftwaffe engaged in retraining, mostly older cohorts that were supposed to be assigned to infantry duty and to anti-tank fighting. Two officers, one sergeant and a corporal among them were keen to defend the village against the approaching enemy. Yet the group had hardly any experience in the use of weapons (rifles and machine guns), had no heavy weapons whatsoever, at most a few hand-held anti-tank weapons, and above all no combat experience. As a result the pointlessness of a defence was obvious to any reasonable person. The unit already had to dig foxholes for the machine-gun placements, while the inhabitants argued with the soldiers mentioned above about the need to defend the village and as a result even were threatened with weapons. Finally, an agreement was reached: the village would be surrendered to the enemy without a fight.[154]

Two village residents were delegated to go to the Americans in nearby Uhingen on the evening of 20 April, carrying a white flag, as 'the inhabitants heaved a sigh of relief'. After some discussion it was agreed that the village would not be bombarded, and the German soldiers remaining within it surrendered.

By the end of April, even in the east Wehrmacht units were disintegrating and the civilian population raising white flags.[155] Probably the most notable decision to surrender a German city to the Red Army without a struggle occurred in Greifswald, when the city commandant, Colonel Rudolf Petershagen, agreed to hand over this small university town to the Russians in order to prevent needless death and destruction. After the enormous bloodshed of the previous months, few people were keen to sacrifice themselves for the Third Reich in its dying hours. The immediate concern of the surviving members of the Wehrmacht was to avoid falling into the hands of the Russians and to get into civilian clothing as soon as possible; the immediate concern of civilians was to survive the transition and prevent, if possible, the destruction of their homes. People were beginning to look to a future after Nazism and war.

In Parchim, in Mecklenburg, it was the old elites who asserted themselves to save their town from destruction at the beginning of May.[156] While the Nazi Party leadership still demanded that Parchim be defended to the last, the local military commandant (who had at his disposal mainly men who had not been regarded as fit for military service, elderly men in the *Volkssturm* and 14–15 year-olds of the Hitler Youth) had doubts. The men under his command could no longer be counted on to fight; the mayor was concerned to prevent a needless battle that would destroy his town, and the commander of the *Volkssturm* regarded as absurd that his men be sacrificed in a lost cause. A group of local notables formed a delegation to ask the military not to mount a defence, and the military commander reached an agreement with the mayor that the town would not be defended. The *Volkssturm* was disbanded, and work on the anti-tank defences ceased. However, not everything unfolded peacefully. On 2 May the Wehrmacht supply stores in the town, previously heavily guarded, were left open, and the local population promptly set about looting food and clothing. Using bicycles, children's buggies, hand-carts and horse-drawn wagons, they carried away as much as they could from the Wehrmacht stores, the railway goods station and factory ware-houses. In the event, there was fighting when the Russians took the town; a number of men were killed, including untrained members of the Reich Labour Service who had been drafted into the fight before the mayor and the city commandant agreed to surrender. Those still in uniform had only a 'single thought: to get away from the Russians and over to the Americans',[157] while the civilian population displayed their eagerness to hang out white flags. In the end, as the Third Reich succumbed to the pressure of Allied military might, what mattered was survival, one's local community and one's family.

When it came, the collapse of the Nazi dictatorship was remarkable in its speed and its thoroughness. Seemingly overnight, the hold of the regime evaporated. Despite expectations to the contrary, despite the remarkable grip which National Socialism had had on the German people across twelve years of indoctrination in the schools, the media and public institutions of all kinds, and despite police terror and wide-spread complicity in the crimes of the Nazi regime, when German cities and towns were occupied by Allied forces Nazism disappeared. Once a city or town had surrendered, almost no one continued to fight fanatically for the Nazi cause. The promised underground of 'Werewolf' guerrilla fighters proved little more than a mirage painted by Goebbels' propaganda machine (and, subsequently, a pretext for the Soviet secret police to arrest many Germans in the Soviet Occupation Zone). Instead, the representatives of the regime tended either to flee, to seek some accommodation with the occupying forces, or to kill themselves, while those they had ruled generally retreated into their own private worlds. Of a fanatical 'people's community' determined to fight on in order to preserve Germany's 'honour' there was hardly a trace.

The utter lack of commitment to Nazism after the Allies arrived was reflected in reactions to the news of Hitler's death. In the rapidly shrinking area remaining under German control, the death of the dictator meant that people were relieved of any residual requirement to maintain (as Hitler had put it in his message of 15 April to the soldiers on the eastern front) 'a blood brotherhood [. . .] for the defence of your Heimat, your women, your children and thereby of our future'. In the rapidly expanding areas under Allied control, the news of Hitler's death seemed strangely irrelevant and hardly worth comment. Most Germans were too concerned with their own survival, with their search for food and shelter, and with shielding themselves and their property from predatory Allied troops to give much thought to the departure of the 'Führer'.[158] In Göttingen, which had been surrendered to the Americans without a fight on the 8th of April, one woman wrote of the reactions after news of Hitler's death had been broadcast:

> On the following morning [i.e. on 2 May] [. . .] I was standing in a long queue of people who wanted to buy meat and listened to the conversations being held around me. Hitler's name was not mentioned a single time! This people who a few years ago still were cheering him effusively, who months ago still placed their entire trust in him, who weeks ago still were inclined to give credence to his slogans, who today to some extent still regard him as a decent personality – this people takes hardly a notice of his end! [. . .] One forgets from one day to the next! No one mourns him![159]

Reactions among the men in uniform were similar. Gerd Schmückle, who later became a general in the West German Bundeswehr and Deputy Supreme Commander of NATO, recalled the moment when he heard over the radio that Hitler had 'fallen': 'If – instead of this announcement – the inn-keeper had come to the door and said that an animal of his had died in the stable, the sympathy could not have been less. Only one young soldier leapt up, extended his right arm and called out 'Hail to the Führer!' All the others continued to eat their soup as though nothing of importance had occurred.'[160]

The dominant feeling was one of relief that the war would be over. As Germans hastily disposed of their pictures of the 'Führer', their Party badges and uniforms before Allied soldiers arrived on the doorstep, it was as if they were awakening from a bad dream, after which their own involvement in, and perhaps former enthusiasm for, Nazism had became an embarrassment best forgotten.[161]

This strange and opportunistic disappearance of Nazism reflected the extent to which Nazi rule had eroded before the final surrender. Even before the Wehrmacht capitulated, the forces available to its commanders often hardly merited the designation of military formations in the last weeks. The lack of ammunition, fuel and, in particular, food, together with the realization that the war was well and truly lost and the fact that many of those in uniform were but children, meant that by late April Germany scarcely had a coherent military organization left. The authority and legitimacy of the Nazi regime – a legitimacy which had rested on the ability of that regime to enable Germans to profit from plunder and murder – had faded before the Allied occupiers arrived. In an intriguing passage in his diary, from 25 April, Victor Klemperer described the Hitler Youth billeted in the village in Upper Bavaria where he spent the last day of the war:

> They are very diverse. Since they are going around begging for food everywhere – they are said to be very badly or not at all supplied with rations, today we overheard one group: 'When the Americans come, at least we'll get something proper to eat!' – we have been able to exchange a couple of words with a few of them. Two [. . .] appear to me to be from good homes and decent, innocent boys. I asked one of them, who was given a couple of potatoes here, how old he was: 'Fifteen.' – 'Are you about to be sent to the Front?' – 'Only the volunteers.' – 'Are you a volunteer?' – Quite unheroic: 'No.'[162]

The need to find enough to eat pushed all else into the background, and even before the surrender the Americans were associated with plenty.

The arrival at least of the Western Allies – and with them the end of Nazi rule – generally was greeted with a sense of relief. Life after defeat might be difficult, but the constant threat of violent death or

injury was largely lifted. On 14 April the author Annemarie Meckel
wrote in her diary in Erfurt:

> In the morning the first Americans. At first they come slowly,
> with machine guns on all sides, driving down the streets. Yet
> soon they are playing football on the corner. First of all deliver-
> ance from the quite primitive fear. Above all the children are
> liberated and full of keen interest in everything that is happening.
> 'Now it's peace', they say in a daze.[163]

However, the arrival of the Americans did not mean that the problems
were over. Meckel went on:

> Immediately there begins a disgusting struggle for food. I
> attempt to get something by standing in a queue. The city, a
> depressing impression, a true Babylon, a mixture of indescribable
> characters, the Germans not the best among them. Great uncer-
> tainty about rumours that the Russians are coming here. It
> appears that calm is something that never will return.

Even where the Americans were destined to stay, their presence did
not necessarily mean that law, order and calm arrived with them.
The heavily armed and nervous occupiers could be quick to resort
to their weapons even where there was no resistance, sometimes
firing their machine guns at nothing in particular.[164] And although
they did not lack material goods, the Americans too sometimes
looted and they hardly conformed to German conceptions of order
and propriety. A schoolboy in the village of Brend, in the district of
Schwäbisch Gmünd, described how his house appeared after the GIs
had visited:

> In our yard [. . .] cooking utensils with half-eaten food, cutlery,
> the odd spoon and pieces of white bread that had been bitten
> into lay all round. Inside the house it was no different. In the
> kitchen a frying pan with butter was on the cooker and next to
> it was the egg-basket. They also did not deny themselves cider.

On the floor lay cigarette packets, chewing gum, and also chocolate all round. In the bedroom the beds were soiled. The soldiers
had laid on the beds with their shoes on. Everywhere everything
was stained and soiled. The Amis [Americans] also had stolen.
We lost a camera, three silver necklaces and a pretty armband. In
the excitement we had not hidden these.[165]

Liberation meant looting; in Mainz American soldiers were seen carrying off watches, cameras, binoculars, perfume and bicycles; houses
were broken into and the wine cellars (in this wine-growing region)
were emptied.[166] Of course, this was mild compared to the fate of
families further to the east whose houses were burned down, but it left
a deep impression. It was not only the soldiers of the Red Army for
whom conquered Germany was a country full of watches and bicycles
for the taking.

The ways in which the war and the Third Reich ended varied
greatly from one locality to another. In some places, particularly
where the Western Allies came through relatively remote villages, the
moment when the Third Reich ended and Allied occupation began
was hardly noticed. In others, the onset of occupation was accompanied by violence, rape, drunkenness, theft and the destruction of
property. In some cases, the occupying forces rounded up men not in
uniform, believing them to be escaped Wehrmacht soldiers, and
imprisoned them; in others, they let captured German soldiers go
home. Much depended on how a village or town fell: whether it had
been given up without a fight or whether the Germans had insisted
on putting up resistance. Where the latter occurred, it was more
common for violence to take place after Allied occupation and for
unfortunate civilians to be beaten or killed for minor infractions. One
such case is that of a 70-year-old man in the village of Genkingen, in
the district of Reutlingen, who was beaten by the French when he
could not keep his arms above his head when ordered to do so and
was taken behind the town hall and shot; and there were instances
where Germans were forced to clear minefields, with the inevitable
result that some lost limbs or their lives.[167]

In contrast with what had occurred in November 1918, in April and May 1945 there were few signs of revolutionary activity aimed at bringing down the regime. The attempted rising by the small resistance group 'Freedom Action Bavaria' in Munich on 28 April, limited though it was, stands out as the exception which proves the rule. This brave, ill-fated attempt to hasten the end of the war in Bavaria was led by Rupprecht Gerngross, the head of an army translation company, who managed to seize the radio transmitters in Erding and Munich-Freimann for a few hours. Announcing themselves as the 'Transmitter Freedom Action Bavaria', Gerngross and his comrades broadcast a call for German forces to cease fighting and for the civilian population to resist the Nazis, as well as demands for an end to National Socialism and militarism. The attempt was noteworthy more for its aims and the bravery of the conspirators than for its effects. It failed when the Nazi 'Reich Governor' in Bavaria, General Franz Ritter von Epp, refused to collaborate, the Nazi Gauleiter in Munich, Paul Giesler, and the local military commanders determined to crush the rising, and SS units succeeded in retaking the two radio transmitters within a few hours.[168] Two days later, on 30 April, the Americans occupied the Bavarian capital and former 'capital of the [Nazi] movement'.

Generally, the German population reacted passively to the end of the Third Reich, knowing that their fate was not in their hands. Accordingly, most kept their heads down and waited for events to unfold. On 6 May, the Wehrmacht reported how the civilian population was looking forward to the imminent end of the war, and noted that the population did not appear particularly downcast; instead a calm and resigned attitude prevailed 'that is disturbed only by a certain nervousness with regard to the expected occupation of the territory that still is free'.[169] This was the moment of a profound shift in German mentalities and public culture – away from nationalism and admiration for the military to more pacifist and personal perspectives. The mentalities that had made possible the establishment of the Third Reich and had provided the basis for broad popular support for National Socialism evaporated. The shock of the extreme violence in early 1945, the catastrophic end to Nazi Germany's war, the successful invasion of the country by vastly powerful Allied armies, and the overwhelming challenges to personal survival shattered perspectives that millions of Germans had hitherto shared.

In the end, and contrary to the fears of the Nazi and military leadership, there was no repeat in 1945 of what had happened in 1918. On the eve of the German surrender, the Wehrmacht, surveying the information received about popular opinion, reported that 'thus far there are no parallels whatsoever to draw with the occurrences of 1918', and that 'destructive elements form an infinitely small minority among all strata of the population'.[170] While in captivity, Dönitz drew similar conclusions, attributing the favourable comparison with 1918 to the better distribution of food to Germans. In a statement remarkable for its myopia and repetition of Nazi phraseology, Dönitz asserted:

> In this war there was a just, clean distribution of food up to the end. Nobody starved. Everyone received his share and no one received more. No black market. In the last war 1914–1918 there was profiteering everywhere in this regard. Ask the housewives who went through both wars. The state food-purchasing organizations of the First World War were Jewish profit enterprises. [. . .] There was an atmosphere of sabotage, soldiers loitering about who did not salute properly, overflowing with profiteers and Jews, God knows that was not clean.[171]

The degree to which the trauma of November 1918 remained an obsession among the political and military leadership of the Third Reich to – and, in the case of Dönitz, beyond – the bitter end is remarkable. However, the terrible events of 1945 served to purge memories of 1918. Given the genocidal policies of the Nazi regime, there was not much prospect of a Germany 'overflowing with Jews' in 1945. Given the Nazi terror and the extreme privations which war had brought to the German people, there was little energy left to stage a repeat of November 1918. And given the success of the Nazi regime in leading the nation to total defeat, there remained little scope for nurturing a belief this time round that Germany had not been defeated on the battlefield but had been stabbed in the back at home.

May 1945 marked the great turning point in the history of modern Germany. When the Second World War ended in Europe, National Socialism – a political movement that had attracted broader support than any other in Germany and which had inspired campaigns of violence, war and murder which were breathtaking in their scope – disappeared. When it was all over, the overwhelming feeling was at once of exhaustion and relief; Germans reacted almost as though Hitler and the Third Reich belonged to a distant past. Coming on top of the shock of the extreme violence during the previous months, the grotesque, bloody end of the Third Reich completely undermined its legitimacy and popular support for Nazism. The way had been cleared, through a catastrophe of unparalleled proportions, to build a new world on the ashes of the old.

6

REVENGE

After looking at the cremated bodies you just feel like killing every German alive. A corporal in the U.S. Army[1]

The history of the Third Reich is a history of violence – violence against supposed racial inferiors, the violence of an imperialist war of annihilation which brought most of the European continent temporarily under German control, violence against Germans who resisted Nazi rule or failed to display a commitment to fight and die. Nazism did not so much offer Germans participation in the political process as it did participation in violence; the citizen of Nazi Germany was the person able to commit, and profit from, violence against others. However, when the regime collapsed in the spring of 1945, it left the people identified with it to face the vengeance of those who had suffered under Nazism for years. Germans found themselves transformed from practitioners of violence to objects of violence – violence committed by Allied soldiers, whose lands often had been laid waste and many of whose relatives and friends had been killed; by foreign workers in Germany who had been exploited for the benefit of the Third Reich, by Poles and Czechs who moved into regions previously settled by Germans, and by occupation authorities who arrived to rule what many of them regarded as a barbarous, fanatical and indoctrinated population, and who had been shocked particularly by what was revealed when the concentration camps were liberated.

Nazism and the war left vast reservoirs of hatred in their wake. Millions had suffered as a result of Nazi rule and at the hands of Germans acting in the name of their regime or profiting from its policies. Of course, in many instances, it was not solely or necessarily Germans who were the guilty parties; Nazism and war put just about all of those involved into difficult and morally ambiguous positions.[2] It was not only Germans who had behaved appallingly during the conflict, and it was not only Germans who had profited from the war unleashed by Hitler. Yet in 1945 vengeance against Germans provided an acceptable framework for expressing the anger and bitterness that war and dictatorship had left in their wake. Germans, no longer in positions of power and privilege, were obvious targets. The urge to humiliate the once powerful and now powerless 'master race' was very strong. It was this, and not simply unbridled sexual desire, that seems to have fuelled much of the sexual violence by invading troops in Germany in 1945, and helps to explain the frequency with which German women were raped by Soviet soldiers in front of husbands or in public.[3] As the war ended in central Europe, taking revenge against Germans was socially acceptable and widely expected. Anger and resentment found an outlet that could be justified as paying the Germans back in kind for what they had done during the war, whether or not those against whom the violence was now directed had themselves actually been responsible.

In no case was this more in evidence than with the behaviour of Soviet soldiers who streamed into Germany in 1945. During the war members of the Red Army had been encouraged constantly to focus their 'hatred on the German-fascist conquerors'; Soviet Army front newspapers had printed numerous accounts of atrocities committed by German forces on Soviet territory; and before the first Russian incursion into East Prussia in October 1944 the soldiers of the 11th Guard Army had been reminded by their commander, General Kusma Galickij, of their 'holy oath to avenge themselves against the enemy for all the atrocities committed on Soviet soil'.[4] When they arrived in the Reich, Soviet troops were admonished not to forget what had been done to their homeland and their families; soldiers' newspapers urged their readers to think of the harm that had been done to them, and to keep a 'book of revenge' that would remind them of the need to 'repay the Germans for their evil'.[5] History too was invoked. Prussia was depicted as a bulwark of militarism and the launching pad for aggression against Slavic peoples down the ages; Soviet propagandists reminded their readers that 'every metre of this land [i.e. Prussia] is soaked in the blood of Slavic peoples who were exterminated here by the Teutonic Knights'.[6] The east Prussian capital of Königsberg, where once Prussia's kings had been crowned, came in for special attention as the historic fount of German militarism. That the old eastern heartlands of Prussia were the first German territories occupied by Soviet troops gave such propaganda all the more resonance.

Of all the Soviet anti-German propaganda, most famous were the calls of the novelist Ilya Ehrenburg to wreak revenge, calls which were repeated so often that they became a standard Soviet mantra of hatred: 'We shall not speak any more. We shall not get excited. We shall kill. If you have not killed at least one German a day, you have wasted that day. . . . If you kill one German, kill another – there is nothing funnier for us than a pile of German corpses.'[7] As Soviet troops first approached the borders of the Reich in August 1944, Ehrenburg famously wrote in an article entitled 'Woe to Germany!':

> Until we reached Germany's borders we were liberators. Now we shall be judges. And never shall we mistake the home of a child slayer for an orphan asylum. [. . .]
>
> We are coming to Germany, having left behind us the Ukraine, Belorussia, the ashes of our cities, the blood of our children. Woe to the country of the assassins!
>
> Not only our troops, the shadows of the slain too, have come to the borders of Germany. Who is hammering at the gates of Prussia? The slaughtered old men from Trostyanets; the children from the Babi Yar ravine: the martyrs of Slavuta.
>
> The children drowned in wells are hovering like angels of vengeance over Insterburg. Old women, whom the Germans tied to horses' tails, are stretching out their hands to Tilsit.[8]

As Soviet troops flooded into German territory in January 1945, Ehrenburg (as Manfred Zeidler has put it) 'remained true to his uncompromising line of hatred and revenge', and his calls for vengeance were published in the Soviet Army newspaper *Krasnaya Zvezda* ('Red Star') to be read by Soviet soldiers streaming into the Reich. On 30 January, under the headline 'The Reckoning Has Begun', he admonished: 'The soldiers who are now storming German cities will not forget how the mothers of Leningrad pulled their dead children on sledges. [. . .] Berlin has not yet paid for the sufferings of Leningrad.'[9]

Ehrenburg's strident calls for revenge were echoed by Soviet generals in orders to their troops as they prepared the final onslaughts on the Reich in early 1945. When Marshal Zhukov issued his orders on the eve of the Soviet offensive of January 1945, he wrote that 'we will get our terrible revenge for everything'; and when Soviet soldiers crossed into East Prussia, the Main Political Administration of the Army stated that 'on German soil there is only one master – the Soviet soldier'. The Soviet soldier, the directive went on, 'is both the judge and the punisher for the torments of his fathers and mothers, for the destroyed cities and villages'; the people he would meet there were not his friends but 'next of kin of the killers and oppressors'.[10] The call issued by Zhukov's colleague Chernyakhovsky to the troops of the Third Belorussian Front massing to attack East Prussia on the eve of the January offensive was even more explicit:

> There will be no mercy – for no one, just as no mercy was given for us. It is unnecessary to expect that the soldiers of the Red Army will exercise mercy. They are burning with hatred and thirst for revenge. The land of the fascists must be made into a desert, just like our land that they devastated. The fascists must die, like our soldiers have died.[11]

Marshal Rokossovsky used similar language in his order to the troops of the Second Belorussian Front (which was poised to attack the southern half of East Prussia) on 13 January: 'The time has come to get completely even with the worst enemy of our homeland, with the fascist conquerors, for all their atrocities and crimes, for the sorrows and sufferings of our people, for the blood and tears of our fathers and mothers, wives and children, for the Soviet cities and villages destroyed and ransacked by the enemy.'[12] When they arrived on German soil, Soviet soldiers knew what was expected – or at least that they would not face penalties for violence against the German civilian population. One former Soviet soldier reflected in an interview 45 years later: 'Had not the Germans raped our women? Yes, and we knew that from the press. The mechanism functioned without a hitch. Therefore blood for blood. If they had done it, now we do the same.'[13]

It was not just the encouragement of their commanders and the death and destruction caused by the Wehrmacht in the USSR which fuelled the furious revenge of Soviet soldiers in 1945. The nature of the combat during the last months and weeks of the war also contributed. The bitterness of the fighting in the last months of the war, fighting which cost the lives of hundreds of thousands of Soviet troops at a time when Nazi Germany already obviously faced imminent defeat and when, therefore, continued fighting made no sense, heightened the desire for revenge.

Thus the stage was set for a terrible outburst of revenge-fuelled violence across eastern Germany. The occupation of town after town by Soviet troops was followed by sickeningly similar scenes. The rapes which accompanied the Soviet conquest of Berlin at the end of April and the beginning of May 1945 stand out due to the large numbers of victims and the prominence of the city, but similar outrages occurred in cities, towns and villages all along the eastern front as the Third Reich fell apart. In villages across East Prussia, the first German province reached by the Red Army, Soviet soldiers often raped every woman over the age of twelve, leaving many dead; houses were looted and villages set alight.[14] Frequently Soviet soldiers took the opportunity to destroy whatever structures had remained standing in German villages they occupied. Lev Kopelev, who was arrested soon afterwards for the 'propagation of bourgeois humanism' and 'sympathy with the enemy', described what happened when his Red Army unit moved into East Prussia with the offensive of January 1945:

We reached the first East Prussian villages: Groß-Koslau and Klein-Koslau – they were burning. The driver had to keep to the middle of the road. On both sides the houses were aflame under their tiled roofs. The tall tree in front of the burning church was smouldering and smoking. There were no people in sight. [. . .]

A horse-cart stood in the village square, next to it a couple of soldiers. We stopped: 'Was there heavy fighting here?'

'Fighting? Why? They just took off before we came – not a civilian remained.'

'So they laid mines and set them off?'

'Who? The Germans? No – there were no mines here at all, the fires were started by our side.'

'Why that then?'

'Ah, who the hell knows why? They just did it, for fun.'

A bearded, surly soldier growled with a casual anger: 'That's just it: here is Germany   so: smash everything up, burn everything! Take revenge!'[15]

During the mid-1950s it was suggested in the West German government's 'Documentation of the Expulsion' that the violence of Soviet troops 'was seen quite intentionally' as a means to pave the way for a subsequent expulsion of the eastern German population.[16] However, there is little evidence to support this claim, which may have reflected political narratives in the postwar Federal Republic more than what actually had motivated Soviet troops in 1945. In fact, Soviet commanders themselves were taken aback by the ferocity of the violence, which made their task of subduing Nazi Germany more difficult.[17] The vengeful violence of Soviet soldiers against German civilians not only provided apparent confirmation of Nazi propaganda about the alleged bestiality of the 'Asiatic' hordes from the east. It also served to stiffen German resistance to the Russian advance long beyond the point when continued fighting held out any prospect of success, and to slow the progress of a Red Army whose soldiers often were busy getting drunk and raping women rather than single-mindedly pressing on towards Berlin. This orgy of violence seems more likely to have been half-controlled expressions of revenge, undertaken by battle-hardened troops who, for a short period, had the opportunity to do what they liked to German civilians, than a strategy calculated to terrify the German population in order to facilitate population transfer.

Such a conclusion is reinforced by the fact that the violence did not ebb once Soviet troops reached central Germany. The conduct of Soviet soldiers after the April offensive which led to the capture of Berlin was little different than their behaviour across eastern Germany during the previous months, not just in the capital but all across the areas occupied by the Red Army. Germans were keenly aware that Soviet soldiers arrived thirsting for revenge. In Görlitz, according to the Catholic priest Franz Scholz, the first encounters of the civilian population with the Soviet troops who entered the city on 6 May 1945 had seemed peaceful: 'Everything looks very disciplined. The Russians appear to take no notice of civilians who now are surfacing more and more.' A few hours later, however, things suddenly changed: the citizens of Görlitz now experienced 'the hard retaliation of revenge for everything that Hitler did with his SS to the peoples of the east'. 'Now', Scholz observed, 'it's our turn to pay the bill'. And pay they did, as it became 'ghastly to have to live in Görlitz', with Soviet troops 'swarming around looking for women and booty'.[18]

What happened to the civilian population in Austria was similar to what took place in eastern and central Germany. Officially, the Red Army was supposed to differentiate 'Austrians' from 'Germans'. Stalin had stipulated that Soviet troops were 'not to insult the population of Austria, to behave correctly and not to confuse the Austrians with the German occupiers', and Soviet forces had been informed that Austria was 'the first state that was the victim of Hitlerite aggression'.[19] However, Soviet soldiers did not necessarily distinguish the 'Germans' they encountered in Austria from the Germans they encountered elsewhere. In Austria too the arrival of the Red Army was accompanied by sexual violence on a large scale, and the NKVD attached to Soviet troop formations in Austria admitted that 'there have been cases of excesses by individual members of units of the Red Army against the local population'.[20] In the Steiermark (in the south of

Austria), for example, thousands of women sought medical help after being raped by Soviet soldiers, and in Graz alone more than 600 cases of rape were reported to the police – a number which no doubt comprised only a fraction of the sexual attacks which had occurred in the city.[21]

As Lev Kopelev's account of the behaviour of Soviet troops in East Prussia indicates, rape and looting were not the only expressions of desire for revenge by Soviet troops after they entered German towns and villages. In numerous places they also unleashed an orgy of wanton destruction. Of course the fighting itself, particularly where (as in Königsberg, Berlin and Breslau) the Red Army had to battle through a German city street by street, led to tremendous damage. However, it did not end there: after the battle was over and the Soviet forces had occupied a town, the victorious soldiers frequently then set about destroying whatever had been left standing. Eyewitnesses in Königsberg, for example, noted how houses damaged during the fighting to take the city, were subsequently set alight and burnt to the ground.[22] There could be no motive for such destruction other than revenge against a now helpless German population. Indeed, in the case of Königsberg, the wanton destruction in the spring of 1945 would make life much harder for the Russian inhabitants of the city, renamed Kaliningrad, in the years thereafter. Upon seeing the obviously better conditions, compared with what they had known in the Soviet Union, in which the German population had lived – well-presented and well-stocked houses, towns with the infrastructure of a developed industrial society, prosperity beyond the dreams of most Soviet citizens at the time – it was common to react with anger. How could people who had so much have brought themselves to attack and destroy the meagre possessions of people who had so little? 'Why', as a Russian sentry in Berlin asked the American journalist Alexander Werth, 'did these people who were living so well have to invade us?'[23] It was not difficult, once the fighting was over and a town was in Russian hands, to justify plunder and destruction. As one officer of the First Belorussian Front put it, 'the deeper we penetrate into Germany the more we are disgusted by the plenty we find everywhere. . . . I'd just love to smash my fist into all those neat rows of tins and bottles.'[24]

For Soviet soldiers the hostility towards the conquered Germans had a further dimension: the language of class and class hatred, in which Soviet politics and propaganda were framed. For the Russians, not only were Germans 'fascists' and the murderers of their country-men; they also often were 'capitalists'. Franz Scholz observed in his diary of events in Görlitz in mid-May that 'Russian soldiers regard a German worker's flat with running water, electric light and gas, cur-tain, radio, porcelain dishes and sewing machines as a capitalist's flat. How often do I hear: Capitalists! The class comrades remove every-thing with the innocent explanation: "We only [from] capitalists take everything."'[25]

Some of the worst examples of the campaigns of needless destruc-tion by Red Army soldiers occurred in the territories east of the Oder–Neiße, which were destined to become part of postwar Poland and where Polish settlers were expected to build a new life. Here, in the new Polish 'western regions' the collapse of the Third Reich, the end of the war and the arrival of Soviet troops was fol-lowed by waves of looting, vandalism and arson as both Poles and Soviet soldiers expressed their anger and hatred after six years of brutal occupation and war of annihilation.[26] In Breslau, for days after the German capitulation, fires broke out across the city, claim-ing hundreds of buildings and cultural treasures that had survived the terrible siege: between the 7th and 10th of May, it seemed as though the entire city were in flames; on 11 May a major fire broke out on the 'Sand Island' in the city, apparently beginning with the former Eastern Europe Institute and spreading to the major churches nearby; on the 17th fire broke out in the Maria-Magdalena Church in the old city centre – one of the symbols of Breslau and one which had survived the fighting largely intact – destroying the inte-rior decoration, one of the church's towers, and the 500-year-old church bell which fell and then melted in the heat.[27] In Liegnitz, one of the first Polish settlers to arrive in the city later described his impressions:

A vast, rich city devoid of people. Clean, almost spruced up. [. . .] The city stood open. [. . .] One could take possession of a flat, a villa, a block of flats left behind by a doctor, a banker, a general. One also could set a house on fire. [. . .]

This affluence, from which one could take as much as one wanted and which nevertheless had the proverbial value of diamonds in the desert, made many people go wild. [. . .] Even I, who came from a doctor's family, sometimes lost healthy common sense at the sight of these objects which had been collected over centuries – what were the poor people supposed to feel who came from basement flats and mud huts and who in their lives had known little more than hard work and a meagre income.

They [the Soviet soldiers] threw luxury objects from the top floor onto the street for their amusement. Lampshades, crystal vases, earthenware chamber-pots. Everything smashed to bits when it hit the asphalt. Chairs, armchairs and everything that fell into their hands went flying through the air. And when they threw a harpsichord down from a balcony – what a final note it gave out when it hit the street![28]

For the first time the military forces of a significantly poorer country had occupied a significantly richer one. German affluence and order seemed almost an affront to people who had suffered under Nazi occupation, but now the boot was on the other foot.

The outbursts of violence by Soviet forces in 1945 have framed the perception of German suffering and victimhood ever since: of German civilians at the mercy of drunken, violent and sexually predatory Soviet soldiers with a thirst for revenge. Given the scale of the violence, the apparent confirmation of images conjured up by Nazi propaganda, the commonly held prejudices about Russians and 'Mongols', and awareness of the conduct of German forces in the USSR and consequent expectations of retribution (the 'revenge for everything that Hitler did with his SS to the peoples of the east'), this comes as no great surprise. However, it was not only Soviet soldiers who behaved in such a manner. The conduct of the French, when they arrived in south-western Germany in April, was not always much better.

Although the violence in the south-west never reached the intensity of what occurred when the Red Army arrived in eastern Germany, there too the arrival of foreign troops was sometimes followed by a 'reign of terror with looting and rape that lasted for days'.[29] The most notorious outburst of vengeful violence in western Germany took place in Freudenstadt in mid-April. The only really important transport junction in the Black Forest region, Freudenstadt had assumed a key position in the campaign of the French commander, General de Lattre de Tassigny, to occupy the south-western corner of the Reich. After French forces had converged on Freudenstadt from the north and east and taken the town on 17 April, three days of looting, arson and violence ensued.[30] According to one account, some 500 women reported having been raped when the French occupied the town and then set much of it alight, allegedly chanting 'we are the avengers, the SS of the French Army'.[31] The intensity of this violence may have been due to the presence of units of the 'Forces Françaises de l'Interieur' (which were composed in large measure of people who had taken part in the *résistance*); memories of the massacre at Oradour and the destruction of the village of Geradmer in the Vosges by a company of German soldiers in November 1944 also may have played a role, although subsequent German accounts point to the behaviour of Moroccan troops (which conjured up images of what had occurred in western Germany after the First World War and which still feature in right-wing propaganda).[32] Whatever the truth, the fear was widespread that German women now were at the mercy of marauding dark-skinned soldiers in French uniform.[33] It was not until the local French commandant threatened those guilty of looting and rape with the death penalty, three days after the French had taken the town, that the violence subsided.

Like the Russians, the French had experienced German occupation, and hundreds of thousands of their citizens had laboured for the benefit of the Nazi war economy. While conditions in wartime France and those faced by French foreign workers in Germany were not as dreadful as those endured by their Soviet counterparts, the French too had been subjected to arrogant, often violent, sometimes murderous Nazi rule. Now they were among the occupying powers, and they too would be able to enjoy a measure of revenge. However, there were certain features peculiar to the French occupation of south-western Germany. Unlike many of the British, American or Soviet armies, the First French Army under Lattre de Tassigny (a part of the U.S. Sixth Army Group under General Jacob Devers) had been constituted only recently, and contained a large proportion of 'colonial' troops, in particular from North Africa. Consequently, fears and fantasies combined with actual violence, as Germans referred repeatedly to the actual and supposed excesses of North African troops. At the same time, much of the area occupied by the French, particularly in the Black Forest, had hardly had been touched by the war; ill-supplied French soldiers from North Africa, who often had been less than well-treated by their own French officers, thus suddenly found themselves in conquered enemy territory where the locals still enjoyed a good standard of living and in a world which appeared largely undisturbed.

Vengeful violence against Germans by occupation troops was not exclusive to the Russians and the French. Members of the British and American armed forces did not always conduct themselves with probity either. Among the Americans, the widely publicized massacre of over 70 American prisoners by soldiers of an SS tank unit at Malmedy on 17 December 1944 (which earned an editorial in the U.S. Army newspaper *Stars and Stripes* on 3 January 1945 headlined 'Murder on the Western Front'), as well as awareness of the killing of Allied airmen shot down over Germany, had hardened attitudes.[34] As one American soldier expressed it in a letter home: 'The Germans have had orders to kill all airborne prisoners. We've found a number of our boys shot in the back so turn about is fair play.'[35] Consequently, German prisoners too were sometimes killed after their surrender or capture. Members of the Waffen-SS in particular were targets for revenge, in large measure because of the Malmedy massacre:

As it was, the only men that we shot on sight were the SS. The young men educated entirely under Hitler's regime, who were responsible for the most atrocious crimes required by the Nazi Party. Although it can never be officially admitted, since it is a direct violation of the Geneva Convention, we killed these men, whether they had surrendered to us or not. Incidentally,

American troops violated this convention in many other ways besides shooting SS men under white flags.[36]

SS-men taken prisoner, who were identified by the tattoos which gave their blood group, were frequently treated more harshly than members of the German Army and the Luftwaffe.[37]

Most German prisoners of the Americans, of course, were not killed. However, many were robbed and beaten. Letters home from American soldiers, picked up by the American military censors, testify to 'souvenir hunting' and physical attacks:

> I got two watches the other day from two German prisoners also a pen. I got 346 marks off another one a while back. I also have a kraut pistol.
>
> Say Beautiful you should see some of the things that the boys has taken from the Jerries. Watches, rings, Bill folds, pistols, knives, helmets, and one of the boys even has a German skull.[38]

Some American soldiers took pleasure in abusing the German prisoners at their mercy:

> I mail you and daddy a watch I hope you like it [. . .] it is a nice watch. Also the one I got it off was a German Cpt Ha Ha he did not like it so I got mad and let him have it all if you get what I mean [. . .] he force me to shoot him and for me I love to shoot him.[39]

Another wrote:

> We did see many, many prisoners these few past days – yes, a delightful sight. A sidelight: always did want to boot one of those Heinies in the pants and I did to my heart's content.[40]

Accounts of the war's end in the west also contain their share of references to instances in which American and British soldiers attacked German women.[41] When Würzburg, for example, was occupied at the beginning of April 1945, the behaviour of some American soldiers left a lot to be desired: they engaged in looting, destroyed a portion of the city's collection of antique vases, tended to look the other way when 'displaced persons' engaged in looting, occasionally attacked and robbed Germans, and committed the occasional rape; violent behaviour on the part of African-American soldiers drew particular attention, and occupied a more prominent place in German memories of this period.[42] Altogether 487 American soldiers were tried for rapes allegedly committed in March and April 1945.[43] The British were not entirely innocent either. For example, after the town of Soltau (roughly mid-way between Hamburg and Hannover) was occupied, British soldiers got drunk, robbed German civilians of watches, rings and other possessions, sometimes at gunpoint, and raped a number of women (one of whom was raped by an officer).[44] Nevertheless, although there were numerous isolated instances of violence against the civilian population in the areas conquered by the Anglo-Saxon armies, the behaviour of the British and the Americans never resembled the mass rape and vengeful wanton destruction which accompanied the Soviet advance into Germany.

What clearly did provoke desire for vengeance among the Western Allied forces, however, were the scenes that greeted the liberators of the concentration camps in the spring of 1945. By the time that the British and Americans arrived in western and central Germany, the once coldly efficient concentration camp system had largely broken down, with huge numbers of prisoners crammed into camps which had no provision for them. As the territory under Nazi control shrunk during the last months of the war and the concentration camp empire shrunk with it, hundreds of thousands of desperately ill, undernourished, ill-treated prisoners had been herded into camps in areas still under German control – camps which had become massively overcrowded, filthy, disease-ridden, and with spiralling mortality. This was what greeted the British who liberated Bergen-Belsen, the Americans who liberated Dachau, and the soldiers who liberated dozens of other camps large and small: emaciated survivors, piles of corpses, the stench of death, the evidence of mass murder.

Allied soldiers reacted with tremendous anger at what they saw. The most striking example was what occurred at Dachau. Conditions in the camp during early 1945 were horrible; between the beginning of the year and the time the camp was liberated by American troops on the afternoon of 29 April 1945 an average of over 100 people daily died of disease.[45] When the Americans arrived, slightly over 32,000 prisoners were still alive in the camp.[46] Thousands more were found dead. The rooms of the crematorium and gas-chamber complex were piled two metres high with 'neatly stacked' naked corpses, some 2000 altogether; in the medical services area and elsewhere a further 1500 corpses were discovered.[47] A U.S. Army sergeant, an illustrator for the Sixth Army Group Headquarters, described the camp when he visited it on 3 May:

The air [. . .] was filled with the smell of lime and the unforgettable smell of the dead. Facing us was a big grey building with a grey wall, about 10 feet high, all around it. To the left of this building and wall were fifty rail cars. [. . .] In at least 40 of the cars including the four open ones, there were dead, starved, emaciated bodies lying in every conceivable position. They wore striped suits (prisoner's uniform) parts of which seem to have been torn from their bodies in their death throes, thus revealing that wax-like skin of the dead. In a plot of grass, opposite the train, were three dead SS guards, evidently beaten to death, because there were terrific bruises all over their bodies. They were dressed in civilian clothes which were partly ripped from their bodies. One of the bodies had part of its skull ripped open but in general they looked very well fed compared to the starved dead bodies of their victims opposite them in the train. [. . .]

We left the open space and entered one of the houses and then one of the rooms. The room we saw was approximately 11 feet square and 10 feet high. In it were four triple decker bunks [. . .]. This meant that there were 12 bunks in this room. Each bunk was occupied by no less than 3 to 4 persons, meaning that there was an average of 45 to 48 underfed, sick, and diseased people in one room. There was one small window. The room was occupied by these people when we looked in. They looked beyond any help and were dying. The stench was horrible and we had to leave very quickly to keep from vomiting. [. . .]

We walked into a fenced-in portion of ground which housed the crematorium.

The rooms where the bodies were kept were about 10 feet high and 17 feet square filled 3/4 full with layer upon layer of human bodies. They were piled as you would pile cord wood ready for burning. The stench was horrible. In back of this crematorium were pile upon pile of clothes all neatly arranged in bales. The coats were separate, the pants separate, and so on. We could see little children's clothes and shoes, girls and women's dresses, shoes and hats. The piles of clothing (less shoes) were put side by side to occupy a space approximately 200 feet long, 10 feet high and 4 feet wide. The place where people were shot was right next to the crematorium. We saw a big blood spot on each side of the earth bank.[48]

The shock at seeing the 'Hell of Dachau' led American troops to gun down many of those they regarded as responsible.[49] One American corporal wrote in a letter:

I've just had the occasion to see one of the worst horrors of the war. I went to one of the crematories – this is where the Nazis burned people alive. Saw some of the half cooked bodies. They were awful [. . .]. I saw rows and rows of bodies that these Germans had killed just before they retreated. After looking at the cremated bodies you just feel like killing every German alive.[50]

And kill they did. The men of the American 45th and 42nd Divisions who liberated Dachau had experienced tough fighting during the previous weeks, and they expected bitter resistance from the SS at the camp. After taking that camp – against little opposition as it turned out – and seeing thousands of dead and dying prisoners, many GIs went berserk with rage; subsequent reports spoke of their unbridled hatred and thirst for revenge.[51] According to Jack Hallett, one of the camp's liberators, interviewed decades later:

> Control was gone after the sights we saw, and the men were deliberately wounding guards that were available and then turned them over to the prisoners and allowing them to take their revenge on them. And, in fact, you've seen the picture where one of the soldiers gave one of the inmates a bayonet and watched him behead the man. It was a pretty gory mess. A lot of the guards were shot in the legs so that they couldn't move and . . . and that's about all I can say.[52]

Germans were gunned down while surrendering; captives were shot at the slightest provocation; in one instance, men guarding over a hundred captured Germans turned their machine guns on their prisoners and killed them all;[53] and American soldiers stood by as camp prisoners turned on their former guards and tormentors. After what they had seen, their reactions were sadly understandable.

The effect of the camps on Allied soldiers' attitudes extended beyond their anger towards the guards. Often little attempt was made to differentiate between Germans who had supported the Nazi regime and Germans who had opposed it. This was what Max Gorbach, a German Communist and former camp inmate, discovered after the Americans arrived at Dachau. Gorbach, who was among those who sought to organize food and labour distribution after the liberation, attempted to dissuade the Americans from evicting Germans from their homes in order to house Poles and other displaced persons. For his troubles he was told bluntly by American soldiers that the foreigners had lost everything 'because of you', and that he was lucky that the Americans did not shoot him.[54] For the British, Bergen-Belsen had a similar effect to that which Dachau had had on the Americans, and some commanders – such as Colonel J. Spottiswoode, the British Military Commander who was put in charge of the district of Münster and who had taken part in the liberation of Bergen-

Belsen[55] – were inclined initially to take a punitive attitude towards
the German population due to their personal experiences of liberat-
ing the camps.

The reactions of Allied soldiers who saw the horrors of the concentration camps in the spring of 1945 were mild compared with
those of the prisoners who had been subjected to the horrors of camp
life for months or years. They emerged with a burning hatred of the
people who had put them through such hell. Saul Padover, an
American intelligence officer, recounted conversations that he had had
with prisoners he met when Buchenwald was liberated. After speaking with a German Communist who had been imprisoned in the
camp, 'a Belgian inmate came over and asked ironically why we
wasted time with Germans, even German Communists. "A good
German", he said, "is a dead German."'[56] Padover also spoke with a
Pole, a former teacher from Kattowice, who had survived Auschwitz
and then been evacuated to Buchenwald:

> He burst forth into such a flood of imprecations against the
> German race as I have never heard. He raised his arms and cried
> out to God to bring down His vengeance upon the German
> nation; to exterminate every German man, woman and child; to
> strike to death every living German being; to cleanse the earth of
> all German blood unto eternity. I was tempted to say Amen, and
> I felt like crying.[57]

Scarcely less intense were the feelings of many of the foreign labourers who had been brought, often against their will, to work in
Germany and who now saw their opportunity to pay back their
former masters. The collapse of the Nazi police state was followed
by a wave of looting and violence, frequently committed by (and
even more frequently blamed on) 'displaced persons'. Allied soldiers,
after occupying a city or town, often looked on as foreign workers
plundered German shops – something made easier when curfews
were decreed for Germans but not for Polish or Ukrainian workers.[58] Germans stood in fear as foreigners 'passed through the
country looting, robbing and murdering'.[59] In Munich 'displaced

persons', who comprised 4 per cent of the population, were held responsible for three quarters of the crimes committed.[60] From Görlitz the priest Franz Scholz wrote of how, soon after the war ended, 'hordes of foreign workers' were encamped everywhere, the city was littered with the debris left from their looting, the German population remained out of sight and fearful, and 'the foreigners dominate the scene'.[61] No doubt the Germans' fears were exaggerated in some cases, and the streets of occupied Germany were not all as dangerous as supposed. And no doubt there were many instances where the end of the war was peaceful and accompanied by cooperation, even friendship and solidarity, among Germans and foreign workers.[62] However, more than a few 'displaced persons' shared the sentiments of one man who had worked in the Ruhr region during the war and who told me in Kiev in 1975, with a broad grin, that he had managed to acquire a firearm and shoot Germans when the war ended.

The collapse of the Third Reich presented not only foreign soldiers, foreign labourers and concentration camp inmates with opportunities to take revenge on Germans. It also offered many Germans the opportunity for reprisals against their countrymen for injustices suffered under Nazi rule. The Third Reich left behind a residue of hatred not only among non-Germans across the European continent but also among Germans themselves. Many had suffered at the hands of the regime, the police and their neighbours; and just about all now suffered as a result of the catastrophe that Nazi rule and a lost war had brought. The magnitude of the hatred which Nazism and war left in their wake would be difficult to overestimate.[63] Shortly before his death in 1947, Gustav Stolper (economic journalist, liberal Reichstag member from 1930 to 1932, and advisor to the Hoover mission to central Europe) wrote that 'millions had been waiting [. . .] millions had made up lists of their enemies, thought out catalogues of measures to eliminate those at whose hands they had suffered'.[64] Others focused their anger more generally on the former Nazi leadership. One woman, in the rubble of Frankfurt am Main, wrote in a letter a couple of weeks after the war ended:

I often am asked if I would not like to leave Germany, and I often have posed the question to myself. In so doing I have come to the realization that I nevertheless am very rooted here and would like to take part in the reconstruction. That does not in any way mean that my hatred against those responsible has become milder. On the contrary, I even would like to help string the criminals up on the gallows.[65]

The desire for revenge by Germans against Germans found particularly sharp expression in the wave of denunciations which accompanied the establishment of foreign military rule. Germany's new rulers often were quite willing to give credence to accusations against people who had been members of Nazi organizations. The new authorities, like their predecessors in the Gestapo, received letters of denunciation from members of the public, this time aimed against people who a few years previously may have been seen in SS uniform or who had taken advantage of positions as local Nazi bosses to bully and terrorize their neighbours.[66] The authors of denunciations comprised, according to one observer, 'especially those people who had not held any special positions [during the Nazi period] and thereby avoided membership in Nazi organizations and then [in 1945] suddenly presented themselves as anti-fascists'. The result, for example in western Mecklenburg after Soviet troops arrived to establish their occupation regime at the beginning of July 1945, was a 'great wave of denunciation' after the war.[67]

The vengeful hatred vented against Germans in 1945 contributed greatly to the victim mentality which developed once the war came to an end. The fact that violence often was aimed at people who themselves had committed no crimes, who became targets of revenge for things that *others* had done, amplified the sense of victimhood and injustice with which millions of Germans emerged from the inferno of 1945. The exercise of revenge against Germans in 1945 thus performed a key role in the profound change in mentalities that occurred as Germans constructed a post-Nazi identity as innocent victims in an unfair world. The hundreds of thousands of German women who were raped in 1945, the millions of Germans who were forced to flee from their homes, the thousands of civilians who were injured or killed by Allied soldiers, were not necessarily the people who had been responsible for the cruelty, barbarity and crimes associated with the Nazi occupation of Europe. They were easy, available targets, whose humiliation could give satisfaction to people who had regarded themselves – or had been encouraged to regard themselves – as victims of Nazi Germany and now saw themselves as agents of retribution. The obvious injustice of this violence made the trauma of 1945 all the greater, and in the immediate postwar years made it easier for Germans to avoid facing what their nation had done to others, and to concentrate instead on what had been done to them.

7

THE BEGINNING OF
OCCUPATION

Perhaps never before in modern history have victorious invaders been faced with such a problem as confronted the Allies in Germany. War always must be expected to produce confusion and some breakdown, but a complete disintegration in a major nation seems to be something new under the sun. Howard Zink[1]

Military Government will control the civilian population so as best to facilitate and promote the success of military operations. The administration will be firm, but just. SHAEF Handbook[2]

When the Allies arrived in Germany, they faced what they assumed was a people schooled in militarism, indoctrinated by Nazi ideology and fanatically committed to continued struggle. They behaved accordingly. They did not see themselves as liberators but as victors in an enemy country; they had come to Germany, as Eisenhower announced, 'as a victorious army'.[3] Allied commanders arrived determined to take an uncompromising stance towards the conquered people; Allied forces put sections of German towns off-limits to the native population, restricted contact between soldiers and German civilians, requisitioned (or simply stole) supplies from the Germans, and evicted them from homes and offices. They imprisoned tens of thousands of Germans who had held positions of responsibility or were believed to have been involved in the crimes of the Nazi regime, and launched a series of war-crimes trials, most famously the Trial of the Major War Criminals that opened in Nuremberg in November 1945. Yet the millions of foreign soldiers in Germany could not and did not remain cut off from the people whose country they occupied, whatever the initial intentions of their commanders. As Allied military administrations took responsibility for alleviating the catastrophic conditions they found when they arrived in Germany, they necessarily had to work together with Germans. The shock of conquest and the initial confrontation between victorious Allied troops and vanquished Germans eventually gave way to accommodation in countless everyday interactions. Both these developments – the violence and clamp-down which accompanied the arrival of the Allies and the subsequent routinization of military occupation – framed how the postwar order began to be imposed, in differing ways and with differing aims, in the various occupation zones.

At the outset, when Allied forces arrived in a German village or town, they were not inclined to be gentle. The first consideration, as had been spelled out in the 'SHAEF Handbook for Military Government in Germany', was 'to control the civilian population so as to facilitate and promote the success of military operations'.[4] This they did. In Marburg, for example, the American military were, from the outset, determined to prevent both German civilians and displaced persons from getting in the way of U.S. army units. The Americans concentrated on tasks necessary for their own operations: the burial of corpses, the prevention of the spread of disease, the repair of water and sewerage works, the requisitioning of food, fuel and motor vehicles. They mobilized German civilians to clear rubble from the streets, and arrested those believed to threaten security. The reconstruction of civil administration, at least initially, was of secondary importance.[5]

There was not much sympathy for the conquered population among the Western Allies, to say nothing of the Russians. Attitudes towards the Germans had been hardened by the discovery of conditions in the concentration camps. Consequently, Allied commanders frequently forced Germans from nearby towns to view the corpses piled up at camps which had just been liberated – at Bergen–Belsen, Weimar/Buchenwald, Dachau, and elsewhere.[6] Townspeople, both men and women, were frequently conscripted to bury the corpses found in the camps.[7] For example, in Ludwigslust (between Berlin and Hamburg) at the beginning of May, the commander of the American 82nd Airborne Division, General James Gavin, ordered all the town's inhabitants over ten years of age to view the horrors on display at the nearby camp at Wöbellin; then able-bodied residents ('the leading German citizens', according to Gavin) were made to re-bury the dead at a park in front of Ludwiglust's palace in the presence of the town's entire population.[8] The Germans, collectively, were viewed not just as a conquered people but also as morally bankrupt and guilty of unspeakable crimes.

For their part, German civilians generally reacted passively to the arrival of occupation forces: 'One raised the white flag, in order to be safe from further surprises; one became more and more conscious that the war with its dreadful air attacks was over; one felt rescued as from a bad dream and was happy about the end of the brown [i.e. Nazi] dictatorship.'[9] In the Ruhr region the American 9th Army reported how 'the attitude of the German people toward American occupation and military government can best be described by a single word – "docile". For the most part, after they got over their initial fright, they were easily controlled and obedient.'[10] Across the country the occupation troops found that the Germans, overwhelmed by the destruction all round them, tended to be passive, apathetic, and preoccupied with their own private affairs.

Once they occupied a locality, Allied commanders were faced immediately with practical and logistical problems of enormous proportions. In some cases they found themselves in cities and towns from which a large proportion of the population had fled in order to avoid the fighting and/or because the bombing had destroyed so much housing. In Würzburg, for example, which on 16 March 1945 had experienced one of the worst bombing raids of the entire Allied air campaign, only about 2000 civilians were left when American forces took the city at the beginning of April; the rest had been evacuated or had fled.[11] In other cases, the population had swollen enormously, often with homeless refugees. When the Americans took Leipzig on 19 April, the city's normal population of roughly 700,000 had grown to more than 1,000,000 as a result of the influx of foreign 'displaced persons' and German refugees.[12] The population of Göttingen, which emerged from the war almost completely undamaged, had increased from the normal figure of 50,000 to 70,000, as evacuees from Kassel and Berlin sought refuge in this small university town.[13] Inevitably, after the battle for a city or town had ended, large numbers of German civilians returned. In Münster, for example, only about 23,000 people remained in the city when Allied forces arrived (as compared with a 1939 population of 140,000); by August, however, the number of people in Münster had doubled.[14]

Upon their arrival, the first task of Allied forces was to ensure their own safety. Items which might be used for continued resistance – weapons, ammunition, binoculars, cameras, radios – were removed from the conquered population.[15] Rigid curfews were imposed, and movement of citizens severely restricted. In Würzburg, the Americans imposed a curfew from seven in the evening to seven in the morning; no one was allowed to travel further than six kilometres, and everyone over the age of 16 had to carry identity papers with them at all times.[16] Then there were the questions of where to house the occupiers, often in towns where a large proportion of the housing had been destroyed, where to set up an occupation administration, how to work with the Germans in the locality and to decide who to work with, and how to suppress any popular resistance – something expected from a supposedly fanaticized Nazi population. The initial responses of the Allied occupiers, with different emphases in the different zones, involved a considerable degree of improvization and pragmatism, together with great reluctance, particularly on the part of the Americans, to allow anything but the most necessary and limited official contact between themselves and the local population.

Speed was of the essence. There was little time to give careful and detailed attention to each and every decision which needed to be made. The determination to take swift, pragmatic action had been reflected in the recommendations contained in the 'SHAEF Handbook for Military Government in Germany' with regard to setting up local administrative structures:

> If the Bürgermeister or the Head of the local government unit is on the 'Black List' or on the list to be suspended, take appropriate action. If not, and you think he may be reliable, send for him. If he is not available or will not serve, send for the next senior official against whom nothing unfavourable is known. Order this official to remain at his post until further orders, and inform him that you will hold him responsible for running the government and for the proper character and performance of all officials under his jurisdiction. Outline Military Government policy to him in so far as it affects his task.[17]

The only clear criterion for appointment to public office was that the person in question had not been a National Socialist. This offered the military authorities rather little guidance for choosing suitable individuals to head local and regional administrations and left them dependent on advice from the German community, but gave them considerable leeway in filling posts. Generally, in small towns and villages the military authorities were more likely to allow Germans to remain at their desks than in the cities.[18] Nevertheless, the purge of Nazi Party members from local government was often abrupt, leaving town administrations suddenly denuded of trained staff. The Americans were particularly determined to remove Nazis from local government, and the Germans newly installed by the military government to run local administrations could themselves be quite zealous in purging their countrymen. In Marburg, within a week of the Americans' arrival, the city's mayor had removed 26 people from their posts at his own initiative and another half dozen on the orders of the military government, and the city's first military governor claimed that he had dismissed three quarters of the municipal and district officials above the rank of clerk or labourer.[19] In Würzburg the mayor dismissed over 250 former Nazi Party members from the city administration at the insistence of the Americans; by the end of the year the number was 320.[20]

In the areas they occupied, the Red Army also took quick decisions about local administration. Although 'Initiative Groups' of leading German Communists had been flown from Moscow to Germany at the end of April with the aim of setting up post-Nazi administrations, initially the Russians lacked a clear idea of what structures they should put in place and were not necessarily so rigorous when it came to sacking former Nazis as were the Americans. During the early weeks of the occupation, the Soviet authorities urged the reconstitution of local 'self-government' in order to maintain basic services.[21] That could mean taking a rather pragmatic approach: as the newly-appointed head of the district administration in Demmin (in Pomerania) reported, 'some former members of the Nazi Party had to be called upon as trained personnel' (although 'they soon were removed from all public offices and leading positions in the economy and replaced with anti-fascists'.)[22] This is not to say that policy towards former Nazis was consistent. In Brandenburg, for example, in some places local Soviet commanders were keen on harsh treatment for erst-while Nazis, while elsewhere they impeded the purging of former Nazi Party members – including one case where a Soviet comman-dant ignored information about the past of a mayor who had been a member of the NSDAP and who, in his role as a teacher, permitted children to continue to use the 'Hitler greeting'.[23] Generally, the Russians were keen to involve Germans in the reorganization of public life, but kept them well removed from decisions involving security.[24]

In each of the zones, with different emphases and in different ways, the objective was to establish German administrations to which a mil-itary government could give orders. The Germans were to restrict their activities to administrative tasks; the real decisions would be taken by the occupation authorities and, as the SHAEF Handbook spelled out, 'political activity of any kind will be prohibited except [where] expressly permitted by Supreme Commander'.[25] Although

German civilians build an anti-tank barrier on the Charlottenburg Bridge
in Berlin, March 1945.

The dictator's last public appearance: Adolf Hitler with his boy soldiers, members of the Hitler Youth in the *Volkssturm*

A British soldier stands guard in front of the former offices of the local Nazi Party group in the town of Rotenburg, to the east of Bremen

Soviet soldiers arrive in the East Prussian village of Kussen, near Gumbinnen,
on 18 January 1945

The death march of prisoners towards the Dachau concentration camp,
Hebertshausen, near Dachau, 27 April 1945

British troops (on foot) greet an American soldier (in a Jeep), in Issum (near the Dutch border) on 6 March 1945

British and Soviet soldiers meet at Wismar, on the Baltic Sea coast, 3 May 1945

A delegation of the inhabitants
of a village near Landsberg, in
Bavaria, approach an American
tank carrying white flags,
late April 1945

White sheets hanging, as a sign
of capitulation, from apartment
windows in Berlin, 2 May 1945

An African–American soldier poses for the camera with German prisoners

Displaced persons flood the streets of Dillenburg in April 1945
after the liberation of the area by American forces

German civilians looting a train in Frankfurt, 7 May 1945

Surrender: Admiral Hans-Georg von Friedeburg signs surrender documents in Field Marshal Bernard Montgomery's field headquarters in the Lüneburg Heath at 6 p.m. on 4 May 1945. Three days later General Alfred Jodl signed the general capitulation of the Wehrmacht at Eisenhower's headquarters in Reims

The American flag is raised over the swastika at the former Nazi Party rally grounds in Nuremberg, 21 April 1945

according to the SHAEF Handbook, 'Military Government will be effected, as a general principle, through indirect rule',[26] it was to be absolutely clear who was in charge. As Charles Keegan, a colonel with the American Third Army bluntly informed one German: 'Rights? You got no rights. You're conquered, ya hear?'.[27]

The attitudes of the occupation forces towards the subjected civilian population also reflected fears of continued Nazi-inspired resistance. Although 'Werewolf' resistance to Allied occupation never really materialized (except for the assassination of the American-installed mayor of Aachen, Franz Oppendorf, on 28 March 1945), the threat was taken extremely seriously. Indeed, fear of the 'Werewolf' among the Americans took on what one historian has described as 'hysterical characteristics'.[28] There were dire predictions about how harmless-looking German youths and fresh-faced German girls would lure unwitting Allied soldiers to their deaths.[29] 'Intelligence Information Bulletins' issued by the American 6th Army Group reckoned on a guerrilla war once the Allies had subdued the Wehrmacht, with a core of 30,000 Werewolf members continuing the struggle, supported by some 400,000 to 500,000 activists; American soldiers were warned of explosives being concealed in hay wagons and cigarette packets, of German agents wearing belts filled with explosive, and of Werewolf members having hidden supplies and prepared strongholds in anticipation of the coming struggle. It was the spectre of an insurgency which never happened. In short, while the German population were to be treated fairly, under no circumstances were they to be trusted.[30]

The Russians treated the supposed 'Werewolf' threat rather differently. The Soviet secret police, the NKVD, also convinced themselves that a 'Werewolf' organization had been created 'on the territory of Germany' in the dying days of the Third Reich; that members of the Nazi Party and the Hitler Youth had been trained in 'terror methods' in order to continue the struggle after the country was occupied, and that 'trained "Werewolf" underground groups had been given the task of carrying out acts of diversion and terror on territory occupied by units of the Red Army and the troops of the Allied armies'.[31] Despite the fact that these 'acts of terror' never actually materialized, suspicions of supposed 'Werewolf' activity provided the pretext for large numbers of arbitrary arrests of young people – for the most part youths aged between 15 and 17 – and harsh prison sentences handed down by Soviet military tribunals, often on the basis of confessions extracted under pressure. In the Soviet zone, accusations and suspicions of 'Werewolf' activity were used to tighten police control, and to secure forced labour.

When the Allied military authorities arrived in Germany, they found themselves in unfamiliar surroundings, often spoke little or no German (at a time when few Germans spoke English, let alone Russian). Yet almost overnight they had to set up complex administrative machinery and address the daunting problems facing the communities for which they now were responsible. They obviously would be dependent upon the cooperation of the local population, and could look in two directions for German personnel: to opponents of the Nazi regime, often Social Democrats and Communists who had been freed from imprisonment and who had banded together in many areas to form 'Anti-fascist Committees'; and to members of the professional civil service who had not been prominent in the Nazi regime and did not appear to have been involved in war crimes. The latter often had little sympathy with their co-nationals on the political left, and looked upon hopes of establishing an 'anti-fascist' political order and of restructuring the capitalist economy with scepticism. For the Allies, the question of where to seek reliable German partners was answered differently in the different zones. The Americans often looked not only to prominent opponents of the Nazis but also to experienced German civil servants – such as the conservative Ernst Reichard, who had been forced into retirement after refusing to join the Nazi Party in 1933 and who was nearly 70 years old when placed at the head of the regional administration in Franconia in May 1945.[32] The Russians, by contrast, looked more to committed German 'anti-fascists' – not so much to the local 'anti-fascist' committees which had sprung up spontaneously once Nazi rule collapsed as to the leadership of the German Communist Party (particularly those members who had been in exile in the USSR during the Nazi period). While Social Democrats might be placed in prominent positions in the Soviet zone – e.g. at the head of a *Land* administration – the key posts, in particular those dealing with security matters, were filled with Communists, who could be relied upon to discipline their followers and loyally serve their Soviet comrades.[33] In all the zones, the appointment of Germans to run local and regional administrations was accomplished remarkably quickly.

The ways in which military government functioned at the local level after German surrender varied greatly from place to place, even within a single occupation zone. In the British zone, some officers insisted on strict formality when dealing with the locals – on one occasion even threatening with military court German bureaucrats who failed to stand up when a British officer entered their office – and treated German personnel almost as servants. Others, however, demonstrated a willingness to work harmoniously with Germans in the local administration in a joint effort to deal with such urgent problems as securing food supplies for the urban population.[34] Sometimes Allied military government personnel could be quite rude and hostile. There were instances in the American zone where Jewish emigrants in the military government refused to converse in German with the civilians in local administration although they were native German speakers; in Ansbach (in Franconia) the newly installed director of the labour office, a Social Democrat, was confronted with an American officer who, smoking Havana cigars, turned his back on the German while issuing orders.[35] During the early weeks of occupation many Germans were treated almost as messenger boys for the military government. Yet for all their power, the local representatives of military government themselves often felt overwhelmed. One detachment officer in Marburg, when asked about the policy of the military government, was recorded as responding: 'Brother, I don't know. Maybe the big wheels in Frankfort [sic] can tell you. They snow me under with all sorts of papers. How'm I going to read them when I'm doing forty-eleven different things to get this burg running again?'[36] Confusion and improvization, alongside an overwhelming show of force, characterized the imposition of Allied control over occupied Germany.

Allied military government brought immediate changes to the physical environment in which Germans lived. Among the first was the renaming of streets and public buildings. Not only did the ubiquitous Adolf-Hitler-Straßen, Hermann-Göring-Straßen and Horst-Wessel-Straßen disappear, but street names which commemorated First World War battles (Langemarckstraßen, Tannenbergstraßen) or nationalist heroes (Litzmannstraßen, Schlageterstraßen) also vanished.[37] More disruptive was the removal of inhabitants from dwellings that the Allies decided to use for offices and housing and the exclusion of Germans from areas where military government headquarters were set up. The most notorious example was Karlshorst, a suburb in the east of Greater Berlin, where the Soviet Military Administration established its headquarters on 9 July.[38] The entire district became in effect a Russian colony in Berlin and off limits for Germans.

In all four zones, the occupation forces arrived with a determination to keep their distance from the conquered Germans. In the west, the watchword was 'non-fraternization', defined in the SHAEF Handbook as 'the avoidance of mingling with Germans upon terms of friendliness, familiarity or intimacy, whether individually or in groups, in official or unofficial dealings'.[39] The Americans were particularly rigorous in their determination to prevent fraternization. American soldiers were instructed, in 'Special Orders for American-German Relations', never to forget that the Germans had supported National Socialism; GIs were forbidden contact with the conquered population: forbidden to shake hands with Germans, visit their homes, play games or sports with them, exchange gifts, take part in social events with them or walk with them on the streets or elsewhere.[40] What is more – and this was especially disruptive for the local population – in the U.S. zone Germans were prohibited from inhabiting any part of a building in which Americans were housed. In any event, neither German civilians nor Allied soldiers were keen to have much to do with one another at the outset.[41] Even the French, who did not forbid Germans from remaining in a building partly inhabited by members of the occupation forces, tended to keep themselves to themselves and separate from the local population.[42] Nevertheless, practice on the ground varied considerably from place to place. While some local military governors were quite strict, others took a more relaxed approach. While in some areas former Nazi Party members might be kept in camps at night and made to do clean-up work under guard by day, in others – particularly in villages where occupation troops were not stationed – restrictions on the local population were conspicuous by their absence and curfew regulations frequently were ignored. The same was true of the 'non-fraternization' policy, which soon became a farce and was abandoned.[43]

The takeover of homes and offices occurred in all the occupation zones and was enormously disruptive for the Germans who were ejected. The sealing off of Karlshorst may have made a particularly lasting impression, but it was far from unique. Military governments in all four occupation zones requisitioned properties, demonstrating a particular liking for villas in the better parts of town. In Frankfurt am Main, which had been captured by U.S. forces on 29 March, the Americans immediately set about requisitioning large numbers of dwellings and offices for their own use, with little thought for the people who lost their homes. On 16 April, only two and a half weeks after the Americans had arrived, the Frankfurt Surveyor's Office reported that 1115 buildings, housing 3654 families, had already been vacated on the orders of the American Military Commission.[44] Whole sections of the city were declared 'off limits' to Germans; the entire area of the Palmengarten and the large Grünburg Park to the north of the city centre, together with the streets to the east of the park, were turned into a restricted American zone from which all German inhabitants had to move. The former I.G. Farben headquarters, which had survived the war unscathed and was taken over by the American Military for their headquarters, was encircled with barbed wire; Germans in the area had to make substantial detours when going about their day-to-day business. Altogether, according to the city's Statistical Office, at the beginning of February 1946 3675 buildings containing 9181 dwelling units had been requisitioned. These had been the homes of 36,668 people.

As a result of the requisitions, newly homeless civilians, moving what belongings they could take with them on hand-carts and baby-buggies as they went to emergency quarters, became a common sight on city streets. Germans saw large portions of their own towns become 'off limits'. In Frankfurt one woman noted on the 1st of May how the Americans 'have requisitioned entire city districts and fenced them off with barbed wire. Unfortunately my aunts' flat also fell victim to this action. It was a miserable scene as they and many others had to leave their home within a few hours. Furniture, carpets, beds, kitchen utensils etc. had to be left behind, they could take only personal clothing, duvets and small items with them.'[45]

In small towns as well as large cities properties were requisitioned and their inhabitants ejected. According to an official account (written in 1948) of the Americans' arrival in the small town of Frankenbach, to the west of Heilbronn:

> The American troops were billeted here in such a way that they took over entire terraces of houses. The inhabitants often had scarcely half an hour's time to leave their flats with the most essential belongings and to seek often quite miserable shelter among relatives or acquaintances. [. . .] A lot of valuables were lost at this time.[46]

At a time when housing was in desperately short supply and when it was virtually impossible to purchase consumer goods to replace what had been lost, these evictions could be quite traumatic, and 'the confiscation of dwellings and the various, numerous and often arbitrary requisitionings did not create the best basis for an understanding'.

The British were hardly less rigorous than the Americans. When they arrived in the city of Gladbeck (in the Ruhr) on 31 March, the British immediately imposed strict curfews, allowing the local population on the streets only between the hours of 7:00 and 8:00 in the morning, 10:00 in the morning and 1:00 in the afternoon, and 5:00 and 6:00 in the evening – though on 2 April this was relaxed to between 7:00 in the morning and 6:00 in the evening.[47] In Berlin it was not only the Russians who took over large amounts of desirable real estate; the Western Allies also liberally requisitioned properties after they arrived in July to take up their positions in the German capital. The musician Karla Höcker described the scene in Berlin-

Charlottenburg at the beginning of August, shortly after the British occupied their sector of the city. 'Whole blocks of houses and streets' were seized:

> Hundreds, perhaps thousands of people are suddenly without furniture, beds, ovens. No one asks where they are going, who is taking them in, how they will survive. But mysteriously it 'works' somehow. One does not hear of anyone who is left outdoors at night. And yet these sudden seizures are unsettling and create a new kind of insecurity: one already knows the other kind, the Russian kind, somewhat. This is more precise, more bureaucratic, but also not exactly pleasant.[48]

Among the Western occupying powers, the French often adopted a particularly punitive approach, as in the district of Böblingen (to the west of Stuttgart), occupied by the First French Army in the second half of April 1945. The arrival of the French was followed by strict curfews, the usual confiscation of radios, weapons and cameras, and also of clothing and foodstuffs; if the civilian population failed to obey French orders, they faced penalties ranging from fines to hostage-taking.[49] In Stuttgart, the French military immediately imposed the standard curfew, from 7:00 in the evening to 7:00 in the morning, entering or leaving the city was forbidden without a special pass from the local police, and Germans were not allowed to ride bicycles.[50] There too the French resorted to hostage-taking: after a black French soldier had been shot in Weilimdorf (a suburb to the north of Stuttgart) on the night of 29 April – by another black French soldier, as it turned out – 20 Germans were arrested in reprisal and imprisoned for ten weeks, and a collective fine was levied on the inhabitants of the community. In another case of collective punishment in Stuttgart, 11 people were arrested arbitrarily, kept in custody for three days and collectively fined 1000 Reichsmarks after a telephone line had been damaged.[51] Not surprisingly, the local population felt some relief when, on 7 July, the French occupation ended in the northern part of Württemberg and the Americans took over – even though expectations of better treatment by the Americans were not always met.[52]

In the university town of Tübingen, which became the civil administrative centre for the French occupation of Württemberg, the occupation authorities engaged in the wholesale requisitioning of property, seizing former military buildings, schools, sports halls and administrative buildings. Although the French were less obsessed with preventing 'fraternization' than were the Americans, and therefore did not necessarily seize entire blocks of housing but rather individual flats, they could be extremely callous in their treatment of the local population. According to Hermann Werner, who chronicled the occupation of the town:

> Up to the end of 1945 roughly 450 flats and 1050 single rooms were seized, as well as offices, hotels, student hostels, storage depots, garages, etc. [. . .] Especially distressing was the demand on 23 April by French medical officers for the handover of the Surgical Clinic [together] with all its inventory and with all the medical instruments. Overnight this, the most modern clinic in the university, had to be cleared of all patients, those seriously ill and having just undergone operations also had to be removed at this time, although scarcely any motor vehicles or ambulances were available.[53]

The requisitioning was not limited to real estate, but extended to furniture, beds, sheets, kitchen utensils, office equipment, tables, chairs, filing cabinets, bicycles and motor vehicles. Every family in Tübingen was ordered to surrender a complete suit and set of underwear and shoes, for the use of Allied prisoners of war waiting to return home – an action which netted between 3000 and 4000 suits. Local food offices carefully registered the foodstuffs that had been requisitioned in the city by the end of 1945, which included 525,087 kilos of bread flour, 52,513 kilos of butter, 33,690 kilos of cheese, 143,760 kilos of meat, 58,456 litres of milk, 83,322 eggs, 585,617 kilos of potatoes and 263,865 kilos of fresh vegetables.[54]

Across the country the occupation authorities also drastically restricted travel by German civilians. By the spring of 1945 the railways and local public transport were at a virtual standstill, and such long-distance railway transport as came back into service was reserved largely for the Allied military.[55] This limited most Germans to the areas that they could reach on foot, and even within the hours permitted by curfew restrictions they were not allowed to move about as they wished. After arriving in Lower Saxony in April, the Americans banned all travel by Germans outside their own locality unless they had special permission from the military government;[56] not until late May was the radius within which German civilians in and around Hannover were allowed to travel on foot or by bicycle extended to 30 kilometres from their own homes.[57] In Tübingen, all travel outside the town initially was prohibited, and allowed later only with the special permission of the military authorities; not until 15 June was travel within the local district beyond the town permitted again, and not until 1 August was this extended to the neighbouring district of Reutlingen.[58] For travel from the French zone to the American zone i.e. from one part of Württemberg to another, a special pass was required. However, within the zones, travel restrictions were gradually eased during the summer, and although travel remained difficult the Germans became 'a relentlessly mobile people'.[59]

Restrictions on travel were not just limited to movement around the cities and towns where German civilians lived, but also along and across the borders of the occupied country. To the east, the new Oder-Neiße border with Poland was sealed off to Germans, creating a barrier for those who had fled westwards during the early months of 1945 and wanted to return to their old homes once the war was over. In the west as well, the borders of occupied Germany were off-limits. On 25 April 1945 the British Military Government ordered that Germans vacate a five-kilometre strip along the border between Westphalia and Holland by 3 May; hundreds of families were uprooted, including the entire village of Suderwick (to the west of Bocholt). It was not until October that the strip was reduced to 500 metres and local farmers allowed to return to their farms.[60] (For the remainder of the German population entry into the border area was permitted only with a special pass.)

★

Allied distrust of Germans also, naturally enough, was reflected in the approaches taken to policing. The breakdown of the Nazi regime during its last months had been accompanied by a huge upsurge in crime.[61] However, the Allies were not about to place their confidence in the German police, many of whom were subject to 'automatic arrest' and large numbers of whom were dismissed in the course of 1945. In Augsburg, in the American zone, at the end of June dismissals left the city's police force at half strength, and by the end of 1945 in Lower Franconia 85 per cent of the police inherited from the Nazi state had been dismissed by the military government.[62] In Recklinghausen, in the Ruhr region, British distrust of the Germans even led to the establishment of an 'Allied police' consisting of foreigners (11 Dutch, 10 French, two Poles, two Russians, three Belgians, five Italians, four Yugoslavs and a Czech) under the command of a Dutchman.[63] The Allies were understandably reluctant to allow the new postwar German police forces to be armed, something that created further problems. Despite pleas that they be given pistols – in June 1945 police in the Ruhr claimed that without firearms 'under the present circumstances an intervention by [police] officers against criminals (no matter whether they are German or foreign) means suicide, as the criminal is always armed' – the military authorities initially limited German police officers to rubber truncheons.[64] In the Soviet zone, where a nearly complete turnover of personnel brought thousands of 'anti-fascists' (in the main, members of the Communist and Social Democratic Parties) into police ranks, there was a similar reluctance to rearm the Germans. As late as November 1945 the firearms available to the entire police force of Magdeburg, which comprised some 950 people, consisted of only 13 7.65mm pistols, none of which were given to officers on the beat.[65] Consequently, the reconstituted German police formations could do rather little to ensure public safety. The power to intervene forcefully remained with the occupation troops, but these were often the source of insecurity in the first place, especially in the Soviet zone.

Another huge problem was that posed by rubble. Faced with enormous problems in getting basic services working once again and clearing up the millions of tonnes of rubble left by the bombing and the fighting on the ground, Allied military authorities looked to the German population to clean up the mess. In the weeks and months after the capitulation, this frequently meant that German civilians were compelled to work for the local authorities to which the Allies now assigned the tasks of administration. Across Germany, people who had been members of Nazi organizations – the Nazi Party, the SA, SS, Hitler Youth and the League of German Girls, the Nazi 'Pilots Corps' and the Nazi 'Motorists Corps', and Nazi women's organizations – were called up for work. For example, in Tübingen the French military administration made daily demands for labour; on 26 April they decreed that the entire male population between the ages of 17 and 80 were required to work, and from 15 May the same went for the entire female population between the ages of 15 and 44. Workers with experience in the building trade were conscripted to prepare offices for the French and dwellings earmarked for French officers and civil servants. Men were conscripted for short periods of clearing up rubble, women for peeling potatoes in kitchens for foreigners awaiting repatriation. 'One even could be picked up off the street and that even happened to university professors.'[66] The costs of all this were met not by the occupier but by the occupied. In nearby Reutlingen, political prisoners were rounded up during the spring and summer – in September, 162 were being held at the 'Camp de prévention de Reutlingen' – and sent out daily to perform tasks ranging from scrubbing down railway cars to building barracks; former Nazi Party members who had not been arrested were required, until April 1946, to appear on Mondays for work assignments; failure to show up was punishable by imprisonment.[67] In the Soviet zone, where former Nazi Party members were targeted for particularly harsh treatment, at the end of November the Military Administration issued an order requiring former Party members to perform 'above all, especially dirty and unpleasant work' such as agricultural labour, removing rubble, repairing railway tracks and digging graves.[68] The Americans were not much more sympathetic. As they put it in an order in August 1945 compelling Germans to work for the city of Mannheim one day a week without pay, 'amputations comprise no excuse for absence from work'.[69]

★

Not surprisingly, the Allied military authorities were particularly keen to put to work those Germans taken into custody in the wake of occupation. The arrival of Allied forces had been followed not only by the arrest of the surviving top leadership of the Third Reich. The arrests had included hundreds of thousands of people who had been prominent locally in the Nazi regime and/or were suspected of having committed war crimes. Fear of a Nazi-inspired insurgency after the surrender of the Wehrmacht also led to the imprisonment of tens of thousands of Germans. Armed with SHAEF's 'Arrest Categories Handbook', the Western occupation forces were to secure the 'two main objects of safeguarding the security of Allied Forces and accomplishing the destruction of Nazi Organizations'.[70] Germans who fell within the categories listed were to be treated to 'automatic arrest'. The categories of people destined for 'automatic arrest' were quite broad: they included those who had served in most of the divisions of the Reich Security Main Office, in military intelligence, in the Secret Field Police and in the Reich Security Service; also, people who had been employed above a certain rank of the Gestapo and the criminal investigative police, the regular police and paramilitary organizations (including the SA and SS), Nazi Party officials down to the level of local group leader (*Ortsgruppenleiter*) and officials of other Nazi organizations such as the Hitler Youth, the League of German Girls, the National Socialist Motorists Corps and the Reich Labour Service, and senior civil servants in the state bureaucracy.[71] Altogether it was envisaged that between 200,000 and 250,000 Germans would be interned under the provisions of automatic arrest.[72]

Thus armed with a remarkably broad set of categories for potential suspects, the new rulers of occupied Germany took tens of thousands of people, mostly men, into custody as political prisoners. Most zealous were the Americans – whose policy was based on a mistaken assessment of what was necessary for 'the safeguarding [of] the security of the Allied Forces' and on fears of an insurgency after the demise of the Nazi regime – and the Russians, whose secret police were active from the moment they set foot in Germany. By the end of 1945, the American Counter Intelligence Corps (the security service of the U.S. Army, armed with copies of the 'Arrest Categories Handbook - Germany' which had been issued in April 1945) had taken some 117,500 people into custody; the British, whose zone was the most heavily populated, interned rather fewer, between 90,000 and 100,000 altogether between 1945 and 1949 (71,250 of whom were arrested in the first year after the war, some 65,000 of whom because they fell into an automatic arrest category); the French interned roughly 21,500 altogether; and in the Soviet zone, according to figures released in 1990, 122,671 were interned (of whom 42,889 died in the internment camps and 756 were sentenced to death and executed).[73] In terms of arrests per head of population, the Americans, who interned altogether one of every 142 inhabitants in their zone, were most assiduous. The Russians were not far behind: in the Soviet zone one of every 144 inhabitants was arrested. In the French zone one of every 263 inhabitants was arrested; and in the British zone, where the military administration took a more relaxed approach overall, the corresponding figure was one of every 284. However, those arrested in the Soviet zone were less likely to be released quickly: whereas in the American, British and French zones nearly half of those who had been interned by the beginning of 1947 already had been released in the meantime, in the Soviet zone the comparable figure was fewer than one in nine.[74]

The arrests were carried out in various ways. In the American zone, the Counter Intelligence Corps (CIC) sometimes sent out letters to people on their arrest lists, demanding that they appear before the military authorities. In many cases people on wanted lists were sought out and arrested as soon as the Allied forces arrived, put into the nearest prison and from there sent on to an internment camp. Most were arrested in their home towns and then sent directly to an internment camp. Generally, either a squad of the CIC would go to their homes and arrest them there, or they were arrested when attempting to acquire official papers such as work permits. An example of the former is what occurred in Plön in Schleswig-Holstein (in the British zone), where prominent local Nazis were rounded up from their homes: the head and all the teachers of the local elite Nazi school ('Napola'), the deputy district leader of the Nazi Party, a head of the local Nazi 'Motorists Corps', men who had served as mayors of the town, the head of the local 'Strength through Joy' organization, a Hitler Youth leader and a local poet. An example of the latter is the case of Erich Möllenhoff, a doctor and former SS officer, who was arrested by the Americans in June 1945 when he tried to get a permit to work in a hospital and was handed over to the British in Recklinghausen.[75] In some cases the intelligence organizations acted on information supplied by Germans themselves, some of whom used the opportunity to settle scores. And in some cases the CIC used extreme pressure: for example, when searching for three Gestapo members hiding in Weimar, the CIC arrested the men's wives and held them until two of the three men appeared (the third was arrested immediately thereafter).[76]

While the arrest of loathed Nazi big-wigs was greeted with approval by the majority of the German population, it was another matter when lesser figures were rounded up. After all, if people regarded as harmless were arrested, then anyone might find themselves taken into custody. Thus, when a Wehrmacht soldier who had been a local Hitler Youth leader before his military service was taken into custody by the American CIC in a village in Franconia, or when the CIC arrested people apparently indiscriminately, treated them badly and then shipped them off to internment camps, or when individuals who had been persecuted by the Nazis were arrested following a denunciation – then the civilian population was dismayed by the Allies' rough justice. It was not only in the Russian zone that Germans felt themselves victims of arbitrary arrest. In the American zone it was not long before people began speaking of the 'American Gestapo'.[77]

The guidelines for automatic arrest, combined with the determination to capture suspected war criminals and the need to ensure public security, gave remarkably wide scope for taking Germans into custody. Just about anyone who had been in a position of some authority or who might be regarded as a security risk could be imprisoned. In the west, the overwhelming majority of the German civilians interned were taken into custody under the terms of automatic arrest. According to a tally of the 4811 Germans held by the Americans in their internment camp at Garmisch-Partenkirchen on 15 October

1945, 4500 had fallen within the framework of automatic arrest, 243 were held because they were considered to be security threats, 37 internees were in the camp because they were on a 'blacklist' and, in 23 cases, the reasons for arrest were not precisely defined, while 8 were suspected of having committed war crimes.[78] In the British zone over 90 per cent of internees had been apprehended because they fell within an automatic arrest category.[79]

The internees were housed in camps, often of a makeshift character and frequently lacking adequate food supplies, clothing or medical care. Often the sites used had been created by the Nazi regime for its own purposes, including camps which the Germans had used to keep prisoners of war, former barracks for German soldiers, and even former concentration camps.[80] Germans were interned at Buchenwald and Sachsenhausen in the Soviet zone, at Neuengamme and Esterwegen in the British zone, and at Dachau in the American zone. In the American camps as well as the British, the large numbers of internees and the problems of supply meant that the prisoners' diet was spartan, generally limited to tea, substitute coffee, bread and soup; although the prisoners did not starve, they lost a considerable amount of weight, became susceptible to disease, and spent a good deal of the hard winter of 1945/46 in bed in order to conserve precious calories.[81] The internees were largely cut off from the outside world: in the American camps, not until the summer were they allowed to receive letters and packages, not until the autumn were they permitted to send postcards to their families, and not for a year and a half were they allowed visitors.[82] Altogether, theirs was an existence which promoted passivity, depression and often hatred towards their captors.

Although arrest was richly deserved in many cases, in many others it was not. Courts were understaffed and overwhelmed, and those arrested often had a long internment in unpleasant surroundings before going to trial.[83] The automatic arrest guidelines provided a rather blunt instrument with which to cleanse German society of Nazism; interning people on the basis of their formal position within the hierarchy of the Hitler regime could mean that relatively harmless, or even quite innocent, officials might be arrested because they had occupied a particular position in the bureaucracy, while someone who, although lower down the formal pecking order, had terrorized his neighbours, might well escape punishment. The Allied forces carrying out the internment campaigns often lacked an understanding of what particular job titles signified and were unfamiliar with a uniform that a German happened to be wearing; they were overly willing to act on unfounded denunciations, made hasty decisions that did not conform strictly to the automatic arrest guidelines, and arrested people on the basis of mistaken identity. Those picked up in Allied sweeps had no avenue for registering complaint, and weeks or months might pass before a mistake was recognized and those falsely interned were released. Furthermore, the tendency of the British in particular to take a pragmatic approach to internment meant that practice on the ground was inconsistent: where they were needed, even well-known local Nazis might keep their freedom and jobs; in some areas the heads of district administrations (*Landräte*) remained at their desks while elsewhere their counterparts were subject to automatic arrest.[84] Even more open to error was the rounding up of 'security suspects'. Although only about 2100 security suspects were taken into custody in the British zone, and although the British were the least harsh of the four occupying powers, this thoroughly elastic category was an invitation to inconsistency and injustice. For automatic arrest there were at least objective criteria for internment, even if these were somewhat flexible and inconsistently applied; for security suspects there were no fixed criteria at all, and someone might even find himself interned – as occurred in one case – for nothing more than having hitched a lift with a lorry that happened to be heading for a camp.[85]

Given the speed and scale of the arrest campaign and the problems facing the occupation authorities generally, a degree of injustice was no doubt inevitable. On the one hand, people in a position to obtain false papers or with enough money to leave Germany were able to evade internment; on the other, many people found themselves interned due to mistakes and misunderstandings by the occupying forces or as a result of denunciation. In some districts, all innkeepers and artisans might find their past scrutinized and some were banned from continuing their trade; in other areas, people regarded as important for the local economy were permitted to remain at their jobs despite previous membership of the Nazi Party.[86] Such arbitrary practice and obvious injustice predictably aroused misgivings about the denazification campaigns imposed by the Allies and provided an easy excuse for Germans to avoid facing their own, perhaps criminal, past. Nevertheless, glaring errors were the exception rather than the rule, and the contrast with what was happening in the Soviet zone – where arbitrary arrest often led to deportation to the USSR, hard labour, years of imprisonment and, in many cases, death in the camps – helped to reconcile the German population in the west to their new rulers, despite the mass arrests which followed the arrival of Allied forces.

Soviet practice differed significantly from that of the Western Allies. This stemmed both from the paranoid politics of the USSR and from the fact that the Red Army already had conquered large tracts of German territory before entering what was to be their occupation zone. In January and February 1945, the head of the Soviet secret police, Lavrenti Beria, had issued secret decrees setting out the broad categories of people who were to be arrested and delivered to the camps of the NKVD. The categories included not only German military commanders, police and concentration camp personnel and leading members of the civil administration, but also newspaper editors, authors of 'anti-Soviet publications' and 'other enemy elements'.[87] These guidelines were initially applied in the erstwhile German territories east of the Oder–Neiße, and this set the precedent for the approach taken in what would become the Soviet Occupation Zone of Germany. Between January and April 1945, in the wake of the great offensives which brought the Red Army from the Vistula to the Oder, Soviet forces made large numbers of summary arrests in East Prussia, Pomerania, Posen and Silesia, and before the end of the war the NKVD had established internment camps ('Speziallager' – 'special camps') across the territories east of the Oder–Neiße.[88] By mid-April (according to a report presented by Beria to Stalin on 17 April 1945), in the course of the 'purging of enemy territory', 215,540 people – among them 138,200 Germans along with roughly 38,000 Poles and 28,000 Soviet citizens – had been rounded up and placed in the newly established NKVD camps east of the Oder before being deported to the USSR.[89]

This wave of arrests, which occurred while war still was raging, had little to do with denazification. It was aimed at preventing German resistance to the advancing Soviet armies and at securing prison labour for the Soviet Union (although, in fact, Beria reported in April that only about half those taken prisoner were capable of work). According to Soviet sources, between 11 February and 16 April 1945, 96,408 people were deported from these camps to the USSR.[90] Yet many camps remained in operation, to be transferred by the NKVD to the Polish authorities. (Not until the beginning of 1946 does it appear that the NKVD handed over all its camps on Polish territory to the Polish secret police, and sent the 'hard core' of the prisoners to its camps in the Soviet Occupation Zone.) After the German capitulation in May, detention camps and prisons holding German civilians were dotted across what had been eastern Germany as well as in Polish cities and towns.[91] Herded into them were not only Nazis but also many Germans who had not been directly involved in the Nazi system: elderly people, women and children, and Poles believed to be Germans, now awaiting deportation to the Soviet Union.

It was not until 18 April that Beria issued a decree halting this practice and laying out more precise criteria for the arrest and internment of Germans 'in the execution of Chekist measures for the purging of the hinterland of the fighting troops of the Red Army'.[92] These criteria put 'spies, diversionists and terrorists of the German secret services' and 'members of all organizations and groups' that allegedly had been placed behind Soviet lines by the Germans at the top of the list for arrest. People suspected of spying, operating illegal radio stations, printing anti-Soviet literature, 'active members of the NSDAP' and local leaders of the Hitler Youth all came within the net of the NKVD operating in Germany. The spectre of the 'Werewolf' was used to intern young men in particular, although young women were not immune from arrest for alleged 'Werewolf' membership. Often, these were teenagers who may have held a position in a local Hitler Youth group and who had no thought of resisting the Russian occupation forces, but nevertheless were interned in camps in the Soviet Occupation Zone or deported to the USSR.[93] And, as elsewhere, some Germans found themselves arrested solely because they had been denounced by others.

However, for most Germans targeted by the occupation administrations in 1945, the main threat was not arrest but dismissal from their jobs. After having expressed their commitment at Yalta to 'remove all Nazi and militarist influences from public office and from the cultural and economic life of the German people',[94] at the Potsdam Conference the leaders of the U.K., U.S. and USSR agreed that:

> All members of the Nazi Party who have been more than nominal participants in its activities and all other persons hostile to Allied purposes shall be removed from public and semi-public office, and from positions of responsibility in important private undertakings. Such persons shall be replaced by persons who, by their political and moral qualities, are deemed capable of assisting in developing genuine democratic institutions in Germany.[95]

This general framework for denazification was, however, open to various interpretations and provided a basis for different practices in the four occupation zones.

In the Soviet zone, the denazification process was used in the first instance to remove people and groups which stood in the way of fundamental social and economic change: capitalists, large landowners, anti-Communists of various hues, people hostile to the Soviet experiment. Among the Americans, denazification tended to be viewed as a moral crusade, to be pursued with rigour and based on a belief in the collective guilt of the German people. The British, while initially adopting a rigorous approach, based on the notion of collective guilt similar to that of the Americans, were quicker to retreat from a rigid programme of wholesale dismissal.[96] Faced with responsibility for the zone with the largest population, the largest concentration of industry and the greatest degree of damage due to the bombing, the British tended to be more willing to allow people to remain at their jobs for the sake of economic recovery. The French, whose zone was not so damaged as that of the British, were interested less in a moral crusade than in the decentralization and weakening of Germany. They largely limited their denazification to purging public administration bodies, and on occasion were willing to employ senior civil servants in southern Baden and southern Württemberg whom the Americans had just removed from their posts in northern Baden and northern Württemberg.[97]

Central to the denazification process, at least in the Western zones, was the task of distinguishing between active Nazis and people who had only passively acquiesced ('Mitläufer') – a process undertaken in different ways in the different zones. Frequently armed with more prejudice than knowledge, those charged with cleansing German society of 'all Nazi and militarist influences' sometimes engaged in rather rough justice. Initially at least, the process was open to denunciations, sometimes made in order to remove an unwelcome business competitor, sometimes to take a measure of revenge on a political opponent. In the early months of the occupation, denunciations often were taken on trust by occupation authorities willing to believe the worst.[98] As the Americans subsequently admitted, the initial cooperation of the CIC with local German officials, who passed on the denunciations, 'at times [. . .] was "overenthusiastic" as the authorities strove to arrest individuals simply because they have been local Nazis or because of petty jealousies'.[99]

'Overenthusiasm' caused problems. The high number of arrests and tough denazification policy created serious obstacles for the smooth running of postwar administration. As one American major reported from Augsburg in July 1945, 'great difficulty has been encountered in finding competent and politically clean personnel for Civil Administration'.[100] From Fürth, the mayor observed at the beginning of August that the wholesale dismissals as a result of denazification 'will mean the greatest possible difficulties for the city administration in carrying out its business in an orderly manner'.[101] Such a situation was replicated in countless towns during the summer of 1945. Obviously, many German government employees who knew and understood their country's bureaucratic structures and practices, had been members of the Nazi Party; some had owed their positions to their Party membership, while others had joined the Nazi Party in order to protect their employment or to improve their career prospects. Their wholesale dismissal in the interests of denazification not only made it difficult to operate an effective civil administration; it also comprised a huge change in the character of German bureaucracy. The turnover of personnel was far greater in 1945 than when Hitler took power in 1933 – in Franconia half of all civil servants and white- and blue-collar workers in the public sector were dismissed – and amounted to a major rupture in the history and traditions of the German civil service.[102]

The gaps left by the dismissals were particularly large in the schools. When the Allies arrived, Germany's education system was at a standstill: large numbers of schools had been damaged by the bombing and/or the fighting on the ground, and many of those still in one piece had been used for military purposes or to house refugees; in many places schools had been shut since the previous winter. Even in cities which had escaped large-scale war damage, schools remained closed from the spring of 1945. School buildings then were used to billet Allied soldiers and to provide shelter for the many foreigners in Germany at the end of the war.[103] Before the schools could reopen, the teaching staff had to be assessed, which left many teachers in the precarious position of not knowing whether they would be reinstated.[104] Large numbers were dismissed. In the American zone 65 per cent of all primary-school teachers were removed, and of those left in post most were approaching retirement.[105] In many towns almost all the teaching staff lost their jobs. In Würzburg, where only one primary school survived the bombing of 16 March in reasonably good shape (and then was seized by the American military government in April), over 90 per cent of the city's teachers were removed, the highest proportion in the entire American Occupation Zone.[106] Everywhere, acceptable new textbooks had to be acquired, and new teachers had to be found to replace the many dismissed for political reasons (or who had died during the war or were in prisoner-of-war camps). Despite the widespread concerns voiced about adolescents running out of control, the schools would not reopen until the autumn of 1945.

*

Nevertheless, during the summer of 1945 denazification appeared successful in many respects. That large numbers of suspect Germans were removed from positions of responsibility generated approval even among the German population.[107] No doubt many Germans were pleased that the fortunes of people who had profited from the Nazi dictatorship now were being reversed. However, the many problems that arose as a result of the process, caused concerns to be raised about over-zealous purges of Germans in public life, at least in the west. The most celebrated calls to relax the denazification process came from General George S. Patton, at that point the Military Governor of Bavaria. In mid-August Patton suggested that Eisenhower press for a less rigorous approach, claiming that trained staff were being removed from their administrative posts and replaced with less experienced and less capable personnel. He asserted: 'It is no more possible for a man to be a civil servant in Germany and not to have paid lip service to Nazism than it is for a man to be a postmaster in America and not have paid lip service to the Democratic Party or Republican Party when it is in power.'[108] But Eisenhower stuck to the agreed policy: rooting out Nazism had been a major war aim; the guidelines that the Military Government had to follow did not permit retaining ex-Nazis in post just because their dismissal might cause problems; and the issue was 'a most delicate subject both here and at home' and there-fore best not raised. The last point was particularly telling. After Patton's views surfaced in the *New York Times*, and newspapers across America reported that the flamboyant general had equated Republicans and Democrats with Nazis, he was transferred.

The immediate response to such concerns was not a relaxation of denazification but rather its opposite. In late September the American Military Government issued its Law Nr. 8, which banned the employ-ment of former Nazi Party members in any capacity other than as ordinary workers.[109] At the same time, the law permitted individual appeals to be lodged with the local military government. The conse-quences were disturbing for all those involved, and reveals a great deal about the denazification process as a whole. On the one hand, wholesale dismissals in both the public and the private sector fol-lowed, with doctors, dentists, teachers, postmen, policemen and, reportedly, even cleaning women, losing their jobs. On the other, in order to keep their managers, firms often employed them nominally as lowly office assistants or as porters, so that (as one German advisor noted) 'Law 8 has meant merely a change in official signatures and a large number of highly competent clerks'.[110] The law aroused fear and anger among a population many of whom regarded it as a vengeful attempt to throw the economy into chaos. The American authorities were taken aback by the opposition that the measures provoked. According to one American commander, 'never before have Military Government measures been received with as much open hostility and their wisdom questioned as today.'[111] The paperwork involved threatened to overwhelm the bureaucracy, and there followed an avalanche of appeals to local German appeals boards, most of which were upheld. What had been intended as an attempt to make denazification more rigorous turned into a process whereby huge numbers of individual cases were reviewed and the people examined effectively rehabilitated. (In early 1946 the Americans modified the law to exempt firms employing less than ten people.)[112] Instead of a vigorous stride being taken towards creating a democratic Germany, thoroughly cleansed of Nazism, a process was put in place whereby hundreds of thousands of people could be classified as having been only nominal Nazis.

In late 1945 both the British and Americans began to relax their occupation regime. The pursuance of denazification become more systematic and orderly, as guidelines became more detailed and explicit. Administrative capacity was expanded to deal with the huge numbers of questionnaires which Germans were expected to complete detailing their past affiliations, and military governments came to rely more on the Germans themselves.[113] In the British zone, whereas the first sweeps of Nazis had been made without German help, by the end of 1945 the authorities decided to involve German advisory committees. Experience had demonstrated that a broad-based purge was simply unworkable unless the occupation authorities relied on the Germans for information.[114] These committees were not allowed to initiate investigations on their own; they were limited to advising the authorities (who were not bound to accept the advice) in cases where the latter were uncertain about how to proceed and needed further information about individuals or about conditions in the Third Reich. Although they remained advisory, the committees served both to prevent errors being made by over-enthusiastic denazifiers and to blunt the thrust of the denazification process. In the American zone too the military authorities came to rely increasingly on Germans, realizing that overly rigorous denazification practice caused serious problems for running the occupation regime. As responsibility for district administration (in November) and regional administration (in December) was handed over to the Germans, the Americans backed away from their earlier harsh posture and welcomed the new policy of 'turn it over to the Germans'.[115]

During 1945 the process of denazification brought considerable insecurity into the lives of millions of Germans who had been members of the Nazi Party, and those who had had various degrees of involvement in the Nazi regime, and therefore were uncertain whether they would be able to continue in their jobs. However, as time went on the threat eased. After the shock of the early months, with their mass arrests and dismissals, Germans had progressively less to fear from the denazification programme, which underwent a change in its function. Whereas the initial purpose of denazification had been to root out Nazism from German life, and to ensure that the Germans never again would be in a position to threaten their neighbours, after 1945 it in effect offered hundreds of thousands of Germans a ticket back into respectable society and the possibility of rebuilding a normal life. As Lutz Niethammer pointed out some time ago, the process of denazification, in which the vast majority of those complicit in the Nazi regime were classified as nominal members (*Mitläufer*), became a matter more of rehabilitation than of removing the guilty from public life.[116] Armed with their 'certificate of cleanliness' (*Persilschein*), Germans who had passed through the 'Mitläufer' factory could begin rebuilding their lives in the wake of Nazism and war.

Perhaps surprisingly, denazification in the Soviet zone served a similar function. To be sure, the Russians and their German Communist allies had been determined to use the denazification process to neutralize not only former Nazi Party leaders and war criminals, but anyone who might challenge the politics of the 'anti-fascist democratic' transformation in the Soviet zone; and the Soviet approach was coloured by a politics of paranoia which was ever on the lookout for spies, subversives, 'Werewolf' activists and the like. However, like its parallels in the Western zones, denazification in the Soviet zone offered rehabilitation to nominal members of the Nazi Party if they would 'break with their political past' and devote themselves to the task of reconstruction.[117] For tens of thousands of former Nazis, denazification spelled discrimination, hardship and punishment; for millions of others it offered a path to rehabilitation and reintegration.

During the first couple of months after the German capitulation, the Soviet authorities relied heavily on local 'anti-fascist committees' and German Communist cadres to determine who should be dismissed and to supply new personnel for public administration. Until German *Land* and provincial administrations were established in July 1945, denazification in the Soviet Occupation Zone was largely spontaneous, improvized and based on different criteria from place to place – uncoordinated local initiatives that only later gave way to central control.[118] Even after July, practices in the different *Länder* varied considerably. In Thuringia, as late as December 1945, nearly three fifths of the people still working in the *Land* administration had been Nazi Party members.[119] In Mecklenburg, by contrast, denazification was particularly rigorous and thorough. There Wilhelm Höcker, the President of the *Land* administration in Schwerin, was able to report to the Soviet Military Administration at the end of November that the removal of all former Nazi Party members (including those who had joined the new anti-fascist parties) 'has been carried out in all the administrative sections subordinate to me'.[120] In the Soviet zone the denazification was neither the expression of a moral crusade nor a pragmatic attempt to deal with the problems of the postwar transition; it was primarily a means to cement political control.

Such concerns were as yet of little importance for the millions of German soldiers who found themselves in prisoner-of-war camps after the war ended. The great majority of them were in the west. The collapse of the Wehrmacht in April 1945 and the desire during the last days of the war that as many German soldiers as possible surrender to the Western Allies rather than to the Red Army (or to the French, particularly where 'colonial troops' were rumoured to be involved),[121] meant that the British and Americans suddenly found themselves responsible for millions of German prisoners. As the war came to a close, American troops rounded up the remnants of the Wehrmacht in south-western Germany while their British counterparts found themselves in charge of Wehrmacht troops in northern Germany, Holland and Denmark.[122] In Schleswig-Holstein alone, the British held some 700,000 members of the Wehrmacht together with 2,000 members of the Waffen-SS and a few hundred army and navy officers.[123] The British tended to be remarkably easy-going in the way they handled their German prisoners. In Schleswig-Holstein the British left many of the POWs more or less under the control of their own junior officers, which saved the occupiers the task of having to set up camps for hundreds of thousands of prisoners. The Americans, on the other hand, drove their prisoners into some 20 huge makeshift camps, 'Prisoner of War Temporary Enclosures', where conditions were often initially dreadful.[124] Altogether roughly five million German soldiers were taken prisoner by the Western Allies, some three million of them by American forces (who tried in vain to get the British to take some of the prisoners off their hands).[125] According to the Military Governor of the U.S. zone, between 8 May and 15 July American forces had to deal with a total of 7.7 million German military personnel (including members of the *Volkssturm* and other paramilitary groups, as well as prisoners bought back from Norway, Italy, the United States and Britain).[126]

German soldiers had high expectations of the Americans.[127] As one subsequently put it, 'because of the leaflets that had been dropped on us, we expected [. . .] shelter and warm meals in American captivity, proper treatment, at least a real chance of survival'.[128] Frequently, however, such expectations were bitterly disappointed. American forces were unprepared for the huge numbers of Germans who fell into their hands in April and May 1945, and the conditions in the massive makeshift enclosures they set up reflected this. In the vast collection camp at Rheinberg am Niederrhein (to which the British also sent some of their internees) some quarter of a million people – prisoners of war, internees, civilians arrested because they perhaps happened to be wearing the cap of some Nazi organization, transport workers, women who had been in the Nazi Labour Service or had operated anti-aircraft guns, and nurses – were herded together to sleep in an open field surrounded by barbed wire, without latrines and without enough to eat.[129] (Conditions improved after June, when the British assumed responsibility for the Rheinberg camp, which remained in existence for four months.) The claim has since been made that the Americans deliberately allowed somewhere in the region of a million German prisoners to die in these camps but, dreadful though conditions may have been, to suggest that a million Germans died in the camps as a result of illness and starvation is absurd; of the roughly two million Wehrmacht soldiers listed as missing at the end of the war at most only 100,000 had been stationed on the western front.[130] American forces may have been guilty of neglect, but they were not guilty of mass murder.

The challenges facing German prisoners of war were not limited to inadequate food, shelter, and sanitary facilities. They also included the psychological difficulties of insecurity and helplessness that often set in after the initial relief at knowing that the war was over. One German soldier, interned by the Americans near Heilbronn, stated: 'When you are taken prisoner you stand face-to-face with ruin. The war was lost – something that many of us could not have believed – you had no sign of life from your relatives and all things considered you were dreadfully disappointed.' According to another:

> The fact of being taken prisoner as a soldier by the enemy certainly was a shocking experience for everyone. Usually a phase of great stress as a result of the fighting preceded capture. Then, when the captivity started, worries and fears suddenly came tumbling out. [. . .] The connection to family, to relatives, friends, to everything that was near and dear to one, was radically no longer there. The feeling of uncertainty [. . .] burdened the soul terribly.[131]

For millions of German soldiers, the collapse of the Third Reich ushered in a period during which they became the passive objects of the Allied occupation forces. All initiative, all ability to determine their own fate, had been stripped away. Until their captors chose to release them, they could only sit and wait to be allowed to begin rebuilding their lives.

Those taken prisoner by the British and Americans were relatively fortunate. While conditions in the makeshift camps often were poor and the uncertainty about the future and the fate of family members and friends was depressing, most of the British and American prisoners would survive and – although they did not know it yet – be released in the not too distant future. Although the periods they spent in captivity varied considerably, most of the German POWs were freed relatively quickly; between the third and fourth quarters of 1945, the number of German soldiers in Allied captivity fell from 8.7 million to 5.5 million (and by the end of 1946 it stood at 2.6 million).[132]

German soldiers taken prisoner by the Red Army generally were not so lucky. While some were released relatively quickly, others were deported to the USSR and put to work repairing Soviet cities and/or incarcerated in Soviet labour camps, sometimes for years; hundreds of thousands died in captivity. (Although the mortality of German soldiers in Soviet captivity was very high, it nevertheless should be remembered that the number of Soviet soldiers who died during the war in German captivity – more than three million – was greater than the *total* number of German soldiers taken prisoner by the Russians.) Altogether, the Soviet prisoner-of-war administration registered nearly 2.4 million German soldiers taken prisoner during the course of the 'Great Patriotic War'.[133] Although significant numbers of soldiers had been captured by Soviet forces during the earlier stages of the war, especially after the defeat at Stalingrad at the beginning of 1943 when roughly 110,000 surrendered to the Red Army, the vast majority of POWs who landed in Soviet captivity were taken prisoner in the first five months of 1945.[134] Indeed, between January and the summer of 1945, the number of German soldiers in Soviet hands more than quadrupled. In order to handle the huge numbers of enemy troops taken, Soviet forces set up a network of POW camps which were near the front lines and run by troops of the NKVD. In East Prussia and the Courland between 200,000 and 250,000 German troops were captured, the great majority (180,000) of whom were members of the Army Group Courland taken into captivity when the Wehrmacht capitulated in May; in Poland and eastern Germany (between the Vistula and the Oder rivers) some 800,000 were taken prisoner between January and April; in Saxony and Bohemia the number was about 630,000 and in the Berlin-Brandenburg region about 330,000.[135]

Like their counterparts in the west, Soviet forces were overwhelmed by the numbers of German prisoners that suddenly fell into their hands. Unprepared to provide for them, they herded them into makeshift detention camps; in just the two huge collection camps near Breslau some 300,000 men were gathered together. It was these camps that saw the highest prisoner mortality rates. Not only the relatively high number of deaths but also the extent of the deportations distinguished the fate of Germans in Soviet captivity from those captured by the Western Allies. Although the British and French also used German POW labour for reconstruction work back home, it was in the USSR that POW labour was used most extensively and for the longest time. Whereas all the Germans taken prisoner in the west had been released by the end of 1948, it would not be until 1955 that the last surviving German POWs returned from the USSR.

Holding millions of German soldiers prisoner, imposing harsh occupation regimes with their strict curfews and restrictions on movement, and arresting tens of thousands of German civilians may have seemed necessary to pacify a hostile enemy people. However, contrary to expectations, once the Americans, British, French and Russians had set up their occupation regimes they were confronted not by continued German resistance but by a beaten and cowed population. The end of the war spelled the end of Nazism. The military defeat had been so complete, the shock of violence so great, and the dislocation suffered so profound, that very few Germans continued to identify with the Nazi cause – and many of those who did were among the people who committed suicide in such large numbers in the spring of 1945. In his account of Tübingen in 1945, Hermann Werner observed:

> It was as if the National Socialist Party had disappeared from the face of the earth. Nowhere was there serious insubordination, no longer was one aware of any preference for National Socialism. The petty Party functionaries who remained also overwhelmingly had completely enough [of Nazism], again and again one heard from them that they in fact were the ones who had been cheated the most.[136]

Thus, it was not defiant supporters of Nazism but a self-pitying people eager to turn their backs on the Third Reich that greeted the victorious Allies. Instead of the fanatical, militaristic, Nazi-indoctrinated populace they had expected, the Allies found a vulnerable people who desperately wanted peace after years of war, who were focused largely on their own immediate needs, and who, largely, had jettisoned thoughts of political involvement or activism. Friction between occupiers and occupied had little to do with any residue of Nazism. Whereas in the Soviet zone the military administration, the secret police and the new German police forces cultivated a paranoid fixation on potential subversion by former Nazis, in the west the concerns expressed were rather different. In Augsburg, for example, the local military government reported in September that 'subversive activities primarily included sporadic threatenings, slander and bill-posting by young men (usually former members of the HJ [Hitler Youth]) against German girls who have been seen with American soldiers.'[137] Similarly, in Würzburg, while Nazi-inspired 'Werewolf' resistance never materialized, in August 1945 three local residents formed a secret society, the 'Black Panthers', with rather more modest aims: although the three were arrested and imprisoned before they could put plans into action, their aim had been (in the words of one of the accused) to cut the hair off 'all German girls who go walking with coloured soldiers'.[138] Of overtly political resistance there was hardly a trace.

Occupation meant that there necessarily would be increasing contact between occupier and occupied. Military administrations had to employ Germans to repair, rebuild and manage public services, to fill the ranks of police forces, to teach in the schools, to work in the hospitals and on public transport. Increasing numbers of Germans found work with the occupation forces, which often brought privileged access to goods in short supply as well as day-to-day contact with those who shortly before had been the enemy. (Employment by the American forces was particularly desirable since it provided access to food and to American cigarettes, which became the most valuable currency in the occupied country.)[139] Consequently, attitudes towards one another began to change. Whereas the terrible behaviour of many Russians upon their arrival in Germany left a poisonous and enduring legacy of hostility and crippled attempts by German Communists to bolster their popular support, the British and Americans were more successful in breaking down animosity. Getting services up and running again helped, as did the relaxing of the initial restrictions placed upon the civilian population. Reporting on conditions in occupied Augsburg in July 1945, the American commanding officer noted progress in a number of areas – from the completion of the registration of the city's population to the re-introduction of street lighting on Augsburg's main thoroughfares – and was able to observe that 'the attitude of the population is friendly'.[140] In November 1945, a survey of American soldiers' opinions provided some astonishing results: nearly four fifths of those interviewed said they had positive impressions of the Germans, making particularly favourable comments about Germans' supposed cleanliness and industriousness; when asked what nationality they liked best, the English came out on top (half saying they preferred them), but more than twice as many preferred the Germans (28 percent) as preferred the French (only 11 percent); fewer than half (43 per cent) blamed the Germans for the war, and only a quarter regarded the German people as responsible for the atrocities in the camps; and more than half (56 per cent) had spent time 'talking' with German girls.[141] It did not take very long before the occupation forces were sleeping with the enemy.

★

The positive attitudes that developed among American soldiers towards the German population contrast sharply with the determination of the Allies in general and the Americans in particular to bring Germans to trial for crimes committed during the war. The Allies had arrived in Germany with a commitment not only to root out Nazism and militarism, but to deal with crimes committed by their defeated enemy. This meant the use of military courts to try Germans and the creation of a new body of international law to prosecute the rulers of a sovereign state for war crimes. Nevertheless, until Germany's capitulation, the preparations for war crimes trials remained embryonic. At the end of 1944 the American War Department had ordered the establishment of a War Crimes Group, which had its office in the headquarters of the American Forces in Paris; at the end of February 1945 the U.S. Army command ordered the creation of 'war crimes branches' with the various armies in the field, in order to collect evidence.[142] Nevertheless, it was not until the fighting ceased that the work of the War Crimes Group and its investigation teams really got going; the War Crimes Group itself was moved from Paris to Wiesbaden, the 'war crimes branches' received more personnel, and a centre for the investigation of war crimes was set up in July to coordinate the prosecution of war crimes with the other Allies.

The prosecution of the major war criminals had been foreseen during the war, with the Moscow Declaration of 30 October 1943. However, not until the Charter of the International Military Tribunal was agreed by the four powers in London on 8 August 1945 was the institutional framework created for what would be the trial of the century: the Trial of the Major War Criminals that opened in Nuremberg, in the American Occupation Zone, on 20 November 1945.[143] The Nuremberg Trial would be the most important expression of the Allied campaign to impose morality through legal proceedings, and simultaneously to establish a record of what the Nazi regime had done. Successor trials, however, would come before an American military court. The commanders of the Third and the Seventh American Armies had been empowered to set up special military courts to deal with alleged war criminals who would not come before the International Military Tribunal in

Nuremberg and for whom there existed no extradition request from another country. Therefore, in both of the military districts in the American zone, 'Central Suspect and Witness Enclosures' and military courts were established: in the region of the Seventh Army in the Camp Nr. 78 in Ludwigsburg-Zuffenhausen; in the region of the Third Army in the former concentration camp at Dachau.[144] (In both cases, the American military courts were set up within the camps.)

Trials of Germans did not begin with the Trial of the Major War Criminals in Nuremberg in November, however. The first already had taken place while the Allies were fighting their way into Germany, well before the Wehrmacht surrendered in May 1945: on 7 April, in the bombed-out Rhineland town of Düren (between Cologne and Aachen), an American military commission convicted a German officer of responsibility for the murder of two American prisoners of war during the Ardennes Offensive.[145] In June, American military commissions in Ahrweiler tried a number of Germans for their role in the murder of an American airman downed in the village of Preist in August 1944. (Two civilians had beaten the airman to death at the urging of a neighbourhood Nazi Party leader, with a policeman standing by; the Party leader and the two civilians received death sentences for their part in the murder, and the policeman a sentence of life imprisonment.) The killing of downed airmen occasioned the largest category of trials involving crimes against the Americans, and investigation teams gathered evidence for some 800 such cases during the summer of 1945.

Soon, the scope of war crimes trials initiated by the Allies broadened to include consideration of crimes which had nothing to do with military operations. On 2 June, General Eisenhower asked the Combined Chiefs of Staff (CCS) to approve the prosecution of concentration camp personnel for war crimes. Eisenhower, who was deeply affected by what had been revealed when the camps were liberated, believed that such prosecutions would have 'a salutary effect on public opinion both in Germany and in Allied countries'. The CCS agreed, lifting all 'previous restrictions' on war crimes trials, 'whether the offences were committed before or after the occupation . . and regardless of the nationality of the victim'.[146] In the months that followed, thousands of suspects and witnesses were taken into custody, and a number of high-profile trials before military commissions were initiated in the autumn, in the British as well as in the American zone. These included the trial of camp personnel at Bergen-Belsen by a British military court on 7 October, the trial of medical personnel accused of the murder by injection of 45 Poles and Russians at Hadamar on 8 October, and the trial of 40 people accused of involvement in thousands of killings at Dachau on 16 November. In Lüneburg on 17 November a British military court sentenced 44 former members of the SS for their part in crimes that had been committed at Bergen-Belsen and Auschwitz, 11 of whom received the death penalty.[147]

The prosecution of people for crimes committed by and for the Nazi regime was not exclusively a matter for the Allies, however. German courts had begun to be reopened in the late summer and early autumn of 1945 and the basis of much Nazi legal practice had been annulled. By the end of 1945, German courts were also involved as, in all four zones and in Berlin, the Allies began to turn Germans over to German courts for prosecution.

The main show, however, was in Nuremberg. With the London Agreement of 8 August, the American, British, French and Soviet representatives agreed to recognize four categories of crimes: war crimes, crimes against peace, crimes against humanity, and membership in criminal organizations. This provided a substantial broadening of the scope of the Tribunal, allowing prosecution for crimes no matter where they were committed or against whom. National sovereignty would offer no protection. International law and morality would trump national sovereignty. This involved an expansion of categories of crime which has held a central place in international law and the concept of war crimes ever since, and cleared the way for the trial of 22 major figures of the Nazi regime at Nuremberg.

When the Trial of the Major War Criminals opened for its first session on 20 November, it attracted tremendous attention both within Germany and around the world. Given prominent coverage in the Allied-controlled newspapers and newsreels, during the early weeks at least it was observed closely by the German public. Whatever worries the Allies may have had about lingering popular support for the defeated Nazi elite, this did not materialize. The sight of Göring, Hess, Ribbentrop, Speer, Keitel, Streicher and their comrades in the dock did not produce waves of sympathy among Germans for their former rulers. As one German put it at the time, 'we are simply too hungry' to worry much about legal niceties and, as for the men in the dock, 'even a death sentence is too lenient'.[148] The defendants were regarded not as German patriots or martyrs unjustly accused by vengeful enemies so much as men who were responsible for the dreadful conditions in which Germans now found themselves. The shock of what had occurred in 1945 removed any lingering admiration for the Nazi bosses now on trial, for the regime they had directed or for the cause they had espoused.

Memories of the immense relief felt by the German population when the war ended and the gradual relaxation of the occupation regime, at least in the British and American Occupation Zones, have tended to overshadow the degree to which the initial imposition of Allied control over Germany in 1945 was accomplished by force and the threat of force. It was not just the Soviet Army and Military Administration that had been tough with the conquered German people; the French were in some instances scarcely less brutal than the Russians, and neither the Americans nor the British were inclined initially to be charitable towards the Germans. The Allies arrived with overwhelming force, with millions of soldiers, determined to impose control over a defeated people and unwilling to tolerate any opposition. They arrived convinced that the German people had been indoctrinated with the Nazi message, feared a continuation of resistance, and underestimated the degree to which the collapse of the Third Reich had destroyed popular support for rabid German nationalism. What they found was a people desperate just to get on with their own lives in terribly difficult circumstances. The Allied imposition of order was not carried out with kid gloves, at least not in 1945; Allied justice was often rough; the Germans were treated as a conquered people; and ample grounds existed for Germans to regard themselves as victims, first of war and dictatorship and then of occupation regimes imposed at a time of extreme hardship. The imposition of Allied military rule was shock therapy. Few would have thought, in 1945, that such an approach would constitute the first step towards the successful reconstruction of a civilized society and a democratic polity. But it did.

8

THE LOSS OF THE EAST

*On the 6th of July Szczecin/Stettin finally was declared a Polish city.
Since that time the behaviour of the Germans has altered completely,
they have become more docile and subservient vis-à-vis the Poles.*
Teofil Konar[1]

*It was as though the German language suddenly had become extinct.
Everyone had to speak Polish. German periodicals disappeared and
in the cemeteries the Poles even smashed the gravestones with German
inscriptions.* Theodor Jurok[2]

The defeat of the Nazi regime in 1945 altered forever what constituted 'Germany'. Core regions of historic Prussia ceased to be
German. These regions had been strongholds of the Junker landowning class. Their main cities had been central to the development of
modern Germany: Königsberg, the birthplace of the philosopher
Immanuel Kant; the Hanseatic port of Danzig, where the first shots
of the Second World War were fired; Breslau, where the population
rose against the French in 1813 and Prussian King Friedrich
Wilhelm III issued his famous appeal 'To My People' and instituted
the Iron Cross. In 1945 one of the largest forced removals of human
beings in world history brought centuries of German settlement in
the former Prussian provinces east of the Oder-Neiße and in the

Sudetenland to an end. As a result of the devastation in eastern Germany during the last months of the war, mass flight and expulsion, and the redrawing of her eastern borders, Germany became a much more western country. Regions whose populations once had been predominantly German became Polish, Russian and Czech. A fifth of pre-war Germany was severed from the country, and its German population removed. Of all the shocks which accompanied Germany's defeat in the Second World War, this was perhaps the greatest.

Among the wartime Allies there had been a widespread conviction that eastern Germany, the home of the Junkers – who A.J.P. Taylor once described as 'ruthless exploiters of conquered lands . . . untouched by European civilization'[3] – formed the cradle of 'Prussianism' and German militarism which had to be rooted out.[4] Germany's eastern neighbours readily agreed. After the brutal wartime population transfers undertaken by the Nazi regime, and given the perception that German minorities (e.g. in Czechoslovakia in 1938–1939) had acted as a 'fifth column' to destroy Slav states, exiled Polish and Czech politicians viewed expulsion as an appropriate and necessary response.[5] Although the millions of Germans who had called East Prussia, Pomerania, Silesia and the Sudetenland home up to 1945 could not have imagined that they would be removed from these regions permanently, that outcome was almost inevitable after the war was over.

During the second half of the Second World War, support among Allied governments grew for the expulsion of Germans from eastern Europe once the war had been won. The Soviet Union came to favour shifting Poland's borders westwards, to the Oder and Neiße rivers, and expelling Germans from lands which would form the western territories of the postwar Polish state, and from the Sudetenland. From 1942 the British government too had shown interest in having the Germans expelled, and the American government came to agree. With regard to the Sudetenland, there was no doubt that the territorial settlement agreed at Munich in 1938 would be reversed after the war. No Germans should be left to undermine a postwar Czechoslovak state: the support shown for Nazism, and the incorporation of the Sudetenland into Germany, by the Sudeten Germans during the 1930s, and the Munich Agreement and subsequent dismemberment of the country, had convinced Edvard Beneš and his fellow Czechs that the German minority could not be trusted to be loyal citizens of a postwar Czechoslovak state.[6] With regard to Poland, the Allies had as good as agreed during the war that Germans would have to be removed from the eastern Prussian provinces destined to be incorporated into the postwar Polish state, i.e. at least from East Prussia and Upper Silesia. This, it was believed, would eliminate Poland's vulnerability to German military attack inherent in the pre-war borders and provide homes for Poles who lived to the east of the Curzon line and who themselves were destined for expulsion. Altogether, it was envisaged in January 1945 that, unless something were done, the return of the Sudetenland to Czechoslovakia and the transfer of most of East Prussia, Danzig, German Upper Silesia and eastern Pomerania to Poland would leave some 4.1 million Germans in a postwar Poland and some 1.5 million Germans in Czechoslovakia. The Polish Government in exile, the Lublin Government and the Czechoslovak government-in-exile all wanted these people expelled; and the Allies were not inclined to stand in the way.[7] The Czechs, the Poles and the British, American and Soviet governments were determined that the map of post-1945 Europe would not resemble the unstable configuration that had emerged from the First World War – a determination that ensured the removal of millions of Germans from their homes.[8]

By the time that Churchill and Roosevelt met with Stalin at Yalta in February 1945 – as hundreds of thousands of Germans were fleeing westwards ahead of the Red Army – both the British and American governments had already expressed (at Teheran in 1943, repeated at Yalta) their general understanding that Poland should be shifted westwards. However, it was at Potsdam in July and August 1945 that formal agreement was reached, both about the supposedly provisional borders of a postwar Germany – in the east along the Oder and western Neiße rivers – and about the removal of German populations from regions outside postwar Germany. Article XIII of the Potsdam Agreement made explicit that there would be a 'transfer to Germany of German populations, or elements thereof, remaining in Poland, Czechoslovakia, and Hungary'. According to the Agreement, 'any transfers that take place should be effected in an orderly and humane manner',[9] but this was window dressing. Given the context within which the transfers took place, such pious statements could have little relation to reality.

In fact, neither were the expulsions 'effected in an orderly and humane manner' nor did they start only after the Potsdam Agreement had been signed. Large numbers of Germans already had fled from the eastern regions of the Reich during the last months of the war, and many fled on their own initiative from regions that came under Polish control for fear that otherwise they would be interned or shipped off to perform forced labour.[10] Then, after the German surrender but before the 'Big Three' met at Potsdam, Poles and Czechs had begun forcing remaining Germans to leave their homes in areas destined to become parts of the postwar Polish and Czechoslovak states. The late spring and early summer of 1945 was the period in which the expulsion of Germans from eastern Europe was most violent. In Czechoslovakia this phase of what the Germans referred to as 'wild expulsions' began immediately after the German surrender, and was particularly brutal; in the territories east of the Oder-Neiße, this phase began in June, after the Soviet authorities handed control of these regions over to the provisional Polish government.

In what became postwar Poland, the worst of the violence occurred between mid-June and mid-July, particularly in the districts bordering the Oder-Neiße demarcation line, an area designated by the Polish Army Command as a military settlement area.[11] The commander of the Polish Second Army expressed the position with brutal clarity in his order of 24 June 'on the continuation of the rapid transfer of the Germans':

We are transferring the Germans out of Polish territory and we are acting thereby in accordance with directives from Moscow. We are behaving with the Germans as they behaved with us. Many already have forgotten how they treated our children, women and old people. The Czechs knew how to act so that the Germans fled from their territory of their own volition.

One must perform one's tasks in such a harsh and decisive manner that the Germanic vermin do not hide in their houses but rather will flee from us of their own volition and then [once] in their own land will thank God that they were lucky enough to save their heads. We do not forget Germans always will be Germans.[12]

The Germans to be resettled usually were permitted to take 20 kilograms of baggage with them, and were escorted to the border by squads of Polish soldiers. Within a few days in late June roughly 40–45,000 people were transferred.[13] In his study of the immediate postwar period in Silesia, Andreas Hofmann describes what this meant to the Germans living near the Oder–Neiße frontier:

> The evacuation of individual localities usually began in the early morning hours. The population, torn from their sleep, had scarcely fifteen to twenty minutes to snatch the most necessary belongings, or else they were driven directly onto the street without any ceremony. Smaller localities and villages were evacuated at gunpoint by small numbers of soldiers, frequently only a squad or a platoon. Due to the proximity of the border, for the sake of simplicity the Germans were marched on foot to the nearest bridge over the river, driven over to the Soviet side [i.e. into the Soviet Occupation Zone of Germany] and there left to their own fate.[14]

For Polish politicians in the 'recovered' western territories the expulsions were a handy way to generate popular support. Poles generally felt little sympathy for Germans, and often were far from unhappy to see them cringe in fear. From one district in Silesia the Polish authorities observed that the evacuation of a few dozen German families had prompted a 'complete transformation of the mood of the Polish population [. . .] while fear and panic spread among the local Germans'.[15]

Evacuation was fraught with danger. Germans frequently were

robbed by members of the Polish militia and military units that carried
out the expulsions, and, when they arrived in the Soviet Occupation
Zone, the uprooted Germans were often destitute and exhausted. A
farmer from the district of Liegnitz in Lower Silesia wrote of how
members of Polish military units demanded watches and other valuables, threatening to shoot anyone caught hiding things; once the
Germans had been marched to the river Neiße, the Poles 'declared
that we were free. We could go where we wanted, they even said that
we could go back, but we no longer trusted the Poles and crossed the
Neiße to Görlitz, where we arrived on 3 July.'[16] For him, at least, the
trek was over. However, in the towns straddling the Oder-Neiße
frontier – in Görlitz, Frankfurt on the Oder, Cottbus, Stettin,
Küstrin – refugees and expellees gathered in huge numbers and conditions were dreadful.[17] With so many refugees, expellees and people
hoping to return to their Heimat congregating along the Oder-Neiße,
food supply became an acute problem. What is more, the expellees
became easy prey for Soviet occupation troops, who often stole the
few belongings that they had managed to take with them. Germans
who, just a few months earlier, had enjoyed a seemingly secure existence in communities east of the Oder-Neiße now found themselves
(as in Görlitz at the beginning of June) 'sleeping in parks in vast numbers with their tattered possessions, searching for their relatives among
the countless notices fastened onto trees'.[18]

During the weeks immediately after the Wehrmacht surrendered,
the violence directed against the German populations in postwar
Poland and Czechoslovakia was often spontaneous and the expression
of local initiative. This changed in mid-July.[19] Not only did uncoordinated expulsions cause economic disruption, with German skilled
labourers often removed without thought to their replacement; they
also threatened to tarnish Poland's image ahead of the meeting of the
'Big Three' at Potsdam. Nevertheless, it was largely due to the intervention of Soviet military commanders that uncoordinated expulsions
of Germans came to an end in mid-July. By that time, however, the
Czechs and Poles had made great strides towards achieving a *fait accompli* – former German regions without Germans – before the Allied
leaders would meet at Potsdam to determine the shape of postwar

Europe. The bland phrases of the Potsdam Agreement were less an instruction for 'transfers' to come than an expression of a hope to end the uncontrolled violence which had already taken place.

For those expelled, the experience was traumatic. Often accompanied by physical and sexual violence, expulsion followed patterns not all that different from what the Nazi regime had done to Poles and others during the war. In Czechoslovakia and Poland, Germans were beaten and raped, forced to perform humiliating tasks, subjected to sadistic violence in labour camps (sometimes in the same places – as in Theresienstadt – where the Nazis had run concentration camps), and compelled to wear armbands or letters on their sleeves identifying their ethnicity. Some were randomly killed, others marched out of their homes and herded onto railway cattle cars for long journeys in dreadful weather.[20] The worst of the violence appears to have been aimed at the Germans in Czechoslovakia. In 1947 a 70-year-old described his expulsion from the Sudetenland, together with his 61-year-old wife and 59-year-old sister-in-law:

On 16 June we were [. . .] driven out of our own house in Leitmeritz and had to appear at a barracks in two hours without valuables, without savings books, with only a little money and very limited baggage. Here our suffering began. Here what little we still possessed was taken from us almost completely, whoever had something forbidden with him was beaten, and almost all money was taken. We stayed there without food for two nights [. . .] and we laid on wooden boards. At night shots were fired, doors were smashed in, girls and women raped and men bloodily beaten. [. . .] Not until the third day were we taken to the railway station and brought in an open coal car to Teplitz, where we 72 people remained with [our] baggage in this open car, exposed to all weather conditions until the morning of the fourth day. That same day we were deliberately driven for many hours on foot in the blazing sun to Geising on the other side of the border. There was no food and also no water. We had to depend on the meagre supplies that we had been able hurriedly to take with us from home. We called the incredibly exhausting

march from Teplitz to Geising the death march and it took place
in dramatic conditions that are indescribable. Whoever could
carry on no longer and remained behind was driven on with
whip and revolver, and people exhausted to the point of death
had to throw away their last possessions in order just to come
through with their lives.[21]

Such stories frame a German narrative of victimhood at the end of the
war, of suffering at the hands of violent, cruel and pitiless tormentors.
It was these 'death marches' – not the death marches of Jews and other
prisoners organized by the collapsing Nazi regime during the early
months of 1945, and not Germans' experiences during the previous
years of the war (when life had been relatively pleasant for many of
them) – that were remembered.

The Soviet offensive of January 1945 marked the beginning of the end
of the German east. Until that time, Nazi Party and state officials had
tried to prevent westward movement by German civilians, regarding
it as a sign of defeatism and fearing that popular anxiety might fuel a
stampede should Germans become convinced that the front could not
be held. In the event, a stampede was what occurred. Stalin was not
far off the mark when, at Yalta on 7 February 1945, in response to
Churchill's concerns about the transfer westwards of millions of
Germans, he claimed that 'there will be no more Germans there, for
when our troops come in the Germans run away and no Germans are
left'.[22] By the time that the Nazi regime surrendered in May 1945, the
former eastern regions of Germany held less than half their former
German population. That is to say, much of the removal of Germans
from the eastern Prussian provinces had taken place before the war
ended. Afterwards, however, hundreds of thousands of Germans
moved (or were moved) temporarily back eastwards across the Oder
and Neiße.[23]

The West German documentary history of the expulsion, published by the German Federal Ministry for Expellees, Refugees and
War-Disabled in the 1950s, referred to the first phase of removal ('this
east–west movement of around five million east Germans') as 'initially

nothing other than one of the war-related evacuations of population within Germany of which there already had been numerous examples'.[24] (These 'examples' included the wartime evacuation of 1.5 million Berliners to escape the bombing, many of whom had gone to East Prussia and Silesia.) However, it soon became clear that this 'war-related evacuation' was something quite different from the previous wartime migrations of Germans within the Reich. Before the Allies confirmed their decision to sever East Prussia, most of Silesia and Pomerania, and much of Brandenburg from postwar Germany, the de-Germanization of the German east was well under way.

De-Germanization of the east proceeded at different tempos in different regions. Nevertheless, in the end the result was the same. In some regions, fear of the Red Army had led almost the entire German population to flee by the end of January 1945. In others, the speed of the Soviet advance caught German civilians by surprise; almost overnight they found themselves in Soviet-occupied territory where they fell victim to looting and violence by soldiers of the Red Army. In areas which had been inhabited by Poles as well as by Germans, the Germans often fled while the Poles mostly remained.[25] Generally, Poles had not been compelled by the German authorities to leave ahead of the Russian advance, and the Poles did not obstruct the flight or evacuation of the Germans. In this way, within a matter of days, areas of previously mixed settlement became regions with essentially Polish populations. Thus, 1945 saw a shift of ethnic boundaries which had taken shape over centuries.

In Poland, the expulsion of Germans began in April 1945, before the German capitulation at Reims and Karlshorst, and gathered pace during the summer. The determination to remove Germans from what had been pre-war Poland (which had been home to a German minority of some three-quarters of a million in the 1930s)[26] and from the eastern Prussian provinces was fuelled both by desire to create a *fait accompli* ahead of the Potsdam conference and by concern that Germans who had fled ahead of the Red Army in early 1945 would return to their old homes. The fate of individual Germans in what had been eastern Germany was often quite arbitrary. In some places German men were arrested and put to work; newly installed Polish authorities received permission to remove Germans from the towns and farms where they had lived in order to make room for Poles expelled from the parts of pre-war Poland being annexed by the USSR; and until 28 June, when a Polish civil administration was appointed for the 'recovered' western territories, the Polish army forcibly removed German nationals. Friction arose between Poles keen to shunt Germans westwards and Soviet military commanders to the west of the Oder unwilling to accept the expellees into areas for which they were responsible. As a result many Germans were left stranded along the banks of the Oder, unable to go west and unable to return east.[27] By the autumn, however, the contours of the population transfer became clearer. In November 1945 a Polish Ministry of the Recovered Territories was created in order to organize the removal of Germans, the settlement of Poles, the establishment of local administration, and the integration of the western territories into the postwar Polish state; it was headed by Władysław Gomułka – who had been advised by Stalin that 'you should create such conditions for the Germans that they want to escape themselves'.[28]

Although the desire to expel Germans was clear enough, it was not always easy to determine who was a 'German'. As the Polish authorities sought to register people in the areas under their control, they had to decide who was Polish and who was German – that is, who would be forced to leave for the west and who would be allowed to remain. Many Silesians, Kashubians (in West Prussia) and Masurians (in East Prussia) could not easily be assigned either Polish or German ethnicity or nationality. Yet, in the immediate aftermath of the Second World War, the Polish administrators responsible for verifying people's nationality were neither much concerned with, nor aware of, the complexities of ethnic identity. Instead, their actions tended to be coloured by hatred and grievance, and consequently many people were classified incorrectly as German, removed from their farms and badly treated by incoming Poles.[29]

At the same time, the Polish authorities had an interest in assimilating people who could be regarded as 'Germanized Poles' – Poles who had taken German citizenship in order to survive during the war, Polish-speaking Silesians in the south, Kashubians and Masurians in the north. Although the Polish state viewed the expulsion of the German population from the 'recovered territories' as necessary to make room for the more than two million Poles being transferred from the east[30] and to ensure that no nationalist German minority could undermine Polish sovereignty in the future, they also needed some to remain in order to prevent a collapse of infrastructure.[31] In addition, their presence as re-Polonized Poles could buttress a claim that (as proclaimed on signs in former German territory near the Baltic coast) 'this land was and always will remain Polish'.[32] These 'Germanized Poles' found themselves under pressure to speak Polish and to polonize their German names (e.g. changing Georg to Jerzy or adding endings such as 'ski' or 'wicz' to surnames). The rough and ready processes by which Germans were removed from the 'recovered' western territories led to a homogenization of the postwar Polish state in more ways than one.

In many respects, what occurred to the east of the Oder-Neiße in early 1945 was similar to what happened in the regions which were to constitute the Soviet Occupation Zone. The arrival of the Red Army was accompanied by scenes of terrible violence, the deliberate burning of buildings, mass rapes, arrests and deportations. It was not uncommon for buildings still standing after battle to be torched by Soviet troops after the Germans surrendered. In Breslau, the scene of some of the worst destruction, once the German garrison had surrendered Soviet soldiers began to roam the streets, loot, pour petrol on buildings and set them alight; the fires burned for days – the first days of 'peace'.[33] Although the Allied political leaders were planning to hand these areas over to Poland, as far as Soviet soldiers were concerned this was still Germany. However, the story was not simply one of destruction. Initially, and in a manner similar to what took place west of the Oder-Neiße, Soviet commandants looked to German Communists to establish local administrations, remove Nazis from positions of responsibility and deal with the dreadful conditions facing the defeated German population. For their part, the Poles were increasingly active, with the beginnings of Polish immigration into the 'recovered' territories and with the first Polish administrations set up alongside the German ones. On 9 and 10 May, a group of Polish

administrators sent by the Soviet-backed government of Poland
arrived in Breslau/Wrocław and set up a rudimentary Polish municipal administration (headed by the 'City President' Bolesław Drobner
and complete with an 'Office of Public Security').[34]

Between the German capitulation at the beginning of May and the
beginning of July, many tens of thousands of Germans returned to
their old homes, in the hope or expectation that their homelands
would continue to form part of postwar Germany. The places to
which they returned were often scenes of terrible destruction. Their
homes had been plundered and in many cases destroyed, and their
livestock slaughtered;[35] they faced disease – in particular, typhoid,
which reached epidemic proportions in the former German east –
crime and administrative chaos. Rudimentary German administrations, often headed by German Communists, did what they could to
mitigate the worst, expecting support from their Soviet comrades and
apparently assuming that the regions in which they were working – at
least in Pomerania and Silesia – would remain German. They were to
be profoundly disappointed. In the summer of 1945 the German
administrations were shut down and responsibility for running the
civil administration handed over to Poles.

In the former German territories which became Polish, the beginning
of July 1945 marked something of a turning point. Agreement was
reached with the Soviet Military Administration in Berlin ceding the
'recovered' western territories to Poland. These areas were declared
part of Poland, and a concerted campaign began to make them physically, visually Polish. Traces of German presence were systematically
removed: German books, German monuments, street signs, inscriptions on buildings, in churches and on storefronts disappeared. The
language of public administration became Polish and the following
year, from 17 April 1946, the speaking of German was prohibited not
only in public but also in the home.[36] Attempts by Germans to return
from the west were restricted, and Polish migration into the 'recovered' regions was promoted. Germans often found themselves evicted
from what had been their homes, which were then occupied by destitute Poles who had been expelled from their own homes further to

the east, or compelled to live in one room of their dwelling while a Polish family inhabited the rest. Germans who remained in Poland and Czechoslovakia were subjected to systematic discrimination. They received poorer food rations, had to perform forced labour for eight to ten, and sometimes twelve, hours per day, and received wages at levels generally between one quarter and one half of that paid to Polish workers – wages insufficient to feed a single person, let alone a family.[37] In order to buy the food necessary for survival, Germans frequently had to sell their possessions to Poles, who were convinced that Germans were wealthy and were probably hiding their valuables.[38] Germans were drafted into work brigades to clean up the mess left behind after the fighting – clearing rubble from the streets, repairing broken infrastructure (sewerage, transport, utilities), defusing mines, and burying the thousands of corpses left behind.[39]

The number one problem, which now dominated the everyday lives of Germans, was the lack of physical security. Effectively, until well into 1946 the former eastern Prussian provinces were beyond the rule of law. Poles, in the main refugees from former Polish territories annexed by the USSR, who arrived in the former German east referred to these regions in 1945 as the 'wild west'.[40] As the most vulnerable group, Germans offered an easy target. Bands of Poles, many from central Poland, descended on the 'recovered' territories determined to steal as much as they could from the now defenceless Germans, who were robbed of food, clothing, furniture and valuables. There was little that Germans could do to prevent Poles from entering their homes and taking whatever they chose, 'even the dwelling itself'.[41] For many Poles, one of the main attractions of postwar Poland's 'wild west' was the prospect of helping themselves to German belongings. In Gdańsk (Danzig), the creation of a Polish administration had, according to its provisional head, 'triggered a "gold rush" among the population: on all roads and with all means of transport everyone from all regions of Poland is heading for this Klondike, and their sole aim is not work but robbery and looting'.[42] In Wrocław, Bolesław Drobner (the Polish City President) reckoned that three fifths of the Poles who arrived in the city in 1945 had come to loot.[43] Indeed, in 1945 there were not many other attractions in this battle-scarred city, described by a Polish printer who arrived from Lwów as one of 'endless ruins, the stink of burning, countless huge flies, the clouded faces of occasionally encountered Germans, and most important, the emptiness of the desolate streets'.[44]

The Germans could not expect much help or sympathy from the new Polish (or Czech) administrations. Not only Soviet and Polish soldiers but also the newly employed and poorly paid Polish police preyed on German civilians. According to a Soviet report describing conditions in Silesia, 'the Polish authorities do absolutely nothing to stop the plundering of the [German] population' and indeed sometimes participated in it.[45] A German from Breslau described experiences that were typical of many:

> We had to stand in a queue of expellees in front of the railway station. The Poles who were doing their jobs there took what they liked from our baggage and threw the things they took onto a large pile. They also took from us what we were carrying. My father had a satchel with our birth certificates. They took these from him and threw them with the papers on the pile.[46]

Resistance could be dangerous. If Germans tried to defend themselves or their property they risked being beaten and sent to internment camps. If they turned to the Polish security forces they found that 'the main investigative methods of those days was to beat the Germans' and that threats of internment were used to extort food and money.[47]

Despite the atrocious conditions, large numbers of Germans returned to the eastern regions in the months following the defeat of the Third Reich. Indeed, many attempted to return to their old homes soon after the fighting ceased. Most of those who had fled westwards ahead of the Red Army during the previous months assumed that once the fighting was over they would be able to go back, and many Germans who found themselves in the Soviet Occupation Zone once the Nazi regime had surrendered then attempted to return 'home'. Initially the Soviet authorities, overwhelmed by the huge numbers of destitute people arriving in their occupation zone, frequently welcomed the desire of Germans to return east. Not only did they not prevent refugees and expellees from returning, but during May and June 1945 some Soviet military commandants actually sent Germans back eastwards over the new Oder-Neiße demarcation line.[48] Altogether, after the fighting stopped at the beginning of May 1945 more than a million Germans, unable to imagine that the loss of their homes was permanent, journeyed back to their old places of residence in the east – sometimes willingly, sometimes not. Immediately after the Wehrmacht surrendered on 8 May 1945 many Germans from the east were organized into what may be described as treks in reverse, often on the orders of Soviet military commanders and newly installed German mayors in the Soviet Occupation Zone.[49] Such orders frequently were met with considerable relief among the 'native' population in the regions where the refugees had arrived.

Such was the reception offered to the members of a trek from Schwanenbeck in the Pomeranian district of Saatzig, after they arrived on the island of Rügen in early 1945: the local authorities called upon them to leave the island; and the local Rügen population was 'happy to get shot of the burdensome billeting' of the refugees, who for their part 'also wanted to return home'. So the Schwanenbeck trek was re-assembled and horses and wagons distributed for the return trip east.[50] Although the weather was warmer, which meant that at least the travellers would not freeze, the return trip eastwards was scarcely less difficult and dangerous than the earlier flight westwards had been. Of those on the Schwanenbeck trek in reverse, 'everyone knew' that they were 'completely defenceless' in the face of gangs roaming around the territory and Soviet soldiers. After they had left Rügen for Schwanenbeck, the hapless Germans were often detained along the way, as Russians took their horses and pressed them into forced labour.[51] The trek had set off from Rügen in two groups. One, which left on 18 May, was turned back by Polish military at the Oder, and found respite in villages to the west of Stettin. The other, which had set out a day earlier, managed to reach Schwanenbeck, only to find their village partly destroyed and partly occupied by Polish settlers. After a few days, they were expelled from the village and their baggage brought from Rügen taken from them. Stripped of their belongings, they now had to make the journey westwards for a second time.

The re-migration of Germans eastwards slowed once the Polish authorities closed the Oder-Neiße border to potential returnees, first at Görlitz at the end of May and then all along the new frontier by late June/early July.[52] Nevertheless, even after Polish military units closed the border and were authorized to shoot people trying to cross, a substantial number of Germans – estimated at some 300,000 – managed to return temporarily across the Oder-Neiße.[53] For German Silesians who had fled south over the Sudeten mountains it proved easier to head back northwards to their old homes soon after the war, and many did. In Lower Silesia some three quarters of a million Germans who had fled then returned after the fighting stopped – some 500,000 coming back from Czechoslovakia and between 200,000 and 300,000 from Saxony and Brandenburg during May and June 1945; by mid-June the region contained more than half its pre-war population, and in some villages (in the foothills of the Sudeten mountains, where the war damage had been limited) almost the entire German population returned.[54] In Wrocław Germans outnumbered Poles by more than two to one (with some 110,000 Germans in the city and about 50,000 Poles) in early 1946.[55] At the beginning of 1946 nearly three quarters of those employed in industry in Lower Silesia (some 53,300 workers) were German.[56] In the Lower Silesian coal region, in and around Waldenburg/Wałbrzych, Germans comprised over four fifths of the employees, and it was not until 1947 that Poles formed a majority.[57] However, their days in Silesia were numbered, and those Germans who had not been induced to leave during 1945 by insecurity, discrimination, dreadful conditions and terror would find themselves expelled soon thereafter.

Despite the eastward return of Germans soon after the war, during the second half of 1945 the territories that had constituted eastern Germany were becoming less and less German. Despite conditions that made it advisable (as one Polish government 'inspector for settlement questions' wrote in June) to send Polish settlers 'who possess a strong pioneer spirit',[58] the ethnic balance was shifting in favour of the Poles. Polish civil authorities encouraged the German population to leave for the west, offering transport for those prepared to quit and making it clear that Germans would not have much of a future if they tried to remain. The Polish population in the 'recovered territories', their numbers swelling as tens of thousands of destitute settlers arrived from former Polish territories ceded to the USSR, added to the pressure as they sought shelter; with the support of the nascent Polish civil administration, they often made life difficult for Germans who had remained or had returned. Not surprisingly, many Germans now chose to abandon their eastern German Heimat for good. However, getting out was not always easy. The dire state of the railway network left Germans stuck at stations for weeks, often without food, waiting for a train to take them westwards. Some were conscripted into labour battalions or labour camps; some were forced out of their homes and into ghettos, with their schools closed, compelled to wear the letter 'N' to identify themselves as German (*Niemiec*), given meagre rations, banned from restaurants and theatres, and left to survive as best they could.[59] For those who remained despite the hostility of the Poles and the dreadful privations, tenacity brought no reward. Beginning in early 1946, they too would be expelled.

The transformation of eastern Germany into western Poland may be understood best by looking in detail at what occurred in a single town. One well-documented example is that of Stettin, which had been pre-war Germany's main Baltic port near the mouth of the Oder and which became Szczecin. Conditions in Stettin/Szczecin were particularly difficult in 1945, with catastrophic problems of food supply, wartime destruction and postwar criminality. Like most German cities, Stettin had been bombed repeatedly during the war: on 21 April 1943 the RAF attacked the city and the 'Vulkan' Dockyard went up in flames; on 6 January 1944 348 British bombers dropped over a thousand tonnes of bombs on the city; and on 17 August 1944 a major bombing raid caused substantial damage in the old city.[60] Continued bombing in early 1945 and then intense fighting in the eastern suburbs of the city during March and April caused further devastation. By the time that the Red Army occupied Stettin on 26 April, much of the city lay in ruins.

The exodus of Stettin's German population had begun in earnest during the second half of February. On 20 February, as the front drew closer to the city, the Nazi Party *Gauleitung* ordered the evacuation of pregnant women and mothers with small children; some 2500–3000 people daily were to leave by ship for Überkmünde, and from there to travel into western Pomerania by rail.[61] By March the Red Army was in the eastern suburbs of Stettin, and the city itself came under artillery fire and continued bombing; on 20 March Stettin was declared a 'fortress', and Germans began sealing up their businesses and dwellings and leaving the city however best they could.[62] By the time that Stettin fell to the Soviet Army on 26 April, few Germans remained: in a city which had had roughly 275,000 inhabitants when the war broke out, some 20,000 Germans at most were present when the Russians arrived.[63] Three days later, on 29 April, control of the city was handed over formally to the Republic of Poland by Soviet forces under Marshal Rokossovsky and the military commandant of the city of Stettin, Colonel Fedotow, and Piotr Zaremba named the city's Polish 'President'.[64] One day later a Polish municipal administration was in place, the Polish flag was raised over government buildings and the first call made for Poles to settle in the city.[65] (The first group of Polish settlers, some 900 people, arrived from Poznań a week later.) At the same time, the Soviet military appointed a German city administration, with the Communist Erich Wiesner named by the Soviet military commandant as mayor from 26 May until the beginning of July.[66] Thus began a period of parallel government, during which German and Polish city administrations both operated alongside the Soviet military authorities.

During early May, Germans who had been evacuated or had fled the city during the previous months began to return, between 2000 and 3000 arriving daily in the weeks which followed. Some came back voluntarily; others, such as Felix Grosser (who had fled the city at the end of the war) did not:

I myself fled to the west with my family nearly as far as Schwerin, where we were stopped by the Americans. [. . .] The next day the Russians came and chased us back home again, that is to Altdamm [a suburb of Stettin, on the eastern side of the Oder]. [. . .] The return journey with a horse-drawn wagon took roughly 14 days. [. . .] I had arrived with my family back in Altdamm and immediately had to work for the Russians, without pay, but at least the Russians gave us bread to eat. The rest we had to look for ourselves. We found shelter in ruins of houses and cellars, since where a house still was standing it was requisitioned by the Russians.[67]

By the beginning of June over 40,000 Germans were living in Stettin again. In mid-June the number of German inhabitants registered in the city, stood at 60,975, with an estimated further 10,000 (largely from East and West Prussia) who had not been recorded.[68]

Conditions in the city were dreadful. The return of tens of thousands of Germans placed huge demands on a limited food supply, and during the first months of 'peace' Stettin was an extremely dangerous place. Germans were arrested, attacked and raped by Soviet soldiers and by Poles. The city offered little personal security, little to eat, and little in the way of housing. According to the head of the German city administration in mid-June, 70 per cent of the city's housing stock had been lost through war damage and a further 10 per cent had been taken over by the Red Army and Polish immigrants; 'the general food-supply situation' was described as 'catastrophic'.[69] Like their comrades elsewhere in eastern Germany, the German Communists in Stettin, who had counted on support from the Soviet authorities, were bitterly disappointed. Of revolutionary or class solidarity there was scarcely a trace. On 17 May the local German Communist Party organization made the following assessment:

A new situation arose when the Red Army entered Stettin. We had imagined this quite differently. While a few Social Democrats raised the white flag from the City Hall and the Soviet general who marched in addressed these people as mayor, our Communist functionaries who placed themselves at the disposal of the Commandant's office were taken into custody. Thus during the first days after the arrival of the Red Army almost all of our functionaries found themselves in detention. When someone has spent 10 years in the gaols and prisons of the militarists and fascists, it is especially hard to be kept under guard as a prisoner of the Red Army with Soviet-Russian machine guns. In addition, where they appeared in public our women were raped and even workers robbed of their last possessions as a result of the constant looting. [. . .]

Our difficulties here in Stettin are enormous. On the one hand, the great insecurity [means] that even comrades who work in the mayor's office are arrested as soon as they leave our city district despite [having] identity cards issued by the City Commandant's office. Then the Polish question in particular is unresolved. Precisely these [i.e. Poles] are committing the gravest acts against the [German] population. A few days ago such a large amount of rape and looting occurred that I explained to the City Commandant on behalf of the Communists in the mayor's office that if this does not cease we will have to deny responsibility. In the last few days a small improvement has taken place.

Now we have further rays of hope, apparently Stettin will remain a German city.[70]

The 'rays of hope' proved a mirage, but the threats to the safety of the German population in the city did not. Three days later the Communists (including Erich Wiesner) in the German municipal administration drafted a bitter protest to the Soviet Command in the city, describing 'the simply indefensible conditions under which the population is suffering':

The series of rapes of women and girls is not abating. [. . .] In addition flats occupied by Germans are continuing to be looted. Arrests and the day-long detention of inhabitants on their way to work, or on the streets, without any or any valid justification are continuing.

The food supply is completely insufficient and is heading irresistibly towards catastrophe. [. . .] Our infants are dying because we cannot give them milk in sufficient quantity, as the cows provided were requisitioned,

Numerous diseases cannot be treated, as neither doctors nor medicines are available.[71]

According to Stettin's German Communists, the returnees who had fled westwards earlier in the year and who now were streaming back to Stettin from western Pomerania, Mecklenburg, Rügen and Berlin reported that conditions were far better in the Soviet Occupation Zone from whence they had just come. According to one returnee:

The lives of the returnees in Stettin are indescribable. Many people live in half-burned buildings, some burrowed into the terraces of the Hakenterasse [where Stettin's representative government buildings were lined up overlooking the Oder] and were living there like the most primitive humans. Living in intact buildings was too dangerous because day and night the Russians were searching for women, for objects of value or, as they said, for soldiers. [. . .] The Germans lived pitifully from a ration of Russian bread – but that was distributed only to working people – from the black market on the Hohenzollernstraße and the Barnimstraße [in the west of the city], from fruit from abandoned allotments and old potatoes. Many people came down with typhoid fever, dysentery, or got dreadful eczema. Every day countless people died who quickly were buried somewhere.[72]

Stettin was becoming an increasingly inhospitable place for its fearful German inhabitants; and the German municipal administration, which had hoped that its anti-fascist credentials would count for something with the Soviet military, was becoming increasingly desperate. On 6 June the German administration petitioned the Soviet Government to recognise Stettin as a German city, to release all dwellings in the city for 'Stettin residents returning home' and to support the planned repatriation of Germans who had been evacuated westwards over the previous months.[73] This was a wasted effort: a week later the German administration reported that, while their countrymen continued to stream back into the city from the west, 'for the past few days groups of Polish civilians, some of whom are armed, again have been coming into Stettin. In various streets German inhabitants are being forced by Poles to leave their flats. Public buildings also are being occupied again by the Poles.'[74] One Ernst Schmidt, in a report to the (German) police administration in mid-June, described how, building by building, Stettin was being transformed into Szczecin:

> On 13 June I took over my old flat and wanted to move in today. The things in the flat belong to me. I had locked up the flat. When I got there today the flat had been broken into; who broke in I do not know. Poles (6–8 people) already were living on the first floor. When I [. . .] asked the German-speaking Poles whether they had a permit for the flat, they said: 'What do you want, you have nothing to say, the Russians have allocated the flat to us.' They were not able to present a written certificate to me.[75]

While Poles were creating new facts on the ground, the Polish administration busied itself with transforming Stettin/Szczecin into a Polish city. On 16 May the first Polish newspaper (the *Glos Nadodrzanski*) appeared.[76] (Between 20 May and 10 June the Red Army published a German-language newspaper, the *Deutsche Zeitung, Frontzeitung für die Deutsche Bevölkerung*, in the city.) The Polish authorities, aware that thousands of Germans were returning, were 'doing everything, not only in western Pomerania but in the territory of the entire Republic of Poland, to bring as many Poles as possible to Szczecin'.[77] Their efforts were given a boost when, at the end of June, the interim period of parallel administration came to an end: on 28 June Erich Wiesner was informed by the Soviet city commandant of a new order from Berlin; accordingly all the activities of the city's German administration (e.g. to organize food distribution, restore infrastructure, reopen schools) were to cease. The next day Wiesner was told officially that the city 'would be handed over to the Poles', and that he 'should submit a list of the most important anti-fascist functionaries, who were to leave Stettin with their families'.[78]

The running of the city was handed over exclusively to the Poles at the beginning of July, after the Soviet Military Administration in Germany agreed to its transfer to Poland. Marshal Zhukov informed Leonard Borkowicz (the Plenipotentiary of the Government for Western Pomerania), Piotr Zaremba, and the City Commandant Colonel Aleksandr Fedotow of the decision on the evening of 3 July.[79] Two days later the Polish administration (with Zaremba as its President) assumed control. A ceremony took place at the headquarters of the Soviet military, led by the Soviet commandant, with prominent members of both the German and the Polish administrations present; the commandant read out the order of Marshal Zhukov and formally handed the administration over to the Poles.[80] (The harbour, however, remained under Soviet control, and Poles were not allowed to enter.) The German administration headed by Erich Wiesner had to cease functioning, as did German political parties. On the following morning the Polish flag was flying over all municipal buildings. A few days later, on 9 July, Zaremba decreed that 'because of the overcrowding of the city' only those people of German nationality who had been registered in the city up to 6 July had the right of abode in Szczecin – thus removing that right from any German who might return to the city subsequently. At that time the number of Germans in the city was estimated at about 100,000.[81]

The transfer of power to the Polish administration created enormous unease among the German population. Wiesner wrote in his 'concluding report':

[News of] the fact that Stettin shall become Polish spread very quickly and the concern about this was very great. It grew as the first motor vehicles with the property of our [i.e. German Communist] comrades left Stettin. As a result a very difficult and uncomfortable situation arose for the Party, as voices were heard that first the fascists ran away and now the [German] Communists are doing the same thing. [. . .]

Among the [German] population themselves there was the deepest depression about the course of events, and only the fact that the entire region was filled to capacity with refugees from eastern Pomerania prevented a mass flight of the Stettin population. Occupation by the Red Army was a hundred times preferable to rule by the Poles, that was the opinion of the [German] population at this time.[82]

The Poles in the city reacted quite differently. With Polish flags flying, on 7 July posters appeared, bearing Zaremba's signature, announcing to the city's Polish population that 'our efforts, our work and toil were not in vain' and that on 6 July Szczecin had become part of the Republic of Poland.[83]

Szczecin may have become Polish officially, but there still were relatively few Poles present to celebrate. According to Zaremba, only 2400 Poles were registered in the city in mid-July, with a total number estimated to be 3500; the registered German population, by contrast, stood at 84,000. This, however, was the high watermark of the German presence in postwar Szczecin. Once the Polish administration had taken control, Germans began to leave for the west. According to Zaremba, 'no obstacles were put in their path'.[84]

It was not only the political transformation that undermined the position of the German population. There were also huge problems of disease and malnourishment. Particularly serious was typhoid, which during the summer claimed many lives in the city – as it did throughout what had been eastern Germany, where the refugees and expellees spread disease as they travelled, where little or no medical care was available, where drinking water often was polluted and where people 'were practically starving'.[85] According to one German, who looked back nearly four decades later:

There was no food to buy. Money was worthless in any case. How people survived at all is a mystery. [. . .] As a result of the poor food supply the amount of illness among the population was very high. During the summer of 1945 typhoid was rampant. [. . .] Entire families were wiped out by it. [. . .]

One could not bury the dead properly. There were no coffins. At the cemetery a large, wide ditch was prepared into which the dead were laid as they were found.[86]

Quite literally, the German population was dying out. In some cities and towns, the toll taken by disease was even higher than in Stettin/Szczecin. In Breslau/Wrocław it was reported that by July 1945 between 300 and 400 people daily were dying of starvation.[87] Perhaps the worst conditions were in East Prussia as a result of the collapse of public-health facilities and a terrible typhoid epidemic: in one doctor's estimate, of roughly 100,000 people left in Königsberg when German forces finally capitulated to the Red Army on 9 April 1945, nearly three quarters had died due to malnutrition and disease by the spring of 1947.[88] Across what had been eastern Germany the pattern was similar. At the end of August 1945 the Political Section of the Soviet army observed that in Poland's 'recovered territories':

[. . .]the German population is starving in many places, in other areas they are under the immediate threat of starvation in the near future. Not only does the plundering of the Germans on the part of the Poles not stop, but it gets greater all the time. There are more and more cases of unprovoked murders of German inhabitants, unfounded arrests, long prison confinements with deliberate humiliation.[89]

Such was the background against which the transformation of Stettin into Szczecin now rapidly proceeded. On 8 July military sovereignty was transferred officially from the Soviet commandant to his Polish counterpart; on the following day any further movement into the city by Germans from west of the Oder was prohibited; and on 10 July a provisional demarcation line between Poland and the Soviet Occupation Zone of Germany was fixed along the city's western boundary.[90] (The permanent border was agreed by representatives of the Soviet Military Administration in Mecklenburg-Vorpommern and of the Polish Republic on 21 September and came into force on 4 October.) After the Polish authorities had taken charge in July, Polish refugees began to move into the city in large numbers. Their arrival increased the hazards for the Germans. More dwellings were requisitioned; more Germans were arrested for minor infractions or found themselves on the receiving end of violence by Polish militia members; more Germans were called up for forced labour, particularly to bring in the harvest.

In the autumn, after agreement had been reached about repatriation of Poles eastwards from Germany and Germans westwards from the greater part of Pomerania which now lay in Poland, the transfer of population began in earnest. The first groups of Poles reached Szczecin from the west on 14 October. On 9 November posters appeared announcing 'to the German population of the city of Szczecin' that they would be able to leave by train for Greifswald; from there they could go wherever they chose. The train trip would be free and 'every resettler can take 50 kilograms of baggage'.[91] On 19 November the first trainload of Germans left Szczecin for Greifswald. It was made clear that for Germans the traffic was to be one way: those who wanted to travel westwards were not to be obstructed, while 'Germans who want to enter the territory of the Polish state may under no circumstances be allowed in'.[92]

Initially, the new border between Poland and Mecklenburg-Vorpommern in the Soviet Occupation Zone was neither completely sealed nor strictly controlled, and Germans continued to attempt a return eastwards during the autumn of 1945.[93] Nevertheless, the hardships facing the Germans and the efforts of the Poles to get them to leave were having their effect, and some 15,000 Germans now opted to depart for what remained of Germany.[94] By the autumn the number of Germans remaining in Szczecin had declined considerably from its summer peak: in late September there were 23,625 Poles and 60,293 Germans in the city, for a total of 83,918.[95] What is more, the Polish population was overwhelmingly male while the German population was overwhelmingly female: among adults between the ages of 19 to 60,

Polish men far outnumbered Polish women (14,315 to 6,926), while German women far outnumbered German men (21,867 to 10,435).

While the 'healthy and able-bodied German population' were required to work, in particular to bring in the potato harvest, the Polish authorities were keen that Germans unfit for labour – children, the ill, the elderly – be among the first to leave for the west. The ill (especially those with venereal disease), the elderly and those unable to work and who lacked support were to be placed into 'special isolation centres that would prevent the spread of diseases among the Polish population', while 'at the same time the German population should be reminded that they have the right of voluntary departure into Reich territory'.[96] For those who took up the offer to leave, a collection point was set up in the suburb of Scheune (Gumience), from whence they were to be taken away by train. Although the Polish militia was supposed to offer protection, the Germans awaiting transport frequently were attacked by members of military formations, their baggage stolen and the women raped.[97]

Efforts to pressure Germans to leave voluntarily formed the first phase of the exodus. The second began in the latter half of February 1946, with the systematic forced removal of Szczecin's remaining German population and their transfer to the British Occupation Zone. For the next six months 1000 Germans daily were supposed to be sent by ship to Lübeck or by rail to the west.[98] At the same time, Poles continued to arrive in the city. By the end of 1946, Szczecin contained 100,000 Poles and only 17,000 Germans.[99] The history of Stettin, and of eastern Pomerania, as part of Germany had come to an end.

For the Polish settlers who took the place of the Germans, transforming their new surroundings into a decent place to live was anything but easy. Nearly three decades later Jerzy Brinken, a Polish teacher and geographer, described his arrival in the 'new, strange world' that was to be his home:

> After a three-day journey I finally reached Altdamm, where the train stood for a rather long time. I therefore had a lot of time to

have a look round in the area. Everywhere there were signs of war, burnt-out houses, endless boarded-up buildings, destroyed artillery, abandoned tanks and derailed railway cars – everywhere disorder and destruction. [. . .]

For me the first steps in Szczecin were [like] a first walk for a moon traveller [. . .]. I remember only a few fragments of what I saw and felt then . I know only that I was very agitated. In front of me spread a new, strange world – heavy German architecture, broad avenues with lots of green, a few groups of fearful Germans and the realization that I will live here. Everywhere emptiness and quiet. At every turn signs of war: burnt walls, water tanks, shelters and bunkers, trenches and anti-tank obstacles, mounds of earth beside the trenches. On the pavements scattered piles of ash, paper and rubbish. Everywhere furniture and household appliances that had been left behind. There was a smell of decay in the air. In short: not a scene and not an atmosphere that created an especially inviting impression.[100]

The first impressions of the Polish military commandant of Altdamm (on the eastern bank of the Oder) were similar: 'In front of the railway station a heap of burnt-out ruins, destroyed houses. Ruins on the right and on the left, the ruins stretched out far into the city. What is this then, a city of ruins? Is this still a city? The first impression is terrible.'[101] This was what remained of the former 'German' east.

The prospect of living in the burnt-out shell of a German city was made all the more daunting by the fact that in 1945 it was dangerous not only for Germans. Lack of food, rampant disease, armed bands of looters and the paucity of police presented challenges for the new Polish inhabitants as well. According to one Polish observer, food supplies were largely exhausted and 'ever more frequently' one saw the warning 'typhoid' written on the doors of buildings. He went on:

Increasingly one could stumble upon the corpses of people who had died or been killed on the streets and in the entrances to houses. Gunfights were a nightly occurrence, and caused no stir even in broad daylight. For a long time the sound of gunfire

indeed dominated Szczecin, [which] was named the 'Wild West'.
[. . .] There even was a restaurant with the name 'Texas'.[102]

Violent crime remained a serious problem throughout 1945, and
became even worse towards the end of the year. Unlucky Polish settlers arriving in the city found themselves greeted by looters, and
some were killed while being robbed. Bombed and burned-out buildings and former German bunkers offered ideal hiding places for those
who had come in order to prey on the rest of the population; armed
bands terrorized railway passengers and made the city's railway stations
dangerous places indeed; and a small and poorly trained police force
was all but powerless to stop the violence.[103]

Another hazard was arson, the 'plague of fire [. . .], that tormented
and destroyed the city of Szczecin for months on end'.[104] Some of the
fires were started deliberately, some were started carelessly by 'looters
who felt no connection of any kind with the city, who regarded the
city as German property and believed that everything that is Germanic
can be destroyed'. Not all the perpetrators of this orgy of destruction
were Polish. Understandably, Germans leaving the city during late
1945 were ill-disposed to hand their property over to the Poles in per-
fect condition. Instead, they frequently demolished whatever they
could not take with them, smashing up their old flats, breaking the
windows and doors, destroying the ovens.[105] As Stettin became
Szczecin, many of its inhabitants were keen to destroy as much of the
city as they could. Things had reached such a pass that in December
1945 the Polish State Repatriation Authority, whose task it was to
bring Poles to the city, warned that conditions there were 'altogether
very difficult and require workers who are clearly aware of this. One
must not steer weak, ill people or women with children without male
help towards Szczecin.'[106] The once-prosperous German port city
had become a burnt-out outpost of Poland's 'wild west'.

The physical destruction of the German past made it all the more
urgent for the new authorities to put a Polish stamp on the present. As
throughout the 'recovered' western territories, once Stettin formally
became Szczecin all traces of German language and culture were
removed and replaced by Polish cultural expressions. On 15 July, a few

days after the city had become part of the Polish Republic, a ceremony was held to mark the 535th anniversary of the Polish victory
over the Teutonic Knights at the Battle of Grunwald in 1410. The
ceremony, at which City President Zaremba spoke, was held on what
had been the Kaiser-Wilhelm-Platz, renamed the Plac Grunwaldzki.
Parallels were drawn between the victory over the Teutonic Knights
in 1410 and the victory over 'the crusaders of the twentieth century'
in 1945, and the assembled crowd sang the Polish national anthem
along with the patriotic song *Nie rzucim ziemi skad nasz ród* ('We are
not leaving the land from whence our fathers came').[107] A week later
the Polish city administration ordered that, from 1 August, signs and
street addresses be in Polish and that German inscriptions be removed.[108]
As more Poles arrived in the city, Polish social and cultural institutions sprang into life; German Protestant churches – German Stettin,
like the rest of Pomerania, had been overwhelmingly Protestant –
became sites of Catholic worship for the new Polish population;[109]
Polish doctors began arriving and taking up positions in what was
left of the city's hospitals;[110] in November Germans were prohibited
from working in restaurants, cafés and shops so that they no longer
would be so visible in public;[111] and on Christmas day 1945, Polish
radio began broadcasting and the first Polish theatre performance
was staged.

Not all communities in the former German east witnessed quite so
rapid a suppression of German culture and German public presence in
1945 as did Szczecin. In the district of Stolp in eastern Pomerania,
where Germans remained the overwhelming majority for some
time, German theatre and cinema were made available and German
schools were reopened.[112] Nevertheless, whether it proceeded
rapidly or at a more leisurely and considerate pace, the eradication of
German life and culture was only a matter of time throughout former
eastern Germany.

The dissolution of eastern Germany was accompanied by huge
amounts of violence and suffering. Countless Germans, many of
whom had not been involved in the crimes committed in their
name, lost their homes and possessions, succumbed to disease, and

suffered brutal treatment at the hands of people many of whom had suffered terribly themselves. There was seldom inclination on either side to empathize or sympathize with the predicament of the other. Of course, not all encounters between Germans and Poles were characterized by callousness, hostility and brutality. In some cases, they could and did come to an accommodation with one another. Poles employed Germans – not least since German labour was cheap and Germans often worked without pay, just for room and board – and in many instances new Polish settlers were dependent upon cheap German labour, for example on farms.[113] In areas where Germans and Poles had lived together before the war, the 'old-established Polish population' often was 'allied and related with the German population in manifold ways' and shared a hostility towards newly arrived Polish 'colonists'.[114] However, such supportive relationships were at odds with how both Poles and Germans subsequently viewed events. For the former, the Germans were often regarded as arrogant, heavy-handed, work-shy and unclean.[115] For the latter, the Poles appeared violent and rapacious, and the treatment of Germans by Poles reinforced their belief that they were innocent victims.

The German sense of victimhood was widespread, and drew on old prejudices. One Protestant minister reported from the Pomeranian town of Rummelsburg in October that, 'while the Russian is like a big, sometimes quite naughty child, the Pole constitutes a type of humanity that one only can regard as sub-human. [. . .] People with such natural criminal instincts [. . .] are destined only to destroy and cause chaos.'[116] Even more disconcerting are descriptions by a parish priest of what occurred after Soviet troops arrived in the Silesian town of Reichenbach:

> In addition to the many cases of rape that occurred, those houses belonging to inhabitants of the town which were untenanted were ransacked and looted by foreigners and Jews who had been released from concentration camps. They not only stole the possessions of the German owners, but also damaged and smashed the fittings with hatchets, etc.

During the first weeks of the Russian occupation a Communist German municipal administration was installed, under Russian protection, but it was removed from office by the Poles a few weeks later.

In June the Poles began to arrive in Reichenbach. They did away with the German administration, and the Polish terrorist regime now began.

[. . .] The Poles then began to turn [the Germans] out of their houses and apartments, and by the beginning of 1946 practically no German family had a home of their own. [. . .] The Russians, too, evicted the German inhabitants from entire districts of the town. The people were turned out of their homes at such short notice that they had to leave most of their belongings behind. [. . .]

The Polish Jews in Reichenbach were a great source of trouble. There were about 5,000 of them, as compared to a German population of about 16,000. They soon took possession of all the shops and charged what prices they pleased. In fact, very soon Reichenbach began to be referred to as 'Jewtown'. The Jews undermined the last trace of any morale there still had been, and made mischief between the Russians and the Poles, with the result that the Germans were the poor victims. [. . .] The daily hardships to which the Germans were subjected soon became almost unendurable, and it was with some relief that they learnt that they were to be expelled by the Poles.[117]

It may seem astonishing to us that, after the Second World War and the revelations of the grisly work of the extermination camps, Germans could feel that they were the victims of Jews, and the lack of understanding of what the Jewish survivors had endured is remarkable. However, desperate and fearful Germans who were losing their homes and living in terror did not concern themselves with the plight of others. Their focus, understandably perhaps, was on their own troubles, and the victims of the Nazi regime – Russians, Poles, Jews – now appeared as tormentors in a cruel and unjust world.

German belief in their own victimhood was amplified by their treatment at the hands of Polish authorities, who arrested people accused of war crimes and of having collaborated with the Nazi regime. The process of verification of German nationals often degenerated into rough justice, with membership in a Nazi youth group or cultural association often regarded as confirmation of Nazi sympathies, and large numbers of Germans were imprisoned.[118] Of course, hundreds of thousands of Germans also were arrested in the four occupation zones west of the Oder-Neiße. However, what interned Germans faced in postwar Poland was especially severe. Former Nazi concentration camps and detention centres were used as labour camps for Germans suspected of a Nazi past; over 100,000 Germans (men and women, young and old) were interned by the Poles and endured disease, physical abuse and malnutrition.[119] Among the worst cases was the camp at Lambinowic (Lamsdorf) south west of Opole (Oppeln) in Upper Silesia. There the director had taken up his post in order to 'exact revenge' for treatment that he had suffered during the war; the camp guards were not paid regular wages and consequently took money from the imprisoned Germans; and the unfortunate German prisoners found themselves in the hands of Polish security forces beyond the reach of the Polish civil administration.[120] A large proportion of the German internees died. Some succumbed to starvation and disease; others were cut down by execution or injuries. They formed a community without rights, and without a home.

The millions of Germans from the former German east who survived these traumatic events were affected by their experiences for the rest of their lives. Whether they landed in the Federal Republic of Germany or the German Democratic Republic, they were always from somewhere else, their identity shaped by violence, suffering and loss. The accommodation of the refugees from the east within what was left of Germany posed enormous problems. The need suddenly to house millions of refugees ensured that regions that otherwise had been relatively untouched by the war – rural districts that had escaped the bombing, areas that had not been fought over during the last months of the war – and therefore had not lost so large a proportion of their housing stock, were inundated with destitute refugees and expellees. The loss of the German east ensured that the disruption which accompanied the end of the war affected most of Germany, whether or not the area in question had suffered directly as a result of the fighting. With the exception of rural regions in the French Occupation Zone in the south-west, where the occupation regime resisted accepting expellees, scarcely a corner of postwar Germany escaped this disruption. Where the dispossessed landed was often a matter of chance, and many areas that had received the largest numbers of refugees struggled to cope.[121] Across rural northern Germany formerly sparsely settled districts saw their populations double. Despite wartime losses (in particular, of soldiers who died in combat), the population of postwar Mecklenburg was half as high again after the war as it had been before.[122] The incomers could feel relief that they had left many horrors behind, but new challenges lay ahead. A 'travelling trade inspector' described to the Central Administration for German Resettlers for the Soviet zone in Berlin what he saw among the homeless arrivals from the east in Schwerin in October 1945: 'No opportunity to wash. No possibility to warm oneself. No warm drinks, not even soup for refugees and returning soldiers. The filth at every corner and on the roadsides piled up into little mountains. No one was on hand who would have ensured order and cleanliness. An inferno of human misery in the smallest space.'[123] This was what was left of the German east.

In November 1945, the Allied Control Council officially permitted the transfer of all the Germans remaining in Poland (estimated at 3.5 million) as well as those in Czechoslovakia, Hungary and Austria (estimated at 3.15 million).[124] Germans from Poland were to be transferred to the Soviet and British zones; Germans from Czechoslovakia, Hungary, and Austria (i.e. Germans who had come from Poland, Czechoslovakia etc., and were in Austria at the time), were to go to the American, French and Soviet zones. Provisionally, the Soviet zone was to receive 2 million expellees from Poland and another 750,000 from Czechoslovakia; the British Zone was to take 1.5 million from Poland; the American Zone was to accept 1.75 million from Czechoslovakia; and the French Zone was to take 150,000 people coming from Austria, but only from mid–April 1946. (In addition, the French zone was to accept 250,000 refugees from the American zone who previously had been resident in the French zone.) The transfers were to take place gradually, from December 1945 through July 1946. Altogether, what remained of Germany had to accommodate more than 11 million refugees and expellees after the Second World War.

In what had become Poland's 'recovered territories', the problem in the immediate postwar period was not overcrowding but its opposite. The number of Poles who settled in these territories was far below the number of Germans who had left. In the towns, many of which had been largely destroyed in the war, the lack of housing in any case limited the numbers of people who could resettle; for decades after the war, Wrocław contained fewer inhabitants than Breslau had had in 1939. However, in the countryside population levels also often remained far below what they had been under German rule. Shortly after the end of the war, as plans for settling these regions with Poles were taking shape, Edward Ochab (then the General Plenipotentiary for the Recovered Territories) admitted bluntly that 'we are not in a position to resettle the recovered territories completely', and that there were insufficient numbers of Poles qualified to take over the farms left by the Germans.[125] For decades the 'recovered' territories would have something of an empty feel about them.

By the end of 1945, the former Prussian provinces east of the Oder–Neiße no longer were German. They still held a fairly substantial number of German inhabitants, but the vast majority of these would be compelled to leave over the next couple of years. The Polish population, less numerous than the German population they had replaced, began the hard work of building a new life amidst the ruins, and of transforming territories which had been German into territories that were Polish. The loss of the German east also meant the gain of the Polish west, and both processes were accompanied by profound social and economic breakdown. Neither Germany nor Poland would be the same again.

9

SOCIETIES OF THE UPROOTED

In April 1945, as United States armies were cutting their way through western Germany, Lewis Gittler and Saul Padover, captains with the American Psychological Warfare Department, observed:

> On the German highways and byways one sees a veritable *Voelkerwanderung* – thousands, tens of thousands of men, in small groups and large, carrying bundles, carrying suitcases strapped to their backs, carrying bulging handbags, are marching east and marching west. Many wear shabby green uniforms – they are Red Army POWs, Frenchmen and Belgians who still wear their old army uniforms, now almost in tatters. Poles and Dutchmen and Serbs wear any kind of rags. Their German masters had not kept them in clothes. They were surprisingly cheerful, surprisingly orderly.
> Now they all march . . . in the direction of home.[1]

At about the same time, the German military postal censorship office in Franconia reported that 'in almost all letters' people expressed 'the wish to survive the final phase [of the war] in good health, in order to be reunited afterwards with relatives'.[2] As the Second World War finally reached its end in Europe, millions of people who had been uprooted, torn from their communities and their families, desired nothing more than to return home and pick up the pieces of their former lives.

Others were less purposeful. Many emerged profoundly disoriented and depressed, and did not find it easy to set about rebuilding their lives, no matter how much they yearned to return 'home'. In particular, German refugees and expellees from the east, and Jewish survivors of the Nazi campaign of genocide, often emerged deeply dispirited and scarcely capable of initiative. In September 1945 the Social Democratic politician and former Buchenwald prisoner Hermann Brill (whom the Americans installed as the first postwar head of the German administration in Thuringia, before the Russians arrived as the occupying power in July 1945) observed of the German refugees arriving from the east: 'They have fully lost the ground from under them. That which is taken for granted by us, a sense of security from life experience, a certain personal feeling for their individual freedom and human worth, that is all gone.'[3] The catastrophe of 1945 left millions of people in Germany – Germans, Jews, foreign labourers, refugees, children – profoundly uprooted and with a desperate longing for that 'sense of security' which is bound up with a 'personal feeling [. . .] for human worth'.

When the Second World War ended, Germany had become a land of the homeless, the dispossessed and the displaced. Never before in its history had the country contained so many people who had lost their homes, who had been evacuated, expelled, uprooted, imprisoned. Some sense of the dimension of this dislocation may be seen in the area to the west of the Oder occupied by the Red Army in April/May 1945. After the war this area contained between 14 and 16 million people, roughly twice the number who had lived there before the war.[4] The newcomers, half the entire population, had been uprooted from somewhere else: foreigners who had been either forced labourers or prisoners of war, German soldiers being held in POW camps, and refugees from east of the Oder-Neiße. At the same time many of the 'natives' of this area were absent, having fled westwards in order to escape the advancing Red Army

Across the defeated country, the fixed points which framed people's lives had been erased, communities scattered, settlements and neighbourhoods destroyed, families torn apart. Millions of Germans had been evacuated from the cities to escape the bombing or had been bombed out of their homes; hundreds of thousands of German children, sent from the cities into the countryside (often hundreds of kilometres distant) with the 'Kinderlandverschickung' programmes, were separated from their families at the end of the war in a country where transport infrastructure had been smashed and the way home was uncertain. During the last months of the war millions of Germans had fled ahead of the advancing Allied armies to escape the fighting as the Allies pushed into Germany and, particularly, to escape violence at the hands of soldiers of the Red Army; millions more were expelled from regions which became parts of postwar Poland and Czechoslovakia, or were uprooted from German settlements from the Balkans to the Baltic; millions of German soldiers had been taken prisoner; millions of foreign labourers remained in Germany, awaiting the chance to return home; tens of thousands of Jews, who had survived the attempts of the Nazi regime to murder Europe's entire Jewish population, found themselves in the 'waiting room' of 'displaced persons' camps (mostly in Bavaria), hoping to leave for Palestine or the United States.[5] The term 'displaced persons' was coined for the more than 10 million people – forced labourers, Allied prisoners of war, concentration-camp survivors – awaiting repatriation from occupied Germany at the end of the war,[6] but in a sense Germany as a whole had become a land of the displaced.

In a culture where a sense of place, of Heimat, had been so important, this came as a deep shock. People in Germany were left desperately seeking permanence, rootedness, place. 'Society' and 'community' had been linked intimately with a sense of permanence and place; now contemporary descriptions often referred to the 'vacuum', the 'no man's land' of Germany immediately after the war.[7] Settled society and community seemed to have been obliterated, leaving uprooted people whose wishes, in the words of the philosopher and former editor of the *Frankfurter Zeitung*, Dolf Sternberger, 'are only one and the same: "to go home"' – although for millions 'home' had disappeared.[8] For Germans, the railway station became the focal point of an often miserable, transient, provisional existence: the place where, despite the collapse of rail transport in the spring of 1945, refugees arrived, notes were left by people seeking lost family members, and the black market thrived. The entire country seemed to be waiting for a train to arrive: a train that would bring their families together, a train that would enable them to go home.

'Home' was no less important for the millions of non-Germans who, mostly against their will, found themselves in Germany when the war ended. For many, the homes that they had left no longer existed, their family members and friends no longer were alive. They too had a deep longing for permanence, for a sense of security, often after years of displacement. One voice may speak for many, as related by Saul Padover when he described arriving in Halle, in central Germany, in April 1945:

> When we reached the industrial city of Halle late in the afternoon, we found its undestroyed houses occupied by combat troops. We looked for a place to spend the night, but nothing was available. A Russian girl walked up to me and in mangled German asked where the Kommandantur was. She had just come to the city after escaping from the farm where she was enslaved, and was looking desperately for somebody to help her. She possessed nothing whatever except what she had on her back, and her eyes were wet from weeping. 'I want to go home', she sobbed, 'please help me get home. I am only seventeen.'[9]

For societies of the uprooted, the hoped-for peace meant not simply the cessation of military conflict and an absence of violence; it also meant being able to settle, to build a stable life in secure circumstances. Amidst all the divisions, fears, resentments and hatreds left by Nazism and war, one thing which millions of people shared was displacement.[10]

Few things better illustrate the depth of the social disruption in Germany than the account of nomadic existence offered by a member of a youth gang in the Rhineland when questioned in March 1946 by the British military police:

On 3 August I was released from being a prisoner of war in Tönningen, in the district of Eidelstadt. From there I went to Cologne to my parents, and then learned that they both were dead and my sister as well. I then stayed for 14 days with acquaintances in Cologne. From Cologne I went to Duisburg and stayed there for two months. I also lived there with friends and helped out a bit. Then I went with three comrades to Hannover because they told me that in Hannover there was a lot going on. When we arrived in Hannover we slept in a bunker at the railway station. I stayed for one month in Hannover and slept in the bunker every night. From Hannover I went to Braunschweig for two days and then came via Helmstedt Marienthal into the Russian zone. In Eberswalde near Berlin I visited my aunt Gertrud. . . . I stayed there until December and worked around the house. From there I went back towards Hannover and stayed for two days in Marienthal in a refugee camp, where I let myself be registered as a refugee from the Russian zone. All my papers were stolen in the bunker in Hannover. . . . I stayed four weeks in Hannover. I then registered for work at the camp at Bremerode, where I stayed for three weeks. Then I went back to Hannover.[11]

This youth found himself uprooted in just about every conceivable sense, with no direction home. His family had been wiped out; he had no fixed abode; he drifted from one city and one occupation zone to another; his social milieu was transient and unstable; he was without identification papers and took advantage of his anonymity in the post-war confusion. His focus was on day-to-day survival.

Day-to-day survival was the pre-occupation too of the millions of defeated German soldiers in 1945, most of whom wanted nothing more than to get rid of their military uniforms and return to civilian life. Some achieved this, managing to evade or escape capture and to find their own way home. Most, however, did not, and ended up in Allied prisoner-of-war camps for varying terms of detention. How long they were kept captive, and in what conditions, was largely a matter of chance – of where they were captured and, most importantly, by whom. Soldiers captured by the British and the Americans generally were relatively lucky. The British and, particularly, the Americans were keen to release large numbers quite quickly, so many of their prisoners were set free during 1945. The result, at least in southern Germany, was a flood of former Wehrmacht soldiers returning home. When in mid-June the Americans announced their decision to release all their prisoners, with the exception of about 660,000 men who included former members of the Waffen-SS, the newspaper *Bayerischer Tag* (published in Bamberg by the American Army) reported that 'on every street, in every city and village in Germany one meets German prisoners of war coming home'.[12]

To the east, despite the Wehrmacht's efforts to ensure that as many German soldiers as possible surrendered to the British and the Americans rather than face capture by the Russians, when the war ended the USSR held probably more than three million enemy soldiers prisoner.

The men who landed in French captivity tended to be less fortunate than those taken prisoner by the Anglo-Saxons, but it was those captured by Soviet forces who generally suffered the roughest treatment and for the longest time. Of the Germans taken prisoner by Soviet forces during the course of the war, at least 700,000 died in captivity.[13] According to the Geneva Prisoner-of-War Convention of 1929, POWs were to be released immediately after the end of a conflict. However, in millions of cases this did not occur. The destruction left in the wake of German occupation led the victorious Allies to put German POWs to work rebuilding cities and towns across Europe, both east and west.[14] In particular, the USSR looked upon the enemy troops they had taken prisoner as a source of labour, and between December 1944 and August 1945 the number of 'western' prisoners of war (the majority of whom were Germans) registered as working for the Russians grew from 418,979 to 1,623,137.[15] Many would spend years in captivity, in camps in the USSR or rebuilding destroyed cities and towns in the Soviet Union.[16] Altogether, the German soldiers of the Second World War would spend more man-years in captivity than they had in active service.[17]

★

Thus, at the end of the war, the majority of German males between the ages of 16 and 40 saw their lives turned upside down, but they experienced the dislocation in very different ways. Seventeen-year-old Ewald L. from Saarbrücken, for example, found himself drafted into the Wehrmacht straight from school on 16 April 1945, only about three weeks before the end of the war; he was captured by the Americans and did not emerge from captivity until May 1946.[18] Wolfgang S. from Gelsenkirchen, not yet 17, volunteered for military service in early 1945, was captured by the Americans but released at the end of the year and was able to resume his apprenticeship as an electrician.[19] Alfred B., born in 1921, spent the entire war in the Navy, mostly on the heavy cruiser *Prinz Eugen*, and at the war's end in a submarine; in May 1945 he was taken prisoner by the British, and was not released until November 1946.[20] Bruno A. (born 1923) had worse luck. A soldier since June 1942, he was taken prisoner by the Red Army on 19 January 1945 and was not released until April 1949.[21] Herbert B. (born 1926) was unlucky as well: he had been drafted in December 1944 and sent to the front in March 1945; his penalty for a few months in Wehrmacht uniform was nearly four years of imprisonment by the French and forced labour; he did not return until January 1949.[22] Heinz F. (born 1928) also was unfortunate: drafted in 1945, he served in the military for a mere two months before being taken prisoner by the Russians, and was not released until the beginning of 1950.[23]

German civilians, even those who did not lose their homes east of the Oder-Neiße, were scarcely less likely to have their lives disrupted in 1945 than were German soldiers. Particularly hard hit were those who had lived in the cities which had been bombed day and night and whose population at the end of the war was only a fraction of what it had been in 1939. Among the most extreme examples of this urban depopulation was Cologne. A major transport, industrial and commercial centre in western Germany and within easy reach of Allied air forces, Cologne had been bombed repeatedly during the war – 262 times altogether.[24] The last of these raids occurred on the morning of 2 March 1945 and sent some 80,000 of the city's inhabitants fleeing in panic.[25] By the time the city was taken by American forces four days later, it was largely devoid of people. A registration ordered by the Americans of the city's population in the central districts on the left bank of the Rhine revealed that, as of early April, only a little more than 44,000 civilians remained – less than 8 per cent of the area's pre-war population of 557,658.[26] The rest had fled, been evacuated, or had died.

Over the following weeks and months people returned to their home towns in steady streams from the places to which they had fled or been evacuated. In Cologne, during the summer some 6000 people weekly were returning to the city; by July its population reached a quarter of a million, and by December 1945, 447,000 residents were registered.[27] The city to which they returned was scarcely recognisable. Half of it had been destroyed. Structures which previously had served to orient people in their daily routines – shops, buildings, homes, restaurants – were gone. Once familiar streets were buried under tonnes of rubble, and were it not for the fact that the cathedral with its huge towers was left standing, many people would have had difficulty recognizing the city as Cologne at all. In the midst of this, the speed and magnitude of the return of the displaced civilians created huge problems for a city where more than half of all dwellings (by some reckonings three quarters) had been destroyed and in which only about a fifth were readily habitable. Such was the enormity of the housing shortage that the British military authorities – Cologne was in the British zone – even considered plans (not put into effect) for compulsory evacuation as the first postwar winter approached. Altogether more than 90 per cent of Cologne's population experienced physical displacement, even if only temporarily, in 1945.

Germans faced similar challenges in city after city, town after town. In Trier, which had been severely bombed and then fought over on the ground, only about 2000 people were living amidst the ruins when the 10th American Tank Division took the city on 2 March 1945. At the end of March the city's population, which before the war had been over 75,000, stood at a mere 5,839; by the end of May it had increased to 19,872.[28] In Würzburg, which endured a massive bombing raid on 16 March 1945 and which had been home to over

100,000 people before the war, only about one third that number
(32,493 – 12,467 males and 20,046 females) were registered in the first
postwar count on 24 May; in December 1945, although many more
had returned, at 52,912 (23,726 males and 29,168 females) the city's
population still was only about half what it had been before the war.[29]
In Munich, which in 1939 was home to 824,000 people, only
479,000 were present when the war ended.[30] In Stuttgart, the population at the end of April stood at 266,067, only a little more than half
what it had been three years earlier; the number of evacuees (including children sent away during the war to escape the bombing) was
estimated to be over 130,000 in the spring of 1945.[31] In Hannover, in
June 1945 the city contained 289,000 inhabitants as compared with
471,000 in May 1939 – a decline of nearly two fifths.[32] In Berlin, the
first postwar census in August 1945, recorded 2,807,405 inhabitants –
less than two-thirds of the 4,338,736 recorded in May 1939;[33] in July
1945 there were 48 transit camps in Berlin holding 537,000 expellees,
and in the course of the year, despite the attempts by both Allied and
German authorities to prevent people from coming into the bombed-
out metropolis, 1,537,000 refugees, expellees and released POWs
moved into the city.[34]

While many German cities contained only a fraction of their prewar
population in 1945, in much of the countryside the situation was
quite the opposite. Germans who had been evacuated from the cities
into the countryside in order to escape the bombing now found it
difficult to return home. With transport largely at a standstill and the
Allied military authorities reluctant to allow hundreds of thousands of
German civilians to return to cities where housing and infrastructure had been laid waste, many of those evacuated to the countryside
in wartime had to remain there through the summer of 1945. Some
examples from the district of Reutlingen, near Tübingen in south-
western Germany, illustrate the situation. In the spring of 1945 the
small town of Dettingen on the Erms held some 600 evacuees –
mostly from other places in Württemberg and the Pfalz – many of whom
were housed in a local school; on 20 September, the number of evacuees
in Dettingen still stood at 521.[35] In the nearby village of Grabenstetten

more than 100 evacuees, from Berlin, Stuttgart, the Pfalz and the Rhineland, had been billeted privately in 'almost every house'; on 20 September 83 still remained.[36] In Metzingen (to the north of Reutlingen) almost all of the more than 700 evacuees who had sought refuge in the town during the war – many of whom were living with friends and relatives – were present in late September.[37] Similarly in Urach, which had taken in over 1000 evacuees (roughly half from elsewhere in Württemberg, but 113 from the Rhineland and 154 from the east), almost all still remained in late September.[38]

The obstacles to returning home were formidable. The most important means of long-distance transport, the railways, had been crippled by the bombing of tracks, marshalling yards and bridges, and the lack of railway carriages, locomotives, and coal to fuel the engines.[39] With trains running only intermittently if at all and terribly overcrowded, for months it was difficult if not impossible for many German evacuees to get home. Bans imposed by occupation authorities on people moving into bombed-out cities where there was no provision for them, combined with the general restrictions on travel created further impediments. Munich, for example, prohibited all new migration into the city from 1 August and placed severe restrictions on former residents who wanted to return to the Bavarian capital; those who nevertheless attempted to move into the city received no food ration cards.[40] The collapse of the postal service and the telephone network added to the sense of dislocation, as it was nearly impossible even to send messages to relatives or friends to let them know that one was alive. In Cologne, regular postal deliveries did not resume until 2 July, after having been disrupted since the previous October; the railways did not start operating again until 23 May, and it was not until 24 July that the first train for four and a half months made the trip from Cologne to Koblenz, some 100 kilometres to the south.[41] After the extreme disruption of the final stages of the war, it took months before Germans could communicate with one another over distance.

Of course, when the war ended, there were millions of uprooted people in Germany who were not German. During the war the Nazi regime had recruited, and in many cases forced, millions of people from across occupied Europe to work in Germany, which became a multi-cultural society created through coercion and violence. These foreign labourers comprised the majority of the foreign 'displaced persons' (DPs) in Germany at the end of the war. In addition, the DPs included Russian soldiers who had fought with General Vlasov along-side the Wehrmacht against the USSR, Italian military personnel who had been deported to Germany, and concentration camp survivors. Altogether, the numbers of DPs awaiting repatriation were huge: SHAEF, the Allied Supreme Command, estimated the number of DPs and refugees in Europe at 11,332,700, of which 7,725,000 were to be found within Germany and 6,362,000 of those in the Western zones of occupation.[42]

Initially, as Allied forces moved into Germany in early 1945, they were determined to keep the hundreds of thousands of freed foreign labourers from interfering with the ongoing military campaigns – in particular, to prevent them from clogging up the roads.[43] However, until they were able to channel the DPs into 'assembly centres', there was little that the Allies could do but keep them out of the line of fire and offer them some meagre rations. For their part, the foreign labourers, at least those who had come from Western Europe, often set out for home immediately, on their own. These 'wandering hordes', as they were described in The New York Times, no longer held in check by the Nazi police state, were desperate to return home and often simply took what they needed from the villages along their way, causing anxiety among both the German civilian population and the Allies.[44]

After the Wehrmacht surrendered, the Allies found themselves responsible for millions of DPs, many of whom were ill and under-nourished. The priority was to establish a firm grip on the situation, which meant in the first instance preventing the vast, uncontrolled movement of masses of foreigners. On 5 May, shortly before the German surrender, Eisenhower broadcast a radio message instructing them to stay where they were for the time being: 'Do not move out of your district. Wait for orders. Form small groups of your own nationality and choose leaders who will deal for you with the Allied military authorities.'[45] But the military authorities initially were ill-equipped to deal with the huge numbers of foreign labourers that the Nazi regime had left stranded in the Reich, and weeks passed before these DPs could be gathered into the assembly centres, fed and housed as the Allied leadership had envisaged.[46] At first under the control of the military, later, after the mass of the DPs had been repatriated, the assembly centres were taken over by the United Nations Relief and Rehabilitation Administration (UNRRA) – on 15 November 1945 in the American zone and at the beginning of 1946 in the British.[47]

Nevertheless, despite the scale of the problem, the Allies succeeded in repatriating the vast majority of the DPs very quickly. They had every incentive to do so, for each repatriated individual was one less person to house and feed in the devastated country for which they were responsible. By the beginning of September 1945, the British military authorities had returned nearly 1.5 million displaced persons; by the end of the month, almost six million had been repatriated from the Western zones. General Clay, at the time Deputy Military Governor in the American Zone of Occupation and responsible for 'the care and protection of displaced persons', subsequently observed:

> In an unbelievable operation, by rail, highway, and air, more than 4,000,000 had been repatriated by July 31, 1945, and of the remaining 2,200,000 almost 2,000,000 were collected in assembly centers. [. . .] By November 1945 continued repatriation had reduced this number in the United States Zone to less than 500,000 and they were being adequately fed and housed.[48]

By the end of September 1945, when only 600,000 DPs were left in the American zone, General Eric Wood felt able to report that the problem of repatriation was 'substantially solved'.[49] In the British zone, the comparable number was roughly the same (596,625, of whom the great majority, 483,504, were Poles). The Soviet authorities, no less keen than their Western counterparts to remove foreign workers and POWs, had repatriated nearly 4.5 million by the end of September.[50]

Almost all the foreign labourers from Western Europe returned home within a couple of months of the German surrender; in the British zone, on 1 July 1945 there were only 6,000 French DPs, 3,400 Belgians and 1,100 Dutch remaining in camps, alongside 570,000 'Russians' and 505,000 Poles.[51] Thus while most of the DPs had left Germany by the autumn of 1945, of those who remained almost all were from eastern Europe, a fact which had significant implications for the attitudes to the DPs of both the German civilian population and the occupation authorities. Many, if not most, were keen to return home, volunteered for repatriation, and left Germany quite quickly. Of the more than 2 million Soviet DPs in western Germany, almost 1.4 million had been handed over to Soviet forces by July 1945, and 98 per cent by the end of the year.[52] However, things were not always straightforward for DPs from the USSR: a substantial number of them – men who had fought with Nazi Germany as soldiers under Vlasov or in Cossack units, and members of nationalities (Estonians, Latvians, Lithuanians, Ukrainians), many of whom in 1941 had welcomed the Germans as liberators from Soviet tyranny – rightly feared what might be in store for them should they be sent back to Stalin's empire. Those who found themselves in the parts of Germany conquered by the Red Army in 1945 had no possibility of avoiding repatriation to the USSR; those in the Western zones may have hoped for a different fate but, in fact, generally fared little better. The Western powers repatriated Soviet DPs whether they wanted to return to the USSR or not, a policy which provoked resistance among some Soviet DPs in western camps, where people scheduled to be repatriated sometimes fled and sometimes greeted Soviet repatriation officers with rocks. In one particularly awful incident, at Dachau in January 1946, an attempt by American soldiers to force DPs onto trains bound for the Soviet Occupation Zone met with fierce opposition. When the GIs finally managed to storm the DP barracks after using tear gas, they found that some of those inside had hanged themselves from the rafters rather than be returned to the Soviet Union while others pleaded with the soldiers to shoot them.[53]

The eagerness of the Allies to repatriate the DPs stemmed not only from the logistical problems of feeding and housing the displaced foreigners. People also remembered the aftermath of the First World War: fear that DPs were carriers of disease and would cause epidemics, as after the 1914–1918 conflict, made the occupation authorities keen to delouse and dust with DDT these populations previously classed as 'vermin'.[54] Old prejudices found seeming confirmation in new circumstances. More worrying than DPs as a source of typhoid was DPs as a source of crime. During the final months of the war German control over the foreign labourers had eroded and foreign labourers increasingly committed violent crime and theft, in many cases to get the food they needed to survive. Thus when the war ended the German population feared what the foreign labourers might do. For example, in the Württemberg town of Metzingen (where American and French troops had arrived in late April) local inhabitants were anxious that the foreign labourers would riot on 1 May.[55] After the German defeat, DPs roamed the streets by day and slept where they could by night – in workers' housing that had been provided during the war, in unoccupied dwellings, in empty warehouses. For example, after Frankfurt am Main was taken by American forces, some 10,000 foreign workers were found living in the huge I.G. Farben office building (which soon was to serve as the SHAEF headquarters).[56] After German civil administration had collapsed, little could be done at first to prevent foreign labourers from looting and engaging in violent crime. Thus when the Allied armies took responsibility, criminality among the displaced foreign population posed a conspicuous problem, and it was widely assumed that a disproportionate amount of reported crime (in particular robbery, rape, murder and manslaughter) in occupied Germany was being committed by foreigners.[57]

Of course, not all of the millions of foreign labourers in Germany in the spring of 1945 engaged in violent crime. Had they done so, the occupation authorities would have found it impossible to establish order. Nevertheless, many foreign labourers, in particular the Soviet DPs, took advantage of the collapse of the Nazi police state to prey on the Germans, who were reported 'to have shown a disregard for authority and for the property of others'.[58] Not all were keen to stay in the DP camps which had been set up for them, and some formed armed gangs and effectively turned to banditry.[59] Immediately after the surrender, the German population comprised an easy target for displaced persons, particularly in the countryside where roaming gangs of displaced persons preyed on German farmers. However, it was not long before Germans retaliated with their own violence, and moving about singly or in small groups, became dangerous for DPs.[60]

Occupation authorities in all the zones viewed the deterioration of social order and personal security with alarm. They restricted the movement of DPs, attempted to confine them to the centres set up to house them temporarily and surrounded them with barbed-wire, imposed strict night-time curfews, placed the centres under police and military guard, and set up summary military courts to deal with infractions. (German courts had no jurisdiction over crimes committed by the DPs.) Animosities grew between Germans and eastern European DPs, each convinced they were victimized by the other. The DPs resented the harsh restrictions placed on them by the occupation authorities (as well as the re-arming of some German police), and the military authorities increasingly regarded the remaining DPs as troublesome criminal elements.[61]

Alarm about the behaviour of DPs agitated the highest reaches of the British and American military in Germany. In the British zone, Field Marshal Montgomery announced in a proclamation on 21 August that he was 'determined to put an end to the serious crimes committed by displaced citizens of the United Nations', and went on to 'warn those of you who are tempted to commit reprehensible crimes against the German population that I have ordered my troops to take drastic measures against all persons caught in the act of rape or murder or those who are committing acts of deliberate looting'.[62] In the American zone, General Clay saw the occupation forces facing 'wandering bands of displaced persons, dressed in United States Army uniforms given to them to replace their rags, [who] engaged in robbery and pillage'.[63] The author of the American Army's official history of the occupation maintained that 'the Germans attributed all violent crimes to the DPs, and military government reluctantly came close to agreeing with them': in Munich, the 'DPs constituted 4 percent of the population but were responsible for 75 percent of the crimes'; in

Bremen from June through October 'a DP population of 6000 – 3500 of them males over fourteen years of age – committed 23 murders, 677 robberies, 319 burglaries, and 753 thefts, with gangs operating from the camps armed with automatic weapons'.[64] The threat of violent crime committed by DPs was the 'chief reason' for arming German police in the American zone in November. (Until that time they were permitted to carry only truncheons.) A British officer recollected of Soviet deportees:

> They just made mayhem. They broke into all the houses, raped all the women and drank the place dry. The Germans were quite docile and just tried to hide. The Russians weren't organized. They were just individuals on the rampage. They'd been quite brutalized by what they'd been through as prisoners.[65]

According to the official history of the British Military Government:

> For those awaiting their turn for repatriation, there was often little or no work. [. . .] A great boredom and uncertainty filled the lives of these people. Many were uneducated, of poor mentality, and of crude outlook. Seeing around them the now defenceless Germans, for whom they had long been compelled to work, and at whose hands numbers had greatly suffered, it was not surprising that many took the opportunity for revenge, particularly when this could be combined with acquisition of some of the things for which they had hungered. There were attacks upon Germans, particularly upon residents of lonely farmhouses, in search of food, alcohol, and women. The Germans resisted. Murder, rape and looting followed. British military patrols restored order.[66]

Reflecting widespread prejudices, a British military government officer wrote at the time:

> It may help you to visualise the situation if I tell you that, at this time, I, on my frequent and long trips about our Zone, always had a loaded pistol at hand, and my driver with a loaded rifle!

Russians and Poles; Poles and Russians; and both are worse than any kind of wild beast.[67]

All this fit quite neatly with the prejudices of Germans, who viewed themselves as victims of primitive foreigners now running wild. For Germans the postwar crime wave was evidence of a world turned upside down: they had become the impotent targets of people who not so long before they had been able to order about; the victims of the Nazi regime now could victimize their erstwhile masters. This picture proved remarkably durable. When Germans interviewed in the Ruhr more than 35 years later looked back on their postwar encounters with foreign workers, in most cases they referred to looting. Foreigners generally appeared as a threat, reacting in a perhaps understandable way after what had happened to them during the war but who now, without the Nazi police state to control them, engaged in violence and theft. One man recalled how, after the war, Ukrainians in Essen would pull people from motorcycles, saying 'Motorcycle mine! Nothing for you, motorcycle ours!' Another, a woman who made a point of noting how Germans often had come to the aid of foreigners, recalled that foreign workers were 'on the streets every day with wheelbarrows full of goods' and that she had witnessed a foreign worker hit a cyclist with a club, grab the bicycle and disappear with it. 'Certainly', she admitted, for some looting was 'a means of survival', but for others it was a way of demonstrating power and 'when one considers everything that was done to these people one can understand this'. However, she lamented, 'only it often was aimed at the wrong people'.[68]

Whether the foreign labourers really were quite the threat that Germans and the occupation authorities assumed is open to question. As both the occupation forces and the German population took it for granted that displaced persons were responsible for the lion's share of crime, it was DPs who were the first to be accused[69] – and the accusers tended to overlook the extent to which Germans themselves were engaged in looting, theft, black-marketeering and violent crime. Indeed, there are indications that at least in the major cities – the countryside was another matter – the DPs may not have been the disproportionate threat that Germans, at the time and in retrospect, believed them to be. An investigation of crime in Bremen from May through November 1945, carried out by Wolfgang Jacobmeyer, suggests that with regard to capital crimes (murder, manslaughter) there probably was little difference between the DPs and Germans and that levels of property crime committed by DPs appear to have been considerably lower than that committed by Germans.[70] (It should be noted that the occupation forces tightened their guard of DP camps in order to prevent crime, and that property crime in large cities increased rapidly during 1946 and 1947, when the DP population already had declined substantially.) In rural Lower Saxony, despite the widespread conviction that looting by foreigners, often accompanied by the threat of violence, had led to serious losses of food and livestock, surveys detailing stocks of livestock from April to July 1945 tell a rather different story: the decline in the numbers of cattle, pigs, sheep, poultry and horses as compared with December 1944 was only minimal (some 3.7%), and probably reflected the illegal slaughter of livestock by German farmers themselves, as much as it did theft by roving bands of foreigners.[71] As the American author of a SHAEF Field Intelligence Study had observed in mid-April 1945, while it was clear that foreign workers took advantage of the collapse of the Third Reich to loot on a considerable scale, the extent of this was 'exaggerated' as much of the looting ascribed to foreigners actually had been committed by Germans.[72]

However, perceptions are at least as important as reality, if not more so. The spectre of 'hordes' of foreigners roaming through occupied Germany and attacking a now defenceless native population – and it is worth noting that in these accounts the foreigners almost always are men, and that the German civilian population at the time was overwhelmingly female – played a significant role in creating feelings of insecurity. Germans, who desperately sought stability and order, saw themselves threatened by transient people who the Nazi regime had uprooted, denigrated and demonized through its propaganda. During the spring and summer of 1945, the presence of, and assumptions about, the DPs contributed mightily to the sense of a society uprooted and displaced.

★

The repatriation of the mass of displaced persons coincided with the huge influx of Germans from the east. Thus as one group of the uprooted was leaving occupied Germany, another group was in effect taking its place. It was not really until the great majority of DPs had been repatriated that the Allied occupation authorities developed ideas about how Germans who had been uprooted from their former homes in the east (and who were not officially designated as 'displaced persons') were to be housed. In the British zone, plans began to be developed in mid-September 1945.[73] Collecting camps and transit camps were to be set up in Lower Saxony, from which the refugees and expellees would be distributed throughout the British zone; the running of the camps themselves was to be left to the Germans. In late September 1945 the famous Friedland transit camp opened, on land which had been used by the University of Göttingen for agricultural experimentation. Consisting initially of three pig stalls and ten tents, by the beginning of December these had been replaced with 19 nissan huts. By the end of 1945, 553,095 people, almost all of whom were German refugees and expellees, had been fed in and passed through the Friedland camp, usually spending no more than a couple of days there before moving on.[74] In the years that followed, the camp became a channel for hundreds of thousands of POWs returning to West Germany, followed by Germans fleeing from the German Democratic Republic and, more recently, 'late-resettlers' coming from eastern Europe.

Of all the people displaced in Germany in 1945, those whose predicament was most difficult were the Jews who somehow had managed to survive the murderous Nazi onslaught during the war. The great majority of Jews in Germany in 1945 were of eastern European origin, primarily from Poland and Hungary, and had been brutally evacuated from the east shortly before the end of the war.[75] Altogether, after the war ended there were roughly 50,000 Jewish survivors in Germany.[76] Unlike most of the other DPs in Germany at the war's end, the liberated Jews — often the only surviving members of their families — had no homes to which to return. Often in dreadful physical condition, their families murdered and their communities extinguished, they were alone, and uprooted more profoundly than just about anyone else in postwar Germany. And – unlike the foreign labourers and prisoners of war who had been held by the Germans – the surviving Jews in the main would not be repatriated in 1945. Where could they be repatriated to? One survivor described the dilemma:

> The Jews looked at themselves. Who are we? Where shall we go? Everything was unclear for them. Go back to Poland? To Hungary? To wander about in these countries in the streets that the Jews had left behind, alone, without a home, always with the tragedy before their eyes . . . in order then to meet a former friendly neighbour who would ask ambiguously with wide eyes and with a smile, 'What, you Yankel! Are you still alive?'[77]

During the course of 1945 and 1946, as the great majority of the non-Jewish displaced persons found their way back to their countries of origin, the number of Jews in Germany actually increased. The largest contingent were the roughly 100,000 Polish Jews who had survived in Nazi-occupied Poland or else had spent the war in the USSR.[78] They felt they could not return to – or remain in – a postwar Poland in which their communities had been wiped out and in which there had been ugly upsurges of violent antisemitism after the Nazis had been driven out.[79] With their communities annihilated and seeing no future in the lands which before the war had been the centres of Jewish life in Europe, surviving eastern European Jews headed for western Germany, above all for the American Occupation Zone. Most of the major camps for Jewish displaced persons in 1945–1946 were to be found in the American zone of Germany (i.e. in Bavaria, Hesse and parts of Württemberg) and in those parts of Austria which bordered on Bavaria.[80] Precise numbers are impossible to reconstruct, not least because when counting the DPs after the war a distinction was not made initially between Jews and non-Jews.[81] Altogether, however, roughly a quarter of a million Jewish survivors would find temporary refuge in the American and British Occupation Zones after the war.[82]

Initially, the Jewish 'Displaced Persons' tended to be housed in

camps with other groups.[8] This often left them as a minority amidst
DPs of various nationalities; for example, in the DP camp set up in
Neustadt on the Baltic (in the British zone, some 25 kilometres north
of Lübeck), of the 4000 inhabitants 800 were Jews. Jewish DPs thus
frequently found themselves housed together with people – for example, from Hungary, Ukraine and the Baltic states – who had
collaborated with the Nazi regime. After recent events, to be thrown
together (and treated on an equal basis) with people who had helped
maintain the Nazi 'New Order' in Europe was deeply disturbing.
Furthermore, animosities did not evaporate just because Jews and
other DPs were, temporarily, in the same boat. Tensions often erupted
into violence. In Dachau in early May 1945 non-Jewish Poles threatened to break up Jewish Sabbath celebrations, and a football match
between Jews and Poles ended in a knife fight when it appeared that
the Jewish side was going to win; and in Hohne-Belsen, Polish DPs
demolished the Jewish prayer house in the camp, destroyed the Torah
scrolls, and shot at the rabbi.[84]

Such frictions, together with the fact that the 'repatriation' problems involving Jews were different from those involving most of the
other DPs, meant that it became necessary to create separate camps for
Jews. The first camp exclusively for Jews was set up in Feldafing, on
the Starnberg Lake to the south of Munich. The Feldafing camp was
established at the end of April to provide shelter for Jews who had
been liberated around Bad Tölz in Upper Bavaria; by July its non-
Jewish (Hungarian) population had been transferred to other camps
and the surviving Jews from Dachau were moved to Feldafing; and by
August the camp held 6000 people, almost all of them Jews. Within
their camps, the Jewish DPs were able largely to run their own affairs,
with their own camp administrations, courts and police. However,
living conditions were generally very poor: the camps were dreadfully
overcrowded and sometimes quite filthy; health-care provision was
often inadequate, all the more so given the terrible physical and psychological consequences of what the Jewish survivors had just
endured. In September 1945 the commandant of the DP camp in
Landsberg am Lech, which at that point housed some 6400 displaced
persons of whom roughly 5200 were Jews,[85] described the camp as

'indescribably dirty' and health-care provision as almost non-existent.[86] Sheltering in overcrowded, often unsanitary camps, their
movements restricted, determined to leave Germany but unable or
unwilling to return to eastern Europe, the Jewish DPs were among
the most profoundly uprooted and traumatized people in a continent
full of uprooted and traumatized human beings.

Not all the Jews in postwar Germany were DPs from eastern
Europe, however. Some 15,000 German Jews emerged alive when the
war ended – some had been in hiding, some (the largest group) had
been married to non-Jewish spouses, and some had managed to survive the horrors of the concentration camps.[87] As soon as it was
possible, they re-established Jewish communities in Germany. The
first of these, revived before the war was over, was in Cologne where,
on 11 April, the British gave permission for religious services to be
held and where the community was re-established officially on 29
April. Jews in other cities soon followed suit: in Munich on 19 July, in
Hamburg on 18 September, in Mainz on 17 October, in Bonn on 3
November.[88] These German Jews had little in common with their co-
religionists from eastern Europe. Indeed, there was friction between
German Jews – who spoke 'the language of the murderers', looked
down upon eastern European Jews, and feared that they would lose
control of their communities – and eastern European Jews, most of
whom were Yiddish-speaking, did not identify with Germany at all
and who wanted nothing more than to emigrate.[89]

Of particular concern was the involvement of eastern European
Jews in black-market activity, especially in Munich, where the greatest
number of Jews were concentrated in Germany after the war ended.
The Bavarian capital, in which 9005 Jews had been counted in the
census of June 1933, contained only a few hundred when the
Americans occupied the city on 30 April 1945; most of these were
baptized Jews or Jews who owed their survival to the fact that they had
non-Jewish spouses.[90] In mid-June, 297 Jews, 120 of them originally
from Munich, arrived from the Theresienstadt concentration camp,
and by the end of June some 430 German Jews were living in the city.
But these German Jews formed only a small proportion of the Jews in
and around Munich after the war. Far more numerous and far more

conspicuous were the east European Jews, who spoke a different language and often were of different appearance, who frequently engaged in black-market trading, and who seemed to correspond to the anti-semitic stereotypes which had been peddled for years in Nazi propaganda – much to the consternation of the German Jews who before 1933 had been for the most part integrated into German society. One German-Jewish woman expressed a mix of self-pity and contempt for her eastern European co-religionists thus: 'If there is a God, why, after making us suffer so terribly in the past, has he punished us with the Möhlstrasse [the street in the Bogenhausen district of Munich which became a centre of East European Jewish life and black-market trading in the city], which is a disgrace to us before the world and which must make every decent Jew blush with shame?'[91]

Unlike the German population and, presumably, 'every decent Jew', the eastern European Jewish DPs were without steady jobs, salaries, bank accounts or property. They had to survive on the charity of Jewish relief organizations; they often received items otherwise unavailable on the open market, and so some turned to black-market trading. Although the Jewish DPs were probably no more involved in black-market trading than the German population or occupation soldiers had been, their conspicuous presence seemed to confirm the stereotype that Jews engaged in illicit trading and shied away from supposedly honest, constructive work. According to the *Landrat* of the district of Wolfratshausen in Upper Bavaria (which contained the Föhrenwald Jewish DP camp), writing to his superiors in Munich in December 1945, 'especially the inhabitants of the camps, over-whelmingly eastern European Jews [*Ostjuden*] . . . engage in black-market and illicit commerce to an incredible degree. The amounts of money that each one of them has can be counted in the tens of thousands.'[92] Given such attitudes, it is hardly surprising that the eastern European Jews met with hostility among the German police, who raided DP camps, as well as among the German civilian population.

The eastern European Jewish DPs did not only arouse antipathy among Germans. While some American camp commanders themselves were Jews and sympathetic to the Jewish DPs in their care, others were not. Even I.F. Stone, the American Jewish left-wing journalist, wrote of the DPs he had observed in the camps that 'they were an unattractive lot'.[93] This was mild in comparison with other reactions. It is one of the more unpleasant coincidences of the time that the majority of the Jewish DPs in the American zone were to be found in the very region – Upper Bavaria – that fell under the command of an American general known for his antisemitic attitudes: George Patton, the Military Governor of Bavaria and Commanding General of the American 3rd Army headquartered in Bad Tölz. In Patton's opinion, unless the Jewish DPs were kept under guard in the camps they would spread over the countryside 'like locusts'.[94] He ordered that every DP camp be surrounded with barbed wire and armed guards; the DPs were permitted to leave the camps only if they had a substantial reason for doing so and then only with a pass.[95] After a visit to the Feldafing DP camp in September 1945, Patton recorded in his diary:

We entered the synagogue which was packed with the greatest stinking bunch of humanity I have ever seen. . . . Either the Displaced Persons never had any sense of decency or else they lost it all during their period of internment by the Germans. My personal opinion is that no people could have sunk to the level of degradation these have reached in the short space of four years.[96]

In Patton's opinion, while others might believe the DPs to belong to the human race, the Jews especially were 'lower than animals'.[97]

Although he was far from alone in his feelings of disgust, fortunately not all those involved in managing the challenges thrown up by the eastern European Jewish DPs were as extreme as Patton. In areas which fell to the American 7th Army under the command of General Alexander Patch (including Württemberg, Baden and part of Bavaria), the Jewish DPs were treated more humanely, and could come and go from the camps as they chose.[98]

In the British Occupation Zone, it was not so much the attitudes or prejudices of the soldiers involved but rather the difficult situation which the British Government faced in Palestine that determined policy. The displaced Jews attracted little sympathy among the occupation authorities, but that was because the British were concerned not to exacerbate an already tense situation between Arabs and Jews in the Palestine Mandate for which they were responsible. This meant that the British were not keen to help Jewish DPs do what many wanted to do more than anything else: emigrate to Palestine. Nor were they keen to see large numbers of eastern European Jews arrive in their zone. Although, after the German surrender, the British initially allowed the migration of eastern European Jews into their zone, they became more restrictive as time went on; and at the beginning of December 1945 the British banned Jewish migration into their zone via Berlin and also put a stop to migration into the DP camps altogether.[99]

However tragic the plight of the Jews, it was rather marginal to the concerns of most Germans in 1945, particularly those who themselves were uprooted and who remained preoccupied with their own problems as they emerged from the rubble left by the Nazi regime. The sense of dislocation among the Germans was perhaps greatest for those who lost their homes in the east – not only the civilians who fled westwards in the treks, but also the soldiers who had come from East Prussia, Pomerania, Silesia or the Sudetenland, who were taken prisoner towards the end of the war and who, upon their release, had no home in Germany to which to return. A typical example was Günter G., born in 1927 in Danzig-Langfuhr, who was taken prisoner by the British at the end of the war, released in July 1945, and then went to Schleswig-Holstein since, as he later wrote, 'my Heimat was under Polish administration'.[100] Similarly, for Franz H., born in eastern Brandenburg in 1925 and released from captivity at the end of June 1945, the end of the war also meant finding work in the west (on a farm near Cologne).[101] For Herbert S, born in Danzig in December 1928, 1945 spelled one drastic change after another: just 16 years old, on 6 January he had been drafted into the Reich Labour Service and then into the Wehrmacht one month later; in May he was taken prisoner by the British, released in August near Euskirchen, where he worked first repairing bridges, then in a sugar factory and then in a textile factory. He never returned to Danzig.[102]

Another group of Germans separated from their homes in 1945 were the children who had been evacuated from cities threatened by bombing. Despite the dangers caused by the approach of enemy armies in early 1945, returning the children to their parents had really been not an option. Hamburg, for example, from which some 80,000 children already had been evacuated by early 1941, remained a bombing target almost until the war ended; the homes of many evacuated children had been destroyed during the war and their parents often transferred to other regions.[103] In any event, the means of transport needed to bring back the children were unavailable; observing that the formerly safe regions to which the children had been sent were in danger of enemy occupation drew the charge of defeatism; and the return of children without authorization drew the threat of the death penalty. Nevertheless, as the war approached its end, anxiety mounted among both the children and their parents. In early March the director of a camp for child evacuees in Oberhaselbach (between Regensburg and Landshut) in Lower Bavaria caught up with three youths who had tried to set off on their own from the camp back to Hamburg. Giving their reasons for the attempt, they referred to the arrival of the Americans in Düsseldorf, the constant pressure on the eastern front, and the 'terror attack' on Hamburg: 'All the youths are very agitated. They fear being separated from their parents.'[104] However, they were relatively fortunate. The children who had been evacuated to eastern Germany — the rural regions of Pomerania and East Prussia, which until late 1944 had appeared to be the safest areas of the Reich — faced the same fate as did the millions of Germans whose homes had been east of the Oder-Neiße: some were re-evacuated westwards; some were left to find their own way back home; and some died along with hundreds of thousands of eastern Germans whose homes were overrun.[105]

For those who did manage to get back home, their problems were far from over. Some, such as Gerhard T. (born in Gelsenkirchen in 1930), were lucky. He had been evacuated to Braunsberg in East Prussia in 1940, finished his schooling there in 1944 and then worked on the farm of his foster parents before returning to Gelsenkirchen to find work as a mining apprentice.[106] The miner's son Günter P., born in Bochum in 1930, was sent to Prague when war broke out in 1939 and to Pomerania in 1942; in early 1945, aged 14, he left school and fled back to Bochum, but because of the lack of food in the Ruhr left again in May 1945 to work as a farm apprentice in Salzkotten (near Paderborn) until the following spring.[107] For others who had been evacuated, whose dwellings had been destroyed and whose parents were killed in the bombing, there was no way home. They often had to remain in institutions, with friends or with relatives, and were not able to return to their home towns when the war came to an end in 1945. One such was Kurt L., who, as an 11-year-old had been evacuated from Hamburg after his mother was killed in the bombing; after the war he went to the Soviet zone, to live with his grandparents in Mecklenburg, and attended school there until Easter 1946 (when he had reached the age of 14); he would not return to West Germany until 1951 (when he fled the GDR after spending a year with the east German 'People's Police').[108]

The dislocation of Germans at the end of the war had yet another, often overlooked dimension: the loss of identity, and not in some vague metaphorical sense. Millions of people who had been displaced, who had fled or been expelled from their homes east of the Oder-Neiße, often found themselves without any documentation which might confirm who they were. The wartime destruction, particularly in the last terrible months, the loss of the former German east (and, with it, the loss of access to official documents), and the administrative barriers created by the division of Germany into four separate occupation zones, meant that it often became impossible to check the identities or previous activities of millions of Germans. For many, this created enormous problems when it came to verifying their identities and qualifications, for establishing claims to assets, and for dealing generally with officialdom. For others, however, the postwar chaos created opportunities for deliberate misrepresentation, deception and fraud. The difficulties involved in confirming German identities led to an upsurge in identity-related crime after the war.

Among the more revealing transgressions which became more frequent in postwar Germany was bigamy. The increase in bigamous marriages had a number of causes: the many hasty wartime marriages, marriages entered into by German soldiers in occupied foreign countries, and an absence of personal documentation for many refugees from the east which left registry offices dependent upon assurances given by the parties that they had not been married before. Men of marriageable age were in short supply in postwar Germany. In the 'Province of Saxony' (i.e. Sachsen-Anhalt), for example, at the end of 1945 there were twice as many women as men between the ages of 30 and 40 and three times as many between the ages of 20 and 30.[109] As a scarce commodity, men found it relatively easy to find partners and, given that it was difficult to check whether they were already married, it was relatively easy for married men to marry again. Professor Karl Bader (Chief State Prosecutor in Freiburg i.Br.) observed in his contemporary study of German postwar criminality: 'Today bigamy is that offence which, alongside robbery, has presented the highest relative increase. One can characterize it as a genuine offence of our postwar era.'[110]

The overwhelming majority of people convicted of bigamy were men. (Women almost never were prosecuted for the offence.) Of these the largest proportion consisted of former soldiers. The motives could vary tremendously, but war-related dislocation was a common motif. Not all the bigamists' motives were necessarily dishonourable. One such was the case of a married but separated soldier who found himself in a POW camp at the end of the war. During the war he had met a Norwegian woman and wanted to marry her; their relationship survived his internment and, partly in order to prevent her from being treated badly by her co-nationals, he claimed to be single and married her.[111] The second largest proportion of convicted bigamists consisted of refugees and people from other occupation zones, and it is hardly surprising that the greatest increases in convictions for bigamy occurred in regions with high proportions of refugees.[112]. In Osnabrück, for example, of 30 postwar cases of bigamy only two involved local people.[113] Contracting a second, bigamous marriage was viewed as one way to get a dwelling in a society where housing

was extremely scarce, to obtain permission to move into a city, to provide for children who were the product of a liaison with a second
woman, or to evade responsibility for the maintenance of children
from a first marriage.

The chaotic conditions at the end of the war created opportunities
for forging papers and establishing new identities, and opened up
fresh possibilities for fraud and embezzlement. In the immediate aftermath of the war, many people turned up in unfamiliar places to claim
identities that were not theirs, qualifications that they did not possess,
pasts that they did not have. In one case in 1945, a former mayor and
Nazi Party official from Saxony obtained false papers, and got his
wife to launch proceedings to have him declared officially dead –
whereby he himself came forth as a witness, under a false name, to
attest to his own death; after being declared dead he married his wife
a second time – now using his new name – managed to get a job in
the economics ministry in Düsseldorf in the British zone dealing with
inter-zonal trade, and then proceeded to make a nice living from
bribes and black-market activity.[11]

One common practice was for men to masquerade as medical doctors. This was facilitated by the fact that many soldiers had had contact
with the medical services while in the Wehrmacht, often as assistants
in military hospitals, where they became familiar with medical terminology. For some – such as a 25-year-old tram worker from the Ruhr
who described himself as a 'surgeon and obstetrician', pocketed consulting fees and committed thefts in south-western Germany
throughout 1945 – a newly concocted professional identity could be
a nice earner. Others, who emerged from the war addicted to mor-
phine, used false identities as doctors to gain access to drugs.[115]
Occupied Germany was awash as well with phony lawyers, counter-
feit civil servants, and fake police officers – professions which gave
considerable scope for committing fraud and extortion.

Two further false identities proved particularly attractive proposi-
tions for fraudsters: clergy and nobility. Those pretending to be men
of the cloth could take advantage of the confusion created by the division of the country into occupation zones and often were looked to
by desperate people in search of comfort. In one case, a 35-year-old

mechanic managed to make contact with the Land Bishop in Mecklenburg and get himself employed as a Protestant vicar in a community near Schwerin through to the end of 1945; he then travelled throughout the various occupation zones maintaining that he was a vicar – even claiming on occasion to be Martin Niemöller – and defrauding people who believed him.[116] Occupation and division also facilitated the impersonation of aristocrats. Men turned up in the Western zones claiming to be sons of expropriated noble families from east of the Oder–Neiße or the Soviet Occupation Zone. The fact that the regions which had been strongholds of the landed aristocracy fell under Soviet control made it all the more plausible for fraudsters to claim noble birth and to take advantage of the social prestige still associated in the west with that status.[117]

Altogether, it was only to be expected that the year 1945 would figure as the great rupture in the biographies of many Germans born before the Second World War. Nineteen forty-five marked the end, indeed the destruction, of previous lives, and the beginning of new ones – what often was perceived as a personal 'zero hour'. The shock of events at the end of the war laid the foundation for a subsequent establishment of reasonably stable, grounded and ordered lives, in environments often very different from those where people had lived before the war. People who had come from the Sudetenland found new homes in Bavaria. People who had grown up on farms in eastern Germany found new lives as miners in western Germany. A few examples, taken from the files of men who signed up for six-week courses offered by the mining trade union in the Ruhr during the late 1950s and the 1960s, illustrate the point. One such was Konrad B., the son of a farmer born in East Prussia in 1925. He had volunteered to join the Navy in 1943; by the end of the war four brothers and his father had been killed; in 1945, after a short period as a prisoner of war he was released to go to western Germany 'since I could not return to the Heimat', and there he worked for a time in agriculture before getting a job in mining in Neunkirchen in 1948.[118] For Ernst B., born in Marten near Dortmund in 1919 and an infantryman from 1940 to 1945, 1945 meant being captured by the Russians in Königsberg in April, managing to escape captivity, and then reaching his wife and finding work in Heiligenstadt in Thuringia (in the Soviet zone) in September.[119] For Franz H. the end of the war also meant displacement: born in 1925 in the village of Pommerzig in Brandenburg, east of the Oder, he had been drafted into the Wehrmacht in 1943, served on the eastern front, was wounded three times, spent short periods in British and American captivity when the war ended and was released at the end of June 1945; 'since my Heimat is under Polish administration', he wrote, 'I took up work on 1 July 1945 as a coachman and tractor-driver on a farm near Cologne'.[120] Günther T., born in 1927 and drafted into the Wehrmacht in July 1944, was seriously wounded on 20 April 1945 (Hitler's final birthday) and then taken captive by the Red Army; the Russians, however, released him as an invalid in October, whereupon he managed to get a job as a guard on the trams.[121]

For another refugee, who had been born in Königsberg in 1929 and after leaving school was sent out to do 'agricultural service' with the aim of becoming a 'soldier-farmer' (*Wehrbauer*) in the Nazi east, 1945 meant first being signed on hastily with the merchant marine, then flight from East Prussia to Copenhagen, captivity in Scotland and Hamburg and, finally, release, after which he went to Schleswig-Holstein where he found a job in agriculture.[122] Yet another sketched his life as follows:

I was born on 26 November 1929 in Lasswitz, the district of Grottkau in Upper Silesia, as the son of the miner Josef B. I spent my youth in the hills near Waldenburg, as my parents lived there until their expulsion in 1945. [. . .] After completing primary school I began [working] as an apprentice with the railways. Because of the war and the developments that followed I could not complete the training. Afterwards I then became an anti-air-craft assistant and [a member of the] *Volkssturm*. When the war came to an end I set out on foot towards Memmingen to my parents. From September 1945 until April 1946 I worked in a cheese factory. After that until March 1947 as an unskilled build-ing worker. Since March 1947 I have been employed in coal-mining in Upper Bavaria.[123]

In almost all these short autobiographical sketches, 1945 figures as a time of displacement. The stories are typical of of the postwar fate of millions of Germans. Their experiences would shape they way they thought about themselves and their world for the rest of their lives.

The lasting legacy of the uprooting which affected millions of Germans in 1945 was a deep desire for place, stability, permanence. People who had been made homeless emerged from the war with a longing for a home, for a secure place in which they could rebuild their lives. This was reflected in the importance of the idea of Heimat among returning POWs, who often saw their return as not so much to the nation as to a particular locality that offered a vision of stability and meaning in a world turned upside down.[124] It was reflected too in a renewed emphasis on the family, after family life had been so disrupted by the war and its aftermath. The postwar sociologist Helmut Schelsky observed: 'The family bond is emphasized because it is or was endangered, what is more it is above all a compensation for the loss of general societal support that took place because of the collapse of the state and economic orders.'[125] In the words of one observer, 'familial self-help took the place of public security, welfare and assistance benefits . . . in short, the family stepped in where the state and society fell away'.[126] Of course, with millions of men having been killed in action or sitting in prisoner-of-war camps, with tens of thousands of children separated from their parents, and with millions of Germans having lost their homes, the German family was hardly a guaranteed source of tranquillity and stability. Nevertheless, the profound social and economic dislocation in 1945 enhanced the utilitarian role of family as the institution which could offer the best chance for individuals to meet at least some of their daily needs for food and shelter and a refuge from the shattered world around them. People uprooted in their public lives cultivated roots in their private lives all the more intensely.

The premium placed on stability helped to shape the successful conservative culture of 1950s West Germany and to undermine the politics of continued upheaval and government-driven transformation in the German Democratic Republic. The uprooting of millions of people in central Europe left deep social, cultural and psychological scars, a hunger for community, for order, permanence, rootedness: for a home. Paradoxically, perhaps in this way the shock of 1945 helped lay foundations for the conservative normality and political stability of West Germany during the 1950s. Once the worst of the postwar hardships were behind them, West Germans were able to channel tremendous energy into rebuilding 'normal' family life and stable communities. Spared the overt politicization of daily life and the constant mobilization foisted on their cousins in the GDR, and benefiting from economic recovery, West Germans could begin to leave the dislocation of 1945 behind them.[127]

Thus the unexpected stability of postwar West German democracy rested upon, among other things, the insecurities left by the greatest displacement of Europeans in their history. A key element of the culture of postwar West Germany was the quest for security. Germans came to accept rearmament in the name of security;[128] they devoted themselves to building the 'economic miracle' in order to construct economically secure lives;[129] they put enormous energy into their private family lives in pursuit of personal security;[130] they built huge numbers of dwellings, which provided homes for millions of people who had been uprooted at the end of the war. After the profound displacement which those millions experienced in 1945, it is hardly surprising that a burning desire for security and place proved one of the most important and resonant legacies of Nazism and the Second World War.

10

VISIONS OF A NEW WORLD

The Third Reich is already almost as good as forgotten, everyone was opposed to it, 'always' opposed to it; and people have the most absurd ideas about the future. Victor Klemperer[1]

W hile most Germans emerged from the chaos and destruction left by Nazism and war with a deep desire to be left to put their own lives back in order, their new masters had other ideas. At Yalta Churchill, Roosevelt and Stalin had agreed:

It is our inflexible purpose to destroy German militarism and Nazism and to ensure that Germany will never again be able to disturb the peace of the world. We are determined to disarm and disband all German armed forces; break up for all time the German General Staff that has repeatedly contrived the resurgence of German militarism; remove and destroy all German military equipment; eliminate or control all German industry that shall be used for military production; bring all war criminals to just and swift punishment and exact reparation in kind for the destruction wrought by the Germans; wipe out the Nazi Party, Nazi laws, organizations and institutions, remove all Nazi and militarist influences from public office and from the cultural and economic life of the German people; and take in harmony such

other measures in Germany as may be necessary to the future
peace and safety of the world. It is not our purpose to destroy the
people of Germany, but only when Nazism and Militarism have
been extirpated will there be hope for a decent life for Germans,
and a place for them in the comity of nations.[2]

The vision of the 'Big Three' at Yalta was of a Germany stripped of
her military capability and cleansed of Nazism. It was essentially a negative vision – a catalogue of what would *not* be permitted in a future
Germany – rather than a blueprint for what was to take the place of
the Third Reich. It was shaped by the conviction that 'German militarism' lay behind the launching of two world wars, and that future
peace in Europe depended upon putting an end to the German armed
forces and everything that had supported them. Germany was to be
demilitarized, deindustrialized in so far as the demilitarization
required, and stripped of all vestiges of Nazism. What, exactly, would
follow remained uncertain.

The end of the Third Reich gave rise to many ideas about what
should take its place. When Allied authorities arrived to administer the
occupied country, German exiles returned after the collapse of the
Nazi regime and German public figures emerged from concentration
camps, prisons or 'internal exile', they had various (and often con-
flicting) visions of what a 'new Germany' could and should be.
Among these were visions of a pastoral country, incapable of making
war again; of a country divided into a number of smaller states, none
sufficiently large to threaten its neighbours; of a democratic country in
which representatives of the 'better Germany' would guide development; of an end to Prussia and with it of 'Prussian militarism'; of a
socialist Germany in which political power would be wrested from
capital and placed in the hands of the working class; of a 'Soviet
Germany' purged of nationalistic German capitalism; of an 'anti-fascist–democratic' order which would banish the dangers of Nazism and
dictatorship; or of a country and society which, 'purified as if by
fire', would return to genuine Christian faith. Of course, the realities
of occupied Germany were terribly messy, and none of the visions for
its future could be realized undiluted. Nevertheless, they would be of

great importance in shaping Germany and Europe in the decades which lay ahead.

Once the German government headed by Karl Dönitz had surrendered its armed forces, the most important ideas about Germany's future were those of the Allied powers that now occupied the defeated country. The agreement reached at Yalta in February 1945 contained general points of principle about Germany's future – in effect the lowest common denominator acceptable to the Allies. How the general principles would be put into practice could be decided later, after the war was won. All four occupying powers (the 'Big Three' – the United Kingdom, the United States and the Soviet Union – plus France, whose occupation zone in south-western Germany was agreed with the British and Americans on 25 July 1945, while the Big Three were meeting in Potsdam) were convinced that Germany posed a danger to world peace and that their primary task was to ensure that the Germans be prevented from ever attaining a position from which they could launch another war. All four powers arrived with prejudices about the country over which they now held sway, and each had its assumptions and designs for Germany's future. The Soviet Union was preoccupied with gaining reparations and ensuring that Germany never again be in a position to attack as she had done in 1941. The British and the Americans were determined to wipe out what they regarded as the German militarism that had led to two world wars and to re-educate the Germans and turn them into democrats; the Americans, particularly, arrived in Germany determined to cleanse the country of Nazism and militarism, while the British were concerned to minimize the expenditure which occupation would entail. The French came determined to exact compensation, if not revenge, for what France had suffered at German hands during the occupation of their country between 1940 and 1944.

Of all the Allies, it was the Americans whose wartime visions of Germany's future had aroused the most controversy. During the war the Americans had given considerable thought to how they would administer a conquered Germany. From 1942 through 1944 people designated for the future occupation administration were sent on training courses to prepare them for the task ahead: the first 'School for Military Government' was set up on 2 April 1942 at the University of Virginia at Charlottesville; nine others followed at other universities, and later a joint training centre, the Civil Affairs Centre, was established in Britain at Shrivenham, near Swindon.[3] The extent to which this training actually helped American and British forces deal with the challenges they faced when actually administering postwar Germany is debatable, and already during the war the effectiveness of the training was questioned. In March 1943 a committee of the American Office of Strategic Services observed:

> It is unrealistic to assume that we can wisely control large parts of Germany with the handful of men now going through the School for Military Government at Charlottesville, many of whom know no German and most of whom have no more training in the problem than they can absorb in sixteen weeks and no greater knowledge of contemporary Germany than can be supplied in a single military handbook.[4]

No doubt a fair amount of the planning for postwar Germany was inspired by ignorance. However, it is difficult to imagine any degree of discussion or planning for future occupation that could have prepared personnel adequately for the challenges ahead.

During the war, various ideas for the coming occupation were discussed. The best known was the 'Program to Prevent Germany from Starting a World War III', presented to President Roosevelt's Cabinet in early September 1944 by the Secretary of the Treasury, Henry Morgenthau, and which became known as the 'Morgenthau Plan'. Morgenthau urged a harsh peace, proposing that conquered Germany be deindustrialized as well as demilitarized; that, essentially, it be turned into an agrarian country. Convinced that the Germans were incorrigible and an inherent danger to the peace of the world, Morgenthau regarded the agrarianization of Germany as necessary to prevent that country ever again being able to wage aggressive war; in addition, he called for extreme measures to be taken against German war criminals, including the summary execution of the 'arch criminals'.[5] In this, he could feel confident of a sympathetic hearing from the President. Roosevelt's own views about Germany and the Germans were far from complimentary, and in 1944 he had agreed with his Treasury Secretary that 'we have to be tough with Germany, and I mean the German people and not just the Nazis. We either have to castrate the German people or you have got to treat them in such a manner so that they can't just go reproducing people who want to continue the way they have in the past'.[6]

In the event, less extreme views prevailed. The Morgenthau Plan was opposed by Secretary of State Cordell Hull and, particularly, War Secretary Henry L. Stimson and, after being reported in major American newspapers (including The New York Times on 24 September 1944, in the middle of the presidential election campaign), it caused embarrassment to Roosevelt, who promptly distanced himself from the proposals.[7] The Morgenthau Plan thus never became official American policy and had little or no influence on the actual occupation other than to provoke disagreement between the British and the Americans. However, it did cause alarm, and provided Goebbels with a welcome propaganda theme for stiffening resistance to the Western Allies during the last months of the war. According to Colonel T. R. Henn, the British deputy head of the Psychological Warfare Division of SHAEF, the publicity given to the Morgenthau Plan confirmed 'to the last detail every statement of enemy propaganda for the past five years';[8] and during October 1944 the Völkischer Beobachter gave prominent attention to the plan of the 'Jew Morgenthau' and how it revealed a readiness to allow 30 million Germans to starve.[9]

The actual framework for American occupation policy between a German capitulation and the establishment of a single Allied control commission for the whole of Germany was provided by the Joint Chiefs of Staff directive 'Regarding the Military Government of Germany in the Period Immediately Following the Cessation of Organized Resistance' – JCS 1067 – drafted in September 1944. The aim was to establish a 'stern, all-powerful military administration of a conquered country, based on its unconditional surrender, impressing the Germans with their military defeat and the futility of any further aggression'.[10] According to Lucius Clay, the directive foresaw Germany being 'occupied as a defeated nation under a just, firm, and aloof administration which would discourage any fraternization' and 'contemplated the Carthaginian peace which dominated our operations in Germany during the early months of the occupation'.[11] Although punitive in aim and tone, unlike the Treasury Department's Morgenthau Plan, JCS 1067 was not a blueprint for Germany's long-term future; rather it was a military directive that served to provide the theatre commander with instructions upon which to base detailed plans.[12] As Walter Dorn, who was involved in the preparation and execution of the American occupation and who served as a personal advisor to Clay, observed, American wartime planning for a postwar occupation regime was characterized by 'the absence of a long-range policy'.[13]

On the ground, the Americans had been the first Allied power to confront the practical problems of setting up an occupation regime, after they had taken Aachen in October 1944 (the first German city to fall to the Allies). On 30 October they appointed Franz Oppendorf, a prominent local Catholic who had the backing of the city's bishop, as *Oberbürgermeister*. Oppendorf organized and ran a city administration under the overall supervision of the American military, until he was assassinated during the night of 25 March by Werewolf agents. The Americans found their first experience of occupation difficult: Oppendorf's practice of employing former Nazi Party members in the city administration drew harsh criticism (leading to a wave of dismissals in February and March 1945); and without clear guidelines, it was uncertain just what the aim of the civil administration was to be – to bring democracy to Germany, or to tolerate authoritarian behaviour in order to manage the huge problems facing German communities at the end of the war.[14]

Roosevelt had been reluctant to authorize firm plans for the occupation before the war against Germany was won. Not until 23 March 1945 (i.e. after the Yalta Conference) did Roosevelt sign JCS 1067. After Roosevelt died, Morgenthau's influence in the American administration waned; American occupation policy rested primarily with the War Department rather than with the Treasury; and the longer-term objectives for the American occupation eventually coalesced around re-educating and re-orienting the Germans, while at the same time trying to manage logistical problems of mammoth proportions. The man chosen to carry out the daunting task was Major General Lucius Clay, who was appointed Deputy Military Governor on 24 March 1945, as Eisenhower's forces were crossing the Rhine in large numbers.[15] The aims of the occupation regime were summed up by the four 'D's': denazification, democratization, demilitarization, and decartelization. The American vision of a postwar Germany was of a country re-educated, its political and economic structures reformed and decentralized, so that it would become more like the United States – or, at least, what the Americans imagined the United States to be.

British perspectives on a post-Nazi, postwar Germany bore many similarities to those of the Americans: a combination of harsh opinions about the nature of Germans and Germany and, when they actually found themselves faced with the problems of an occupying power, a healthy dose of pragmatism. The British name associated most prominently with extreme anti-German views – a British counterpart to Henry Morgenthau – was that of Robert Gilbert Vansittart, who had been Permanent Under-Secretary at the Foreign Office from 1930 to 1938 and then the Chief Diplomatic Advisor to the British Government between 1938 and 1941. Vansittart, whose 1941 pamphlet 'Black Record. Germans Past and Present' (the text of a series of radio talks broadcast by the BBC in December 1940) went through three printings in the space of two months and sold over a million copies, had referred to the Germans as a 'race of hooligans' and 'a breed which from the dawn of history has been predatory and bellicose'.[16] However, far more important than the attitudes of Vansittart were those of Churchill who, addressing the House of Commons on 21 September 1943, had maintained that the Germans:

> [. . .]combine in the most deadly manner the qualities of the warrior and the slave. They do not value freedom themselves, and the spectacle of it in others is hateful to them. Whenever

they become strong they seek their prey, and they will follow with an iron discipline anyone who will lead them to it. The core of Germany is Prussia. There is the source of the recurring pestilence. [. . .] Nazi tyranny and Prussian militarism are the two main elements in German life which must be absolutely destroyed. They must be absolutely rooted out if Europe and the world are to be spared a third and still more frightful conflict.[17]

The task of the Allies in shaping a future Germany was an essentially negative one: to ensure that the allegedly innate German urge for domination and the Prussian virus were extinguished and thus to eliminate a major threat to the peace of the world.

It was one thing to fulminate against Prussian militarism and assert one's iron determination to root it out; it was quite another to take practical steps to bring this about and to prepare the ground for a Germany which might again join the community of nations. During the war a Directorate of Civil Affairs was to plan for administering a defeated, occupied Germany. However, like its American counterpart, the Civil Affairs Division which had been established in the War Department in March 1943, its impact was limited. Until May 1945 the main focus was on the military campaign, and those planning for 'civil affairs' after the war were not necessarily able to command the attention of the decision makers.[18]

In any event, when it actually came to implementing policy for the administration of occupied Germany, practical considerations prevailed. German local administrations were revived very quickly under the supervision of the British Military Government. However, in the absence of German central and regional government, and with the collapse of the transport and communications infrastructure, local administrations 'were like so many independent governments'; in some places the pressures were so great that there was (as in the district of Wesermünde in May and June 1945) 'nearly a standstill of the district administration'.[19] The commanding officer of the Duisburg Detachment 617 described experiences common among those put in charge of German towns after their capture:

25 April . . . Great flood of people at office. Food and displaced persons are greatest worry. . . 26 April . . . Pressure of work continues. Area is far too large to be properly administered. [. . .] 27 April . . . All offices working sixteen to eighteen hours a day. The amount of paperwork is so terrific that the practical things that should be done, have to suffer . . . 30 April . . . Pressure of business very heavy. [. . .] 18 May . . . Much confusion exists to who is Military Government: practically every officer considers he is empowered to consult Burgermeister and dictate policy. [. . .] 20 June . . . Hundreds of passes are issued from this office every day. It would seem that the essential business of Mil. Gov. – supervision – is being ignored. Instead it is losing itself in a matter of pettifogging detail.[20]

Given the problems, it perhaps was inevitable that the occupation regime would become bogged down in 'pettifogging detail'. It also perhaps was inevitable that the occupation authorities quickly became milder than originally envisaged. At the outset the British approach was to be characterized 'by the issue of orders, obedience to which will be exacted', and a determination that 'Germany will be made to realize that this time she has been well and truly beaten in the field of arms, and must now do as she is ordered'. The Germans did, however, generally do as they were told, and consequently the British administration 'soon acquired a less forbidding, more British character' than had been envisaged originally.[21]

For the British, the challenges of administering their occupation zone were compounded by financial constraints arising from the economic exhaustion of the United Kingdom after six years of war, and exacerbated by the cancellation in August 1945 of the Lend-Lease Agreement with the United States. The U.K., which desperately needed to husband its depleted foreign-currency reserves, was not in a position to provide hefty subsidies for the British Occupation Zone in Germany – which, with the heavily bombed Ruhr industrial region, was the zone facing the most severe problems of housing and food supply. It was no surprise, therefore, that the basic objectives of the British occupation regime, as laid out in the Directive on Military

Government of September 1945, concerned economic considerations and the problem of food supply.

However, the longer-term goal was the establishment of democracy. In the eyes of the British this required that flaws in what they
viewed as the German national character – absence of independent
thought, lack of a sense of civic responsibility, attachment to an
authoritarian state – should be corrected.[22] The key to this transformation would be the introduction, along British lines, of democratic
government, particularly at the local level; the authoritarian methods
of the German civil service were to be replaced by a British-style
administration whose employees regarded themselves as responsible to
the citizenry. New structures for local government would be introduced, with the office of mayor transformed and a position introduced
akin to an English town clerk, that of 'city director', to be filled by a
non-political civil servant.[23] Raymond Ebsworth, who worked for the
British Control Commission for Germany (CCG), later observed that
'in the British Zone, we envisaged authorities like the more rural
county councils in our own country, to which until recently only
independents were elected and where politics was taboo'.[24] The
Germans were to be re-educated through exposure to British-style
local democracy, something which the British viewed with a 'missionary pride'.[25] Although British democracy was seen as a product of
the British character, the British were proud to export it. As the
CCG reminded its staff, British democracy was 'the most robust in the
world: It is on British soil that it flourishes best, but we do export it,
and, tended carefully, it grows and flourishes in diverse lands, even if
it takes a long time to acclimatise itself'.[26] This vision of postwar
Germany was, in short, of a country which would become more like
the United Kingdom (or, at least, what the British imagined the
United Kingdom to be).

The motivations driving the French in setting up their occupation
regime in south-western Germany were rather different. They had less
of the missionary zeal that framed the American desire to cleanse
Germany morally, or of the British desire to remake German civic
culture into something more like their own; they felt less of an urge

to re-make Germany in their image. During the war, French thoughts about Germany's future had focused largely on their own security, on ensuring that the 'restless neighbour' to the east of the Rhine never again would threaten France. On the political left the instinct was to look to a system of collective security in which national powers would be superseded. Writing from prison in 1941, the Socialist former prime minister of France, Léon Blum, had called for a strong international organization into which a new Germany would be integrated;[27] and in 1943 Emile Laffon (who at that time was with the Free French in London, would be appointed 'Général adjoint' to the French Commander-in-Chief in Germany in mid-1945, and who did believe that France had a mission to democratize Germany) drew up a programme for a future occupation policy which would combine economic and social reforms with anchoring Germans in a supranational community.[2] Others – not least Charles de Gaulle – were less prepared to be generous. From the summer of 1944 de Gaulle (President of the French Committee of National Liberation from 1943 and head of the provisional government of the French Republic from August 1944) called for a postwar Germany to be federalized (i.e. divided up into autonomous regions), for the Rhineland to be detached from Germany, for the Ruhr region to be placed under international control, and for the Saar region to be integrated into France.[29] De Gaulle was determined to safeguard France's security, and in January 1945 he had stated that France did not want to see an end to the war before being assured of control along the entire Rhine.[30] Although de Gaulle's views did not go unchallenged, such notions played a central role in shaping the French approach to occupation. For the French, whose zone was carved out of the Western zones, joining the Big Three as an occupying power meant reasserting their power and status after the occupation of their own country by the Germans. Their main concerns were to ensure their own security and to use the occupation to facilitate the postwar economic recovery of France itself.

During the war it had been the British who first supported French demands for a share in the occupation – not least due to fears that, as Churchill had written to Roosevelt in November 1944, 'there will be a time not many years distant when the American armies will go home and when the British will have great difficulty in maintaining large forces overseas'.[31] This concern was openly discussed at the Yalta Conference: in Churchill's view 'it was problematical how long the United States forces would be able to stay in Europe, and, therefore, it was essential that France be relied upon to assist in the long term control of Germany'; Roosevelt replied that he 'did not believe that American troops would stay in Europe much more than two years'.[32] Once France had been liberated and a French army restored to fight alongside the Americans and British, the French in general and de Gaulle in particular were keen to take a substantial place in the occupation condominium, not least to detach if possible the territories on the left bank of the Rhine from a postwar Germany.[33] As things turned out, the French zone was rather more modest than de Gaulle had wanted. Demands that the Americans hand over Frankfurt, Kassel, Karlsruhe, Mannheim and Darmstadt to the French were rejected.[34] Cologne, which was essential to any plans to control the Rhineland, remained part of the British zone, so the boundaries of the French zone agreed with the British and Americans on 25 July included no really major cities. However, the area under French control did include the Saar region, with coal reserves that the French regarded as vital for their own postwar economic recovery, as well as the Black Forest, which had been left relatively untouched by the wartime destruction.

The French arrived in Germany less concerned to democratize the country than to re-assert their own prestige and status as a major power. General Jean de Lattre de Tassigny, the commander of the First French Army (which had participated, under Eisenhower's overall command, in the invasion of south-western Germany in 1945), became Commander-in-Chief of the French Occupation Zone for the first eleven weeks, until he was promoted to chief of the French General Staff by de Gaulle. In de Lattre de Tassigny's opinion, the French participation in the invasion of Germany 'was for our country a duty and a right [. . .] this surest means of demonstrating her resurrection – and, even more, of making it a lasting resurrection by taking possession of some of the real symbols of her future security. [. . .] In

the eyes of the leader of the government [de Gaulle] it was a historical necessity, as much to raise our world prestige as to lay out the basis
of our postwar position on the Rhine'.[35] Aside from impressing the
German population with their military displays, the French seemed
initially to have had little idea of how the occupation regime itself
would be organized. As in the other zones, the hallmark of the first
few months of administration was improvization.

General Pierre Koenig, who replaced de Lattre de Tassigny at the
head of the French occupation administration in August 1945, was
rather more visionary. A close associate of de Gaulle and military
governor of Paris after its liberation in August 1944, Koenig agreed
that the objective of the French in Germany was to punish the guilty
and secure France's 'traditional guarantees'. But he went further,
describing the aims of his administration in the following terms:

> To free the German population, and above all its young people,
> from its illusions; to give to a Germany plunged into chaos a
> suitable organization for this order-loving country; to be inspired
> in setting up this organization by the principles of the democratic
> countries in the West and America; to attempt to orient toward
> our ideas the teeming youth which tomorrow will take charge of
> the revival of this country; to lay down with an indestructible
> firmness the bases of a Franco-German *rapprochement*, which is
> indispensable for the reconstruction of Europe.[36]

This was, altogether, a remarkable set of objectives, which rather
accurately described what would take shape in the years to come: a
democratic (West) Germany anchored in the West, and a Franco-
German *rapprochement* which would lie at the centre of the postwar
order in Western Europe.

That, however, was for the future. In 1945 there was one thing
about which the French occupiers agreed: there should be no resurrection of a unified Germany which might again threaten France.
Consequently, the French favoured political structures which were
as decentralized as possible, and during 1945 it was the French who
repeatedly threw up obstacles to a united approach to Germany

among the occupying powers. The French, who had not been invited
to the table at Potsdam, were not keen that (as stated in Clause 2 of the
Potsdam Agreement) 'so far as is practicable, there shall be uniformity
of treatment of the German population throughout Germany'; and
the French government objected to the establishment (as spelled out
in Clause 9) of centralized institutions, of 'essential German administrative departments, headed by State Secretaries [. . .] particularly in
the fields of finance, transport, communications, foreign trade and
industry [. . . which would] act under the direction of the Control
Council'. They also opposed the terms of Clause 14, which stipulated
that 'during the period of occupation, Germany shall be treated as a
single economic unit', and of Clause 15 (c) which called for the
'equitable distribution of essential commodities between the different
zones so as to produce a balanced economy throughout Germany and
reduce the need for imports'.[37] French commanders, in common
with the military authorities in the other zones, ignored the clause
about the 'uniformity of treatment of the German population
throughout Germany' when it suited them.

In addition to fear of a united Germany again threatening France,
two general considerations informed French opposition to a unified
postwar occupation regime. One was economic. For the French,
occupation offered the opportunity to use German resources – in
particular, the coal and steel of the Saar region – to aid French recovery. The Saar was to be, more or less as it had been between 1919 and
1935, fused economically with France in a customs and currency
union.[38] Unlike the British or the Americans, the French actually
managed to extract a surplus from their occupation zone. By encour-
aging the development of export industries (the vast majority of
whose production went to France), the French were able to prevent
their zone, which was largely agricultural and therefore less dependent on food imports, from becoming a financial liability as the British
and American zones were for the U.K. and the U.S.[39] The other
consideration was strategic: that an occupied Germany treated as a
unity would allow the Soviet Union to gain access to the resources of
western Germany, especially of the Ruhr, and that a united Germany
might someday join with the USSR to threaten the West.[40] There also

was French public opinion to consider. After the experience of two world wars and four years of German occupation, the prospect of a tough occupation policy met with overwhelming popular approval within France: according to a public-opinion poll in August 1945, 78 per cent of the French wanted to see Germany divided and 71 per cent wanted to see it turned into an agricultural state.[41] (This is not to say that British or American public opinion had been much more positive towards Germany. In February 1945 more than half the British population (54%) had admitted feelings of hatred towards the German people, and in November 1944 three fifths of Americans had been convinced of German preparations for a third world war.)[42]

However, as the comments of Pierre Koenig demonstrate, the attitudes of the French were not exclusively punitive. The picture of a harsh and unsympathetic French occupation regime may be in some need of revision, and it can be argued that the French path to German democracy was not worse but just different than that mapped out by the Americans.[43] Even for de Gaulle, national interests were not simply a matter of military control and economic extraction. On his first visit to the occupation zone, in October 1945, he declared in Trier that 'France is not here in order to take, but to renew, and for you to renew with her'.[44] Behind de Gaulle's thoughts about postwar Germany lay a vision of a Europe in which Germany and France would work together (no doubt with France as the senior partner).

The objectives which framed how the Soviet Union dealt with its zone of occupation were of a different nature from those of the Western occupying powers. In theory at least, the USSR was a socialist state inspired by a Marxist ideology, and in April 1945 Stalin had stated, in an oft-quoted remark recorded by Milovan Djilas: 'This war is not as in the past; whoever occupies a territory also imposes on it his own social system. Everyone imposes his own system as far as his army has the power to do so. It cannot be otherwise.'[45] In fact, however, the USSR did not impose its own system immediately; indeed, in 1945 the Soviet Military Administration and its handmaidens among the German Communist Party leadership sought to restrain their more enthusiastic German supporters, who regarded the collapse of the Third Reich and occupation by Soviet forces as an opportunity to create a 'Soviet Germany'. The Soviet occupiers worked closely with German Communists from the outset and regarded the democratic transformation of Germany agreed by the Allies at Yalta and Potsdam rather differently than did the United Kingdom or the United States. Like that of the French, the Russian attitude was framed by two main concerns: to prevent Germany from being able ever again to attack their country; and to extract reparations in order to compensate for at least some of the damage that the Germans had caused to them during the war. Overall, the Soviet government did not have a really clear vision of a postwar Germany, other than that it should be punished for its aggression and compelled to pay reparations.

During the war, Stalin had agreed, in somewhat vague terms, with the British and American leaders that Germany ought to be dismembered after it was defeated. Churchill had informed Stalin that he (Churchill) viewed as necessary 'the complete dismemberment of Germany for at least a full generation and the dismemberment of Germany into individual parts, above all the severing of Prussia from the other parts of Germany';[46] shortly thereafter, at his first meeting with British Foreign Secretary Anthony Eden in December 1941, the Soviet dictator agreed. And at Teheran in late 1943 Stalin concurred with Roosevelt, who was also pressing for Germany's dismemberment. However, Stalin remained deliberately vague about his intentions, and by the time the war ended he had changed his mind – at least publicly.[47] Whereas at Yalta he had appeared willing to see Germany broken up – pressing the British and Americans for 'an agreement in principle that Germany should be dismembered' but leaving the details to be worked out later by a commission of the Foreign Ministers[48] – it soon became obvious that (like the British and the Americans) the USSR did not possess a clear vision for a dismembered postwar Germany. According to Fedor Gusev (the Soviet representative on the European Advisory Commission), writing at the end of March: 'The Soviet government understands the Yalta resolution not as an absolute commitment but, rather, as a possibility to put pressure on Germany in the event that other means do not prove effective enough in rendering that nation harmless.'[49] Dismemberment no longer framed plans for postwar

Germany; it would, in the words of the British Chancellor of the Exchequer, Sir John Anderson, 'greatly impair Germany's capacity to make reparation'.[50] Dismemberment now was merely a possibility, to be implemented – as the British now put it – 'if necessary'.[51]

The more concrete proposal made by the Soviet delegation at Yalta, that Germany be compelled to pay reparations of 20 billion dollars, half of which would go to the USSR, militated against dismemberment. (This proposal was accepted only insofar as it was to provide the basis for subsequent negotiations to decide the matter.) In order that the USSR could extract substantial reparations from Germany, the defeated country had to be treated as a single entity. Never firmly committed to chopping Germany up, once the war in Europe had ended in May 1945 Stalin jettisoned the idea. In his victory proclamation on 9 May, he stated that the Soviet Union had no intention of dividing or destroying Germany. Practical considerations had prevailed: the Generalissimus now envisaged a postwar Germany kept in one piece from which the USSR could extract reparations – not just from a part of the country but from the whole (including from Germany's largest industrial region, the Ruhr),[52] and in which a resuscitated Communist Party of Germany would be a dominant political force at the head of a broad anti-fascist 'bloc'. How this was to be accomplished remained unclear. Although it appears that Soviet officers and specialists had been trained for future employment in the occupation,[53] the leaders of the Soviet Military Administration (SMAD) arrived in Germany with little idea about how to set up a German administration, the tasks it was to perform or its relationship to the SMAD.[54] In the event the Soviet Union failed either to gain access to the resources of western Germany or to create a unified Germany in which the left would be in a strong position. Instead, the policies of the SMAD, its support for the Communist Party of Germany and the pressure brought to bear on those who disagreed with its course, served to increase divisions between east and west and to undermine support for Communist politics in western Germany. Instead of realizing a vague vision of a neutral, socially transformed and united Germany, the Soviet Union would eventually settle for the establishment of a Socialist state in part of postwar Germany.

Given the dictatorial regime established in the Soviet Occupation Zone during the late 1940s, it may seem surprising that the USSR was the occupying power initially most willing to allow a revival of German political activity. On 10 June 1945, just two months after the German capitulation, the Soviet Military Administration in Germany permitted the activity of 'anti-fascist' political parties and organizations in its zone – the first of the occupation zones where this occurred; while in the Western zones the authorities remained committed to enforcing a 'political quarantine' in Germany and limiting political activity to the local level, German political parties were formed in Berlin under the supervision of the SMAD.[55] The Soviet formula – a swift process of denazification and the licensing of political parties – signalled a readiness to introduce a parliamentary system in Germany as a whole. But that did not mean a readiness to relinquish control. The SMAD kept a tight rein on the Germans and allowed local government officials little room for independent action.[56] Furthermore, the Soviet occupation authorities were determined to engineer, with the assistance of their German Communist allies, a social and economic revolution from above: to carry through a rigorous programme of land reform (drawn up in the summer of 1945) involving the complete expropriation of large landed estates, and to impose direct control over much of the economic activity in the zone. They closed the major banks and insurance companies in July 1945, and seized property formerly belonging to the German state, the Wehrmacht, the Nazi Party and its various organizations, and to leading Nazi politicians. The Soviet conquerors may have arrived without a detailed blueprint for postwar Germany, and initially they may have been committed to an 'anti-fascist, democratic' transformation rather than a socialist one; however, the course they charted in the summer of 1945 immediately set their zone apart from what was happening in the west.

As for the Germans themselves, the end of the war and the Nazi regime also created opportunities to realize new visions of the future. However, the obstacles and challenges before them were enormous. Their ideas about their future were often vague and contradictory, and suspicions about their own people who had supported Hitler so enthusiastically and had committed such terrible crimes were considerable. The position of German politicians who looked forward to rebuilding their broken country after its unconditional surrender was difficult, and they had only limited power to realize their hopes.

Unlike what had occurred at the end of the First World War, there was no popular rising in Germany as the Nazi regime collapsed and the war ended. There were no mass demonstrations; Germans did not take to the streets demanding a new political agenda. Mostly, they were too tired and too preoccupied with day-to-day survival for such action, and after unconditional surrender and with the country occupied by foreign armies, the scope for popular politics was limited indeed. Thus the period immediately following the defeat of German military forces saw something of a political vacuum. Political activity by Germans initially was banned, and while the formation of political parties was first permitted in the Soviet zone on 10 June, in the three Western zones this did not occur until after the Potsdam Conference: on 27 August the U.S. Military Government permitted the establishment of parties at district level, and on 23 November at *Land* level; the British Military Government allowed the formation of parties on 15 September; while the French Military Government did not permit the formation of political parties in its zone until 13 December.

Nevertheless, across Germany, in all the occupation zones, local initiatives surfaced in the interval between liberation and occupation. In the spring of 1945, during the short period after German forces had been defeated but before Allied military forces had established their own administration in a particular locality, groups of local activists – the 'activists of the first hour' – mainly Communists, Social Democrats and former trade-union activists, spontaneously formed local 'reconstruction commissions' or 'anti-fascist committees'. These committees, the self-styled representatives of the 'other Germany' that had not succumbed to the attractions of Nazism, sprang up in all four occupation zones, and formed what has been described as a sort of 'collective self-help'.[57] As could have been expected, they were strongest in those areas which, before the Nazi capture of power in 1933, had been strongholds of the labour movement.[58] The reception of these 'anti-fascist committees' varied in the different occupation zones. In the Soviet zone, where the military administration and its allies in the German Communist Party had little desire to see independent left-wing organizations flourish and where political parties were permitted within a few weeks of the German surrender, these independent groups were dissolved relatively quickly; and in a few isolated cases, in Rostock and Greifswald, members of these committees were arrested.[59] In the British and American zones, they were viewed as difficult to control, and the occupation powers preferred to focus on the development of political parties with which they could deal more easily. Perhaps paradoxically, given the often punitive views of the French, they seem to have had their greatest effect in the French zone (where they met with the approval of Emile Laffon and where the French military authorities supported their work), in particular in South Baden.[60] The numbers of people involved could be substantial: for example, in Rastatt in Baden, a town of about 15,000 inhabitants before the war, the anti-fascist committee numbered 600 people. It was headed by a member of the Communist Party, a skilled worker at Rastatt's Leitz factory and a survivor of five years in a concentration camp, who ran the committee together with a former member of the SPD and a former member of the Catholic Centre Party.

The aims of these local anti-fascist committees were similar throughout: to purge local government of Nazis, to get local services up and running, and to defend the interests of the labour movement and working people. Accordingly, they sought to arrest local Nazis and compel them to perform tasks such as clearing up rubble 'for the community', organize food supply, allocate available housing, organize the repair of damaged infrastructure, and set up provisional auxiliary police forces. The committees were radically anti-Nazi and favoured punishing guilty Nazis with forced labour, but they lacked a clear social or economic programme. Their members desired an end to the division between the Communist and Social Democratic Parties (which in the eyes of many had helped Hitler to achieve power in 1933) and favoured the formation of a single, united working-class political movement; they sought to involve people from across the political spectrum in the tasks of reconstruction; and they assumed that politics in postwar Germany would see a swing to the left.[61] They saw themselves as champions of a new politics rather than a resurrection of what had been buried when the Weimar Republic collapsed. As a member of the managing committee of the 'Antifa' in Mühlheim in southern Baden (near Tuttlingen, in the French zone) expressed it to the local *Landrat* in November 1945, 'as a matter of principle the old former parties should not be resuscitated. I far prefer a union of all the people who in the past years of Hitler's rule have maintained a clear head and a decent position.'[62] The destruction of the Nazi regime had given many 'activists of the first hour' hope that a peace-loving Germany could be built on the basis of cooperation among all those who had 'maintained a clear head and a decent position' during the hard years of Nazi oppression. After the catastrophes of Nazi dictatorship and military defeat, and against the background of the conflict-ridden partisan politics of the Weimar Republic, the watchword now was 'unity'. When Haselhorst, in the west of Berlin near Spandau, was liberated, the local anti-fascist committee proclaimed:

> Hang your flags! Today is your birthday; the day on which we have the right to demonstrate our political maturity. Let's form *one* large 'German Workers' Party'. Show the International that you are worthy of the great gift which you have received today – namely the right to express openly your political opinion through the founding of a large strong Workers' Party [which has been] tested through misery and distress. Prove that we finally have come to the long cherished goal – 'Unity'   There can be no more 1919s and no 1933s . . . Long live the International![63]

After the terrible experiences of the previous twelve years, the socialist grass roots were convinced that their hour had come and that the divisions of the past would be overcome.

Such convictions were not limited to Socialists and Communists. In early 1946 – not long after General Koenig allowed the formation of political parties in the French Occupation Zone – the *Südkurier* newspaper in Konstanz (on the Swiss border) asserted:

The horrors of fascism may lie behind us, but we all must endure its catastrophic consequences together in the future as well, peacefully ward off the disturbances that already can be observed. Education for democracy, for peace and for freedom remain the common tasks of as broad as possible an anti-fascist unity front. We do not know which and how many parties will emerge in the French Zone. But whether Christian Democratic Union, whether Liberal Democrats, whether Socialists or Communists, they all will recognize that cooperation and unity are the most powerful motor for the reconstruction of our economy and our new state. [This is] the only guarantee for the fulfilment of the Allied resolutions of Potsdam, indeed for the existence of the German nation. For never again must the old militarist imperialist reactionary Nazi Germany rise from the dead; a new Germany of work, powerful democracy and honest peace must be constructed. The free anti-fascist block of all democratic forces will be and will remain its firm foundation.[64]

If this language sounds similar to that employed by Communists and Socialists in the wake of the collapse of Nazi Germany, that is a reflection of the degree to which anti-fascist perspectives were shared across the political spectrum. The editor of the *Südkurier*, Eduard Sütterli, was no socialist but rather a member of the Catholic upper-middle class and the main organizing force among the Christian Democrats in and around Konstanz.[65] The article was also a reflection of the 'tabula rasa syndrome' present after the collapse of the Nazi regime: the general conviction that it was not possible to return to where one had left off in 1933; that the challenges facing Germany required new political formations and a broad coalition of democrats in order to clear the political, material and moral wreckage left behind by Nazism.

More important than the local figures who sought to rebuild their communities in 1945 were the exiles who had fled the country during Hitler's rule and now returned, and the German politicians who emerged from the concentration camps or 'internal exile' after the Nazi years. Many, if not most, of the men – and they were men – who became leading political figures in postwar Germany had spent much of the period of Hitler's 'thousand-year Reich' either in exile or in prison; others – for example, Konrad Adenauer – had spent the Nazi years in Germany, sometimes persecuted and certainly cut off from public life. Many, particularly on the Left, were convinced that when the Hitler regime collapsed their hour would come – a conviction that had been expressed by the Social Democratic politician Rudolf Breitscheid during the turbulent election campaigns of 1932: 'After Hitler – Us!'.[66] Breitscheid did not survive to see the end of the Third Reich. Arrested in France in 1941 and delivered up to the Gestapo, he died in Buchenwald during an air raid in August 1944. However, those who did survive to surface in a defeated, destroyed and occupied Germany in 1945 brought with them their hopes and ideas about how the future might be shaped.

The German exiles and those who had emerged from the concentration camps or 'internal exile' generally held a number of assumptions in common. They were committed to building a democratic Germany. They tended to assume that the economic problems facing the country were so overwhelming, and that the capitalist system had proved itself so incapable of providing a basis for stable growth and stable politics, that Germany's future would be socialist. Although committed to maintaining the unity of postwar Germany, many favoured a federal structure for a future German Republic. And they tended to think in European dimensions, seeking an end to destructive German nationalism within a supra-national European framework. One example of this was the programme of 'Democratic Germany' (a group of German emigrants in Switzerland), which was published as a brochure in the spring of 1945. Although the group itself – which included the former Reich Chancellor and left-wing Centre Party politician Joseph Wirth, the former SPD Prussian Prime Minister Otto Braun, and the Bavarian SPD politician Wilhelm Hoegner – never achieved political influence, it expressed thoughts which had wide resonance at the time: that 'the reconstruction of the entire economy has to take place according to the needs of the broad strata of the people and according to plan', and that, 'If one really wants to safeguard the freedom of the spirit and the cultural achievements of Europe, one must solve the social question from the ground up'.[67]

Among the clearest left-wing visions of a future Germany was the 'Buchenwald Manifesto' of 13 April 1945. This 'Manifesto of the Democratic Socialists of the Former Concentration Camp' had been drafted by the Social Democratic politician Dr Hermann Brill (whom the Americans were to instal as head of the Weimar city administration at the end of April, and then as head of a provincial administration of Thuringia in early May).[68] The ten-point manifesto was read out at a memorial gathering of 21,000 survivors of the Buchenwald camp on 19 April, and thousands of copies were printed subsequently.[69] In it, Brill laid out the claim to the moral authority of 'democratic social- ists', who had 'endured gaol, prison and concentration camp because we believed that under the dictatorship we had to work for the ideas and goals of socialism and for the maintenance of peace', to set the agenda for the future. Their comrades had 'died at the hands of the Hitlerite hangmen'; they regarded themselves as 'therefore author- ized and obligated to tell the German people what measures are necessary in order to save Germany' from the 'historically unprece- dented' collapse and 'to obtain for her respect and trust in the council of nations once again'. To this end, predictably, 'fascism and militarism in Germany' had to be eliminated and the institutional apparatus of the Nazi system had to be rooted out in its entirety. 'This gigantic task', the Manifesto went on, could be accomplished 'only if all anti- fascist forces join together in an unbreakable alliance' and a 'new type of democracy' established that was 'not limited to empty formulaic parliamentarianism, but enables the broad masses in the cities and the countryside to be involved in politics and administration'. Freedoms of speech, thought, belief and association were to be restored, and the old professional civil service was 'to be abolished and replaced by a highly qualified, clean, socially modern people's civil service'. As regards the economy, it seemed self-evident that its organization would be socialist:

Convinced that the basic cause of this most terrible of all wars lies in the predatory nature of the capitalist economy, of finance-capital imperialism and in the consequent moral and political demoralisation of the lumpenproletariat and petty bourgeoisie, we demand that societal crises be brought to an absolute end through a socialist economy. Germany can be reconstructed economically only on a socialist basis. Building our destroyed cities as a capitalist enterprise is just as impossible as a reconstruction of industry out of the pockets of the taxpayers.

This vision also was a European one, of a socialist Germany that would reject chauvinistic nationalism and make a positive contribution to a new world order and thus help secure peace and security – a vision much of which (minus the socialist rhetoric) would be realized over the next half century. The 'highest goal' was, 'in cooperation with all socialist-governed states', to form 'a European community of states' that would 'guarantee order and prosperity through a European community'. For this a 'new spirit' was needed, 'embodied in the new model of the German European'.

In many respects, the programme of the Buchenwald 'democratic socialists' was more radical than were the (tactical) public statements of German Communists at this time. The Soviet occupation authorities were not enthusiastic about it, and in July 1945 the call in the Manifesto for the socialization of the economy and the transition to a people's democracy through parliamentary elections was criticized harshly by the head of the Soviet Military Administration in Thuringia, Lieutenant General I.S. Kolesnichenko.[70] However, the tone of the Manifesto was significant. The experience of Nazi rule had reinforced the sense of rectitude and moral authority among Germany's 'democratic socialists' and the conviction that the hour to realize their visions for a postwar Germany had arrived.

German Socialists and Communists emerged from the long years of Hitler's rule convinced that the German Left must be united in future. They had, they believed, learned the hard way that division invited disaster. The question of 'unity' on the Left therefore was at the top of the agenda for Social Democrats and Communists alike, although obviously there were differences of opinion about where the blame for past divisions lay. The desire for unity was heartfelt among some, a tactical consideration for others. Communists, who during the final Weimar years had been shrill in their condemnation of the Social Democrats – 'social fascists' in their rhetoric of the time – emerged from Nazism and war publicly committed to the re-unification of the Left. During the war, after Germany had attacked the Soviet Union, many of the obstacles to a 'unity front' on the left were removed. The establishment, on 12/13 July 1943 in Krasnogorsk, near Moscow, of the 'National Committee of Free Germany' had been a clear signal – not just of a public commitment to create a 'strong democratic state power that has nothing in common with the impotence of the Weimar regime'[71] but also of an opening by the Communists both to Social Democrats and to liberals and bourgeois democrats, with the professed aim of creating a united front to bring down the Nazi regime.[72] This is not to say that misgivings about collaborating within a broad front of anti-Nazis evaporated. Social Democrats remained suspicious of Communists and their sub-servience to Moscow, and the conflicts of the past could not simply be forgotten. The support drawn in the Western zones by the Social Democratic leader Kurt Schumacher, who rejected collaboration with the Communists, was a reflection of bitter memories and well-founded suspicions. Nevertheless, the extent of the desire for a united socialist party, which could appeal to bourgeois voters as well as to workers, should not be underestimated.[73]

Among the socialist exiles – Social Democrats and, to differing degrees, members of smaller groups such as the left-wing Socialist Workers Party and the 'New Beginning Group' – there was a shared commitment to parliamentary democracy and to the idea of state economic planning. The aim was not a state takeover of the economy along Soviet lines but 'social democracy', a 'synthesis of Western capitalism and the state socialism of the Soviet Union',[74] which would involve significant state intervention in the economy as well as a major role for the trade unions in decision-making. The economic power of the 'monopolies' would be broken, major industrial concerns as well as banks and insurance companies would be nation-alized, the holdings of large landowners expropriated, and worker participation introduced into the running of the factories.[75] A future Germany was to be democratic and social, and it was to include the whole country: the Social Democrats regarded themselves as German patriots for whom a rapid restoration of German unity was essential, and to whom the loss of the eastern Prussian provinces to Poland was unacceptable. Kurt Schumacher, who emerged as SPD leader in the Western zones and who himself had been born in West Prussia, declared in Cologne in October 1945 that 'Germany will never recognize the Oder-Neiße line, as it was determined by the four [sic] victorious powers in Potsdam, as the German border'.[76] Schumacher vehemently opposed any division of the country, claiming that it would create the basis for future wars; he condemned the handing over of the territories east of the Oder-Neiße as unwise; and he resisted suggestions that the Rhineland or the Ruhr region should be placed under international control.[77]

Although Germany's Communists took a very different public line towards the demarcation line along the Oder-Neiße, many of the hopes that were widespread among Social Democrats had their parallels among German Communists. The German Communists who managed to survive within Nazi Germany or in exile also emerged with a conviction that 'after Hitler it's our turn'.[78] The destruction of the Third Reich, many believed, would allow the dismantling of a capitalist system which, as they saw it, lay at the root of Nazism; the catastrophe which had befallen Germany would, it was felt, show Germans the error of their ways and provide new reservoirs of support for left-wing politics; and with the support of a victorious Soviet Union occupying a large portion of their country, the end of the war would be followed by the building of socialism in Germany. Nevertheless, the Communist leadership that returned to Germany from exile in 1945 did not jump at the chance to impose a socialist system immediately. Rather than support the hopes of supporters within the country who were impatient to realize sweeping visions of a socialist future, the Communist leadership was determined to rein in the radicals, impose discipline on their followers, and take their lead from the Soviet occupiers.

★

The most important Communist exiles who returned to Germany in the spring of 1945 were the members of the 'Initiative Groups' flown back to their homeland by the Russians at the end of April. Three groups of Communist functionaries arrived in Soviet-occupied Germany shortly before the surrender: the 'Gruppe Subbotka' for the north of the area occupied by Soviet forces (led by Gustav Subottka and sent to Mecklenburg-Vorpommern), the 'Gruppe Ackermann' for the south (led by Anton Ackermann and sent to Saxony), and the 'Gruppe Ulbricht' for the centre (led by Walter Ulbricht and sent to Berlin). The most important group was that headed by Ulbricht, who returned to his homeland as a colonel in the Soviet Army. They landed near Kahlau and were driven on to Bruchmühle near Straußberg (to the east of Berlin) on 30 April, the day on which Hitler committed suicide. The Initiative Groups worked together with the local Soviet military authorities, and over the coming weeks they played a key role in setting up the German administration of the Soviet zone and bringing local Communist groups into line with the wishes of Moscow. Their task was less to impose a Communist vision of Germany's future than to create a disciplined, strictly hierarchical organization which effectively would prevent the comrades on the ground from realizing their own ideas about how a postwar order might develop. On the 11th of June, 16 leading veterans of the German Communist movement, 13 of whom had just returned from a short trip to Moscow, formed a 'central committee' and made a public call for the re-establishment of the Communist Party of Germany (KPD) in Berlin. Its main centre of activity was in the Soviet zone, where it could count on the support of the Soviet Military Administration; however, the KPD associations in the Western zones also fell into line, and accepted the leadership in Berlin.

The situation faced by the Social Democrats in 1945 obviously was different. Unlike the Communists, the Social Democrats had no occupation power that regarded them as its political foot soldiers and from whom they were prepared to take orders. Many were convinced that they had emerged with moral credit and therefore had a right to shape Germany's future, whatever the Allies might think. For example, Social Democratic politician Carl Severing (who had been

Prussian Interior Minister until Franz von Papen deposed the Prussian government in July 1932, and who had remained in Bielefeld, living on a government pension, during the Nazi period) re-emerged as an influential figure in his native eastern Westphalia in 1945. There, he collided with the British military authorities, due not least to his conviction that as someone who had steadfastly defied the Nazis he deserved to be regarded not as a supplicant from a nation guilty of war and mass murder but as a claimant, pointing an accusatory finger at the Allies for their actions at Versailles in 1919 and thus their share of responsibility for the rise of Hitler.[79]

Such attitudes were understandable in the circumstances. Unlike the members of the bourgeois political parties during the Weimar Republic, the Social Democrats had not compromised with the Nazis; and unlike the Communists, who had made common cause with the Nazis during the Berlin transport strike of autumn 1932, they had maintained their commitment to democratic politics. Many had suffered in concentration camps or in exile, and felt that they had emerged with considerable moral credit, which ought to be recognized. As Otto Grotewohl, who became the leading figure in the SPD in the Soviet Occupation Zone (and who in April 1946 would lead his party into a union with the Communists in the Soviet zone to form the Socialist Unity Party of Germany), asserted in a speech to Social Democratic functionaries in September 1945, the Social Democrats regarded themselves as the sole uncompromised political force in postwar Germany.[80]

The man who quickly became the dominant figure in the SPD in the Western occupation zones was Kurt Schumacher. Schumacher, a native of Culm in West Prussia (which had become part of Poland after 1918) and a veteran of the First World War (during which he had lost his right arm), had been an outspoken Social Democratic Reichstag deputy during the dying days of the Weimar Republic, and was well-known for his uncompromising opposition to the Nazis. Now he had surfaced after a dozen years of persecution, including a decade of imprisonment in various concentration camps, which had ruined his health. On 6 May 1945, the day before General Alfred Jodl signed the unconditional surrender document at Reims, Schumacher spoke before a meeting of Social Democrats who had gathered in

Hannover to re-establish a local group of their party. While rejecting the idea of fusing with the Communists (for which there was considerable sympathy among his party comrades), Schumacher asserted that the National Socialists had been the 'servants of big capital' whose rule had led to the 'moral decay of the German people' and that 'the complicity of large sections of the population with the bloody rule of the Nazis lay in their belief in dictatorship and violence'. According to Schumacher, 'because the Germans allowed their control over their government to be removed, therefore today they are controlled by others' – control which he considered to be a prerequisite for the spiritual and moral regeneration of the German people.[81] To bring about that regeneration required 'above all, political principles of a moral nature, according to which Germany will be reorganized'.[82]

However, those who had been persecuted by the Nazis emerged in a Germany that was not necessarily keen to honour their sacrifice. Many Germans had been involved in the criminality of the Nazi regime, and many more had profited from it before the war turned against the Third Reich, leaving little popular enthusiasm for dwelling on guilt for Nazi crimes. Then, too, in 1945 most Germans were too preoccupied with the challenges of finding food, shelter, employment and missing loved ones to care very much about demands for moral or political renewal, presented by men returning from abroad or emerging from imprisonment. As a result, the reception of those who felt they offered recipes for a new, enlightened democratic future often left a lot to be desired. Decades later, Wilhelm Hoegner, who had been a Social Democratic member of the Reichstag between 1930 and 1933 and who was named Bavarian Minister President in 1945, wrote of his return to Germany from exile:

During the emigration I never doubted that the Third Reich would collapse. I prepared myself in Switzerland over a long period for the return to Germany. However, it brought a great disappointment. We emigrants had expected that the German people would welcome those persecuted by National Socialism with open arms. Instead of that we experienced only distrust, depression and bitter complaints about misery and destitution.[83]

The emotional gulf between the public figures who cherished visions of a 'new Germany' and the mass of the German people, caught between preoccupation with the challenges of everyday life amidst the ruins of their country and guilt over their involvement in the Nazi regime, was considerable. And, if they were being honest, the politicians would have had to admit that the distrust flowed in the opposite direction as well. For alongside the conviction that they had emerged from the Nazi period with a clean vest and moral credit was the recognition that millions of their fellow Germans had supported the Nazi dictatorship as long as things appeared to be going well.

Such feelings were, if anything, even stronger among the Communists, many of whom looked with suspicion on a people that, only a few years before, had supported Hitler so enthusiastically. For Walter Ulbricht, who quickly established himself as the dominant personality among the German Communists after the war, the German people were deeply suspect. They were a people with whose sons Ulbricht had spoken in Soviet prisoner-of-war camps, the young Wehrmacht soldiers who had, in Ulbricht's words, 'fantasized about "German socialism"', who had declared 'categorically that Germany had to have more "living space"', and had shown themselves generally convinced by the racist and imperialist National Socialist 'world view'.[84] They were not to be trusted. The bitterness of German Communists towards the people who had cheered Hitler so loudly until just recently oozed from the proclamation issued by the KPD when it re-emerged on 11 June 1945:

> All the more is it necessary that in every German individual the consciousness and the shame burns that the German people bear to a significant extent guilt and responsibility for the war and its consequences.
>
> Not only Hitler bears guilt for the crimes that were committed against humanity! Also bearing their portion of guilt are the ten million Germans who in 1932 cast their votes for Hitler in free elections although we Communists warned: 'He who votes for Hitler votes for war!'

Bearing their portion of guilt are all those German men and
women who spinelessly and meekly looked on as Hitler gathered
power in his hands, as he smashed all democratic organizations,
above all the working-class organizations, and let the best
Germans be locked up, tortured and decapitated.[85]

This was not simply a political manifesto after a catastrophic lost war
and occupation by foreign military powers; it also was a declaration of
mistrust and, indeed, hatred towards a people who had failed their historic test and had supported the brutal suppression of 'the best
Germans'.[86]

From the perspective of the Communist Party leadership it was not
simply the German people in general who could not be trusted.
Ulbricht and his comrades in the Soviet-sponsored Initiative Groups
were also suspicious of those – principally Communist and Social
Democrat veterans of the labour movement – who had formed the
independent anti-fascist committees in the spring of 1945.[87]
Independence of initiative was precisely what Ulbricht and his comrades, flown in from the Soviet Union, were determined to suppress.
Their main aim was to establish control, first over the Communist
movement and then, faithfully doing the bidding of the Soviet leadership, over the Soviet Occupation Zone.

It came as a surprise to many veterans of the labour movement,
who after years of persecution by the Nazi police state were eager to
realize their dreams of a new socialist order on German soil, that in
1945 the German Communist leadership resisted calls for a radical
social and economic transformation. It was not the communist rank-
and-file, or even the German leadership that had the final say about
Communist Party policy. It was Stalin.

The one novel political party to emerge in 1945 was the Christian
Democratic Union, which would become the dominant force in West
German politics in the 1950s and 1960s. During the Weimar period
and before, non-socialist politics in Germany had been divided among
a large number of 'bourgeois' parties and the Centre Party, which
regarded itself as representing the interests of Germany's Catholic

minority. The CDU, which drew together former members of the
Centre Party as well as of liberal and conservative groups and
(Christian) trade unionists, coalesced during the summer of 1945 out
of numerous local and regional initiatives. Particularly important
were those in the British zone: in Düsseldorf under the leadership of
the Christian trade unionist Karl Arnold, in Cologne by former
Centre Party politicians, in Wuppertal led by men who had played
a leading role in the (Protestant) Confessing Church, in Münster by
Archbishop Clemens August von Galen and Centre Party politician
Hermann Pünder, who had been State Secretary in the Reich
Chancellery from 1926 to 1932. The other important locus of
activity was in the Soviet zone in Berlin. There, the leading figures
were Andreas Hermes, a former Centre Party politician who had
been Reich Food Minister and Reich Finance Minister in the early
1920s; Jakob Kaiser, also from the Centre Party; and Ernst Lemmer,
who had been a member of the left-liberal German Democratic Party
during the Weimar years. Unlike the SPD and KPD, the CDU initially was more a confederation than a centralized and disciplined
political party – a 'union' rather than a 'party'. Indeed, it was not until
its first 'Reich Conference' in Bad Godesberg on 14–16 December
1945, attended by some 200 Christian Democrats from the British,
American and Soviet zones, that it finally christened itself the
CDU; and it was not until October 1950 – a year after its leading
figure, Konrad Adenauer, had become the first postwar Chancellor of
West Germany – that the CDU really became a unified party across the
Federal Republic.

The CDU looked toward a democratic society guided by social
and Christian principles. In the 'Provisional Draft for a Programme of
the Christian Democrats of Germany, submitted by the Christian
Democrats of Cologne in June 1945' – the 'Cologne Leading Principles' – a general vision for a future Germany emerged: a Germany in
which 'the spiritual worth of human beings will be recognised' (point
one), in which the family would be 'the foundation of the social order'
(point two), and in which 'justice' would be 'the fundament of the
state' (point three). Germany was to be democratic, and organized on
a federal basis: 'centralism will be rejected as un-German'. And while

'the right to property will be safeguarded', 'the dominance of big capital, of the private monopolies and concerns will be broken'. The draft
ended with the call: 'Help to construct a new and more beautiful
Germany upon the unshakeable fundament of Christianity and of
Western culture'.[88] In his memoirs, Adenauer later referred to the
'necessity of establishing a party which [. . .] stood on ethical principles
[. . .] in order to confront materialist thinking in political questions and
in order to make possible a healthy political life in Germany based not
only on the interest of individual strata and classes but on all strata of
the people'.[89]

No less important than the ideas of political groups were the perspectives offered by the clergy themselves. After the recent catastrophe,
people were increasingly prepared to look to the churches for guidance and comfort. In western Germany the immediate postwar
period saw something of a religious revival, with Catholic processions
filling the streets and the clergy enjoying considerable influence
both locally and regionally. As Damian van Melis and Joachim Köhler
have put it in a memorable phrase, with its 'proud processions
through cities destroyed by war' the Catholic Church could regard
itself as the 'victor among the ruins'.[90] As was asserted in the minutes
of the Catholic Church's Fulda Bishop Conference in August 1945,
the destruction of the Nazi regime signified 'the elimination of an
enormous danger for the Church'.[91] No less than their Catholic
counterpart, the Protestant churches emerged from Nazi dictatorship and military defeat with their belief in the correctness of their
positions and their importance strengthened. The loss of the trappings of modern industrial society served to promote the idea that
all essential problems could be solved if people would return to God
under the leadership of the church.[92] On both sides of the confessional
divide, Protestants and Catholics believed that it was necessary and
possible to create a new society on the basis of a return to religious
faith, a comprehensive 're-Christianization' of society, or the realization
of a 'Christian socialism'.[93]

The combination of the liberation of the churches from the restrictions and pressures exerted by the Nazi dictatorship on the one hand,

and of profound popular disillusionment with secular ideologies after the war on the other, meant – so leading clergy believed – that the 'hour of the church' had arrived.[94] The German population appeared to be turning away from secularism and back towards faith. The Catholic city dean in Cologne wrote in his diary on 5 November 1945, 'I have the impression that the religious consciousness that we expected in vain during the war is now slowly appearing'.[95] The clergy basked in new-found confidence. 'Does the church still have anything to tell us?' asked the Protestant Bishop of Hamburg, Franz Tügel, in his last 'war letter' on 28 May 1945: 'With one blow this question [. . .] has found a tremendously clear answer.' 'In fact', he asserted, the church was the 'only power' that had survived in one piece and, 'what is more important', was called upon to speak out in the knowledge of the 'superiority' of its message.[96] The churches had survived the Third Reich and the Second World War, while other institutions had been shattered. As Otto Fricke, who had been a vicar in Frankfurt am Main and a leading figure in the struggles of the Protestant Church with the Nazi regime, put it in August 1945, 'there simply is nothing else left but the church'.[97]

As well as the importance of religious faith during a time of extreme need, naturally the clergy now chose to emphasize the differences which had existed between the churches and the Nazis. According to the Catholic Archbishop of Freiburg, Conrad Gröber, in his pastoral letter of 8 May 1945 entitled 'Looking Back and Looking Forward', the main cause of Nazism had been secularization – a thesis which, coming from a man whose support for the Nazis and whose antisemitic utterances had earned him the nickname 'brown Conrad', neatly absolved the Church of responsibility for what had happened, and implicitly accused liberals, socialists and communists of being spiritually related to Nazism.[98] Josef Frings, the Catholic Archbishop of Cologne, maintained in his first pastoral letter after the war, on 27 May 1945, that the clergy and the devout population had kept their distance from Nazism while those in power had ignored the voice of the Church: 'Untold injustice was committed in the name of the German people by those in responsible positions as a result of their erroneous fundamental idea', and 'the entire people has suffered an untold amount for this and already has atoned for it'.[99] The German people as a whole could not be considered guilty, but the lesson of recent events was clear: 'Our German people must hear the voice of God and willingly set out on the path to a return [to the Church]'. The horrors of the recent past had demonstrated what could happen when people lost their way and ignored religious teachings. As the German bishops asserted on 23 August 1945, in their first joint pastoral letter after the war: 'An era of pure secularism has collapsed and has left us with an enormous expanse of ruins. Let us overcome these ruins, above all in penance and in a return to the Lord, our God.'[100]

Once the war was over, the clergy looked forward to a 're-Christianization' of Germany which would halt the pernicious long-term trend towards secularism. This was to be achieved not through direct political involvement by the Church but rather (in the case of the Catholic Church) on the basis of a 'Catholic mentality' generated among the laity.[101] The mood of triumphalism extended to the Church's youth work, despite the fact that the organizational structure of Catholic youth groups was in shreds.[102] This triumphalism did not necessarily encompass an appreciation of democratic participation or democratic government. A number of senior Catholic clergy, including the archbishops of Münster (Galen) and Munich (Faulhaber) remained sceptical of democracy, which some thought had opened the door to demagogy and Nazism and now threatened to do the same with regard to Communism. For them, the re-Christianization of Germany was compatible with conservative or even (in the case of Galen) aristocratic conceptions of politics.[103] For others, however, 1945 appeared to offer the opportunity to realize a 'Christian socialism'. Looking back nearly two decades later at the immediate postwar period, Walter Dirks, one of the most prominent postwar advocates of 'Christian socialism' in Germany, observed: 'Never in our lives did the opportunities and the tasks of a Christian renewal appear so great to us. Only the Allies were applying the brakes, but that, we assumed, would not last forever. Many Catholics even dreamt back then of a Christian society, of a renewal of the Christian occident.'[104] Altogether, for the Catholic Church in Germany, as one of the few institutions which emerged from the

Nazi dictatorship and the Second World War more or less intact, 1945 did not really mark a fundamental break with the past. Rather, it reinforced the self-image of a venerable institution which had survived war and Nazism and now saw the underlying truth of its teachings confirmed and its prospects for the future enhanced – a 'victor among the ruins'.

Similar opinions were expressed by leading Protestants who had been active in the Confessing Church during the Nazi period, and who also attached great importance to the idea of 're-Christianization' after the war. Protestant clergy and theologians who had voiced opposition to Nazi policies and who, in many cases, had been persecuted as a consequence, emerged in 1945 with a powerful sense of the rectitude of their path and a conviction that their time had come. The Württemberg Land Bishop – the 77-year-old doyen of German Protestants and Chairman of the Council of the newly-formed Protestant Church in Germany (*Evangelische Kirche in Deutschland* = EKD) from 1945 to 1949,[105] Theophil Wurm – spoke in October 1945 of 'a great hour for the re-Christianization of the European world' which should not be allowed to pass.[106] On 22 August 1945, shortly after his liberation from eight years in concentration camps, Martin Niemöller declared: 'The era of ideas, ideals and ideologies is at an end. We have no alternative now to building on the soil of Christianity.' Otto Fricke maintained, 'Today we stand at the end of the death dance of the ideologies. [. . .] We have a metaphysical catastrophe behind us. There is simply nothing remaining but the church.'

The triumphalism was tempered by a degree of breast-beating and introspection, however. In the Declaration of the Council of the Protestant Church in Germany – the 'Stuttgart Declaration of Guilt' of 19 October 1945 – prominent figures in the EKD (among them Wurm and Niemöller) publicly berated themselves for not having done more to assert Christian values during Nazi rule:

Certainly we fought in the name of Jesus Christ through long years against the spirit that found its expression in the National Socialist rule of violence, but we indict ourselves for not having professed our beliefs more courageously, not having prayed more faithfully, not having behaved more joyously, and not having loved more intensely.[107]

Thus the churches faced a challenge and an opportunity for a 'new beginning'. Catastrophe would lead the people back to Christ. The time had come for a 're-Christianization' of Germany and Europe and for rolling back the tide of secularism. In this, in the conviction that the 'hour of the church' had arrived, Protestant and Catholic clergy were in agreement.[108] Although hopes for a postwar 'religious renaissance' were to be disappointed, and the obsession with re-Christianization faded during the 1950s and, particularly, the 1960s, when Germans arose from the ashes of defeat in 1945 the Church offered a potent vision of the future.[109]

Not everyone was prepared to accept the self-critical approach voiced in the 'Stuttgart Declaration of Guilt'. Indeed, the evidence suggests that among the laity in the Western occupation zones (who had read press reports to the effect that the Protestant Church had recognized Germany's guilt for starting the war) the Declaration met with 'incomprehension, dismay and embittered rejection'.[110] Many regarded it as an admission of 'war guilt' which amounted to a 'second Versailles'.[111] Not all the Protestant clergy were willing to subscribe to an admission of guilt either. Many agreed with the self-reverential sentiments expressed by a group of leading clergy in Braunschweig (including the future bishop, Martin Erdmann) that 'no other estate in Germany fought against National Socialist rule so resolutely and irrespective of the associated disadvantages, distress and dangers as did the German clergy'.[112] It was conveniently overlooked that over a quarter of the Protestant clergy had joined the Nazi Party before Hitler captured power in 1933.[113] However, whether or not they were prepared to admit guilt, the clergy emerged in 1945 with little doubt in the correctness of their own position and its relevance for the future.

Although it aroused strong emotions, the Stuttgart Declaration had been rather less than a full recognition of the crimes committed in Germany's name. The Declaration was a compromise, which went too far for some and not far enough for others. The clergy, Catholic as well as Protestant, were resistant to any idea of the 'collective guilt' of the German people and were generally critical of Allied denazification campaigns – as for example when, in July 1945, the Protestant Bishop Hans Meiser and the Catholic Cardinal Michael Faulhaber in Munich made common cause to protest to the American Military Government against mass dismissals of former Nazis from public service and industry, and against the blanket condemnation of former members of the SS.[114] They chose to focus more on those who had 'suffered' as a result of denazification than those who had suffered at the hands of the Nazi regime, and it was not until 1950 that the EKD referred directly to what had been done to Europe's Jews.[115] Nevertheless, the Declaration was a sign that the centre of gravity of German Protestantism, as well as the role of the churches in German public life and politics generally, had shifted. The challenges created by Nazi dictatorship, military defeat and economic collapse, together with the occupation of the core regions of (conservative) German Protestantism by the Red Army, provided the context in which the Stuttgart Declaration could be issued (and for Protestants and Catholics jointly to support the Christian Democratic Union).[116]

Among Christian Democrats in 1945 the conviction was widespread that the 'bourgeois era' had come to an end; that, as the Catholic trade unionist Theodor Blank put it, they were entering a 'social era of a Christian character'.[117] Jakob Kaiser, who became the most prominent postwar CDU politician in Berlin, may have been exceptionally outspoken in his belief that the bourgeois, capitalist era was at end and would be replaced by a new, labour-dominated social and economic order.[118] But he was not alone. At their 'Reich Conference' in Bad Godesberg on 14–16 December 1945, the language was distinctly socialist: the resulting resolution spoke of 'nationalization', of the 'equal participation of employees in the steering of the economy', and of 'socialism based on Christian responsibility'.[119] Calls for 'Christian socialism' and for the 'extensive nationalization' of industry[120] drew broad support among those who formed the CDU in 1945. Although the party turned away from such rhetoric in the years to come – Konrad Adenauer, the CDU's leading figure in the Western zones, had never had much time for 'Christian socialism', and observed perceptively in 1946 that 'we win five people with the word socialism and twenty run the other way'[121] – the rhetoric played an important role in the formation of what proved to be the most successful political party during the first two decades of the Federal Republic.

The visions of Germany's future which emerged in 1945 and which guided many Germans in their political and their religious lives in the aftermath of Nazism and war, reflected two sets of attitudes. On the one hand, as among the Allied occupation authorities, among German politicians and, to some extent, church leaders, a strong current of distrust coloured attitudes towards the German people – a people many of whom had endorsed militarism and imperialist conquest, abandoned civilized values, engaged in crimes without parallel in modern European history, supported a dictatorial regime (at least until the tide turned against it), had betrayed the true interests and representatives of the working class, and turned their backs on the churches and the word of God. So, the argument went, the creation of a brave new world on German soil after the demise of Nazism would require safeguards to ensure that this would not happen again. On the other hand, the 'zero hour' of 1945 offered an unprecedented opportunity to create a better world in which German militarism could be rooted out, civilized Western values and democracy be reimposed, socialism be built upon, the interests of working people be properly represented, and a moral and religious renewal achieved. The determination to build a new Germany – democratic, peaceful, socialist, and morally regenerated – rested on a deep conviction on the part of anti-Nazi German politicians, Allied political leaders, local activists and clergy that they had been proved right: that the cataclysm which had engulfed Germany and Europe had confirmed the correctness of their beliefs.

This combination of distrust and hope, of deep-seated fears and optimistic visions of the future, framed the ways in which people imagined and planned Germany's future in 1945. In the event, neither the worst fears about the future nor the most optimistic hopes for fundamental renewal were realized. In the years that followed, Germans proved themselves neither so dangerous nor so visionary as many had imagined in 1945. However, the visions of the future that circulated in Germany in 1945 shaped the ways in which German societies and politics developed in the second half of the twentieth century.

11

THE GREAT DISORDER

The collapse of 9 November 1918 was a storm in a teacup compared with the typhoon of the year 1945. Rudolf Paul[1]

Every couple of minutes, every couple of lines, no matter where I start I end up with the same sentence: everything is uncertain, everything is in suspense, there is nothing solid under one's feet, in one's hands. Victor Klemperer[2]

Traditionally, Germans had associated themselves and their country with order. In 1945, however, they were confronted by disorder at every turn: through the violence of the last months of the war, the destruction of infrastructure, the collapse of public administration, the huge influx of refugees and the arrival of millions of foreign occupation troops. Germany was a country in which conventional family and sexual relations were undermined, crime was epidemic, and youth were perceived to be running wild. The population was 'defeated, disillusioned, demoralized'.[3] In almost every respect, it seemed – in Victor Klemperer's words – that 'everything is uncertain, everything is in suspense'; that there was 'nothing solid under one's feet, in one's hands'.

Fundamental to this feeling of uncertainty was the lack of public safety. The German police may have terrorized their own people as well as foreigners before the Third Reich collapsed, but they did constitute a significant disincentive to commit ordinary crime. Now that check on criminal behaviour was swept away, quite literally: the German police largely vanished as Allied troops arrived. In the Ruhr region, for example, few policemen were left when Allied forces appeared: in Essen only 470 of 1670 remained, in Duisburg only 147 of 1230, in Oberhausen all 500 left, and in Wattenscheid the police fled, taking police vehicles, typewriters and other equipment with them. In Cologne, whose police force had numbered 2,700, 'not a single policeman was found remaining' when the Americans occupied the city in March 1945.[4] Generally, in the weeks immediately after the war the police suffered a huge loss of status and authority.[5]

The immediate consequence of the disappearance of the Nazi police state was the wave of looting committed not only by the foreign labourers who emerged to take advantage of their erstwhile masters but also by Germans themselves.[6] While Germans may have expected such behaviour from foreigners, their image of themselves had been rather different – that of an orderly, law-abiding people. Now they not only had to fear foreigners and occupation soldiers; they also had to fear one another. Altogether, those charged with combating criminality after the collapse of the Third Reich faced a crime wave without modern precedent in Germany. Looking back at the challenges they faced between 1945 and 1948, the 'new democratic police' in Saxony, in the Soviet zone, reported that the extreme social hardship after the war had brought 'an increase in criminality to four to five times the criminality before the war'.[7]

No less than the threat of crime, the acute housing shortage contributed mightily to the sense of there being 'nothing solid under one's feet'. Millions of Germans had lost their homes as a result of evacuation or bombing, or because they fled the onslaught of or, later, were removed by Allied military authorities. The loss of homes was invariably accompanied by the loss of household effects, from furniture to cutlery, which in many cases could not be replaced for years. The lack of space which people could call their own made it difficult if not impossible for Germans to reconstruct orderly lives. Consider the predicament of one family in the city of Darmstadt, which had largely been destroyed by the British bombing raid in September 1944, leaving some 12,000 people dead and 70,000 homeless:

> The father was conscripted and the boy, Willy [who was five years old when the war ended], lived together with the mother and a sister who was two years older than he. During the major attack on [the night of] 11/12 September 1944 the family fled from the cellar of the bombed house. The mother and Willy gathered the next morning with a sister-in-law and the grandmother, who also were bombed out. Enquiries about the sister remained fruitless, she was not found again. The family salvaged nothing; only the sister-in-law still possessed some bed-sheets and two suitcases. During the day they stayed out in the open, at night they slept in a cellar. The mother brought the boy and the grandmother to relatives in the countryside in Württemberg. She herself came back, worked in Darmstadt, and together with the sister-in-law got a room in a house whose occupants had been evacuated.
>
> The place where Willy lived with the grandmother was shelled during the fighting [in 1945], and both became homeless and were sent back to Darmstadt. The city refused to accept them. After lengthy disputes, permission was granted. The thus expanded family – sister-in-law, grandmother, mother and Willy, now live together in one room, they have two beds among them.
>
> When the house [in which they had the one room] was occupied by [Allied] soldiers, the boy lost his accommodation for the third time. The family moved into a [. . .] cellar in the neighbourhood, that with difficulty was made somewhat liveable. In the autumn [of 1945] the father returned from captivity.[8]

For the remainder of 1945, nine months altogether, the family lived in that cellar, until they finally managed to move into a flat. One may argue that homelessness as a consequence of war was the sad fate of millions around the globe during the twentieth century, and that what Germans experienced in 1945 was not unique, as many of them may have felt. However, it is difficult to imagine a greater contrast than that between the extreme disorder of 1945 and what most Germans had enjoyed in the years prior to 1942 (when the bombing started in earnest) and which they continued to regard as normal. How could families which had been split up during the war, had lost their homes and possessions, and been forced to live in cellars after the war, re-establish order in their everyday lives?

The challenge of recovering a sense of order and normality was all the greater in a society which had been largely denuded of young men and become overwhelmingly female. Colossal military losses had turned millions of German women into widows. In the summer of 1945 nearly 8.7 million German POWs were officially in the hands of the Allies; roughly 40 per cent, or nearly 3.5 million, of them were married.[9] Once released from POW camps, by no means did they all return home. Some were interned by the Allies for denazification, while others were among the thousands of civilians sent off to the USSR at the end of the war; and some decided not to return to their families but chose instead to start new lives elsewhere. Thus, when the war came to an end millions of couples were separated, millions of families were incomplete, and millions of German households were headed by women.

This provided the context in which a desperate search for 'normality' in family life and sexual relations ensued.[10] Such normality was not easy to find. As was recognized at the time, defeat had led to what might be termed a crisis of masculinity. German men had fought and lost a world war; if they survived, returning husbands did not necessarily find a welcoming, intact family ready to embrace them. German women, in the meantime, had had to get used to living without men, managing their households, providing for their families. Not a few husbands returned home to discover that their wives were living with other men or had given birth to children that could not have been theirs.[11] Some women had taken up with soldiers of the occupying armies; others had set up households with 'uncles'.[12] Years apart had often dissolved emotional bonds between husbands and wives, and for small children who had never really known their fathers, there were no bonds to be dissolved. In households which had been run by women, the return of a man who may have been ill, disabled and emotionally disturbed, was not necessarily welcome; the one-time 'head of household' was frequently a burden rather than a support in a time of desperate need. Instead of re-integration into family, household and community, for many men who survived the war the postwar transition brought new dislocation and a shattering of hopes to re-establish roots. As one woman, 14 years old when her father returned after the war, recalled: 'He could have stayed away; . . . he'd been away for six years; . . . he was, so to say, superfluous for us.'[13]

Not long after the end of the war one observer noted :

Six years of war, during which wives had to shift for themselves and increasingly replaced men in almost all fields of economic activity, had gone a long way in developing their self-confidence and self-reliance, in violation of the Nazi-fostered traditional subordination of the German wife to the husband. The military defeat of the regime which had stressed 'manly virtues' automatically decreased the respect women held for men in general and for their husbands in particular. The returned soldiers themselves were largely dispirited and unable to orient themselves in the chaotic post-defeat conditions, thus further impairing their prestige, but still expected their wives to revert to pre-war patterns of the German husband-wife relationship. Men having been indoctrinated to feel as 'supermen' were, in varying degrees, unable to deal in a dignified manner with the occupation forces in the role of subordinates, often discrediting themselves in the eyes of their wives through awkward obsequiousness.[14]

Defeat, imprisonment, loss of employment, and the presence of millions of foreign men in uniform meant that the habits and values that had framed male-female relationships in Germany were shaken. Perhaps most disconcerting were the effects of sexual relations –

whether rape or 'fraternization' – between German women and occupation soldiers. Whether they took German women by force or by favours, foreign soldiers undermined the position of German men.

More generally, the field of sexual relations seemed to offer ample evidence of a disintegration of the social and moral order. One observer later described the immediate postwar period as a time of 'anarchy in Germany';[15] 'the complete dissolution of all order' had led, so it seemed, to an epidemic of 'indiscriminate sexual intercourse'. Far from (re-)constructing conventional households, many people cut themselves loose from the moorings of orthodox morality. According to one physician, looking back in the mid-1950s at the behaviour of his compatriots in the wake of the war, 'In these conditions it was often people who had barely met, who never again in life would see one another . . . who engaged in unrestrained sexual intercourse'.[16] Apparent confirmation of this 'unrestrained sexual intercourse' and the general moral decline was the sharp postwar rise in illegitimate births. As after the First World War, the percentage of births in Germany that occurred out of wedlock increased noticeably after the Second: in 1946 the proportion of illegitimate births – the product of liaisons during 1945 – stood at 16 per cent, twice the level recorded in 1945. In January 1946, 27.4 per cent of all births in the Western occupation zones were illegitimate, in February 25.6 per cent and in March 20.9 per cent.[17] (By the end of the year the figure had fallen back to 14.5 per cent.) In fact, however, the rise in illegitimate births was rather less shocking than it seemed: a substantial proportion, estimated at between 30 and 40 per cent, of the children born to couples unmarried at the time of the birth were made legitimate by the subsequent marriage of the parents. (In addition, about one sixth of the children born out of wedlock in western Germany during 1946 were 'occupation children' – children whose fathers were in the occupation forces – and their numbers declined sharply in subsequent years.)

Alarm about the social and moral order was exacerbated by the spread of venereal disease. This was nothing new. Concern about a breakdown in morality and about an alleged epidemic of venereal diseases had been widespread in Germany during and after the First World War.[18] After the Second World War, when conditions were far more chaotic than after the First, such concern was as predictable as it was prominent. Typical was the assessment contained in a report from the district of Anklam (in the Soviet Occupation Zone), in which it was alleged that 'after the war the number of people with venereal disease grew almost without limit, brought about by the licentious lifestyle and the immorality which had spread generally'.[19] Occupation authorities were anxious that German women, having lost their moral compass and in severe economic distress, would infect soldiers; and German police formations, set up under Allied control, devoted considerable energy to making raids on places where people gathered who were the prime suspects for spreading sexually transmitted diseases.[20]

Allegedly immoral and criminal behaviour, and the alarm it provokes, is typical of the aftermath of war, and memories of what had occurred in Germany after defeat in the First World War were revived after defeat in the Second.[21] One German judge in Saxony-Anhalt (who wrote that he was 'familiar with the conditions from the year 1919'), asserted that the overcrowding of prisons – which, in the Soviet zone, had mostly been taken over by the NKVD – was 'a consequence of the sunken morality of a people after the war'.[22] Police in the Baltic Sea resort of Kühlingsborn, in the district of Rostock in Mecklenburg, writing in December 1945 attributed the postwar increase in crime to both the 'overcrowding of the community with refugees' and 'the general lack of restraint' among those who, faced with hardship, lacked inhibitions about stealing food and household goods.[23] In his study of 'German postwar criminality', published in 1949, Karl Bader wrote of the 'disintegration of all orderly running of the state' that had undermined the rule of law.[24] Military collapse, economic paralysis and the 'complete decomposition of the running of the state' had, in Bader's opinion, led to a collapse of authority and morality.

Not surprisingly, much of the anxiety about 'the general lack of restraint' centred on the young. Raised in the Third Reich, indoctrinated in Nazi schools and the Hitler Youth, having experienced dislocation and violence during the war, having lost homes and family members, and with millions of fathers either dead, missing or in prisoner-of-war camps, roughly one quarter of all German children grew up after the Second World War without fathers (among the refugees from the east the proportion was even higher)[25] – the young, it seemed, had been cut loose from their social and ethical moorings. Particularly worrying were the consequences of the collapse of the school system. Across Germany schools had been closed down in the last months of the war as children were evacuated from cities and towns; school buildings were destroyed in the bombing or requisitioned by the military or as housing for refugees from the East. In many places school buildings no longer were usable when the war ended, and in some towns few if any children remained who might attend school. School directors and local-government officials voiced concerns about the 'demoralization of youth' while the schools remained closed.[26] In the extreme case of Cologne, the schools had been closed at the beginning of October 1944. When the greater part of Cologne (i.e. on the left bank of the Rhine) was captured by American forces on 6 March 1945, almost no children were left in the city; and while Cologne's elementary schools re-opened in July and August, high schools did not reopen until late November and middle schools not until 20 December.[27] (Cologne's vocational schools did not open their doors again until March 1946.) There also were few teachers available. At the end of the war many had been rounded up by Allied forces and put into prison camps, where they had to wait for their cases to be heard by denazification tribunals before being allowed to teach again.[28] This often meant that after the schools re-opened in the second half of 1945 and schoolchildren returned to cities from which they had been evacuated, the shortage of teachers grew more acute.[29] In addition, little was available in the way of school materials – notebooks, pencils, textbooks. Tremendous efforts were made to re-open German schools at the beginning of October, but even then huge problems remained. In Stuttgart, for example, at the end of 1945 there were 35,000 pupils in the city's schools but only

368 teachers and 418 classrooms, creating a pupil-teacher ratio of nearly 100 to one.[30]

The absence of educational provision exacerbated what many regarded as an epidemic of criminality and a loss of moral bearings among a younger generation devoid of hope for the future or trust in their elders.[31] The police, reflecting public concern, targeted young people regarded as in danger of embarking on a life of crime and immorality, and devoted particular attention to young women believed likely to become involved in prostitution.[32] In the British Occupation Zone, social services were empowered to place 'roaming' minors, and those who could demonstrate no fixed abode, into 'labour camps' designed to provide adequate oversight and 'educative development' while preventing 'large masses' from negatively influencing one another.[33] Justifying draft legislation for work-education in 1946, the 'Youth Office' in Hamburg cited 'the constantly increasing demoralization of youth and juvenile criminality [which] today after the Second World War has taken on infinitely greater and more crude forms': youths did not register promptly with the authorities as they should; they showed up at work only long enough to get ration cards; they did not bother to work at all and instead lived from the black market; they engaged in theft of food and in burglary, which 'served to finance a life beyond law and order'. Dangerous habits had become ingrained as a result of separation from family and leading a nomadic existence: 'They already have become so very used to vagrancy and vagabondage that they know how to avoid all rules and order from the outset'.[34]

It was deeply disturbing that young Germans displayed little inclination to behave as their elders and political leaders may have hoped – in the Soviet Occupation Zone no less than in the Western zones. In Saxony, a Communist youth secretary bemoaned the 'regrettable desire of young people just to dance'; and in Berlin, Communists were so appalled by the numbers of young people 'hanging around' bars and dance halls that they sought to ban those under 16 from entering drinking establishments.[35] At a conference of some 55 Communist 'youth functionaries' in Berlin in late July 1945 Heinz Keßler, who had spent 1941 to 1945 in the Soviet Union and was destined to become the last Defence Minister of the German Democratic Republic, complained:

> The level among young people is so low; we have to find new ways to approach the youth. It is clear that the youth are not yet enthusiastic about what we want. Every girl mainly is preoccupied with the thought 'how will I get a man, where can I best spend my evening?' (Dance, variety shows, etc.) Among the male youths it is similar. They don't want to work at all.[36]

While German youth appeared to be running out of control and crime was reaching epidemic proportions, the new German police formations permitted to operate by the Allies remained undermanned, ill-equipped and largely untrained. They lacked weapons, motor vehicles, fuel, working telephones, or police files. In Braunschweig, in the British zone, at the beginning of June 1945 the regular municipal police numbered only 464 as compared with 621 during the war, and only 31 of them (7 per cent) had been trained as police; the criminal investigative police numbered only 43, as compared with 75 during the war; and the postwar police did not gain access to firearms until mid-December.[37] In Magdeburg, in the Soviet zone, during the autumn of 1945 a German police force of slightly over 1300 people possessed a mere 13 firearms altogether, and the number of police officers who were dismissed between the occupation of the city in mid-April and late September was greater than the total strength of the force.[38] This was hardly a recipe for effective law enforcement. Furthermore, where crime was perpetrated by soldiers of the occupying armies, the German police were powerless to intervene. Although violence and theft by occupation soldiers was most pronounced in the regions occupied by the Red Army, the problem was not by any means limited to the Soviet zone. In the Western zones as well the police remained unarmed during the second half of 1945, were empowered only to deal with the German population, and therefore could offer little protection to Germans against acts of violence committed by members of the occupation forces or by displaced persons.[39]

But it was the conduct of the occupying troops in the Soviet zone that left the lasting memories of violence and disorder. Ralf Dahrendorf has spoken of the 'supreme, horrible moment of lawlessness' in the Soviet sector of Berlin in the summer of 1945.[40] This shocked and dismayed German Communists, who had hoped for class solidarity rather than wanton violence from the soldiers of the socialist motherland. One local Communist Party group in Berlin complained in late June that 'the occupation by the Red Army has developed into a real scourge. Not a day and not a night passes but that bands of bandits in Red Army uniform perpetrate attacks like looting, rapes. [. . .] The "police" responsible here constitute a "farce" and, as they are unarmed, can do nothing to counteract it!'[41] From Köpenick, in the south-east of Greater Berlin, the local Communist Party complained in July that the Soviet military authorities were not doing enough to control their troops, that 'the looting of flats in which predominantly workers and minor white-collar workers live, is a daily occurrence'; fruit was being stolen off the trees, cyclists were shot and their bicycles stolen, German police guarding coal stores had been fired upon, and 'rapes too are a daily occurrence'.[42] The result was 'a feeling of insecurity among the population'. German women found that going about their daily affairs and doing their jobs could be very dangerous. In Dresden, the director of the local transport company complained to the city's mayor in December 1945 about the dangers that women conductors faced when working in the evenings on the city's trams, where 'both they and female passengers have been threatened with guns: Recently a woman passenger was dragged from the car and away into the darkness. A female conductor was threatened with a gun and dragged to an apartment, where she was raped. After finally being released at 1.30 at night, she encountered a group of soldiers and was again raped three times.'[43] In the weeks and months after the Nazi regime collapsed, Germany remained a disorderly and dangerous place.

The hazards facing the German population during the second half of 1945 were not only a matter of physical violence. Scarcely less threatening were the consequences of the dire state of Germany's health care system. Hospitals had been bombed and medical staff killed – or dismissed by the Allied military authorities; poor nutrition left the population vulnerable to disease. In Stuttgart, for example, by the end of the war almost half the city's hospital beds had been lost as a result of wartime destruction, and of those remaining the American military government requisitioned more than 200 for its own use at the end of July 1945; medical equipment and drugs (in particular, sulpha drugs) often were lacking; doctors were in desperately short supply, leaving many hospital wards with no medical staff; the incidence of infectious diseases such as diphtheria, tuberculosis and – especially among returning prisoners of war – typhus, rose alarmingly; diabetics faced a shortage of insulin on the one hand and a diet which consisted of carbohydrates on the other; drug addiction was on the rise.[44] And, perhaps most disturbing of all, infant mortality rose steeply, with some places reporting a doubling or trebling of the numbers of infants who died in 1945 as compared with 1939.[45]

A lack of institutional anchors marked the 'interregnum',[46] the roughly six months during which Allied military forces were establishing their occupation administration but before the future shape of occupied Germany became clear. Rather than being able to depend on the orderly functioning of a state bureaucracy and service sector, Germans were thrown back on their own meagre resources. Social services and educational provision collapsed, the German criminal justice system and courts were, effectively, abolished, and the prisons were removed from German control.[47] During the weeks after the German surrender banks remained closed, and for months after they finally reopened the amounts which people could withdraw from their savings remained restricted. (The accounts of government and Nazi Party organizations remained closed, as did the accounts of people who had been taken into custody by the occupation authorities.)[48] Uncertainty about the future, the lack of a firm foundation upon which to build, was debilitating. Ludwig Vaubel, of the chemical concern Vereinigte Glanzstoff Fabriken, noted in his diary at the end of August 1945 that 'the political uncertainty' left no room for 'initiative to be taken'; people were unable to adapt to the new necessities. 'There has been too much disappointment', he wrote; 'after the mobilization of the last emotional reserves', people had sunk into 'apathy'.[49] Similarly, Karl Bader observed that 'the tension that became unbearable in the last months of the war [had been] replaced by a depression that bordered on lethargy'.[50] Many Germans had little energy to do anything beyond what was necessary to keep their own heads above water.

Nevertheless, for all the difficulties that Germans faced in the wake of war, it would be mistaken to picture their country uniformly as a site of utter chaos, in which everyone sank into apathy and depression. In some parts of occupied Germany – in rural regions which had neither been bombed nor laid waste in the fighting in 1945 (e.g. in the countryside in the south west) – life continued more or less as before. More generally, the fact that the war was over, that the bombing had ceased, that the killing largely had stopped and, not least, that the weather was warm, gave grounds for a certain optimism. No longer did everyone constantly have to fear for his or her life. At last it seemed possible to rebuild. The summer months saw a number of improvements in daily life: Restrictions on the movement of Germans began to be lifted; the first trains began to run, even if intermittently, and local transport resumed service; churches again opened their doors to the faithful; newspapers began to appear under Allied military control; the first radio broadcasts were made; cinemas, insofar as they had not been destroyed during the war, re-opened for business and the first postwar theatre performances were held; postal and telephone services were reintroduced.[51] Life was far from normal, but the first steps were being taken towards recovering a sense of normality.

In Hildesheim in Lower Saxony, the Social Democratic head of the regional government administration, Wilhelm Backhaus, described the rather optimistic popular mood that had followed the end of hostilities:

During the spring everyone who looked at things candidly and impartially had to come to the conclusion that the immediate future would bring nothing but distress, grief and tremendous deprivations to our people. [. . .] The summer and the early autumn appeared to disprove these dismal prognoses – at least in our region. The forces of reconstruction were making them-

selves felt everywhere. Many industries started peacetime production surprisingly quickly. Things were available in the shops
that one had not seen for years. Traffic revived, the railway was
operating everywhere. Liberated from the depressing fear of
death and from the paralyzing political pressure [of Nazism], the
people began to be happy to be alive.[52]

Yet there remained a dark side to this upbeat assessment: the sum-
mertime mood reflected not just the warmer weather and the
resumption of economic activity; it also revealed an element of xeno-
phobia and hostility towards the 'unwelcome guests' who were
blamed for much of the upsurge in crime: 'Again and again people
have said during this summer, it would be better only if the foreigners would disappear.'

Of course, the most important determinant of popular morale
was – and would continue to be during the coming months and
years – the 'stomach question'. As Backhaus reported for the
Hildesheim district, 'in the summer many of us have eaten better
than in past years'. However, that happy circumstance, and with it the
public mood, soon changed. The 1945 harvest was extremely poor,
one of the worst for decades.[53] The causes were manifold: the fighting during early 1945 which had damaged large amounts of
farmland, lack of fertilizer and farm machinery, the sudden exodus of
foreign farm labourers, the loss of farm animals, and heavy rains in
late August which left potatoes and grain rotting in the fields.
Furthermore, after the loss of the largely agricultural provinces east of
the Oder-Neiße, western and central Germany no longer could draw
upon the agricultural surplus from the east. It has been estimated that
in the Soviet zone roughly 30 per cent of all farm machinery had
been either destroyed or so damaged as to be unusable as a result of
the fighting;[54] and Anton Ackermann memorably described the desperate conditions in parts of the countryside in the Soviet zone when
he returned to Germany from the USSR in 1945: 'Entire villages
were deserted, the livestock driven away or dead, the barns empty or
burnt out.'[55] In the British Zone, where the problem of feeding the
population of the Ruhr industrial region was particularly acute, the

rye harvest of 1945 was 44 per cent below that recorded in 1943, wheat 42 per cent down, oats 35 per cent and potatoes 45 per cent.[56] The forecasts were dire. In Hildesheim Wilhelm Backhaus claimed that 'now one already can calculate when the German people will starve if its former enemies do not come to its aid'. Similar predictions were made in the Soviet zone. In Leipzig in August 1945, the veteran Communist, Fritz Selbmann (then First Secretary of the Communist Party in Leipzig), noted anxiously that 'today we do not yet know whether we can feed our people during the coming winter. Today we literally are fighting one day to the next for our daily bread.'[57]

Everywhere one turned during the autumn months, there seemed to be increasing grounds for pessimism. The considerable achievements of the summer months – the rapid repatriation of the majority of the foreign labourers in Germany, the fact that occupation had been accompanied by neither guerrilla warfare nor mass starvation – were either overlooked or taken for granted. Instead, it was the mounting problems that drew attention: the numbers of German refugees coming from the east grew; the already acute housing shortage became steadily worse as the population increased; thanks to the poor harvest, the quantity of available food diminished. Industry lacked the energy supplies necessary to guarantee production, and shortages of heating fuel became critical as the weather grew colder; unemployment mounted as prisoners of war began returning home; and now there was an 'iron curtain' separating the Western occupation zones from neighbouring regions to the east. Not surprisingly, popular morale plummeted. Backhaus reported from Hildesheim:

The flood of bad news has turned many of our inhabitants into desperate pessimists. Precisely those people who previously did not want to see the difficulties have lost their heads. Again and again one hears of suicides, nervous breakdowns and hopeless depression.

Hopes, which had risen during the summer, that one might begin to build again and bring some order to profoundly disordered lives, were

Young German soldiers are marched off to Soviet prisoner of war camps,
Berlin, early May 1945

Corpses are taken from the Dachau concentration camp compound to town on farmers' carts for burial as American soldiers look on, May 1945

The remains of dead concentration-camp inmates from the camp at Wöbbelin are reburied on 8 May 1945 in nearby Schwerin with the German population looking on

Soviet soldiers pose for the camera in Adolf Hitler's office in the Reich Chancellery in Berlin

American soldiers are awarded combat medals in Germany after the war. Here General Jacob Devers, commander of the Sixth Army Group, presents the author's father with the Bronze Star in the centre of Heidelberg, 29 May 1945

An American prisoner of war camp near Regensburg, May 1945. Here female Wehrmacht employees as well as male soldiers were kept prisoner in the open air, with separate compounds for men and women

Cleaning up afterwards: women clear the street after a bombed-out building is detonated on Unter den Linden

The end of the last Nazi government: Alfred Jodl, Albert Speer and Karl Dönitz are taken to the Flensburg Police Presidium after their arrest on 23 May 1945

Former Nazi leaders in Allied captivity. From left to right: Hermann Goering, Alfred Rosenberg, Baldur von Schirach (in the background) and Karl Dönitz

The new American President Truman meets Stalin and Churchill at Potsdam, July 1945

French Prime Minister Charles de Gaulle reviews a military parade in the centre of
Freiburg in Breisgau, 4 October 1945

Refugees carting their belongings through the streets of Berlin, 23 August 1945. Note that the group is composed of women and children

Graves in the courtyard of a block of flacks near the Kurfürstendamm in Berlin, 1945

One of many children in the children's centre at Kloster Indersdorf whose photographs were published in newspapers in the hope that surviving family members might locate them. The Indersdorf centre was established by UNRAA for homeless children in an abandoned cloister near Priem am Chiemsee in Bavaria dashed. The disorder of 1945 was not simply a matter of the chaos and destruction left when the war ended in May 1945; it also reflected the problems that grew in seriousness during the last months of the year.

In early 1946, Backhaus drew a sketch of popular feeling among the German population in his region at the beginning of the year, which provides something of a balance sheet for 1945:

Characteristic for the majority of them is a feeling of profound numbness; emotionally they have not yet got over the collapse of last spring, indeed one can say that they have not yet comprehended the significance of those events at all. They still frantically cling to the more than vague hope that the former familiar rhythm of life will return, and regard what is unfolding at the moment more as a bad dream from whose gloomy images they can escape again when they awake. This is entirely understandable, as the misfortune that has befallen every individual is so unspeakable that it exceeds all measure. The people appear so tired and without hope [that] most are devoid of any emotion, to say nothing of being in a condition to make plans again for the future.

Thrown into the maelstrom of a general collapse, the individual sees only his own fate. The city-dweller stands before the ruins of his house, laments the loss of his furnishings that for him, in most cases, were not only the external trappings of his existence but an indissoluble part of his own life as a result of the memories associated with them. Even worse for families is loss of relatives who have not returned from the war, the death of fathers, brothers and sons as well as the agonizing feeling of uncertainty about the fate of the prisoners of war and the missing, of those about whom there often has been no news for years. Added to this pain about what has been lost irretrievably is the agonizing worry about their own future. Countless people have had to give up their former occupations, in part for political reasons, in part, however, also as a result of the complete dislocation of economic conditions. [. . .] Precisely when one appreciates what work signifies for most Germans does one grasp

the emotional condition of these people. For their vocation was
not only a means for them to earn money but was at the same
time the essential content of their life.[58]

For refugees from the east, and for soldiers who survived the war but
could not return to former homes east of the Oder-Neiße frontier
or in the Sudetenland, the prospects for bringing order back to their
lives appeared even more remote. For millions of Germans, torn
from their moorings, 1945 really did constitute a 'zero hour'; for a
people who had been addicted to order, the great disorder of 1945
seemed a bad dream from which, try as they might, they could not
yet awake. We now know that Germans would be able to dig themselves out from their 'zero hour' during the coming years, but the
shadow left by the disorder of 1945 could not be swept away easily
or in only a few months. Small wonder then that the German
people focused almost completely on their own suffering, and gave
little thought to the terrible consequences of Nazism and war for
others.

   One might have thought that the preoccupation with their own
difficulties at least would have promoted a sense of social solidarity
among Germans themselves. However, rather than drawing them
together, the chaos of 1945 appears rather to have had the opposite
effect. Largely cut off from the wider society and faced with huge
challenges in their daily lives, people looked out for themselves and
cast suspicious eyes on others. The struggle to find enough to eat,
shoes and clothing, and fuel to heat draughty overcrowded
dwellings, fostered not solidarity but envy. Germans kept a jealous
watch on what their neighbours received: 'everyone had the feeling
that they themselves had got the short straw, that they had been
treated unjustly'.[59] The ubiquitous resort to the black market, the
need to 'organize' the acquisition of food and other scarce
commodities, the frequent forays of urban dwellers into the countryside to steal from farmers' fields, meant that the normative
constraints and moral codes of ordered society were eroded and
transgressed. Self-discipline seemed to have evaporated; money (as
after the First World War) lost its value; the black market replaced

orderly and regulated exchange; greed replaced morality. Heinrich
Böll wrote of this period:

> Everyone possessed just their lives and, in addition, whatever fell
> into their hands: coal, wood, books, building materials.
> Everyone justifiably could have accused everyone else of theft.
> Whoever did not freeze in a destroyed city had to have stolen his
> wood or his coal, and whoever did not starve had to have
> obtained food or had food obtained for him in some illegal
> manner.[60]

Theft became a way of life, accepted as necessary while at the same
time eliciting deep unease. The black market became an essential element in the daily struggle of a hungry population for survival in the
ruins of their cities, and was beyond the power of either the occupation authorities or the newly formed German police forces to control.
Raids against black-market traders in public places merely succeeded
in driving illicit trading into cellars, pubs, people's homes and back
gardens. It is no wonder that Germans emerged from the upheaval of
1945 with a craving for security, stability, property and the satisfaction
of their own material needs.

The hardship and disorder that confronted Germans in 1945 not
only undermined social solidarity and led people to focus almost
exclusively on their own individual, personal horizons.[61] This also
allowed them to bury their memories of the earlier stages of the war
when Germany had conquered, exploited and profited from an entire
continent whose inhabitants had been treated with indescribable brutality. A report of a Communist Party activist in Berlin from October
1945, in which she described attitudes among returning German
POWs, offers a revealing picture of how Germans viewed their frac-
tured world and their own place in it:

> While speaking with returned prisoners of war [. . .] I observed
> how demoralized these people were. I regard it as my duty to
> report this. [. . .] The prisoners of war feel absolutely no guilt for
> the present-day conditions; they claim for their part only to

have done 'their duty'. Had they refused to do so, the same thing would have been done to them as was done to the political prisoners of the concentration camps. The interest in discussing this is very low. In the first instance they are interested in their dwellings: Are the windows glazed, the walls repaired, the doors firm, is the roof covered? Then comes the stomach question. What have we got to eat? Are we getting enough food? Why don't we get our rations of fats? For them it is important: Do we have enough fuel? How do I get some? For the time being they are not interested in doing work. They want to have 'their rest'; we still have money and can bide our time. The incidents by the Red Army with women, the looting of dwellings, etc. they do not at all regard as reaping what was sowed by the Nazi hordes in the countries they attacked. Mention of the incidents [*Vorkommnisse*] in the course of the Jew-action [*Judenaktion*] is brushed aside as completely misrepresented and exaggerated. The call about the importance of a trade union or political organization is completely rejected by many with the remark 'we want nothing more to do with politics'.[62]

The experience of Nazism and war, and particularly of the hardships in 1945, did not inspire most Germans to seek to build a better world, as some idealists may have hoped. Instead Germans concentrated largely on their own problems, and viewed themselves as powerless and innocent victims of forces beyond their control – of the arbitrary and sometimes violent behaviour of the Allied occupation troops, of desperate shortages of food and housing, of the upsurge in crime which accompanied the end of the war, of the seeming collapse of a social and moral order. The profound disorder that faced the German people after the Nazi regime collapsed, allowed them to leave the Third Reich behind without having to confront their own role in it. The historian Bernd Martin, in a personal account of the end of his and Germany's Second World War, summed it up well fifty years later: 'In the way they regarded themselves and in the stories of older people, at the end of the war the Germans were only victims and never previously perpetrators as well. Their own crimes were repressed in the chaos of the upheaval and subsequently kept secret.'[63] In this sense, 1945 was indeed a 'zero hour' for millions of Germans. The 'chaos of the upheaval', the great disorder of 1945, swept away uncomfortable memories of the Nazi period and left Germans with an overwhelming desire for order and normality in their own lives. In the event, it was the great achievement of the West German Republic to be able to satisfy that desire in the years to come.

12

PAYING FOR WAR AND PEACE

As soldiers we said with gallows humour, one should enjoy the war; as the peace would be terrible. Egon Bahr[1]

What manner of Germany can emerge from so much confusion and uncertainty? Economically there can be little doubt that ruin lies ahead. Ruin there will be whatever the Allies do, for probably not even the most superb organization could avoid disaster this winter. The Economist[2]

Everyone's primary duty is to work. Düsseldorfer Mitteilungsblatt[3]

When the Second World War ended in Europe, the German economy was at a standstill. During the preceding three decades Germans had experienced hyperinflation and a savage depression, but never had they experienced anything like this. On 11 May 1945, the 72-year-old Theodor Spitta (soon to be installed as deputy mayor in Bremen) wrote in his diary:

Astounding that so large a city as Bremen can live for weeks without public utilities, without means of transport, without news transmission, without supplies of food and fuel, as good as without shops and workmen, without schools and without courts. One does not spend any money because there is nothing to buy, the banks and financial institutions also are closed. In addition there also is uncertainty about the currency.[4]

In May 1945, economic activity in Germany appeared to have come to a complete stop.

It was against this background that the Germans now faced the unenviable prospect of having to pay for a lost world war. The cost was enormous. The victorious Allies were determined that Germany would pay for the damage caused by her aggression, and that she would never again be allowed to develop an economic base from which she could launch another war. At Yalta, Churchill, Roosevelt and Stalin had agreed in general terms that a defeated Germany would have to pay for the damage caused to the Allied nations during the war; and at Potsdam agreement was reached that 'the German economy should be decentralized for the purpose of eliminating the present excessive concentration of economic power as exemplified in particular by cartels, syndicates, trusts and other monopolistic arrangements'; the 'primary emphasis' was to 'be given to the development of agriculture and peaceful domestic industries', and 'average living standards' in occupied Germany were to be maintained at levels 'not exceeding the average of the standards of living of European countries'.[5] A more agricultural, decentralized postwar economy was to provide a basic standard of living and allow Germans to deliver reparations, but no more.

Unlike after the First World War (when Germany had retained her unity and her sovereignty), this time reparations were to be paid in goods rather than money. At Yalta, general agreement had been reached that Germany 'pay in kind for the war losses caused by her to the Allied nations in the course of the war' and that these reparations would be extracted from Germany's national assets, from the delivery of goods from German production, and from the use of German labour. At Potsdam agreement was reached as to how this should be carried out. Soviet reparation claims were to be met in the main by 'removals' of assets from the Soviet Occupation Zone and 'from appropriate German external assets'; the reparation claims of the United Kingdom and the United States were to be met from resources in the Western zones and from foreign assets. In addition, '15 per cent of such usable and complete industrial capital equipment [. . .] as is unnecessary for the German peace economy' was to be removed from the Western zones in exchange for food and raw materials, and another 10 per cent was to be transferred to the Soviet Government without payment.[6] (The Potsdam Agreement stipulated that 'reparations should not be extracted from Austria', although reparations could be extracted from German 'external assets' in Austria.)

Although the extraction of reparations and the dismantling of industrial capacity is associated in the popular mind with the Soviet occupation, factories in the Western zones would not be left untouched. Following from the Potsdam Agreement, towards the end of 1945 some dismantling of plant and equipment took place in the British and American zones for shipment to the USSR. (This ceased in 1946, as relations between the USSR and the West deteriorated.) The distribution of reparations was hammered out at the Paris Reparations Conference, which sat from 9 September until 21 December 1945 and in which 18 countries – but not the USSR or Poland – participated. However, Germany's new masters did not wait until December before carrying off plant and machinery: not just the Russians but also the French – who were not present in Potsdam and did not regard themselves bound by the provisions of the Potsdam Agreement – engaged in 'wild' removals during 1945.[7] In the years that followed, the dismantling of industrial plant took place with varying intensity in all four occupation zones, but most assiduously in the French and, especially, the Soviet zones.[8]

The costs of a lost war made themselves felt in other ways as well. The Nazi regime had financed its war not only by raising taxes, but also by resorting to printing money and, of course, to the brutal exploitation of a conquered continent.[9] In August 1942 Hermann Göring famously declared: 'The Führer repeatedly said, and I repeat after him: if anyone has to go hungry, it shall not be the Germans, but other peoples.'[10] But Germany's extraction of resources from a conquered continent came to a crashing end in 1945. Now the Germans would go hungry – although they would not face mass starvation as the Nazi regime had envisaged for millions of inhabitants of a conquered eastern Europe. After their country was occupied by the victorious Allies, not only were the Germans no longer able to profit from the exploitation and misery of other Europeans; they now would have to meet the costs of Allied occupation and to pay reparations at a time when not just German industry but also German agriculture were at rock bottom.

What followed was a food crisis of major proportions. That Germany would face a crisis of food supply had been foreseen before the Wehrmacht collapsed. During early 1945 there had been anxious discussions and dire predictions within the civil and military leadership of the Nazi regime. In mid-February, while millions of hungry refugees were streaming into what remained of Germany, urgent concerns were raised about the consequences of the loss of eastern regions – East and West Prussia, the 'Wartheland', Silesia, Pomerania and the Courland – which comprised more than 30 per cent of the agricultural land at Germany's disposal.[11] It was reckoned that, with significant cuts in their rations, Germans could be fed into the summer; however, the prognosis for the period thereafter was 'considerably more unfavourable'.[12] Hinrich Lohse, Nazi Party Gauleiter of Schleswig-Holstein, Reich Commissar in the Baltic and 'Reich Defence Commissar', summed up the discussions with the observation that 'we no longer can prevent that the people go hungry, only [prevent] that they starve'.[13] The Reich Food Ministry calculated in late February that, even should the Wehrmacht manage to re-capture Germany's eastern regions, the extent of war-related damage was such that cuts in food rations of roughly a quarter would be unavoidable.[14] And Germany was not about to get the eastern regions back. In so far as they were able, Germans – both civilian and in uniform – drew the obvious conclusions: they hoarded food as the end approached. A Security Service report from early April noted: 'What is happening at the moment is real hoarding, like we know from the wretched memories from the time of the [First] World War.'[15] Germans' memories of the First World War still framed their perceptions of the Second.

★

The grave threat to the country's food supply emerged as predicted once the Nazi regime collapsed. On 11 May 1945, just a few days after the Wehrmacht's unconditional surrender, the 'Leading Minister of the Caretaker German Reich Government', Schwerin von Krosigk, sent an 'aide mémoire' to the Supreme Commander of the Allied Armed Forces, Dwight Eisenhower. In it he listed 'those questions [. . .] whose immediate tackling and sorting out appear necessary to the caretaker Reich Government'. At the top of the list was the food situation, in particular the threat of a 'food catastrophe' in areas of southern and western Germany that had been dependent on food arriving from agricultural regions in the east.[16] As after the First World War, when Germany had lost large tracts of agricultural land in the east, after the Second Germans were convinced that without the agricultural surplus regions in what had been eastern Germany it would be difficult, if not impossible, to feed the population.[17]

In the weeks immediately following the German surrender, however, food rations could be met by using up the existing stocks of wholesalers, farmers' shipments, and supplies previously distributed or confiscated from Wehrmacht stores. Furthermore, although the amounts of food distributed via official channels were not great, they could be supplemented by what people themselves had put by.[18] Indeed, at the time of the surrender many Germans (at least in the west) saw things in a remarkably positive light – which made the sharp decline in food supplies and in living standards which set in from late 1945 all the more disconcerting. In Bremen Theodor Spitta observed in early June that popular attitudes, particularly with regard to food supply, were 'dominated by illusions':

Because the population was furnished with some supplies in April and salaries, pensions and benefits for surviving dependants mostly were paid out some time in advance, and there also was hardly a chance to spend money, the population felt tolerably well for some weeks after the conquest, the more so since the air attacks ceased – at least in so far as people were not totally robbed of their homes or robbed by the Americans.[19]

However, the illusions soon were to evaporate. Spitta went on to note that 'now the defeat is starting to have its effects in its entire dreadfulness'. But that was only the beginning. As had been predicted in February 1945, once winter approached food shortages became critical. Disrupted transport links left some regions desperately short of food. For example, the area around Trier was particularly hard hit in the winter of 1945/46, when all transport links to the Rhine were cut, rations were reduced to 600–800 calories per person, and local inhabitants trekked to Koblenz (some 140 kilometres distant) on foot or by bicycle in order to buy bread.[20]

Behind the acute local or regional problems lay a chronic food deficit. At the beginning of the war, Germany had been able to meet 83 per cent of her food requirements from domestic production, with the rest supplied through imports. During the war, the shortfall was met by taking food from territories occupied by the Wehrmacht. After the war, however, occupied Germany was not in a position to trade industrial products for food and no longer was able to extract agricultural produce by force from the rest of Europe. At the same time, the loss of the provinces east of the Oder-Neiße meant that what remained of Germany was cut off from regions of agricultural surplus – regions which, while they had been home to only 13.8 per cent of the population of the German Reich in 1939, had contained 26.7 per cent of the agricultural land and had provided 25.4 per cent of the country's grain, 25 per cent of its sugar beets and 29.7 per cent of its potatoes.[21] Furthermore, millions of German refugees had fled from the Sudetenland and territories east of the Oder-Neiße (with more to come), and they had to be fed.

The looming 'food catastrophe' stemmed both from the loss of farmland in the former eastern Prussian provinces and the need to feed the millions of German refugees. Another contributing factor was the decline in the amount of land being cultivated in what remained of Germany. During the war, the amount of land in Germany sown to crops had been reduced by the building of roads, military exercise grounds and airfields. With more mouths to feed and less land in cultivation, the number of people to be fed per hectare of cultivated land increased substantially after the war – in 1946 by roughly 16 per cent in the British zone and in the American zone by nearly 26 per cent, as compared with 1939.[22] In Bavaria, 671,000 hectares were sowed with grain in 1945/46 as compared with 796,000 in 1937/38; the land sown for potatoes in Bavaria fell during the same period from 316,000 hectares to 264,000.[23] In Brandenburg, in the Soviet zone, broad areas in the vale of the Oder could not be cultivated because they had been laid with land mines, and some 20,000 hectares of fertile farmland could not be cultivated for lack of draught animals and machinery.[24] Across the country farm buildings had been destroyed, fields had been mined, and the number of working farms had declined.

In addition, agricultural production was hampered by severe shortages of fertilizer, machinery, fuel, and farm animals. For example, in the French Occupation Zone – which, of the four zones of occupation, had suffered the least war damage – the number of horses in December 1945 was some 8 per cent less than it had been in December 1938; the number of cattle was down by more than 14 percent; and the number of pigs was barely two fifths what it had been seven years previously.[25] The figures for the (much larger) British and American zones were similar: while the number of cattle in 1945 had declined somewhat (by nearly 8 percent, as compared with 1935/1938, in the British zone, and by about 3 per cent in the American zone), the numbers of pigs had dropped sharply (by 55 per cent in the British zone and 44 per cent in the American zone).[26] In the three Western zones taken together, the number of pigs and chickens in December 1945 was less than half what it had been before the war (although the number of sheep and horses was rather greater).[27] The amount of fertilizer used in the Western occupation zones in 1945/46 was a mere fraction of what it had been in 1938/39 – in the case of nitrogen and phosphorous fertilizers in the British and American zones it stood at barely one tenth of the 1938/39 levels.[28]

It is no surprise that the size of harvests plummeted. In the French zone in 1945, the total harvest of bread grain was less than half that in 1938, and of potatoes only slightly more than half (56.6 per cent). Altogether the 1945 harvest was sufficient to cover only little more than half of the zone's food requirements (in an area which, before the war, could meet three quarters of its food needs).[29] To the east the decline in the harvest was no less drastic. In many parts of Saxony, the fighting in early 1945 had interrupted spring cultivation, and the resulting harvest of grain stood at only 51 per cent, of potatoes at 49 per cent, and of sugar beets at 50 per cent of the average during the years 1935/1939.[30] No doubt these figures are underestimates; the thriving black market cannot be explained otherwise, and it is clear that German farmers withheld a substantial amount of their produce from the compulsory deliveries demanded of them. For example, in November 1945 the Land President of North Baden, Heinrich Köhler, informed the French Military Government in Karlsruhe that, among other things, milk deliveries were less than half what they should have been, farmers were slaughtering cattle without permission, and 'the delivery of eggs is so poor that in cities the sale of eggs for practical purposes does not exist'.[31] Nevertheless, the overall harvest figures point to a sharp decline in agricultural production, and the efforts of farmers to evade making compulsory deliveries only contributed further to the food crisis which was enveloping Germany.

More difficulties arose during the second half of 1945 from shortages of farm labour. This might seem odd, since the population in the British, American and Soviet occupation zones grew substantially after May 1945 with the arrival of millions of Germans from the east. However, the refugees consisted disproportionately of women, children and the elderly, rather than people necessarily capable of heavy farm work. The sudden departure of the millions of foreign labourers who had toiled in Nazi Germany, some 2.7 million of them on farms (comprising almost half the employed labour force in agriculture in August 1944),[32] left a huge gap at a time when millions of young German men were either dead or in POW camps. This made it difficult to bring in the 1945 harvest on farms often run by women without sons, husbands, or the help of foreign labourers who had played so important a role during the war.

The problems of food supply were not limited to poor harvests. It also proved difficult to get the food which had been harvested to the consumers who needed it. The disruption of transport infrastructure – the paralysis of the rail system and, particularly, the lack of motor vehicles – hampered delivery from the surrounding countryside of desperately needed food to the hungry inhabitants of Germany's bombed-out cities. For example, in June 1945 potatoes could not be brought into Hamburg because only a fraction of the required vehicles were available for use.[33] The creation of borders between the occupation zones made the problem worse – as in Lübeck in the British zone, which suddenly found itself cut off from the nearby agricultural regions of Mecklenburg which, from July 1945, lay in the Soviet zone.

It was in the British Occupation Zone that the problems of food supply were most critical. Not only was it the most populous of the four zones; it also contained the largest concentration of heavy industry and many of the most important targets of the Allied bombing campaign. What is more, as Germans returned to cities from which they had been evacuated or fled, the population of devastated industrial regions increased rapidly: in the Rhine Province the number of people in receipt of food ration cards grew from 3,979,000 to 5,473,000 between the beginning of July and September 1945.[34] Somehow they had to be fed. Emergency measures needed to be taken. Unlike their Soviet counterparts, the British were neither politically predisposed to impose radical changes on the ownership of agricultural property nor were they prepared to implement policies which might undermine food production. Therefore, in the summer of 1945 the British implemented 'Operation Barleycorn', releasing roughly 300,000 German POWs to gather in crops – a programme which proved so successful that it was repeated soon thereafter to release POWs for work in mining and transport. In consequence, more than a million German POWs had been released in the British zone by August 1945 (and almost all of the roughly three million POWs in the British zone had been freed by June 1946)[35] – a policy in marked contrast to the actions of the Soviet or French military, who kept many of their German POWs captive for years. For the British, the desperate need for labour to deal with the three key areas of bottleneck in the postwar economy – agriculture, mining and transport – took priority. Economic pragmatism trumped politics, and it proved remarkably successful.

★

Despite the fears expressed during the early months of 1945 and despite the economic paralysis which accompanied the end of the war, in the immediate aftermath of the German military collapse the food situation had appeared relatively favourable. In many rural regions, the fighting on the ground and the destruction of railway lines had prevented farmers from delivering up all their 1944 harvest, which meant that many held considerable stocks in reserve. Perhaps more important, especially for inhabitants in the cities and towns, was the fact that the stores which the Wehrmacht had located throughout the country had not been emptied by the rapidly retreating German troops. In some areas, for example in Schleswig-Holstein, extra rations were distributed to the civilian population out of military stores as the front came nearer, to ensure that the supplies did not fall into the hands of the Allies.[36] After the surrender, former Wehrmacht stores provided foodstuffs which local administrations, installed by the Allies, were able to distribute.[37] During the late spring of 1945 these supplies provided an important source of food for the civilian population.

However, the civilian population did not wait patiently to receive its allocation of food. Once their towns had fallen to Allied armies, many Germans stocked up by looting. With the end of a police state which had enforced draconian penalties for looting, Germans (as well as foreigners in Germany) raided Wehrmacht stores, warehouses and shops, taking as much as they could carry. Accounts of the end of the war from across the country all tell a similar story. On 18 April 1945 an officer with the American Psychological War Department (PWD), Lt. Daniel Lerner, submitted a report to the head of the intelligence service of the PWD at SHAEF on conditions in areas in western Germany which just had been liberated; in it he surveyed the vast extent of the looting by both foreign workers and Germans, observing that 'in every town' one could see German men and women carrying shopping bags full of spoils taken from homes or shops.[38] Germans did not wait for the Allies to arrive before they began stealing. In Munich, for example, the plunder had started a couple of days before the Americans arrived: the city's Food Office gave the green light for the Volkssturm-Battalion 101 to remove 500 bottles of brandy and 1000 kilograms of cooked meats from city stores, and a 'Fighting

Group Schwarz' managed to make off with 4000 tins of sausage meat.[39] Without an Anti-fascist Committee able to keep looting in check (as had been the case elsewhere, for example in Leipzig), people took advantage of the power vacuum at the end of the Nazi regime to steal huge amounts of food. A year later the *Süddeutsche Zeitung* in Munich described the scene at the end of April 1945:

> In the food storerooms during this brief period they were wading in sugar, spirits, rice, barley, wheat, coffee, milk; the supplies of entire armies wandered out of the warehouses into the hands of looters of all nationalities. The [looting] campaign took place [. . .] in all parts of the city wherever supplies were stored: cheeses were rolled out from railway goods stations through the streets, the Arzberg Cellar stood knee-deep in wine in which drunken women were lying. The greed no longer could be restrained.[40]

Greed it may have been, but this also meant that when the war came to an end many Germans were surprisingly well fed.

The epidemic of looting was accompanied by an upsurge of hoarding – what Germans labelled as acting like hamsters (*Hamsterwesen*). Prohibited under the Nazi regime, hoarding emerged as a national habit amidst the breakdown in security and order during the immediate postwar period[41] Often ill-disposed to obey the decrees of German administrators working under Allied supervision, and in the absence of armed and effective German police forces, people looked to the considerable stocks held by farmers, whose access to the market otherwise was limited due to the dire state of the transport network. Farmers, who under-reported their harvest (which, if fully reported, they would have had to deliver to the authorities), and town dwellers with large amounts of paper money in their pockets, together undermined Allied attempts to impose a measure of economic planning and order. As a result a large, if undetermined, proportion of the postwar German economy was covert.

Of course, the food gained by looting and hoarding at the end of the war would not last forever, and domestic food stores were soon

exhausted. Consequently, the food catastrophe which had been predicted in the first half of 1945 began to materialize in the second half.
The unhappy change was described in stark terms by Wilhelm
Backhaus when he reported on popular morale in the Hildesheim
region in this part of the British Occupation Zone during the last
quarter of 1945:

> During the summer many of us have eaten better than in recent
> years. Through the distribution of [food from] the stores, people
> got many things that provided a welcome improvement on the
> meagre official menu. In addition, for a few weeks the produc-
> ers and distributors no longer believed that the [compulsory]
> delivery and ration-card economy would remain in place. Much
> produce that one should have saved for the winter was given
> away or eaten up with irresponsible imprudence. Now the extra
> supplies and [reserve] stocks are absent. One again has to make
> do with the prescribed rations. People will find that the more
> difficult the better they have eaten during recent months. Thus
> one suddenly can hear people again talking everywhere about
> the meagre diet. Worries are returning that one believed had
> been forgotten.[42]

Germans now would have to survive on the inadequate amounts of
food allotted to them by their ration cards. Initially, the Allies maintained the food-rationing system inherited from the Nazi regime.
This had divided the population into three groups: those who could
provide completely for themselves, those who could provide partly for
themselves, and those – in the main city-dwellers – who were termed
'normal consumers'.[43] Over and above this, the Nazi regime had
allotted additional rations for people doing heavy physical work and
those working long and night shifts. However, after the Allies arrived
the German economy was largely at a standstill and in some places
little was available to distribute as rations.[44] What is more, the administrative machinery needed to operate a ration programme had largely
collapsed: government employees no longer were at their desks and
government offices were without windows, doors, electricity, water,

furniture or typewriters.[45] Thus, it was not really until the autumn of 1945 that new schemes for food rationing could be put into practice.

As during the war, postwar rations were fixed according to what people required in order to work (with those engaged in heavy labour entitled to more generous amounts) and, in some cases, according to where people lived (with city dwellers receiving more generous rations).[46] The introduction of postwar rationing programmes coincided with the marked deterioration of the food supply, while the official rations provided barely enough to live on – and that only if people could supplement the amounts from other sources. In August 1945 the Americans set an official ration for normal consumers of 1550 calories per day; however, despite imports of grain from abroad, the amount of food actually distributed soon fell to less than 1000 calories per person per day.[47] In the French Occupation Zone, rations were to provide 1100 calories for the 'normal' person in October 1945, 1339 in November (as the weather grew colder) and 1350 in December. Yet this did not necessarily mean that these rather meagre amounts were available. In late 1945 and early 1946 only a portion of the amounts foreseen in the ration scheme actually were delivered: in Trier this stood at just 893 calories per person in November, 1100 in December and a mere 616 in January 1946.[48] In the Soviet Occupation Zone, refugees from the east faced a particularly difficult time: there the distribution of ration cards to refugees initially was forbidden, and they were forced to purchase food at high prices on the black market; when refugees in camps finally did get ration cards (from October 1945), they received only children's rations – which in November stood at about 1200 calories per day in Berlin and 1040 calories per day in Brandenburg.[49]

The combination of rationing and growing food shortages had a number of important consequences. It meant that Germans were constantly hungry and often incapable of hard physical labour.[50] It lowered people's resistance to disease; many Germans (especially 13–18-year-olds) were chronically underweight;[51] and there were large increases in infant mortality. (In Trier, for example, during 1945 nearly one third of infants died in their first year.)[52] It also meant that people in each region tried to keep as much food as possible for themselves, thus undermining cross-regional economic cooperation and integration, a phenomenon described as 'food separatism' during the postwar period.[53] And the situation allowed the distribution of ration cards to be used to discipline people. In Berlin, for example, the decree on compulsory labour and registration issued by the city administration on 29 May threatened the removal of ration cards from those who failed to register with the police; police raids resulted in the 'unemployed' being picked up on the street and delivered to labour offices or to places of work; women who declined to take up paid work were left with the paltry rations they might receive as a housewife – the 'hunger or ascension [ration] card' – which did not really provide enough for survival;[54] and, in October, the Berlin city administration announced that food ration cards would be removed from anyone who did not obey the instructions of the labour office and that anyone who failed to appear at work without an adequate excuse would have their food-ration category reduced.[55] These measures caused considerable popular discontent – discontent which, however, could not find effective public expression because of the absence of any political forum for its articulation. Germans were not only without food, but also without rights.

The food crisis that had been predicted in early 1945 did not really materialize until the winter of 1945/1946, when it came to overshadow almost everything else. During the summer of 1945, with the vast majority of surviving Wehrmacht soldiers still in Allied captivity, with Germans still eating what they had acquired from Wehrmacht stores and other illicit sources, and with warm weather and the fruits of the 1945 harvest becoming available, the full force of the economic collapse had not yet made itself felt. Instead, there was a time-lag; the hunger that was a consequence of the war arrived during the following winter.[56] Germans would not really face the economic costs of fighting and losing a world war until their first postwar winter.

Alongside the problems of food supply, another huge obstacle to economic recovery and threat to living standards was the acute shortage of coal. The German economy, like most European industrial economies during the first half of the twentieth century, was largely coal-based. Coal was the main fuel both for German industry and for domestic heating. Lack of coal, combined with the severe damage done to a rail network necessary to shift coal from where it was mined to where it was burned, crippled the German economy in 1945. Indeed, when the fighting stopped in May, in the British zone – which held Germany's most important coal reserves – only 1000 of 13,000 route-kilometres of railway track were serviceable and not a single permanent bridge had been left intact across the Rhine.[57] During the first four months of 1945, as Allied bombing reached its peak and Allied armies captured Germany's coal-producing regions (beginning with Upper Silesia in the east and then the Ruhr and Saar regions in the west), German coal production declined rapidly, and by the time the Wehrmacht surrendered it had almost collapsed. Whereas in May 1944 monthly extraction of anthracite had amounted to 13,247,000 tonnes, by January 1945 the figure had fallen to 6,591,000 tonnes and by April to a mere 715,000 tonnes.[58] By the end of the year it had recovered to 4,946,000 tonnes, but still was only about two fifths what it had been a year and a half earlier.

A principal cause of low coal production during 1945 was the sharp drop in labour productivity. At the end of 1945, the number of workers employed in coal-mining in the British and American zones was marginally higher than it had been in 1936.[59] Yet the quantities of coal extracted remained far below pre-war levels. In December 1945 the average daily coal production in the British and American zones was less than half what it had been in 1936 (and that after a near trebling of production as compared with July); and in 1946, output per employee in the British and American zones was still just slightly more than half what it had been in 1936. Efforts were made to attract men to the pits with promises of better food rations, in the Soviet zone no less than in the British zone.[60] Yet the problems remained. Not only were workers tired and undernourished; they also tended to be older than their pre-war counterparts had been, and the new miners attracted to the pits with offers of better food rations were often poorly qualified for the task.[61]

Despite the disruptions that closed down businesses, and despite the

influx of millions of refugees from the east, labour shortages in various areas were a problem during the immediate postwar period. Huge
amounts of repair work needed to be carried out, particularly in the
cities, and it could prove difficult to find the necessary skilled workers – bricklayers, carpenters, roofers and the like.[62] Many things
contributed to the problem: the internment of millions of German
prisoners of war, the lack of transport facilities which made it difficult
for people to get to work, the shortage of housing in bombed-out
cities where coal needed to be extracted and repairs needed to be carried out, the movement of Germans from cities into the countryside
where they might more easily find something to eat, the attractions of
living from black-market trading rather than from productive employment, and the desire of many people to rebuild shattered personal lives
before taking up paid work. Although the receipt of ration cards was
made dependent upon registering at labour offices, there remained
sizeable numbers of 'shirkers' and 'loafers' who used false papers and
avoided lawful employment. In 1945 it was not always easy to per-
suade Germans to return to steady work.

Nevertheless, during the second half of 1945 those who would not
work were more than outnumbered by those who could not work.
Altogether, the loss of the former eastern regions of Germany, combined with the wartime destruction of industry and transport
infrastructure, effectively removed an estimated 4.7 million jobs from
the German economy – that is, about 15 per cent of the positions in
Germany when war was launched in 1939.[63] Allied dismantling of
German industry led to further losses of employment opportunities –
although, it should be remembered, the dismantling itself provided
work for substantial numbers of Germans, both in the Soviet zone and
in the Western occupation zones, as German workers were frequently
compelled to dismantle their own factories for delivery to the Allies.[64]
While labour shortages arose in some cities and, not least, on farms,
the collapse of transport infrastructure, coal shortages and the closure
of many factories in the spring of 1945 meant that large numbers of
Germans were without work whether they liked it or not.

Large firms now engaged only a tiny proportion of their former
employees. In Ludwigshafen, when the giant BASF chemical works

resumed production on 15 May, the number of its employees stood at a mere 800 as compared with 37,400 two years previously.[65] Uncertainty, and interference by the occupation authorities – not only in the Soviet zone – undermined efforts to get businesses up and running again and made it difficult for them to offer steady employment. To take one example, that of Giulini in Ludwigshafen and Wutöschingen (in the French zone, near the Swiss border), an aluminium smelting company which had profited considerably from the armaments boom under the Nazis: Giulini had employed roughly 500 workers in 1936, a figure which rose to 1570 by 1944. On 26 June 1945 production started again on a modest scale, but a couple of weeks later, on 12 July, raw materials held by the firm were seized by the French. Production of aluminium pots and pans began again at the end of August with what raw materials remained. However, Giulini fell into difficulties once again in October, when the occupation authorities seized more than half its aluminium stocks and shipped them off to France.[66] Such disruption, caused by seemingly arbitrary actions on the part of the occupation powers, together with the enormous problems left when the Nazi regime came crashing down, played havoc with business, production and the labour market.

Things were not made any easier by the fact that, after the defeat, payment in Reichsmarks offered poor reward when set against high black-market prices or, as was often the case after the German surrender – when there was little or nothing to buy. In mid-July, when the question of raising wages for building workers was discussed in the Senate in Bremen, one member noted that 'the problem of the aversion to work cannot be solved from the wage side but only from the goods side. A worker now works two days [per week] for food and one day for the rent; for what he earns on the three remaining days he cannot buy anything.'[67] The erosion in the value of the Reichsmark meant that working for wages lost much of its incentive. One contemporary observer noted:

> Wages in Reichsmarks therefore no longer are an incentive to working. Qualified skilled workers seek out and find employment for example with the occupying power, which attracts

[them] with goods in kind, but in positions which in no way correspond to the worker's training. Many youths, whose training in any event is deficient as a result of the long period of war, initially do not even try to get a job but instead tread the same path as the older comrades or to the black market. The employees who actually work in the places allocated to them skip shifts because otherwise they do not find the time to get additional food and the fuel necessary to maintain a household, something that is vastly [more] complicated than before the war. Standing in queues, making repairs to household utensils that normally would have been thrown away, and to dwellings, swallow up a quarter of the normal working and leisure time of employees. Many devote themselves only to [their] domestic circumstances, avoid any work, live from savings or are supported by relatives.[68]

The disorder in the labour market also reflected the geographical shifts of the German population as the war came to its end. Although Germany's war losses had been enormous, the flight of millions of Germans from the Sudetenland and the territories east of the Oder-Neiße meant that in much of occupied Germany the population was substantially greater after the war than it had been before: in 1946 the population of occupied Germany totalled roughly 65,930,000, as compared with 59,764,000 on the same territory in 1939.[69] Alone of the four occupation zones, the French zone contained marginally fewer people after the war than before: whereas in the British zone the population was 11.3 per cent higher in 1946 than it had been in 1939, in the American zone 17.1 per cent greater, and in the Soviet zone 22.7 per cent greater, in the French zone it had diminished by 4.1 per cent.[70] However, even where the postwar population grew substantially, Germans capable of doing heavy work – healthy men in their twenties and thirties – were in short supply. In the British and American zones the proportion of the population in 1946 comprised by men between 25 and 29 years of age was roughly half what it had been in 1939, and among men from 30 to 39 it had declined from 18.0 to 12.9 per cent;[71] and in the Soviet zone, the total proportion of the population classified as capable of work in 1946 stood at 60.1 per cent, as compared with 67.1 per cent in 1939, while the absolute number had declined from 11,244,000 to 10,865,000 during the same period.[72]

To turn from human capital to plant and machinery, it should be remembered that, despite the damage caused by bombing and dismantling by the Allies, German industrial capacity remained substantial when the war ended, but precisely how substantial is impossible to determine, and available estimates are far from exact. The dreadful scenes of destruction in 1945 gave an impression of far greater damage than was necessarily the case; the fact that a factory building was largely destroyed, for example, did not always mean that the machinery which had been housed in that building was no longer usable. Those who made estimates of the losses often had their own interests to protect. For their part, the Allies had a stake in underestimating the degree of destruction of manufacturing capacity, not least because by doing so they would have greater scope for demanding reparations. German entrepreneurs and trade unions, on the other hand, had an interest that was just the opposite, for the greater the estimates of the damage the less attractive a factory would be as a candidate for dismantling.

For western Germany, when all the losses caused by the war and its aftermath were taken into account – the damage caused by bombing and military action on the ground, the return of property which had been stolen by the Germans from other countries during the war, material looted at the war's end, the disruption caused by the shifts to and then away from war production, and the consequences of the war-related damage and labour shortages for the optimal use of productive capacity – it has been estimated that between 10 and 25 per cent of industrial capacity was destroyed, depending on the industry. Even in the heavily bombed Ruhr region the losses amounted to probably no more than 30 per cent.[73] These are not insubstantial losses, but they are lower than many people assumed, and suggest that most of Germany's industrial capacity survived the war. Such was the conclusion reached by Ludwig Erhard, later the architect of West Germany's 'social market economy' and Konrad Adenauer's successor as Federal Chancellor, when he surveyed conditions in his native town of Fürth in May 1945. Erhard noted that Fürth's industry had suffered 'relatively minor damage' from Allied bombing and on the whole remained 'immediately serviceable': 'The factories that had been partly damaged are, after being overhauled at short notice and after bringing up stocks from elsewhere, [. . .] ready for production.'[74] This was an assessment which no doubt could have been made in many German towns in 1945.

In the immediate postwar period it was less the wartime destruction of plant and machinery than the problems of transport and shortages of raw materials, in particular of coal, that held back industrial production. For example, despite massive bombing, the giant Krupp factories emerged in the spring of 1945 with their production capacity largely intact. A director of the Krupp works in Essen informed American occupation officers in May 1945 that steel production in the Ruhr could increase to two thirds or even three quarters of wartime levels if the necessary coal, transport facilities and labour were available; according to Moses Abramovitz (who later became a Professor of Economics at Stanford University), the American who drafted a report of impressions gathered during travels through western Germany at the time, the 'surprisingly good' condition of the Krupp factories made such positive assessments appear 'not unrealistic'.[75] (This happy state of affairs at Krupp would not last for long, however: at the end of the year, Krupp's steel works in Essen–Borbeck, one of its most modern, was dismantled and shipped off to the USSR.)[76] Similarly, Abramovitz observed that the three major industrial installations of I.G. Farben in Frankfurt, including the Hoechst chemical factories, showed almost no damage.

Another German industrial giant that emerged from the war in remarkably good shape was Daimler-Benz. Despite the effects of intensive Allied bombing, the dispersal of machinery from the company's main factories in and around Stuttgart meant that, according to one estimate, only about 15 per cent of its machine tools had been destroyed and the substance of the company essentially remained intact.[77] Although Daimler-Benz received permission to resume motor-vehicle production on 11 December 1945, the firm did not produce motor vehicles again until 1946; it had to restrict itself during the second half of 1945 to car-repair work and the manufacture of household goods, engaging only a fraction of the numbers employed a year earlier. However, it had retained large amounts of capital and was in a strong position from which to recover.[78] A similar picture emerged at the giant motor-vehicle factory at Wolfsburg, which in the 1950s would become the flagship of West Germany's 'economic mir=acle', producing the Volkswagen beetle. Although bomb damage had been substantial, it had not really affected the factory's productive capacity since much of its machinery had been dispersed and the looting in April 1945 had been limited; altogether, it was estimated at the time that more than 90 per cent of its machinery had remained usable and more than 80 per cent had not been damaged at all.[79] Production re-started gradually, and between the end of the war and the end of the year the Volkswagen factory produced 1785 cars. At the end of the year it was employing over 6000 people.[80]

Smaller companies were disrupted in the same ways as larger ones. A revealing example of the ups and downs of smaller industrial firms during 1945 is the case of the Cologne firm of Felten & Guilleaume, which manufactured cables. According to an assessment by the management, its factories had been up to 70 per cent destroyed. Nevertheless, the management drew some rather astounding conclusions about what remained after the dust had settled: 'Despite the many heavy air attacks and the incessant artillery fire during the period from 5 March to 11 April no machines in the Cable Factory 1 were destroyed'. They went on: 'As a result of the large stocks of supplies [. . .] that were saved almost without loss [. . .], there were no particular difficulties with regard to raw materials for the year 1945.'[81] Felten & Guilleaume received permission from the occupation authorities to resume production on 15 July 1945, and appears to have started operating again the following day. The biggest problems facing the company during the second half of 1945 were recovering the machinery dispersed during the war, finding sufficiently skilled labour, and acquiring the building materials necessary to repair the factory (including glass for windows as winter approached). The fortunes of the firm were reflected in the numbers of people it employed: At the beginning of 1945, on 2 January, 318 people (177 men and 141 women) had been employed in its Cable Factory 1; on 28 February the number was 304 (174 men and 130 women); when production resumed in mid-summer the factory employed only 56 people (53 men and 3 women); but at the end of the year, on 29 December, 235 people (157 men and 78 women) again were working in the plant.[82]

For many industries and many towns, the greatest economic disruption in 1945 resulted not from the wartime destruction but from the sudden stop to war production and the intervention of the occupying powers. When the war ended, firms that had expanded substantially to meet the requirements of the Nazi war economy suddenly had to shift their focus to civilian goods, in so far as this was permitted by the Allies. In the process large numbers of employees lost their jobs. For some this was hardly a tragedy: the German war machine had relied on the labour of millions of foreign workers, both civilians and prisoners of war, who now could return home. Some Germans who lost their jobs in industry in the spring of 1945 were able to find temporary employment in agriculture.[83] However, for many the end of the war meant – alongside an end to daily threats to life and limb – unemployment and economic insecurity.

For both businesses and their employees the changes that occurred in 1945 were substantial and abrupt. In Hamburg the giant Blohm & Voss shipyards had been sealed off immediately after the arrival of the British on 3 May; on 21 May they re-opened with 500 workers, who busied themselves with removing armaments from ships and renovating them as fishing vessels, repairing steam turbines, and producing cooking pots, weigh scales and suitcases; and by August Blohm & Voss was employing 2500 workers.[84] However, the strategy of the brothers Rudolf and Walther Blohm of making their firm 'interesting for the English' and 'indispensable as soon as possible' did not succeed: Blohm & Voss had to close in December, and began to be dismantled in the spring of 1946. In Stuttgart, the firm of Bosch also abruptly shifted its manufacturing in May 1945, from war production to 'simple household utensils', including cooking pots, frying pans, plates, meat mincers and sieves for making Swabian noodles (*Spätzle*). By the end of the year, Bosch had dismissed not only 5510 foreign labourers but also 8528 Germans and granted leave of absence to a further 2412. Those on the margins were most likely to face dismissal. As the company expressed it in its business report for the period from 1 January 1945 to 30 June 1946: 'Above all those who had been conscripted for work, those working half-time, pensioners, those who entered the company work force during the war and those who were politically incriminated were dismissed.'[85]

Bosch was far from unique in its postwar human-resources policies. The temporary standstill of German industry at the end of the Second World War offered companies the opportunity to dismiss particular categories of employees (including former Nazi Party members, whose presence now was an embarrassment rather than an advantage) while retaining those regarded as the core work force. In the months after the surrender many firms carried out massive staff reductions, in part to make room for former employees returning from military service and Allied captivity.[86] Employers tended to reserve jobs during the postwar transition for their 'own employees', while shedding large numbers of men and women hired during the war (and not always adhering to employment law when doing so); thus they sought to ensure the presence of a loyal core of skilled workers in anticipation of postwar recovery.[87] In addition, employers were pressured by local-government officials to re-hire former employees who had been in the Wehrmacht.[88] At a time when the German population was disproportionately female, employers dismissed the less well qualified, older employees, foreigners and women.

The extent of the disruption in the spring and summer of 1945 meant that, even with the best will in the world, German employers would have been hard pressed to retain all those who had been working for them before the Allies arrived. In the immediate aftermath of the war, many factories were shut, awaiting permission from the occupation authorities to resume operation. When they did re-open they often could operate for only a few hours per week.[89] The factories allowed to resume production quickly were frequently those which carried out work for the occupation administration. During the second half of 1945 production started to recover more generally, but even so the level of German industrial production during the last quarter of 1945 was barely one fifth what it had been in 1936, and during the first quarter of 1946 it still stood at only about two fifths of its level ten years earlier.[90] The hard winter of 1945/46 intensified problems, with productivity undermined by cold weather, lack of fuel and inadequate food supply. Shortages of coal and electricity meant that factories sometimes had to operate without heating – and without windows! – during the winter months; an undernourished and poorly housed work force easily fell victim to illness; and stocks of raw materials which had been left with factories at the end of the war needed to be replaced.[91] In effect, the fat which had remained in the summer of 1945 was largely used up by the winter of 1945/1946. If Germans were going to see their living standards recover, they now would have to work much harder.

That said, some aspects of economic activity resumed remarkably quickly after the German surrender. At local level, traders often got back to business immediately after the cessation of hostilities, despite seemingly overwhelming obstacles. In the Rhineland-Palatinate, for example, despite the destruction of communications infrastructure, fuel shortages and the obstacles thrown up by zonal borders, businesses were able to revive links remarkably quickly – not just across the region but also in southern Germany and even in the Soviet zone.[92] Some industries, such as breweries, were surprisingly quick off the mark. In Cologne, the city's breweries were brewing beer again in the summer of 1945; and in Rostock, the Mahn & Ohlerich brewery, which had halted production in early 1945 for lack of coal, emerged from the war largely undamaged, began producing beer for Soviet forces on 2 May, and continued to do so in the following weeks as far as the sporadic supply of coal and electricity permitted.[93] There also appears to have been – and this can be seen in the American zone – a widespread desire to start up in business on one's own after the war.[94] People who had been unable to establish their own businesses due to legal hurdles under the Nazi regime, former Nazi Party members who lost their employment in the public sector as a result of denazification, and refugees from the east who wanted to take up their old trades in new circumstances, now sought to register as independent traders. Independent, local business initiatives often were of great importance in enabling the population to meet basic needs in the aftermath of the war.

Business organization was not just a local matter, however. Despite the hostility of the Allies towards German big business, despite the division of the country into occupation zones largely cut off from one another economically, and despite the prohibition of employers' associations that had represented German business at national level, German entrepreneurs began to organize themselves again very quickly after the war.[95] Both the British and the Americans permitted the establishment of local economic associations soon after the Wehrmacht surrendered, and German businessmen were quick off the mark. By the autumn of 1945, associations of the chemical and pharmaceutical industries and of metallurgical industries had formed in the Rhine and Ruhr regions, and an 'Association of the Bavarian Chemical Industry' had been established in the south.

Despite the arrest of many leading figures, particularly in the British zone economic elites were able to enjoy considerable influence with a military administration that sought their advice and valued their expertise.[96] For the British Military Government, which was desperately concerned to increase coal production in the Ruhr, practical considerations were more important than political ideology – although the work force often saw things rather differently. One report of the Military Government observed bluntly that although the 'miners wish to eject all management as Nazis [. . . the Ruhr Coal District is] in favour of their retention as irreplaceable technical experts, who can obtain coal'.[97] In November 1945 a trade unionist from Bochum complained bitterly that while the employers' organizations had been dissolved officially:

[. . .] the political representatives of these organizations and the spiritual authors of activities which brought ruin on humanity nevertheless still are sitting in the administrations and directorates of the mining company. They are the ones who advise the offices of the NGCC [North German Coal Council]

through their directors and works managers, who provide information about the hitherto existing social-political conditions
and influence the district leaders [of the British administration]
and their decrees through their close contact. The miner has the
impression that behind the broad back and the smoke-screen of
the Military Government these people still carry out their disastrous activity even today.[98]

In western Germany the rupture of 1945 was, in so far as the influence of industrial interests was concerned, perhaps not quite so much
of a rupture with the past after all.

Particularly remarkable was the continued and almost uninterrupted
operation of local Chambers of Industry and Commerce in the
Western zones. While political parties and trade unions had to apply
to Allied military authorities for permission to operate (frequently not
granted), the Chambers of Industry and Commerce often continued
to function without a break after the German surrender, and in the
British zone worked closely with the Military Government. In
Hamburg, the Chamber met again on 7 May, just four days after the
city had been occupied by the British and before the Germans surrendered at Reims; in Bremen, Lübeck and Wetzlar the Chambers
continued without interruption; and across western Germany – in
Düsseldorf, Osnabrück, Hannover, Lüneburg, Braunschweig,
Oldenburg, Hildesheim, Neuß and other cities – the Chambers
resumed their work within a few days of the arrival of Allied troops.[99]
In the American and French zones as well as in the British, often it
was the occupation forces that urged the formation (or re-formation)
of the local Chambers. All three Western occupation powers were
keen that these forums for business representation should function,
and were disposed to give them extensive responsibility for economic
reconstruction.[100]

It was not long before the local Chambers began to organize
regionally, and in the eyes of their members served as a substitute for
employers' associations that were not yet permitted to form. For
example, in June 1945 representatives of the Chambers met from

across the Düsseldorf region, and in July from across the entire North-Rhine Province; and an association of Chambers from North Rhine and Westphalia existed from the beginning of 1946.[101] The Chambers of Industry and Commerce gave business a platform from which to represent their interests from the outset of the occupation, and thus were able to maintain their traditional twin functions as a support to government (now Allied military government) and as a forum for local and regional business leaders to meet and coordinate their interests.[102] Not only did they provide an important element of continuity during 1945; they also formed a base from which the business organizations of the Federal Republic of Germany would develop in the years to come.

Nevertheless, despite the successful re-establishment of business links in 1945, the overwhelming impression with regard to economic affairs remained one of rupture. Not only had the central government, including the ministries and agencies responsible for economic planning and regulation, been abolished, but leading figures in the economy had lost their positions and the companies they had directed no longer were capable of strategic planning in a country which was prostrate, occupied and divided. Furthermore, the Allies were convinced to a greater or lesser extent that German big business had worked hand-in-glove with the Nazi regime and needed to be broken up and its directors prosecuted. Accordingly, many of Germany's big industrial firms were taken over by the occupying powers and many leading figures in the economy were taken into custody after the war. Assets that had been owned by Germany's largest industrial companies were confiscated in both the Western and Soviet zones. In the Western zones the property of the largest industrial trusts was confiscated under the terms of SHAEF law Nr. 52.[103] Some targets were obvious, chief among them Krupp and the giant I.G. Farben chemicals trust: on 16 November, the British took control of the Krupp works, and two weeks later the Allied Control Council seized the assets of I.G. Farben (which had been dissolved at the end of August by the American Military Government). Given its central importance for both German and European recovery, coal-mining in particular attracted the attentions of the occupying powers. On 22 December the British Military Government took direct control of all the coal mines in the British zone, which meant the expropriation of 68 mining companies with 225 mines; and on the following day the French Military Government announced the seizure of coal mines in the Saar region.[104]

Obviously, German private enterprise could expect the least friendly reception in the Soviet Occupation Zone, where the Russians were concerned less with specific responsibility for crimes committed by and under the Nazi regime than they were with the general proposition that Nazism was a product of capitalism. A sign of what lay ahead was the Soviet Military Administration's order of 23 July on the 'Re-organization of German Financial and Credit Firms', which effectively spelled the nationalization of banking and insurance.[105] But the more immediate threat for individual businessmen was arrest and internment, whereby a call for police questioning might lead to years of imprisonment. This is what happened to Oswald Rösler, a member of the board of Deutsche Bank, who was taken from the bank's Berlin headquarters by Soviet soldiers in mid-June 1945; he did not emerge from Soviet custody until January 1950.[106] Consequently, the second half of 1945 saw the beginnings of a migration westwards of German businesses, to escape the Soviet occupation regime and to find what they hoped would be a more congenial welcome from the British and Americans. For example, Germany's largest insurance firm, Allianz, moved its general headquarters from Taubenstraße in Berlin-Mitte (in the Soviet sector) to Jebenstraße in Berlin-Charlottenburg (in the British sector) in October 1945.[107]

Yet the Western Allies were not necessarily that well disposed to German big business either, and a considerable number of prominent businessmen were taken into custody in the Western zones. Among the first was Alfred Krupp von Bohlen und Halbach, who had been arrested in his mansion, the Villa Hügel on the southern outskirts of Essen, on 10 April. Another figure who had been prominent in German armaments production, Wilhelm Messerschmidt, was arrested in Murnau (to the south of Munich) on 1 May, taken to London for questioning, brought back to Murnau, re-arrested, and then interned in a series of detention camps for roughly a year.[108] Kurt

Schmitt, a leading figure in Allianz, found himself in a civilian internment camp at Moosberg, presumably because he had held the
honorary rank of SS-*Brigadeführer*.[109] During the second half of 1945
the Western Allies, determined to break the power and concentration
of German industry, decided to arrest members of the boards of major
industrial firms and other leading industrialists. At the beginning of
July the directors of the machine-building firm MAN, Otto Meyer
and Heinrich Riehm, were arrested in Augsburg;[110] on 6 September
Hugo Stinnes was arrested together with 39 other members of the
Rhine-Westphalian Coal Syndicate, the cartel of the coal industry in
the Rhineland and Westphalia; on 30 November/1 December some
70 steel entrepreneurs were sent for internment at Bad Nenndorf, to
the east of Hannover.[111] Generally, these (often elderly) businessmen
were treated rather more gently than the great mass of Germans
rounded up under the 'automatic arrest' provisions with which the
Western Allies had entered Germany; usually, they were held in local
gaols rather than in mass internment camps, and often they were
released after a relatively short period. However, the arrests and the
threat of arrest added to their insecurity, even in the Western zones.

Allied campaigns aimed at denazification affected not only the captains of industry and finance but middle management as well. The
screening and dismissal of employees for previous membership in
Nazi organizations, a process carried out particularly rigorously in the
American zone, could cut deeply into company ranks. Businesses (as
well as public-sector administrations) lost experienced staff and found
it difficult to plan against the possibility that key employees might be
dismissed at short notice, or arrested due to previous involvement – or
presumed involvement – in the activities of the Nazi regime, as happened with the Bayerische Versicherungsbank in Munich (in the
American zone): of the 51 people who had been employed in mana-
gerial positions below the level of the bank's managing board (five of
whose members were dismissed) and its deputies, 17 were dismissed in
the summer of 1945 (while three had retired, another had died and
another had not returned from the front).[112] In Bremen, 200 of 400
civil servants and white-collar workers in the public sector had been
dismissed in early November, and among those removed from their

jobs were people whose task it was to lay electric cables in a city where such work was urgently required.[113] During the autumn, newspapers were filled with announcements of dismissals of the owners of businesses; in Würzburg alone roughly 500 heads of businesses had been dismissed by the end of 1945.[114] The Bremen deputy mayor, Theodor Spitta, reflected widespread concern when he complained in mid-September of the 'scant understanding of the Americans for the difficulties of the economy [created] by the dismissals of works managers'.[115] German local business associations protested against the dismissals, but to little effect; in the American zone, where the denazification was being carried out most rigorously, Eisenhower and Clay (mindful of opinion in the United States) were determined to press ahead regardless of German objections.[116] During the second half of 1945, the denazification process and the dismissals which followed from it caused considerable difficulties for German businesses attempting to get back on their feet.

Allied interference with German business was not limited to splitting up the giant trusts or dismissing and/or arresting people believed to have been complicit with the Nazi regime. Businesses needed permission to re-open, and each occupying authority handled this matter in its own way with different types of business treated differently. In the west, the French were most restrictive. Initially, they did not allow any firms to operate save municipal services, transport, and those supplying French troops; they then issued permits to operate only for businesses with up to 12 employees.[117] The British proved rather less severe, demonstrating great concern to get production re-started, and in some cases (e.g. in Cologne) provided transport to bring entrepreneurs back to their factories and helped to return machinery that had been dispersed during the war.[118] German businessmen could be checked later, for example to determine whether there were political objections (i.e. that the businesses might serve as refuges for National Socialists) or whether criminal charges were outstanding.[119] The British left it to the German Chambers of Industry and Commerce to issue permits to re-open for small businesses (i.e. businesses with 25 employees or fewer and with small energy requirements). The Americans, on the other hand, were less inclined to allow Germans to manage this themselves, and either issued their 'Permissions to Re-Open' directly or delegated the task to the local authorities under their control.[120]

While some businesses were able to re-open in the summer of 1945 and to re-start production provided that their equipment was usable and the necessary raw materials were available, others had to wait. For example, like other large firms in the British zone, the iron-and-steel concern Otto Wolff (headquartered in Cologne) needed permission from the *Land* Economics Office in Düsseldorf to resume production in its factories in Essen and Oberhausen, but it did not receive the necessary permits until December 1945.[121] Permits could be quite restrictive, specifying what could be produced and the number of employees allowed. Generally, however, all the parties concerned had an interest in a revival of economic activity, and most firms appear to have received permission to re-open during the summer of 1945. In Stuttgart, of the 1740 businesses which submitted requests to the Americans to resume operations at the end of July, 1423 had been approved by the end of August (and 1566 by mid-November).[122]

Receipt of a permit did not necessarily clear the path for a smooth resumption of production. The materials – such as cement, wood, glass and so on – needed to repair damaged shops, warehouses and factories were in short supply. During the summer and autumn of 1945 businesses sometimes had to enter into barter arrangements in order to acquire necessary materials. In some instances plant and machinery had been dispersed during the war, away from the most obvious targets for Allied bombing; if they had not been moved too far or had remained within the same occupation zone, the chances of recovery were relatively good, but machinery which had ended up in the Soviet zone or in Austria effectively was lost to firms in the Western zones and had to be written off.[123] Closer to home, theft of raw materials, tools and machinery, typewriters, employees' bicycles – anything that could be flogged on the black market – posed a serious problem, and firms often had to employ guards to prevent goods from being 'shifted'.[124]

In addition, German companies faced a fundamental rupture of their trading links. With the defeat and occupation, the country's for-

eign trade came to a standstill, and in September 1945 the Allied
Control Council formally prohibited any activity by German consular
and trade representatives abroad – leaving the military government
with a monopoly on foreign trade.[125] German officials and citizens
were banned from contact with foreign countries; doing business
with foreigners was virtually impossible, and required special permission from the military government.[126] In 1945, as its borders became
insurmountable barriers to trade, Germany largely disappeared from
the world trading system.

Trade arrangements within the country were not much better.
Inter-zonal trade began in the autumn of 1945, but was hampered by
bureaucratic hurdles and the divergent economic policies being
pursued by the different occupation regimes. The once integrated
German national economy was divided into islands whose trading
ties with one another were being severed. Traditionally close links
between Franconia in the American zone and Thuringia in the
Soviet zone, or between the Ruhr industrial region in the British
zone and Württemberg, split between the French and the American
zones, were ruptured. The American zone found itself cut off
from the main German sources of coal, which lay in the British and
Soviet zones. Businesses were cut off from suppliers and customers.
For example, in late 1945 a bicycle factory in Nuremberg (in the
American zone), which formerly had supplied bicycles across
Germany, found itself in considerable difficulties when sufficient
supplies of pedals, spokes and, especially, tyres, could no longer be
acquired from the Rhineland (in the British zone).[127] In Bremen,
shortages of matches – a particularly important item when electricity
supply was intermittent – and of building materials needed for urgent
repairs to the city's sewers, were attributed to a British decision to
prohibit exports from their zone, which surrounded the American
enclave of Bremen.[128] A unified, integrated German economy appeared
to be a thing of the past.

One problem shared in all four occupation zones was inflation. For a
second time in little over a quarter of a century, a lost world war led
to a collapse of the German currency. In part this was a consequence

of the huge increase in the money supply which had taken place during the war. Increasingly, the Nazi regime had financed its war through borrowing and recourse to printing money. In January 1945 Otto Ohlendorf, Permanent Secretary in the Reich Economics Ministry at the time, had noted that the currency in the pockets of the civilian population had 'increased tremendously' and that the Reich had had to 'resort ever more to the currency printing press'.[129] As a result, the amount of German currency in circulation in 1945, 73 billion Reichsmarks, was seven times greater than it had been in 1938; the amount of bank balances had increased by more than five times (from 18.7 to 100 billion Reichsmarks), and savings deposits by almost five times (from 27.3 to 125 billion Reichsmarks).[130] At the same time, few goods were available to buy. Thus large quantities of cash were chasing small quantities of goods. This resulted in rapidly rising prices, attempts by the occupation administrations to implement price controls and rationing, and a thriving black market.

The black market was a ubiquitous feature of the social and economic landscape of postwar Germany. However, it had not emerged suddenly in May 1945. During the war, rationing had been accompanied by a growing black market, and during the last months of the war black-market activity – and prices – skyrocketed as rationed goods became scarce and Germans assumed that the Reichsmark soon would become worthless.[131] The explosion of the black market and its prices, which at the beginning of 1945 had climbed in some cases to 100 times the prices of 1939, was a reflection of the popular conviction that Germany's war was lost. Nevertheless, it is the period between the military collapse in 1945 and 1948, when new currencies were introduced in Germany both east and west, that is referred to as the 'black-market time'. After the war just about everyone looked to the black market in order to meet daily needs; according to one contemporary estimate from 1947, up to 95 per cent of Germans were involved, participating directly or indirectly either in barter or in the black market.[132]

Although the end of the war brought a marked decline in black-market prices from the extortionate levels they had reached in the last months of the conflict,[133] they generally remained quite high in relation to wage rates, and were considerably above official price levels. In the autumn of 1945 the price of potatoes on the black market in the Trier region was more than double the official price: 8.00 RM per hundredweight as compared to the official price of RM 3.50, at a time when an average industrial wage officially stood at less that RM 0.90 per hour.[134] In Bremen, a pound of cocoa was reported to cost 450 RM on the black market in late October 1945 and a pound of butter 120 RM.[135] Black-market prices varied significantly from region to region; in areas where people had more money in their pockets – in particular large cities in northern Germany (Hamburg, Berlin) – prices tended to be higher than in regions where people earned less (such as in rural regions in south-western Germany, where black-market prices tended to be lowest).[136] Given the lack of confidence in the old paper currency and the importance of the black market, it is not surprising that cigarettes became a more readily accepted currency than Reichsmarks. To a significant degree it was barter and the black market that formed the real economy of occupied Germany, rather than exchange at controlled, official prices.

This indicates that the actual level of economic activity in Germany after the war was higher than that reflected in official statistics, and the black market had a profound effect on people's everyday lives. Not only did it mean that millions of Germans engaged in law-breaking; it also meant that people who tried to earn a living through honest labour, as well as the weaker members of society – the old, the ill, the poor – lost out.[137] It was the latter who, in effect, were paying disproportionately for the lost war. Whatever people may have imagined subsequently, economic relationships in 1945 had a hard edge, leading to accusations of greed, profiteering and cheating. Public social and economic relationships reflected not a pulling together during a period of hardship, but rather ill-will, mutual suspicion between town-dwellers and country-dwellers, belief that the occupying powers were exercising revenge against the Germans, conviction that people elsewhere were being treated better than oneself, jealousy towards those – especially foreigners and former victims of the Nazi regime – who enjoyed better rations.[138] The root causes of the postwar hardships often were forgotten or ignored. In early September 1945 a certain Dr Ludwig wrote to the Catholic Archbishop of Cologne, Josef Frings, with a revealing description of life in a police state that had fed its own people while letting others starve:

> Back then [i.e before 1945] we always had enough to eat. Trade and traffic proceeded without restriction, as there was enough fuel of all kinds and also everything else that one needed to live . . . Today these products are rolling out over the borders of our province. Back then there was no robbery, looting, theft, murder and intimidation by Russians, Poles, Serbs and criminal Germans; there was no profiteering caused by the food situation in the purchase of foodstuffs of all kinds and articles for everyday use (. . .), back then civil servants and white-collar workers were thoroughly proper in their contact with the public, and it did not happen that a department head had to summon his subordinates and threaten the most severe measures and legal penalties for civil servants etc.[139]

The postwar economy was a tough school, in which goods and services were worth what people would pay for them and where each individual was on his or her own in a desperate scramble to get the necessities of life. Of a moral economy there appeared hardly a trace. As one woman put it when being interviewed some 35 years later, 'that was bad, the hunger. There one learned to know one's fellow human beings. Among the people I know there was not one who would have helped without getting something in return. That did not exist.'[140]

It followed that calls for economic controls, for harsh measures against profiteers who made a handsome living from the black market, had considerable resonance.[141] And German civilians were not the only people alarmed at the postwar resurgence of the black economy in all its ugliness. Faced with severe shortages and the threat of economic collapse, the occupation authorities in all four zones looked to economic controls. With food, fuel and raw materials in desperately short supply, Allied military authorities were concerned to manage access to and distribution of scarce commodities. Most critical was food. In mid-July 1945 the British, in whose zone the problem of food supply was most severe, called together a group of German agricultural specialists to form the 'German Interregional Food Allocation Committee' (GIFAC) to advise on food distribution. The GIFAC produced a food distribution plan in mid-October, and this was followed by the introduction of uniform ration scales and the creation of a German 'Central Food Administration' for the British zone.[142] More generally, there was concern to rein in inflation, which led to the declaration of wage and price freezes. In the French zone, in June 1945 the military commandant in Baden prohibited price rises, and at the beginning of September 1945 the Military Government officially assumed responsibility for fixing and monitoring prices.[143] However, such measures inevitably proved inadequate because administrative controls could not stem the rapid rise of prices on the black market, and might even have exacerbated them.

Allied military governments were also keen to control the German labour force. The challenge was enormous, with millions of Germans having fled westwards ahead of the Soviet Army, millions of foreign labourers awaiting repatriation, and vast numbers of Germans thrown temporarily out of work as factories were shut. However, very soon the Allies re-opened German labour offices and used them to channel people towards employment. Most rigorous were the measures taken in the Soviet zone. There, in mid-September the Military Administration ordered the introduction of the 'work-book' (actually, its re-introduction, since the 'work-book' had been a feature of Nazi labour controls), in which one's employment history could be logged and which served as a means for directing labour; from 1 October, registration with labour offices was made mandatory for all males between the ages of 14 and 65 and females between 14 and 50.[144]

Despite the willingness to impose economic controls in the various zones, there was no comparable readiness to coordinate economic policy for occupied Germany as a whole. At Potsdam, the Allies had agreed that 'during the period of occupation Germany shall be treated as a single economic unit',[145] but, as with many of the stated intentions of the victors, it soon became apparent that this would not happen. Even before the leaders of the U.K., the U.S. and the USSR met in Potsdam in July, decisions had been taken on the ground that pointed towards the break-up of the German economy. The principle agreed at Potsdam that 'common policies shall be established in regard to [. . .] currency and banking, central taxation and customs' was a dead letter even before it had been written. In a move with far-reaching consequences, on 5 June the Soviet Military Administration ordered the Reichsbank shut and re-opened it as the Berliner Stadtbank (Berlin City Bank) under the control of the Berlin municipal administration, which had a banking monopoly in the city. This measure, made without consultation with the Western Allies, left Germany without a central bank to issue currency. In the west, the Reichsbank's offices in Hamburg and Speyer took over its functions for the British and French zones respectively, and in the American zone separate offices of the Reichsbank were set up in each of the individual *Länder*. By the time that the Allied leaders had agreed to the establishment of common policies in regard to currency and banking, the institutional framework through which to put this into practice had already been abolished.

The USSR was not the only occupying power to ignore the principle that Germany be treated as a single economic unit. The French also went their own way. Not only did they largely seal their occupation zone off from the others and seek to tie it closely to the economy of France; they also torpedoed proposals put before the Allied Control Council in the autumn of 1945 that envisaged the creation of five central administrations (economics, finance, transport, food and foreign trade) for the whole of occupied Germany. However, it quickly became apparent that Soviet intentions with regard to a future economic order in Germany were quite different from those of the Western powers, France included. The closure of the Reichsbank in Berlin was followed on 23 July by the decision of the Soviet Military Administration to embargo bank-account assets, to prohibit the repayment of loans made before the German capitulation, and to close the banks and savings institutions in the Soviet zone.[146] In stark contrast with what occurred in the west, the Soviet occupation authorities also shut down the German Chambers of Industry and Commerce and replaced them with new institutions in which entrepreneurs comprised only one third of the membership and the remainder consisted of representatives of the trade unions and the local and regional government administrations. These new chambers were intended to mediate between central planning and local businesses rather than to represent business interests.[147]

Most importantly, the USSR was determined to extract maximum reparations from Germany. Thus Soviet economic policy in occupied Germany was always reparations policy. Colonel Sergei Tjulpanov, the head of the Administration for Censorship and Propaganda (Information) within the Soviet Military Administration in Germany and a key figure with the SMAD, wrote in a newspaper article published in May 1948: 'The Russians are also taking reparations. Yes, we are taking them. We have a moral right to take them. Every honest German democrat understands that the German population [has] a moral duty to make good the damage caused, even if only in part.'[148] The main mechanism for extracting reparations was the dismantling of German industry and infrastructure and its transport to the USSR, where the factories were reassembled and the machinery put to use. The decisions taken at Potsdam to restructure the German economy so that it could not provide a basis for rearmament, and to allow the Russians to extract what they wanted from their occupation zone, opened the door to dismantling on a massive scale.[149] To be sure, dismantling occurred in the Western zones as well, and the Americans removed materials from factories in Thuringia and Saxony-Anhalt (for example, from the Zeiss optics works at Jena and the Agfa photographic-film factory at Wolfen) before handing these regions over to the Russians in July 1945.[150] However, their activity was on nothing like the scale of that undertaken by the Soviet occupiers.

In fact, the USSR began dismantling German industrial plant before the final text of the Potsdam Agreement was signed.[151] The first wave, during the summer and autumn of 1945, was rather chaotic. Various Soviet ministries organized their own dismantling teams with little reference to the wishes of the Soviet Military Administration in Germany, with results that brought little benefit to the Russians and much harm to the Germans.[152] The greatest amount of dismantling took place in 1945 and 1946, and initially was aimed at removing the Germans' capacity to produce armaments. The principal targets were metallurgical plants, the oil industry, machine-tool building and optics – which would cause problems for the east German economy for years to come.[153] Sometimes Soviet soldiers carried out the dismantling – altogether, some 70,000 Soviet personnel came to Germany to work as 'dismantlers'[154] – and sometimes German workers were compelled to take apart and pack the contents of their own factories for despatch to the USSR (in some cases being beaten and abused by Soviet officers while they did so). The aim was to remove as much as possible as fast as possible.

The cost to the economy and inhabitants of areas occupied by the Red Army was enormous. When the Americans arrived in West Berlin at the beginning of July 1945, they estimated that the Russians already had removed 85 per cent of all undamaged factory equipment in the city's U.S. sector.[155] According to contemporary estimates, nearly half (45 per cent) of the industrial capacity in the Soviet Occupation Zone had been dismantled by the end of 1946.[156] The railways were a prime target and the Russians removed a substantial portion of German rolling stock before turning to the infrastructure itself. (The dismantling of the railway lines took place primarily during 1947 and 1948, leaving half of all track in the Soviet Occupation Zone gone by the end of 1947. Single-track railways where once there had been two tracks remained a common sight for the entire life of the GDR.)[157] German workers often tried to restore production capacity with what was left behind after the Soviet dismantling teams had done their work, only to have the results of these efforts dismantled and carted off as well.[158] Not just the dismantling itself, but the threat of further dismantling undermined efforts to revive the economy. Reporting 'on the current situation' in Mecklenburg, the Economics Ministry in Schwerin observed in November 1945 that 'at the moment everyone is afraid of drawing attention to themselves by an increase in production and thereby [provoking] dismantling'.[159] As a consequence of the dismantling, the Soviet zone experienced what can be described as a process of de-industrialisation.

Reparations were extracted not just through the removal of plant and machinery but also, increasingly, in the form of goods that Germans produced in the Soviet zone. Initially there had not been much scope for this, since economic activity was extremely low immediately after the surrender. However, during the second half of 1945 the Soviet authorities displayed a growing interest in taking what the Germans could manufacture. On 21 July Marshal Zhukov, the Chief of the Soviet Military Administration in Germany, issued an order demanding the rapid re-starting of important German factories in the zone, and the first Soviet plans for extracting goods from current German production were drawn up in the autumn.[160] The focus was on delivering what the USSR required – in particular cement, and machinery for energy and food industries – rather than what the Germans most easily could produce. The process initially was chaotic and poorly coordinated; Soviet reparations demands often involved sweeping up the stocks left in German factories; and during 1945 the shipment of goods still comprised only a small proportion of reparations payments. Rainer Karlsch estimates that German payments to the USSR in 1945 consisted altogether of roughly two billion Reichsmarks as a result of dismantling, 500 million in occupation costs paid to the Russians, 100 million in deliveries from German production, and one billion in the form of the removal of 'trophies' and booty.[161] Gradually the delivery of goods as reparations became better organized, after the Soviet Military Administration moved in October 1945 to centralize and coordinate the issuing of contracts for reparations goods. (This also had advantages for German firms, as such contracts appeared to offer protection from the threat of dismantling.)[162] Consequently, from a small start in 1945, the shipment of goods would gradually replace dismantling as the main means by which the USSR extracted reparations from occupied Germany.

The Soviet authorities did not only remove German factories; they also seized them *in situ*. At the end of October 1945, the Soviet Military Administration issued a decree for the 'sequestration and provisional takeover of some categories of property', which led to the seizure of property of the Reich and Prussia, of former leading figures in the Nazi Party, as well as of 'persons who are specified by the

Soviet Military Command through special lists or otherwise'.[163] This set the stage for the expropriation of large sections of industry, effectively leaving only small and medium-sized firms in private hands. It was not until 1946, however, that the 'Soviet Joint Stock Companies', a new form of economic organization designed to facilitate the delivery of reparations to the USSR, were formed. Eventually the 200 most important industrial plants in the Soviet zone became Soviet companies, owned by the Soviet Ministry of Foreign Trade and various Soviet industrial ministries and controlled directly through a Soviet office in Berlin-Weißensee (under the overall direction of the 'Main Administration of the USSR Council of Ministers for Soviet Property Abroad'). They produced for the USSR, and their operation was integrated into the Soviet planned economy.[164] By the end of 1946 the USSR owned nearly 30 per cent of production in the Soviet Occupation Zone.[165]

Not only German industry was removed from private ownership in the Soviet zone. The authorities also had agricultural enterprises in their sights. Of all the zones, it was in the Soviet Occupation Zone that large landed estates had constituted the greatest proportion of agricultural land. Estates of more than 100 hectares comprised 29.8 per cent of the agricultural land (and fully 45.4 per cent of the entire land area) in the Soviet zone, although they made up a mere 1.5 per cent of farms.[166] Their confiscation had an important political dimension: the land-owning Junker class was regarded as having been a main prop of 'Prussian militarism' and therefore of Nazism. Already at the end of 1944 Anton Ackermann had drafted an 'Action Programme' in which he proposed the confiscation of landed estates of more than 150 hectares;[167] and at a meeting with the German Communist Party leadership in Moscow on 4 June 1945 – well before the conference at Potsdam – Stalin had urged that the power of the large landowners be broken in the Soviet Occupation Zone.[168] In its call of 11 June, therefore, the newly re-established Communist Party of Germany demanded the 'liquidation of large landed estates, of the large estates of the Junkers, counts and princes, and the handing over of their land as well as [their] livestock and other property to the provincial *Land* administrations for distribution to farmers who had been ruined and lost their property as a result of the war'.[169] By mid-August the German Communist leadership, together with the Russians, had drafted land-reform legislation, which was distributed to district organizations of the Party at the end of the month.[170]

Plans were swiftly translated into action. On 2 September the Communist Party Chairman, Wilhelm Pieck, speaking in the small town of Kyritz in Brandenburg, demanded immediate land reform, with the aim of creating 'as many small independent farms as possible'.[171] According to Pieck, 'all of these war guilty and war criminals must be made harmless forever [. . .] the bases of their power, their lands and their possessions, must be taken from them'.[172] The next day, on 3 September, the government of the Province of Saxony issued the first decree for land reform, stipulating that estates of more than 100 hectares would be expropriated without compensation and re-distributed to farmers with either little or no land.[173] In the days that followed, administrations in the other *Länder* of the Soviet zone issued similar decrees: Brandenburg on 6 September, Mecklenburg on 7 September, Saxony on 11 September and Thuringia on 12 September. However, the process of land reform in fact had begun even before these decrees were issued: during the summer of 1945 many large landowners, particularly in the northern regions of the Soviet zone, had either headed westwards or been chased from their estates. Soviet soldiers sometimes attacked German landowners, and estate owners were evicted from their homes at short notice by local Communists and Soviet military authorities. Together with the transfer to Poland of the lands east of the Oder-Neiße frontier, this process of eviction and expropriation spelled the end of the Junker landowning class which had been the backbone of the eastern German rural economy and of German political conservatism.

Like the Russians, the French aimed to extract resources from their zone of occupation. For the French, who wanted both to make good the damage done to their country during the war and to overcome the stagnation which had characterized French economic life during the interwar years, German resources were vitally important.[174] The exploitation of their occupation zone would not only help to avoid economic dependence upon the United States but also to relieve French taxpayers of having to shoulder the expense of the occupation of their old enemy across the Rhine. As Philippe Livry-Level, a Resistance hero and deputy of the *Mouvement Populaire Républicain*, declared in a National Assembly debate in March 1946: 'We have here a land for us to exploit'.[175]

Like the USSR, but unlike either the United Kingdom or the United States, France had been invaded by the Germans, and the French emerged from the war with an overriding concern about the potential threat arising from a resurgent Germany. Also like the Russians but unlike the British and Americans, the French took both agricultural and industrial goods from current production in their zone. Their troops and military administration essentially lived off the resources of the land in their zone of occupation. Unlike the United States, France was in no position to subsidize its zone, which meant that the costs of maintaining the French presence in Germany (roughly 1,000,000 soldiers at the end of the war and still 200,000 at the beginning of 1946, as well as some 10,000 French government bureaucrats and members of their families) had to be met in large measure through requisitioning.[176] While the German population had to pay a substantial proportion of the costs of occupation in all the zones, it was in the French zone where, among the Western occupying powers, their share was the highest.[177] While this reduced the financial burden on the French state, it also reduced the living standards of the German population.

The French, like their Russian counterparts, designed their economic policies in Germany to support their economic policy at home. They turned their zone into an exporter of goods to France, and in 1945/46, 89 per cent of exports from the French Occupation Zone went to France and were integrated into planning for her economic recovery.[178] They also imposed central planning in their zone almost from the outset. With their 'Decree Nr. 5' of 4 September 1945, the entire economy of the zone was placed under the control of the French Military Government, which allowed the zonal commander to set production targets, release goods and control their distribution.[179]

For agriculture, it meant that farmers were required to deliver their entire harvest save only what they required for their own consumption and for seed. The French largely turned their backs on the market economy in their zone, while seeking to cut it off economically from the rest of Germany and to integrate it as far as possible (and at terms disadvantageous to the Germans) with France. French designs went even further in the Saar, a region which they hoped would be fused with France. (Consequently, the Saar enjoyed better provision of food, raw materials and industrial products than did the remainder of French-occupied Germany).[180] Not surprisingly, the French occupation regime left a legacy of resentment among the population of south-western Germany.[181]

Overall, although it is impossible to determine precisely the extent of the economic disaster which enveloped Germany at the end of the Second World War, it is clear that the German people in all four zones faced economic meltdown in 1945. After having benefited from resources plundered from across Europe by the Nazi regime, in 1945 Germans began paying for their lost war with drastically lower living standards, severe shortages of food and fuel, poor health, a catastrophic housing situation, and the delivery of substantial economic resources to the Allies. The population of what had been one of the world's richest countries was reduced to poverty.

Nevertheless, with hindsight, it appears that the condition of the German economy – or, perhaps more accurately, the German economies taking shape in the different occupation zones – was not quite so dire as it seemed immediately after the surrender in May 1945. Germany's industrial capacity, which had expanded massively in the years leading up to the conflict and during the war itself, remained considerable. Although the necessary repair work was daunting, although the extent of reparations and the dismantling of industrial capacity particularly in the Soviet and French zones was substantial, and although the condition of German infrastructure was calamitous, defeated Germany had not become a Third World country. It possessed a highly developed, if battered, industrial economy. Thus the significance of Germany's economic plight in 1945 was as much psychological as it was physical, if not more so. Looking out over the shattered landscapes of Germany's industrial and urban centres, at its smashed rail yards, ports and waterways littered with wrecks of ships, and its burnt-out villages and farmhouses, it was easy to believe that generations would pass before the country could recover. Indeed, many who surveyed this landscape of ruins despaired of the damage ever being made good. Yet, as we now know, after the severe hardship of the immediate postwar years, Germany – first in the west of the country and then, rather less impressively, in the east – did recover. The 'economic miracles' of the 1950s and 1960s were seen against the backdrop of the visible disaster of 1945, which really *had* been perceived by contemporaries as a 'zero hour'. Thus the economic predicament of Germany at the end of the Second World War created the psychological basis for the economic success story which followed.

13

CONCLUSION: LIFE AFTER DEATH

*After midnight, a few minutes in the open air; only a few stars —
memories and thoughts. What a year lies behind us!* Theodor
Spitta[1]

Death is a problem of the living. Norbert Elias[2]

Germany was the first country in modern history to achieve total
defeat. The Nazi regime did not surrender and German soldiers
did not stop fighting, even when foreign armies were approaching the
gardens of the Reich Chancellery in the centre of Berlin. Never
before in modern history had a nation reached the depths plumbed by
Germany in 1945: its sovereignty was extinguished; its infrastructure
was smashed; its economy was paralysed; its cities reduced to piles of
rubble; much of the population was hungry and homeless; its armed
forces were disbanded and their surviving members were in prisoner-
of-war camps; its government had ceased to exist and the entire
country had been occupied by foreign armies. Germany had become
a land of death. During the last year of the Second World War, more
Germans died than in any other year before or since. By the time
that the Wehrmacht surrendered in May 1945, half the population

had lost at least one family member.[3] The bombing, and the fighting on the ground in 1945, much of it taking place within Germany, left behind a landscape littered with corpses.

The 'omnipresence of death'[4] in Germany at the end of the war made a deep and disturbing impression. The scenes that people witnessed would haunt them for the rest of their lives. Franz Scholz, the priest at the Catholic parish of St Bonifatius in the east of Görlitz, wrote in his diary about conditions there during the last weeks of the war:

> The mortuary at the municipal cemetery is bursting at the seams. For some time now the dead no longer could be accommodated. Therefore only the countless corpses of children are brought there. The huge hall of the Nikolai Church is used for the corpses of the adults. Some 100 corpses, placed temporarily in boxes, await burial. [. . .] In the entrance hall one sees a pile of the dead, taller than a man and covered with sackcloth, barely two metres long and two metres wide. At one end a tangle of naked feet, at the other hair and people's heads.[5]

More recently, the German-Jewish violinist Michael Wieck published memoirs of his childhood and adolescence in Königsberg, in which he described his experiences as a 16-year-old in the East Prussian capital after it had been occupied by the Red Army:

> The city still was littered with unburied dead. They buried soldiers, but the troops did not regard themselves responsible for civilians. So it now was our task to search houses and cellars, courtyards and gardens for corpses, in order to 'dispose' of them. One could not really describe it as burying. I have to bring myself to describe what we did: The first removal was of a partly naked young woman with dried streams of blood around the vagina and the mouth, lying on the ground floor of a half-burnt-out house. She had a delicate, tender face. We carried her with gloves – which they gave to us – by the arms and legs out to the street; we had to throw her into the nearest bomb crater.

Others brought a man who had been shot. They threw him on top of the woman. The corpses were about a week old, and had already begun to decompose. [. . .] I can still remember almost all of these poor murdered women and men; I see not just their faces but also their various positions and sometimes also the objects that surrounded them. Children as well as old people; most of them shot, some stabbed or strangled. There also were a number of suicides. They had taken poison or hanged themselves on the staircase. In one case there was an entire family that had killed themselves. In [the district of] Hufen there was one street with an especially large bomb crater – I have forgotten the name of the street. Into this crater I dragged people who had been shrivelled up by the heat of the house that had burned down on top of them.[6]

The documentary collection on 'The Expulsion of the Germans from the Regions east of the Oder-Neiße', edited by Theodor Schieder on behalf of the West German government during the 1950s, contains numerous descriptions of encounters with corpses. To cite but two, both from the end of the war in Lower Silesia: Fritz Schmidt, a vicar from Marschwitz in the district of Ohlau, described what was left of his village after the fighting had ended – shot-up and burnt-out houses, streets littered with broken agricultural machinery and smashed domestic possessions, 'dead soldiers and cadavers' – and how he had been compelled by the Russians to remove and bury rotting corpses.[7] Another vicar, Georg Gottwald, described the scene in Grünberg, where he had to bury the mutilated corpses of women: of the 4000 inhabitants (out of a former population of 35,000) who remained in the town after the surrender:

[. . .] in the first 14 days [after the Russians arrived] over 500 people (entire families, men, women and children) ended their lives by suicide, including doctors, senior court officials, factory owners and prosperous citizens. The corpses of those who had killed themselves must have remained unburied for two weeks.

They had to remain in people's flats or were left on the pavement in order to frighten others.[8]

Germans were confronted with the dead in the west also. Not only did Allied commanders parade German civilians in front of the dead found in liberated concentration camps; they too sometimes left corpses in public view as a warning to anyone who might be tempted to resist the occupation.[9] In the first half of 1945 carrying out one's daily tasks frequently meant encountering the dead on the streets – corpses of soldiers and civilians, of strangers and acquaintances, of people who no longer could be recognized. As never before, death became part of everyday life.[10]

It was not just the physical remains of the dead that haunted the living. Enormous numbers of people were missing – the hundreds of thousands whose deaths had gone unconfirmed or unrecorded at the front, in the bombings, in the course of flight from the east, in the battles waged on German soil during the last months of the conflict. Huge numbers of soldiers had been reported 'missing in action';[11] millions of family members had been separated in the flight ahead of the Red Army in early 1945; men, women and children had been blown apart or burnt beyond recognition in the bombings. While the exact number of casualties will never be known, the total of German dead that resulted from the Second World War probably approaches 6.5 million.[12] This was the dark shadow under which the German survivors of Hitler's war had to begin a new life amidst the ruins of their country. The story of Germany after the cataclysm of 1945 is, quite literally, a story of life after death.

The violence that visited Germans with such intensity during the first half of 1945 framed their memory of the Second World War long into the postwar period. For Germans, the ferocity of the last months of war and the privations of the first months of peace pushed the experiences of the previous years of war and dictatorship, as well as consciousness of what the Nazi regime had done to other peoples during the earlier phases of the conflict, into the background. Not Auschwitz but Dresden; not the battle for Warsaw in 1939 but the battle for Berlin in 1945; not the atrocities committed against the civilian populations across Nazi-occupied Europe but the rape of hundreds of thousands of German women in the spring of 1945; not the expulsion of Poles from their homes in areas annexed by the 'Greater German Reich' in West Prussia and the 'Warthegau' but the expulsion of Germans from their homes in East Prussia, Pomerania, Silesia and the Sudetenland; not the creation of 'dead zones' in German-occupied Belarus but the devastation of wide stretches of the countryside around Berlin during the battles in spring 1945 – *these* were the experiences that Germans came to regard as their Second World War. As a consequence of the terrible shock of 1945, the German people emerged preoccupied almost exclusively with their own cares and concerns.[13]

Conditions in Germany in 1945 did not appear to offer many grounds for optimism about the future. Yet the stark landscape of political, economic, social and moral devastation that constituted Germany at the end of the Second World War provided the unlikely base for a remarkable recovery: within a generation of 1945, Germans (at least those in the west) were enjoying unprecedented prosperity and stable parliamentary democracy. It would be easy enough to conclude this book by stressing again the horrors and devastation that characterized life in Germany at the end of the war, to emphasize the dreadful plight of its people in 1945. This, indeed, is the message delivered by countless volumes published during the postwar years describing the terrible events at the end of the war in one German town after another. However, to leave it at that would be to miss the most important point: that, for all the horrors of events in Germany during 1945, they form part of an underlying story of longer-term success. And that success, one can reasonably argue, was built upon what happened during 1945. That said, without the iron tutelage of the Allies, without the benefits of the greatest economic boom in world history, without the establishment of a stable currency and a firm constitutional order, and without the forty years of division and limited sovereignty which made it impossible for Germans to repeat after the Second World War the sorts of mistakes they had made after the First, that success would not have been achieved. However, that achievement was also made possible through the profound shock of 1945 – a shock that not merely allowed but *compelled* Germans to leave racist imperialism behind, and made possible the German odyssey from catastrophe to democracy during the second half of the twentieth century.

One can identify five main features of the cataclysm of 1945 that paved the way to Germany's postwar success. The first was the *completeness of the German defeat*. The very fact that the defeat of Germany was total, that the war ended not with an armistice but with unconditional surrender, was an essential precondition for the positive transformation that followed. The fact that Nazi Germany had been completely crushed by the time the Wehrmacht finally surrendered left no room for a second stab-in-the-back legend of the sort that had gained acceptance after the First World War. The failure of the German people to rise up against the Nazi dictatorship as it headed towards total defeat may have left them with little moral and political credit at the end of the war, but it did serve to confirm that surrender had been unavoidable – and that responsibility for defeat lay with a regime that had launched a world war that could not be won. Failure ensured that there would be no continuity of government in Germany after the war, that there would be no one with whom the Allies might make a deal. It also ensured that no one was left to whom Germans might turn for a continuation of the struggle and no external source of support which might enable traces of the Nazi regime to survive beyond the end of the war. Total defeat meant that, constitutionally, politically and, to a considerable extent, psychologically, 1945 marked a fundamental break with the past. The completeness of the defeat gave substance to the idea of the 'zero hour'.

Closely associated with the conclusive quality of the German defeat was *the complete and obvious bankruptcy of National Socialism*. Nazism had been a disaster for the peoples of Europe long before 1945, but in 1945 it also was revealed to the German people, unmistakably, as a catastrophe. It had proved itself bankrupt in every conceivable sense. In terms of its own values, it had failed miserably. A racist political ideology that asserted the alleged superiority of the German people and glorified war had guided Germany to a defeat the like of which had never before been experienced – and at the hands of allegedly inferior peoples: the Slavs and 'Mongols' from the east, and the 'mongrel' nation across the Atlantic. The triumphant Soviet soldiers celebrating their victory at the Reichstag and the gum-chewing American GIs driving their jeeps across Germany provided confirmation of the bankruptcy of Nazi racism. At the end of a war launched by men convinced that life consisted of ruthless struggle, that might made right and that the strong had a right to exploit (and a duty to kill) the weak, the enemies of Nazi Germany had proved themselves the stronger. Far from showing themselves capable of leading the German people to glorious victory, for the most part the Nazi leadership either committed suicide, leaving their followers to face the consequences of the disaster that they had unleashed, or scrambled about trying to save their own skins. In the summer of 1945 there was little left of National Socialism that could provide heroic legends capable of inspiring a Nazi revival.

Nazism was not only exposed to the German people as a catastrophic failure on its own terms, but was also revealed to all as an assault on civilized values. As long as the German people had profited from the Nazi adventure, as long as they had benefited from Nazi racism and imperialist plunder, it had been possible to ignore the crimes that underpinned 'Aryan' privilege. However, in 1945 the privilege had evaporated and the crimes were exposed for all to see. It was one thing to snap up bargains at the auctions of property taken from Jews who had emigrated or had been deported to their deaths in the east[14] – after all, Germans who had lost their own property when bombed out of their homes did not necessarily give much thought to the origins of the goods on offer – but it was quite another thing to be confronted with the corpses of people murdered in the camps when Allied commanders forced Germans to view the handiwork of the Nazi regime. The revelation of the full extent of the depravity and inhumanity of National Socialism not only increased the self-confidence of those who had opposed it, and of church leaders who saw in the collapse of the Third Reich a confirmation of the wisdom of church teachings, but also removed any claim to moral or political leadership which deranged supporters of Nazism still might have held. It was one thing to support a leader at the head of a military struggle against Germany's enemies; it was quite another to support a regime that had created Dachau, Belsen and Auschwitz – all of which were exposed to the world when liberated by Allied troops in 1945.

The obvious bankruptcy of National Socialism also undermined the appeal of German nationalism generally. That the Nazi regime did not crumble until the very end, that Germans continued to follow their leaders until the eleventh hour, had had as much to do with German nationalism as it did with the appeal of National Socialism. On the defensive, Germans identified with their nation more than with Nazism; in the end they were fighting for their country rather than for the National Socialist 'idea'. The defeat of Nazi Germany, however, discredited German nationalism, which the Nazi regime had hijacked with such disastrous results. If this was where nationalism led, then better not to follow. This helps explain the appeal of various forms of internationalism in Germany after the Second World War: the appeal of religion, the appeal of Socialism and even Communism, the appeal of America, the appeal of European integration. For the time being at least, German nationalism would have little allure for the German people.

The third main feature of 1945 that subsequently contributed to the surprising success of postwar Germany was *the harshness with which the Allies imposed their occupation*. When Allied forces arrived in Germany in 1945, they were not disposed to handle the Germans with kid gloves. As Eisenhower had made clear, they arrived not as liberators but as victors. And they arrived in their millions. Their task in the first instance was to occupy an enemy country and to control its inhabitants, and that they did. Although it was the Red Army, and then the Soviet secret police apparatus which accompanied the Soviet Military Administration, that imposed the harshest occupation regime, beginning with an orgy of violence against a fearful and impotent civilian population, it was not just the Russians who came determined to stamp their authority on the occupied enemy country in no uncertain terms. Although the Americans and the British arrived with somewhat less punitive attitudes than did the

French and the Russians, all shared the view that their task was to control a conquered people who had fought a murderous war tenaciously and for years. Even the Americans, who in retrospect were remembered for handing out chewing gum and chocolate to German children and cigarettes and nylons to German women, were determined to impose order and to allow the defeated population to take no liberties. For tens of thousands of Germans, the arrival of the victors from the west meant not chewing gum but automatic arrest. The harshness of the occupation in its initial months left no room for successful resistance. Nazi fantasies of an insurgency created by 'Werewolf' fanatics remained just that: fantasies. A battered, exhausted, disillusioned and impoverished German people faced the overwhelming might of millions of Allied troops who were not prepared to tolerate any resistance to their rule.

The fourth important feature of the events of 1945 was *the vast extent of the losses*, both human and material, suffered by Germany and its people by the end of the war. These losses were so overwhelming, the numbers of dead and injured so large, the damage to the infrastructure and economy so extensive, the damage to cities and the loss of territory so great, that the resources no longer existed which might have fuelled revanchism during the postwar period. It should be remembered that, unlike in certain more recent conflicts, during the Second World War military strategists sought to inflict maximum damage and cause maximum death. As a result, by the time that the Wehrmacht surrendered, almost all German cities had been reduced to rubble, hundreds of thousands of people had been killed in bombing campaigns designed to cause maximum casualties, and millions of soldiers lay dead. While injury often leaves bitterness and a desire for revenge, the overwhelming scale of the losses suffered by Germans by the end of the war, left them profoundly disoriented and without the energy for much more than a struggle for individual survival.

This brings us to the fifth major consequence of the catastrophe of 1945, *the overwhelming focus of Germans upon their day-to-day concerns*. This had a number of causes: the destruction of the transport and communications infrastructure, which limited people to their immedisate surroundings; the catastrophic housing shortage, which left millions of Germans desperately seeking shelter; the severe food shortages, which meant that much of their time was devoted to the search for something to eat; the lack of fuel, which made keeping warm a constant preoccupation as the weather turned cold in late 1945; the pervasive threat of crime, which required unceasing vigilance; and the absence of family members, especially of men, who either were dead or languishing in Allied POW camps, which increased the demands on those who remained. All of this left Germans with little time or energy to deal with the wider world.

Here one really could speak of a 'zero hour'. The German people now had to start again from scratch. Nineteen forty-five was a year of catastrophe and, as a result, it also was a year of new beginnings. In a letter to his daughter in late September 1945, Robert Niebatz, a 70-year-old blacksmith, described conditions in Cottbus after the city had been occupied by the Red Army during the previous April:

> Arnold killed his entire family on the Wednesday before the Russians marched in, and now I am living over the forge as a tenant. Lotte has been living with me since 5 May, as her flat was confiscated. My old flat and the entire neighbourhood was burned down on Sunday, 22 April. The day of the entry [of the Soviet Army] was quite a drama. Your flat is half occupied . . . There are no more pensions. 10 Marks welfare payments per month is sufficient to buy what no longer is available . . . Even if I do everything possible to shield you from hunger, there will be little in the way of fats except for fresh eggs. . . . I have, thank God that I stayed here, saved four of Arnold's hens, from which I have two layers which have produced 18 chicks.[15]

By the time that Cottbus was captured by Soviet forces on 22 April, it had been bombed repeatedly, and in a city whose population had numbered roughly 51,000 before the war fewer than 8000 were left.[16] More than 1000 German soldiers had died in the senseless final battle for Cottbus, leaving the city ringed with mass graves. One hundred and eighty-seven Germans (including the 'fortress commandant' *Generalleutnant* Ralf Sodan) had committed suicide. Cottbus had become a field of ruins, littered with corpses. Nevertheless, in the midst of this terrible scene survivors felt the need to re-establish everyday routines which were life affirming: caring for hens, which, in a landscape of wartime destruction, would provide eggs and chicks.

During the last stages of the war 'a large portion of the people [had] become accustomed to live just for the day',[17] and after the tidal wave of violence had left their country in ruins, surviving Germans had little but their daily routines to cling to. The following observations, from an article published in 1995, were clearly intended to emphasize the dreadful nature of conditions immediately after the war. What emerges, however, is how important it was to piece together the constituents of everyday life:

'When we came back on 28 April [1945], a great hole yawned in the wall of our living room', remembers Minna Massalski. 'We repaired it with rocks, cardboard and wood . . . Thus the room became habitable once again.' Dr Kurt Elze experienced even worse: 'When I returned, I learned that our house no longer existed. As a result of the fire of the neighbouring [shop] our house was burned down as well. After that I placed myself at the disposal of . . . Dr Steinhäuser . . . That same day Mayor Döring issued a handwritten certificate in Russian and German according to which I could transport medicines with a hand-cart.'[18]

What mattered after the devastation was being able to retrieve fragments of a normal existence, whether that meant having a habitable living room once again or being able to exercise one's profession as a doctor.

Historians have been understandably reluctant to lend too much credence to the idea of a zero hour. 'Zero hour' was the description of 1945 widely used by Germans, and appeared to draw a line neatly between themselves and what had occurred (and, by extension, what they had been involved in) during the years of Nazi rule. Remarking on observations raised in interviews conducted in the Ruhr region during the early 1980s, Lutz Niethammer referred to 'the so-called "zero hour"' as the 'wishful thinking of the Germans' that consisted of the idea that 'everything was over and forgotten'.[19] To speak of a 'zero hour' was to deny the structural and personal continuities which extended from the Nazi period into the postwar world. It served to let Germans off a hook on which many historians, who have regarded it as their duty not to allow a nation of perpetrators to evade their moral responsibility, wanted to keep them skewered.

However, our task is less to judge than to understand. Of course many Germans were keen in 1945 to leave an unedifying and tarnished past behind, but that is part of the story and not the point of telling it. By refusing to acknowledge the terminology employed by the people who lived through those awful times, we risk failing to comprehend fully what happened, and its significance. If, seduced by the desire to emphasize the importance of continuities over the 1945 divide, we risk losing sight of the extent to which 1945 *was* a break, of the extent to which discontinuities rather than continuities framed people's experiences, and the ways in which they understood those experiences. While the concept of a 'zero hour' may have offered a convenient escape route from the nightmare of war and Nazism, that does not mean it should be dismissed out of hand. After what had happened to them, Germans desperately wanted to believe that 1945 marked a fundamental break with the past. It did – and that was no bad thing.

As a result of the horrors they endured – particularly in the last months and weeks of the war – Germans emerged with a powerful sense of their own victimhood. They did so following a war launched by a Germany which had invaded and conquered much of the European continent, enslaved millions of people, destroyed cities and towns from Rotterdam to Minsk, caused the deaths of millions of soldiers, and murdered innocent civilians on a hitherto unimaginable scale. After the shock of their experiences during the last days of the Reich, Germans became preoccupied almost exclusively with their own problems and sorrows, and hardly possessed the mental energy to concern themselves with the problems and sorrows of others. This enabled them to emerge from war and Nazism with a belief in their own moral rectitude, despite the crimes that had been committed in their name and, in many cases, with their involvement, whether active or passive. After the war there was a tension between the German wish to remember their own suffering and loss and the readiness to forget what they had inflicted on others.[20] In this they were not unique. The Japanese also emerged from the war with a pervasive sense of victimhood, preoccupied with their own suffering and giving little thought to the suffering they had caused to others.[21] Victim consciousness after mass death and total defeat, in Japan as well as Germany, profoundly shaped the manner in which people constructed their postwar identities.

It was not only the total military defeat and the end of national sovereignty; not only foreign military occupation, destruction of the political system, and paralysis of the economy; not only the loss of the former German east and the division of what remained of the country that left the German people with a challenge of monumental proportions in 1945: it was also the trauma caused by the unimaginable violence of mass death. Histories of post-1945 Germany have, understandably, focused on the transition from dictatorship to democracy, from economic crisis to economic miracle, from Nazi barbarism to European civilization.[22] This transition was an achievement unparalleled in modern European history: never before had a nation recovered so successfully from such terrible political, military, economic, social and moral wreckage as that left by Nazism and war. Yet for the individuals who emerged from that wreckage to build a life after death, the fundamental achievement − one that framed their memories of the end of the Second World War − was survival.[23]

The horrors of 1945 and the low expectations which people held about prospects for recovery made the subsequent successes of Germany during the second half of the twentieth century seem all the more astonishing. Many people, casting their eyes over the wreckage left when the Nazi regime collapsed, wondered if the damage could ever be repaired. It is revealing that, when reflecting on their postwar recovery, Germans often described it as a miracle. As the authors of a volume (published in 1964), describing the history of a 'world sinking into senseless destruction and into darkness and death' – the district of Kleve, along the Dutch border, during the last months of the war – concluded with almost lyrical prose:

> Life began again. Today one still hardly knows how people man-aged it. They had to bear untold privations; a people which had been tormented to the point of bleeding to death supplied an excess of victims yet again. However, a resolute will inspired everyone. The citizenry and administration achieved what was almost unbelievable during these early days. And they succeeded! Gradually order displaced chaos.[24]

It indeed appeared little short of miraculous that 'life began again', such was the degree of destruction and privation in 1945. But this was a man-made miracle: by dint of discipline and industry, so the story went, Germans were able to embark on a virtuous journey from catastrophe and victimhood to recovery and success. The shock of violence, destruction and death on a hitherto unimaginable scale was central to how Germans emerged into a postwar world where their country was occupied, divided and at the centre of the Cold War. The price they had paid was unprecedentedly high but, eventually, the Germans were able to rebuild 'normal' lives – albeit in the abnormal circumstances of a divided country in a divided Europe enjoying unparalleled prosperity and fearing nuclear annihilation.

Among the most remarkable aspects of the transformation of German mentalities that stemmed from the catastrophe of 1945 was the turn away from war and from the glorification of things military in the second half of the twentieth century. Whereas the French and the British had emerged from the First World War with a deep sense of the horrors of war and a conviction that in future war was to be avoided if at all possible, in Germany a parallel development did not really occur until after the Second World War. The events of 1945 led to a profound change in German popular and political culture. Finally an antiwar consensus came to dominate in German society and culture. In German eyes, the extreme violence of 1945 made the Second World War 'the war to end all wars'.[25]

This offers a stark contrast with the prevalence (but not monopoly) of a war-affirming 'myth of the war experience' which (in the widely applauded view of George Mosse) served after the First World War to prepare the cultural and political ground in Germany for embarking on the next conflict.[26] The German experiences at the end of the Second World War left little scope for a repeat of the war-affirming revanchism that followed the First. In this respect, Hitler was proved right when he declared to the assembled members of the Reichstag on 1 September 1939 that 'a November 1918 will never be repeated in German history'[27] – but not in the way he had envisaged. In the last days of the Reich, Hitler and his more fanatical followers may have hoped that to continue the militarily hopeless, suicidal conflict would inspire future generations to take up the struggle again.[28] However, the total defeat which the Third Reich bequeathed to the German people achieved just the opposite. It converted a nation once renowned for its reverence of the military into a nation which took a fundamental turn to pacifism.[29] This was reflected in popular attitudes in the postwar Federal Republic of Germany where, in the autumn of 1951, public-opinion polls revealed that nearly half the population – and more than half of former Wehrmacht soldiers – supported conscientious objection.[30] In this, attitudes had come to resemble those in interwar France. War was seen not as a glorious crusade but as a terrible cataclysm which created only victims and was to be avoided at all costs. War was remembered not as the German victories and jubilation of 1940 but the defeat and privations of 1945.

It is remarkable, but hardly surprising, that the terrible experiences of 1945 loomed large in German popular consciousness and in the popular history and literature of the immediate postwar period. During the late 1940s and through the 1950s vast numbers of books and pamphlets were published in (West) Germany, which vividly described the extent of the misery and destruction at the end of the war, usually graphically illustrated with photographs of towns and cities reduced to burned-out buildings and rubble-strewn streets. Only relatively recently, with new waves of studies published about the end of the war and the immediate postwar years, have German historians caught up with the preoccupations of their parents and grandparents. Yet for all the attention they now devote to it, historians have had some difficulty in dealing with the subject, as if to focus on the misery experienced by Germans might appear to minimize or trivialize the suffering that the Nazis inflicted on others, and sometimes feel obligated almost to issue a health warning when describing the conditions faced by Germans in 1945.[31] However, with the postwar era now behind us, with a united democratic Germany firmly anchored in a united Europe, it no longer is necessary to feel so circumscribed when trying to understand how Germans emerged from Nazism and war and how they began to build a future very different from their past.

Building life after death was not easy. The choices that Germans had to make and the ways they dealt with (or avoided dealing with) their past were often ambiguous. Confusion, despair, self-pity, hope and immense challenges formed a shaky foundation on which to build. Contemporaries could be forgiven for believing that their future would not be rosy. However, with the benefit of hindsight we can see that their world in fact had changed for ever, and for the better. At least from the perspective of the early twenty-first century, the result of what happened in 1945 appears to have been a remarkable, surprising success.

How did Germans at the end of 1945 look back upon the terrible, momentous year that had just passed? On the last night of 1945, the actor and cabaret artist Werner Finck remarked: 'Can we Germans shed a tear for this 45th product of the twentieth century? No, since we no longer have any more.'[32] No doubt his sentiments were shared by many Germans, preoccupied as they were with their own tribulations and sorrows. Yet, for the first time in many years one could say with some justification that at the end of the year life held more promise than it had at the beginning. On New Year's Day 1946, Hermann Hesse looked back on the year that had just passed, and wrote:

> And this time, so it appears, the new, the welcome, the as yet so unblemished year is something quite special and important. After years of slaughter and destruction it is the first New Year night for us in which there is no war.[33]

NOTES

1. Introduction: To Hell and Back

1 Victor Klemperer, *To the Bitter End. The Diaries of Victor Klemperer 1942–1945* (London, 2000), p. 484 (entry for 27 January 1945).

2 Letter from Gerda J., Hamburg/Altona, to Gerda T., Buchholz, Krs. Harburg (Niedersachsen), 7 May 1945, printed in Jörg Echternkamp, *Kriegsschauplatz Deutschland 1945. Leben in Angst – Hoffnung auf Frieden: Feldpost aus der Heimat und von der Front* (Paderborn, 2007), p. 252.

3 Hitler's message was broadcast at midnight on 1 January 1945 and the complete text was published in the daily newspapers on 1 January. For the text of the message, see Herbert Michaelis and Ernst Schraepler (eds.), *Ursachen und Folgen. Vom deutschen Zusammenbruch 1918 und 1945 bis zur staatlichen Neuordnung Deutschlands in der Gegenwart*, vol. 22 (Berlin, 1976), pp. 319–326 (doc. 3581a).

4 See Marlis Steinert, *Hitler's War and the Germans. Public Mood and Attitude during the Second World War* (Athens, Ohio, 1977), p. 293.

5 Rüdiger Overmans, *Deutsche militärische Verluste im Zweiten Weltkrieg* (Munich, 1999), pp. 265–6.

6 'Bericht aus Akten der Geschäftsführenden Reichsregierung Dönitz vom Ende März 1945', in Heinz Boberach (ed.), *Meldungen aus dem Reich. Die geheimen Lageberichte des Sicherheitsdienstes der SS 1938–1945*, Vol. 17 (Herrsching, 1984), pp. 6734–6740, here p. 6737. This report also may be found in Bundesarchiv Militärarchiv (BA-MA), RW44, Nr. I/11.

7 Ian Kershaw, *Hitler 1889–1936: Hubris* (London, 1998), p. xxx.

8 See Jörg Friedrich, *Der Brand. Deutschland im Bombenkrieg 1940–1945* (Munich, 2002); Ralf Blank, 'Kriegsalltag und Luftkrieg an der "Heimatfront"', in Jörg Echternkamp (ed.), *Die deutsche Kriegsgesellschaft 1939 bis 1945. Erster Halbband. Politisierung, Vernichtung, Überleben*

(Munich, 2004), pp. 357–461; Dietmar Süß (ed.), *Deutschland im Luftkrieg. Geschichte und Erinnerung* (Munich, 2007).

9   For an outline of the argument, see Richard Bessel, 'The War to End All Wars. The Shock of Violence in 1945 and its Aftermath in Germany', in Alf Lüdtke and Bernd Weisbrod (eds.), *No Man's Land of Violence. Extreme Wars in the 20th Century* (Göttingen, 2006), pp. 71–99.

10 See esp. Frank Bajohr, *'Arisierung' in Hamburg. Die Verdrängung der jüdischen Unternehmer 1933–1945* (Hamburg, 1997); Götz Aly, *Hitlers Volksstaat. Raub, Rassenkrieg und nationaler Sozialismus* (Frankfurt am Main, 2005); Adam Tooze, *The Wages of Destruction. The Making and Breaking of the Nazi Economy* (London, 2006).

11 Otto Dietrich, *Auf den Straßen des Sieges. Erlebnisse mit dem Führer in Polen* (Munich, 1940), p. 180.

12 Cited in Hans-Erich Volkmann, 'Von Blomberg zu Keitel – Die Wehrmachtführung und die Demontage des Rechtsstaates', in Rolf-Dieter Müller and Hans-Erich Volkmann (eds.), *Die Wehrmacht. Mythos und Realität* (Munich, 1999), p. 63.

13 Fritz Stern, *Verspielte Größe. Essays zur deutschen Geschichte des 20. Jahrhunderts* (Munich, 1996), p. 285 ('Verlorene Heimat', lecture given in Berlin on 1 June 1995).

14 Michael Wildt, *Generation des Unbedingten. Das Führungskorps des Reichssicherheitshauptamtes* (Hamburg, 2002).

15 On this theme, see Nicholas Stargardt, *Witnesses of War. Childrens' Lives under the Nazis* (London, 2005).

16 Manfred Uschner, *Die zweite Etage. Funktionsweise eines Machtapparates* (Berlin, 1993), pp. 28–9.

17 Quoted in Hans Dieter Schäfer, *Berlin im Zweiten Weltkrieg. Der Untergang der Reichshauptstadt in Augenzeugenberichten* (Munich, 1985), p. 309: 'Bericht über den "Sondereinsatz Berlin" für die Zeit vom 30.3.-7.4.1945', dated 10 April 1945.

18 Bundesarchiv Berlin, SAPMO-BA, NL 182, Nr. 1084, Bl. 85–90: Willi Barth, "Entwicklung und Tätigkeit der Beratenden Versammlung des Landes Thüringen", Berlin, 18 July 1946.

2. A World in Flames

1   Elke Fröhlich (ed.), *Die Tagebücher von Joseph Goebbels, Vol. 15, Januar-April 1945* (Munich, 1995), p. 34.

2   Testimony of Albert Speer on 20 June 1946, *Der Prozess gegen die Hauptkriegsverbrecher vor dem Internationalen Gerichtshof Nürnberg 14. November 1945 – 1. Oktober 1946* (Nuremberg, 1948), vol. xvi, p. 553.

3   Fröhlich (ed.), *Die Tagebücher von Joseph Goebbels, Vol. 15*, pp. 32–33.

4   See Rüdiger Overmans, *Deutsche militärische Verluste im Zweiten Weltkrieg* (Munich, 1999), p. 238. See also the suggestive comments in Andreas Kunz, 'Die Wehrmacht in der Agonie der nationalsozialistischen Herrschaft 1944/45. Eine Gedankenskizze', in Jörg Hillmann and John Zimmermann (eds.), *Kriegsende 1945 in Deutschland* (Munich, 2002), p. 107.

5   John Erickson, *The Road to Berlin* (London, 2003, first published 1983), p. 622. According to Erickson, of the roughly half million military and civilian casualties resulting from the Battle of Berlin, the three Soviet 'Fronts' (army groups) involved in the fighting lost 304,887 men killed, wounded and missing between 16 April and 8 May 1945.

6   *Die Wehrmachtberichte 1939–1945. Band 3: 1. Januar 1944 bis 9. Mai 1945* (Cologne, 1989), p. 450 (17 Feb. 1945), p. 540 (16 Apr. 1945), p. 542 (17 Apr. 1945). See also Günter Böddecker, *Der Untergang des Dritten Reiches. Mit den Berichten des Oberkommandos der Wehrmacht vom 6. Januar – 9. Mai 1945 und einer Bilddokumentation* (Munich, 1995), p. 90.

7   Lothar Gruchmann, *Der Zweite Weltkrieg. Kriegführung und Politik* (Munich, 1967), p. 414.

8   Karin Orth, 'Kampfmoral und Einsatzbereitschaft in der Kriegsmarine 1945', in Jörg Hillmann and John Zimmermann (eds.), *Kriegsende 1945 in Deutschland* (Munich, 2002), p. 140. See also Gottfried Hoch, 'Zur Problematik der Menschenführung im Krieg', in Günter Luther et. al., *Die Deutsche Marine. Historisches Selbstverständnis und Standortbestimmung* (Bonn, 1983), pp. 200–201, 207.

9   Quoted in Heinrich Schwendemann, 'Strategie der Selbstvernichtung: Die Wehrmachtführung im "Endkampf" um das "Dritte Reich"', in Rolf-Dieter Müller and Hans-Erich Volkmann (eds.), *Die Wehrmacht. Mythos und Realität* (Munich, 1999), p. 228.

10 See Schwendemann, 'Strategie der Selbstvernichtung', p. 227.

11 See Charles W. Sydnor, Jr., *Soldiers of Destruction. The SS Death's Head Division, 1933–1945* (Princeton, 1977), pp. 308–310.

12 'Auszug aus den "Niederschriften über Teilnahme des Oberbefehlshabers der Kriegsmarine aus den Führerlagen", 23.1. [1945], 16.00 Uhr', in Percy Ernst Schramm (ed.), *Kriegstagebuch des Oberkommandos der Wehrmacht (Wehrmachtführungsstab), Band IV: 1. Januar 1944 – 22. Mai 1945* (Frankfurt am Main, 1961), p. 1601.

13 Manfred Zeidler, *Kriegsende im Osten. Die Rote Armee und die Besetzung Deutschlands östlich von Oder und Neiße 1944/45* (Munich, 1996), p. 94.

14 According to General Jodl's diary, towards the end of January 1945 the central military commands still were receiving 120,000 telephone calls and 33,000 telexes on a single day. See Andreas Kunz, 'Die Wehrmacht in der Agonie der nationalsozialistischen Herrschaft', pp. 107–8.

15　*Reichsgesetzblatt* 1944, I, p. 253 (20 October 1944). (Also published in *Völkischer Beobachter*, 20 Oct. 1944.) See Hermann Jung, *Die Ardennen-Offensive 1944/45. Ein Beispiel für die Kriegführung Hitlers* (Göttingen, 1971), pp. 78–79; Rolf-Dieter Müller and Gerd R. Ueberschär, *Kriegsende 1945. Die Zerstörung des Deutschen Reiches* (Frankfurt am Main, 1994), pp. 42–47.

16　See Klaus Mammach, *Der Volkssturm. Das letzte Aufgebot 1944/45* (Cologne, 1981), pp. 31–74; David K. Yelton, *Hitler's Volkssturm: The Nazi Militia and the Fall of Germany 1944–1945* (Lawrence, Kansas, 2002), pp. 7–88. See also Roland Müller, *Stuttgart zur Zeit des Nationalsozialismus* (Stuttgart, 1988), pp. 519–20. By this point, Germans were far from enthusiastic to become cannon fodder for an obviously lost cause, particularly in formations which were ill-equipped, and it was not uncommon for men to seek to avoid being organized into the *Volkssturm*.

17　Quoted in Andreas Kunz, 'Die Wehrmacht in der Agonie der national-sozialistischen Herrschaft', p. 105.

18　See Bernd Wegner, 'Hitler, der Zweite Weltkrieg und die Choreographie des Untergangs', *Geschichte und Gesellschaft*, vol. xxvi (2000), no. 3, pp. 492–518; Michael Geyer, 'Endkampf 1918 and 1945. German Nationalism, Annihilation, and Self-Destruction', in Alf Lüdtke and Bernd Weisbrod (eds.), *No Man's Land of Violence. Extreme Wars in the 20th Century* (Göttingen, 2006), pp. 54–55.

19　Bundesarchiv-Militärarchiv (=BA-MA), RW 4/793: 'Hitlers Aufruf an die deutsche Wehrmacht anläßlich des Heldengedenktages 1945', Hauptquartier, 11 March 1945.

20　General Hellmuth Reymann, 'Grundsätzlicher Befehl für die Vorbereitungen zu Verteidigung der Reichshauptstadt', Berlin-Grünewald, 9 March 1945, printed in Reinhard Rürup (ed.), *Berlin 1945. Eine Dokumentation* (Berlin, 1995), pp. 25–26.

21　See Schwendemann, 'Strategie der Selbstvernichtung', p. 232; Klaus-Dietmar Henke, *Die amerikanische Besetzung Deutschlands* (Munich, 1995), pp. 802–813.

22　Manfred Overesch, *Das III. Reich 1939–1945. Eine Tageschronik der Politik, Wirtschaft, Kultur* (Düsseldorf, 1983), p. 582.

23　Hans Wrobel, *Verurteilt zur Demokratie. Justiz und Justizpolitik in Deutschland 1945–1949* (Heidelberg, 1989), p. 95.

24　Quoted in Manfred Messerschmidt and Fritz Wüllmer, *Die Wehrmachtsjustiz im Dienste des Nationalsozialismus. Zerstörung einer Legende* (Baden Baden, 1987), p. 127.

25　Geyer, 'Endkampf 1918 and 1945', p. 61. See also Messerschmidt and Wüllmer, *Die Wehrmachtsjustiz*; Stephen G. Fritz, *Endkampf. Soldiers,*

Civilians, and the Death of the Third Reich (Lexington, Kentucky, 2004), pp. 41, 130–139, 147.

26 Messerschmidt and Wüllmer, *Die Wehrmachtsjustiz*, p. 131. Messerschmidt and Wüllmer write that one must reckon with 'a few hundred thousand'.

27 See Kunz, 'Die Wehrmacht in der Agonie der nationalsozialistischen Herrschaft', p. 109.

28 For example, on 3 January 1945 the Wehrmacht reported: 'Yesterday all telephone connections to the west were interrupted sporadically.' See Schramm (ed.), *Kriegstagebuch des Oberkommandos der Wehrmacht. Band IV*, p. 981: 'Lagebuch 3.1.45'.

29 Schramm (ed.), *Kriegstagebuch des Oberkommandos der Wehrmacht. Band IV*, pp. 1305–1306.

30 Alfred C. Mierzejewski, *The Collapse of the German War Economy, 1944–1945. Allied Air Power and the German National Railway* (Chapel Hill and London, 1988), p. 173.

31 Wilhelm Michels and Peter Sliepenbeek, *Niederrheinisches Land im Krieg. Ein Beitrag zur Geschichte des Zweiten Weltkrieges im Landkreis Kleve* (Kleve, 1964), pp. 101–102.

32 BA-MA, N 648/1: Dethleffsen Erinnerungen, Kriegsgefangenenlager Allendorf, Winter 1945/46.

33 Schwendemann, 'Strategie der Selbstvernichtung', p. 232.

34 MacGregor Knox, *Common Destiny: Dictatorship, Foreign Policy, and War in Fascist Italy and Nazi Germany* (Cambridge, 2000), p. 187.

35 "Erlebnisbericht eines Angehörigen des Volkssturmbataillons 7/108 Franken über den Einsatz an der Oderfront", in Richard Lakowski, 'Das Ende der Naziherrschaft in Brandenburg. Mit einer Dokumentation', in Dietrich Eichholtz und Almuth Püschel (eds.), *Brandenburg in der NS-Zeit. Studien und Dokumente* (Berlin, 1993), p. 428.

36 See, for example, BA-MA, RW4, Nr. 495, f. 28: 'Anlage Nr. 1 zu Chef des NS-Fuehrungsstabes d.H. Nr. 304/45 g.Kdos. vom 19.3.45'.

37 'Ortsbericht Aalen', in Hansmartin Schwarzmaier (ed.), *Der deutsche Südwesten zur Stunde Null. Zusammenbruch und Neuanfang im Jahr 1945 in Dokumenten und Bildern* (Karlsruhe, 1975), pp. 114–15.

38 Quoted in Christoph Studt, *Das Dritte Reich in Daten* (Munich, 2002), p. 244.

39 Angus Calder, *The People's War. Britain 1939–1945* (London, 1969), p. 565; Toby Thacker, *The End of the Third Reich. Defeat, Denazification & Nuremberg. January 1944 – November 1946* (London, 2006), p. 83.

40 Mierzejewski, *The Collapse of the German War Economy*, p. 175. See also Alfred C. Mierzejewski, 'When Did Albert Speer Give Up?', *Historical Journal*, vol. 31, no. 2 (1988), pp. 391–7; Henke, *Die amerikanische Besetzung Deutschlands*, pp. 429 430.

41 Mierzejewski, *The Collapse of the German War Economy*, p. 172. Mierzejewski notes that 'by the end of March, overall car placings were only 11 percent of normal', and that in the Ruhr 'coal car placings were a mere 10 percent of normal in February and by the end of March had ceased altogether'.

42 In the first three months of 1945, the British and Americans dropped over 293,000 tons of bombs on Germany and German-occupied territory, considerably more than the 201,000 tons dropped in the whole of 1943. The British concentrated their bombing on oil targets and on towns and factories, while the Americans concentrated their bombing on railways and canals. See L.F. Ellis and A.E. Warhurst, *Victory in the West. Vol. II. The Defeat of Germany* (London, 1968; reprinted Uckfield, 2004), p. 219–228.

43 Heinrich Schwendemann, 'Endkampf und Zusammenbruch im deutschen Osten', in *Freiburger Universitätsblätter*, vol. 34, no. 139 (Dec. 1995), p. 15; Zeidler. *Kriegsende im Osten*, pp. 81–2; I.C.D. Dear and M.R.D. Foot (eds.), *The Oxford Companion to the Second World War* (Oxford and New York, 1995), p. 447.

44 Schwendemann, 'Strategie der Selbstvernichtung', pp. 224, 225.

45 Heinz Guderian, *Erinnerungen eines Soldaten* (Stuttgart, 2003) (first published in Heidelberg, 1951), p. 346.

46 Max Hastings, *Armageddon. The Battle for Germany 1944–45* (London, 2004), p. 153.

47 When he was interrogated in the summer of 1945, Speer remarked that roughly 1500 German tanks were available for action at the time but were 'immovable' due to the shortage of fuel. See Ulrich Schlie (ed.), *Albert Speer. Die Kransberg-Protokolle 1945. Seine ersten Aussagen und Aufzeichnungen (Juni-September)* (Munich, 2003), pp. 400–401. According to Speer, similar problems had condemned the Ardennes Offensive to failure: 'The transport difficulties were decisive for the rapid collapse of the Ardennes Offensive.' See *Die Kransberg-Protokolle*, p. 406.

48 Guderian, *Erinnerungen eines Soldaten*, p. 347. See also Müller and Ueberschär, *Kriegsende 1945*, p. 60; Böddecker, *Der Untergang des Dritten Reiches*, pp. 20–28; Raymond Cartier, *Der Zweite Weltkrieg*, Bd. 3: 1944–1945 (München, 1982); Werner Haupt, *1945. Das Ende im Osten. Chronik der Kampf in Ost- und Mitteldeutschland* (Dorheim, 1970); Heinz Magenheimer, *Abwehrschlacht an der Weichsel 1945. Vorbereitung, Ablauf, Erfahrungen* (Freiburg, 1976); Wolfgang Paul, *Der Endkampf um Deutschland 1945* (Esslingen, 1976). The Wehrmacht leadership, however, had recognized the threat of a Soviet offensive from the Baranow bridgehead and had attributed its delay in early January to the weather (as, among other things, a good frost was needed for a tank offensive). See Percy Ernst Schramm (ed.), *Die Niederlage 1945. Aus dem Kriegstagebuch des*

Oberkommandos der Wehrmacht (Munich, 1985), pp. 55–6: 'Lagebuch 9.1.45'.

49 Schramm (ed.), *Kriegstagebuch des Oberkommandos der Wehrmacht. Band IV*, p. 1010: 'Lagebuch 13.1.45'. See also Norman Davies and Roger Moorhouse, *Microcosm. Portrait of a Central European City* (London, 2003), p. 17.

50 Schramm (ed.), *Kriegstagebuch des Oberkommandos der Wehrmacht. Band IV*, p. 1010: 'Lagebuch 13.1.45'.

51 Hitler returned to his quarters in the Reich Chancellory on 16 January, while the Chief of the Wehrmacht High Command, Field Marshal Wilhelm Keitel, and the Chief of the Operations Staff of the OKW, Colonel General Alfred Jodl, moved into quarters in Berlin-Dahlem. The Operations Staff, which had been in Bad Nauheim during the Ardennes Offensive, now was located in the 'Maybach I' camp near Zossen, to the south of Berlin.

52 Zeidler. *Kriegsende im Osten*, p. 83; Heinz Magenheimer, 'Die Abwehrschlacht an der Weichsel 1945. Planung und Ablauf aus der Sicht der deutschen operativen Führung', in Militärgeschichtliches Forschungsamt (ed.), *Operatives Denken und Handeln in deutschen Streitkräften im 19. und 20. Jahrhundert* (Herford-Bonn, 1988), pp. 161–182 (here p. 178).

53 Rudolf Kabath, 'Die Rolle der Seebrückenköpfe beim Kampf um Ostpreussen 1944–1945', in Friedrich Forstmeier, Helmuth Forwick, Rudolf Kabath and Karl Köhler, *Abwehrkämpfe am Nordflügel der Ostfront 1944–1945* (Stuttgart, 1963), p. 285; Davies and Moorhouse, *Microcosm*, p. 17.

54 According to Soviet sources, the Soviet attack had moved forward twice as fast as the military leadership had predicted. See Lakowski, 'Das Ende der Naziherrschaft in Brandenburg', p. 412; John Erickson, '*Poslednii Shturm*: The Soviet Drive to Berlin, 1945', in Gill Bennett (ed.), *The End of the War in Europe 1945* (London, 1996), p. 18. See also Vassili Chuikov, *Das Ende des Dritten Reiches* (Munich, 1966), p. 105.

55 Schwendemann, 'Endkampf und Zusammenbruch im deutschen Osten', p. 15; Schwendemann, 'Strategie der Selbstvernichtung', p. 230.

56 Erickson, '*Poslednii Shturm*', p. 18.

57 Danuta Czech, *Kalendarium der Ereignisse im Konzentrationslager Auschwitz-Birkenau 1939–1945* (Reinbek bei Hamburg, 1989), pp. 992–995; Robert Jan van Pelt, *The Case for Auschwitz. Evidence from the Irving Trial* (Bloomington and Indianapolis, 2002), pp. 158–9; Sybille Steinbacher, *Auschwitz. A History* (London, 2005), p. 128.

58 Schramm (ed.), *Kriegstagebuch des Oberkommandos der Wehrmach. Band IV*, p. 1052: 'Lagebuch 29.1.45'. On the witness stand in Nuremberg a year and a half later, Speer put the position as follows:

With the successful offensive of the Soviet armies on the Upper
Silesian coal field from mid January, here too the greatest part of
coal supplies were eliminated. With that it could be calculated
precisely when the economy had to collapse. With that a situation had been reached in which, even were enemy military
operations to cease, the war would be lost within a short time, as
the Reich would collapse economically from being starved inter-
nally of coal.

See the testimony of Albert Speer on 20 June 1946, *Der Prozess gegen die
Hauptkriegsverbrecher vor dem Internationalen Gerichtshof Nürnberg 14.
November 1945 – 1. Oktober 1946* (Nuremberg, 1948), vol. xvi, p. 539.

59   Guderian, *Erinnerungen eines Soldaten*, p. 369. Guderian also noted that at
this point Speer drafted a new memorandum beginning with the sentence
'the war is lost'. When being interrogated in the summer of 1945, Speer
stated that 'The final collapse of armament and war production then
became unavoidable due to the loss of the great part of Upper Silesian coal
at the end of January 1945'. See Schlie (ed.), *Albert Speer. Die Kransberg-
Protokolle 1945*, p. 407.

60   Schwendemann, 'Strategie der Selbstvernichtung', p. 232.

61   Richard Lakowski, 'Das Ende der Naziherrschaft in Brandenburg. Mit
einer Dokumentation', in Dietrich Eichholz (ed.), *Brandenburg in der NS-
Zeit. Studien und Dokumente* (Berlin, 1993), p. 412.

62   The 'Fortress' Küstrin, with its 9000 defenders, held out until 29 March.
See Lakowski, 'Das Ende der Naziherrschaft in Brandenburg', p. 413.

63   Chuikov, *Das Ende des Dritten Reiches*, pp. 101–109; Zeidler, *Kriegsende im
Osten*, p. 94. It was Chuikov who received the surrender of the Berlin city
garrison in May 1945.

64   Zeidler, *Kriegsende im Osten*, pp. 83–87.

65   See Kabath, 'Die Rolle der Seebrückenköpfe beim Kampf um Ostpreussen',
pp. 286–290.

66   See Schramm (ed.), *Kriegstagebuch des Oberkommandos der Wehrmacht. Band
IV*, p. 1033. Subsequently, stone from the German memorial was used to
build the Soviet war memorial in the centre of nearby Olsztyn
(Allenstein).

67   Zeidler, *Kriegsende im Osten*, pp. 85–87.

68   Quoted in Schwendemann, 'Endkampf und Zusammenbruch im
deutschen Osten', p. 17.

69   Schwendemann, 'Endkampf und Zusammenbruch im deutschen Osten',
p. 16.

70   Lakowski, 'Das Ende der Naziherrschaft in Brandenburg', p. 413.

71   Zeidler, *Kriegsende im Osten*, p. 94. Goebbels rushed to visit Lauban on 11

March, in order to squeeze what propaganda value he could from this temporary German military success. See Wolfram Wette, Ricarda Bremer and Detlef Vogel (eds.), *Das letzte halbe Jahr. Stimmungsberichte der Wehrmachtpropaganda 1944/45* (Essen, 2001), pp. 354–5: 'Bericht des Wehrmacht-Propaganda-Offizieres des Wehrkreiskommandos III. Berlin, Oberstleutnant Wasserfall, über den "Sondereinsatz Berlin" für die Zeit vom 30.3. bis 7.4.1945', Berlin, 10 Apr. 1945.

72 The Wehrmacht recorded two figures, one totalling 81,834 casualties (12,652 dead, 38,600 wounded and 30,582 missing), the other totalling 98,024 (not broken down further). See Schramm (ed.), *Kriegstagebuch des Oberkommandos der Wehrmacht. Band IV*, p. 1362.

73 Schramm (ed.), *Kriegstagebuch des Oberkommandos der Wehrmacht. Band IV*, p. 977: 'Lagebuch 2.1.45'; Hermann Jung, *Die Ardennen-Offensive 1944/45. Ein Beispiel für die Kriegführung Hitlers* (Göttingen, 1971), p. 186. In December the Germans had managed to down 611 Allied aircraft in the West, but lost 795 of their own. See Schramm (ed.), *Kriegstagebuch des Oberkommandos der Wehrmacht. Band IV*, p. 980: 'Lagebuch 3.1.45'.

74 Henke, *Die amerikanische Besetzung Deutschlands*, p. 340.

75 Ellis and Warhurst, *Victory in the West. Vol. II*, pp. 256–257.

76 Henke, *Die amerikanische Besetzung Deutschlands*, p. 344. Henke quotes the SHAEF Weekly Intelligence Summary from 11 February 1945.

77 Henke, *Die amerikanische Besetzung Deutschlands*, pp. 316–318.

78 Hastings, *Armageddon*, pp. 420–421.

79 Ellis and Warhurst, *Victory in the West. Vol. II*, p. 283.

80 Henke, *Die amerikanische Besetzung Deutschlands*, pp. 348.

81 Ellis and Warhurst, *Victory in the West. Volume II*, p. 296.

82 See Martin Kitchen, *The Silent Dictatorship. The Politics of the German High Command under Hindenburg and Ludendorff, 1916–1918* (London, 1976), pp. 247–70.

83 See Schwendemann, 'Strategie der Selbstvernichtung', p. 228.

84 BA-MA, RW4, Nr. 704, ff. 3–6: Wehrmachtführungsstab, 'Rücksprache mit dem Sachbearbeiter der Parteikanklei für Evakuierungsfragen', F.H.Qu., 6 Jan. 1945 (initialled by Keitel, 8 Jan. 1945).

85 Quoted in Schwendemann, 'Strategie der Selbstvernichtung', p. 238.

86 Schwendemann, 'Strategie der Selbstvernichtung', pp. 238–9.

87 'Aktennotiz einer Besprechung über die Versorgungslage der 2. Armee, 9 March 1945', printed in Gerhard Förster and Richard Lakowski (eds.), *1945. Das Jahr der endgültigen Niederlage der faschistischen Wehrmacht* (Berlin, 1985), pp. 201–202 (Dokument 96).

88 Quoted in Schwendemann, 'Strategie der Selbstvernichtung', p. 240. As Schwendemann notes, while in his best-selling memoirs Speer devoted attention to his alleged, unsuccessful attempts to stir Hitler's concern for

'the miseries of the refugees', he neglected to make any mention of this order. See Albert Speer, *Inside the Third Reich* (London, 1975), p. 566.

89 BA-MA, RW4, Nr. 709, f. 160: 'Notiz für Gen. Lt. Winter!', 'Betr. Schutzzonen für die Zivilbevölkerung in Berlin', dated in pencil '16/4'. Keitel's comments added in pencil.

90 Böddecker, *Der Untergang des Dritten Reiches*, pp. 109–110.

91 Schwendemann, 'Endkampf und Zusammenbruch im deutschen Osten', pp. 16–17.

92 Schwendemann, 'Strategie der Selbstvernichtung', p. 235. See also Friedrich Hoßbach, *Die Schlacht um Ostpreußen. Aus den Kämpfen der deutschen 4. Armee um Ostpreußen in der Zeit von 19.7.1944 – 30.1.1945* (Überlingen, 1951), pp. 67–73.

93 The decision was made public in the Wehrmacht report of 12 April, with the observation that Lasch had been 'sentenced by the military court to death by hanging for the cowardly surrender to the enemy. His family is made liable.' See *Die Wehrmachtberichte 1939–1945. Band 3: 1. Januar 1944 bis 9. Mai 1945* (Cologne, 1989), p. 532.

94 For thoughts along these lines, see David Keith Yelton, '"Ein Volk steht auf". The German Volkssturm and Nazi Strategy 1944–1945', *The Journal of Military History*, vol. 64 (2000), pp. 1068–70. See also Gerhard L. Weinberg, 'German Plans for Victory, 1944–1945', in his *Germany, Hitler and World War II: Essays in Modern German and World History* (Cambridge, 1994), pp. 274–86.

95 See Bernd Wegner, 'Hitler, der Zweite Weltkrieg und die Choreographie des Untergangs', *Geschichte und Gesellschaft*, vol. xxvi (2000), no. 3, pp. 492–518; Michael Geyer, 'Endkampf 1918 and 1945. German Nationalism, Annihilation, and Self-Destruction', in Alf Lüdtke and Bernd Weisbrod (eds.), *No Man's Land of Violence. Extreme Wars in the 20th Century* (Göttingen, 2006), pp. 49–67.

96 The front page of the Nazi Party's Gau newspaper, the *Schlesische Tageszeitung*, for 22 January 1945 is printed in Sebastian Siebel-Aschenbach, *Lower Silesia from Nazi Germany to Communist Poland 1942–49* (New York, 1994), p. 62. See also Davies and Moorhouse, *Microcosm*, p. 15. For a contemporary account of the evacuation of civilians from Breslau, and the panic which ensued, see Paul Peikert, *'Festung Breslau' in den Berichten eines Pfarrers 22. Januar bis 6. Mai 1945* (Berlin, 1971), pp. 23–44.

97 Siebel-Aschenbach, *Lower Silesia*, p. 61.

98 These are the figures given in Böddecker, *Der Untergang des Dritten Reiches*, p. 91.

99 Böddecker, *Der Untergang des Dritten Reiches*, pp. 95–6; Siebel-Aschenbach, *Lower Silesia*, p. 75.

100 See Hans von Ahlfen and Hermann Niehoff, *So kämpfte Breslau. Verteidigung und Untergang von Schlesiens Hauptstadt* (Stuttgart, 1991), pp. 74, 83.

101 Schwendemann, 'Strategie der Selbstvernichtung', pp. 240–241.

102 See Peikert, *'Festung Breslau'*; Davies and Moorhouse, *Microcosm*, pp. 13–37.

103 See Hastings, *Armageddon*, pp. 332–336.

104 Michaelis and Schraepler (eds.), *Ursachen und Folgen*, vol 22, p. 349, doc. 3584d.

105 See Karl-Heinz Frieser, 'Die Schlacht um die Seelower Höhen im April 1945', in Roland G. Foerster (ed.), *Seelower Höhen 1945* (Hamburg, 1998), pp. 128–143.

106 Ian Kershaw, *The 'Hitler Myth'. Image and Reality in the Third Reich* (Oxford, 1987), pp. 221–225.

107 See the suggestive comments in Thomas Kühne, *Kameradschaft. Die Soldaten des nationalsozialistischen Krieges und das 20. Jahrhundert* (Göttingen, 2006), p. 203.

108 Generally, see Messerschmidt and Wüllner, *Die Wehrmachtsjustiz*.

109 Förster and Lakowski (eds.), *Das Jahr der endgültigen Niederlage*, p. 129.

110 In February 1945 the Feldjägerkommando II, operating behind the lines of the Army Group Centre under the command of Ferdinand Schörner, reported that it had picked up 136,000, of whom more than half imme- diately were sent back to the front. See Jürgen Förster, 'Die Niederlage der Wehrmacht: Das Ende des "Dritten Reiches"', in Foerster (ed.), *Seelower Höhen 1945*, pp. 10–11.

111 Quoted in Messerschmidt and Wüllner, *Die Wehrmachtsjustiz*, p. 117.

112 Text in Schramm (ed.), *Kriegstagebuch des Oberkommandos der Wehrmacht. Band IV*, pp. 1589–1590. See also Förster, 'Die Niederlage der Wehrmacht', p. 11.

113 Schramm (ed.), *Kriegstagebuch des Oberkommandos der Wehrmacht. Band IV*, p. 1364 (Meldung des OB West vom 7.2.1945).

114 Quoted in Förster, 'Die Niederlage der Wehrmacht', p. 11.

115 BA-MA, RW4, Nr. 495, ff. 23–27: Der Chef des NS-Fuehrungsstabes, 'Truppenbesuch im Bereich OB West und Ersatzheer', 19 March 1945.

116 BA-MA, RW4, Nr. 495, ff. 23–27 (here f. 26): Der Chef des NS-Fuehrungsstabes, 'Truppenbesuch im Bereich OB West und Ersatzheer', 19 March 1945.

117 BA-MA, RW4, Nr. 495, ff. 23–27 (here f. 25): Der Chef des NS-Fuehrungsstabes, 'Truppenbesuch im Bereich OB West und Ersatzheer', 19 March 1945. 'Since the German soldier does not fight as well in the presence of the civilian population', the suggested answer to this dilemma was to evacuate the civilian population if possible.

118 Speer, *Inside the Third Reich*, p. 585.

119 Speer, *Inside the Third Reich*, p. 586.

120 Fröhlich (ed.), *Die Tagebücher von Joseph Goebbels. Band 15*, p. 569 (entry from 22 March 1945). See also Marlis Steinert, *Hitler's War and the Germans. Public Mood and Attitude during the Second World War* (Athens, Ohio, 1977), pp. 308–309; Richard Overy, *Why the Allies Won* (New York and London, 1996), pp. 132–133; Jörg Echternkamp, *Kriegsschauplatz Deutschland 1945. Leben in Angst – Hoffnung auf Frieden: Feldpost aus der Heimat und von der Front* (Paderborn, Munich, Vienna and Zürich, 2006), pp. 57–61.

121 Schwendemann, 'Strategie der Selbstvernichtung', p. 241.

122 See Richard Bessel, 'The War to End All Wars. The Shock of Violence in 1945 and its Aftermath in Germany', in Alf Lüdtke and Bernd Weisbrod (eds.), *No Man's Land of Violence. Extreme Wars in the 20th Century* (Göttingen, 2006), pp. 69–99.

123 The decision to launch this last offensive in Hungary, although Allied forces were poised to capture central Germany and Berlin, had its origins in Hitler's conviction (expressed to Dönitz on 23 January) that without the Hungarian oil fields and the Vienna basin the war could not be continued. See Förster, 'Die Niederlage der Wehrmacht', p. 6.

3. Murder and Mayhem

1 Ursula von Kardorff, *Berliner Aufzeichnungen 1942–1945* (Munich, 1976), p. 253f. Quoted in Klaus-Dietmar Henke, *Die amerikanische Besetzung Deutschlands* (Munich, 1995), p. 840.

2 Hugo Gryn, with Naomi Gryn, *Chasing Shadows* (Harmondsworth, 2001), pp. 238–239, 120f.

3 On the death marches, see Yehuda Bauer, 'The Death Marches, January – May 1945', in Michael Marrus (ed.), *The Nazi Holocaust: Historical Articles on the Destruction of the European Jews* (Westport and London, 1989), vol. 9, pp. 491–511; Daniel Jonah Goldhagen, *Hitler's Willing Executioners: Ordinary Germans and the Holocaust* (New York, 1996), pp. 327–371; Daniel Blatman, 'Die Todesmärsche – Entscheidungsträger, Mörder und Opfer', in Ulrich Herbert, Karin Orth and Christoph Dieckmann (eds.), *Die nationalsozialistischen Konzentrationslager. Entwicklung und Struktur* (Göttingen, 1998), vol. ii, pp. 1063–1092; Saul Friedländer, *The Years of Extermination. Nazi Germany and the Jews 1939–1945* (London, 2007), pp. 648–652.

4 On 15 August the total had stood at 524,286: 379,167 men and 145,119 women. See Martin Broszat, 'Nationalsozialistische Konzentrationslager 1933–1945', in Martin Broszat, Hans Buchheim, Hans-Adolf Jacobsen and Helmut Krausnick, *Anatomie des SS-Staates* (Munich, 1967), vol. ii, p. 132; Daniel Blatman, 'Die Todesmärsche', pp. 1066–1067.

5   Martin Broszat estimated in the 1960s that 'at least a third of the over 700,000 prisoners registered in January 1945 died on the exhausting evacuation marches, in the transport trains which wandered about for weeks, and (above all) in the completely overcrowded reception camps during the months and weeks immediately before the end of the war'. See Broszat, 'Nationalsozialistische Konzentrationslager 1933–1945', pp. 132–133. More recently, Yehuda Bauer has estimated that as many as half the prisoners could have died. See Bauer, 'The Death Marches', p. 1069; Jan Erik Schulte, *Zwangsarbeit und Vernichtung. Oswald Pohl und das SS-Wirtschafts-Verwaltungsamt 1933–1945* (Paderborn, Munich, Vienna and Zürich, 2001), p. 405.

6   Harry Stein, 'Funktionswandel des Konzentrationslagers Buchenwald im Spiegel der Lagerstatistiken', in Herbert, Orth and Dieckmann (eds.), *Die nationalsozialistischen Konzentrationslager*, vol. i, pp. 186–187.

7   Michel Fabréguet, 'Entwicklung und Veränderung der Funktionen des Konzentrationslagers Mauthausen 1938–1945', in Herbert, Orth and Dieckmann (eds.), *Die nationalsozialistischen Konzentrationslager*, vol. i, pp. 202, 209.

8   Broszat, 'Nationalsozialistische Konzentrationslager 1933–1945', p. 132; Jens-Christian Wagner, *Produktion des Todes, Das KZ Mittelbau-Dora* (Göttingen, 2001), pp. 201–208.

9   Wagner, *Produktion des Todes*, p. 268.

10 Quoted in Wagner, *Produktion des Todes*, p. 332. Mittelbau-Dora received roughly 4000 prisoners from Auschwitz in early 1945, followed by more than 10,000 from Groß-Rosen. See Wagner, *Produktion des Todes*, pp. 269–70.

11 Wagner, *Produktion des Todes*, p. 272–73.

12 Hermann Kaienburg, 'Funktionswandel des KZ-Kosmos? Das Konzentrationslager Neuengamme 1938–1945', in Herbert, Orth and Dieckmann (eds.), *Die nationalsozialistischen Konzentrationslager*, vol. i, pp. 270–271; Detlef Garbe, 'Institutionen des Terrors und der Widerstand der Wenigen', in Forschungsstelle für Zeitgeschichte in Hamburg (ed.), *Hamburg im "Dritten Reich"* (Hamburg, 2005), pp. 550–551.

13 Wilhelm Lange, *Cap Arcona. Dokumentation* (3nd ed., Eutin, 1988); Kaienburg, 'Funktionswandel des KZ-Kosmos?', p. 270: Garbe, 'Institutionen des Terrors', p. 554.

14 See Nikolaus Wachsmann, *Hitler's Prisons. Legal Terror in Nazi Germany* (New Haven and London, 2004), pp. 323–338.

15 Quoted in Wachsmann, *Hitler's Prisons*, p. 326.

16 Quoted in Gabriele Lotfi, *KZ der Gestapo. Arbeitserziehungslager im Dritten Reich* (Stuttgart and Munich, 2000), pp. 292–293.

17 Lotfi, *KZ der Gestapo*, p. 295.

18   For a table of some 30 instances of executions carried out by the Security
     Police in the Rhine-Westphalian military district alone – almost of them
     in February, March and April 1945, see Lotfi, *KZ der Gestapo*,
     pp. 304–306.

19   Lotfi, *KZ der Gestapo*, pp. 298–300.

20   Tables in Ulrich Herbert, *Hitler's Foreign Workers. Enforced Foreign Labor in
     Germany under the Third Reich* (Cambridge, 1997), pp. 297, 298.

21   'Bericht über den "Sondereinsatz Berlin" für die Zeit vom 25.12.-
     31.12.1944', dated 3 Jan. 1945. Quoted in Hans Dieter Schäfer, *Berlin im
     Zweiten Weltkrieg. Der Untergang der Reichshauptstadt in Augenzeugenberichten*
     (Munich, 1985), p. 248.

22   Report of the Regierungspräsident of Swabia, quoted in Joachim
     Brückner, *Kriegsende in Bayern 1945. Der Wehrkreis VII und die Kämpfe
     zwischen Donau und Alpen* (Freiburg, 1987), pp. 51–2.

23   See Herbert, *Hitler's Foreign Workers*, pp. 364–70. Already during the
     autumn of 1944, as the bombing increasingly disrupted daily life and pro-
     duction, some foreign workers had fled the camps in which they had
     been housed and formed gangs, captured firearms and engaged in robbery
     and looting. See Bernd-A. Rusinek, '"Maskenlose Zeit". Der Zerfall der
     Gesellschaft im Krieg', in Ulrich Borsdorf and Mathilde Jamin (eds.),
     Über Leben im Krieg. Kriegserfahrungen in einer Industrieregion 1939–1945
     (Reinbek bei Hamburg, 1989), pp. 189–190.

24   'Mitteilungsblatt' of the NSDAP Kreisleitung in Küstrin, 5 Feb. 1945,
     reproduced in Hermann Thrams, *Küstrin 1945. Tagebuch einer Festung*
     (Berlin, 1992), p. 47.

25   Quoted in Lotfi, *KZ der Gestapo*, pp. 277–278.

26   Quoted in Lotfi, *KZ der Gestapo*, p. 277. See also Gerhard Paul and
     Alexander Primavesi, 'Die Verfolgung der "Fremdvölkischen". Das
     Beispiel der Staatspolizei Dortmund', in Gerhard Paul and Klaus-Michael
     Mahlmann (eds.), *Die Gestapo – Mythos und Realität* (Dusseldorf, 1995),
     pp. 399–401.

27   See Herbert, *Hitler's Foreign Workers*, pp. 370–74; Rusinek, '"Maskenlose
     Zeit"', pp. 190–191. See also Gerhard Paul, '"Diese Erschießungen haben
     mich innerlich gar nicht mehr berührt." Die Kriegsendeverbrechen der
     Gestapo 1944/45', in Gerhard Paul and Klaus-Michael Mallmann (eds.),
     Die Gestapo im Zweiten Weltkrieg. 'Heimatfront' und besetztes Europa
     (Darmstadt, 2000), pp. 552–562.

28   For these and the following cases, see Paul, '"Diese Erschießungen haben
     mich innerlich gar nicht mehr berührt"', pp. 553–562.

29   Lotfi, *KZ der Gestapo*, pp. 279–292.

30   See Gerhard Paul, *Landunter. Schleswig-Holstein und das Hakenkreuz*
     (Münster 2001), pp. 298–300.

31 Paul, '"Diese Erschießungen haben mich innerlich gar nicht mehr berührt", p. 543.

32 Paul, '"Diese Erschießungen haben mich innerlich gar nicht mehr berührt", p. 561.

33 For example, as American artillery was shelling Hemer (on 9 April) and Iserlohn (on 11 April) and at least 13 foreign prisoners (who had been caught stealing food or looting) were executed, see Lotfi, *KZ der Gestapo*, p. 309.

34 For example, at the end of 1944 the former head of the Security Police in Warsaw, the SS-Standartenführer D. Ludwig Hahn, took command of the Security Police in Münster; at the beginning of February 1945 the SS-Standartenführer Rudolf Batz, who had headed the Security Police in Krakow, arrived to command the Security Police in Dortmund. See Lotfi, *KZ der Gestapo*, p. 278.

35 Quoted in Rusinek, '"Maskenlose Zeit"', p. 189.

36 See Jörg Friedrich, *Der Brand. Deutschland im Bombenkrieg 1940–1945* (Munich, 2002), pp. 488–489.

37 Telegram of the Reich Justice Ministry to the Public Prosecutor at the Special Court in Hirschberg, re: Death sentence on town official Otto S. from Dombrowa on 6 Feb. 1945, in Jeremy Noakes (ed.), *Nazism. Volume 4. The German Home Front in World War II* (Exeter, 1998), p. 655.

38 *Reichsgesetzblatt* 1945, I, p. 30: 'Verordnung über die Errichtung von Standgerichten vom 15. Februar 1945'. This also is printed in Herbert Michaelis and Ernst Schraepler (eds.), *Ursachen und Folgen. Vom deutschen Zusammenbruch 1918 und 1945 bis zur staatlichen Neuordnung Deutschlands in der Gegenwart*, vol. 22 (Berlin, 1976), pp. 366–367, doc. 3585d. For a translation of the text of the decree, see Noakes (ed.), *Nazism. Volume 4*, pp. 655–6. See also Hans Wrobel, *Verurteilt zur Demokratie. Justiz und Justizpolitik in Deutschland 1945–1949* (Heidelberg, 1989), pp. 94–97.

39 Quoted in Henke, *Die amerikanische Besetzung Deutschland*, p. 845. See also Wrobel, *Verurteilt zur Demokratie*, pp. 94–97.

40 See Alois Stadtmüller, *Maingebiet und Spessart im Zweiten Weltkrieg. Überblick – Luftkrieg – Eroberung* (3rd edn., Aschaffenburg, 1987), p. 554.

41 Henke, *Die amerikanische Besetzung Deutschlands*, p. 853.

42 Quoted in Hans-Martin Stimpel, *Widersinn 1945. Aufstellung, Einsatz und Untergang eines militärischen Verbandes* (Göttingen, 1998), p. 68.

43 'Warum ich nach sechzig Jahren mein Schweigen breche. Eine deutsche Jugend: Günter Grass spricht zum ersten Mal über sein Erinnerungsbuch und seine Mitgliedschaft in der Waffen-SS', *Frankfurter Allgemeine Zeitung*, 12 Aug. 2006, no. 186, p. 33.

44 See Henke, *Die amerikanische Besetzung Deutschlands*, pp. 844–861.

45 On the terror in Heilbronn, see Friedrich Blumenstock, *Der Einmarsch der*

Amerikaner und Franzosen im nördlichen Württemberg im April 1945 (Stuttgart, 1957), pp. 29–34; Henke, *Die amerikanische Besetzung Deutschlands*, pp. 847–851. On Richard Drauz, see Susanne Schlösser, "'Was sich in den Weg stellt, mit Vernichtung schlagen". Richard Drauz, NSDAP-Kreisleiter von Heilbronn', in Michael Kißener and Joachim Schlotyseck (eds.), *Die Führer der Provinz. NS-Biographien aus Baden und Württemberg* (Konstanz, 1997), pp. 143–159. Drauz was tried by a U.S. Army court for shooting at least one American prisoner of war, and was executed in Landsberg on 4 December 1946.

46   Henke, *Die amerikanische Besetzung Deutschlands*, pp. 851–852.

47   Sixth Army Group, G-2, Weekly Intelligence Summary Nr. 32, from 28 April 1945, NA, RG 407, Operations Reports, Box 1742. Quoted in Henke, *Die amerikanische Besetzung Deutschlands*, p. 853.

48   Manfred Messerschmidt and Fritz Wüllner, *Die Wehrmachtsjustiz im Dienste des Nationalsozialismus. Zerstörung einer Legende* (Baden-Baden, 1987), p. 131.

49   See, for example, Blumenstock, *Der Einmarsch der Amerikaner*, pp. 28–34.

50   Details in Andreas Kunz, 'Die Wehrmacht in der Agonie der national-sozialistischen Herrschaft 1944/45', in Jörg Hillmann and John Zimmermann (eds.), *Kriegsende 1945 in Deutschland* (Munich, 2002), p. 103, fn. 26.

51   Quoted in Rudolf Absolon (ed.), *Die Wehrmacht im Dritten Reich* (Band 6: 19. Dezember bis 9. Mai 1945) (Boppard am Rhein, 1995), p. 604.

52   Adolf Hitler, *Mein Kampf* (Boston, 1943) (trans. by Ralph Mannheim), p. 524. See also Wolfram Wette, *Die Wehrmacht. Feindbilder, Vernichtung, Legenden* (Frankfurt am Main), p. 165.

53   Steven R. Welch, "'Harsh but Just"? German Military Justice in the Second World War: A Comparative Study of the Court-Martialling of German and U.S. Deserters', *German History*, vol. 17, no. 3 (1999), p. 389.

54   Wilhelm Langenbach, 'Bedrohung – Entbehrung – Drangsalierung . Bestrafung. Erinnerungen an die Not- und Leidenszeit von 1939–1948', in *Krieg und Elend im Siegerland. Das Inferno an der Heimatfront in den 1940er Jahren* (Siegen, 1981), p. 17.

55   Wolfgang Franz Werner, *'Bleib übrig'. Deutsche Arbeiter in der national-sozialistischen Kriegswirtschaft* (Düsseldorf, 1983), pp. 329–333.

56   On looting by German civilians in Tübingen, see Manfred Schmidt (ed.), *Tübingen 1945. Eine Chronik von Hermann Werner* (Tübingen, 1986), p. 86; for a general description of the looting in Franconia, see Karl Kunze, *Kriegsende in Franken und der Kampf um Nürnberg im April 1945* (Nürnberg, 1995), pp. 185–7, 353. For reports of Wehrmacht soldiers looting the homes of German civilians in western Germany in February 1945, see BA-MA, RW 4/722, f. 57: Chef OKW to Wehrmachtführungsstab III

(Org.), [undated, received 21 Feb. 1945], 'Betrifft: Erschwerung von Räumungen in frontnahem Gebiet durch disziplinloses Verhalten von Truppenangehörigen'. For reports of looting by Wehrmacht soldiers of German property on the eastern front, see BA–MA, RW 4/722, ff. 80–1: Feldpostprüfselle b.d. Armeegruppe Heinrici to OKW/WFSt/Abt. Truppenabwehr, E.O., 12 March 1945. Oral testimony of looting by Germans of Wehrmacht supply depots at the end of the war, was presented on the television programme 'Kriegskinder in Mitteldeutschland', broadcast on MDR on 19 April 2005.

57 See, generally, Patrick Wagner, *Hitlers Kriminalisten. Die deutsche Kriminalpolizei und der Nationalsozialismus* (Munich, 2002), pp. 113–28.

58 'Rundschreiben 16/45 des Leiters der Partei-Kanzlei Martin Bormann zur Schließung von Schulen, 21.1.1945', printed in Karl-Heinz Jahnke, *Hitlers letztes Aufgebot. Deutsche Jugend im sechsten Kriegsjahr 1944/45* (Essen, 1993), p. 122; 'Schreiben der Partei-Kanzlei an den Reichsminister für Wissenschaft, Erziehung und Volksbildung Bernhard Rust, die Schließung von Schulen und den Kriegseinsatz der HJ betreffend, 9.2.1945', printed in Jahnke, *Hitlers letztes Aufgebot*, p. 136–7.

59 See Götz Aly, *Hitlers Volksstaat. Raub, Rassenkrieg und nationaler Sozialismus* (Frankfurt am Main, 2005).

4. Fleeing for their Lives

1 E. Müller, on the flight from Cosel in Upper Silesia, quoted in Wolfgang Schwarz, *Die Flucht und Vertreibung Oberschlesien 1945/46* (Bad Nauheim, 1965), p. 231.

2 *Dokumentation der Vertreibung der Deutschen aus Ost-Mitteleuropa. Band I/1*, pp. 35–37: 'Bericht des ehemaligen Bürgermeisters der Stadt Löbau, Kreis Neumark, Original, 28. Juni 1952'.

3 For a comparative history of forced removals, see Richard Bessel and Claudia Haake (eds.), *Forced Removal in the Modern World* (Oxford, 2009).

4 Michael Schwartz, *Vertriebene und 'Umsiedlerpolitik'. Integrationskonflikte in den deutschen Nachkriegsgesellschaften und die Assimilationsstrategien in der SBZ/DDR* (Munich, 2004, 1958), pp. 50–51.

5 Statistisches Bundesamt (ed.), *Die deutschen Vertreibungsverluste. Bevölkerungsbilanzen für die deutschen Vertreibungsgebiete 1939/50* (Wiesbaden, 1958), p. 33.

6 The numbers continued to rise, but more slowly, during the late 1940s, and it was estimated that in 1950 the total number of refugees and expellees in the Federal Republic and the GDR together amounted to 12,448,000, of whom 7,374,000 were 'Reichsdeutsche' (i.e. from regions which formerly had been German) and 5,074,000 were 'Volksdeutsche'

(i.e. who had been citizens of non-German countries). See Chauncy D. Harris and Gabriele Walker, 'The Refugee Problem of Germany', *Economic Geography*, vol. 29, no. 1 (January 1953), p. 11; Schwartz, *Vertriebene und 'Umsiedlerpolitik'*, pp. 50–55..

7   Protocol of the Proceedings at Potsdam, 1 August 1945, XII. Orderly Transfer of German Populations. Source: <http://www.cnn.com/SPECIALS/cold.war/episodes/01/documents/potsdam.html>.

8   Statistisches Bundesamt (ed.), *Die deutschen Vertreibungsverluste*, p. 37.

9   Hans W. Schoenberg, *Germans from the East. A Study of their Migration, Resettlement, and Subsequent Group History since 1945* (The Hague, 1970), p. 32. However, as Schoenberg notes, these figures were challenged by the Czechs and Poles. See Radomir Luza, *The Transfer of the Sudeten Germans – a Study of Czech-German Relations, 1933–1962* (New York, 1964); Stanlisaw Schimitzek, *Truth or Conjecture? German Civilian War Losses in the East* (Warsaw, 1966).

10 See Rüdiger Overmans, 'Personelle Verluste der deutschen Bevölkerung durch Flucht und Vertreibung' in *Dzieje najnowsze*, vol. xvi (1994), no. 2, pp. 51–65.

11 Elizabeth Harvey, *Women in the Nazi East. Agents and Witnesses of Germanization* (New Haven and London, 2003), p. 79.

12 Andreas Hofmann, *Nachkriegszeit in Schlesien. Gesellschafts- und Bevölkerungspolitik in den polnischen Siedlungsgebieten 1945–1948* (Cologne, Weimar and Vienna, 2000), p. 15.

13 Interview with Wolfgang Schieder, Berlin, 12 March 1999, printed in Rüdiger Hohls and Konrad H. Jarausch (eds.), *Versäumte Fragen. Deutsche Historiker im Schatten des Nationalsozialismus* (Stuttgart and Munich, 2000), p. 281. A similar example is that of Lothar Gall, born in 1936 in Lötzen in East Prussia, whose family also fled in 1944 – 'in a rather adventurous manner through the Reich – Bochum, Stuttgart, München' – and also fetched up in Bavaria at the end of the war. See the interview with Gall (Frankfurt am Main, June 1999), also in Hohls and Jarausch, *Versäumte Fragen*, p. 300. The same is true for Heinrich August Winkler, who was born in Königsberg in 1938 and who left the city together with his mother and grandmother in August 1944. See the interview with Winkler (Berlin, March 1999), in Hohls and Jarausch, *Versäumte Fragen*, p. 369.

14 Bundesministerium für Vertriebene (ed.), *Dokumentation der Vertreibung der Deutschen aus Ost-Mitteleuropa. Band I/1. Die Vertreibung der deutschen Bevölkerung aus den Gebieten östlich der Oder-Neiße. Dokumente. Die Flucht vor der Roten Armee. I. Die Fluchtereignisse in Ostpreußen, Westpreußen und Pommern* (Bonn, 1953–1957), p. 15E; Bernadetta Nitschke, *Vertreibung und Aussiedlung der deutschen Bevölkerung aus Polen 1945 bis 1949* (Munich, 2004), p. 67.

15 Marlis Steinert, *Hitler's War and the Germans. Public Mood and Attitude during the Second World War* (Athens, Ohio, 1977), p. 287. Generally, see Bernhard Fisch, *Nemmersdorf, Oktober 1944. Was in Ostpreußen tatsächlich geschah* (Berlin, 1997). The events at Nemmersdorf also have been the subject of television investigation in Germany, e..g. the ZDF television programme, 'Die Wahrheit über Nemmersdorf', broadcast on 25.11.2001: <http://www.zdf.de/ZDFde/inhalt/0,1872,2004695,00.html>.

16 *Dokumentation der Vertreibung der Deutschen aus Ost-Mitteleuropa. Band I/1*, pp. 7–8: 'Erlebnisbericht des Volkssturmmannes K.P. aus Königsberg i. Ostpr. Original, 14. Januar 1953'.

17 *Dokumentation der Vertreibung der Deutschen aus Ost-Mitteleuropa. Band I/1*, 'Einleitung', p. 16E.

18 *Dokumentation der Vertreibung der Deutschen aus Ost-Mitteleuropa. Band I/1*, 'Einleitung', p. 33E.

19 'Erlebnisbericht des ehemaligen Bürgermeisters von Insterburg i, Ostpr., Dr. Wander' from 7 Nov. 1952, in *Die Vertreibung der deutschen Bevölkerung aus den Gebieten östlich der Oder-Neiße*, vol. 1, Nr. 5, ('Die letzten Monate und Tage vor der Einnahme Insterburgs durch die Russen'), p. 10.

20 'Erlebnisbericht des ehemaligen Bürgermeisters von Insterburg i, Ostpr., Dr. Wander' from 7 Nov. 1952, in *Die Vertreibung der deutschen Bevölkerung aus den Gebieten östlich der Oder-Neiße*, vol. I/1, Nr. 5, ('Die letzten Monate und Tage vor der Einnahme Insterburgs durch die Russen'), pp. 13–14. In Insterburg, some plans for an eventual evacuation nevertheless had been made by the local authorities and kept secret from Koch.

21 *Die Vertreibung der deutschen Bevölkerung aus den Gebieten östlich der Oder-Neiße*, vol. I/1, 'Einleitung', p. 33E.

22 Quoted in Schwendemann, 'Tod zwischen den Fronten', in Stefan Aust and Stephan Burgdorff (eds.), *Die Flucht. Über die Vertreibung der Deutschen aus dem Osten* (Munich, 2005), p. 72.

23 Friedrich Hoßbach, *Die Schlacht um Ostpreußen* (Überlingen, 1951), p. 43.

24 *Vertreibung und Vertreibungsverbrechen 1945–1948. Bericht des Bundesarchivs vom 28. Mai 1974. Archivalien und ausgewählte Erlebnisberichte* (Bonn, 1989), p. 138: Document 2, 'Maschinenschriftlicher Bericht der Frau Herta Bluhm aus Königsberg i. Pr. vom 25. Februar 1952'.

25 *Dokumentation der Vertreibung der Deutschen aus Ost-Mitteleuropa. Band I/1*, pp. 149–150: 'Erlebnisbericht des A.S. aus Pillau, Kreis Samland i. Ostpr. Original ohne Datum'.

26 Schwendemann, 'Tod zwischen den Fronten', pp. 77–79.

27 Nitschke, *Vertreibung und Aussiedlung*, pp. 69–71. See also Alfred M. de Zayas, 'Die Flucht', in Frank Grube and Gerhard Richter (eds.), *Flucht und Vertreibung. Deutschland zwischen 1944 und 1947* (Hamburg 1980), pp. 136–138.

28   Heinz Nawratil, *Vertreibungsverbrechen an Deutschen. Tatbestand, Motive, Bewältigung* (Munich, 1982), p. 36; Nitschke, *Vertreibung und Aussiedlung*, p. 70. See also Heinz Schön, *Ostsee '45. Menschen, Schiffe, Schicksale* (Stuttgart, 1998); Heinz Schön, *SOS Wilhelm Gustloff. Die größte Schiffskatastrophe der Geschichte* (Stuttgart, 1998); and the recent novel by Günter Grass, *Crabwalk* (London, 2003).

29   Nitschke, *Vertreibung und Aussiedlung*, p. 69.

30   *Dokumentation der Vertreibung der Deutschen aus Ost-Mitteleuropa. Band I/1*, 'Einleitung', p. 5E.

31   Sebastian Siebel-Aschenbach, *Lower Silesia from Nazi Germany to Communist Poland 1942–1949* (Basingstoke and London, 1994), p. 120; *Dokumentation der Vertreibung der Deutschen aus Ost-Mitteleuropa. Band I/1*, 'Einleitung', p. 59E.

32   Hofmann, *Nachkriegszeit in Schlesien*, p. 20.

33   *Dokumentation der Vertreibung der Deutschen aus Ost-Mitteleuropa. Band I/1*, p. 411: 'Bericht des Hauptlehrers i. R. Waldemar Birkhoven aus Eichhagen, Kreis Cosel i. Oberschles.' Original, 10. April 1951.

34   Hofmann, *Nachkriegszeit in Schlesien*, p. 20.

35   Nitschke, *Vertreibung und Aussiedlung*, p. 72.

36   de Zayas, 'Die Flucht', in Grube and Richter (eds.), *Flucht und Vertreibung*, p. 138.

37   Z. Dulczewski and A. Kwilecki (eds.), *Pamietniki osadników Ziem Odzyskanzch* (Poznań, 1970), p. 30; quoted in Nitschke, *Vertreibung und Aussiedlung*, p. 73.

38   BA-MA, RW4, Nr. 705, ff. 6–14: 'Anlage 1 zur Tagesmeldung vom 20.3.1945. Bericht über die Lage in den besetzten deutschen Ostgebieten'.

39   *Die Vertreibung der deutschen Bevölkerung*, Bd. I/1, Introduction, p. 55; Nitschke, *Vertreibung und Aussiedlung*, p. 73.

40   Paul Peikert, *"Festung Breslau" in den Berichten eines Pfarrers 22. Januar bis 6. Mai 1945* (ed. by Karol Jonca and Alfred Konieczny) (Berlin, 1971), pp. 25–26.

41   Peikert, *"Festung Breslau"*, p. 30; Hofmann, *Die Nachkriegszeit in Schlesien*, p. 22.

42   Peikert, *"Festung Breslau*, p. 31.

43   Hofmann, *Die Nachkriegszeit in Schlesien*, pp. 22–3. Of the 530,000 civilian inhabitants of Breslau in the autumn of 1944, only between 150,000 and 180,000 still were in the city when it was cut off by Soviet forces in February 1945.

44   See Klaus Scheel, 'Veränderungen der Lebenslage der deutschen Zivilbevölkerung in der Provinz Brandenburg vor dem Kriegsende 1945', in Fritz Petrick (ed.), *Kapitulation und Befreiung. Das Ende des II. Weltkriegs in Europa* (Münster, 1997), p. 32; Kurt Adamy and Kristina Hübener,

'Provinz Mark Brandenburg – Gau Kurmark. Eine verwaltungs-geschichtliche Skizze', in Dietrich Eichholtz und Almuth Püschel (eds.), *Brandenburg in der NS-Zeit. Studien und Dokumente* (Berlin, 1993), p. 27; Gerd Heinrich, *Berlin und Umgebung. Handbuch der historischen Stätten Deutschlands*. Bd. 10 (Stuttgart, 1985), p. LXXXVII. Scheel gives the proportion killed as 38.9%, Adamy and Hübener as 39%, and Heinrich as 41.7%.

45   *Dokumentation der Vertreibung der Deutschen aus Ost-Mitteleuropa. Band I/1,* 'Einleitung', pp. 26–27E. See also Nitschke, *Vertreibung und Aussiedlung,* p. 75.

46   *Dokumentation der Vertreibung der Deutschen aus Ost-Mitteleuropa. Band I/1,* pp. 386–387: 'Erlebnisbericht des Bauern Hans Rünger aus Bärfelde, Kreis Soldin i. Brandenbg. Original, 2. November 1952'.

47   On looting by German soldiers during the last weeks of the war, see above, Chapter 3, p. 64.

48   *Vertreibung und Vertreibungsverbrechen* 1945–1948, pp. 38–40; Nitschke, *Vertreibung und Aussiedlung,* pp. 73–74. When one adds to this the rough estimates of the over 100,000 Germans from the east who died in Soviet camps and prisons in the former German territories and the roughly 200,000 who did not return from deportation to the USSR, the total estimate of dead exceeds 400,000. See *Vertreibung und Vertreibungsverbrechen* 1945–1948, p. 41.

49   On looting by Poles and Czechs, see below, Chapter 8.

50   Nawratil, *Vertreibungsverbrechen an Deutschen,* p. 52.

51   *Dokumentation der Vertreibung der Deutschen aus Ost-Mitteleuropa. Band I/1,* pp. 35–37: 'Bericht des ehemaligen Bürgermeisters der Stadt Löbau, Kreis Neumark, Original, 28. Juni 1952'.

52   Table in Rüdiger Overmans, *Deutsche militärische Verluste im Zweiten Weltkrieg* (Munich, 1999), p. 239.

53   Nitschke, *Vertreibung und Aussiedlung,* p. 66.

54   On this process, see Hans Mommsen, 'The Indian Summer and the Collapse of the Third Reich: The Last Act', in Hans Mommsen (ed.), *The Third Reich between Vision and Reality. New Perspectives on German History 1918–1945* (Oxford and New York, 2001), pp. 115–117.

55   Nitschke, *Vertreibung und Aussiedlung,* p. 66.

56   Martin Holz, *Evakuierte, Flüchtlinge und Vertriebene auf der Insel Rügen 1943–1961* (Cologne, 2003), pp. 76–77.

57   Nitschke, *Vertreibung und Aussiedlung,* p. 66.

58   See Holz, *Evakuierte, Flüchtlinge und Vertriebene auf der Insel Rügen,* pp. 74–75.

59   See Holz, *Evakuierte, Flüchtlinge und Vertriebene auf der Insel Rügen,* p. 78.

60   See Holz, *Evakuierte, Flüchtlinge und Vertriebene auf der Insel Rügen,*

pp. 79–83. Von Schlieffen's luck was short-lived. He later was arrested on Rügen by the Russians and taken to Grudiadz (Graudenz) in Poland, where he died in captivity in 1947. See http://home.foni.net/~adels-forschung/lex57.htm

61 Generally see Alfred Karaseck-Langer, 'Volksturm im Umbruch', in Eugen Lemberg and Friedrich Edding (eds.), *Die Vertriebenen in Westdeutschland. Ihre Eingliederung und ihr Einfluß auf Gesellschaft, Wirtschaft, Politik, Geistesleben*, vol. 1 (3. vols., Kiel, 1959), p. 625; and Marion Frantzioch, *Die Vertriebenen. Hemmnisse und Wege ihrer Integration* (Berlin, 1987), pp. 68–70.

62 *Dokumentation der Vertreibung der Deutschen aus Ost-Mitteleuropa. Band I/1*, p. 157: 'Erlebnisbericht des Gutsbesitzers Franz Adalbert Frhr. von Rosenberg aus Kloetzen, Kreis Marienwerder in Westpr. Original, April 1951'.

63 Quoted in Frantzioch, *Die Vertriebenen*, p. 69.

64 Holz, *Evakuierte, Flüchtlinge und Vertriebene auf der Insel Rügen*, pp. 82–83.

65 See Schwartz, *Vertriebene und 'Umsiedlerpolitik'*, p. 423.

66 Quoted in Elizabeth Harvey, *Women and the Nazi East. Agents and Witnesses of Germanization* (New Haven and London, 2003), pp. 287–288.

67 Quoted in Wolfgang Schwarz, *Die Flucht und Vertreibung Oberschlesien 1945/46* (Bad Nauheim, 1965), p. 89.

68 Quoted in Harvey, *Women in the Nazi East*, p. 289.

69 Altogether, according to the *Dokumentation der Vertreibung*, some 218,000 German civilians from the eastern provinces and the annexed territories of Poland were marched off into Soviet captivity; the deportations of Germans east of the Oder-Neiße began in January, continued in a systematic fashion during February and reached their high point in March and early April 1945. See *Dokumentation der Vertreibung der Deutschen aus Ost-Mitteleuropa. Band I/1*, 'Einleitung', pp. 79–83E.

70 BA-MA, RW4, Nr. 705, ff. 6–14: 'Anlage 1 zur Tagesmeldung vom 20.3.1945. Bericht über die Lage in den besetzten deutschen Ostgebieten'.

71 Peikert, *"Festung Breslau"*, p. 108: entry for 28 February 1945. The text of Goebbels' speech, broadcast over the radio on 28 February, was printed in the Breslau newspaper *Schlesische Zeitung* on 1 March under the headline, 'We will break the Mongol storm!'.

72 Peikert, *"Festung Breslau"*, p. 27.

73 See Chauncy D. Harris and Gabriele Walker, 'The Refugee Problem of Germany', *Economic Geography*, vol. 29, no. 1 (January 1953), pp. 14–17; Schwartz, *Vertriebene und 'Umsiedlerpolitik'*, pp. 50–55.

74 Harris and Walker, 'The Refugee Problem of Germany', p. 16.

75 See Rainer Schulze, 'Nicht alle, die kamen, blieben auf Dauer. Zuwanderungen in den Landkreis Celle im 20. Jahrhundert', in Rainer

Schulze (ed.), *Zwischen Heimat und Zuhause. Deutsche Flüchtlinge und Vertriebene in (West-) Deutschland 1945–2000* (Osnabrück, 2001), p. 42.

76 Mecklenburgisches Landeshauptarchiv (= MLHA), Kreistag/Rat des Kreises Demmin, Nr. 46, ff. 62–64: Landrat des Kreises Demmin to the Präsident des Landes Mecklenburg-Vorpommern, Demmin, 21 Nov. 1945. The 'resettlers' first were housed in three transit camps and then distributed among the villages in the district.

77 MLHA, Landesbehörde der Volkspolizei, Nr. 400, f. 110: The Bürgermeister der Stadt Ostseebad Kühlungsborn, Ortspolizeibehörde, to the Landrat des Kreises Rostock, Kühlungsborn, 18 Dec. 1945.

78 Quoted in Schulze, 'Nicht alle, die kamen, blieben auf Dauer', p. 43.

79 Albrecht Lehmann, *Im Fremden ungewollt zuhaus. Flüchtlinge und Vertriebene in Westdeutschland 1945–1990* (Munich, 1991), p. 91.

80 Interview with Katharina Hassel, quoted in Lehmann, *Im Fremden ungewollt zuhaus,* p. 90.

5. The Last Days of the Reich

1 Wilfried von Oven, *Finale Furioso. Mit Goebbels bis zum Ende* (Tübingen, 1974), p. 610. (diary entry for 17 March 1945)

2 'Bericht über die infolge der feindlichen Besetzung der Umgegend in der Pfarrgemeinde Obernsee eingetretenen Kriegsereignisse' to the Evangelische-Lutherische Dekanat Bayreuth, mid-June 1945. Quoted in Klaus-Dietmar Henke, *Die amerikanische Besetzung Deutschlands* (Munich, 1995), p. 842.

3 BA-MA, RW 44 II, Nr. 8, ff. 19–24: 'Versorgungsbericht für den Raum des Bevollmächtigen Generals B', 21 April 1945.

4 Quoted in Major L. F. Ellis, *Victory in the West. Volume II. The Defeat of Germany* (London, 1968), p. 326.

5 See John Erickson, *The Road to Berlin* (London, 2003), pp. 528–534.

6 'Aufruf und die Soldaten der Ostfront (15 April [1945])', in Percy E. Schramm (ed.) *Kriegstagebuch des Oberkommandos der Wehrmacht (Wehrmachtführungsstab)* [=*KTB*], Vol. 4: 1. Januar 1944 – 22. Mai 1945 (Frankfurt am Main, 1961), pp. 1589–1590.

7 Ian Kershaw, *Hitler 1936–45: Nemesis* (London, 2000), pp. 797–799; Joachim Fest, *Inside Hitler's Bunker. The Last Days of the Third Reich* (London, 2004), pp. 44–46.

8 Wilhelm Keitel, *Mein Leben. Pflichterfüllung bis zum Untergang. Hitlers Generalfeldmarschall und Chef des Oberkommandos der Wehrmacht in Selbstzeugnissen* (ed. by Werner Maser) (Berlin, 1998), p. 378. See also Manfred Overesch, *Das III. Reich 1939–1945. Eine Tageschronik der Politik, Wirtschaft, Kultur* (Augsburg, 1991), p. 606.

9 Traudl Junge, *Until the Final Hour. Hitler's Last Secretary* (London, 2004), p. 159.

10 Fest, *Inside Hitler's Bunker*, pp. 16–17.

11 Fest, *Inside Hitler's Bunker*, p. 17.

12 For a description of the bunker, see Junge, *Until the Final Hour*, pp. 157–158.

13 BA-MA, N 648, Nr. 1, f. 8: 'Dethleffsen Erinnerungen', Kriegsgefangen-lager Allendorf, Kreis Marburg, Winter 1945/46.

14 BA-MA, N 648, Nr. 1, ff. 12–14: 'Dethleffsen Erinnerungen'.

15 For Heinrici's account of his 'surprising' appointment to head the Army Group Vistula, see BA-MA, N 265/109, ff. 1–3: undated postwar obser-vations by Heinrici, probably from May 1945 (quotation from f. 3). At this time the Army Group Vistula was responsible for the eastern front from the Baltic to the confluence of the Oder and Neiße south of Frankfurt. (The front to the south of this point, to the Riesengebirge, was the responsibility of the Army Group Schörner. Military forces in Berlin were commanded by Hitler directly.)

16 BA-MA, N 265/108, ff. 2–9: Generaloberst Heinrici, 'Bericht ueber Erlebnisse bei der Heeresgruppe Weichsel im April 1945', May 1945 (quotation from f. 9).

17 BA-MA, N 265/109, f. 3: undated postwar observations by Heinrici, probably from May 1945.

18 BA-MA, N 648, Nr. 1, f. 14: 'Dethleffsen Erinnerungen'.

19 BA-MA, N 648, Nr. 1, f. 15: 'Dethleffsen Erinnerungen'.

20 BA-MA, N 648, Nr. 1, f. 18: 'Dethleffsen Erinnerungen'.

21 BA-MA, N 648, Nr. 1, f. 19: 'Dethleffsen Erinnerungen'; Fest, *Inside Hitler's Bunker*, pp. 54–55.

22 BA-MA, N 648, Nr. 1, f. 10: 'Dethleffsen Erinnerungen'.

23 BA-MA, N 648, Nr. 1, f. 39: 'Dethleffsen Erinnerungen'; Jacob Kronika, *Der Untergang Berlins* (Flensburg and Hamburg, 1946), p. 134.

24 Ansgar Diller, *Rundfunkpolitik im Dritten Reich* (Munich, 1980), p. 441.

25 Antony Beevor, *Berlin. The Downfall 1945* (London, 2002), p. 274.

26 See Fest, *Inside Hitler's Bunker*, pp. 29–30.

27 BA-MA, N 648, Nr. 1, f. 5: 'Dethleffsen Erinnerungen'.

28 BA-MA, N 648, Nr. 1, f. 8: 'Dethleffsen Erinnerungen'.

29 BA-MA, N 265/108, ff. 2–9: Generaloberst Heinrici, 'Bericht ueber Erlebnisse bei der Heeresgruppe Weichsel im April 1945', May 1945.

30 See John Erickson, *The Road to Berlin* (London, 2003), pp. 538–539; Max Hastings, *Armageddon. The Battle for Germany 1944–1945* (London, 2004), pp. 532–533.

31 On the presence of *Volkssturm*, Hungarian SS men and Vlassov soldiers, see BA-MA, N 265/108, ff. 2–9: Generaloberst Heinrici, 'Bericht ueber Erlebnisse bei der Heeresgruppe Weichsel im April 1945', May 1945.

32 Christopher Duffy, *Red Storm on the Reich* (New York, 1993), p. 297;
    Hastings, *Armageddon*, pp. 532–533.

33 Karl-Heinz Frieser, 'Die Schlacht um die Seelower Höhen im April 1945',
    in Roland G. Foerster (ed.), *Seelower Höhen 1945* (Hamburg, 1998),
    p. 142.

34 BA-MA, N 265/109, f. 4: undated postwar observations by Heinrici,
    probably from May 1945.

35 BA-MA, N 648, Nr. 1, f. 33: 'Dethleffsen Erinnerungen'. Altogether, some
    15–16,000 members of the Reich Labour Service were given rudimentary
    military training, put under Wehrmacht command and thrown into battle.
    See Kiran Klaus Patel, *'Soldaten der Arbeit'. Arbeitsdienste in Deutschland und den
    USA 1933–1945* (Göttingen, 2003), p. 375.

36 See Richard Lakowski and Karl Stich, *Der Kessel von Halbe 1945. Das letzte
    Drama* (Berlin, 1998); Tony Le Tissier, *Slaughter at Halbe. The Destruction of
    Hitler's 9th Army, April 1945* (Stround, 2005).

37 Hans George Kampe, *Zossen-Wünsdorf 1945. Die letzten Kriegswochen im
    Hauptquartier des OKH* (Berlin, 1997), pp. 71–72.

38 Keitel, *Mein Leben*, pp. 382–383; Kershaw, *Hitler 1936–1945*, pp,
    802–804; Beevor, *Berlin. The Downfall*, pp. 275–276; Fest, *Inside Hitler's
    Bunker*, pp. 62–66.

39 See Fest, *Inside Hitler's Bunker*, pp. 62–63.

40 Nicolaus von Below, *At Hitler's Side. The Memoir's of Hitler's Luftwaffe
    Adjutant 1937–1945* (London, 2004), p. 236.

41 BA-MA, N 265/109, f. 5: undated postwar observations by Heinrici,
    probably from May 1945.

42 Keitel, *Mein Leben*, pp. 382.

43 BA-MA, N 648, Nr. 1, f. 35: 'Dethleffsen Erinnerungen'.

44 Keitel, *Mein Leben*, pp. 382–383.

45 Keitel, *Mein Leben*, pp. 386–387.

46 Quoted in Overesch, *Das III. Reich 1939–1945*, p. 607.

47 Elke Fröhlich (ed.), *Die Tagebücher von Joseph Goebbels*, Section II, vol. 15
    (Munich, 1995), p. 478.

48 See Bernd Wegner, 'Hitler, der Zweite Weltkrieg und die Choreographie
    des Untergangs', *Geschichte und Gesellschaft*, vol. xxvi (2000), no. 3,
    pp. 492–518.

49 BA-MA, N 539/1: 'Fragen an Grossadmiral Dönitz im Lager Mondorf
    (Lux) 1945', dated 23 July 1945.

50 Account of the military briefing on the evening of 24 April, in BA-MA,
    N 648, Nr. 1, f. 44: 'Dethleffsen Erinnerungen'. Keitel's references to
    1918, which reflected the clichés broadly accepted among the Nazi and
    military leadership, echoed what he, then a captain who had served in the
    general staffs of various units during the war and had marched back to

Germany from Belgium in November 1918, himself had written to his father-in-law shortly thereafter. See his letter written to his father-in-law on 10 December 1918, printed in Keitel, *Mein Leben*, p. 150.

51 Gerhard Förster and Richard Lakowski (eds.), 1945. *Das Jahr der endgülti-gen Niederlage der Faschistischen Wehrmacht* (Berlin, 1985), pp. 319–320: Dokument 186: 'Aktennotiz eines Ferngesprächs zwischen dem Oberbefehlshaber der 3. Panzerarmee, General der Panzertruppe Hasso v. Manteuffel, und dem Chef des Generalstabes der Heeresgruppe Weichsel, Generalmajor Thilo v. Trotha, über Auflösungserscheinungen bei der Truppe'. See also Andreas Kunz, *Wehrmacht und Niederlage. Die bewaffnete Macht in der Endphase der nationalsozialistischen Herrschaft 1944 bis 1945* (Munich, 2005), pp. 285–286.

52 Quoted in Kunz, *Wehrmacht und Niederlage*, p. 286.

53 Fest, *Inside Hitler's Bunker*, pp. 68–69.

54 Fest, *Inside Hitler's Bunker*, p. 83.

55 See Fest, *Inside Hitler's Bunker*, pp. 66–67.

56 See Keitel, *Mein Leben*, pp. 386–390.

57 'Führerbefehl betr. Befehlsgliederung im Nord- und Südraum im Falle einer Aufspaltung (15. April [1945])', in *KTB*, vol. 4, pp. 1587–1589.

58 BA-MA, RW 44 I/1, f. 6: unsigned account of Dönitz's actions between 20 April and 9 May 1945.

59 See von Below, *At Hitler's Side*, pp. 236–237.

60 BA-MA, RW 44 I/33, f. 167: FRR-Funkspruch, Jodl to Kesselring, Vietinghoff, Schörner, Rendulic, Lohr and Winter, F.H.Qu., 24 April 1945.

61 von Below, *At Hitler's Side*, p. 238.

62 BA-MA, RW 44 I/33, f. 166: Hitler to Großadmiral Dönitz, 25 April 1945.

63 Keitel, *Mein Leben*, p. 391; Fest, *Inside Hitler's Bunker*, p. 85.

64 Quoted in Overesch, *Das III. Reich 1939–1945*, pp. 608–609.

65 BA-MA, N 648, Nr. 1, f. 48: 'Dethleffsen Erinnerungen'.

66 BA-MA, RW 44 I/33, f. 121: Op (H)/Nordost, 28 April 1945.

67 BA-MA, RW 44 I/1, f. 6: unsigned account of Dönitz's actions between 20 April and 9 May 1945.

68 BA-MA, N 265/109, f. 11: undated postwar observations by Heinrici, probably from May 1945.

69 BA-MA, N 265/108, ff. 10–58: Generaloberst Heinrici, description of the Battle for Berlin, Hürup, 20 May 1945 (quotation from f. 22). According to Heinrici, Keitel, to whom Heinrici had reported these conditions, 'completely closed his mind to my arguments, clung to his viewpoint, appealed to my obligation to rescue the Führer and demanded attacks on Berlin from all sides'.

70 BA-MA, N 265/109, f. 11.

71 BA-MA, N 265/108, ff. 10–58 (quotation from f. 29).

72 BA-MA, N 648, Nr. 1, ff. 48–49: 'Dethleffsen Erinnerungen'. On 29 April the person designated to succeed Heinrici to command the Army Group Vistula, General Hasso von Manteuffel, refused to accept the post. Keitel finally named General Kurt Student to head the army group, with Dethleffsen as his Chief of Staff. See BA-MA, RW 44 I/33, f. 93: WFST/Op, FRR-Funkspruch Keitel an General d. Inf. Krebs, 30 April 1945; BA-MA, RW 44 I/33, f. 119: Chef OKW. Keitel, to Generaloberst Heinrici, 28 April 1945.

73 *Die Wehrmachtberichte 1939–1945. Band 3. 1. Januar 1944 bis 9. Mai 1945* (Cologne, 1989), p. 559 (report for 28 April 1945).

74 Keitel, *Mein Leben*, pp. 398.

75 BA-MA, RW 44 I/1, f. 34: v. Puttkammer to Dönitz, 29 April 1945, 23:07.

76 Hanna Reitsch, *Fliegen – mein Leben* (Munich and Berlin, 1979), pp, 321, 325. See also Fest, *Inside Hitler's Bunker*, p. 95; Kershaw, *Hitler 1936–1945*, pp. 817–819.

77 See Fest, *Inside Hitler's Bunker*, pp. 97–100.

78 Recollections of Flight Captain Hans Bauer, in Peter Gosztony (ed.), *Der Kampf um Berlin 1945 in Augenzeugenberichten* (Munchen, 1970), pp. 327–328.

79 'Befehl Nr. 1 des Chefs der Besatzung der Stadt Berlin, Generaloberst Nikolai E. Bersarin, an die Berliner Bevölkerung vom 28.4.1945', printed in Rolf-Dieter Müller and Gerd R. Ueberschär, *Kriegsende 1945. Die Zerstörung des Deutschen Reiches* (Frankfurt am Main, 1994), pp. 193–195. Shortly thereafter, on 16 June, Bersarin, who acted with great energy to get services in Berlin functioning again, was killed in a motorcycle accident.

80 See Erich Kuby, *Die Russen in Berlin 1945* (Munich, 1965); Erika M. Hoerning, 'Frauen als Kriegsbeute. Der Zwei-Fronten-Krieg. Beispiele aus Berlin', in Lutz Niethammer and Alexander von Platow (eds.), *'Wir kriegen jetzt andere Zeiten'. Auf der Suche nach der Erfahrung des Volkes in nachfaschistischen Landern* (Bonn, 1985), pp. 327–344; Norman M. Naimark, *The Russians in Germany. A History of the Soviet Zone of Occupation, 1945–1949* (Cambridge, Mass., and London, 1995), pp. 68–140, esp. 78–83; Ingrid Schmidt-Harzbach, 'Eine Woche in April. Berlin 1945', in Helke Sander and Barbara Johr (eds.), *BeFreier und Befreite. Krieg, Vergewaltigung, Kinder* (Frankfurt am Main, 2005), pp. 21–26.

81 Quoted in Schmidt-Harzbach, 'Eine Woche im April', p. 23.

82 Gerhard Junger, *Schicksale 1945* (Reutlingen, 1991), pp. 101–102, 139, 148–19, 234. See also Edward N. Peterson, *The Many Faces of Defeat. The*

German People's Experience in 1945 (New York, Bern, Frankfurt am Main and Paris, 1990), pp. 131–132.

83   Hansmartin Schwarzmaier, *Der deutsche Südwesten zur Stunde Null. Zusammenbruch und Neuanfang im Jahr 1945 in Dokumenten und Bildern* (Karlsruhe, 1975), pp. 99–101; Jochen Theis, *Südwestdeutschland Stunde Null* (Düsseldorf, 1979), p. 26; Peterson, *The Many Faces of Defeat*, p. 130.

84   Manfred Schmidt (ed.), *Tübingen 1945. Eine Chronik von Hermann Werner* (Tübingen, 1986), p. 86. Werner's manuscript remained unpublished for 35 years. At the time it was completed, in 1951, the author was told that for it to be published 'in the foreseeable future' the 'sections that deal with the conduct of the French during the early weeks must be gone over again and shortened'; what he had written about the 'looting, assaults and violence against women cannot yet be said so openly today'. See the introduction by Manfred Schmidt, p. 11.

85   Lothar Burchardt, *Konstanz zwischen Kriegsende und Universitätsgründung. Hungerjahre, 'Wirtschaftswunder', Strukturwandel* (Konstanz, 1996), p. 48.

86   Sibylle Meyer and Eva Schulze, *Wie wir das alles geschafft haben. Alleinstehende Frauen berichten über ihr Leben nach 1945* (Munich, 1984), p. 216.

87   See BA-MA, RW 4/703, ff. 146–147: WFSt/Qu to Chef OKW, 'Betr.: Staatssekretärbesprechung am 18.4.1945. Vortragsnotiz', 19 April 1945.

88   Interview quoted in Hoerning, 'Frauen als Kriegsbeute', p. 333.

89   Interview quoted in Hoerning, 'Frauen als Kriegsbeute', p. 334.

90   *KTB*, Band IV: 1. Januar 1944 – 22. Mai 1945, p. 1272.

91   Fest, *Inside Hitler's Bunker*, p. 105.

92   BA-MA, RW 44 I/33, f. 69: WFSt/Op, Nr. 88 868/45 g.K.Chefs., Funkspruch an Reichskanzlei [signed by Keitel], 30 April 1945, 01.00 Uhr. Copies of Hitler's telegram may be found in BA-MA, RW 44 I/33, f. 70 and 108: Telegram to Chef WFSt. Gen. Obst. Jodl, 29 April 1945, 2300. See also Kershaw, *Hitler 1936–1945*, p. 826; Fest, *Inside Hitler's Bunker*, p. 108.

93   BA-MA, RW 44 I/1, f. 102: Bormann to Dönitz, 29 April 1945.

94   For Göring's comments – 'we always knew that the Führer would kill himself if things were coming to an end' – see Richard Overy, *Interrogations. The Nazi Elite in Allied Hands, 1945* (London, 2001), p. 312.

95   See Kershaw, *Hitler 1936–1945*, pp. 828–830.

96   A translation of the text of Hitler's personal and political testaments may be found in Jeremy Noakes (ed.), *Nazism 1919–1945. Volume 4. The German Home Front in World War II* (Exeter, 1998), pp. 667–671.

97   BA-MA, RW 44 I/1, f. 46: Funkspruch Dönitz to Führerhauptquartier, sent 1 May, 3:27. This is published in Herbert Michaelis and Ernst Schrapler (eds.), *Ursachen und Folgen. Vom deutschen Zusammenbruch 1918*

und 1945 bis zur staatlichen Neuordnung Deutschlands bis in der Gegenwart, vol. xxiii (Berlin, 1975), p. 201, doc. 3636f.

98 BA-MA, RW 44 I/1, f. 46: Funkspruch Bormann to Dönitz, received 1 May 10:53.

99 BA-MA, RW 44 I/1, ff. 46–47: Funkspruch Goebbels to Dönitz, received 1 May 15:18.

100 Quoted in Overesch, *Das III. Reich 1939–1945*, p. 611. See also Kershaw, *Hitler 1936–1945*, p. 832.

101 *Die Wehrmachtberichte 1939–1945. Band 3. 1. Januar 1944 bis 9. Mai 1945* (Cologne, 1989), p. 563 (report for 2 May 1945). See also Kershaw, *Hitler 1936–1945*, p. 832.

102 BA-MA, RW 44 I/33, ff. 79–82: Der Chef des Oberkommandos der Wehrmacht, OKW/WFSt/Nr. 00 4003/45 g. Kdos., 30 April 1945.

103 BA-MA, RW 44 I/33, ff. 83–84: WFSt/Op Nr. 66 868/45 g.K.Chefs., Keitel, FRR-Funkspruch an Generalleutnant Winter, Führungsstab B, 30 April 1945.

104 The text may be found in Noakes (ed.), *Nazism 1919–1945. Volume 4*, pp. 671–672.

105 See Kershaw, *Hitler 1936–1945*, pp. 832–833.

106 'Der Endkampf in Berlin (23.4.-2.5.1945)', *Wehrwissenschaftlichte Rundschau* Nr. 1/1962, p. 171.

107 Quoted in Kershaw, *Hitler 1936–1945*, p. 832.

108 BA-MA, N 265/108, ff. 10–58: Generaloberst Heinrici, description of the Battle for Berlin, Hürup, 20 May 1945 (quotation from f. 38). In his other, somewhat more detailed account, Heinrici quoted Jodl as saying, 'As long as the Führer is alive, there will be no negotiations!' See BA-MA, N 265/109, f. 8: undated postwar observations by Heinrici, probably from May 1945.

109 BA-MA, RW 44 I, Nr. 58, f. 265: Oberkommando der Wehrmacht, response to demands for information by Colonel Barenkov of the Soviet Army, H.Qu.OKW, 20 May 1945.

110 BA-MA, RW 44 II, Nr. 8, ff. 38–41: Gruppe IVa, 'Verpflegungsversorgungslage im Bereiche Festung "Alpen"', 1 May 1945.

111 See Müller and Ueberschär, *Kriegsende 1945*, pp. 101–104; Ian Kershaw, *Hitler 1936–1945*, pp. 834–835.

112 BA-MA, N 539/1: 'Fragen an Grossadmiral Dönitz im Lager Mondorf (Lux) 1945', dated 23 July 1945.

113 BA-MA, N 265/109, f. 7: undated postwar observations by Heinrici, probably from May 1945.

114 Müller and Ueberschär, *Kriegsende 1945*, pp. 107–8; Kershaw, *Hitler 1936–1945*, p. 835. The Wehrmacht estimated that at the time the fighting ended, at midnight on 8/9 May, roughly 1.5 million German soldiers were on the eastern front altogether, of whom 600,000 were with the

Army Group Centre, 100,000 still were in East Prussia and 200,000 in Courland. See BA-MA, RW 44 I/54: 'Beilage 1 zu Anlage 6 zu OKW/WFSt Einsatz Abt (H) Nr 010 040/45', 11 May 1945.

115   BA-MA, N 539/1: 'Fragen an Grossadmiral Dönitz im Lager Mondorf (Lux) 1945', dated 23 July 1945.

116   BA-MA, N 648, Nr. 1, f. 73: 'Dethleffsen Erinnerungen'.

117   See Walter Lüdde-Neurath, *Regierung Dönitz. Die letzten Tage des Dritten Reiches* (Göttingen, 1951), pp. 89–90; Karl Dönitz, *Memoirs. Ten Years and Twenty Days* (New York, 1997), p. 470.

118   Dönitz, *Memoirs*, p. 471.

119   BA-MA, N 648, Nr. 1, f. 74: 'Dethleffsen Erinnerungen', Kriegsgefangenlager Allendorf, Kreis Marburg, Winter 1945/46.

120   BA-MA, RW 44 I/33, ff. 26–27: WFSt/Op(H)/Nordost an Obkdo. der Wehrmacht Führ. Stab Oper (H)/Nordost, 4 May 1945.

121   BA-MA, N 648, Nr. 1, f. 52: 'Dethleffsen Erinnerungen'.

122   BA-MA, N 648, Nr. 1, f. 55: 'Dethleffsen Erinnerungen'.

123   BA-MA, N 539/1: 'Fragen an Grossadmiral Dönitz im Lager Mondorf (Lux) 1945', dated 23 July 2005.

124   BA-MA, RW 44 I, Nr. 58, ff. 49–50: Oberst Franz Blätterbauer, 'Gedanken zur Lage', Flensburg, 6 May 1945.

125   BA-MA, RW 44 I/33, f. 53: Oberstleutnant i. G. de Maiziere, 'Punkte für den mündlichen Vortrag bei den Ob. und Chefs der H. Gr. Kurland und des A.OK. Ostpreußen', 3 May 1945.

126   Dönitz, *Memoirs*, p. 453.

127   BA-MA, RW 44 I/1, f. 6: unsigned account of Dönitz's actions between 20 April and 9 May 1945.

128   See *KTB*, Band IV: 1. Januar 1944 – 22. Mai 1945, p. 1437. Vietinghoff-Scheel's own acount may be found in BA-MA, N 574/5: Heinrich v. Vietinghoff-Scheel, 'Lebenslauf', Hainstadt/Baden, Kr. Buchen, 29 Sept. 1948.

129   Kerstin von Lingen, *Kesselrings letzte Schlacht. Kriegsverbrecherprozesse, Vergangenheitspolitik und Wiederbewaffnung: Der Fall Kesselring* (Paderborn, 2004), p. 47; Dönitz, *Memoirs*, p. 457.

130   BA-MA, RW 44 I/33, f. 57: OKW/WFSt, Dönitz to Kesselring, 3 May 1945.

131   Dönitz, *Memoirs*, p. 457.

132   BA-MA, RW 44 I/33, f. 66: OKW/WFSt op H.B.Nr.g.k. 004200/45, O.U., 2 May 1945.

133   Dönitz, *Memoirs*, p. 459.

134   *Die Wehrmachtberichte 1939–1945. Band 3. 1. Januar 1944 bis 9. Mai 1945* (Cologne, 1989), p. 566. Keitel's order to continue the struggle in the east may be found in BA-MA, RW44 I/33, f. 17: OKW/WFSt, 4 May 1945.

135 BA-MA, RW 44 I/33, f. 40: OKW/WFSt, Nr. 003007/45 g.k.II.Ang., 4 May 1945.

136 BA-MA, RW 44 I/36, ff. 237–238: FRR-Fernschreiben, Oberste Befehlshaber der Wehrmacht to Ob. Nordwest, W.B. Dänemark, Reichsführer SS, Reichsminister Speer, H. Qu., 5 May 1945.

137 Dönitz, *Memoirs*, pp. 458–459.

138 Quoted in L. F. Ellis, *Victory in the West. Volume II. The Defeat of Germany* (London, 1968), p. 343.

139 Quoted in Dönitz, *Memoirs*, p. 463.

140 BA-MA, RW 44 II, Nr. 3, f. 85: Dönitz to Ob. Südost Ge, Oberst Löhr, Ob, H-Gr. Ostmark, Gen. Oberst Rendulic, and Ob. H.Gr. Mitte, Gen. Feldm. Schörner.

141 Printed in *KTB*, vol. iv, pp. 1680–1682. See also Gerhard Paul, '"Wir brachten den letzten Wehrmachtsbericht dieses Krieges". Der "Reichssender Flensburg" im Mai 1945 und die Leitideen der bundesdeutschen Nachkriegsgesellschaft', in Gerhard Paul, *Landunter. Schleswig-Holstein und das Hakenkreuz* (Münster, 2001), pp. 312–314.

142 Paul, '"Wir brachten den letzten Wehrmachtsbericht dieses Krieges"', p. 314.

143 Printed in Walter Lüdde-Neurath, *Regierung Dönitz. Die letzten Tage des Dritten Reiches* (Göttingen, 1951), pp. 160–161.

144 BA-MA, RW 44 I, Nr. 58, f. 265: Oberkommando der Wehrmacht, response to demands for information by Colonel Barenkov of the Soviet Army, H.Qu.OKW, 20 May 1945; BA-MA, RW 44 I, Nr. 58, f. 258: OKW/WFSt/Org Abt (Heer), 'Ist Stärken des Feldheeres', II.Qu.OKW, 19 May 1945.

145 *Die Wehrmachtberichte 1939–1945. Band 3*, p. 569.

146 BA-MA, RW 44 II, Nr. 3, f. 158: Fernschreiben an Funkstab B Gen. Winter, 15 May 1945.

147 Quoted in Paul, '"Wir brachten den letzten Wehrmachtsbericht dieses Krieges"', p. 317.

148 Dönitz, *Memoirs*, p. 466.

149 BA-MA, RW 44 I/33, f. 74: Fernschreiben from Gen.Lt. Winter, sent 29 April 1945, 2315.

150 Diary entry for 21 April 1945, quoted in Thomas Berger and Karl-Heinz Müller (eds.), *Lebenssituationen 1945–1948. Materialien zum Alltagsleben in den westlichen Besatzungszonen 1945–1948* (Hannover, 1983), pp. 12–13.

151 The order to blow up the bridges across the Dreisam was not carried out, since electricity, gas and water lines ran underneath them. The officer charged with the defence of Freiburg, Rudolf Bader, had allowed only explosive charges without fuses and detonators to be placed under the bridges, and local inhabitants removed these fuseless charges from the

bridges when the French arrived. See Gerd R. Ueberschär, 'Freiburgs letzte Kriegstage bis zur Besetzung durch die französische Armee am 21. April 1945', in Thomas Schnabel and Gerd R. Ueberschär, *Endlich Frieden! Das Kriegsende in Freiburg 1945* (Freiburg, 1985), pp. 32–34.

152   Quoted in Gerhard Hirschfeld and Irena Renz (eds.), *"Vormittags die ersten Amerikaner". Stimmen und Bilder vom Kriegsende 1945* (Stuttgart, 2005), pp. 142–143: Tagebuch von C.F.W. Behl, Freitag, 20. April – Donnerstag, 26. April, Berndorf bei Kemnath/Oberpfalz.

153   Victor Klemperer, *To the Bitter End. The Diaries of Victor Klemperer 1942–1945* (London, 2000), pp. 576–577 (diary entry for 3 May 1945).

154   Schwarzmaier, *Der deutsche Südwesten zur Stunde Null*, p. 111: Ortsbericht Bünzwangen Krs. Göppingen: Übergabe durch Parlamentäre (HStA Stuttgart J 170).

155   See, for example, the report of developments in Malchim, near Demmin in western Pomerania, on 30 April: BA-MA, RW 44 I/53, f. 87: WFSt/Op, Meldung H.G. Weichsel, 30 April 1945 (initialled by Keitel).

156   Kurt Stüdemann, 'Parchim 1945 – Am Rande des Abgrundes. Teil I: Ereignisse bis zum 3, Mai 1945', in *Parchimer Heimathefte*, no. 19 (1994), pp. 24–32.

157   Christoph Bretschneider, 'Wie ich in Parchim am 3. 1945 das Ende der Kampfhandlungen im 2. Weltkrieg im Bereich von Mecklenburg erlebte' (Manuscript, 1994), quoted in Kurt Stüdemann, 'Parchim 1945 – Am Rande des Abgrundes. Teil I, p. 32.

158   Marlis Steinert, *Hitler's War and the Germans. Public Mood and Attitude during the Second World War* (Athens, Ohio, 1977), p. 313.

159   Hannah Vogt, 'Aus meinem Tagebuch', in *Göttingen 1945. Kriegsende und Neubeginn. Texte und Materialien zur Ausstellung im Städtischen Museum 31. März – 28. Juli 1985* (Göttingen, 1985), p. 63 (diary entry for 4 May 1945)

160   Gerd Schückle, 'Mitgegangen, mitgefangen . . .', in Gustav Trampe (ed.), *Die Stunde Null. Erinnerungen an Kriegsende und Neuanfang* (Stuttgart, 1995), p. 57.

161   Ian Kershaw, *The 'Hitler Myth'. Image and Reality in the Third Reich* (Oxford, 1987), pp. 224–225.

162   Victor Klemperer, *To the Bitter End. The Diaries of Victor Klemperer 1942–45* (abridged and translated by Martin Chalmers) (London, 2000), p. 569 (diary entry for 25 April 1945).

163   Annemarie Meckel, *Das Bild des Gefangenen. Tagebuchauszüge 1944–1947* (Freiburg i. Br., 1982), p. 27 (entry for 14 April 1945).

164   E.g. in Mainz. See Peterson, *The Many Faces of Defeat*, p. 127.

165   Quoted in Schwarzmaier, *Der deutsche Südwesten zur Stunde Null*, p. 113.

166   Peterson, *The Many Faces of Defeat*, p. 127.

167   Gerhard Junger, *Schicksale 1945* (Reutlingen, 1971), p. 124. See also
      Peterson, *The Many Faces of Defeat*, pp. 131–133. (Peterson mistakes the
      name of the village where the 70-year-old was shot.)
168   See Rupprecht Gerngross, *Aufstand der Freiheits Aktion Bayern 1945.
      'Fasanenjagd' und wie die Münchner Freiheit ihren Namen bekam* (Augsburg,
      1995).
169   BA–MA, RW 44/15: 'Tagesmeldung Nr. 1, Betr.: Haltung und Mein-
      ungsbildung der Bevölkerung', 6 May 1945.
170   BA–MA, RW 44/15: 'Tagesmeldung Nr. 1, Betr.: Haltung und Mein-
      ungsbildung der Bevölkerung', 6 May 1945.
171   BA–MA, N 539/1: 'Fragen an Grossadmiral Dönitz im Lager Mondorf
      (Lux) 1945', dated 23 July 2005.

6. Revenge

1   Headquarters ETOUSA, Office of the Assistant Chief of Staff, G-2: Cen-
    sorship Report on Observance of Rules of Land Warfare for Period 1–15
    May 45, in: NA, RG 338, ETOUSA, Historical Division, Administrative
    File; Box No. 9; Folder 58 (Censorship). Quoted in Christof Strauß,
    *Kriegsgefangendschaft und Internierung. Die Lager in Heilbronn-Böckingen
    1945–1946* (Heilbronn, 1998), p. 100.
2   This is shown particularly well in the impressive book by Nicholas
    Stargardt, *Witnesses of War. Children's Lives under Nazi Rule* (London,
    2005).
3   See, especially, Norman M. Naimark, *The Russians in Germany. A History
    of the Soviet Zone of Ocupation 1945–1949* (Cambridge, Mass., 1995),
    pp. 114–115. Naimark notes that 'the Russian soldier's desire for revenge
    was fed by his desire to restore his honor and manhood, to erase doubts
    about inferiority that were exacerbated by German well-being and self-sat-
    isfaction'.
4   Manfred Zeidler, *Kriegsende im Osten. Die Rote Armee und die Besetzung
    Deutschlands östlich von Oder und Neiße 1944/45* (Munich, 1996), p. 70.
5   Naimark, *The Russians in Germany*, p. 72.
6   This is from an article on 'conquest adventures in the history of Germany
    and the Hitler clique', by B. V. Porshnew in *Bolshevik* in 1943, quoted in
    Ruth Kibelka, *Ostpreußens Schicksalsjahre 1944–1948* (Berlin, 2000), p. 31.
7   Quoted in Naimark, *The Russians in Germany*, p. 72.
8   Ilya Ehrenburg, 'Woe to Germany!', in *Soviet War News* (published by the
    press department of the Soviet Embassy in London), no. 941, 22 August
    1944. Reproduced in Zeidler, *Kriegsende im Osten*, p. 217.
9   Ilya Ehrenburg, 'Nastala rasplata', in *Krasnaya Zvezda*, 30 January 1945,
    p. 3. Quoted in Zeidler, *Kriegsende im Osten*, p. 124.

10   Naimark, *The Russians in Germany*, p. 72.
11   Printed in Herbert Michaelis and Ernst Schraepler (eds.), *Ursachen und Folgen. Vom deutschen Zusammenbruch 1918 und 1945 bis zur staatlichen Neuordnung Deutschlands in der Gegenwart. Eine Urkunden- und Dokumentensammlung zur Zeitgeschichte*, vol. xxii (Berlin, 1976), p. 343 (doc. Nr. 3584a).
12   Institut für Marxismus-Leninismus beim Zentralkomitee der Kommunistischen Partei der Sowjetunion (ed.), *Geschichte des Großen Vaterländischen Krieges der Sowjetunion*, vol. v (Berlin, 1976), p. 124.
13   Quoted in Heike Sander and Barbara Johr (eds.), *BeFreier und Befreite. Krieg, Vergewaltigung, Kinder* (München, 1992), p. 129 (script of the film 'BeFreier und Befreite').
14   Naimark, *The Russians in Germany*, pp. 72–73.
15   Lev Kopolev, *Aufbewahren für alle Zeit!* (Munich 1979), pp. 95–96.
16   Bundesministerium für Vertriebene, Fluchtlinge und Kriegsgeschädigte (ed.), *Dokumentation der Vertreibung der Deutschen aus Ost-Mitteleuropa* (Munich, 1984), vol. i, 1, p. 138 E.
17   Naimark, *The Russians in Germany*, p. 72. See also Ruth Kibelka, *Ostpreußens Schicksalsjahre 1944–1948* (Berlin, 2004), pp. 31–33.
18   Franz Scholz, *Wächter, wie tief die Nacht? Görlitzer Tagebuch 1945/46* (3rd edn., Eltville, 1986), p. 32 (diary entry for 6 May 1945).
19   Stefan Karner, Barbara Stetzl-Marz and Alexander Tschubarjan (eds.), *Die Rote Armee in Österreich. Sowjetische Besatzung 1945–1955. Dokumente* (Graz, Vienna and Munich, 2005), pp. 74–77 (Doc. Nr. 8: 'Directive Nr. 110055 of the Stavka of the Supreme Command to the Commanders of the Troops of the Second and Third Ukrainian Fronts about the Proclamation to the Population of Austria', 2 Apr. 1945), and 168–169 (Doc. Nr. 39: 'Report of the Political Secton of the 336th Guard Regiment of the Troops of the NKVD', undated, before 15 May 1945).
20   Karner, Stetzl-Marz and Tschubarjan (eds.), *Die Rote Armee in Österreich*, pp. 144–145 (Doc. Nr. 30: 'Report of the Leader of the 17th Border Regiment of the troops of the NKVD Rozkov, to the Leader of the Political Section of the Troops of the NKVD for the Protection of the rear territory of the Third Ukrainian Front, Namejšvili, about the political and economic situation in Jennersdorf', 1 May 1945).
21   Stefan Karner, *Die Steiermark im 20. Jahrhundert. Politik – Wirtschaft – Gesellschaft – Kultur* (Graz, Vienna and Cologne, 2000), p. 318.
22   Michael Wieck, *Zeugnis vom Untergang Königsbergs. Ein "Geltungsjude" berichtet* (Munich, 2005), pp. 238, 260.
23   Alexander Werth, *Russia at War* (New York, 1964), p. 963.
24   Quoted in Naimark, *The Russians in Germany*, p. 78.

25 Scholz, *Wächter, wie tief die Nacht?*, p. 39 (diary entry for 19 May 1945).

26 Gregor Thum, *Die fremde Stadt. Breslau 1945* (Berlin, 2003), p. 172.

27 Thum, *Die fremde Stadt*, p. 173.

28 Quoted in Thum, *Die fremde Stadt*, pp. 172–173.

29 Thus in Reutlingen. See Gerhard Junger, *Schicksale 1945. Das Ende des 2. Weltkrieges im Kreise Reutlingen* (2nd edn., Reutlingen, 1977), p. 234.

30 See Elmar Krautkrämer, 'Das Kriegsende in Südwestdeutschland', in Horst Buszello (ed.), *Der Oberrhein in Geschichte und Gegenwart. Von der Römerzeit bis zur Gründung des Landes Baden-Württemberg* (Freiburg im Breisgau, 1986), pp. 213–217; Gerhard Hertel (ed.), *Die Zerstörung von Freudenstadt. Das Schicksal von Freudenstadt am 16./17. April 1945* (Horb am Neckar, 1987).

31 Hansmartin Schwarzmaier, *Der deutsche Südwesten zur Stunde Null. Zusammenbruch und Neuanfang im Jahr 1945 in Dokumenten und Bildern* (Karlsruhe, 1975), pp. 99–101; Jochen Theis, *Südwestdeutschland Stunde Null* (Düsseldorf, 1979), p. 26; Edward N. Peterson, *The Many Faces of Defeat. The German People's Experience in 1945* (New York, Bern, Frankfurt am Main and Paris, 1990), p. 130.

32 This is mentioned by Heide Fehrenbach in her article, 'Rehabilitating Fatherland: Race and German Remasculinization, *Signs: Journal of Women in Culture and Society*, vol. 24, no. 1 (1998), p. 111 (footnote 10). Fehrenbach refers to 'the notorious local history of Freudenstadt' by Hans Rommel, *Vor Zehn Jahren. 16.-17. April 1945. Wie es zur Zerstörung von Freudenstadt gekommen ist* (Freudenstadt: *Freudenstädter Heimatblätter Beiheft I*, 1955). That the events in Freudenstadt in April 1945 continue to provide a focus for right-wing propaganda can be seen in the leaflet of the 'Deutschland-Bewegung' on the occasion of the 60th anniversary of the end of the war, under the title 'Freudenstädter Leidenstage' (http.//www.swg-hamburg.de/Geschichtspolitik/freudenstadt.pdf). This leaflet speaks of 'murder, looting, arson and the mass violation of women and girls'.

33 See the diary entry of Gerhard Hertel for 20 April, in Hertel, *Die Zerstörung von Freudenstadt*, p. 31.

34 See Tom Maloney, *U.S. Camera 1946, Victory Volume* (n.p., 1946), pp. 206–207; Henke, *Die amerikanische Besetzung Deutschland*, pp. 326–328; Strauß, *Kriegsgefangenschaft und Internierung*, p. 99.

35 Headquarters ETOUSA, Office of the Assistant Chief of Staff, G-2: Censorship Report on Observance of Rules of Land Warfare for Period 1–15 April 45, quoted in Strauß, *Kriegsgefangenschaft und Internierung*, p. 99.

36 Quoted in Strauß, *Kriegsgefangenschaft und Internierung*, p. 107.

37 Understandably, many tried to remove these tattoos. See Strauß, *Kriegsgefangenschaft und Internierung*, pp. 107–108.

38   Quoted in Strauß, *Kriegsgefangenschaft und Internierung*, p. 97.

39   Quoted in Strauß, *Kriegsgefangenschaft und Internierung*, p. 98.

40   Quoted in Strauß, *Kriegsgefangenschaft und Internierung*, p. 98.

41   See, for example, Albert Deibele, *Das Kriegsende 1945 im Kreis Schwäbisch Gmünd* (Schwäbisch Gmünd, 1966), p. 18.

42   Herbert Schott, *Die Amerikaner als Besatzungsmacht in Würzburg (1945–1949)*, p. 159. On how the spectre of rape figured in subsequent memories of 1945, see Lutz Niethammer, 'Privat-Wirtschaft. Erinnerungsfragmente einer anderen Umerziehung', in Lutz Niethammer (ed.), *'Hinterher merkt man, daß es richtig war, daß es schiefgegangen ist'. Nachkriegs-Erfahrungen im Ruhrgebiet* (Berlin and Bonn, 1983), pp. 22–34.

43   Earl F. Ziemke, *The U.S. Army in the Occupation of Germany 1944–1946* (Washington, 1975), p. 220.

44   Willy Klapproth, *Kriegschronik 1945 der Stadt Soltau und Umgebung, mit Beiträgen zur Kriegsgeschichte 1945 der Süd- und Mittelheide* (Soltau, 1955), pp. 204–205.

45   See the table of month-by-month mortality in the camp in Günther Kimmel, 'Das Konzentrationslager Dachau. Eine Studie zu den national-sozialistischen Gewaltverbrechen', in Martin Broszat and Elke Fröhlich (eds.), *Bayern in der NS-Zeit. Herrschaft und Gesellschaft in Konflikt*, vol. ii (Munich and Vienna, 1979), p. 385.

46   At the last roll-call in the camp, on the morning of 29 April, the number of prisoners was recorded at 32,335. See Kimmel, 'Das Konzentrationslager Dachau', p. 410f.

47   Henke, *Die amerikanische Besetzung Deutschlands*, p. 869.

48   Report by Master Sergeant Jack Bessel, Sixth Army Group History, Section I, Narrative, S. 350; (United States) National Archives, RG 332, ETO, Historical Division Program Files, Sixth Army Group 1944–45. See also Henke, *Die amerikanische Besetzung Deutschlands*, pp. 869–870.

49   See Robert H. Abzug, *Inside the Vicious Heart. Americans and the Liberation of Nazi Concentration Camps* (New York and Oxford, 1985), pp, 90–95; Henke, *Die amerikanische Besetzung Deutschlands*, p. 920; Harold Marcuse, *Legacies of Dachau. The Uses and Abuses of a Concentration Camp, 1933–2001* (Cambridge, 2001), pp. 50–52.

50   Quoted in Strauß, *Kriegsgefangenschaft und Internierung*, p. 100.

51   Henke, *Die amerikanische Besetzung Deutschlands*, p. 922.

52   Quoted in Abzug, *Inside the Vicious Heart*, p. 94.

53   Abzug, *Inside the Vicious Heart*, p. 93.

54   Tony Barta, 'Antifaschismus und demokratischer Neubeginn. Die Stadt Dachau im ersten Jahr nach dem Nationalsozialismus', *Dachauer Hefte. Studien und Dokumente zur Geschichte der nationalsozialistischen*

Konzentrationslager, vol. 1, no. 1 (December 1985), p. 71.

55 Gisela Schwarze, *Eine Region im demokratischen Aufbau. Der Regierungsbezirk Münster 1945/46* (Düsseldorf, 1984), pp. 18, 293.

56 Saul K. Padower, *Experiment in Germany. The Story of an American Intelligence Officer* (New York, 1946), p. 359.

57 Padower, *Experiment in Germany*, p. 358.

58 This occurred, for example, in Aschaffenburg. See Alois Stadtmüller, *Aschaffenburg im Zweiten Weltkrieg. Bombenangriffe, Belagerung, Übergabe* (2nd. edn., Aschaffenburg, 1971), p. 344.

59 Thus the description by a local historian of the activities of Polish labourers in the district of Schwäbisch Gmünd. See Deibele, *Das Kriegsende 1945 im Kreis Schwäbisch Gmünd*, p. 19. For a similar example in the area occupied by the British, see Klapproth, *Kriegschronik 1945 der Stadt Soltau und Umgebung*, pp. 206–207.

60 Ziemke, *The U.S. Army in the Occupation of Germany*, p. 358.

61 Scholz, *Wächter, wie tief die Nacht?*, p. 39 (diary entry for 18 May 1945).

62 For example, the village of Würtingen, in Württemberg: Würtingen emerged from the war with no damage whatsoever. When French soldiers arrived on 27 April, the six French prisoners of war who had been working in the village as farm helpers informed the French servicemen that no German soldiers were in the village, that the villagers deserved decent treatment, and that it was not really necessary for the military to occupy the village. These French POWs, who had worked and eaten together with the German farmers' families for years, had no thoughts of revenge, and continued to enjoy good relations with the villagers for years after the war. See Junger, *Schicksale 1945*, pp. 291–292.

63 See Richard Bessel, 'Hatred after War: Emotion and the Postwar History of East Germany', *History & Memory*, vol. xvii, nos. 1 and 2 (Autumn 2005), pp. 195–216.

64 Quoted in John Gimbel, *A German Community under American Occupation. Marburg 1945–1952* (Stanford, 1961), p. 52.

65 Emilie Brach, *Wenn meine Briefe Dich erreichen können. Aufzeichnungen aus den Jahren 1939–1945* (ed. by Birgit Forchhammer) (Frankfurt am Main, 1987), p. 238 (letter from 19 May 1945). Quoted in Frolinde Balser, *Aus Trümmern zu einem europäischen Zentrum. Geschichte der Stadt Frankfurt am Main 1945–1989* (Sigmaringen, 1995), p. 18.

66 For the Soviet Occupation Zone see Kurt Stüdemann, 'Parchim 1945–47: Vom Leben in jenen Tagen, Teil II', *Parchimer Heimathefte*, No. 25 (1996), p. 29. For the French Zone see Junger, *Schicksale 1945*, p. 234.

67 Karl Schomaker, "Die Besetzung West-Mecklenburgs am 1. Juli 1945 durch die Sowjetarmee", quoted in Joachim Schultz-Naumann, *Mecklenburg 1945* (Munich, 1989), p. 151.

7. The Beginning of Occupation

1 Howard Zink, *American Military Government in Germany* (New York, 1947), p. 89.

2 *SHAEF Handbook for Military Government in Germany*, § 71. Quoted in Gisela Schwarze, *Eine Region im demokratischen Aufbau. Der Regierungsbezirk Münster 1945/46* (Düsseldorf, 1984), p. 16.

3 In his 'Proclamation Nr. 1' to the German people, Eisenhower as Supreme Commander of Allied Forces famously announced that 'we come as a victorious army; but not as oppressors'. The proclamation was distributed on posters by American troops as they marched into Germany in the spring of 1945, and is reproduced in Wolf-Arno Kropat, *Hessen in der Stunde Null 1945/47. Politik, Wirtschaft und Bildungswesen in Dokumenten* (Wiesbaden, 1979), p. 14.

4 *SHAEF Handbook for Military Government in Germany*, § 71. Quoted in Schwarze, *Eine Region im demokratischen Aufbau*, p. 16.

5 John Gimbel, *A German Community under American Occupation. Marburg 1945–52* (Stanford, 1961), p. 33.

6 See Harold Marcuse, *Legacies of Dachau. The Uses and Abuses of a Concentration Camp, 1933–2001* (Cambridge, 2001), pp. 55–9.

7 Thus, for example at Belsen, where one of those involved described in an interview in July 1946 how 'every day 100 men and women were sent to Belsen in order to bury corpses, clean toilets, etc'. See Rainer Schulze (ed.), *Unruhige Zeiten. Erlebnisberichte aus dem Landkreis Celle 1945–1949* (Munich, 1990), p. 83 (document 6: interview with Oskar Stillmark, Winsen, 25 July 1946).

8 James M. Gavin, *On to Berlin. Battles of an Airborne Commander 1943–1946* (New York, 1978), pp. 288–289; Dagmar Barnouw, *Germany 1945. Views of War and Violence* (Bloomington and Indianapolis, 1996), pp. 12–13; Marcuse, *Legacies of Dachau*, p. 56.

9 Stadt Gelsenkirchen, *Jahres-Chronik für das Jahr 1945*, p. 75. Quoted in Hartmut Pietsch, *Militärregierung Bürokratie und Sozialisierung. Zur Entstehung des politischen Systems in den Städten des Ruhrgebiets 1945 bis 1948* (Duisburg, 1978), p. 11.

10 Quoted in Pietsch, *Militärregierung Bürokratie und Sozialisierung*, p. 11.

11 Herbert Schott, *Die Amerikaner als Besatzungsmacht in Würzburg (1945–1949)*, pp. 24–25.

12 Earl F. Ziemke, *The U.S. Army in the Occupation of Germany 1944–1946* (Washington, 1975), p. 243.

13 Ziemke, *The U.S. Army in the Occupation of Germany*, p. 232.

14 Schwarze, *Eine Region im demokratischen Aufbau*, p. 40.

15 See, for example, Gerhard Junger, *Schicksale 1945. Das Ende des 2.*

Weltkrieges im Kreise Reutlingen (2nd edn., Reutlingen, 1977), pp. 253–254.

16 Schott, *Die Amerikaner als Besatzungsmacht in Würzburg*, p. 20.

17 *SHAEF Handbook for Military Government in Germany*, § 1254. Quoted in Schwarze, *Eine Region im demokratischen Aufbau*, pp. 18–19.

18 For the British Zone, see Schwarze, *Eine Region im demokratischen Aufbau*, p. 16.

19 Gimbel, *A German Community under American Occupation*, p. 63.

20 Schott, *Die Amerikaner als Besatzungsmacht in Würzburg*, p. 78. Of these 320, 207 were civil servants, 92 were white-collar workers in public service, and 21 were workers.

21 Norman M. Naimark, *The Russians in Germany. A History of the Soviet Zone of Occupation 1945–1949* (Cambridge, Mass., 1995), p 44.

22 Mecklenburgisches Landeshauptarchiv Schwerin, Kreistag/Rat des Kreises Demmin, Nr. 46, ff- 62–64: The Landrat des Krieses Demmin to the Präsident des Landes Mecklenburg-Vorpommern, Ableitung Innere Verwaltung, Demmin, 21 Nov. 1945.

23 Timothy R. Vogt, *Denazification in Soviet-Occupied Germany. Brandenburg 1945–1948* (Cambridge, Mass., 2000), p 39.

24 See Damian van Melis, *Entnazifizierung in Mecklenburg-Vorpommern. Herrschaft und Verwaltung 1945–1948* (Munich, 1999), pp. 21–22.

25 Quoted in Schwarze, *Eine Region im demokratischen Aufbau*, p. 20.

26 Quoted in Schwarze, *Eine Region im demokratischen Aufbau*, p. 293.

27 Quoted in Edward N. Peterson, *The American Occupation of Germany. Retreat to Victory* (Detroit, 1977), p. 216.

28 Christof Strauß, *Kriegsgefangenschaft und Internierung. Die Lager in Heilbronn-Böckingen 1945–1947* (Heilbronn, 1998), p. 101.

29 Kurt Schilde, 'Jugendliche unter "Werwolf"-Verdacht. Anmerkungen zu einem schwierigen Thema', in Norbert Haase and Brigitte Oleschinski (eds.), *Das Torgau-Tabu. Wehrmachtstrafsystem, NKWD-Speziallager, DDR-Strafvollzug* (Leipzig, 1993), pp. 177–178.

30 Strauß, *Kriegsgefangenschaft und Internierung*, p. 101; Schilde, 'Jugendliche unter "Werwolf"-Verdacht', pp. 176–179.

31 See the report of 22 June 1945 by the head of the NKVD in Germany, Serov, to L.J. Beria concerning Werewolf activity, printed in Alexander von Platow, 'Sowjetische Speziallager in Deutschland 1945 bis 1950. Ergebnisse eines deutsch-russischen Kooperationsprojektes', in Peter Reif-Spirek and Bodo Ritscher (eds.), *Speziallager in der SBZ. Gedenkstätten mit 'doppelter Vergangenheit'* (Berlin, 1999), pp. 138–139.

32 Hans Woller, *Gesellschaft und Politik in der amerikanischen Besatzungszone. Die Region Ansbach und Fürth* (Munich, 1986), p. 76.

33 For example, the appointment of Wilhelm Höcker (SPD) as President of the Land Administration and Johannes Warnke (KPD) as head of the

'Internal Administration' in Mecklenburg-Vorpommern in the summer of 1945. See van Melis, *Entnazifizierung in Mecklenburg-Vorpommern*.

34 See Schwarze, *Eine Region im demokratischen Aufbau*, pp. 38–39.

35 Woller, *Gesellschaft und Politik*, p. 93.

36 Quoted in Gimbel, *A German Community under American Occupation*, p. 33.

37 For Würzburg, for example, see Schott, *Die Amerikaner als Besatzungsmacht in Würzburg*, p. 80. For Tübingen, the announcement of the 'renaming of the streets' printed in the *Nachrichtenblatt der Militärregierung für den Kreis Tübingen* on 3 August 1945 is reproduced in Manfred Schmid (ed.), *Tübingen 1945. Eine Chronik von Hermann Werner* (Tübingen, 1986), pp. 144–146

38 A chief reason for the choice of Karlshorst was that it had emerged relatively unscathed from the bombing and fighting on the ground and therefore most of the buildings remained intact. This was to be a major consideration of all the Allied powers when choosing where to set up their administrations: the French in Tübingen and Baden-Baden, the British in Bad Oeynhausen, the Americans in Heidelberg, as well as the Russians in Berlin-Karlshorst.

39 'Handbook, No. 629', quoted in Schott, *Die Amerikaner als Besatzungsmacht in Würzburg*, p. 158.

40 Woller, *Gesellschaft und Politik*, p. 70.

41 Schott, *Die Amerikaner als Besatzungsmacht in Würzburg*, p. 158.

42 See Schmid, *Tübingen 1945*, p. 125. Segregation involved not only housing but also retail outlets. In Tübingen, for example, in August the French Military Government ordered that a French department store be opened in what had been a large German shop, with access only for members of the French Military Government and their families. See Schmid, *Tübingen 1945*, p. 151.

43 Gimbel, *A German Community under American Occupation*, pp. 47–49.

44 Cited in Frolinde Balser, *Aus Trümmern zu einem europäischen Zentrum. Geschichte der Stadt Frankfurt am Main 1945–1989* (Sigmaringen, 1995), p. 17.

45 Quoted in Balser, *Aus Trümmern zu einem europäischen Zentrum*, p. 16.

46 'Geschichtliche Darstellung der letzten Kriegstage durch das Bürgermeisteramt der Gemeinde Frankenbach vom Dezember 1948', quoted in Strauß, *Kriegsgefangenschaft und Internierung*, pp. 136–137.

47 See Schwarze, *Eine Region im demokratischen Aufbau*, p. 38.

48 Karla Höcker, *Beschreibung eines Jahres. Berliner Notizen 1945* (Berlin, 1984), p. 91 (diary entry for 1 August 1945).

49 See Reiner Heeb (ed.), *Der Kreis Böblingen* (Stuttgart, 1983), p. 103.

50 Hermann Vietzen, *Chronik der Stadt Stuttgart* (Stuttgart, 1972), p. 47.

51 Vietzen, *Chronik der Stadt Stuttgart*, pp. 39–40.

52 Vietzen, *Chronik der Stadt Stuttgart*, p. 51.

53 Schmid, *Tübingen 1945*, p. 90.

54 Schmid, *Tübingen 1945*, pp. 92–94.

55 E.g. in the American Zone, where 'except for city and suburban lines, which were essential to get the German civilians back and forth to work, the railroads carried only U.S. troops'. See Ziemke, *The U.S. Army in the Occupation of Germany*, p. 351.

56 'Bekanntmachung an die Zivilbevölkerung', *Göttinger Mitteilungsblatt* Nr. 1, 20 April 1945, p. 4; quoted in Thomas Berger and Karl-Heinz Müller (eds.), *Lebenssituationen 1945–1948. Materialien zum Alltagsleben in den westlichen Besatzungszonen 1945–1948* (Hannover, 1983), pp. 40–41. In addition, gatherings of more than five Germans 'in private dwellings for the purpose of discussion' were banned, as was allowing homing pigeons to fly.

57 Order concerning freedom of movement, signed by Major Taft, Hannover, 26 May 1945; quoted in Berger and Müller, *Lebenssituationen 1945–1948*, p. 41.

58 Schmid, *Tübingen 1945*, p. 99.

59 Ziemke, *The U.S. Army in the Occupation of Germany*, p. 351.

60 See Schwarze, *Eine Region im demokratischen Aufbau*, pp. 265–266. In addition, the Dutch Government initially refused entry visas for Germans, some of whom had Dutch spouses and had to wait for months along the border to be reunited. The British refused to intervene, regarding this as a Dutch-German problem which did not concern them.

61 On postwar criminality, see especially Karl S. Bader, *Soziologie der deutschen Nachkriegskriminalität* (Tübingen, 1949).

62 Gerhard Fürmetz. 'Alte und neue Polizisten. Kommunale Personalpolitik in der frühen Nachkriegszeit am Beispiel der Augsburger Stadtpolizei', in Paul Hoser and Reinhard Baumann (eds.), *Kriegsende und Neubeginn. Die Besatzungszeit im schwäbisch-allemanischen Raum* (Konstanz, 2003), pp. 341–342; Schott, *Die Amerikaner als Besatzungsmacht in Würzburg*, p. 77.

63 Schwarze, *Eine Region im demokratischen Aufbau*, p. 43.

64 Schwarze, *Eine Region im demokratischen Aufbau*, p. 43.

65 Landesarchiv Magdeburg, Landesbehörde der Volkspolizei, Nr. 290, ff. 14–15: The Polizeipräsident to the Bezirkspräsident, Magdeburg, 8 Nov. 1945. Not until 1946 did the Soviet Military Administration allow German police in the Soviet Zone to be armed.

66 Schmid, *Tübingen 1945*, p. 94.

67 Gerhard Junger, *Schicksale 1945. Das Ende des 2. Weltkrieges im Kreise Reutlingen* (2nd edn., Reutlingen, 1977), pp. 248–249.

68 Vogt, *Denazification in Soviet-Occupied Germany*, pp. 60–61.

69 *Military Government Gazette*, Mannheim, 11 August 1945. Printed in (Generallandesarchiv, ed.), *Der deutsche Südwesten zur Stunde Null* (Karlsruhe, 1975), pp. 159–160.

70 SHAEF to Commanding Generals vom 13.4.1945, NA, RG 260, 1945–46/44/3, quoted in Christa Horn, *Die Internierungs- und Arbeitslager in Bayern 1945–1952* (Frankfurt am Main, 1992), p. 20.

71 Horn, *Die Internierungs- und Arbeitslager in Bayern*, pp. 20–22.

72 Heiner Wember, *Umerziehung im Lager. Internierung und Bestrafung von Nationalsozialisten in der britischen Besatzungszone Deutschlands* (Essen, 1991), pp. 35–37.

73 Lutz Niethammer, 'Alliierte Internierungslager in Deutschland nach 1945. Vergleich und offene Fragen', in Christian Jansen, Lutz Niethammer and Bernd Weisbrod (eds.), *Von der Aufgabe der Freiheit. Politische Verantwortung und bürgerliche Gesellschaft im 19. und 20. Jahrhundert. Festschrift für Hans Mommsen zum 5.11.1995* (Berlin, 1995), p. 474; Wember, *Umerziehung im Lager*, pp. 31–32, 38; Alexander von Plato, 'Sowjetische Speziallager in Deutschland', pp. 125–132. See also Christof Straub, 'Zwischen Apathie und Selbstrechtfertigung: Die Internierung NS-belasteter Personen in Württemberg-Baden', in Paul Hoser and Reinhard Baumann (eds.), *Kriegsende und Neubeginn. Die Besatzungszeit im Schwäbisch-alemannischen Raum* (Konstanz, 2003), p. 288.

74 Irmgard Lange (ed.), *Entnazifizierung in Nordrhein-Westfalen. Richtlinien, Anweisungen, Organisation* (Siegburg, 1976), p. 12. The numbers are as follows:

Zone	Interned up to 1.1.1947	of those, already released by 1.1.1947
American	95,250	44,244
British	68,500	34,000
French	18,963	8,040
Soviet	67,179	7,214

75 Wember, *Umerziehung im Lager*, p. 38.

76 Horn, *Die Internierungs- und Arbeitslager in Bayern*, pp. 36–39.

77 Woller, *Gesellschaft und Politik*, pp. 69–70.

78 Horn, *Die Internierungs- und Arbeitslager in Bayern*, p. 33.

79 Of the remainder, 4,044 were suspected war criminals and 2,100 were arrested for various reasons as 'security suspects'. See Wember, *Umerziehung im Lager*, p. 38.

80 Schwarze, *Eine Region im demokratischen Aufbau*, pp. 196–197; Marcuse, *Legacies of Dachau*, pp. 68–69.

81 Horn, *Die Internierungs- und Arbeitslager in Bayern*, pp. 217–220.

82 Horn, *Die Internierungs- und Arbeitslager in Bayern*, pp. 220–225.

83 For the British Zone, see Barbara Marshall, 'German Attitudes to British

Military Government 1945–47', *Journal of Contemporary History*, vol. 15 (1980), p. 669.

84 Schwarze, *Eine Region im demokratischen Aufbau*, pp. 196–198; Barbara Marshall, 'German Attitudes to British Military Government 1945–47', p. 669; Wember, *Umerziehung im Lager*, pp. 40–41.

85 Wember, *Umerziehung im Lager*, pp. 42–43.

86 Schwarze, *Eine Region im demokratischen Aufbau*, pp. 198–199.

87 Order Nr. 00100, Moscow, 22 Feb. 1945, printed in Bodo Ritscher, 'Zur Herausbildung und Organisation des Systems von Speziallager des NKVD der UdSSR in der sowjetischen Besatzungszone Deutschlands im Jahr 1945', in *Deutschland Archiv*, vol. 26, no. 6 (1993), pp. 726–727; also Bodo Ritscher, *Speziallager Nr. 2 Buchenwald* (Weimar-Buchenwald, 1995), p. 26.

88 Camps were set up in Posen (Poznań), Danzig, Schneidemühl, Schwiebus, Landsberg, Stargard, Bartenstein, Königsberg, Preußisch Eylau, Oppeln and Tost. See Gudrun Lenzer, *Frauen im Speziallager. Buchenwald 1945–1950. Internierung und lebensgeschichtliche Einordnung* (Münster, 1996), p. 9, note 2; Ritscher, 'Zur Herausbildung und Organisation des Systems von Speziallager', p. 724; von Platow, 'Speziallager in Deutschland', pp. 124–130; Holm Kirsten, *Das sowjetische Speziallager Nr. 4 Landsberg/Warthe* (Göttingen, 2005), pp. 10–11.

89 Niethammer, 'Alliierte Internierungslager in Deutschland', p. 106. Many of the Poles who had been arrested by the NKVD were imprisoned because they were assumed to be Germans on the basis of their identity papers; this was the case particularly in Upper Silesia, and the Polish Embassy in Moscow reported that at least 15,000 Polish miners had been treated unjustly as Germans. See Helga Hirsch, *Die Rache der Opfer. Deutsche in polnischen Lagern 1944–1950* (Berlin, 1998), pp. 193–194.

90 Hirsch, *Die Rache der Opfer*, pp. 194–196.

91 A list of the camps and prisons east of the Oder-Neiße, as reported by the NKVD on 10 May 1945 may be found in von Plato, 'Sowjetische Speziallager in Deutschland', pp. 129–130.

92 Order Nr. 00315, Moscow, 18 April 1945, printed in Ritscher, 'Zur Herausbildung und Organisation des Systems von Speziallagern', pp. 727–728. The title page and a German translation of the complete text of this NKVD order, giving the categories of the people to be arrested, also is reproduced in Achim Kilian, *Mühlberg 1939–1948. Ein Gefangenenlager mitten in Deutschland* (Cologne, Weimar and Vienna, 2001), pp. 227–229.

93 Schilde, 'Jugendliche unter "Werwolf"-Verdacht', pp. 179–181. On the women arrested because of suspected 'Werewolf' activity, see Lenzer, *Frauen im Speziallager Buchenwald*, pp. 41–43, 51.

94   Communiqué issued at the end of the Yalta Conference, printed in *Foreign Relations of the United States. Diplomatic Papers. The Conferences at Malta and Yalta 1945* (Washington, 1955), p. 970.

95   Protocol of the Proceedings at Potsdam, 1 August 1945, II.A.6. Source: <http://www.cnn.com/SPECIALS/cold.war/episodes/01/documents/potsdam.html>.

96   Schwarze, *Eine Region im demokratischen Aufbau*, pp. 195–196; Wolfgang Krüger, *Entnazifiziert! Zur Praxis der politischen Säuberung in Nordrhein-Westfalen* (Wuppertal, 1982), pp. 23, 153.

97   See Irmgard Lange (ed.), *Entnazifizierung in Nordrhein-Westfalen. Richtlinien, Anweisungen, Organisation* (Siegburg, 1976), pp. 11–12. Generally for denazification in the French Occupation Zone, see Klaus-Dietmar Henke, *Politische Säuberung unter französischer Besatzung* (Stuttgart, 1981).

98   For the British Zone, see Schwarze, *Eine Region im demokratischen Aufbau*, pp. 199–200; Krüger, *Entnazifiziert!*, p. 102.

99   Quoted in Horn, *Die Internierungs- und Arbeitslager in Bayern*, p, 37.

100 Bericht des Detachment G1H2 für den Monat Juli 1945: Report by Major Everett S. Cofran, Major AC, Military Government Officer, Commanding, for the period from 1 July 1945 to 31 July 1945. Printed in Karl-Ulrich Gelberg (ed.), *Kriegsende und Neuanfang in Augsburg 1945. Erinnerungen und Berichte* (Munich, 1996), pp. 139–143.

101 Quoted in Woller, *Gesellschaft und Politik*, p. 99.

102 Woller, *Gesellschaft und Politik*, p. 102.

103 For example, in Tübingen: see Schmid, *Tübingen 1945*, pp. 162–163. In addition, the French took over one of the best school buildings in Tübingen and converted it into a French lycée, which opened its doors on 5 November and was named after a martyr of the French Resistance.

104 For the British Zone, see Schwarze, *Eine Region im demokratischen Aufbau*, pp. 240–244.

105 Lutz Niethammer, *Die Mitläuferfabrik. Die Entnazifizierung am Beispiel Bayerns* (Berlin and Bonn, 1982), p. 186.

106 Schott, *Die Amerikaner als Besatzungsmacht in Würzburg*, p. 118.

107 Ziemke, *The U.S. Army in the Occupation of Germany*, p. 383.

108 Quoted in Ziemke, *The U.S. Army in the Occupation of Germany*, p. 384. See also Klaus-Dietmar Henke, *Die amerikanische Besetzung Deutschlands* (Munich, 1995), p. 1000.

109 Ziemke, *The U.S. Army in the Occupation of Germany*, p. 386.

110 Quoted in Niethammer, *Die Mitläuferfabrik*, p. 246.

111 Quoted in Ziemke, *The U.S. Army in the Occupation of Germany*, p. 388.

112 Ziemke, *The U.S. Army in the Occupation of Germany*, p. 390.

113 For the British Zone, see Lange, *Entnazifizierung in Nordrhein-Westfalen*, pp. 14–15.

114   Krüger, *Entnazifiziert!*, p. 23. See also Schwarze, *Eine Region im demokra-
      tischen Aufbau*, p. 198.

115   Woller, *Gesellschaft und Politik*, pp. 107–108.

116   Niethammer, *Die Mitläuferfabrik*.

117   Quoted in Clemens Vollnhals, 'Einleitung', in Clemens Vollnhals (ed.),
      *Entnazifizierung. Politische Säuberung und Rehilitierung in den vier Besatzungs-
      zonen 1945–1949* (Munich, 1991), p, 46.

118   Vogt, *Denazification in Soviet-Occupied Germany*, p. 29. See also Vollnhals,
      'Einleitung', p. 43; van Melis, *Entnazifizierung in Mecklenburg-Vorpommern*.
      pp. 68–70.

119   Vollnhals, 'Einleitung', p. 46.

120   Quoted in van Melis, *Entnazifizierung in Mecklenburg-Vorpommern*, p. 110.

121   According to one German soldier taken prisoner by the Americans, 'under
      no circumstances did we want to fall into the hands [. . .] of the French.
      One heard rumours that above all there were colonial troops serving with
      the French. We wanted to hold out as long as possible in order by all
      means to fall into the hands of the Americans, from whom we expected
      decent treatment.' Eyewitness account quoted in Strauß, *Kriegsgefangen-
      schaft und Internierung*, p. 92.

122   Ziemke, *The U.S. Army in the Occupation of Germany*, p. 291.

123   Wember, *Umerziehung im Lager*, p. 44.

124   Strauß, *Kriegsgefangenschaft und Internierung*, p. 16. The two 'Temporary
      Enclosures' in Heilbronn alone contained roughly 150,000 prisoners,
      double the city's 1939 population and four times its population at the end
      of the war.

125   In 1945, 3,107,000 German soldiers fell into American hands and
      2,319,000 into the hands of the British. Figures in Hermann Glaser, *Beginn
      einer Zukunft. Bericht und Dokumentation* (Frankfurt am Main, 2005), p. 97.

126   Ziemke, *The U.S. Army in the Occupation of Germany*, p. 291, fn 60.

127   For reports of rumours repeated in late 1944 and early 1945 about good
      treatment offered in the U.S. and Canada to captured Germans, see
      Wolfram Wette, Ricarda Bremer and Detlef Vogel (eds.), *Das letzte halbe
      Jahr. Stimmungsberichte der Wehrmachtpropaganda 1944/45* (Essen, 2001),
      pp. 149, 168, 308.

128   Eyewitness account quoted in Strauß, *Kriegsgefangenschaft und Internierung*,
      p. 93.

129   Wember, *Umerziehung im Lager*, pp. 45–46.

130   Wember, *Umerziehung im Lager*, p. 45, note 83. The claim about vast
      numbers of German deaths in American captivity was made in the late
      1980s by James Bacque, *Other Losses* (Toronto, 1989).

131   'Augenzeugenbericht', quoted in Strauß, *Kriegsgefangenschaft und Inter-
      nierung*, p. 93.

132 Bernd-A. Rusinek, 'Der Krieg ist aus, die Freiheit muss noch warten: Deutsche Kriegsgefangene und Zwangsarbeiter', in *Kriegsende in Deutschland* (Hamburg, 2005), p. 126.

133 Andreas Hilger, 'Deutsche Kriegsgefangene im Wiederaufbau der Sowjetunion. Arbeitsorganisation und -leistung im Licht deutscher und russischer Quellen', in Rüdiger Overmans (ed.), *In der Hand des Feindes. Kriegsgefangenschaft von der Antike bis zum Zweiten Weltkrieg* (Cologne, Weimar and Vienna, 1999), p. 444. The Soviet figure of 2,388,443 German prisoners is an underestimate, as it excluded many who had been shot or had died due to poor treatment and inadequate medical provision.

134 Stefan Karner, 'Deutsche Kriegsgefangene und Internierte in der Sowjetunion 1941–1956', in Rolf-Dieter Müller and Hans-Erich Volkmann (eds.), *Die Wehrmacht. Mythos und Realität* (Munich, 1999), pp. 1012–1019; Andreas Hilger, *Deutsche Kriegsgefangene in der Sowjetunion, 1941–1956. Kriegsgefangenenpolitik, Lageralltag und Erinnerung* (Essen, 2000), pp. 100–101, 390–392; Frank Biess, *Homecomings. Returning POWs and the Legacies of Defeat in Postwar Germany* (Princeton and Oxford, 2005), p. 20. On Stalingrad, see Rüdiger Overmans, 'Das andere Gesicht des Krieges: Leben und Sterben der 6. Armee', in Jürgen Förster (ed.), *Stalingrad. Ereignis, Wirkung, Symbol* (Frankfurt am Main, 1992), pp. 419–455.

135 Manfred Zeidler, *Kriegsende im Osten. Die Rote Armee und die Besetzung Deutschlands östlich von Oder und Neiße 1944/45* (Munich, 1996), pp. 178–180.

136 Schmid, *Tübingen 1945*, p. 97.

137 Report by Lt. Col. Richard A. Norton (Bericht des Detachment G1H2 für September 1945), CE, Director for September 1945, printed in Karl-Ulrich Gelberg (ed.), *Kriegsende und Neuanfang in Augsburg 1945. Erinnerungen und Berichte* (Munich, 1996), p. 147.

138 Quoted in Schott, *Die Amerikaner als Besatzungsmacht in Würzburg*, p. 67.

139 Balser, *Aus Trümmern zu einem europäischen Zentrum*, p. 16.

140 Report by Major Everett S. Cofran, Major AC, Military Government Officer, Commanding, for the period from 1 July 1945 to 31 July 1945, printed in Gelberg, *Kriegsende und Neuanfang in Augsburg 1945*, pp. 139–143.

141 USFET, I&E, Research Staff, Study no. 1, The American Soldier in Germany, Nov. 1945, cited in Ziemke, *The U.S. Army in the Occupation of Germany*, p. 327.

142 Horn, *Die Internierungs- und Arbeitslager in Bayern*, pp. 25–27.

143 Annette Weinke, *Die Nürnberger Prozesse* (Munich, 2006), pp. 16–23.

144 Horn, *Die Internierungs- und Arbeitslager in Bayern*, p. 27.

145 Ziemke, *The U.S. Army in the Occupation of Germany*, p. 391. Ziemke notes that this case 'was entirely within the traditional concept of war crimes as

specific acts against the laws and usages of war committed by soldiers during hostilities'.

146 Ziemke, *The U.S. Army in the Occupation of Germany*, p. 391.

147 Martin Broszat, 'Siegerjustiz oder strafrechtliche "Selbstreinigung". Aspekte der Vergangenheitsbewältigung der deutschen Justiz während der Besatzungszeit 1945–1949', *Vierteljahrshefte für Zeitgescichte* (1981), p. 477; Wember, *Umerziehung im Lager*, p. 30.

148 Quoted in Weinke, *Die Nürnberger Prozesse*, p. 41.

8. The Loss of the East

1 'Auszug aus dem Bericht des Leiters der Organisation- und Gebietsabteilung des Ministeriums für Information und Propaganda, Teofil Konar, betreffend die Lage der polnischen und der deutschen Bevölkerung in Pomorze Zachodnie/Pommern', 16 July 1945, printed in Wlodzimierz Borodziej and Hans Lemberg (eds.), *'Unsere Heimat ist uns ein fremdes Land geworden . . .'. Die Deutschen östlich von Oder und Neisse, 1945–1950. Dokumente aus polnischen Archiven*, vol. iii (Marburg, 2004), p. 366.

2 Stadtinspektor Theodor Jurok, Hindenburg-Jabze, quoted in Wolfgang Schwarz, *Die Flucht und Vertreibung Oberschlesien 1945/46* (Bad Nauheim, 1965), p. 109.

3 A.J.P, Taylor, *The Course of German History. A Source of the Development of German History since 1815* (London, 1968), p. 21.

4 While en route to Teheran in November 1943, President Roosevelt had spoken of a possible future tripartite division of Germany, with a southern state which would be largely Catholic and a northwestern state which would be largely Protestant, asserting that 'it might be said that the religion of the Northeastern part is Prussianism'. Quoted in John H. Backer, *The Decision to Divide Germany. American Foreign Policy in Transition* (Durham, N.C., 1978), pp. 22–23.

5 Pertti Ahonen, *After the Expulsion. West Germany and Eastern Europe 1945–1990* (Oxford, 2003), p. 16. Generally, see Detlef Brandes, *Der Weg zur Vertreibung. Pläne und Entscheidungen zum 'Transfer' der Deutschen aus der Tschechoslowakei und aus Polen* (Munich, 2001); Hans Lemberg and Wlodzimierz Borodziej, 'Einleitung', in Wlodzimierz Borodziej and Hans Lemberg (eds.), *'Unsere Heimat ist uns ein fremdes Land geworden . . .'. Die Deutschen östlich von Oder und Neisse, 1945–1950. Dokumente aus polnischen Archiven*, vol. i (Marburg, 2000), pp. 37–55; Klaus-Dietmar Henke, 'Der Weg nach Potsdam – Die Alliierten und die Vertreibung', in Wolfgang Benz (ed.), *Die Vertreibung der Deutschen aus dem Osten. Ursachen, Ereignisse, Folgen* (Frankfurt am Main, 1985), pp. 49–69.

6   Detlef Brandes, *Der Weg zur Vertreiburg 1938–1945*.

7   See, for example, the American 'Briefing Book Paper' of 12 January 1945 on 'The Treatment of Germany', in *Foreign Relations of the United States. Diplomatic Papers. The Conferences at Malta and Yalta* (Washington, 1955), pp. 188–190.

8   Generally, see Norman M. Naimark, *Fires of Hatred. Ethnic Cleansing in Twentieth-Century Europe* (Cambridge, Mass., and London, 2001), pp. 108–111.

9   Protocol of the Proceedings at Potsdam, 1 August 1945, XII. Orderly Transfer of German Populations. Source: <http://www.cnn.com/SPE-CIALS/cold.war/episodes/01/documents/potsdam.html>.

10   Andreas Hofmann, *Die Nachkriegszeit in Schlesien. Gesellschafts- und Bevölkerungspolitik in den polnischen Siedlungsgebieten 1945–1948* (Cologne, Weimar and Vienna, 2000), pp. 190–191.

11   Hofmann, *Die Nachkriegszeit in Schlesien*, p. 192. On 18 June the Supreme Command of the Polish Army issued instructions covering the expropriation and removal of the German population in the military settlement area.

12   'Befehl des Kommandos der 2. Armee des WP Nr. 0150 über die Fortsetzung der raschen Aussiedlung der Deutschen', 24 June 1945, in Borodziej and Lemberg, *'Unsere Heimat ist uns ein fremdes Land geworden . . .'*, vol. i, pp. 160–161.

13   'Der Chef der Abteilung für politische Erziehung der 7. Infanteriedivision an den Chef der Verwaltung für politische Erziehung der 2. Armee des WP in der Frage der Aussiedlung der Deutschen aus dem Grenzstreifen', 26 June 1945, printed in Borodziej and Lemberg, *'Unsere Heimat ist uns ein fremdes Land geworden . . .'*, vol. i, pp. 163–164.

14   Hofmann, *Die Nachkriegszeit in Schlesien*, p. 192. For accounts of these forced removals, see Bundesministerium für Vertriebene (ed.), *Dokumentation der Vertreibung der Deutschen aus Ost-Mitteleuropa. Band I/1. Die Vertreibung der deutschen Bevölkerung aus den Gebieten östlich der Oder-Neiße. Dokumente. Die Zerstörung der Lebensgrundlage der ostdeutschen Bevölkerung seit 1945* (Bonn, 1953–1957), pp. 690–703.

15   'Situationsbericht des Starosten von Groß Strehlitz', quoted in Hofmann, *Die Nachkriegszeit in Schlesien*, p. 195.

16   *Dokumentation der Vertreibung der Deutschen aus Ost-Mitteleuropa*. vol. I/1, pp. 693–694: 'Erlebnisbericht des Landwirts A. N. aus Barschdorf. Kreis Liegnitz i, Niederschles.', Original, 7 Dec. 1952.

17   Hofmann, *Die Nachkriegszeit in Schlesien*, pp. 192–193. On conditions in Görlitz, see Franz Scholz, *Wächter, wie tief die Nacht? Görlitzer Tagebuch 1945/46* (Eltville, 1986), and the report by Richard Süßmuth, dated 20 Aug. 1945, 'Ausgetrieben und ausgeplündert', printed in Herbert

Hupka (ed.), *Letzte Tage in Schlesien. Tagebücher, Erinnerungen und Dokumente der Vertreibung* (5th edn., Munich and Vienna, 1988), pp, 346–351.

18 Scholz, *Wächter, wie tief die Nacht?* p. 45.

19 Hofmann, *Die Nachkriegszeit in Schlesien*, p. 198.

20 Naimark, *Fires of Hatred*, pp. 108–38; Norman Davies and Roger Moorhouse, *Microcosm. Portrait of a Central European City* (London, 2003), pp. 417–425.

21 Bericht 320, from Adelheid, Marie and Karl Uiberla on 28 April 1947, printed in Alois Harasko, 'Die Vertreibung der Sudetendeutschen. Sechs Erlebnisberichte', in Wolfgang Benz (ed.), *Die Vertreibung der Deutschen aus dem Osten. Ursachen, Ereignisse, Folgen* (Frankfurt am Main, 1985), pp. 111–112.

22 Quoted in Naimark, *Fires of Hatred*, p. 109.

23 The *Dokumentation der Vertreibung* offered the following rough estimates of the German population in the east from the end of 1944 to the second half of 1945:

Regions east of the Oder–Neiße	German population at the end of 1944	German population after the flight before the Red Army, April–May 1945	German population after the returns in the summer of 1945 before the expulsion
East Prussia	2,653,000*	600,000	800,000
Eastern Pomerania	1,861,000	1,000,000	1,000,000
Eastern Brandenburg	660,000	300,000	350,000
Silesia	4,718,000	1,500,000	2,500,000
Polish regions	1,612,000	800,000	800,000
Danzig	420,000	200,000	200,000
Total	11,924,000	4,400,000	5,650,000

* Note: This figure includes the roughly 131,000 inhabitants of the Memelland and the roughly 310,000 inhabitants of the *Regierungsbezirk Westpreußen*.

Source: *Die Vertreibung der deutschen Bevölkerung aus den Gebieten östlich der Oder-Neiße*, vol. I/1, 'Einleitung', p. 78.

24 *Die Vertreibung der deutschen Bevölkerung aus den Gebieten östlich der Oder-Neiße*, vol. I/1, 'Einleitung', p. 23.

25 See *Die Vertreibung der deutschen Bevölkerung aus den Gebieten östlich der Oder-Neiße*, vol. I/1, 'Einleitung', p. 32.

26   According to the Polish census of 1921, 1,059,000 people gave their
      nationality as German; in 1931 the number of Germans in Poland stood at
      741,000. See Antony Polonsky, *Politics in Independent Poland 1921–1939.*
      The Crisis of Constitutional Government 1921–1939 (Oxford, 1972), p. 39.

27   'Der Chef der Abteilung für politische Erziehung der 7. Infanteriedivision
      an den Chef der Verwaltung für politische Erziehung der 2. Armee des
      WP in der Frage der Aussiedlung der Deutschen aus dem Grenzstreifen',
      26 June 1945, printed in Borodziej and Lemberg, *'Unsere Heimat ist uns ein*
      fremdes Land geworden . . .', vol. i, pp. 163–164. See also Anita J.
      Prazmowska, *Civil War in Poland, 1942–1948* (Basingstoke, 2004), p. 180.

28   Quoted in Naimark, *Fires of Hatred*, p. 109. Gomułka, who placed police
      along the new border to prevent Germans from returning eastwards, wrote
      that 'the kinds of conditions should be created so that they [Germans]
      won't want to remain [in postwar Poland]'. Quoted in Naimark, *Fires of*
      Hatred, p. 125.

29   Prazmowska, *Civil War in Poland*, p. 181.

30   Altogether by 1948 at least 2.1 million Poles had been transferred from the
      former eastern regions of Poland and from places of deportation in Siberia
      and Central Asia; most of these settled in the former eastern regions of
      Germany. See Philipp Ther, *Deutsche und polnische Vertriebene. Gesellschaft*
      und Vertriebenenpolitik in der SBZ/DDR und in Polen 1945–1956
      (Göttingen, 1998), pp. 44–45.

31   Padraig Kenny, *Rebuilding Poland. Workers and Communists, 1945–1950*
      (Ithaca and London, 1997), p. 153; Naimark, *Fires of Hatred*, p. 131.

32   Naimark, *Fires of Hatred*, p. 133.

33   See Norman Davies and Roger Moorhouse, *Microcosm. Portrait of a Central*
      European City (London, 2002), p. 408.

34   On 13 May, a few days after setting up the nascent Polish administration,
      Drobner travelled to Marshal Koniev's headquarters in Sagan/Zagan and
      secured Soviet acceptance of what had been done. See Davies and
      Moorhouse, *Microcosm*, pp. 409–410.

35   See Naimark, *Fires of Hatred*, p. 125.

36   Naimark, *Fires of Hatred*, pp. 134–136. The prohibition was ineffective,
      however, and served to provoke resentment particularly among Polish
      Silesians who also spoke German.

37   Ther, *Deutsche und polnische Vertriebene*, pp. 62, 102. Katrin Steffen, 'Flucht,
      Vertreibung und Zwangsaussiedlung aus der Wojewodschaft Stettin
      (Województwo Szczecínskie) in den Jahren 1945–1950', in Borodziej and
      Lemberg (eds.), *'Unsere Heimat ist uns ein fremdes Land geworden . . .'*, vol. iii,
      pp. 298–300.

38   See Kenny, *Rebuilding Poland*, pp. 152–153.

39   See Davies and Moorhouse, *Microcosm*, p. 413; Richard Bessel, 'The

Shadow of Death in Germany at the End of the Second World War', in Paul Betts, Alon Confino and Dirk Schumann (eds.), *Between Mass Death and Individual Loss. The Place of the Dead in 20th-Century Germany* (Oxford and New York, 2008), pp. 51–68.

40 Ther, *Deutsche und polnische Vertriebene*, p. 61.

41 Naimark, *Fires of Hatred*, p. 127.

42 'Bericht des Leiters der Vorläufigen Staatsverwaltung für die Wojewodschaft Gdańsk/Danzig, Roman Dabrowski, an Edward Ochab von einer Bereisung der Wojewodschaft Gdansk/Danzig', 24 May 1945, printed in Borodziej and Lemberg (eds.), *'Unsere Heimat ist uns ein fremdes Land geworden . . .'.*, vol. iv, pp. 72–79.

43 Kenny, *Rebuilding Poland*, p. 140. See also Davies and Moorhouse, *Microcosm*, pp. 408–409.

44 Quoted in Kenny, *Rebuilding Poland*, pp. 137–138.

45 Quoted in Naimark, *Fires of Hatred*, pp. 127–128.

46 Quoted in Ther, *Deutsche und polnische Vertriebene*, p. 61.

47 Naimark, *Fires of Hatred*, p. 127.

48 *Dokumentation der Vertreibung der Deutschen aus Ost-Mitteleuropa. Band I/1*, 'Einleitung', pp. 70–74E; Hofmann, *Die Nachkriegszeit in Schlesien*, pp. 192–193; Martin Holz, *Evakuierte, Flüchtlinge und Vertriebene auf der Insel Rügen 1943–1961* (Cologne, 2003), pp. 95–97.

49 See Holz, *Evakuierte, Flüchtlinge und Vertriebene auf der Insel Rügen*, pp. 115–120.

50 Quoted in Holz, *Evakuierte, Flüchtlinge und Vertriebene auf der Insel Rügen*, p. 116.

51 Quoted in Holz, *Evakuierte, Flüchtlinge und Vertriebene auf der Insel Rügen*, p. 116.

52 *Dokumentation der Vertreibung der Deutschen aus Ost-Mitteleuropa. Band I/*, 'Einleitung', pp. 72–73E. See also Klaus-Dietmar Henke, 'Der Weg nach Potsdam – Die Alliierten und die Vertreibung', in Wolfgang Benz (ed.), *Die Vertreibung der Deutschen aus dem Osten. Ursachen, Ereignisse, Folgen* (Frankfurt am Main, 1985), pp. 66–67; Ahonen, *After the Expulsion*, p. 16.

53 Hofmann, *Die Nachkriegszeit in Schlesien*, p. 193.

54 Sebastian Siebel-Achenbach, *Lower Silesia from Nazi Germany to Communist Poland, 1942–49* (London, 1994), p. 120.

55 Kenny, *Rebuilding Poland*, p. 152.

56 Kenny, *Rebuilding Poland*, p. 153.

57 Eufrozyna Maria Piatek, 'Die Entwicklung der Belegschaften im niederschlesischen Steinkohlenbergbau 1945 bis 1945', in Klaus Tenfelde (ed.), *Sozialgeschichte des Bergbaus im 19. und 20. Jahrhundert* (Munich, 1992), p. 153. In February 1946 the population of Wałbrzych consisted of 52,176 Germans, 19,647 Poles and 650 people of other nationalities.

58   'Schreiben eines PUR-Inspekteurs für Ansiedlungsfragen in Tarnów an
      das Staatliche Repatriierungsamt (PUR) in Gdańsk/Danzig über die
      Organisation des polnischen Ansiedlungswesens in Stadt und Kreis
      Elblag/Elbing', 9 June 1945, printed in Borodziej and Lemberg (eds.),
      Unsere Heimat ist uns ein fremdes Land geworden . . .', vol. iv, pp. 79–82.

59   Naimark, *Fires of Hatred*, pp. 128–9.

60   Manfred Overesch, *Das III. Reich 1939–1945. Ein Tageschronik der Politik,
      Wirtschaft, Kultur* (Augsburg, 1991), pp. 363, 445, 524. See also Jörg
      Friedrich, *Der Brand. Deutschland im Bombenkrieg 1940–1945* (Munich,
      2002), pp. 187–189. For a map showing the areas of the city – the old city,
      the port and the districts to the north of the city centre – most damaged
      by the bombing, see Tadeusz Bialecki et. al. (eds.), *Stettin 1945–1946.
      Dokumente – Erinnerungen* (Rostock, 1995), p. 32.

61   'Evakuierung der Bevölkerung. Weisung Nr. 318 der Gauleitung
      Pommern der NSDAP in Stettin vom 20. Februar 1945', printed in
      Bialecki, *Stettin 1945–1946*, pp. 25–27.

62   Testimony of Kazimierz Borowski, a Polish forced labourer in Stettin in
      1945, from 2 October 1975, printed in Bialecki, *Stettin 1945–1946*, p. 41;
      Report of Felix Gosser, printed in Bialecki, *Stettin 1945–1946*, p. 105.

63   'Auszug aus dem Bericht Nr. 1 des kommissarischen Stadtpräsidenten
      Stettins Piotr Zaremba über den Zustand der Stadt vom 28. April 1945',
      printed in Bialecki, *Stettin 1945–1946*, p. 97. Erich Wiesner, who headed
      the German administration in the city in May and June 1945, claimed that
      the number of inhabitants was 380,000 at the outbreak of the war and
      roughly 4–5000 when the Red Army marched into the city. See 'Auszug
      aus dem Bericht des Bürgermeisters Erich Wiesner vom 19. Juni 1945',
      printed in Bialecki, *Stettin 1945–1946*, pp. 155–157.

64   'Übernahme der Macht in Stettin, Bekanntmachung des Stadtpräsidenten
      Piotr Zaremba vom 6. Mai 1945', printed in Bialecki, *Stettin 1945–1946*,
      p. 97.

65   A photocopy of Zaremba's order to raise the Polish flag at 8:15 on the
      morning of 30 April is printed in Bialecki, *Stettin 1945–1946*, p. 98.

66   Wiesner later played a significant role in Mecklenburg, as mayor of
      Schwerin from 1945 to 1952 and a leading member of the regional SED;
      from 1952 he worked on the newspaper *Schweriner Volkszeitung*. See Erich
      Wiesner, *Man nannte mich Ernst. Erlebnisse und Episoden aus der Geschichte
      der Arbeiterjugendbewegung* (Berlin, 1982).

67   Report of Felix Gosser, printed in Bialecki, *Stettin 1945–1946*, p. 105.

68   'Auszug aus dem Bericht des Bürgermeisters Erich Wiesner vom 19. Juni
      1945', printed in Bialecki, *Stettin 1945–1946*, pp. 155–157. According to this
      report, the registered German population consisted of 6616 children up to
      the age of six, 7727 children aged between 6 and 14, 34,983 adults up to 60

years of age and a further 11,649 who were over 65. The numbers of people deemed capable of working were 11,248 men and 15,374 women. A couple of weeks later the Stettin Labour Office reported that the total population on 2 July was 80,980, of whom 19,533 were children; the numbers able to work was given as 14,330 men and 22,586 women. 17,125 men and women were working for the Russian authorities. See 'Arbeitsbericht des Arbeitsamtes vom 3. Juli 1945', printed in Bialecki, *Stettin 1945–1946*, p. 185.

69 'Auszug aus dem Bericht des Bürgermeisters Erich Wiesner vom 19. Juni 1945', printed in Bialecki, *Stettin 1945–1946*, pp. 155–157.

70 'Auszug aus dem Bericht über die Parteisitzung der KPD am 17. Mai 1945', printed in Bialecki, *Stettin 1945–1946*, pp. 111–113.

71 'Nicht signierte Kopie eines Memorandum der Kommunisten in der deutschen Stadtverwaltung Stettins vom 20. Mai 1945', printed in Bialecki, *Stettin 1945–1946*, pp. 113–115.

72 'Auszug aus dem Bericht von Brigitte Manzke', printed in Bialecki, *Stettin 1945–1946*, p. 119.

73 'Petition der deutschen Stadtverwaltung Stettins zur Situation in Stettin an die Regierung der UdSSR vom 6. Juni 1945', printed in Bialecki, *Stettin 1945–1946*, pp. 129–133.

74 'Nachtrag zu der Petition der deutschen Stadtverwaltung Stettins zur Situation in Stettin an die Regierung der UdSSR vom 12. Juni 1945', printed in Bialecki, *Stettin 1945–1946*, p. 135.

75 'Auszüge aus dem Tätigkeitsbericht der Polizei- und Justizverwaltung vom 16. Juni 1945', printed in Bialecki, *Stettin 1945–1946*, pp. 145–147.

76 See the 'Zeittafel' in Bialecki, *Stettin 1945–1946*, p. 371.

77 'Schreiben des Bevollmächtigten der Republic Polen für den Bezirk Westpommern Leonard Borkowicz an das Mitglied des Kriegsrates der I. Weißrussischen Front General K.F. Telegin in Berlin vom 13. Juni 1945', printed in Bialecki, *Stettin 1945–1946*, p. 141. According to Borkowicz, populating Stettin with Poles was a 'task set by Stalin'.

78 'Abschlußbericht des Bürgermeisters Erich Wiesner an das Zentral-kommittee der KPD in Berlin über seine Tätigkeit in Stettin vom 14. Juli 1945', printed in Bialecki, *Stettin 1945–1946*, pp. 187–193.

79 'Bericht des Stadtpräsidenten Stettins vom 7. Juli 1945', printed in Bialecki, *Stettin 1945–1946*, p. 201.

80 'Abschlußbericht des Bürgermeisters Erich Wiesner an das Zentral-kommittee der KPD in Berlin über seine Tätigkeit in Stettin vom 14. Juli 1945', printed in Bialecki, *Stettin 1945–1946*, pp. 187–193.

81 Steffen, 'Flucht, Vertreibung und Zwangsaussiedlung aus der Wojewod-schaft Stettin', p. 307; 'Bekanntmachung des Präsidenten von Szczecin/Stettin, Piotr Zaremba, betreffend die Grundsätze des Aufenthalts und der vorgesehenen Registrierung der deutschen Bevölkerung', 9 July 1945,

printed in Borodziej and Lemberg, *'Unsere Heimat ist uns ein fremdes Land geworden . . .'*, vol. iii, p. 364.

82   'Abschlußbericht des Bürgermeisters Erich Wiesner an das Zentral-kommittee der KPD in Berlin über seine Tätigkeit in Stettin vom 14. Juli 1945', printed in Bialecki, *Stettin 1945–1946*, pp. 187–193.

83   Poster of the President of the City of Szczecin, 7 July 1945, printed (with a fascimile) in Bialecki, *Stettin 1945–1946*, pp. 208–209.

84   'Schreiben des Stadtpräsidenten Stettins an den Minister für Propaganda und Information in Warschau vom 13. Juli 1945', printed in Bialecki, *Stettin 1945–1946*, p. 215.

85   The typhoid epidemic in eastern Germany during the summer of 1945 fig-ures repeatedly in accounts of Germans' suffering at the time. For example: Johannes Kaps (ed.), *The Tragedy of Silesia 1945–46. A Documentary Account with a Special Survey of the Archdiocese of Breslau* (Munich, 1952/53), p. 482: Report No. 163. The Parish of Haynau, near Goldberg. It also was a con-cern for the Polish authorities, who placed part of the blame on Germans who 'in the current living conditions disregard the most basic principles of hygiene'. See 'Tätigkeitsbericht der Stadtverwaltung Gdańsk/Danzig für August 1945. Auszug aus dem Bericht der Gesundheitsabteilung', printed in Borodziej and Lemberg (eds.), *'Unsere Heimat ist uns ein fremdes Land geworden . . .'*, vol. iv (Marburg, 2004), pp. 115–117.

86   'Auszüge aus dem Tätigkeitsbericht von Otto Römling' (written down in February 1982), printed in Bialecki, *Stettin 1945–1946*, p. 171.

87   Observations by Paul Peikert, quoted in Siebel-Achenbach, *Lower Silesia from Nazi Germany to Communist Poland*, p. 127.

88   Wilhelm Starlinger, *Grenzen der Sowjetmacht im Spiegel einer Ost-West-Begegnung hinter Palisaden, von 1945–1954. Mit einem Bericht der deutschen Seuchenkrankenhäuser York und St. Elisabeth über das Leben und Sterben in Königsberg von 1945–1947* (Kitzingen, 1954), p. 38. In his memoirs, Michael Wieck gives the figure of 20,000 survivors out of 130,000. Wieck, *Zeugnis vom Untergang Königsberg*, pp. 264–5.

89   Quoted in Naimark, *Fires of Hatred*, p. 127.

90   See the 'Zeittafel' in Bialecki, *Stettin 1945–1946*, p. 373.

91   'Bekanntmachung des Stadtpräsidenten Stettins vom 9. November 1945', facsimile printed in Bialecki, *Stettin 1945–1946*, p. 295.

92   'Auszug aus der vorläufigen Grenzinstruktion des Stadtpräsidenten Stettins als Bevollmächtigter für den Kreis Stettin vom 6. Oktober 1945', printed in Bialecki, *Stettin 1945–1946*, pp. 266–269.

93   It also took months before the Poles were able to secure the border regions along the western Neiße and the frontier with Czechoslovakia. See Siebel-Achenbach, *Lower Silesia from Nazi Germany to Communist Poland*, pp. 120–121.

94 'Stand der Kriegszerstörungen und Besiedlung der Stadt nach vorläufigen Berechnungen der Stettiner Stadtverwaltung vom 31. Oktober 1945', in Bialecki, *Stettin 1945–1946*, pp. 286–289. In addition to the 15,000 who had left, a further 3,500 Germans had died of typhoid between July and October. See the 'Auszüge aus einem Bericht der Stettiner Stadtverwaltung aus der zweiten Hälfte Oktober 1945', in Bialecki, *Stettin 1945–1946*, pp. 283.

95 'Nachweis der im Gebiet von Szczecin/Stettin wohnhaften polnischen und deutschen Bevölkerung, angefertigt durch die Abteilung für Allgemeine Verwaltung der I. Instanz der Stadtverwaltung von Szczecin/Stettin', 22 Sept, 1945, printed in Borodziej and Lemberg (eds.), *'Unsere Heimat ist uns ein fremdes Land geworden . . .'*, vol. iii (Marburg, 2004), pp. 408–409.

96 'Schreiben des Leiters der gesellschaftlich-politischen Abteilung des Bevollmächtigten der Republik Polen für den Bezirk Westpommern an den Stadtpräsidenten Stettins vom 8. Oktober 1945', in Bialecki, *Stettin 1945–1946*, pp. 266–269.

97 'Bericht des Bevollmächtigten der Regierungsdelegation in Stettin, Januar 1946', printed in Bialecki, *Stettin 1945–1946*, pp. 320–323; 'Auszug aus dem Bericht von Robert Müller', printed in Bialecki, *Stettin 1945–1946*, p. 325.

98 For the planning for this forced population transfer, see 'Schreiben des Abteilungsleiters der Grenzschutzarmee an den Bevollmächtigten der Republik Polen für den Bezirk Westpommern vom 1. Februar 1946', printed in Bialecki, *Stettin 1945–1946*, pp. 326–331; and the 'Abkommen zwischen den britischen und polnischen Vertretern der Vereinigten Repatriierungsexekutive (C.R.X.) über die Umsiedlung der deutschen Bevölkerung aus Polen, geschlossen zwischen der britischen Rheinarmee und der polnischen Regierung in Berlin am 14. Februar 1946', printed in Bialecki, *Stettin 1945–1946*, pp. 330–337.

99 'Zeittafel' in Bialecki, *Stettin 1945–1946*, p. 377.

100 'Auszüge aus dem Bericht von Jerzy Brinken', printed in Bialecki, *Stettin 1945–1946*, pp. 226–229.

101 'Auszüge aus dem Bericht von Marion Wieczorek', written in 1977, printed in Bialecki, *Stettin 1945–1946*, pp. 230–235.

102 'Auszüge aus dem Bericht von Józef Kijowski', printed in Bialecki, *Stettin 1945–1946*, pp. 234–235.

103 'Information der Abteilung für Allgemeines der Stettiner Stadtverwaltung über die Situation in der Stadt, Anfang 1946', printed in Tadeusz, *Stettin 1945–1946*, pp. 302–305.

104 'Auszüge aus dem Bericht von Józef Kijowski', printed in Bialecki, *Stettin 1945–1946*, pp. 234–241.

105 'Schreiben des Inspektors für ländliche Siedlung im Kreis Stettin an den Leiter der Ansiedlungsabteilung des Kreisbevollmächtigten vom 11. Dezember 1945', printed in Bialecki, *Stettin 1945–1946*, pp. 318–319.

106 'Information der Kreisabteilung der Staatlichen Repatriierungsbehörde [P.U.R] in Stettin über den Stand der Besiedlung vom 4. Dezember 1945', printed in Bialecki, *Stettin 1945–1946*, pp. 304–309.

107 'Die Grunwald-Feier am 15. Juli. Auszug aus dem Bericht von Franciszek Buchtalarz', printed in Bialecki, *Stettin 1945–1946*, pp. 216–217.

108 'Verordnung des Stadtpräsidenten Stettins vom 23. Juli 1945', printed in Bialecki, *Stettin 1945–1946*, pp. 218–221 (fascimile on p. 218).

109 'Auszug aus dem Bericht von Fritz Dittner über ein Gespräch mit Charlotte', printed in Bialecki, *Stettin 1945–1946*, p. 245.

110 'Auszüge aus dem Bericht von Jan Kortas', printed in Bialecki, *Stettin 1945–1946*, pp. 252–257.

111 Steffen, 'Flucht, Vertreibung und Zwangsaussiedlung aus der Wojewodschaft Stettin', p. 300.

112 Steffen, 'Flucht, Vertreibung und Zwangsaussiedlung aus der Wojewodschaft Stettin', p. 301.

113 Steffen, 'Flucht, Vertreibung und Zwangsaussiedlung aus der Wojewodschaft Stettin', pp. 300–301.

114 'Bericht des Starosten von Sztum/Stuhm über den Verlauf der Ansiedlungsaktion August 1945', 28 Aug. 1945, printed in Borodziej and Lemberg (eds.), *'Unsere Heimat ist uns ein fremdes Land geworden . . .'*, vol. iv, pp. 111–112.

115 Such descriptions appear repeatedly in the reports of Polish authorities in the 'recovered' territories during 1945. There are numerous examples in the four-volume documentary collection edited by Wlodzimierz Borodziej and Hans Lemberg, *'Unsere Heimat ist uns ein fremdes Land geworden . . .'* (Marburg, 2000–2004).

116 Quoted in Ingo Eser and Witold Stankowski, 'Die Deutschen in den Wojewodschaften Pommerellen und Danzig', in Borodziej and Lemberg (eds.), *'Unsere Heimat ist uns ein fremdes Land geworden . . .'*, vol. iv, pp. 42–43.

117 Kaps (ed.), *The Tragedy of Silesia 1945–46*, pp. 354–356: Report No. 116.

118 Prazmowska, *Civil War in Poland*, p. 181.

119 Naimark, *Fires of Hatred*, p. 129. Helga Hirsch gives the total number of Germans interned by the Poles after the war as 109,189, of whom some 15,000 died. See Helga Hirsch, *Die Rache der Opfer. Deutsche in polnischen Lagern 1944–1950* (Berlin, 1998), p. 203.

120 Naimark, *Fires of Hatred*, p. 130.

121 For example, the district of Rostock. See Michael Schwartz, 'Integration und Transformation. "Umsiedler-Politik und regionaler Strukturwandel in

Mecklenburg-Vorpommern von 1945 bis 1953', in Damian van Melis (ed.), *Sozialismus auf dem platten Land. Mecklenburg-Vorpommern 1945–1952* (Schwerin, 1999), p. 167.

122 In 1939 the population of Mecklenburg(-Vorpommern) had stood at 1,405,403; in 1948, it stood at 2,139,640. See Barbara Fait, 'Mecklenburg(-Vorpommern)', in Martin Broszat and Hermann Weber (eds.), *SBZ Handbuch. Staatliche Verwaltungen, Parteien, gesellschaftliche Organisationen und ihre Führungskräfte in der Sowjetischen Besatzungszone Deutschlands 1945–1949* (2nd edn., Munich, 1993), p. 103.

123 Quoted in Schwartz, 'Integration und Transformation', p. 136.

124 'Auszug aus dem Protokoll des Alliierten Sekretariats beim Kontrollrat vom 17. November 1945', printed in Bialecki, *Stettin 1945–1946*, pp. 301–303.

125 'Protokoll Nr. 37 der Sitzung des Ministerrats', 26 May 1945, printed in Borodziej and Lemberg, *'Unsere Heimat ist uns ein fremdes Land geworden . . .'*, vol. i, pp. 153–155.

9. Societies of the Uprooted

1 Quoted in Earl F. Ziemke, *The U.S. Army in the Occupation of Germany 1944–1946* (Washington, 1975), p. 240.

2 Quoted in Hans Woller, *Gesellschaft und Politik in der amerikanischen Besatzungszone. Die Region Ansbach und Fürth*, (Munich, 1986), p. 49.

3 Quoted in Norman M. Naimark, *The Russians in Germany. A History of the Soviet Zone of Occupation 1945–1949* (Cambridge, Mass., 1995), p. 149.

4 Jan Foitzik, *Sowjetische Militäradministration in Deutschland (SMAD) 1945–1949* (Berlin, 1999), p. 61.

5 Angelika Königseder and Juliane Wetzel, *Lebensmut im Wartesaal. Die jüdischen DPs (Displaced Persons) im Nachkriegsdeutschland* (Frankfurt am Main, 1994); Michael Brenner, *Nach dem Holocaust. Juden in Deutschland 1945–1950* (Munich 1995); Wolfgang Jakobmeyer, 'Jüdische Überlebende als "Displaced Persons"', in *Geschichte und Gesellschaft*, vol. 9 (1983), pp. 429–444.

6 This is the estimate used by Jörg Echternkamp, *Nach dem Krieg. Alltagsnot, Neuorientierung und die Last der Vergangenheit 1945–1949* (Zürich, 2003), p. 61.

7 See Hermann Glaser, *1945 Beginn einer Zukunft. Bericht und Dokumentation* (Frankfurt am Main, 2005), p. 102.

8 Dolf Sternberger, 'Reise in Deutschland – Sommer 1945', in *Die Wandlung* 1/1945/46, p. 8.

9 Saul K. Padover, *Experiment in Germany. The Story of an American Intelligence Officer* (New York, 1946), p. 361.

10 See Wolfram Wette, 'Eine Gesellschaft im Umbruch. "Entwurzelungs-erfahrungen" in Deutschland 1943–1948 und sozialer Wandel', in Robert Streibel (ed.), *Flucht und Vertreibung. Zwischen Abrechnung und Verdrängung* (Vienna, 1994), pp. 257–284.

11 Quoted in Alfons Kenkmann, *Wilde Jugend. Lebenswelt großstädtischer Jugendlicher zwischen Weltwirtschaftskrise, Nationalsozialismus und Währungs-reform* (Essen, 1996), p. 248.

12 *Bayerische Tag*, 16 June 1945. Quoted in Glaser, *1945 Beginn einer Zukunft*, p. 96.

13 See the estimates made by Rüdiger Overmans, in 'Einleitung', in Manfred Zeidler and Ute Schmidt (eds.), *Gefangene in deutschem und sowjetischem Gewahrsam 1941–1956: Dimensionen und Definitionen* (Dresden, 1999), pp. 17–18. The official Soviet prisoner-of-war administration registered 2,388,443 German prisoners taken; the true number of German prisoners taken by the Russians certainly is far higher, as those who were shot, who died while being transported to the camps, who succumbed to disease or died as a result of poor conditions were not registered. See Andreas Hilger, 'Deutsche Kriegsgefangene im Wiederaufbau der Sowjetunion. Arbeits-organisation und -leistung im Licht deutscher und rußischer Quellen', in Rüdiger Overmans (ed.), *In der Hand des Feindes. Kriegsgefangenschaft von der Antike bis zum Zweiten Weltkrieg* (Cologne, Weimar and Vienna, 1999), p. 444; Andreas Hilger, *Deutsche Kriegsgefangene in der Sowjetunion 1941–1956. Kriegsgefangenenpolitik, Lageralltag und Erinnerung*, (Essen, 2000), pp. 389, 392.

14 Frank Biess, *Homecomings. Returning POWs and the Legacies of Defeat in Postwar Germany* (Princeton and Oxford, 2005), pp. 44–45.

15 Hilger, *Deutsche Kriegsgefangene in der Sowjetunion*, p. 196.

16 Hilger, 'Deutsche Kriegsgefangene im Wiederaufbau der Sowjetunion', pp. 441–460.

17 Rüdiger Overmans, 'Ein Silberstreif am Forschungshorizont? Veröffent-lichungen zur Geschichte der Kriegsgefangenschaft', in Overmans (ed.), *In der Hand des Feindes*, pp. 483–484.

18 Archiv für soziale Bewegungen (=AfsB), IGBE-Archiv, Nr. 14096: Ewald L., 'Lebenslauf', Haltern, 18 Feb. 1959.

19 AfsB, IGBE-Archiv, Nr. 14109: Wolfgang S., 'Lebenslauf', Haltern, 27 Feb. 1962.

20 AfsB, IGBE-Archiv, Nr. 14070: Alfred B., 'Lebenslauf', Haltern, 2 Dec. 1963.

21 AfsB, IGBE-Archiv, Nr. 14067: Bruno A., 'Lebenslauf', Haltern, 19 Jan. 1964.

22 AfsB, IGBE-Archiv, Nr. 14071: Herbert B., 'Lebenslauf', Haltern, 22 Oct. 1964.

23 AfsB, IGBE-Archiv, Nr. 14080: Heinz F., 'Lebenslauf', Haltern, 31 Aug. 1965.

24 Jörg Friedrich, *Der Brand. Deutschland im Bombenkrieg 1940–1945* (Munich, 2002), pp. 87–89, 155–160.

25 Ingrid Hege, 'Köln am Ende der Weimarer Republik und während der Herrschaft des Nationalsozialismus', in Otto Dahn (ed.), *Köln nach dem Nationalsozialismus. Der Beginn des gesellschaftlichen Lebens in den Jahren 1945/6* (Wuppertal, 1981), p. 34.

26 Gerhard Braun, 'Köln in den Jahren 1945 und 1946. Die Rahmen-bedingungen des gesellschaftlichen Lebens', in Dahn (ed.), *Köln nach dem Nationalsozialismus*, p. 38.

27 Braun, 'Köln in den Jahren 1945 und 1946', pp. 38–41.

28 Kurt Düwell and Franz Irsigler (eds.), *Trier in der Neuzeit* (Trier, 1988), p. 591.

29 Hans Oppelt (ed.), *Würzburger Chronik des denkwürdigen Jahres 1945* (Würzburg, 1947), pp. 208, 242.

30 Rainer Gries, *Die Rationengesellschaft. Versorgungskampf und Vergleichs-mentalität. Leipzig, München und Köln nach dem Kriege* (Münster, 1991), pp. 146–147.

31 Hermann Vietzen, *Chronik der Stadt Stuttgart 1945–1948* (Stuttgart, 1972), p. 231.

32 Ullrich Schneider, *Niedersachsen 1945/46. Kontinuität und Wandel unter britischer Besatzung* (Hannover, 1984). p. 83. In November 1945 the number had risen to 335,000, which still was 30% below the prewar total.

33 Senat von Berlin (ed.), *Berlin. Kampf um Freiheit und Selbstverwaltung 1945–1946* (Berlin, 1961), p. 144.

34 Senat von Berlin (ed.), *Berlin. Kampf um Freiheit und Selbstverwaltung*, pp. 14, 132.

35 Gerhard Junger, *Schicksale 1945. Das Ende des II. Weltkrieges im Kreis Reutlingen* (3rd edn., Reutlingen, 1991), pp. 113–114.

36 Junger, *Schicksale 1945*, p. 151.

37 Junger, *Schicksale 1945*, p. 178.

38 Junger, *Schicksale 1945*, pp. 276, 318.

39 Gustav W. Harmsen, *Reparationen, Sozialprodukt, Lebensstandard. Versuch einer Wirtschaftsbilanz*, B. *Einzeldarstellungen*, vol 3 (Bremen, 1948), p. 100–102.

40 Text of the ban on people entering Munich is printed in Friedrich Prinz and Marita Kraus (eds.), *Trümmerleben. Texte, Dokumente, Bilder aus den Münchner Nachkriegsjahren* (Munich, 1985), pp. 149–150.

41 Brunn, 'Köln in den Jahren 1945 und 1946', p. 53.

42 Wolfgang Jacobmeyer, *Vom Zwangsarbeiter zum heimatlosen Ausländer. Die*

Displaced Persons in Westdeutschland 1945–1951 (Göttingen, 1985), p. 24;
Herbert, *Hitler's Foreign Workers*, p. 377.

43 Thus Eisenhower's order to all DPs that 'You will stand fast and not
move!' See Jacobmeyer, *Vom Zwangsarbeiter zum heimatlosen Ausländer*,
p. 24.

44 See Jacobmeyer, *Vom Zwangsarbeiter zum heimatlosen Ausländer*, p. 27;
Herbert, *Hitler's Foreign Workers*, p. 377.

45 Message from General Eisenhower, 5 May 1945, in *The New York Times*,
6 May 1945, quoted in Nicholas Bethell, *The Last Secret. Forcible
Repatriation to Russia 1944–1947* (London and Sydney, 1976), p. 90.

46 Herbert, *Hitler's Foreign Workers*, p. 377.

47 Angelika Königseder and Juliane Wetzel, *Lebensmut im Wartesaal. Die jüdischen DPs (Displaced Persons) im Nachkriegsdeutschland* (Frankfurt am Main,
1994), p. 33. The UNRRA-run camps, which housed (particularly
Jewish) DPs who would spend many months or even years in Germany,
offered various services in addition to basic housing and feeding; they also
provided a health service, recreational activities, and vocational training as
well as help with repatriation and the coordination of the activities of
Jewish aid organizations in the camps.

48 Lucius D. Clay, *Decision in Germany* (Garden City, N.Y., 1950) pp. 231–232.

49 Ziemke, *The U.S. Army in the Occupation of Germany*, p. 355.

50 F.S.V. Donnison, *Civil Affairs and Military Government North-West Europe
1944–1946* (London, 1961), pp. 250–251 (fold-out table), 358.

51 By that date 209,532 French DPs, 50,596 Belgians and 53,864 Dutch
already had been repatriated. See Donnison, *Civil Affairs and Military
Government*, pp. 250–251 (fold-out table).

52 Nicholas Bethell, *The Last Secret. Forcible Repatriation to Russia 1944–1947*
(London and Sydney, 1976), p. 96.; Herbert, *Hitler's Foreign Workers*,
p. 380.

53 See Bethell, *The Last Secret*, pp. 80–146, 172–221; Herbert, *Hitler's Foreign
Workers*, pp. 380–381. For the Dachau story, which was reported in the
American soldiers' newspaper *Stars and Stripes* on 23 January 1946, see
Jacobmeyer, *Vom Zwangsarbeiter zum Heimatlosen Ausländer*, pp. 133–134.
Of the 399 inmates of the two barracks in question, 31 attempted suicide
and 11 succeeded.

54 Paul Julian Weindling, *Epidemics and Genocide in Eastern Europe 1890–1945*
(Oxford, 2000), p. 397.

55 Junger, *Schicksale 1945*, p. 181.

56 Malcolm J. Proudfoot, *European Refugees: 1939–52. A Study in Forced
Population Movement* (London, 1957), p. 169, f. 1.

57 See Karl S. Bader, *Soziologie der deutschen Nachkriegskriminalität* (Tübingen,
1949), pp. 168–170; Proudfoot, *European Refugees*, pp. 175–177. Not all

Allied observers were convinced that the DPs were such a problem, however. Saul Padover and Lewis Gittler, of the American Psychological
Warfare Department, observed:

> There is much talk about looting. German farmers say the
> Eastern workers are stealing their chickens. German workers
> say that the Russians are breaking into homes and helping
> themselves to necessities. German middle-class people say that
> Russians are animals. The truth is that the Eastern workers are
> remarkably well-behaved.

Quoted in Ziemke, *The U.S. Army in the Occupation of Germany*, p. 240.

58 This according to American observers in a report prepared for Senator
    Alexander Wiley (the 'Wiley Report', November 20, 1952), quoted in
    Bethell, *The Last Secret*, p. 93.
59 Earl F. Ziemke, *The U.S. Army in the Occupation of Germany*, p. 240.
60 Proudfoot, *European Refugees*, pp. 176–177.
61 Proudfoot, *European Refugees*, p. 177; Ziemke, *The U.S. Army in the
    Occupation of Germany*, p. 358.
62 Quoted in Proudfoot, *European Refugees*, p. 177, f. 1.
63 Clay, *Decision in Germany*, p. 256.
64 Ziemke, *The U.S. Army in the Occupation of Germany*, p. 358.
65 Memoirs of the British officer John Stanton, quoted in Bethell, *The Last
    Secret*, p. 93.
66 Donnison, *Civil Affairs and Military Government*, p. 356.
67 Quoted in Donnison, *Civil Affairs and Military Government*, p. 357.
68 Quoted in Ulrich Herbert, 'Apartheid nebenan. Erinnerungen an die
    Fremdarbeiter im Ruhrgebiet', in Lutz Niethammer (ed.), *"Die Jahre weiß
    man nicht, wo man die heute hinsetzen soll". Faschismus-Erfahrungen im
    Ruhrgebiet* (Berlin and Bonn, 1983), p. 257.
69 Proudfoot, *European Refugees*, pp. 248–249.
70 Wolfgang Jacobmeyer, 'Die "Displaced Persons" in Deutschland
    1945–1952', in *Bremisches Jahrbuch* 59 (1981), pp. 97–98); Jacobmeyer,
    Vom Zwangsarbeiter zum Heimatlosen Ausländer, pp. 48–49.
71 Schneider, *Niedersachsen 1945/46*, p. 78.
72 SHAEF, Field Intelligence Study, 18 April 1945, printed in Ulrich
    Borsdorf and Lutz Niethammer (eds.), *Zwischen Befreiung und Besatzung.
    Analysen des US-Geheimdienstes über Positionen und Strukturen deutscher Politik
    1945* (Wuppertal, 1978), pp. 31–32.
73 See Schneider, *Niedersachsen 1945/46*, p. 85.
74 Manfred Overesch, *Das III. Reich 1939. Eine Tageschronik der Politik,
    Wirtschaft, Kultur* (Augsburg, 1991), pp. 82–83.
75 Juliane Wetzel, '"Mir szeinen doh", München und Umgebung als Zuflucht

von Überlebenden des Holocaust 1945–1948', in Martin Broszat, Klaus-Dietmar Henke and Hans Woller (eds.), *Von Stalingrad zur Währungsreform. Zur Sozialgeschichte des Umbruchs in Deutschland* (Munich, 1988), p. 329.

76 Wolfgang Jacobmeyer, 'Jüdische Überlebende als "Displaced Persons". Untersuchungen zur Besatzungspolitik in den deutschen Westzonen und zur Zuwanderung osteuropäischer Juden 1945–1947', *Geschichte und Gesellschaft*, vol. IX (1983), p. 421; Michael Brenner, *Nach dem Holocaust. Juden in Deutschland 1945–1950* (Munich, 1995), p. 19; Königseder and Wetzel, *Lebensmut im Wartesaal*, p. 14. See also Atina Grossmann, 'Victims, Villains, and Survivors: Gendered Perceptions and Self-Perceptions of Jewish Displaced Persons in Occupied Postwar Germany', *Journal of the History of Sexuality*, vol. xi, no. 2 (January/April 2002), pp. 295–296.

77 Quoted in Königseder and Wetzel, *Lebensmut im Wartesaal*, pp. 18–19.

78 Wetzel, '"Mir szeinen doh"', p. 328. Michael Brenner gives the number of Jews living in Poland in August 1945 as roughly 80,000. See Brenner, *Nach dem Holocaust*, p. 25.

79 For example, in Krakow in 1945, an incident which began with Polish children throwing stones at Jews attending synagogue ended with the synagogue being stormed by a mob and set alight, whereby 10 Jews were killed and another 30 seriously injured. See Königseder and Wetzel, *Lebensmut im Wartesaal*, p. 49.

80 See the map of the 'Major Camps for Jewish Displaced Persons 1945–1946', in the entry on 'Displaced Persons' by Michael Brenner in Walter Laqueur (ed.), *The Holocaust Encyclopedia* (New Haven and London, 2001), p. 155.

81 Königseder and Wetzel, *Lebensmut im Wartesaal*, pp. 14–15.

82 Atina Grossmann, *Jews, Germans and Allies. Close Encounters in Occupied Germany* (Princeton, 2007), pp. 132–133.

83 For this and the following, see Brenner, *Nach dem Holocaust*, pp. 19–25.

84 Jacobmeyer, 'Jüdische Überlebende als "Displaced Persons"', p. 426; Brenner, *Nach dem Holocaust*, pp. 19–20.

85 Figures in Angelika Eder, 'Jüdische Displaced Persons im deutschen Alltag. Eine Regionalstudie 1945 bis 1950', in Fritz Bauer Institut (ed.), *Überlebt und Unterwegs. Jüdische Displaced Persons im Nachkriegsdeutschland* (Frankfurt am Main and New York, 1997), p. 164.

86 Quoted in Brenner, *Nach dem Holocaust*, p. 21.

87 Brenner, 'East European and German Jews in Postwar Germany', in Y. Michel Bodeman (ed.), *Jews, Germans, Memory: Reconstructions of Jewish Life in Germany* (Ann Arbor, 1996), p. 52; Frank Stern, 'German-Jewish Relations in the Postwar Period: The Ambiguities of Antisemitic and Philosemitic Discourse', in Bodeman (ed.), *Jews, Germans, Memory*, p. 79.

88 Brenner, 'East European and German Jews in Postwar Germany', p. 53.

89   Brenner, 'East European and German Jews in Postwar Germany',
      pp. 59–60; Michael Brenner, 'Displaced Persons', in Walter Laqueur (ed.),
      The Holocaust Encyclopedia (New Haven and London, 2001), p. 155.

90   Wetzel, '"Mir szeinen doh"', pp. 330–331, 334.

91   Quoted in Brenner, 'East European and German Jews', p. 60.

92   Quoted in Königseder and Wetzel, *Lebensmut im Wartesaal*, p. 136.

93   Quoted in Atina Grossmann, 'Victims, Villains, and Survivors: Gendered
      Perceptions and Self-Perceptions of Jewish Displaced Persons in Occupied
      Postwar Germany', *Journal of the History of Sexuality*, vol. xi, nos 1/2
      (January/April 2002), p. 299.

94   Quoted in Königseder and Wetzel, *Lebensmut im Wartesaal*, p. 30.

95   Wetzel, '"Mir szeinen doh"', p. 341.

96   Quoted in Brenner, 'Displaced Persons', in Laqueur (ed.), *The Holocaust
      Encyclopedia*, p. 157.

97   Quoted in Königseder and Wetzel, *Lebensmut im Wartesaal*, p. 30, and in
      Grossmann, *Jews, Germans, and Allies*, p. 149. Soon thereafter, at the end of
      September, Eisenhower removed Patton from his command in Bavaria and
      replaced him with Lt. Gen. Lucian K. Truscott. The trigger was not
      Patton's antisemitism but rather his openly expressed scepticism about the
      merits of denazification. On 22 September Patton had told reporters that
      'the Nazi thing is just like a Democratic-Republican election fight', com-
      ments which appeared in American newspapers on the following day and
      provoked controversy. See Ziemke, *The U.S. Army in the Occupation of
      Germany*, p. 386. Patton was made President of the General Board of
      USFET (United States Forces European Theater, and the successor to
      SHAEF, which had been dissolved on 14 July 1945). He died in a motor-
      vehicle accident in Heidelberg on 21 December.

98   Königseder and Wetzel, *Lebensmut im Wartesaal*, p. 30.

99   Königseder and Wetzel, *Lebensmut im Wartesaal*, p. 31.

100   AfsB, IGBE-Archiv, Nr. 14080: Günter G., 'Lebenslauf', Haltern, 17
      Nov. 1961.

101   AfsB, IGBE-Archiv, Nr. 14086: Franz H., 'Lebenslauf', Haltern, 27 April
      1965.

102   AfsB, IGBE-Archiv, Nr. 14108: Herbert S., 'Lebenslauf', Haltern, 2 Dec.
      1963.

103   Fritz Hauschild (ed.), *Das Ende der Kinderlandverschickung. Die Hamburger
      KLV-Lager im Jahre 1945, Briefe, Tagebücher, Berichte* (Norderstedt, 2004),
      p. 12.

104   Quoted in Hauschild (ed.), *Das Ende der Kinderlandverschickung*,
      pp. 106–107.

105   See Nicholas Stargardt, *Witnesses of War. Children's Lives under the Nazis*
      (London, 2005) pp. 275–276, 287–288.

106   AfsB, IGBE-Archiv, Nr. 14117: Gerhard T., 'Lebenslauf', Haltern, 31 Aug. 1965.

107   AfsB, IGBE-Archiv, Nr. 14102: Günter P., 'Lebenslauf', Haltern, 26 Apr. 1962.

108   AfsB, IGBE-Archiv, Nr. 14094: Kurt L., 'Lebenslauf', 22 June 1960.

109   Bundesarchiv Berlin, DO-I-7, f. 58: Statistisches Landesamt an die Abteilung Polizei, Halle/Saale, 8 Oct. 1946. The figures for the 20–30 year olds are 101,878 men and 301,025 women, for the 30–40 year olds 170,681 men and 367,536 women.

110   Karl S. Bader, *Soziologie der deutschen Nachkriegskriminalität* (Tübingen, 1949), p. 57.

111   Bader, *Soziologie der deutschen Nachkriegskriminalität*, p. 58, footnote 28.

112   Bader, *Soziologie der deutschen Nachkriegskriminalität*, p. 58.

1113 Bader, *Soziologie der deutschen Nachkriegskriminalität*, p. 58, footnote 29.

114   This case is described in Bader, *Soziologie der deutschen Nachkriegs-kriminalität*, pp. 59–60.

115   Bader, *Soziologie der deutschen Nachkriegskriminalität*, pp. 92–93.

116   Bader, *Soziologie der deutschen Nachkriegskriminalität*, p. 93, note 99.

117   Bader, *Soziologie der deutschen Nachkriegskriminalität*, p. 96.

118   AfsB, IGBE-Archiv, Nr. 14069: Konrad B., 'Lebenslauf', Haltern, 13 June 1961.

119   AfsB, IGBE-Archiv, Nr. 14070: Ernst B., 'Lebenslauf', Haltern, 8 June 1962.

120   AfsB, IGBE-Archiv, Nr. 14086: Franz H., 'Lebenslauf', Haltern, 27 April 1965. Franz H., whose father had died 'from the consequences of depor-tation by the Red Army', moved to the Soviet Occupation Zone, where his mother was living, in 1946 and returned to the west in early 1948.

121   AfsB, IGBE-Archiv, Nr. 14118: Günther T., 'Lebenslauf', Haltern, 27 Feb. 1962.

122   AfsB, IGBE-Archiv, Nr. 14089: Alfons K., 'Lebenslauf', Haltern, 10 Nov. 1965.

123   AfsB, IGBE-Archiv, Nr. 14070: Josef B., 'Lebenslauf', Haltern, 25 Feb. 1966.

124   Biess, *Homecomings*, p. 66.

125   Helmut Schelsky, *Wandlungen der deutschen Familie in der Gegenwart* (5th edn., Stuttgart, 1967), quotation from p. 90. See also Lutz Niethammer, 'Privat-Wirtschaft. Erinnerungsfragmente einer anderen Umerziehung', in Lutz Niethammer (ed.), *'Hinterher merkt man, daß es richtig war, daß es schiefgegangen ist'. Nachkriegserfahrungen im Ruhrgebiet* (Berlin and Bonn, 1983), pp. 38–55; Gries, *Die Rationengesellschaft*, pp. 202–203; Barbara Willenbacher, 'Zerrüttung und Bewährung der Nach-Kriegsfamilie', and Nori Möding, 'Die Stunde der Frauen? Frauen und Frauenorganisationen

des bürgerlichen Lagers', in Broszat et. al, *Von Stalingrad zur Währungsreform*, pp. 595–618 and 619–647 respectively.

126 Quoted in Gries, *Die Rationengesellschaft*, p. 202.

127 For this argument, see Richard Bessel, 'Catastrophe and Democracy: The Legacy of the World Wars in Germany', in Anthony McElligott and Tim Kirk (eds.), *Working towards the Führer. Essays in Honour of Sir Ian Kershaw* (Manchester, 2003), pp. 15–40.

128 Michael Geyer, 'Cold War Angst. The Case of West-German Opposition to Rearmament and Nuclear Weapons', in Hanna Schissler (ed.), *The Miracle Years. A Cultural History of West Germany 1949–1968* (Princeton and Oxford, 2001), pp. 376–408.

129 See Michael Wildt, *Am Beginn der "Konsumgesellschaft". Mangelerfahrung, Lebenshaltung, Wohlstandshoffnung in Westdeutschland in den fünfziger Jahren* (Hamburg, 1994).

130 See Moeller, *Protecting Motherhood*.

10. Visions of a New World

1 Victor Klemperer, *To the Bitter End. The Diaries of Victor Klemperer 1942–5*, translated by Martin Chalmers (London, 1999), p. 583.

2 *Foreign Relations of the United States. Diplomatic Papers. The Conferences at Malta and Yalta 1945* (Washington, 1955), pp. 970–971.

3 Harold Zink, *American Military Government in Germany* (New York, 1947), pp. 6–21; Earl F. Ziemke, *The U.S. Army in the Occupation of Germany 1944–1946* (Washington, 1975), p. 7; Hermann-J. Rupieper, 'Amerikanische Besatzungspolitik', in Wolfgang Benz (ed.), *Deutschland unter alliierter Besatzung 1945–1949/55* (Berlin, 1999), p. 33.

4 Quoted in F.S.V. Donnison, *Civil Affairs and Military Government North-West Europe 1944–1946* (London, 1961), pp. 11–12.

5 Annette Weinke, *Die Nürnberger Prozesse* (Munich, 2006), p. 13. Generally, see Henry Morgenthau, *Germany is our Problem* (New York, 1945); Harry G. Gelber, 'Der Morgenthau-Plan', in *Vierteljahrshefte für Zeitgeschichte*, vol. xiii (1965), pp. 372–402.

6 Quoted in Edward N. Peterson, *The American Occupation of Germany. Retreat to Victory* (Detroit, 1977), p. 38. Lucius Clay later wrote about how, when he met Roosevelt at the end of March 1945, the President had spoken 'of his youth in Germany, where he had attended school and had formed an early distaste for German arrogance and provincialism'. See Lucius D. Clay, *Decision in Germany* (Garden City, N.Y., 1950), p. 5; also Richard Overy, *Why the Allies Won* (New York, 1996), p. 287.

7 Wolfgang Krieger, 'Die amerikanische Deutschland Planung. Hypotheken

und Chancen für einen Neuanfang', in Hans-Erich Volkmann (ed.), *Ende des Dritten Reiches – Ende des Zweiten Weltkriegs. Eine perspektivische Rückschau* (Munich, 1995), p. 33.

8 Quoted in Ziemke, *The U.S. Army in the Occupation of Germany*, p. 107.

9 Klaus-Dietmar Henke, *Die amerikanische Besetzung Deutschlands* (Munich, 1995), p. 89.

10 Quoted in Ziemke, *The U.S. Army in the Occupation of Germany*, p. 104.

11 Clay, *Decision in Germany*, pp. 17, 19.

12 Ziemke, *The U.S. Army in the Occupation of Germany*, p. 104.

13 Walter L. Dorn, 'The Debate over American Occupation Policy in Germany in 1944–1945', in *Political Science Quarterly*, 72 (1957), p. 501.

14 On the occupation of Aachen and the setting up of a German administration in the city, see Ziemke, *The U.S. Army in the Occupation of Germany*, pp. 147–148, 180–184; Henke, *Die amerikanische Besetzung Deutschlands*, pp. 252–297.

15 See Ziemke, *The U.S. Army in the Occupation of Germany*, pp. 222–224; Henke, *Die amerikanische Besetzung Deutschlands*, pp. 975–978. Clay's career had been in the Engineering Corps, and his specialism was logistics. He had supervized the military production programme as Director of Matériel, Army Service Forces; and for a few weeks he had been in charge of the Normandy Base Section, the task of which was to channel supplies through Cherbourg.

16 Overy, *Why the Allies Won*, p. 288; Lothar Kettenacker, 'Der britische Rahmenplan für die Besetzung Deutschlands und seine unerwarteten Folgen', in Volkmann (ed.), *Ende des Dritten Reiches – Ende des Zweiten Weltkriegs*, pp. 52, 70; Jörg Später, *Vansittart. Britische Debatten über Deutsche und Nazis 1902–1945* (Göttingen, 2003), pp. 127–138.

17 Statement by Churchill to the House of Commons on 21 September 1943, in *Onwards to Victory. War Speeches by the Right Hon. Winston S. Churchill C.H., M.P. 1943*, compiled by Charles Eade (London, 1944), pp. 203–204). See also Lothar Kettenacker, *Krieg zur Friedenssicherung. Die Deutschlandplanung der britischen Regierung während des Zweiten Weltkriegs* (Göttingen, 1989), p. 490; Lothar Kettenacker, 'Der britische Rahmenplan', p. 52.

18 According to the official British historian, while many of those assigned to the Civil Affairs staff were quite able, 'many tended to be eccentrics, skilled in some little-known or faintly ludicrous employment, but hopelessly unmilitary, and some even anti-military. Or else, somewhat naturally, they were the weaker members rejected from more active units. All Civil Affairs officers were likely to be a little elderly.' See Donnison, *Civil Affairs and Military Government*, p. 28.

19 Donnison, *Civil Affairs and Military Government*, p. 227; Wolfgang Rudzio,

Die Neuordnung des Kommunalwesens in der britischen Zone. Zur Demokratisierung und Dezentralisierung der politischen Struktur: eine britische Reform und ihr Ausgang (Stuttgart, 1968), p. 35.

20 Quoted in Hartmut Pietsch, *Militärregierung, Bürokratie und Sozialisierung. Zur Entwicklung des politischen Systems in den Städten des Ruhrgebiets 1945 bis 1948* (Duisburg, 1978), p. 26.

21 Donnison, *Civil Affairs and Military Government*, p. 205.

22 See Harold Ingrams, 'Building Democracy in Germany', in *The Quarterly Review* 572 (April 1947), pp. 208–222; Rudzio, *Die Neuordnung des Kommunalwesens*, pp. 42–50; Pietsch, *Militärregierung, Bürokratie und Sozialisierung*, p. 41.

23 For the example of British planning for local government in Cologne, see Herbert Treiß, 'Britische Besatzungspolitik in Köln', in Otto Dann (ed.), *Köln nach dem Nationalsozialismus. Der Beginn des gesellschaftlichen und politischen Lebens in den Jahren 1945/46* (Wuppertal, 1981), p. 75.

24 Raymond Ebsworth, *Restoring Democracy in Germany. The British Contribution* (London, 1960), p. 22. Quoted in Marie-Louise Recker, 'Westminster as a Model? The Parlamentarischer Rat on the Way to the Basic Law 1948–49', in Arnd Bauerkämper and Christiane Eisenberg (eds.), *Britain as a Model of Modern Society? German Views* (Augsburg, 2006), p. 77.

25 Pietsch, *Militärregierung, Bürokratie und Sozialisierung*, p. 41.

26 Quoted in John Ramsden, *Don't Mention the War. The British and the Germans since 1890* (London, 2006), p. 256.

27 Edgar Wolfrum, 'In napoleonischer Tradition? Die Zukunft Deutschlands in französischer Sicht 1940–1945', in Edgar Wolfrum, Peter Fäßler and Reinhard Grohnert, *Krisenjahre und Aufbruchszeit. Alltag und Politik im französisch besetzten Baden 1945–1949* (Munich, 1996), pp. 32–33.

28 On the 'Laffon project', see Wolfrum, 'In napoleonischer Tradition?', pp. 33–34. Laffon's 1943 proposals never got much beyond the planning stage, as they met with opposition from both the right and the Communist left.

29 Wolfgang Benz, *Potsdam 1945. Besatzungsherrschaft und Neuaufbau im Vier-Zonen-Deutschland* (Munich, 1986), p. 43.

30 See Wolfrum, 'In napoleonischer Tradition?', pp. 34–36.

31 Prime Minister to President Roosevelt, 15 Nov, 1944, in Winston S. Chuchill, *The Second World War. Vol. VI. Triumph and Tragedy* (London, 1954), p.220.

32 *Foreign Relations of the United States. Diplomatic Papers. The Conferences at Malta and Yalta 1945*, p. 617.

33 See Corine Defrance, *La politique culturelle de la France sur la rive gauche du Rhin 1945–1955* (Strasbourg, 1994), pp. 36–40.

34   Georges-Henri Soutou, 'Frankreich und die Deutschlandfrage 1943 bis 1945', in Hans-Erich Volkmann (ed.), *Ende des Dritten Reiches – Ende des Zweiten Weltkriegs. Eine perspektivische Rückschau* (Munich, 1995), p. 92.

35   Quoted in F. Roy Willis, *The French in Germany 1945–1949* (Stanford, 1962), p. 16.

36   Quoted in Willis, *The French in Germany*, p. 78.

37   See Willis, *The French in Germany*, pp. 25–26. The text of the Potsdam Agreement may be found on the internet at: http://www.pbs.org/wgbh/amex/truman/psources/ps_potsdam.html

38   See Soutou, 'Frankreich und die Deutschlandfrage', pp. 97–98.

39   See Willis, *The French in Germany*, pp. 140–141.

40   Soutou, 'Frankreich und die Deutschlandfrage', pp. 100–103.

41   Willis, *The French in Germany*, p. 94; Soutou, 'Frankreich und die Deutschlandfrage', p. 91.

42   H.D. Willcock, 'Public Opinion: Attitudes to the German People', *The Political Quarterly*, vol. xix (1948), pp. 160–66; John L. Snell, *Wartime Origins of the East-West Dilemma over Germany* (New Orleans, 1959), p. 2; Werner Röder, *Die deutschen sozialistischen Exilgruppen in Großbritannien 1940–1945* (2nd edn., Bonn-Bad Godesberg, 1973), p. 218f.

43   Edgar Wolfrum, '"Das Land zu einem geistigen Erwachen führen". Motive der französischen Parteienzulassung', in Wolfrum, Fäßler and Grohnert, *Krisenjahre und Aufbruchszeit*, pp. 89–90. In Wolfrum's view, the French Military Government's delay (relative to developments in the other zones) in allowing German political parties was due to a concern with security and the belief that only after a probationary period, marked by cooperation with the 'anti-fascist committees', should party-political activity be permitted; the French wanted to replicate neither the heavy political pressure which lay behind Soviet policy nor the 'laissez-faire' approach of the Americans.

44   Quoted in Defrance, *La politique culturelle de la France*, p. 41. See also Rainer Hudemann, 'Zentralismus und Dezentralisierung in der französischen Deutschland- und Besatzungspolitik, 1945–1947', in Winfried Becker (ed.), *Die Kapitulation von 1945 und der Neubeginn in Deutschland* (Cologne and Vienna, 1987), pp. 181–209; Rainer Hudemann, 'Französische Besatzungszone 1945–1952', in Claus Scharf and Hans Jürgen Schröder (eds.), *Die Deutschlandpolitik Frankreichs und die französische Zone, 1945–1949* (Wiesbaden, 1983), pp. 205–248.

45   Milovan Djilas, *Conversations with Stalin* (Harmondsworth, 1969), p. 90.

46   Quoted in Wilfried Loth, *Stalin's Unwanted Child. The Soviet Union, the German Question and the Founding of the GDR* (Houndmills and London, 1998), pp. 4–5.

47 Kettenacker, *Krieg zur Friedenssicherung*, p. 234; R.C. Raack, 'Stalin Plans of Post-War Germany', *Journal of Contemporary History*, vol. 28 (1993), p. 58.

48 *The Conferences at Malta and Yalta 1945*, p. 615.

49 Quoted in Loth, *Stalin's Unwanted Child*, p. 5.

50 Quoted in Kettenacker, *Krieg zur Friedenssicherung*, p. 497.

51 Quoted in Loth, *Stalin's Unwanted Child*, p. 5.

52 At the Potsdam Conference in July 1945 Stalin also suggested the internationalization of the Ruhr region. See Raack, 'Stalin Plans of Post-War Germany', p. 59.

53 Jan Foitzik, *Sowjetische Militäradministration in Deutschland (SMAD) 1945–1949* (Berlin, 1999), p. 45.

54 Norman M. Naimark, *The Russians in Germany. A History of the Soviet Zone of Occupation 1945–1949* (Cambridge, Mass., 1995), p. 44. Sergei Tjulpanov later wrote that the Soviet Communist Party possessed 'no worked-out theory of how to organize the occupation', although it did possess a tried and tested idea of liberation. See Foitzik, *Sowjetische Militäradministration in Deutschland*, p. 44.

55 Elke Scherstjanoi, 'Sowjetische Besatzungspolitik', in Wolfgang Benz (ed.), *Deutschland unter alliierter Besatzung 1945–1949/55* (Berlin, 1999), p. 85.

56 Naimark, *The Russians in Germany*, pp. 44–46.

57 Ulrich Borsdorf and Lutz Niethammer (eds.), *Zwischen Befreiung und Besatzung. Analysen des US-Geheimdienstes über Personen und Strukturen deutscher Politik 1945* (Wuppertal, 1976), pp. 79–82.

58 See Lutz Niethammer, Ulrich Borsdorf and Peter Brandt (eds.), *Arbeiterinitiative 1945. Antifaschistische Ausschüsse und Reorganisation der Arbeiterbewegung in Deutschland* (Wuppertal, 1945).

59 See Jeannete Michelmann, *Aktivisten der ersten Stunde. Die Antifa in der Sowjetischen Besatzungszone* (Cologne, Weimar and Vienna, 2002), p. 360.

60 Edgar Wolfrum, 'Selbsthilfe gegen Resignation und Franzosenfeindschaft. Antifas und Gewerkschaften', in Wolfrum, Fäßler and Grohnert, *Krisenjahre und Aufbruchszeit*, pp. 55–57.

61 See, for example, the report written on 22 April 1945 by the American political scientist Hans Meyerhoff for the American Office of Strategic Studies about the anti-fascist organization in Frankfurt-Riederwald, in Borsdorf and Niethammer (eds.), *Zwischen Befreiung und Besatzung*, pp. 83–89.

62 Quoted in Manfred Bosch, *Der Neubeginn. Aus deutscher Nachkriegszeit Südbaden 1945–1950* (Konstanz, 1988), p. 187. The author of this letter also asserted that Germany was 'today certainly no longer a country in which there will be "capitalists"'.

63 Quoted in Naimark, *The Russians in Germany*, p. 256.

64 *Sudkurier*, Konstanz, 26 Feb. 1946. Quoted in Bosch, *Der Neubeginn*, p. 186.

65 See Peter Fäßler, '"Wir fangen nicht da an, wo wir 1933 aufgehört haben". Christliche Partei und Liberale', in Wolfrum, Fäßler and Grohnert, *Krisenjahre und Aufbruchszeit*, p. 92.

66 See Theo Pirker, *Die SPD nach Hitler. Die Geschichte der Sozialdemokratischen Partei Deutschlands 1945–1964* (Berlin, 1977), p. 15.

67 Quoted in Rolf Badstübner, *Vom 'Reich' zum doppelten Deutschland. Gesellschaft und Politik in Umbruch* (Berlin, 1999), p. 33.

68 Herman Brill, who had joined the USPD in 1918 and the SPD in 1920, was a member of the Thuringian Landtag from 1919 to 1932 and of the Reichstag in 1932 and 1933. Repeatedly arrested during the Nazi years for his resistance activities, Brill had been imprisoned for high treason; he spent the years from 1938 until April 1945 first in prison (at Brandenburg-Gärden) and then from late 1943 in the Buchenwald concentration camp (where he organized an illegal German Popular Front Committee). In May 1945 he founded the 'League of Democratic Socialists', and was appointed by the Americans to head of the Thuringian provincial administration. After the Red Army occupied Thuringia at the beginning of July 1945, he was removed from the post. He headed the SPD in Thuringia from May until December, when, facing mounting pressure from the Russians and threatened with arrest, he fled to (west) Berlin during a Christmas trip. He subsequently made his career in the west, serving as Permanent Secretary in the government of Hesse from July 1946 and as a member of the Bundestag from 1949 to 1953. See Helga A. Welsh, 'Thuringen', in Martin Broszat and Hermann Weber (eds.), *SBZ-Handbuch. Staatliche Verwaltungen, Parteien, gesellschaftliche Organisationen und ihre Führungskräfte in der Sowjetischen Besatzungszone Deutschlands 1945–1949* (2nd edn., Munich, 1993), pp. 173–174; Manfred Overesch, *Hermann Brill in Thüringen 1895–1946: Ein Kämpfer gegen Hitler und Ulbricht* (Bonn, 1992), pp. 309–327.

69 The text of the 'Buchenwald Manifesto' may be found in Manfred Overesch, *Deutschland 1945–1949. Vorgeschichte und Gründung der Bundesrepublik. Ein Leitfaden in Darstellung und Dokumenten* (Düsseldorf, 1979), pp. 171–176.

70 Naimark, *The Russians in Germany*, p. 262.

71 Quoted in Manfred Overesch, *Das III. Reich 1939–1945. Eine Tageschronik der Politik, Wirtschaft, Kultur* (Augsburg, 1991), p. 385.

72 See Röder, *Die deutschen sozialistischen Exilgruppen*, pp. 198–199. The 'unity front' perspective is reflected in the volume of essays from exiles across the political spectrum published in London in 1943: Heinrich Fraenkel (ed.), *Der Weg zu einem neuen Deutschland. Gesehen von einem*

Sozialdemokraten, Kommunisten, Liberalen, Wissenschaftler, Pastor und einer Frau (London, 1943). This included contributions from Wilhelm Koenen (Communist), Victor Schiff (Social Democrat), August Weber (Liberal), Arthur Liebert (former philosophy professor at the Berlin University), Irmgard Litten (who represented women) and a clergyman of the Confessing Church.

73 See Röder, *Die deutschen sozialistischen Exilgruppen*, pp. 230–239.

74 Quoted in Röder, *Die deutschen sozialistischen Exilgruppen*, p. 222.

75 Karsten Krieger, 'Parteien', in Wolfgang Benz (ed.), *Deutschland unter alliierter Besatzung 1945–1949/55* (Berlin, 1999), p. 156.

76 Quoted in Pirker, *Die SPD nach Hitler*, p. 43.

77 See the American intelligence report on the national conference of the Social Democratic leadership in Wennigsen near Hannover on 5–6 October 1945, in Borsdorf and Niethammer (eds.), *Zwischen Befreiung und Besatzung*, p. 218.

78 See Peter Erler, Horst Laude and Manfred Wilke (eds.), *'Nach Hitler kommen wir''. Dokumente zur Progammatik der Moskauer KPD-Führung 1944/45 fur Nachkriegsdeutschland* (Berlin, 1994).

79 Thomas Alexander, *Carl Severing. Sozialdemokrat aus Westfalen mit preußischen Tugenden* (Bielefeld, 1992), p. 228.

80 Grotewohl reasoned that the SPD therefore was acceptable to all the occupying powers and could assume a mediating role among them, thus offering the best prerequisities for maintaining German unity. See Markus Jodl, *Amboss oder Hammer? Otto Grotewohl. Eine politische Biographie* (Berlin, 1997), p. 103.

81 Quoted in Franz Osterroth and Dieter Schuster, *Chronik der deutschen Sozialdemokratie. Band II: Vom Beginn der Weimarer Republik bis zum Ende des Zweiten Weltkrieges* (Berlin and Bonn, 1980), pp. 431–432.

82 Quoted in Overesch, *Deutschland 1945–1949*, p. 69.

83 Wilhelm Hoegner, *Flucht vor Hitler. Erinnerungen an die Kapitulation der ersten deutschen Republik 1933* (Munich, 1977), p. 8.

84 Thus Ulbricht, when he spoke with Wehrmacht soldiers in one of the first Soviet prisoner-of-war camps for Germans in August 1941. See Walter Ulbricht, *Zur Geschichte der deutschen Arbeiterbewegung*, vol. ii (Berlin, 1953), p. 258.

85 Quoted in Hermann Weber, *Völker hört die Signale. Der deutsche Kommunismus 1916–1966* (Munich, 1967), p. 241.

86 On the theme of hatred in the wake of Nazism and war, see Richard Bessel, 'Hatred after War: Emotion and the Postwar History of East Germany', *History & Memory*, vol. 17, nos. 1 and 2 (autumn 2005) (Special issue on 'Histories and Memories of Twentieth-Century Germany'), pp. 195–216.

87 Borsdorf and Niethammer (eds.), *Zwischen Befreiung und Besatzung*, pp. 79–133; Michelmann, *Aktivisten der ersten Stunde*.

88 Text of the 'Kölner Leitsätze' in Otto Dann (ed.), *Köln nach dem Nationalsozialismus. Der Beginn des gesellschaftlichen und politischen Lebens in den Jahren 1945/46* (Wuppertal, 1981), pp. 211–215.

89 Konrad Adenauer, *Erinnerungen 1945–1953* (Stuttgart, 1063), p. 50.

90 Joachim Köhler and Damian van Melis, 'Einleitung der Herausgeber', in Joachim Köhler and Damian van Melis (eds.), *Siegerin in Trümmern. Die Rolle der katholischen Kirche in der deutschen Nachkriegsgesellschaft* (Stuttgart, 1998), p. 11. Konrad Repgen also notes that 'the Corpus Christi processions that passed through the ruins of the cities in 1945 and 1946 were huge'. See Konrad Repgen, 'Die Erfahrung des Dritten Reiches und das Selbtstverständnis der deutschen Katholiken nach 1945', in Victor Conzenius, Martin Greschat and Hermann Kochen (eds.), *Die Zeit nach 1945 als Thema der kirchlichen Zeitgeschichte* (Göttingen, 1988), p. 141.

91 Quoted in Norbert Trippen, *Josef Kardinal Frings (1887–1978). I. Sein Wirken für das Bistum Köln und für die Kirche in Deutschland* (Paderborn, 2003), p. 134; and in Repgen, 'Die Erfahrung des Dritten Reiches', p. 131. Repgen, it should be noted, does not see anything triumphalist about the Church's position at Fulda.

92 Martin Greschat, 'Zwischen Aufbruch und Beharrung. Die evangelische Kirche nach dem Zweiten Weltkrieg', in Conzemius, Greschat and Kocher (eds.), *Die Zeit nach 1945 als Thema kirchlicher Zeitgeschichte*, p. 112.

93 Anselm Doering-Manteuffel, 'Die "Frommen" und die "Linken" vor der Wiederherstellung des bürgerlichen Staats. Integrationsprobleme und Interkonfessionalismus in der frühen CDU', in Jochen-Christoph Kaiser and Anselm Doering-Manteuffel (eds.), *Christentum und politische Verantwortung. Kirchen in Nachkriegsdeutschland* (Stuttgart, 1990), p. 90; Greschat, 'Zwischen Aufbruch und Beharrung', pp. 112–114.

94 Greschat, 'Zwischen Aufbruch und Beharrung', p. 112.

95 Quoted in Repgen, 'Die Erfahrung des Dritten Reiches', p. 141.

96 Werner Jochmann, 'Evangelische Kirche und Politik in der Phase des Neubeginns 1945–1950', in Conzemius, Greschat and Kocher (eds.), *Die Zeit nach 1945 als Thema kirchlicher Zeitgeschichte*, p. 195.

97 Quoted in Greschat, 'Zwischen Aufbruch und Beharrung', p. 112.

98 See Heiko Haumann, Dagmar Rübsam, Thomas Schnabel and Gerd R. Ueberschär, 'Freiburg im "Dritten Reich"', in Heiko Haumann und Hans Schadek (ed.), *Geschichte der Stadt Freiburg im Breisgau, Bd. 3: Von der badischen Herrschaft bis zur Gegenwart* (Stuttgart, 1992), p. 310; Peter Fäßler, '"Umkehr durch Verchristlichung". Die Kirchen als Ordnungsfaktor', in Edgar Wolfrum, Peter Fäßler und Reinhard Grohnert, *Krisenjahre und*

Aufbruchszeit. Alltag und Politik im französisch besetzten Baden 1945–1949
(Munich, 1996), p. 78. This was the same Conrad Gröber who had
emphasized at a diocesan synod at the end of April 1933: 'We must not
and we cannot reject the new state, but must welcome it with unwavering
cooperation.' Quoted in Fäßler, '"Umkehr durch Verchristlichung"', p. 79;
Jörg Thierfelder, 'Die Kirchen', in Otto Borst (ed.), *Das Dritte Reich in
Baden und Württemberg* (Stuttgart, 1988), p. 80.

99 Quoted in Trippen, *Josef Kardinal Frings (1887–1978). I*, p. 121. See also
Karola Fings, 'Kriegsenden, Kriegslegenden. Bewältigungsstrategien in
einer deutschen Großstadt', in Bernd-A. Rusineck (ed.), *Kriegsende 1945.
Verbrechen, Katastrophen, Befreiungen in nationaler und internationaler
Perspektive* (Göttingen, 2004), p. 227. In the summer of 1945 Frings succeeded Cardinal Adolf Bertram, the Archbishop of Breslau (who died on
6 July), as Chairman of the German [Catholic] Bishops' Conference, a
post which he retained until 1965. In February 1946 (together with
Konrad Graf von Preysing of Berlin and Clemens August Graf von Galen
of Münster) he was named a Cardinal.

100 Quoted in Martin Greschat, '"Rechristianisierung" und "Säkularisierung".
Anmerkungen zu einem europäischen konfessionellen Interpretations-
modell', in Kaiser and Doering-Manteuffel (eds.), *Christentum und politische
Verantwortung*, p. 6.

101 Wilhelm Damberg, '"Radikal katholische Laien an die Front!" Beobach-
tungen zur Idee und Wirkungsgeschichte der Katholischen Aktion', in
Köhler and van Melis (eds.), *Siegerin in Trümmern*, p. 151. See also Wolfgang Löhr, 'Rechristianisierungsvorstellungen im deutschen Katholizismus
1945–1948', in Kaiser and Doering-Manteuffel (eds.), *Christentum und
politische Verantwortung*, pp. 25–41; Greschat, '"Rechristianisierung" und
"Säkularisierung"', pp. 1–24.

102 Mark Edward Ruff, *The Wayward Flock: Catholic Youth in Postwar Germany,
1945–1965* (Chapel Hill and London, 2005), p. 33.

103 Karl-Egon Lönne, 'Katholizismus 1945: Zwischen gequälter Selbstbehauptung gegenüber dem Nationalsozialismus und Öffnung zur
pluralistischen Gesellschaft', in Volkmann (ed.), *Ende des Dritten Reiches –
Ende des Zweiten Weltkriegs*, p. 754.

104 Walter Dirks, 'Das gesellschaftliche Engagement der deutschen Katholiken
seit 1945', *Frankfurter Hefte* 19 (1964), p. 761; See also Löhr, 'Rechristianisierungsvorstellungen', pp. 35–36.

105 The EKD had been founded in August 1945 at the 'Church Leaders
Conference' in Treysa – now part of Schwalmstadt, to the south of Kassel.
On the Treysa conference, see Armin Boyens, 'Tresa 1945 – Die evangelische Kirche nach dem Zusammenbruch des Dritten Reiches', *Zeitschrift
für Kirchengeschichte*, 82 (1971), pp. 29–53; Martin Greschat, *Die evangelische*

Christenheit und die deutsche Geschichte nach 1945. Weichenstellungen in der Nachkriegszeit (Stuttgart, 2002), pp. 96–131.

106 These and the following quotations from Greschat, '"Rechristianisierung" und "Säkularisierung"', p. 1.

107 'Die Stuttgarter Schuldbekenntnis', printed in Martin Greschat (ed.), *Im Zeichen der Schuld. 40 Jahre Stuttgarter Schuldbekenntnis. Eine Dokumentation* (Neukirchen-Vluyn, 1985), pp. 45–46. Also quoted in Clemens Vollnhals, 'Die Evangelische Kirche zwischen Traditionswahrung und Neuorientierung', in Martin Broszat, Klaus-Dietmar Henke and Hans Woller (eds.), *Von Stalingrad zur Währungsreform. Zur Sozialgeschichte des Umbruchs in Deutschland* (Munich, 1988), p. 135.

108 For the ways in which the Catholic Church approached 're-Christianization' after the war, see Lohr, 'Rechristianisierungsvorstellungen'.

109 Joachim Köhler and Damian van Melis, 'Einleitung der Herausgeber', in Köhler and van Melis (eds.), *Siegerin in Trümmern*, p. 13.

110 Vollnhals, 'Die Evangelische Kirche zwischen Traditionswahrung und Neuorientierung', p. 136.

111 Doris L. Bergen, *Twisted Cross. The German Christian Movement in the Third Reich* (Chapel Hill and London, 1996), p. 209.

112 Quoted in Greschat, *Die evangelische Christenheit*, p. 234.

113 Greschat, *Die evangelische Christenheit*, p. 233.

114 Letter of Bishop Meiser and Cardinal Faulhaber to the American Military Government for Germany, 20 July 1945, printed in Clemens Vollnhals (ed.), *Entnazifizierung und Selbstreinigung im Urteil der evangelischen Kirche* (Munich, 1989), pp. 30–31. See also Greschat, *Die evangelische Christenheit*, p. 206.

115 See Gerhard Besier, 'Die politische Rolle des Protestantismus in der Nachkriegszeit', *Aus Politik und Zeitgeschichte* (B 50/2000). Available on the internet: http://www.bpb.de/publikationen/IA4BB2.html.

116 This line of reasoning is presented by Martin Greschat, 'Weder Neuanfang noch Restauration. Zur Interpretation der deutschen evangelischen Kirchengeschichte nach dem Zweiten Weltkrieg', in Ursula Büttner (ed.), *Das Unrechtsregime. Internationale Forschung über den Nationalsozialismus. Band 2. Verfolgung – Exil – Belasteter Neubeginn* (Hamburg, 1986), p. 349. On the position of the Protestant Churches in eastern Germany in 1945, see Kurt Nowak, 'Christentum in politischer Verantwortung. Zum Protestantismus in der Sowjetischen Besatzungszone (1945–1949)', in Kaiser and Doering-Manteuffel (eds.), *Christentum und politische Verantwortung*, p. 42.

117 Quoted in Doering-Manteuffel, 'Die "Frommen" und die "Linken"', p. 91.

118 See Alfred C. Mierzejewski, *Ludwig Erhard. A Biography* (Chapel Hill and London, 2004), p. 46.

119 Hans-Peter Schwarz, *Adenauer. Band 1. Der Aufstieg 1876–1952* (Munich, 1994), pp. 500–501.
120 So Johannes Albers, quoted in Mierzejewski, *Ludwig Erhard*, p. 46.
121 Quoted in Schwarz, *Adenauer. Band 1*, p. 484.

11. The Great Disorder

1 Dr Rudolf Paul, Minister President of Thuringia, speaking at a rally in June 1946. Quoted in Bundesarchiv Berlin (=BAB), SAPMO-DDR, NL 182, Nr. 1084, ff. 85–90: Willi Barth, 'Entwicklung und Tätigkeit der Beratenden Versamlung des Landes Thüringen', Berlin, 18 July 1946.
2 Victor Klemperer, *The Lesser Evil. The Diaries of Victor Klemperer 1945–1959* (translated by Martin Chalmers) (London, 2003), p. 11. (diary entry from 23 June 1945)
3 David F. Smith, 'Juvenile Delinquency in the British Zone of Germany, 1945–51', *German History*, vol. 12, no. 1 (1994), p. 39.
4 F.S.V. Donnison, *Civil Affairs and Military Government. Central Organisation and Planning* (London, 1966), p. 279; Hartmut Pietsch, *Militärregierung, Bürokratie und Sozialisierung. Zur Entwicklung des politischen Systems in den Städten des Ruhrgesbietes 1945 bis 1948* (Duisburg, 1978), p. 9.
5 Gerhard Fürmetz, 'Alte und neue Polizisten. Kommunale Personalpolitik in der frühen Nachkriegszeit am Beispiel der Augsburger Stadtpolizei', in Paul Hoser and Reinhard Baumann (eds.), *Kriegsende und Neubeginn. Die Besatzungszeit im schwäbisch-alemannischen Raum* (Konstanz, 2003), p. 341.
6 See, for example, the photographs of shops being looted in April 1945 in Ullrich Schneider, *Niedersachsen 1945. Kriegsende, Wiederaufbau, Landesgründung* (Hannover, 1985), p. 38.
7 BAB, DO-1-7, Nr. 23, ff. 34–35: 'Entwicklungspolitischer Bericht der neuen demokratischen Polizei des Landes Sachsen (1945–1948)'.
8 Quoted in Gerhard Baumert, *Jugend der Nachkriegszeit. Lebensverhältnisse und Reaktionsweisen* (Darmstadt, 1952), p. 24.
9 Elizabeth D. Heineman, *What Difference Does a Husband Make? Women and Marital Status in Nazi and Postwar Germany* (Berkeley, Los Angeles and London, 1999), p. 118. Heineman notes that 'of those registered as missing, 47.6 percent were married', but that married men were more likely to be registered since single men 'had no wives to register them'.
10 See Dagmar Herzog, *Sex after Fascism. Memory and Morality in Twentieth-Century Germany* (Princeton and Oxford, 2005), pp. 101–140.
11 Heineman, *What Difference Does a Husband Make?*, p. 119.
12 See Robert G. Moeller, *Protecting Motherhood. Women and the Family in the*

Politics of Postwar West Germany (Berkeley and Los Angeles, 1993), pp. 23–24.

13   Quoted in Heineman, *What Difference Does a Husband Make?*, p. 119; and in Moeller, *Protecting Motherhood*, p. 28.

14   O. Jean Brandes, 'The Effects of War on the German Family', *Social Forces*, vol. 29, no. 2 (Dec. 1950), p. 172.

15   Quoted in Herzog, *Sex after Fascism*, p. 66.

16   Quoted in Herzog, *Sex after Fascism*, p. 66.

17   See Statistisches Bundesamt, *Statistisches Jahrbuch für die Bundesrepublik Deutschland* (Stuttgart and Cologne, 1952), p. 55. See also Barbara Willenbacher, 'Zerrüttung und Bewahrung der Nachkriegs-Familie', in Martin Broszat, Klaus-Dietmar Henke and Hans Woller (eds.), *Von Stalingrad zur Währungsreform. Zur Sozialgeschichte des Umbruchs in Deutschland* (Munich, 1988), p. 600f.

18   See Richard Bessel, *Germany after the First World War* (Oxford, 1993), pp. 233–239.

19   Mecklenburgisches Hauptstaatsarchiv Schwerin (=MLHA), Kreistag/Rat des Kreises Anklam, Nr. 39, ff. 49–57: 'Übersicht über die Leistungs-steigerung vom 1. Juli 1945 bis 1. Oktober 1946 im Kreise Anklam'.

20   For example, in the American Zone. See Dagmar Ellerbrock, 'Die restau-rativen Modernisierer. Frauen als gesundheitspolitische Zielgruppe der amerikanischen Besatzungsmacht zwischen 1945 und 1949', in Ulrike Lindner and Merith Niehuss (eds.), *Ärztinnen – Patientinnen. Frauen im deutschen und britischen Gesundheitswesen des 20. Jahrhunderts* (Cologne, Weimar and Vienna, 2002), pp. 243–266.

21   Willenbacher, 'Zerrüttung und Bewahrung der Nachkriegs-Familie', p. 597.

22   Landeshauptarchiv Sachsen-Anhalt Magdeburg (=LHA-SA), LBdVP, Nr. 309, ff. 60–61: The Präsident des Bezirksgerichts, 'Bericht über das Gefängniswesen im Regierungsbezirk Magdeburg', Magdeburg, 25 March 1946.

23   MLHA, LBdVP, Nr. 400, f. 110: The Bürgermeister der Stadt Ostseebad Kühlingsborn, Ortspolizeibehörde, to the Landrat des Kreises Rostock, Abt. Polizei, Kühlingsborn, 18 Dec. 1945.

24   Karl Bader, *Soziologie der deutschen Nachkriegskriminalität* (Tübingen, 1949), p. 131.

25   See Willenbacher, 'Zerrüttung und Bewahrung der Nachkriegs-Familie', p. 602.

26   MLHA, Rat des Kreises Greifswald, Nr. 51: The Schulrat to the Landrat in Greifswald, Greifswald, 18 Aug. 1945.

27   Gerhard Brunn, 'Köln in den Jahren 1945 und 1946. Die Rahmenbeding-ungen des gesellschaftlichen Lebens', in Otto Dann (ed.), *Köln nach dem*

Nationalsozialismus. Der Beginn des gesellschaftlichen Lebens in den Jahren 1945/46 (Wuppertal, 1981), p. 59.

28 For example, in Stuttgart. See Hermann Vietzen, *Chronik der Stadt Stuttgart 1945–1948* (Stuttgart, 1972), p. 489.

29 Brunn, 'Köln in den Jahren 1945 und 1946', p. 59. Brunn notes that in Cologne the shortage of teachers increased in 1946, as the numbers of pupils rose and as teachers were either dismissed or suspended from service as a result of denazification proceedings.

30 Vietzen, *Chronik der Stadt Stuttgart*, p. 491.

31 Smith, 'Juvenile Delinquency in the British Zone of Germany', pp. 39, 40.

32 For example: in Stuttgart, between 15 May 1945 and the end of February 1946, 469 arrest warrants against children and adolescents were issued and 478 cases of people regarded as endangered were processed; of the latter, 120 were of children, 69 of male adolescents and 289 female. See Vietzen, *Chronik der Stadt Stuttgart*, p. 552.

33 Quoted in Frank Kebedies, *Außer Kontrolle. Jugendkriminalpolitik in der NS-Zeit und in der frühen Nachkriegszeit* (Essen, 2000), p. 219.

34 Quoted in Kebedies, *Außer Kontrolle*, p. 220.

35 Alan McDougall, 'A Duty to Forget? The "Hitler Youth Generation" and the Transition from Nazism to Communism in Postwar East Germany, c. 1945–1949', *German History*, vol. 26, no. 1 (2008), p. 28.

36 BAB, SAPMO-DDR, NL 182, Nr. 852, ff. 43–51: 'Auszug aus der Diskussion zweier Konferenzen der Berliner Jugendfunktionäre der Partei am 28.7.1945 in der Rosenthaler Str. 13'. Keßler also noted with dismay that in Spandau (in the British sector of Berlin) 'the girls go out only with the English and Americans' and 'are alienated from us', and that 'the youth want nothing to do with the Communists'.

37 Schneider, *Niedersachsen 1945*, p. 60.

38 LHA-SA, LBdVP, Nr. 285, f. 62: The Polizeipräsident, Magdeburg, 25 Sept. 1945; LHS-SA, LBdVP, Nr. 290, ff. 14–15: The Polizeipräsident to the Bezirkspräsident in Magdeburg, Magdeburg, 8 Nov. 1945.

39 For example, in Stuttgart. See Vietzen, *Chronik der Stadt Stuttgart*, p. 548.

40 Quoted in Alan Kramer, '"Law-abiding Germans'? Social Distintegration, Crime and the Reimposition of Order in Post-war Western Germany, 1945–9', in Richard J. Evans (ed.), *The German Underworld. Deviants and Outcasts in German History* (London and New York, 1988), p. 257f.

41 BAB, SAPMO-DDR, NL 182, Nr. 852, ff. 132–133: Ortsgruppe der KPD-Tegel-Süd, Kolonie Mäckeritzwiesen to the ZK der KPD, Mäckeritzwiesen, 26 June 1945. The authors of this letter demanded that the Soviet Army leadership act in the spirit of 'Bolshevik discipline' and reign in their troops. They proposed that 'every bandit in Red Army uniform who is caught be hanged publicly', and that 'the organized part

of the revolutionary working class' be allowed immediately to form 'armed self-protection organizations'. They went on to recommend that, 'with regard to the sexual deprivation of the Red Army soldiers', public institutions be set up 'whose inmates are to be gathered from the ranks of bourgeois and fascist females who by their nature are prostitutes anyway'. Walter Ulbricht reacted to this outburst by calling for a meeting of the Communist Party in Tegel-Süd to condemn this 'anti-Party and anti-Soviet declaration'. See BAB, SAPMO-DDR NL 182, Nr. 852, f. 131: Ulbricht to the BL[=Bezirksleitung]-Berlin, [Berlin], 4 July 1945.

42　BAB, SAPMO-DDR NL 182, Nr. 852, f. 134: Kommunistische Partei, 16. Verw. Bez. to the Bezirksleitung Berlin, Köpenick, 10 July 1945. This letter apparently was not actually sent to the district leadership.

43　Dresdner Strassenbahn AG to Bürgermeister Welz, 18 Dec. 1945, quoted in Barbara Schmucki, 'On the Trams. Women, Men and Urban Public Transport in Germany', *The Journal of Transport History*, vol. 23 (2002), no. 1, p. 64.

44　Vietzen, *Chronik der Stadt Stuttgart*, pp. 455–464.

45　For example, in Goßlar in Lower Saxony the number of infants who died in their first year rose from 38 in 1939 to 113 in 1945; in the rural district of Melle the number rose from 23 in 1939 to 88 in 1945. See Schneider, *Niedersachsen 1945*, p. 115.

46　This term was used by an impatient official (Ivor Pink) with the British Control Commission in a letter to the Foreign Office on 13 June 1945. See Schneider, *Niedersachsen 1945*, p. 12f. See also Leonard Krieger, 'The Inter-Regnum in Germany, March–August 1945', in *Political Science Quarterly* 64 (1949), pp. 507–532.

47　In the Soviet Zone, the NKVD took over German prisons and until the autumn almost all the prisons remained in Soviet hands. See LHA-SA, LBdVP, Nr. 309, ff. 60–61: The Präsident des Bezirksgerichts, 'Bericht über das Gefängniswesen im Regierungsbezirk Magdeburg', Magdeburg, 25 March 1946.

48　In Stuttgart, for example, the banks remained shut until 1 June, and then limits were placed on the amounts which could be withdrawn; it was not until the middle of November that the limits on cash withdrawals were lifted. See Vietzen, *Chronik der Stadt Stuttgart*, pp. 573–575.

49　Ludwig Vaubel, *Zusammenbruch und Wiederaufbau. Ein Tagebuch aus der Wirtschaft 1945–1949* (edited by Wolfgang Benz) (Munich, 1985), p. 52: diary entry for 30 Aug. 1945.

50　Bader, *Soziologie der deutschen Nachkriegskriminalität*, p. 132.

51　See, for example, the chronology of developments in Stuttgart during 1945, in Vietzen, *Chronik der Stadt Stuttgart*, pp. 624–630.

52 'Bericht des Regierungspräsidenten [Wilhelm Backhaus SPD] in Hildesheim für die Monate Oktober bis Dezember 1945', printed in Herbert Michaelis and Ernst Schraepler (eds.), *Ursachen und Folgen. Vom deutschen Zusammenbruch 1918 und 1945 bis zur staatlichen Neuordnung Deutschlands in der Gegenwart. Ein Urkunden- und Dokumentensammlung zur Zeitgeschichte*, vol. 24, *Deutschland unter dem Besatzungsregime* (Berlin, 1977), pp. 163–168.

53 H. Barthel, *Die wirtschaftlichen Ausgangsbedingungen der DDR. Zur Wirtschaftsentwicklung auf dem Gebiet der DDR* (Berlin, 1979), p. 49.

54 Barthel, *Die wirtschaftlichen Ausgangsbedingungen*, p. 48.

55 Ackermann in Anton Ackermann, Robert Büchner, Werner Eggerath, Fritz Selbmann, Robert Siewert and Hans Warnke, 'Von der Geburt der neuen Staatsmacht', in *Staat und Recht*, vol. 14 (1965), no. 5, p. 670.

56 Schneider, *Niedersachsen 1945*, p. 113.

57 F. Selbmann, *Reden und Tagebuchblätter 1933–1947* (Dresden, 1947), p. 49. Cited in Rainer Gries, *Die Rationengesellschaft. Versorgungskampf und Vergleichsmentalität. Leipzig, München und Köln nach dem Kriege* (Münster, 1991), p. 48.

58 'Bericht des Regierungspräsidenten in Hildesheim für die Monate Januar bis März 1946', printed in Michaelis and Schraepler (eds.), *Ursachen und Folgen*, vol. 24, pp. 169–173.

59 This is the observation of Hanna Sophia Reich based on evidence in the files of the Economics and Food Office in Konstanz immediately after the war. See Hanna Sophia Reich, 'Studien zum Alltag in Konstanz 1945–1949' (MS, University of Konstanz, 2003), p. 44.

60 Heinrich Böll, 'Heimat und keine', in Heinrich Böll *Aufsätze, Kritiken, Reden* (Cologne, 1967), p. 204.

61 Gries, *Die Rationengesellschaft*, pp. 19–20.

62 BAB, SAPMO-DDR, NL 182, Nr. 852, f. 203: 'Bericht', signed by 'Marg. Schulchen', dated in pencil '15/X.45'.

63 Bernd Martin, 'Die deutsche Kapitulation: Versuch einer Bilanz des Zweiten Weltkrieges', *Freiburger Universitätsblätter*, vol. 34, no. 130 (Dec, 1995), p. 51.

12. Paying for War and Peace

1 Egon Bahr, 'Als rasender Reporter im zerstörten Berlin', in Gustav Trampe (ed.), *Die Stunde Null. Erinnerungen an Kriegsende und Neuanfang* (Stuttgart, 1995), p. 295.

2 *The Economist*, vol. cxlviii, no. 5312 (16 June 1945), p. 800.

3 *Düsseldorfer Mitteilungsblatt* Nr. 13, 21 July 1945. Quoted in Peter Brandt, 'Unternehmerorganisationen im Umbruch', in Lutz Niethammer, Ulrich

Borsdorf and Peter Brandt (eds.), *Arbeiterinitiative 1945. Antifaschistische Auschüsse und Reorganisation der Arbeiterbewegung in Deutschland* (Wuppertal, 1976), p. 673.

4 Diary entry for 11 May 1945, in Ursula Büttner and Angelika Voß–Louis (eds.), *Neuanfang auf Trümmern. Die Tagebücher des Bremer Bürgermeisters Theodor Spitta 1945–1947* (Munich, 1992), p. 121.

5 Section II B, Economic Principles Protocol of the Proceedings of the Berlin (Potsdam) Conference, 1 August 1945, available at http://www.yale.edu/lawweb/avalon/decade/decade17.html

6 Section III, Reparations from Germany, Protocol of the Proceedings of the Berlin (Potsdam) Conference, 1 August 1945, available at http://www.yale.edu/lawweb/avalon/decade/decade17.html

7 Rudolf Laufer, *Industrie und Energiewirtschaft im Land Baden 1945–1952* (Freiburg and Munich, 1979), p. 98.

8 Lists of the plants dismantled in all four zones, together with a list of the 'Soviet Joint Stock Companies' in the Soviet Zone, may be found in G. W. Harmssen, *Reparationen Sozialprodukt Lebensstandard. Versuch einer Wirtschaftsbilanz. Heft 1 A. Allgemeiner Teil* (Bremen, 1948), pp. 99–129.

9 See Adam Tooze, *The Wages of Destruction. The Making and Breaking of the Nazi Economy* (London, 2006), pp. 513–551; Götz Aly. *Hitlers Volksstaat. Raub, Rassenkrieg und nationaler Sozialismus* (Frankfurt am Main, 2005).

10 Quoted in Tooze, *The Wages of Destruction*, p. 546.

11 Bundesarchiv-Militärarchiv (= BA-MA), RW 4, Nr. 703, f. 133: WFSt, 'Notiz für Staatssekretärbesprechung am 17.2.1945', 'Betr.: Maßnahmen zur Verbesserung der Ernährungslage', 16.2.1945. See also BA-MA, RW 4, Nr, 712, ff. 4–7: [WFSt], 14.2.45.

12 BA-MA, RW 4, Nr, 712, ff. 4–7: [WFSt], 14.2.45.

13 Quoted in Gabriele Stüber, *Der Kampf gegen den Hunger 1945–1950. Die Ernährungslage in der britischen Zone Deutschlands, insbesondere in Schleswig-Holstein und Hamburg* (Neumünster, 1984), p. 36.

14 Gustavo Corni and Horst Gies, *Brot Butter Kanonen. Die Ernährungswirtschaft in Deutschland unter der Diktatur Hitlers* (Berlin, 1997), p. 579.

15 Quoted in Corni and Gies, *Brot Butter Kanonen*, p. 580.

16 BA-MA, RW 44, Nr. I/18: Mimeographed copy of 'Aide-Mémoire über sofort zu lösende überregionale Fragen', to the Supreme Commander of the Allied Armed Forces General Eisenhower, Mürwick, 11 May 1945.

17 An additional problem was that the bulk of the seeds for German agriculture had come from the east. See Rainer Gries, *Die Rationengesellschaft. Versorgungskampf und Vergleichsmentalität. Leipzig, München und Köln nach dem Kriege* (Münster, 1991), pp. 177–178.

18 For discussion of how this unfolded in the French Zone, see Karl-Heinz

Rothenberger, 'Ernährungs- und Landwirtschaftspolitik in der Französischen Besatzungszone 1945–1950', in Claus Scharf and Hans-Jürgen Schröder (eds.), *Die Deutschlandpolitik Frankreichs und die französische Zone 1945–1949* (Wiesbaden, 1983), p. 193.

19 Diary entry for 7 June 1945, in Büttner and Voß-Louis (eds.), *Neuanfang auf Trümmern*, pp. 153–154.

20 Rothenberger, 'Ernährungs- und Landwirtschaftspolitik', p. 193.

21 See the table ('Anteil Ostdeutschlands an der Agrarproduktion des Altreichs im 1935/39') in Hans Schlange-Schöningen (ed.), *Im Schatten des Hungers. Dokumentarisches zur Ernährungspolitik und Ernährungswirtschaft in den Jahren 1945–1949* (Hamburg and Berlin), p. 293; Michael Wildt, *Der Traum vom Saatwerden. Hunger und Protest, Schwarzmarkt und Selbsthilfe in Hamburg 1945–194* (Hamburg, 1986), pp. 20–22.

22 Helga Grebing, Peter Pozorski and Rainer Schulze (eds.), *Die Nachkriegsentwicklung in Westdeutschland 1945–1949. a) Die wirtschaftlichen Grundlagen* (Stuttgart, 1980), p. 7.

23 Gries, *Die Rationengesellschaft*, p. 178.

24 Arnd Bauerkämper, 'Strukturumbruch ohne Mentalitätswandel. Auswirkungen der Bodenreform auf die ländliche Gesellschaft in der Provinz Mark Brandenburg 1945–1949', in Arnd Bauerkämper (ed.), *"Junkerland in Bauernhand"? Durchführung, Auswirkungen und Stellenwert der Bodenreform in der Sowjetischen Besatzungszone* (Stuttgart, 1996), p. 72.

25 Figures in Rothenberger, 'Ernährungs- und Landwirtschaft', p. 187.

26 Percentages calculated from the figures in the table in Schlange-Schöningen (ed.), *Im Schatten des Hungers*, p. 309. See also the figures in Conrad F. Latour and Thilo Vogelsang, *Okkupation und Wiederaufbau. Die Tätigkeit der Militärregierung in der amerikanischen Besatzungszone Deutschlands 1944–1947* (Stuttgart, 1973), p. 213 (note 16).

27 Grebing, Pozorski and Schulze (eds.), *Die Nachkriegsentwicklung in Westdeutschland 1945–1949. a) Die wirtschaftlichen Grundlagen*, p. 8.

28 Figures in Rothenberger, 'Ernährungs- und Landwirtschaft', p. 187.

29 See Rothenberger, 'Ernährungs- und Landwirtschaft', pp. 188–190.

30 Ulrich Kluge, '"Die Bodenreform ist in erster Linie eine politische Angelegenheit". Agrarstruktureller Wandel in Sachsen 1945/46', in Arnd Bauerkämper (ed.), *"Junkerland in Bauernhand"?*, p. 104.

31 Landespräsident Köhler to the Militärregierung, 14 Nov. 1945. Printed in Hansmartin Schwarzmaier (ed.), *Der deutsche Südwesten zur Stunde Null. Zusammenbruch und Neuanfang im Jahr 1945 in Dokumenten und Bildern* (Karlsruhe, 1975), pp. 162–163.

32 See figures for August 1944 in Ulrich Herbert, *Hitler's Foreign Workers. Enforced Foreign Labor in Germany under the Third Reich* (Cambridge, 1997), p. 297. Of the 5,919,761 people recorded as employed in agriculture in

August 1944, 2,061,066 were civilian foreign workers and 686,172 were POWS; together they comprised 46.4% of the employed labour force in agriculture.

33 Stüber, *Der Kampf gegen den Hunger 1945–1950*, p. 64.

34 Wolfgang Trees, Charles Whiting and Thomas Omansen, *Drei Jahre nach Null. Geschichte der britischen Besatzungszone 1945–1948* (Düsseldorf, 1978), p. 86.

35 See Robert W. Carden, 'Before Bizonia: Britain's Economic Dilemma in Germany, 1945–46', in *Journal of Contemporary History*, vol. 14, no. 3 (1979), p. 539.

36 Stüber, *Der Kampf gegen den Hunger 1945–1950*, pp. 36–37.

37 Karl-Heinz Rothenberger, *Die Hungerjahre nach dem Zweiten Weltkrieg. Ernährungs- und Landwirtschaft in Rheinland-Pfalz 1945–1950* (Boppard am Rhein, 1980), p. 97.

38 See the report in Ulrich Borsdorf and Lutz Niethammer (eds.), *Zwischen Befreiung und Besatzung. Analysen des US-Geheimdienstes über Positionen und Strukturen deutscher Politik 1945* (Wuppertal, 1976), p. 32.

39 Gries, *Die Rationengesellschaft*, p. 147.

40 *Süddeutsche Zeitung*, 30 April 1946 (Nr. 35/1946), quoted in Gries, *Die Rationengesellschaft*, p. 147.

41 Rothenberger, *Die Hungerjahre nach dem Zweiten Weltkrieg*, p. 98.

42 'Bericht des Regierungspräsidenten in Hildesheim für die Monate Oktober bis Dezember 1945', printed in Herbert Michaelis and Ernst Schraepler (eds.), *Ursachen und Folgen. Vom deutschen Zusammenbruch 1918 und 1945 bis zur staatlichen Neuordnung Deutschlands in der Gegenwart. Ein Urkunden- und Dokumentensammlung zur Zeitgeschichte*, Bd. 24, *Deutschland unter dem Besatzungsregime* (Berlin, 1977), pp. 163–168.

43 Gries, Die *Rationengesellschaft*, p. 43.

44 For example, in Leipzig, which was administered until the beginning of July by the Americans. See Gries, Die *Rationengesellschaft*, pp. 46–47.

45 This in the, admittedly extreme, case of Cologne. See Gries, Die *Rationengesellschaft*, pp. 251–252.

46 E.g. for the Soviet Zone, see Wolfgang Zank, *Wirtschaft und Arbeit in Ostdeutschland 1945–1949. Probleme des Wiederaufbaus in der Sowjetischen Besatzungszone Deutschlands* (Munich, 1987), p. 66.

47 Lucius D. Clay, *Decision in Germany* (Garden City, N.Y., 1950), pp. 264–265; Latour and Vogelsang, *Okkupation und Wiederaufbau*, p. 151.

48 See figures in Rothenberger, *Die Hungerjahre nach dem Zweiten Weltkrieg*, p. 114.

49 Zank, *Wirtschaft und Arbeit in Ostdeutschland*, p. 142.

50 In 1946, when the food situation became even more critical, particularly in the British Zone, there were cases of workers fainting from hunger. See

Carden, 'Before Bizonia, p. 543. Describing conditions in the American Zone, Lucius Clay wrote that 'the effect in Germany was paralyzing. Workers could not produce a full day's work. Economic recovery was stopped and the population was becoming more apathetic each day.' Clay, *Decision in Germany*, p. 266.

51 Rothenberger, *Die Hungerjahre nach dem Zweiten Weltkrieg*, p. 122.

52 Rothenberger, *Die Hungerjahre nach dem Zweiten Weltkrieg*, p. 99.

53 Rothenberger, *Die Hungerjahre nach dem Zweiten Weltkrieg*, p. 116.

54 Sibylle Meyer and Eva Schulze, *Wie wir das alles geschafft haben. Alleinstehende Frauen berichten über das Leben nach 1945* (Munich, 1988), p. 94.

55 Senat von Berlin (ed.), *Berlin. Kampf um Freiheit und Selbstverwaltung 1945–1946* (Berlin, 1961), p. 212.

56 Martin H. Geyer, 'Die Hungergesellschaft', in Jost Dullfer (ed.), *"Wir haben schwere Zeiten hinter uns". Die Kölner Region zwischen Krieg und Nachkriegszeit* (Vierow bei Greifswald, 1996), p. 184.

57 Theodor Eschenberg, *Jahre der Besatzung 1945–1949* (Wiesbaden, 1983), p. 267.

58 Figures in Manfred Overesch, *Das besetzte Deutschland 1945–1947. Eine Tageschronik der Politik, Wirtschaft, Kultur* (Augsburg, 1992), p. 17.

59 See figures in Werner Abelshauser, *Wirtschaft in Westdeutschland 1945–1948. Rekonstruktion und Wachstumsbedingungen in der amerikanischen und britischen Zone* (Stuttgart, 1975), pp. 139–141.

60 In the Soviet Zone coal miners who worked underground were the first group of workers who were allotted extra rations. See Zank, *Wirtschaft und Arbeit in Ostdeutschlan*, pp. 26, 69.

61 Whereas in 1939 45.1% of miners working undergound in the Ruhr were aged 35 and under, in 1946 only 29.2% were. See Abelshauser, *Wirtschaft in Westdeutschland*, p. 141.

62 E.g. in Cologne. See Gerhard Brunn, 'Köln in den Jahren 1945 und 1946. Die Rahmenbedingungen des gesellschaftlichen Lebens', in Otto Dann (ed.), *Köln nach dem Nationalsozialismus. Der Beginn des gesellschaftlichen und politischen Lebens in den Jahren 1945/46* (Wuppertal, 1981), p. 51.

63 Harmssen, *Reparationen Sozialprodukt Lebensstandard*, p. 40.

64 For example, in Bremen, where the dismantling of industrial plant began in the autumn of 1945 and lasted until the spring of 1948 – principal targets were aircraft factories, a torpedo factory, and a power plant – some 2800 people were employed in the dismantling operations at the end of 1945. See Peter Brandt, *Antifaschismus und Arbeiterbewegung. Aufbau – Ausprägung – Politik in Bremen 1945/46* (Hamburg, 1976), p. 81; Büttner and Voß-Louis (eds.), *Neuanfang auf Trümmern*, p. 225f.

65 Overesch, *Das besetzte Deutschland 1945–1947*, p. 23.

66   See Rudolf Laufer, *Industrie und Energiewirtschaft im Land Baden 1945–1952* (Freiburg and Munich, 1979), pp. 128–129.

67   Theodor Spitta, diary entry for 17 July 1945, in Büttner and Voß–Louis (eds.), *Neuanfang auf Trümmern*, pp. 185–186.

68   Harmssen, *Reparationen Sozialprodukt Lebensstandard*, p. 40.

69   Christoph Klessmann, *Die doppelte Staatsgründung. Deutsche Geschichte 1945–1955* (Göttingen, 1982), p. 41.

70   Werner Abelshauser, *Wirtschaftsgeschichte der Bundesrepublik Deutschland 1945–1980* (Frankfurt am Main, 1983), p. 22; Hermann Weber, *Geschichte der DDR* (Munich, 1985), p. 91.

71   See figures in Abelshauser, *Wirtschaft in Westdeutschland*, p. 107.

72   Wolfgang Zank, *Wirtschaft und Arbeit in Ostdeutschland 1945–1949. Probleme des Wiederaufbaus in der Sowjetischen Besatzungszone Deutschlands* (Munich, 1987), p. 33.

73   Grebing, Pozorski and Schulze (eds.), *Die Nachkriegsentwicklung in Westdeutschland 1945–1949. a) Die wirtschaftlichen Grundlagen*, pp. 5–6.

74   Quoted in Hans Woller, *Gesellschaft und Politik in der amerikanischen Besatzungszone. Die Region Ansbach und Fürth* (Munich, 1986), p. 241.

75   'Reise durch den Westen Deutschlands (Mai 1945)', in Borsdorff and Niethammer (eds.), *Zwischen Befreiung und Besatzung*, p. 48.

76   Overesch, *Das besetzte Deutschland 1945–1947*, p. 118.

77   Neil Gregor, *Daimler-Benz in the Third Reich* (New Haven and London, 1998), p. 249.

78   See Michael Fichter, 'Aufbau und Neuordnung: Betriebsräte zwischen Klassensolidarität und Betriebsloyalität', in Martin Broszat, Klaus-Dietmar Henke and Hans Woller (eds.), *Von Stalingrad zur Währungsreform. Zur Sozialgeschichte des Umbruchs in Deutschland* (Munich, 1988), pp. 484–485. In March 1945 the firm's Untertürkheim factory had employed 13,183 people (including 3801 civilian forced labourers and 257 POWs); in June there were only 1000 employees in the factory, occupied mostly with clearing up war damage and accountancy tasks. At the year's end the firm was employing 3740 people.

79   Hans Mommsen and Manfred Grieger, *Das Volkswagenwerk und seine Arbeiter im Dritten Reich* (Düsseldorf, 1996), p. 954 . Generally, see Abelshauser, *Wirtschaft in Westdeutschland*, p. 117.

80   Overesch, *Das besetzte Deutschland 1945–1947*, p. 119.

81   Quoted in Friedrich-Wilhelm Henning, 'Produktionshemmnisse und Produktionsleistungen vom Herbst 1944 bis zum Herbst 1945', in Düllfer (ed.), *"Wir haben schwere Zeiten hinter uns"*, pp. 219–220.

82   Henning, 'Produktionshemmnisse und Produktionsleistungen', p. 224.

83   Ludwig Vaubel, *Zusammenbruch und Wiederaufbau. Ein Tagebuch aus der Wirtschaft 1945* (edited by Wolfgang Benz) (Munich, 1984), p. 35 (diary

entry for 25 May 1945). Vaubel, a director of a chemical firm in Wuppertal, noted that 'many former members of the retinue [i.e. employees] have found emergency employment in agriculture'.

84   Andreas Meyhoff, *Blohm & Voss im "Dritten Reich". Eine Hamburger Werft zwischen Geschäft und Politik* (Hamburg, 2001), pp. 509–510.

85   Quoted in Fichter, 'Aufbau und Neuordnung', pp. 485–486

86   For example, the case of the Allianz insurance company. See Gerald D. Feldman, *Allianz and the German Insurance Business, 1933–1945* (Cambridge, 2001), p. 449.

87   For the example of Bosch, see Fichter, 'Aufbau und Neuordnung', p. 483

88   See, for example, Vaubel, *Zusammenbruch und Wiederaufbau*, p. 36 (diary entry for 25 May 1945).

89   For example, in southern Baden at the end of May 1945 the working hours of factories were limited to roughly 18 hours per week. See Rudolf Laufer, 'Die südbadische Industrie unter französischer Besatzung 1945–1949', in Claus Scharf and Hans-Jürgen Schröder (eds.), *Die Deutschlandpolitik Frankreichs und die französische Zone 1945–1949* (Wiesbaden, 1983), p. 151.

90

Industrial Production in the Occupation Zones in Germany, 1945–1946 (1936=100)

	American	British	French	Soviet
Fourth Quarter 1945	19	22	–	22
First Quarter 1946	41	34	36	44

From Werner Abelshauser, 'Wirtschaft und Besatzungspolitik in der Französischen Zone 1945–1949', in Scharf and Schröder (eds.), *Die Deutschlandpolitik Frankreichs*, p. 122.

91   Henning, 'Produktionshemmnisse und Produktionsleistungen', pp. 216–217.

92   Rothenberger, *Die Hungerjahre nach dem Zweiten Weltkrieg*, p. 98.

93   Andreas Wagner, 'Die Rostocker Brauerei. Zum Wandel industriebetrieblichen Alltags von 1945 bis 1952', in Damian van Melis (ed.), *Sozialismus auf dem platten Land. Tradition und Transformation in Mecklenburg-Vorpommern von 1945 bis 1952* (Schwerin, 1999), pp. 324–326. Things soon changed for the worse, however. In mid-July the brewery's works manager was dismissed due to his involvement in the Nazi regime, and in September the dismantling of the factory began. The brewery's own employees had to take the factory apart for the Soviet dismantling commission, and by the time they were finished all that remained were the building, the large concrete vats in the basement, and 30,000 beer bottles.

94   See Woller, *Gesellschaft und Politik in der amerikanischen Besatzungszone*, pp. 264–265.

95 See Volker Berghahn, *Unternehmer und Politik in der Bundesrepublik* (Frankfurt am Main, 1985), pp. 60–69.

96 Hartmut Pietsch, *Militärregierung, Bürokratie und Sozialisierung. Zur Entwicklung des politischen Systems in den Städten des Ruhrgebietes 1945 bis 1948* (Duisburg, 1978), pp. 108–109.

97 Quoted in Pietsch, *Militärregierung, Bürokratie und Sozialisierung*, p. 106.

98 Walter Schmidt, 'Zeitprobleme im Bergbau', 24 Nov. 1945. Quoted in Pietsch, *Militärregierung, Bürokratie und Sozialisierung*, p. 109.

99 Peter Brandt, 'Unternehmerorganisationen im Umbruch', in Niethammer, Borsdorf and Brandt (eds.), *Arbeiterinitiative 1945*, pp. 664–665; Barbara Marshall, 'The Democratization of Local Politics in the British Zone of Germany: Hanover 1945–47', in *Journal of Contemporary History*, vol. 21 (1986), pp. 418, 422; Rainer Schulze, *Unternehmerische Selbstverwaltung und Politik. Die Rolle der Industrie- und Handelskammer in Niedersachsen und Bremen als Vertretungen der Unternehmerinteressen nach dem Ende des Zweiten Weltkrieges* (Hildesheim, 1989), pp. 31–128.

100 Brandt, 'Unternehmerorganisationen im Umbruch', p. 667. The Americans were rather more keen to reform the Chambers than were the British or the French, and were more rigorous about disbanding the 'Gau Economic Chambers' which had replaced the local Chambers of Industry and Commerce during the Nazi period.

101 Brandt, 'Unternehmerorganisationen im Umbruch', p. 671; Pietsch, *Militärregierung, Bürokratie und Sozialisierung*, p. 108; Jürgen Weise, *Kammern in Not – zwischen Anpassung und Selbstbehauptung. Die Stellung der Industrie- und Handelskammern in der Auseinandersetzung um eine neue politische Ordnung 1945–1946. Dargestellt am Beispiel rheinischer Kammern und ihre Vereinigungen auf Landes-, Zonen- und Bundesebene* (Cologne, 1989), pp. 99–117.

102 Schulze, *Unternehmerische Selbstverwaltung und Politik*, pp. 156–159.

103 Carden, 'Before Bizonia', p. 545.

104 Overesch, *Das besetzte Deutschland 1945–1947*, p. 116.

105 Overesch, *Das besetzte Deutschland 1945–1947*, p. 52; Carl-Ludwig Holtfrerich, 'Die Deutsche Bank vom Zweiten Weltkrieg über die Besatzungsherrschaft zur Rekonstruktion 1945–1957', in Lothar Gall, Gerald D. Feldman, Harold James, Carl-Ludwig Holtfrerich and Hans E. Büschgen, *Die Deutsche Bank 1870–1995* (Munich, 1995), p. 442.

106 Holtfrerich, 'Die Deutsche Bank', p. 440.

107 Feldman, *Allianz and the German Insurance Business*, p. 447.

108 Gerhard Hetzer, 'Unternehmer und leitende Angestellte zwischen Rüstungseinsatz und politischer Säuberung', in Broszat, Henke and Woller (eds.), *Von Stalingrad zur Währungsreform*, p. 573.

109 Feldman, *Allianz and the German Insurance Business*, p. 478.

110 Hetzer, 'Unternehmer und leitende Angestellte',, p. 555.

111 Berghahn, *Unternehmer und Politik*, p. 59.

112 Feldman, *Allianz and the German Insurance Business*, p. 455.

113 Theodor Spitta, diary entry of 6 November 1945, in Büttner and Voß-Louis (eds.), *Neuanfang auf Trümmern*, pp. 270–271.

114 Herbert Schott, *Die Amerikaner als Besatzungsmacht in Würzburg (1945–1949)* (Würzburg, 1985), pp. 82–84.

115 Theodor Spitta. diary entry of 14 September 1945, in Büttner and Voß-Louis (eds.), *Neuanfang auf Trümmern*, p. 235. The dismissals also hit the administrative oversight of business: at the beginning of November Spitta noted that of 26 people employed with the trade police, after the wave of dismissals only three remained. See diary entry of 1 November 1945, *Neuanfang auf Trümmern, p.* 269.

116 See Büttner and Voß-Louis (eds.), *Neuanfang auf Trümmern*, pp. 235–236f; Lutz Niethammer, *Die Mitläuferfabrik. Die Entnazifizierung am Beispiel Bayerns* (Berlin and Bonn, 1982), pp. 229–240.

117 For example, in Stuttgart before the Americans arrived. See Fichter, 'Aufbau und Neuordnung', p. 481.

118 Gerhard Brunn, 'Köln in den Jahren 1945 und 1946. Die Rahmenbedingungen des gesellschaftlichen Lebens', in Dann (ed.), *Köln nach dem Nationalsozialismus*, p. 67. In August the *Kölnische Kurier* newspaper reported that 400 firms in Cologne already had received permission to resume production.

119 Henning, 'Produktionshemmnisse und Produktionsleistungen', ip. 214. Of course, this did not mean that no one was removed, or that German businessmen did not regard it as unjust when they were dismissed for having been members of the Nazi Party.

120 Thus, in Stuttgart, where after replacing the French as occupying power the Americans allotted this task to the municipal economics office. See Fichter, 'Aufbau und Neuordnung', p. 482.

121 Henning, 'Produktionshemmnisse und Produktionsleistungen', pp. 215–216. See also Jürgen Weise, *Kammern in Not*, pp. 90–91.

122 Fichter, 'Aufbau und Neuordnung', p. 482.

123 Henning, 'Produktionshemmnisse und Produktionsleistungen', pp. 216–218.

124 Henning, 'Produktionshemmnisse und Produktionsleistungen', pp. 220–221.

125 Rothenberger, *Die Hungerjahre nach dem Zweiten Weltkrieg*, p. 110. For the text of the proclamation, see Michaelis and Schraepler (eds.), *Ursachen und Folgen. Vom deutschen Zusammenbruch 1918 und 1945*, Bd. 24, pp. 322–334. The relevant section, Section III, is printed on pp. 323–324.

126 Laufer, *Industrie und Energiewirtschaft*, p. 90.

127 Woller, *Gesellschaft und Politik in der amerikanischen Besatzungszone*, p. 243.

128 Theodor Spitta, diary entry for 10 October 1945, in Büttner and Voß-Louis (eds.), *Neuanfang auf Trümmern*, p. 253.

129 Quoted in Aly, *Hitlers Volksstaat*, p. 337.

130 During the same period, the Reich debt rose from 19.1 billion Reichsmarks to 379.8 billions, an increase of nearly 20 times. See Abelshauser, *Wirtschaftsgeschichte der Bundesrepublik Deutschland*, p. 46; Karl-Heinrich Hansmayer and Rolf Caesar, 'Kriegswirtschaft und Inflation (1936–1948)', in Deutsche Bundesbank (ed.), *Währung und Wirtschaft in Deutschland 1876–1975* (Frankfurt am Main, 1976), pp. 414–418.

131 Willi A. Boelcke, *Der Schwarzmarkt 1945–1948: Vom Überleben nach dem Kriege* (Braunschweig, 1986), p. 109.

132 Alan Kramer, '"Law-abiding Germans?" Social Disintegration, Crime and the Reimposition of Order in Post-war Western Germany', in Richard J. Evans (ed.), *The German Underworld. Deviants and Outcasts in German History* (London and New York, 1988), p. 241.

133 Boelcke, *Der Schwarzmarkt 1945–1948*, p. 110.

134 Rothenberger, *Die Hungerjahre nach dem Zweiten Weltkrieg*, p. 98. Two years later the black-market price of potatoes in the Trier region had risen to between RM 200 and RM 300 per hundredweight. For the level of industrial wages in the French Zone, see Laufer, *Industrie und Energiewirtschaft*, p. 84f.

135 Theodor Spitta, diary entry of 30 October 1945, in Büttner and Voß-Louis (eds.), *Neuanfang auf Trümmern*, p. 268.

136 Boelcke, *Der Schwarzmarkt 1945–1948*, pp. 105–106.

137 Kramer, '"Law-abiding Germans?"', p. 241.

138 Geyer, 'Die Hungergesellschaft', pp. 178–180.

139 Letter from 7 Sept. 1945, quoted Geyer, 'Die Hungergesellschaft', pp. 183–184.

140 Quoted in Lutz Niethammer, 'Privat-Wirtschaft. Erinnerungsfragmente einer anderen Umerziehung', in Lutz Niethammer (ed.), *"Hinterher merkt man, daß es richtig war, daß es schiefgegangen ist". Nachkriegs-Erfahrungen im Ruhrgebiet* (Berlin and Bonn, 1983), p. 62.

141 Geyer, 'Die Hungergesellschaft', p. 180.

142 This 'Central Food Administration' was headed from February 1946 by the agricultural expert Dr Hans Schlange-Schöningen, who had been a member of Heinrich Brüning's cabinet and Reich Commissar for Eastern Relief in 1931–1932. See Carden, 'Before Bizonia', p. 544; Latour and Vogelsang, *Okkupation und Wiederaufbau*, p. 151.

143 Laufer, *Industrie und Energiewirtschaft*, pp. 84–86.

144 See Zank, *Wirtschaft und Arbeit in Ostdeutschland*, pp. 86–88.

145 Section II, B. Economic Principles, Protocol of the Proceedings of the

Berlin (Potsdam) Conference, 1 August 1945, available at http://www.yale.
edu/lawweb/avalon/decade/decade17.html

146   Wolfgang Zank, 'Wirtschaftliche Zentralverwaltungen und Deutsche
      Wirtschaftskommission (DWK)', in Martin Broszat and Hermann
      Weber (eds.), *SBZ Handbuch. Staatliche Verwaltungen, Parteien, gesell-
      schaftliche Organisationen und ihre Führungskräfte in der Sowjetischen
      Besatzungszone Deutschlands 1945–1949* (Munich, 1993), p. 254;
      Overesch, *Das besetzte Deutschland 1945–1947*, p. 52; Holtfrerich, 'Die
      Deutsche Bank', p. 422.

147   Hans Herzfeld, 'Berlin und das Berlinproblem', in Der Senat von Berlin
      (ed.), *Berlin. Kampf um Freiheit und Selbstverwaltung* (Berlin, 1957), p. 25;
      Brandt, 'Unternehmerorganisationen im Umbruch', p. 663f.

148   Sergei Tjulpanow, 'Mit Zuversicht in die Zukunft', in *Tägliche Rundschau*,
      3 May 1948, quoted in Sergei Tjulpanow, *Deutschland nach dem Kriege
      (1945–1949). Erinnerungen* (Berlin, 1986), p. 36.

149   See Rainer Karlsch, *Allein bezahlt? Die Reparationsleistungen der SBZ/DDR
      1945–1953* (Berlin, 1993), pp. 21–31.

150   Karlsch, *Allein bezahlt?*, p. 59.

151   Kathrin Möller, 'Industrialisierung in Mecklenburg-Vorpommern. Zur
      Entstehung der ostdeutschen Werftindustrie von 1945 bis 1953', in van
      Melis (ed.), *Sozialismis auf dem platten Land*, p. 344.

152   See Zank, *Wirtschaft und Arbeit in Ostdeutschland*, p. 63; Norman M.
      Naimark, *The Russians in Germany. A History of the Soviet Zone of Occupation,
      1945–1949* (Cambridge, Mass., and London, 1995), pp. 178–180; Karlsch,
      Allein bezahlt?, p. 63.

153   See Karlsch, *Allein bezahlt?*, pp. 84–87.

154   Karlsch, *Allein bezahlt?*, p. 60.

155   Overesch, *Das besetzte Deutschland 1945–1947*, p. 42.

156   Harmssen, *Reparationen Sozialprodukt Lebensstandard*, p. 70. In the French
      Zone, the other occupation zone where a large proportion of plant and
      equipment was removed, roughly one quarter of the industrial capacity
      had been dismantled by October 1947.

157   Karlsch, *Allein bezahlt?*, pp. 81–84.

158   Naimark, *The Russians in Germany*, pp. 179–180.

159   Quoted in Möller, 'Industrialisierung in Mecklenburg-Vorpommern', p. 346.

160   See Karlsch, *Allein bezahlt?*, pp. 167–174.

161   See the table of reparations payments by categories, 1945–1953, in
      Karlsch, *Allein bezahlt?*, p. 230.

162   See Karlsch, *Allein bezahlt?*, pp. 169–170.

163   Overesch, *Das besetzte Deutschland 1945–1947*, p. 97.

164   Zank, 'Wirtschaftliche Zentralverwaltungen und Deutsche Wirtschafts-
      kommission (DWK)', p. 254.

165   Naimark, *The Russians in Germany*, p. 190.

166   Günter J. Trittel, *Die Bodenreform in der Britischen Zone 1945–1946* (Stuttgart, 1975), p. 33.

167   '"Aktionsprogramm des Blocks der kämpferischen Demokratie" – Maschinenschriftliche Abschrift des Entwurfs van Anton Ackermann vom Ende 1944', in Peter Erler, Horst Lauch and Manfred Wilke (eds.), *"Nach Hitler kommen wir". Dokumente zur Programmatik der Moskauer KPD-Führung 1944/45 für Nachkriegsdeutschland* (Berlin, 1994), pp. 295–296; Arnd Bauerkämper, 'Der verlorene Antifaschismus. Die Enteignung der Gutsbesitzer und der Umgang mit dem 20. Juli 1944 bei der Bodenreform in der Sowjetischen Besatzungszone', *Zeitschrift für Geschichtswissenschaft*, vol. xlii (1994), pp. 624–626; Arnd Bauerkämper, 'Strukturumbruch ohne Mentalitätswandel. Auswirkungen der Bodenreform auf die ländliche Gesellschaft in der Provinz Mark Brandenburg 1945–1949', in Arnd Bauerkämper (ed.), *"Junkerland in Bauernhand"? Durchführung, Auswirkungen und Stellenwert der Bodenreform in der Sowjetischen Besatzungszone* (Stuttgart, 1996), p. 73.

168   See Wilhelm Pieck's notes of the meeting of the KPD leadership with Stalin, Molotov and Zhdanov in Moscow on 4 June 1945, in Gerhard Keiderling (ed.), *'Gruppe Ulbricht' in Berlin April bis Juni 1945. Von den Vorbereitungen im Sommer 1945 bis zur Wiedergründung der KPD im Juni 1945. Eine Dokumentation* (Berlin, 1993), p. 470. See also Bauerkämper, 'Strukturumbruch ohne Mentalitätswandel', p. 73.

169   Quoted in Bauerkämper, 'Strukturumbruch ohne Mentalitätswandel', p. 73.

170   Naimark, *The Russians in Germany*, p. 151.

171   Quoted in Overesch, *Das besetzte Deutschland 1945–1947*, p. 72.

172   Quoted in Naimark, *The Russians in Germany*, p. 151.

173   Zank, 'Wirtschaftliche Zentralverwaltungen und Deutsche Wirtschafts-kommission (DWK)', p. 254.

174   Abelshauser, 'Wirtschaft und Besatzungspolitik', p. 113.

175   Klaus-Dietmar Henke, 'Politik der Widersprüche. Zur Charakteristik der französischen Militärregierung in Deutschland nach dem Zweiten Weltkrieg', in Claus Scharf and Hans-Jürgen Schräder (eds.), *Die Deutschlandpolitik Frankreichs und die französische Zone 1945–1949* (Wiesbaden, 1983), p. 67. Livry-Level had fled to Britain in 1941 and spent much of the war as a pilot with the Royal Air Force.

176   For Rheinland-Pfalz, see Rothenberger, *Die Hungerjahre nach dem Zweiten Weltkrieg*, p. 96.

177   In 1946, occupation costs in the French Zone amounted to 86 % of tax receipts, while in the British Zone the figure was 40 % and in the American Zone 34 %. See figures in Institut für Besatzungsfragen

Tübingen, *Sechs Jahre Besatzungslasten. Eine Untersuchung des Problems der Besatzungskosten in den Westzonen und in Westberlin 1945–1950* (Tübingen, 1951), p. 6.

178   F. Roy Willis, *The French in Germany, 1945–1949* (Stanford, 1962), p. 127; Laufer, *Industrie und Energiewirtschaft*, p. 94; Henke, 'Politik der Widersprüche', pp. 70–71.

179   Rothenberger, *Die Hungerjahre nach dem Zweiten Weltkrieg*, p. 112.

180   Abelshauser, 'Wirtschaft und Besatzungspolitik in der Französischen Zone', p. 117.

181   Abelshauser, 'Wirtschaft und Besatzungspolitik in der Französischen Zone, p. 111.

13. Conclusion: Life after Death

1   Theodor Spitta, diary entry for 31 December 1945, in Ursula Büttner and Angelika Voß-Louis (eds.), *Neuanfang auf Trümmern. Die Tagebücher des Bremer Bürgermeisters Theodor Spitta 1945–1947* (Munich, 1992), p. 294.

2   Norbert Elias, *Über die Einsamkeit der Sterbenden* (Frankfurt am Main, 1982), p. 10.

3   In a survey conducted in 1952 by the Allensbach Institute for Opinion Research, of 535 young German men about their experiences during the war, 51 per cent had lost family members. See Elisabeth Noelle and Erich p. Neumann (eds.), *Jahrbuch der öffentlichen Meinung 1947–1955* (2nd edn., Allensbach, 1956), p. 23; quoted in Alice Förster and Birgit Beck, 'Post-Traumatic Stress Disorder and World War II. Can a Psychiatric Concept Help Us Understand Postwar Society?', in Richard Bessel and Dirk Schumann (eds.), *Life after Death. Approaches to a Cultural and Social History of Europe during the 1940s and 1950s* (Cambridge, 2003), p. 30.

4   Bernd-A. Rusinek, *Gesellschaft in der Katastrophe. Terror, Illegalität, Widerstand – Köln 1944/45* (Essen, 1989), p. 115.

5   Franz Scholz, *Wächter. wie tief die Nacht? Görlitzer Tagebuch 1945/46* (3rd edn., Eltville, 1986), pp. 17–18 (entry from 12 Feb. 1945).

6   Michael Wieck, *Zeugnis vom Untergang Königsbergs, Ein "Geltungsjude" berichtet* (Munich, 2005), pp. 238–9.

7   Bundesministerium für Vertriebene (ed.), *Die Vertreibung der deutschen Bevölkerung aus den Gebieten östlich der Oder-Neiße*, Band I/2, p. 380: 'Erlebnisbericht des Pfarrers Fritz Schmidt aus Marschwitz, Kreis Ohlau i. Niederschles. Original, 3. Oktober 1949'.

8   *Die Vertreibung der deutschen Bevölkerung aus den Gebieten östlich der Oder-Neiße*, Band I/2, p. 349: 'Erlebnisbericht des Pfarrers Georg Gottwald, Dechant von Grünberg i. Niederschles. Original, 15. Juni 1949'.

9   See, for example, the photo of British soldiers examining a corpse dis-
    played along a street next to a sign reading 'This man shot at our sentry
    during the night of 3 to 4 May', in Charles Whiting, *Norddeutschland
    Stunde Null April-September 1945. Ein Bild/Text-Band* (Düsseldorf, 1980),
    p. 167.

10 See Richard Bessel, 'The Shadow of Death in Germany at the End of
    the Second World War', in Alon Confino, Paul Betts and Dirk
    Schumann (eds.), *Between Mass Death and Individual Loss: The Place of the
    Dead in Twentieth-Century Germany* (Oxford and New York, 2008),
    pp. 51–68.

11 Some sense of the dimensions of the 'missing' may be gauged by the
    numbers of war dead from Hamburg, which included over 44,000 soldiers
    who had fallen in battle and a further 27,000 who were missing; in addi-
    tion, 41,000 inhabitants of the city had been killed in the bombings. See
    Frank Bajohr, 'Hamburg – Der Zerfall der "Volksgemeinschaft"', in
    Ulrich Herbert and Axel Schildt (eds.), *Kriegsende in Europa. Vom Beginn
    des deutschen Machtzerfalls bis zur Stabilisierung der Nachkriegsordnung
    1944–1948* (Essen, 1998), p. 335.

12 This is the figure given in I.C.B. Dear (ed.), *The Oxford Companion to the
    Second World War* (Oxford and New York, 1995), p. 290.

13 For a development of this argument, see Richard Bessel, 'The War to End
    All Wars. The Shock of Violence in 1945 and its Aftermath in Germany',
    in Alf Lüdtke and Bernd Weisbrod (eds.), *The No Man's Land of Violence.
    Extreme Wars in the 20th Century* (Göttingen, 2006), pp. 71–99.

14 See Frank Bajohr, *"Arisierung" in Hamburg. Die Verdrängung der jüdischen
    Unternehmer 1933–1945'* (Hamburg, 1997), pp. 331–338.

15 Robert Nebatz to Freda Petzold, 28 Sept. 1945, cited in Heinz Petzold,
    'Cottbus zwischen Januar und Mai 1945', in Werner Strang and Kurt Arlt
    (eds.), *Brandenburg im Jahr 1945* (Potsdam, 1995), p. 125.

16 Petzold, 'Cottbus zwischen Januar und Mai 1945', pp. 106–7, 125.

17 Bundesarchiv-Militärarchiv, RW 44, Nr. I/11: 'Volk und Führung', dated
    in pencil, 16/ (1945).

18 Petzold, 'Cottbus zwischen Januar und Mai 1945', p. 125.

19 Lutz Niethammer, 'Privat-Wirtschaft. Erinnerungsfragmente einer
    anderen Umerziehung', in Lutz Niethammer (ed.), *"Hinterher merkt man,
    daß es richtig war, daß es schiefgegangen ist". Nachkriegserfahrungen im Ruhrgebiet*
    (Berlin and Bonn, 1983), p. 28.

20 Sabine Behrenbeck, 'Between Pain and Silence. Remembering the
    Victims of Violence in Germany after 1949', in Bessel and Schumann
    (eds.), *Life after Death*, p. 39.

21 John W. Dower, *Embracing Defeat. Japan in the Wake of World War II* (New
    York, 1999), pp. 29, 119.

22 See Konrad Jarausch, *Die Umkehr. Deutsche Wandlungen 1945–1995* (Munich, 2004).

23 See Konrad H. Jarausch and Michael Geyer, *Shattered Past. Reconstructing German Histories* (Princeton and Oxford, 2003), pp. 317–341.

24 Wilhelm Michels and Peter Sliepenbeek, *Niederrheinisches Land im Krieg. Ein Beitrag zur Geschichte des Zweiten Weltkrieges im Landkreis Kleve* (Kleve, 1964), pp. 6, 166.

25 See Bessel, 'The War to End All Wars'; Richard Bessel, 'Gewalterfahrung und Opferperspektive. Ein Rückblick auf die beiden Weltkriege des 20. Jahrhunderts in Europa', in Jörg Echternkamp and Stefan Martens (eds.), *Der Zweite Weltkrieg in Europa, Erfahrung und Erinnerung* (Paderborn, 2007), pp. 253–267.

26 George L. Mosse, *Fallen Soldiers. Reshaping the Memory of World Wars* (New York and Oxford, 1990).

27 Reichstag speech of 1 Sept. 1939, in Erhard Klöss (ed.), *Reden des Führers. Politik und Propaganda Adolf Hitlers 1922–1945* (Munich, 1967), p. 215.

28 See Bernd Wegner, 'Hitler, der Zweite Weltkrieg und die Choreographie des Untergangs', *Geschichte und Gesellschaft*, vol. xxvi (2000), no. 3, pp. 492–518. See also Sabine Behrenbeck, *Der Kult um die toten Helden. Nationalsozialistische Mythen, Riten und Symbole* (Vierow bei Greifswald, 1996), pp. 580–591.

29 Konrad H. Jarausch, '1945 and the Continuities of German History: Reflections on Memory, Historiography, and Politics', in Geoffrey J. Giles (ed.), *Stunde Null: The End and the Beginning Fifty Years Ago* (Washington, 1997), p. 18.

30 Michael Geyer, 'Cold War Angst: The Case of West German Opposition to Rearmament and Nuclear Weapons', in Hanna Schissler (ed.), *The Miracle Years. A Cultural History of West Germany, 1949–1968* (Princeton, 2001), pp. 386–7.

31 For example, the introduction of the excellent recent popular illustrated account of Freiburg in the immediate postwar period by Robert Neisen: *Und wir leben immer noch! Eine Chronik der Freiburger Nachkriegsnot* (Freiburg, 2004), p. 13.

32 Quoted in Manfred Overesch, *Das besetzte Deutschland 1945–1947. Eine Tageschronik der Politik, Wirtschaft, Kultur* (Augsburg, 1992), p. 118.

33 Quoted in Overesch, *Das besetzte Deutschland 1945–1947*, p. 121.

SELECT BIBLIOGRAPHY

Robert H. Abzug, *Inside the Vicious Heart. Americans and the Liberation of Nazi Concentration Camps* (New York and Oxford, 1985).

Pertti Ahonen, *After the Expulsion. West Germany and Eastern Europe 1945–1990* (Oxford, 2003).

John H. Backer, *The Decision to Divide Germany. American Foreign Policy in Transition* (Durham, N.C., 1978).

Dagmar Barnouw, *Germany 1945. Views of War and Violence* (Bloomington and Indianapolis, 1996).

Antony Beevor, *Berlin. The Downfall* 1945 (London, 2002).

Nicolaus von Below, *At Hitler's Side. The Memoirs of Hitler's Luftwaffe Adjutant 1937–1945* (London, 2004).

Wolfgang Benz (ed.), *Die Vertreibung der Deutschen aus dem Osten. Ursachen, Ereignisse, Folgen* (Frankfurt am Main, 1985).

Richard Bessel, *Nazism and War* (New York, 2004).

Richard Bessel and Dirk Schuman (eds.), *Life after Death. Approaches to a Cultural and Social History of Europe during the 1940s and 1950s* (Cambridge, 2003).

Paul Betts, Alon Confino and Dirk Schumann (eds.) *Between Mass Death and Individual Loss. The Place of the Dead in 20th-Century Germany* (Oxford and New York, 2008).

Frank Biess, *Homecomings. Returning POWs and the Legacies of Defeat in Postwar Germany* (Princeton and Oxford, 2005).

Michael Brenner, *Nach dem Holocaust. Juden in Deutschland 1945–1950* (Munich 1995).

Martin Broszat, Klaus-Dietmar Henke and Hans Woller (eds.), *Von Stalingrad zur Währungsreform. Zur Sozialgeschichte des Umbruchs in Deutschland* (Munich, 1988).

Norman Davies and Roger Moorhouse, *Microcosm. Portrait of a Central European City* (London, 2002).

Karl Dönitz, *Memoirs. Ten Years and Twenty Days* (New York, 1997).

F.S.V. Donnison, *Civil Affairs and Military Government North-West Europe 1944–1946* (London, 1961).

Jörg Echternkamp, *Nach dem Krieg. Alltagsnot, Neuorientierung und die Last der Vergangenheit 1945–1949* (Zürich, 2003).

L.F. Ellis and A.E. Warhurst, *Victory in the West. Vol. II. The Defeat of Germany* (London, 1968; reprinted Uckfield, 2004),

John Erickson, *The Road to Berlin* (London, 2003).

Richard J. Evans, *The Third Reich at War. How the Nazis led Germany from Conquest to Disaster* (London, 2008).

Joachim Fest, *Inside Hitler's Bunker. The Last Days of the Third Reich* (London, 2004).

Jan Foitzik, *Sowjetische Militäradministration in Deutschland (SMAD) 1945–1949* (Berlin, 1999).

Stephen G. Fritz, *Endkampf. Soldiers, Civilians, and the Death of the Third Reich* (Lexington, Kentucky, 2004).

John Gimbel, *A German Community under American Occupation. Marburg 1945–1952* (Stanford, 1961).

Rainer Gries, *Die Rationengesellschaft. Versorgungskampf und Vergleichsmentalität. Leipzig, München und Köln nach dem Kriege* (Münster, 1991).

Atina Grossmann, *Jews, Germans and Allies. Close Encounters in Occupied Germany* (Princeton, 2007).

Elizabeth Harvey, *Women in the Nazi East. Agents and Witnesses of Germanization* (New Haven and London, 2003).

Max Hastings, *Armageddon. The Battle for Germany 1944–45* (London, 2004).

Elizabeth D. Heineman, *What Difference Does a Husband Make? Women and Marital Status in Nazi and Postwar Germany* (Berkeley, Los Angeles and London, 1999).

Klaus–Dietmar Henke, *Die amerikanische Besetzung Deutschlands* (Munich, 1995).

Ulrich Herbert, *Hitler's Foreign Workers: Enforced Foreign Labour in Germany under the Third Reich* (Cambridge, 1997).

Dagmar Herzog, *Sex after Fascism. Memory and Morality in Twentieth-Century Germany* (Princeton and Oxford, 2005).

Jörg Hillmann and John Zimmermann (eds.), *Kriegsende 1945 in Deutschland* (Munich, 2002).

Andreas Hofmann, *Nachkriegszeit in Schlesien. Gesellschafts- und Bevölkerungspolitik in den polnischen Siedlungsgebieten 1945–1948* (Cologne, Weimar and Vienna, 2000).

Martin Holz, *Evakuierte, Flüchtlinge und Vertriebene auf der Insel Rügen 1943–1961* (Cologne, 2003).

Wolfgang Jacobmeyer, *Vom Zwangsarbeiter zum heimatlosen Ausländer. Die Displaced Persons in Westdeutschland 1945–1951* (Göttingen, 1985).

Konrad H. Jarausch and Michael Geyer, *Shattered Past. Reconstructing German Histories* (Princeton and Oxford, 2003).

Traudl Junge, *Until the Final Hour. Hitler's Last Secretary* (London, 2004).

Rainer Karlsch, *Allein bezahlt? Die Reparationsleistungen der SBZ/DDR 1945–1953* (Berlin, 1993).

Padraig Kenny, *Rebuilding Poland. Workers and Communists, 1945–1950* (Ithaca and London, 1997).

Ian Kershaw, *Popular Opinion and Political Dissent in the Third Reich. Bavaria, 1933–45* (Oxford, 1983).

Ian Kershaw, The 'Hitler Myth'. Image and Reality in the Third Reich (Oxford, 1987).

Ian Kershaw, *Hitler, 1936–2000: Nemesis* (London, 2000).

Victor Klemperer, *To the Bitter End. The Diaries of Victor Klemperer 1942–1945* (London, 2000).

Victor Klemperer, *The Lesser Evil. The Diaries of Victor Klemperer 1945–1959* (London, 2003).

Angelika Königseder and Juliane Wetzel, *Lebensmut im Wartesaal. Die jüdischen DPs (Displaced Persons) im Nachkriegsdeutschland* (Frankfurt am Main, 1994).

Andreas Kunz, *Wehrmacht und Niederlage. Die bewaffnete Macht in der Endphase der nationalsozialistischen Herrschaft 1944 bis 1945* (Munich, 2005).

Alf Lüdtke and Bernd Weisbrod (eds.), *No Man's Land of Violence. Extreme Wars in the 20th Century* (Göttingen, 2006).

Harold Marcuse, *Legacies of Dachau. The Uses and Abuses of a Concentration Camp, 1933–2001* (Cambridge, 2001).

Damian van Melis, *Entnazifizierung in Mecklenburg-Vorpommern. Herrschaft und Verwaltung 1945–1948* (Munich, 1999).

Alfred C. Mierzejewski, *The Collapse of the German War Economy, 1944–1945. Allied Air Power and the German National Railway* (Chapel Hill and London, 1988).

Robert G. Moeller, *Protecting Motherhood. Women and the Family in the Politics of Postwar West Germany* (Berkeley and Los Angeles, 1993).

Robert G. Moeller, *War Stories. The Search for a Usable Past in the Federal Republic of Germany* (Berkeley, Los Angeles and London, 2001).

George L. Mosse, *Fallen Soldiers: Reshaping the Memory of the World Wars* (New York, 1990).

Rolf-Dieter Müller and Gerd R. Ueberschär, *Kriegsende 1945. Die Zerstörung des Deutschen Reiches* (Frankfurt am Main, 1994).

Norman M. Naimark, *The Russians in Germany. A History of the Soviet Zone of Occupation 1945–1949* (Cambridge, Mass., 1995).

Norman M. Naimark, *Fires of Hatred. Ethnic Cleansing in Twentieth-Century Europe* (Cambridge, Mass., and London, 2001).

Lutz Niethammer, *Die Mitläuferfabrik. Die Entnazifizierung am Beispiel Bayerns* (Berlin and Bonn, 1982).

Bernadetta Nitschke, *Vertreibung und Aussiedlung der deutschen Bevölkerung aus Polen 1945 bis 1949* (Munich, 2004).

Rüdiger Overmans, *Deutsche militärische Verluste im Zweiten Weltkrieg* (Munich, 1999).

Richard Overy, *Interrogations. The Nazi Elite in Allied Hands, 1945* (London, 2001).

Edward N. Peterson, *The American Occupation of Germany. Retreat to Victory* (Detroit, 1977).

Edward N. Peterson, *The Many Faces of Defeat. The German People's Experience in 1945* (New York, Bern, Frankfurt am Main and Paris, 1990).

Hartmut Pietsch, *Militärregierung Bürokratie und Sozialisierung. Zur Entstehung des politischen Systems in den Städten des Ruhrgebiets 1945 bis 1948* (Duisburg, 1978).

Gisela Schwarze, *Eine Region im demokratischen Aufbau. Der Regierungsbezirk Münster 1945/46* (Düsseldorf, 1984).

Sebastian Siebel-Achenbach, *Lower Silesia from Nazi Germany to Communist Poland 1942–49* (New York, 1994).

Nicholas Stargardt, *Witnesses of War. Childrens' Lives uner the Nazis* (London, 2005).

Marlis Steinert, *Hitler's War and the Germans. Public Mood and Attitude during the Second World War* (Athens, Ohio, 1977).

Toby Thacker, *The End of the Third Reich. Defeat, Denazification & Nuremberg. January 1944 – November 1946* (London, 2006).

Timothy R. Vogt, *Denazification in Soviet-Occupied Germany. Brandenburg 1945–1948* (Cambridge, Mass., 2000).

Hans-Erich Volkmann (ed.), *Ende des Dritten Reiches – Ende des Zweiten Weltkriegs. Eine perspektivische Rückschau* (Munich, 1995).

Clemens Vollnhals (ed.), *Entnazifizierung. Politische Säuberung und Rehabilitierung in den vier Besatzungszonen 1945–1949* (Munich, 1991).

Nikolaus Wachsmann, *Hitler's Prisons. Legal Terror in Nazi Germany* (New Haven and London, 2004)

Gerhard L. Weinberg, *A World at Arms. A Global History of World War II* (Cambridge, 1994).

F. Roy Willis, *The French in Germany 1945–1949* (Stanford, 1962).

Hans Woller, *Gesellschaft und Politik in der amerikanischen Besatzungszone. Die Region Ansbach und Fürth* (Munich, 1986).

David K. Yelton, *Hitler's Volkssturm: The Nazi Militia and the Fall of Germany 1944–1945* (Lawrence, Kansas, 2002).

Wolfgang Zank, *Wirtschaft und Arbeit in Ostdeutschland 1945–1949. Probleme des Wiederaufbaus in der Sowjetischen Besatzungszone Deutschlands* (Munich, 1987).

Manfred Zeidler, *Kriegsende im Osten. Die Rote Armee und die Besetzung Deutschlands östlich von Oder und Neiße 1944/45* (Munich, 1996).

Earl F. Ziemke, *The U.S. Army in the Occupation of Germany 1944–1946* (Washington, 1975).

INDEX

NOTE ON THE AUTHOR

Richard Bessel is Professor of Twentieth Century History at the University of York. He works on the social and political history of modern Germany, the aftermath of the two world wars and the history of policing. He is a member of the Editorial Boards of *German History* and *History Today*. His books include *Political Violence and the Rise of Nazism*, *Germany after the First World War* and *Nazism and War*.